*I*daho Folklife

WITHDRAWN

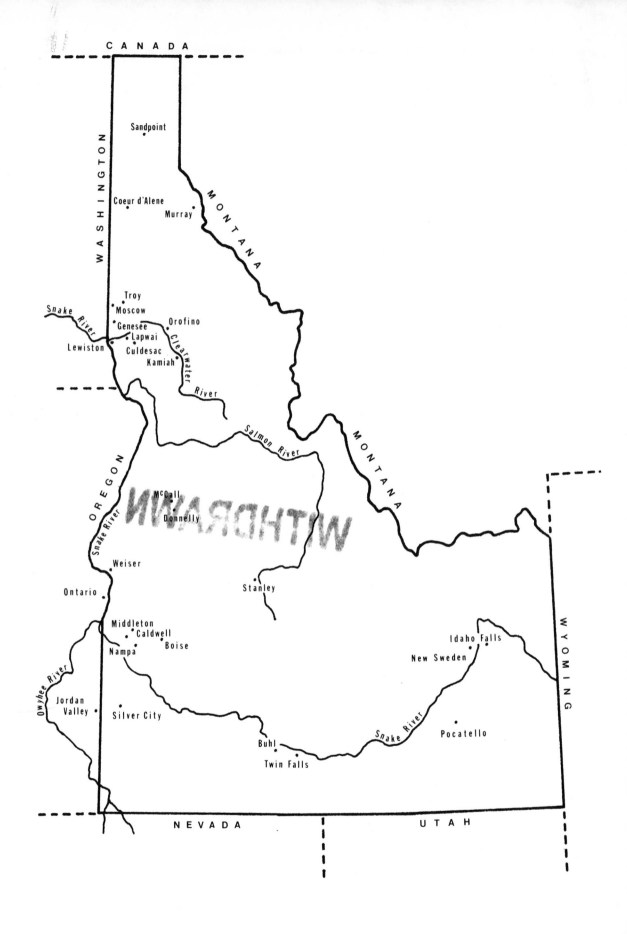

Idaho Folklife

HOMESTEADS TO HEADSTONES

Edited, and With an Introduction by
LOUIE W. ATTEBERY

Foreword by
WAYLAND D. HAND

Contributions by

Brian Attebery, Jennifer Eastman Attebery,
Louie W. Attebery, Jan Harold Brunvand, Madeline Buckendorf, Hal Cannon,
Thomas Edward Cheney, Carol Edison, Austin E. Fife, James M. Fife, Joan H. Hall,
Charlene James-Duguid, Alice Koskela, Sarah Baker Munro, Keith Petersen,
Mary E. Reed, J. Sanford Rikoon, Dennis C. Shaw, Polly Stewart,
Kenneth J. Swanson, Joe Toluse, Frederick L. Walters,
and William A. Wilson

Editorial Assistance by
J. SANFORD RIKOON

University of Utah Press — Salt Lake City, Utah

Idaho State Historical Society — Boise, Idaho

Library of Congress Cataloging in Publication Data

Main entry under title:

Idaho folklife.

Bibliography: p.
1. Folklore — Idaho — Addresses, essays, lectures.
2. Idaho — Social life and customs — Addresses, essays,
lectures.   I. Attebery, Louie W. (Louie Wayne), 1927–   .
II. Attebery, Brian, 1951–   .
GR110.I2I3   1985   390 '.009796   84–17341
ISBN 0–87480–240–7

Contents

Foreword
Wayland D. Hand____vii

Acknowledgments____x

Introduction
Louie W. Attebery____xi

Folklife and Regionalism

Hay Derricks of the Great Basin and Upper Snake River Valley
Austin E. Fife and James M. Fife_____2
A Lexical Survey of the Snake River Region
Joan H. Hall_____12
Finnish Log Homestead Buildings in Long Valley
Alice Koskela_____29
Folk Song Studies in Idaho
Jan Harold Brunvand_____37
The Montgomery House: Adobe in Idaho's Folk Architecture
Jennifer Eastman Attebery, Kenneth J. Swanson,
Joe Toluse, and Frederick L. Walters_____46

Folklife and Group Identity

The Paradox of Mormon Folklore
William A. Wilson_____58
New Sweden Pioneer Day
Hal Cannon_____68
Orofino Lumberjack Days
Charlene James-Duguid_____81
Basque Celebrations in Eastern Oregon and Boise
Sarah Baker Munro_____91
''Prairie Chickens Dancing . . .'': Ecology's Myth
Alan G. Marshall_____101

Folklife and Individual Style

Retention and Change in the Singing Tradition of a Northern Idaho Family
POLLY STEWART_____110

Len Henry: North Idaho Münchausen
JAN HAROLD BRUNVAND_____120

A Contextual Survey of Selected Homestead Sites in Washington County
LOUIE W. ATTEBERY_____129

Folklife and Change

Early Dairy Barns of Buhl
MADELINE BUCKENDORF_____144

Medical Care in Latah County, 1870–1930
KEITH PETERSEN_____160

Folk Ballad Characteristics in a Present-day Collection of Songs
THOMAS EDWARD CHENEY_____171

Motorcycles, Guitars, and Bucking Broncs:
Twentieth-century Gravestones in Southeastern Idaho
CAROL EDISON_____184

Folklife and Folk History

The Story of Molly B'Dam: A Regional Expression of American Ideology
DENNIS C. SHAW_____192

The Narrative of "Chief Bigfoot": A Study in Folklore, History, and World View
J. SANFORD RIKOON_____199

Folklore in Regional Literature: Carol Brink's Buffalo Coat
MARY E. REED_____216

Land Use Attitudes and Ethics in Idaho Folklore
BRIAN ATTEBERY_____223

Appendix

An Annotated Bibliography of Materials on Idaho Folklife
J. SANFORD RIKOON_____231

Foreword

Folklore and folklife studies were late in coming to America and even later in coming to the Rocky Mountain West. It was not until the 1930s and the 1940s that the interest in regional literature and local history broadened to include folklore in its range of concerns about American folk culture. Regionalism in literature and history at that time were the forebears of what by the 1970s became known under the more encompassing term of American Folklife. From the German and Dutch notions of *Volksleben* and *volksleven* in the latter part of the nineteenth century, where verbal lore was a prominent, if not major, component of folklife, through the Scandinavian modulations of the present century (Swed. *folklive*; Dan. *Folkeliv*) where the folklore of material culture and ethnology are emphasized, folklife in the American scholarly lexicon has come full circle. Folklore and folklife (*sachliche Volkskunde*) are back together. Actually, in historical terms, the study of material culture in this country, starting out modestly in the 1940s — half a century after the formal beginnings of folklore study — has now become a full partner with folklore in the study of verbal folk expression, whether it be in a tale or legend, in a joke or anecdote, in custom or belief, or in proverb or riddle. What people *say*, of course, is only part of the repertory of folklore and folklife; what they *do* and they *make* are, in every sense, meaningful expressions of the creative energy of man. The design and usefulness of a fence or hay derrick, the beauty and utility of a hand-tooled saddle, a butter mould carved to keep witches from spoiling the butter, the exuberance of a country dance, or the verve and brilliance of a folk pageant, no less than a sacred folk healing or an impassioned exorcism — all these in their own way are fitting counterparts to the intricate narrative pattern of a folktale, the pointed lesson of a legend, the ancient wisdom of a proverb, the baffling twist of a joke, or the hidden meaning of a riddle.

In his fine anthology of essays, *Idaho Folklife: Homesteads to Headstones*, Louie W. Attebery has sought to bring within the covers of a single volume a broad conspectus of folklife in the Intermountain West and adjacent states. Inasmuch as pedigrees of early workers and the lines of descent of folklore and folklife studies in this sequestered part of the American West are little known, it would be worthwhile to focus on Louie Attebery and the credentials he brings to this challenging assignment. Whereas the task of training up workers in other parts of the country had fallen to trained folklorists, in the Rocky Mountain States during the forties, and even into the fifties, the job rested largely in the hands of professors of English. At a few places around the country folklore studies fitted into the emerging programs in American Studies, and both drew nourishment from the new movement of regionalism which spread throughout the length and breadth of the land, particularly during the period of the highly successful series of state guides in the American Guide Series of the Federal Writers Project. At this same time in the 1940s there were other state and regional series that dealt with rivers, mountains, and lakes, and then the well-known "Country Series" which treated different parts of the country by geographic configuration, economic patterning, or religious orientation, as in Wallace Stegner's classic *Mormon Country*.

In his college days Louie Attebery was close to the fountainhead of this new and eclectic approach to the study of American literature and cultural history that also gripped the West during this period of great intellectual ferment. As a bright and eager young graduate of The College of Idaho (1950), Attebery set out for the University of Montana to take graduate work with Harold G. Merriam, editor of *Frontier*, the first literary and critical journal of its kind in the West. With a Master's degree in English from Montana in hand (1951), and five years of secondary teaching behind him, Attebery headed not to the prestigious graduate schools of the East, but south to the University of Denver, where Levette J. Davidson was making a reputation in Folklore Studies for the rapidly developing Colorado institution. Davidson's annual Western Folklore Conference, which drew scholars from all over the West, and from other parts of the country as well, had been going on for almost a decade when young Attebery arrived in Denver. Arthur L. Campa, noted scholar in Latin American folklore, had come to the university in 1946 and John Greenway by 1953. After Davidson's death in 1957 Campa saw Attebery through to the doctorate in 1961, with a dissertation on *Folklore of the Lower Snake River Valley: A Regional Study*.

The constellation at the University of Denver, augmented by Ben Lumpkin and Marjorie M. Kimmerle from the University of Colorado, nearby, was unmatched, of course, anywhere else in the Rocky Mountain country. Since little is generally known about the precursors of folklore elsewhere in the West, it will be useful for the history of the period to give here at least a roll call of early workers, not only for Montana and Colorado, but for other Mountain and Pacific states as well. Wyoming: Wilson O. Clough; New Mexico: T. M. Pearce, Arthur L. Campa (Spanish), John D. Robb (Music); Arizona: Frances Gillmor: Utah: King Hendricks, Lester Hubbard, Thomas E. Cheney; Idaho: George Morey Miller, Vardis Fisher, Sven Liljeblad (a Swedish folklorist living in Idaho); Washington: Henry A. Person; Oregon: Randall V. Mills, Helen Pearce; California: Walter Morris Hart, Sigurd B. Hustvedt, George R. Stewart, Arthur Brodeur, B. H. Bronson, Arthur Hutson. Except where they chanced to be from the same state, it is doubtful that many of these people knew of each other. They did, however, have one thing in common. In one way or another, most of them were inspired by the work in Anglo-American balladry that had been carried on at Harvard University from the time of Francis James Child and later on during the long and distinguished career of George Lyman Kittredge. There went forth from Kittredge's classes a whole generation of workers to teach courses in "The Ballad" at several eastern and southern universities, and elsewhere. One of them, Professor George Morey Miller, went all the way out to Idaho where he too taught The Ballad at the Gem State's rising university. Among the most important scholars coming from the literary field of balladry and folk song to influence folklore studies in the country, and especially in the Middle States and the West, was Professor Louise Pound of the University of Nebraska. Although she had never been a member of the select "Harvard Circle," Pound, trained at Heidelberg under Johannes Hoops, had impeccable credentials in philology and literature. Louise Pound was the headliner at the first Western Folklore Conference at Denver in 1941 and became the mainstay of the Conference throughout its fifteen-year history which ended in 1955. Other seasoned scholars took part in the Denver conference over the years and helped Davidson and Pound forge the bond between the founders of folklore studies in America and the eager new generation of folklore students who by this time were being trained in regular folklore programs. Among other places, these new workers were starting to come from the graduate schools of the University of Pennsylvania and those of the state universities of Indiana, Texas, North Carolina and California, and from Harvard, Yale, Columbia, and Stanford. Of the contributors to *Idaho Folklife: Homesteads to Headstones*, as things turn out, only Thomas E. Cheney, himself one of the pioneer folklore scholars of Idaho and Utah, fits into the older mould represented by Louise Pound.

Idaho Folklife: Homesteads to Headstones, is a series of twenty-one essays dealing largely with Idaho life and work, but also embracing rural life and pursuits in the eastern part of Oregon and the northern tips of Utah and Nevada. Authors represented in the anthology are mainly Idahoans and former residents of the Gem State. They are bound together professionally as the Idaho Folklife Associates.

The Attebery anthology includes five essays on material culture per se and an additional paper on land use. To these are added titles on folk custom and another couple of studies on occupational lore. All of these papers deal in turn with group identity in one way or another and with local mores and group values.

Several involve ethnic groups (*inter alia* Swedes, Basques, Finns, Germans) and emphasize the problems of cultural adaptation and changing human relations. Attebery's own introduction and contextual survey of homesteading in Washington County gets down to the most basic denominations of early farm life and treats in some detail the transition from horse power on the farm to the coming of motorized farm equipment. The article on hay derricks by the Fife brothers does somewhat the same thing for haying, stopping short, however, of modern methods of stacking and baling hay.

Three excellent papers on folk song and balladry give a good conspectus of song repertories in Idaho, all the way from the Child ballads, as in the Cheney piece, to old favorites and sentimental songs of home and fireside. The workmanlike study by Polly Stewart treats retention and change in the song tradition of a North Idaho family over four generations. This is a theoretical case study in which all of the elements needed for an intergenerational survey are brought together, a rare circumstance.

Folk narrative is represented by four essays. The first is Jan Brunvand's account of Len Henry, a Nez Perce squawman, locally famous around Lapwai as a spinner of tall tales. The other two fall more in the literary tradition, one dealing with the depredations and death of Chief Bigfoot, a notorious Indian half-breed along the Oregon Trail, and the other a regional novel woven together by author Carol Brink from semi-historical accounts of local life and narratives from storytelling legacies. The final account, pieced together from bits of local legend and hearsay, deals with a prostitute in the heart-of-gold tradition, who, among other civic benefactions, rises to selfless heights in joining hands with other citizens of the mining camp at Murray to combat an epidemic of smallpox.

One of the richest genres of folklore and folklife, namely, folk speech, is represented by only one paper, but this article, "A Lexical Survey of the Snake River Region," by Joan H. Hall, deserves special comment. Hall's work grows out of surveys of the American Dialect Society in the 1930s and the later documentations of the *Linguistic Atlas of the United States and Canada*. Specifically, it is based on Carol Reed's and Henry Person's work on the dialectology of the Northwest, including the Snake River region, begun in the late 1940s, and Hall's own work and that of her students, on the *Dictionary of American Regional English (DARE)* in the early 1970s. From a finding list of 105 lexical items, each with variant terms, Hall in her introduction has selected a few for cultural reference and elucidation. Without saying so, Hall has shown that folk speech is truly a resourceful handmaiden of folklife!

Natural history is the basis of Alan G. Marshall's article showing the mythological implication among the Nez Perce of the mating dances of prairie chickens and the Indian ecological practices that relate to hunting and food supply. Connected with human survival, too, is Keith Peterson's paper on medical care in Latah County in the sixty-year period between 1870 and 1930. Taken up are the lack of adequate medical care on the Idaho frontier and the resort of settlers to folk medicine. Oral history accounts of treatments and cures fall into the accepted modes of American folk curative practice. Two estimable local healers are treated; one of them, Robert Foster, was credited with curing skin cancer by what was called a "burner" method.

Like the paper by the Fifes, William A. Wilson's paper on "The Paradox of Mormon Folklore," is reprinted from an earlier publication. What these articles have in common, however, is their matrix in the length and breadth of Mormon country—Utah, Idaho, Arizona, and adjacent states—not only in the inland empire's economy and culture, but particularly, as in the Wilson paper, in the intellectual and spiritual heritage of the whole western country colonized by the Mormons. This piece, among Wilson's best, is an attractive sampler of the treasure trove of Mormon lore.

The writer of these lines is disappointed, of course, that there is no treatment of folk beliefs apart from a few items here and there, notably in the article on folk medical practice. This deficiency is compensated somewhat by Vardis Fisher's *Idaho Lore*, some studies by Brunvand during his Idaho period, and Attebery's own earlier writings on the subject. Rewarding beyond measure however, is a most unusual waif and stray at the end of Attebery's Introduction: After telling about the value of a horse that can turn all the way over in rolling, Attebery underscores the need of local and regional collections for the purposes of comparative study by citing a striking folk belief about horses collected in Filer, Idaho in 1974: "Water goes to sleep sometimes. It makes no noise. If a horse drank sleeping water he would die. That is why a horse always blows before drinking at night, to wake the water." This aetiological folk belief tells its own graphic story, and so be it!

Finally, Sanford Rikoon has drawn together an annotated bibliography of materials on Idaho folklore and folklife, including mention as to where unpublished papers and other documents are to be found. (The Bibliography in Anthon S. Cannon's *Popular Beliefs and Superstitions from Utah*, recently published by the University of Utah Press, contains several items of collateral interest from other western states.)

The Idaho volume is important in American folklore and folklife studies in many ways. First of all, the anthology inventories the folklife resources in the state for the use of scholars elsewhere; but for the Idaho Folklife Associates and their confreres and other interested parties throughout the state, it sets a goal for systematic fieldwork that could one day result in a great state collection, comparable (for a smaller state, to be sure) to the seven sumptuous volumes of the *Frank C. Brown Collection of North Carolina Folklore* and the long series of primary studies in the *Publications of the Texas Folklore Society*. The field is ripe unto the harvest, the reapers and the binders are in the fields, and the day, though weary, is still long.

Wayland D. Hand

Acknowledgments

From the following individuals and organizations came contributions of time, talent, and encouragement without which the appearance of this book would have been delayed by several life spans; they are listed here in no particular order but with profound gratitude: Belinda Henry Davis, drawings of the Buhl barns and an Idaho map; Kris Kendall, typing and photocopying; Fred Walters, drawings of the Montgomery house; Dr. Merle Wells, Arthur Hart, and Judy Austin, editorial suggestions; Guila Ford, typing; Bill Buckendorf, photos of the Buhl barns; the Idaho Historical Society; the Regional Studies Center of The College of Idaho and its director Donna Parsons and secretary Midori Furushiro. Additionally Howard A. Marshall and Suzi Jones made detailed and thoughtful suggestions that improved the book. Finally the roll of present and former Idaho Folklife Associates should be called, for that organization bears a heavy responsibility for the present work: Barbara Rahm, Jackie Day, Madeline Buckendorf, Jennifer Attebery, Brian Attebery, Kathleen Warner, Sandy Rikoon, Elaine Lawless, Steve Siporin, Tom Green, Stacy Ericson, Louie Attebery, Linda Morton, and Louise Ackley.

Introduction

Louie W. Attebery

Idaho is the most easily ignored state in our Union. To the people on the Oregon Trail, the land that is now Idaho was a dry and hostile stretch of discomfort to be crossed as quickly as possible. It was a part of the American Desert, beginning somewhere in what is now western Nebraska and ending somewhere around the Cascades, a barrier to the green and productive Willamette Valley. To the legendary Boston dowager introduced to a young woman from the West it was an enigma: "And where are you from, my dear?" "Idaho." "Oh, my dear," responded the Bostonian, "you must learn that here we pronounce it 'Ohio.'" When the NBC Today show recognized the bicentennial by devoting part of the program to each of the states, many Idahoans cringed to hear Barbara Walters refer to the Gem State as "Iowa." It is a common error.

In introducing to the general reader a collection of essays focusing upon Idaho and the region of which it is a part, the editors realize that they are contending with this vast lack of awareness of both Idaho and the region. This latter includes, after all, the Mountain Time Zone, omitted by television networks when they announce showtimes: 9 P.M. Eastern, 8 Central, and 6 Pacific. In truth, it has not yet been established to what region the state belongs. Is Idaho in the Pacific Northwest group of states along with Washington and Oregon? Or is it a Rocky Mountain state? The state is too large and too varied to make easy generalizations. Much of it is mountainous, much is arid. In the well-watered north, forests of cedar and white pine impress the traveler; in the dry south extensive irrigation is required to make agriculture possible. Great Basin? Columbia Plateau? Each of these designations has proven useful for some purposes. For the purposes of this book, political boundaries are of less significance than geographical and cultural ones. The drainage of the Snake River defines an area of some physical and cultural integrity. It contains most of the state and also bits of surrounding states. That overlap is appropriate, for folklore and material culture are quite indifferent to state lines. Items of Mormon folklife freely cross from northern Utah into Idaho and from Idaho into Utah; traditions of the cattle industry move freely from Owyhee County, Idaho, into Malheur County, Oregon, and from both into northern Nevada. A header puncher in Idaho's Palouse could punch header equally well in southeastern Washington's Palouse. Thus, a statement about Idaho folklife may often apply to persons and communities elsewhere, in some cases, perhaps, throughout the West.

Western traditions are not so well known in other parts of the country as the frequency of Western images in books, films, and advertisements would lead one to believe. A national television commercial for an after-shave product, for example, portrays a buckaroo in a pair of chaps to stimulate feelings about space and freedom, manliness and *virtu*. But the announcer pronounces the name of the product with a *ch* sound, instead of a *sh* sound, evoking in the Westerner the sensation of lip discomfort experienced by people who work under a hot sun in a dry climate.

This book is, then, partly an essay in the correction of ideas. It is an attempt on the part of a group of Idaho residents whose professional interests are connected with folklife studies to offer to the public the results of scholarship that has been going on since the 1930s. In this brief introduction I wish to talk about the study of folklife here and elsewhere and about the origin and purpose of this collection of essays.

First, folklife studies. This book accepts the wisdom of European scholarship in using that term. Folklife studies is an academic enterprise which studies folklore and material culture. Whether consisting of words and sounds uttered and heard (folklore) or of elements shaped by hand and existing in three dimensions (material culture), the elements collected, analyzed, and interpreted by students of folklife share certain characteristics. The essays in this book represent one or more of those scholarly processes, and a careful reading will permit anyone to understand what those characteristics are — to know, in short, what folklife studies are about.

Before I describe these characteristics, let me turn to a question often asked of students of folklife (folklorists): "How did you become interested in this subject?" I will answer from my own experience, because, as Thoreau says, there isn't anyone else whom I know half so well.

Growing up as I did on a small ranch (180 acres, 35 of them irrigable) north of Weiser, Idaho, it was my strange fortune to pass through the remnant years of a dying culture and to emerge into a new one. I refer to the fact that the life I knew on Monroe Creek and Mann's Creek was a life that depended upon horse power; that is *horse power*, not horsepower. It was a horse culture, and it remained so until the onset of World War II. It was another twenty years before the Department of Agriculture signaled the end of the horse culture by declaring that it would henceforth no longer include statistics on the number of work horses in its compilation of farm figures, according to ''RFD 630'' KHOW, Denver, 16 February 1961. Although not so striking as the dictum that generated Frederick Jackson Turner's well-known response to the end of the American frontier, the official signal of the end of a horse culture should have inspired a serious retrospective look at what the presence of the horse had meant to the development of our country. To attempt such a studied look here would be inappropriate, but a glance might be permitted.

One of the qualities of the world of horse power on Upper Monroe Creek in the 1920s and 1930s was silence. The absence of internal combustion engines — except for automobiles — made rural life quiet. If conditions were right, we could hear the steam whistle from the laundry in town some nine miles distant at eight, twelve, one, and five o'clock. It and the whistles of steam locomotives on the Union Pacific line through town created certain weather beliefs. If we could hear them as clearly as if they were just below the schoolhouse a half mile distant, then a storm was coming. In that quiet time we could hear the postmaul of a neighbor building fence two miles away. Livestock could be heard from time to time, and one could tell who was not feeding his animals enough by the cries of animal hunger.

But the work itself, with a few notable exceptions, went on in a remarkably quiet way. Harnesses creaked and butt chains clattered, but the earth turned over by a plow made little noise as it scoured softly over the moldboard. Disking and harrowing and drilling were never too noisy to drown the cries of blackbirds, meadowlarks, and migrating wild geese. It is true that some mowing machines were noisy; we could hear them a mile away. But the rest of haying went on quietly.

I suppose the noisiest traditional activities were grain harvesting — headers and binders and threshers, especially threshers, were noisy — and activities where animals were branded, castrated, earmarked, and so on. And, of course, butchering was sometimes noisy, at the start.

But the point is that the times were quiet and when something made enough noise to be heard, the noise was noticeable and disruptive. I can recall — it must have been in 1938 or '39 — hearing the local cavalry troop firing a machine gun on the range a mile or so north of town. Sensibilities shaped by sounds of nature in a quiet age are pained by the decibels of stereos and portable radios.

Along with the quiet of that time and place went pneumonia, scarlet fever, Rocky Mountain spotted or breakbone fever, smallpox, measles, whooping cough, lockjaw, typhoid, ptomaine, and botulism. This was before antibiotics, and calomel was in most cupboards. Imagine giving a mercury compound to a sick child today! There was neither electricity nor plumbing indoors. It was a time when my grandfather would say, while watching a newly purchased cow bawling for her old surroundings, ''She'll be all right as soon as she gets

ha'nted to the place.'' It was, in short, a time when traditional ways of doing things were the only ways to do them. And when the word *tradition* appears, quite obviously we have moved into the foreground of folklife studies.

But I did not know that when I was growing up. After the Navy, marriage, college, graduate school, and high school teaching, I finally learned that what I had grown up knowing and doing, other people were collecting, classifying, and interpreting. They called it folklore. So, I looked about and selected a university where I could pursue additional graduate work in folklore while supporting my family by teaching in a public high school. At that time the University of Denver, whose faculty included Levette Davidson, Arthur Campa, and John Greenway, offered one of the best American folklore programs, but too soon the gentle Professor Davidson died, and Greenway left. I finished my dissertation with Dr. Campa and returned to my undergraduate college to teach English and folklore and to collect as time permits until such time as I am, in turn, collected.

It would appear, then, that as senior editor of this publication and the senior citizen in the Idaho Folklife Associates, I might be able to reflect upon the quiet time of the horse culture and connect it with the modern times in which we live. It is as mediator between the time of home remedies and the time of *etic* and *emic* analysis of folktales that I have prepared this introduction.

Folklife studies in Idaho cannot be surveyed without mentioning George Morey Miller and Sven Liljeblad. Professor Miller's work is discussed in Brunvand's article on folk music studies in Idaho and in the headnote to Thomas Cheney's article on his folk song collection. Sven Liljeblad, however, requires some introduction.

Liljeblad was a Swedish immigrant who taught folklore at Idaho State University for a number of years and quietly went about satisfying his life's passion — studying the lore and language of the Paiute Indians. One must visit folklore centers in Europe to begin to understand this man's contribution to folklife studies. An account told to me in 1972 by Folke Hedblom of the University of Uppsala clarifies this point.

According to Hedblom, a panel of Swedish folklife professionals assembled at Uppsala in the mid-1930s to try to develop some consistent scheme for classifying the elements of tradition which they were collecting and studying. Heretofore, the University of Lund employed one system, Uppsala another, and so on. The panel worked far into the night before giving up in despair that a consistent system could ever be developed. They did, however, agree to meet the following day. At their next day's gathering, Sven Liljeblad arose and asked the panel to consider something he had worked on all night. He had analyzed their previous day's work, sorted through it, discarded faulty elements, added stronger ones, and virtually single-handedly saved the day. What he presented became the

Uppsala Register, the method for classifying the elements of folklife widely used throughout Europe. Hedblom continued by relating Liljeblad's decision to turn to the New World for a redirection of his energies and move to Idaho. On the walls of the conference room in which my conversation with Hedblom took place were photographs of Swedish folklorists who had made significant contributions to the study of folklore. There with the photographs of other great men — von Sydow, Aake Campbell among them — was the handsome young Sven Liljeblad.

It was quite true that in 1971–72 as I visited with the folklorists in Greece, England, Scotland, Ireland, Norway, and Sweden, without exception they identified Idaho with three things: Frank Church, potatoes, and Sven Liljeblad. It is not inappropriate that the Idaho Folklife Associates recognize and pay tribute to this man — *Tack så mycket!*, Sven.

Jan Brunvand and I began teaching in Idaho colleges the same year, 1961, he at the University of Idaho and I at The College of Idaho. Kathleen Warner began her career at Boise State University in 1968. Others who have contributed to the growth of folklife studies are Lalia Boone and Bacil Kirtley, formerly at the University, and Thomas Green at Idaho State. With a measure of pride I note that four contributors to this book are former students of mine. As for the membership of Idaho Folklife Associates, whose efforts this book reflects, it is made up of scholars — teachers and professionals — in the field of folklife studies or in fields related to it and employing similar methodologies. Steve Siporin is Folk Arts Coordinator for the Idaho Commission for the Arts. Tom Green is State Archeologist for the Idaho State Historical Society. Elaine Lawless was Archivist for the Idaho Folklife Center and now teaches folklore in the anthropology department at Boise State University. Kathleen Warner is Assistant Professor of English at Boise State University. Sandy Rikoon is Director of the Idaho Folklife Center at the Idaho State Historical Society. Madeline Buckendorf is Coordinator of the Oral History Center at the Idaho State Historical Society. Jennifer Eastman Attebery is State Architectural Historian. Brian Attebery directs the American Studies program at Idaho State University. Jackie Day is Program Officer of the Association for the Humanities in Idaho.

Besides planning this book, the members gather each month and listen to papers and presentations on folklife topics ranging from log architecture to traditions among the Venetian Jewry.

As to the book itself, this reader contains a meld of new essays and previously published articles of recognized worth on the rather specific subject of Idaho folklife. Some are representative collections and descriptions of Idaho traditions, and some are interpretations. The essays have been organized into five groups, according to their general concern with or reflection of folklife. The categories are useful, but assuredly neither totally exhaustive nor mutually exclusive.

Folklife and Regionalism. Under this section are placed articles that discuss folk culture as an indicator of cultural regions as distinct from political or geographic regions. In these studies we find that regional culture does not stop at political or occupational boundaries, but rather denotes a shared experience as its common denominator. The diversity of the articles illustrates the variety of cultural expressions that can be used to delimit regions. Further, they point out that regions do not exist in isolation from one another; rather there are similarities and borrowing between them.

Folklife and Group Identity. The folk cultural expressions that are based on shared aspects of group experience are the basis of the essays in this section. To the folklorist, group expressions are one means by which items are classified, e.g., Swedish-American music. To the members of a group, traditions often become consciously maintained in an effort to promote group distinctiveness and solidarity. This latter behavior is especially evident in celebrations and festivals.

Folklife and Folk History. Folk cultural expressions cannot be divorced from the historical contexts in which they arise and are perpetuated. In each of the essays in this section, the authors discuss folk traditions that reflect particular historical circumstances and personages. In all cases, the historical context becomes a key element in determining the function and significance of the presented traditions.

Folklife and Change. As individuals must respond to changes in their lives and the world around them, so also do they alter the content, style, form, and function of their traditions. Folk expressions do not remain stagnant as long as they remain a viable part of peoples' lives. For this reason, there can never be an end to folk culture although some older forms may disappear as they become inappropriate to contemporary life. In the articles included in this section, we note changes in folk traditions caused by new or different life experiences, or as a result of encounters with other forms of cultural expression.

Folklife and Individual Style. Although the term "folklife" denotes a group or shared expression of culture, in almost all instances the performance of a tradition is effected by individuals within a group. For this reason, it is impossible to grasp the significance of folk culture without looking at its carriers and performers. Upon doing so, the folklorist necessarily enters into the realms of sociology and psychology. The essays in this section emphasize the carriers of traditions and how their unique personalities and life experiences shape their particular forms of expression.

It has been the consistent aim of the Idaho Folklife Associates to secure materials appropriate for the use of folklore students at the college level and for teachers of history and English at the secondary level. Additionally, the inquisitive general reader may find in this book certain of those insights that help make life richer and fuller. Each essay is preceded by a brief headnote placing the material in its proper perspective.

Earlier it was claimed that the elements collected, analyzed, and interpreted by students of folklife share certain characteristics. Prominent among these are the following:

(1) The elements are transmitted in an oral, customary, and imitative mode, not in a formal textbook or media dominated mode.

(2) This method of transmission creates variant forms of the elements involved.

(3) The elements are shared by and within a group.

Among the items included under these criteria are jokes (today's form of the folktale), dandling rhymes, weather signs, and the "proper" method of cutting up a fryer. Each item is transmitted — shared — laterally or horizontally by contemporaries within a group, or vertically from, let us say, a grandmother to her daughter who shares the techniques with *her* daughter. Thus the elements of folklife studies are, in Barre Toelken's formidable phrase, dynamically variable in time and space. *Variable* hardly needs clarification; in the nature of the process of transmission some details are likely to be altered, either accidentally or deliberately through the function of the personality of the vector: "My grandmother used to use cream of tartar in vinegar pies but I use. . . ."

Dynamism, however, is a bit more complex. In the first place, the term refers to the context of personal relationships within which folklore and material traditions are shared. It is a living, vital, changing (dynamic as opposed to static) context. In the second place, the term refers to the fact that new life and vitality are somehow grafted upon the items each time they are filtered through a new vector. How many ways are there of telling a good joke, of carving a willow whistle? Some may be better than others; that is, some ways work better than others, and the variants that are dull, inept, or unworkable disappear in the creative evolution of the item of folklore or material tradition. Many adults can recall that as children they were very concerned with the *right* way to do something, and they may observe this same concern in their own children, whether the problem is the making of a paper airplane or the pronunciation of *creek*. This understanding of the elements that are dynamically variable removes the anxiety of always doing things the *right* way and enhances our appreciation of that component of life which we are told is necessary for spice — variety.

As to why folklife should be studied, there are many reasons. If we are to understand the literature, the history, the philosophy of another people in another time, how can we do so without taking into account the beliefs, the traditions, the legends — the world view, in short — upon which the literature is based and from which the history and philosophy proceed? The same

may be said for the study of any group of our own time, for folklore is not always of the past.

Even within our own region, there are unexpected differences in cultural assumptions. For instance, contemporary studies of custom and tradition — at the very heart of folklife — tell us that eye contact is not always appropriate. With some folk groups living within our state, respect and deference, not dishonesty, are manifest in downcast eyes. We note also that when admiration for a Chicano child in a local supermarket is spoken — "What a cute baby!" — the admirer must touch the baby with the hands in order that the child will not sicken and die because of the *mal ojo*, the evil eye. Unless the child is touched, the unexpressed desire to fondle and momentarily appropriate the child will grow within the admirer until the child senses the unrelieved desire and begins to languish, suspended between the natural love of his parents and the natural but unrelieved admiration of the outsider.

Personal satisfaction, insight, and pleasure emerge from knowing things or seeing connections unperceived before. Included here is the personal satisfaction of sensing continuity in the face of technologically inspired discontinuity as, for instance, a family raises, processes, and preserves in traditional ways its own meat and produce. Thus, folklife studies may show how closely we are related to those shadowy ancestors who, first standing erect, looked at a suddenly broader horizon.

Each of us is a better reader when each of us knows something of the folklore and material culture out of which a work of literature has emerged. Indeed, the person who reads Shakespeare or Hawthorne or Robert Frost or Vardis Fisher without knowing something about their beliefs and the world view associated with them is reading with less than half an eye and must find these writers quaint and puzzling. If the "New Critics" have done a disservice to the intelligent reader it is in their attempts to persuade the reader that the text supplies all that is necessary to a successful reading of the work. Nor is structuralism or semiotics or whatever critical theory replaces them a substitute for an understanding of the folklife matrix out of which the work emerged.

Without requiring an undue amount of the reader's time, this point can be illustrated by reference to an alternative reading of Robert Frost's lyric "Mending Wall." (I meant what I said about connections between literary studies and folklife studies.) The reading emerges from an item from the folklife of southwestern Idaho and eastern Oregon, and before the reader despairs of there really being a connection between the traditions of the West and those of the East a word of reassurance is appropriate.

The process of crossing the continent caused the appearance and reappearance of place names the settlers took with them — Springfield and Salem spread from Massachusetts to Ohio, Illinois, Missouri, and

Oregon. Traditions also traveled west with the covered wagons, the handcarts, and later railroad cars. One such tradition is expressed in the proverb "Good fences make good neighbors." How many times I have heard it expressed thus: "He's a good neighbor. He keeps his fences up and his gates shut." An Idaho informant was once asked how his neighbors attended to the problem of keeping a boundary fence in repair. That is, when a fence separates the property of two neighbors, how do they know their respective obligations to keeping up the fence? Without hesitation my ninety-year-old father replied as follows. At an agreed-upon time the neighbors meet at the middle of the common fence, shake hands across the fence, and then each man begins to repair the fence to his left. I later learned that in some communities the tradition is to repair the fence to the right—dynamic variation. Considering that the upkeep of fences was, along with the use of irrigation water, one of the two problems paramount in the West, what a superb way of encouraging neighborliness! When two neighbors have to meet and reestablish human contact through a handshake, reacting to a tradition carrying all the force of law, assuredly the opportunity for neighborliness to develop is present. A good fence is not an accident, it is an artifact created by neighbors. The proverb is almost reversible, for one could just as easily state that good neighbors make good fences. And yet it is not quite the same, for it is the artifact on the cultural landscape that has called the neighborly feeling into being. When I asked Dad if the tradition might really be a law, he replied that if it was he did not know about it. He and his neighbors did it simply because that was the way fences were repaired: tradition with the force of law.

Values deriving from a knowledge of folklife do not, of course, begin and end with literature. Those who are familiar with urban legends recognize as old friends and consequently put in perspective some of the materials reported as fact in the popular press: stories about cement trucks unloading into parked cars, a dentist who drills a loathsome creature out of an aching tooth, a woman bitten by a black wasp hatched from an egg inside a Taiwanese fur coat as reported in the Idaho *Statesman*, and many more. (See Jan Brunvand's *The Vanishing Hitchhiker* for a readable and scholarly treatment of this genre of folklore.)

But the final value to be mentioned here refers to the satisfaction we experience when we finally know what to call something. Bird watchers and taxonomists will understand, and the *caveat* accompanying the naming process provided by folklife studies is applicable to all circumstances in which people are likely to believe that a name given to something is somehow real and essential instead of useful. So we begin with man's capacity or passion, or perhaps mania, to classify. This is partly a human response to that nature (external nature) which exists apart from man.

Among many, if not most—if not *all*—primitive peoples is the well-known belief that control or power over a thing resides in the name of the thing. That is, if you can name the thing, you have mastered an essential part of the thing: "Nimmy nimmy not/You're Tom Tit Tot." So we "name" a meadowlark and rest in a kind of contentment, for that bird is now ours and the apparent disorder of the universe becomes orderly, at least in a small way and at least for a short time. And if we can call the lark *Sturnella neglecta* and give it its *true* name, our power over it is that much greater.

It is quite true that we must label or name things, quite apart from our primitive lust for power over those things in nature that are not-us. The recognition of similar and dissimilar elements in our world is vital to our very survival. And all of this is well and good, provided that we remember that naming is useful rather than necessarily or absolutely true. When we identify a rural legend, an urban legend, a ballad, a memorate, a belief, a folktale, a myth, a worm fence, a buck and rail fence, a rock jack, an A derrick, a patchwork quilt, a fiddle tune, we are gaining the satisfaction that comes from seeing order where disorder was before and perhaps, in the primitive corners of our minds, appropriating the power residing in things outside us to which we can now give their proper names as provided by folklife studies.

This book, then, reflects a broad spectrum of the folklife of Idaho, primarily, but also of northern Utah and Nevada and eastern Oregon. Although the book is not an overt argument for regionalism, quite clearly a regional approach to understanding a culture underlies it. Ideas, attitudes, traditions, and other cultural phenomena are usually quite indifferent to the accidents of history and politics that created states. Thus the folk belief originating in an earlier time, firmly heeded by youthful observers and perhaps their elders, about the worth of a horse that turns completely over as he rolls on the ground after being unharnessed or unsaddled is widely diffused throughout the region represented by this book. In case the belief is unfamiliar, the horse that rolls completely over is a better horse and thus worth more than the one which does not. Questions of the circulation of other beliefs within the state and region need to be answered. Let this introduction conclude with a few examples from the interesting world of folklife studies.

Another belief about horses needs to be studied and variants compared with respect to regional distribution. This belief was collected by folklore student Mildred Fisher in the summer of 1974 from informant Debbie Baker in Filer, Idaho: "Water goes to sleep sometimes. It makes no noise. If a horse drank sleeping water, he would die. That is why a horse always blows before drinking at night, to wake the water."

Does the reader know how to tell whether his grandmother (sweetheart, senator—any noun can be substituted) loves him? The answer comes by burning a wooden match completely from end to end, shifting fingers from the unburned portion to the sometimes still hot end, insulating the fingers with saliva, if necessary. If the burnt match stick does not break, your grandmother loves you. And have you ever played a hand game as a child when it was too cold or too wet to play outside, taught you by your aunt—"Johnny pick it up" or "Let the puppy drink"? And have you ever heard your mother look out at a spring day and say "March winds and April sun/Make linens white and ladies dun"? Or, "You kids quit messin' and gommin' and tearin' up Jack!"?

In this book the reader will find essays touching upon dialect, the Three Nephites, traditional singing and . . . but there is no need to reproduce the table of contents. It is an attempt to show that the enterprise called folklife studies is alive in Idaho, that the local and specific is a road to understanding culture broadly conceived, and that the study of folklore and material culture, like charity, may well begin at home.

The College of Idaho—1983

Folklife and Regionalism

Hay Derricks of the Great Basin and Upper Snake River Valley
Austin E. Fife and James M. Fife

A Lexical Survey of the Snake River Region
Joan H. Hall

Finnish Log Homestead Buildings in Long Valley
Alice Koskela

Folk Song Studies in Idaho
Jan Harold Brunvand

The Montgomery House: Adobe in Idaho's Folk Architecture
Jennifer Eastman Attebery, Kenneth J. Swanson,
Joe Toluse, and Frederick L. Walters

Hay Derricks of the Great Basin and Upper Snake River Valley

AUSTIN E. FIFE AND JAMES M. FIFE

When folklorists turn to the study of material artifacts and regionalism, their interests and those of the cultural geographer overlap. A cultural geographer's primary interest is the regionalization of culture that results in a distinctive cultural landscape of house types, barns, transportation systems, and structures like the hay derrick. The methodology followed by Austin and James Fife in this article is that of the cultural geographer: they identify different types of derricks and map their locations on a transect through the chosen study area. The resulting distribution of derrick types suggests the regionalization and routes of diffusion of this artifact.

Cultural geographer Fred Kniffen first recognized the importance of folk artifacts to the study of United States geography. His article "Folk Housing: Key to Diffusion," Annals of the Association of American Geographers (1965) was a seminal study; Henry Glassie's Pattern in the Material Folk Culture of the Eastern United States (1968) carries Kniffen's methodology clearly into the folklore camp and applies it to such artifacts as banjos, toys, foods, and canoes in addition to folk houses.

Austin Fife, an Idaho-born folklorist, has devoted his career as professor of English at Utah State University to the study of Mormon and Great Basin folklore. In most of his work he has collaborated with Alta Fife. The present essay was done with his brother and fishing partner, James M. Fife, formerly employed by the United States Department of Agriculture as a chemist. Austin is now retired and lives in Logan, Utah; James is also retired and lives in Salinas, California.

This article is reprinted with permission from Western Folklore, where it originally appeared in vol. 7 (1948): 225–39, and vol. 10 (1951): 320–22.

The hay derrick is one of the few pieces of farm equipment in the irrigated sections of the Rocky Mountain area that are almost universally homemade.[1] This fact gives it significance as an item of the folklore of material culture, along with fences of native materials, noncommercial gates and gate locks, and even patchwork quilts. In a recent automobile trip that carried the authors over Highway US 91 and parts of US 191 and US 89 from Bunkerville, Nevada, to Yellowstone National Park—a distance of about a thousand miles—only two commercial stackers were observed among at least fifteen hundred derricks of home construction.

From the farmer's first need of a hay derrick to its completion and initial use, the process is one of folk design and workmanship, without recourse to specialists, published designs, or extracommunity labor. Using the derrick of a neighbor as a model, the farmer draws up his specifications, makes his inventory of necessary materials, and then pays recurrent visits to the model during the process of construction. With teams and the running gear of a wagon or with a truck, he goes to neighboring forests at a season when work with the soil is not pressing, to cut and trim suitable

logs and to bring them to the farmyard where the derrick is actually built. He may seek the help of a local smith to shape the few metal parts that are necessary, but except for this a farmer's derrick is usually the work of his own hands. He takes the pride of a craftsman in the proper performance of the completed stacker, even though the builder's claim to creative workmanship consists only in an unfailing fidelity to his model.

In earlier days, when the first derricks were built, the production of alfalfa was so limited that the entire crop was stacked preferably within the barnyard, where it was easily accessible for winter feeding to milk cows and other livestock. This condition still obtains in most farming communities south of the Utah Valley. The derrick that is required under such farming conditions is quite simple, since it need not be mobile.

With increased acreage of alfalfa, however, a number of problems were encountered. Only a small portion of the yield was needed for the animals kept permanently on the farm. The remainder could more practicably be stacked in the field adjacent to the ground that produced it and there be fed to range cattle which were brought down to the irrigated ranches to be wintered. Under these conditions there was an urgent need for derricks that could be moved with relative ease so that several stacks might be built with the same derrick. The same factors provided an incentive for the farmers to put up their hay with more speed and efficiency. The four tines of the Jackson fork (Figure 2), which was used to carry the hay from load to stack, were increased to six, and this, in turn, necessitated the use of a derrick that could support a greater load. So it is that in the Great Basin and upper Snake River Valley there are hay derricks of most varied design and efficiency, reflecting the alfalfa production of a particular community, or the acreage of alfalfa of particular farms, or representing survivals of earlier conditions. There is an evident lag in some localities between the economic need and the tool that is currently used.

While these facts go a long way to explain why different types of derricks are used in the area which is the subject of this study,[2] they do not explain all the peculiar circumstances under which certain derrick types appear in each valley. The valleys of the Great Basin are isolated by miles of dry land or mountain ranges. This fact would be of no interest in explaining the geographic distribution of quilt patterns, for example, since these are easily carried from one valley to another in complete defiance of natural barriers. But with the hay derrick it is a different matter. The bulk and relative immobility of this piece of farm machinery are such that it is rarely, if ever, transported for more than a few miles. A farmer may take his livestock, wagon, plow, and miscellaneous other farm machinery and settle in another valley, but most certainly he will leave his hay derrick with the permanent installations of his former home. Upon arriving at his new farm he will build another derrick either like his former one, depending upon his memory for the details of construction, or one of a new type, copying a local model the design and operating principle of which may differ from the derrick to which he had been accustomed.

Nearly all the irrigated valleys between Bunkerville, Nevada, and Salt Lake City are narrow and are separated from each other by uncultivated areas that make observations from the highway highly reliable. More than 80 percent of all the derricks in the valleys touched by the highway were counted, except in the Utah and Salt Lake valleys and in the restricted area around St. George, Utah, which we were forced to pass through in darkness. This fact, we believe, gives greater value to the distribution chart in Figure 12 and to our conclusions regarding the generic development of derrick types.

Hay derricks of the alfalfa-growing districts of the Great Basin and upper Snake River Valley (from Pocatello, Idaho, to Yellowstone National Park) use the Jackson fork (Figure 2) to carry the hay from load to stack. This fork grasps a sixth to an eighth of a wagonload at a time. It is carried from load to stack by a cable which travels over pulleys at appropriate points on the derrick and is pulled by a single horse, a team,

or a tractor. When the hay has been raised to a point above the place on the stack where the farmer wants it dumped, the fork is tripped and the hay falls on the stack. Then the derrick horse, team, or tractor is backed up while the hayrack teamster uses the trip rope to pull the empty fork back to his load.

Any efficient derrick must carry the loaded Jackson fork in a natural arc over the stack so that, with only a minimum of redistribution by hand, the hay forms a straight and solid butt.[3] This is accomplished by varied details of construction which take advantage of a mobile boom anchored to a mast in such a way that it tends to swing from any position to which it is pulled, back to a point over the center of the butt. Local designers have worked out ingenious devices to achieve this result and, at the same time, to construct a derrick sturdy enough to support any load.

Most derricks of recent construction have a base sufficiently broad and sturdy to stabilize the weight of the entire superstructure plus a loaded Jackson fork. Not being permanently anchored to the ground, they can be dragged by a tractor or a sturdy team the short distance required to build a new butt or even to build another stack a few hundred yards distant. In areas or on ranches where alfalfa is produced on a large scale, the base structure is sufficiently sturdy to permit moving the derrick an appreciable distance.

We have found six basic types, with from one to four subtypes of each. Our classification identifies derrick types with regard to both their origins and the details of structural or operating principle. We have excluded devices for hoisting hay into a barn or permanent shelter, and the "beaverslide" (also of folk construction), which is so popular wherever timothy and other grasses are produced for fodder. The "beaverslide" is rarely seen in this area.

DERRICK TYPES

Type 1. The simplest derrick which has come to our attention consists of a single upright mast that is planted in the ground and anchored by three or more cables in a slanting position so that its apex is nearly over the center of the butt. A cable which travels through pulleys at the top and bottom of this mast permits the farmer to drag the hay from the load to a fixed position on the stack, whence it is redistributed by hand. Although we saw no derricks of this type, we have been told that such derricks were once used in the vicinity of St. George and in the Utah Valley around Provo. We conjecture that they may also have been used elsewhere when the production of alfalfa was just getting under way.

Type 2 (Figure 2). Structure and function. Derricks of Type 2 are anchored in the same way as the single vertical mast of Type 1. But varying types of booms are suspended on the vertical mast so that the loaded Jack-

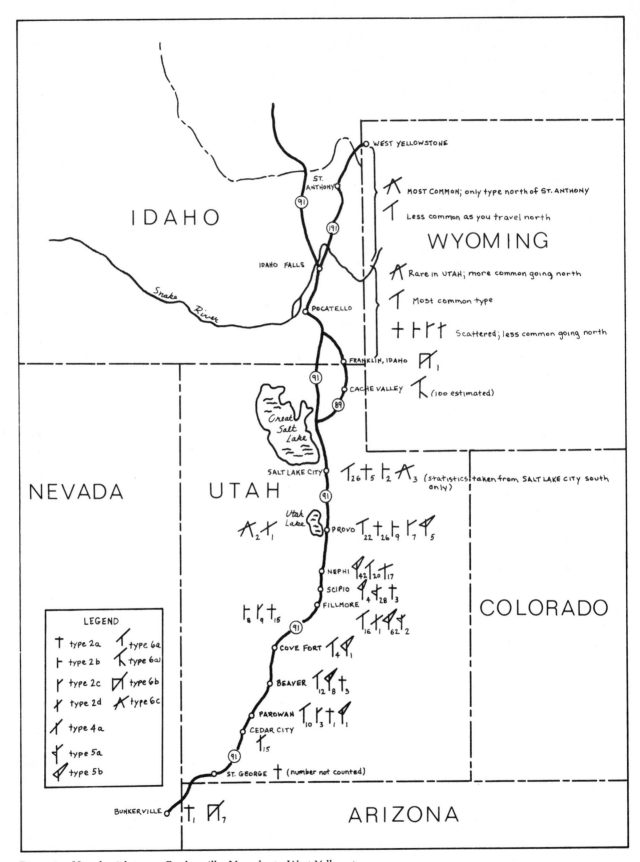

Figure 1.   Hay derrick types, Bunkerville, Nevada, to West Yellowstone

son fork may swing in a suitable arc over the stack and drop the hay at any desired point thereon. Both Subtypes b and c have a single-directional boom and differ only in the angle the boom forms with the mast: a right angle in Subtype b; a 45° to 60° angle in Subtype c. In derricks of Type 2 the boom is suspended so that it will hang naturally over the center of the stack. It is pulled by the load teamster away from this position in order to load the Jackson fork, but, as the hay rises from the load, the boom swings around once more to its natural position.

Subtype d resembles c in every detail except that the single-directional boom extends beyond the vertical mast for three or four feet and is fastened to it by a log chain. This slight difference may seem trivial, but may well have been the point of departure for the innovations which led to most of the modern derricks. The services of a blacksmith, needed to build the metal joint which attaches the booms of Subtypes b and c to the mast, are not required for Subtype d.

Some may think that there is overrefinement in these classifications of derricks of Type 2. Yet a careful examination of the distribution chart which accompanies this article (Figure 1) shows that specific communities adhere to a particular subtype. The uniformity of derrick type in most communities, even to the specific angle formed by the mast and boom, is even more striking than this chart indicates.

Even in derricks of Type 2, farmers began to make changes in the base structure in order to give the vertical mast more rigidity and at the same time to decrease the number of cables required to anchor it. The addition of a lateral base (Type 2c), with braces some ten feet up the mast, decreased the number of supporting cables from three (or even four) to two, and at the same time reinforced the mast.

Distribution of Type 2. Derricks of Type 2 appear in nearly all the irrigated valleys along Highway US 91, from Bunkerville, Nevada, to Idaho Falls, Idaho, and on up the Snake River Valley along US 191 at least as far as Rexburg, Idaho. Of 417 derricks counted between Bunkerville and Salt Lake City, 108, or 26 percent, were of Type 2—a possible exception being made for the fact that derricks seen at a distance may have had the base structure that differentiates derricks of Type 3 from Type 2. However, of the many whose base structure was actually seen, only one was of Type 3. The most casual examination will reveal that Type 2 is characteristic of the area from Salt Lake City south. It is found practical today only where alfalfa is produced in relatively small quantities and is stacked in the barnyard for feeding to dairy cattle or other farm animals. Its use in the Snake River Valley diminishes as the acreage of alfalfa increases, and its present use on small farms represents the survival of stacking conditions that prevailed three to five decades ago.

A total of 55 derricks of Subtype 2a was observed, of which 26 were in the Utah Valley and 5 in the southern part of the Salt Lake Valley where counts were made.

Fifteen derricks of this subtype were observed in Millard County, and the remaining 9 appeared at scattered points from Scipio to Bunkerville.

From a distance it is frequently difficult to distinguish between Subtypes 2b, 2c, and 2d. However, the fact that we assemble our data on these types under a single heading should not be construed to mean that there is random local deviation from one of these types to another. The derricks which we observed at close range seemed to adhere somewhat rigorously to a particular subtype. In the irrigated area around Cedar City, for example, every one of 15 derricks observed was of Type 2d. In Beaver, 19 derricks of the 39 observed were of Type 2; of these, 3 were of Subtype a and the other 16 of Subtype c. Only in Millard County was there a random occurrence of most of the derricks of Type 2: here 15 of Subtype a were observed, and 17 of Subtypes b, c, and d.

Type 3 (Figure 2). We did not positively identify a single derrick of Type 3 during the trip which led to the preparation of this article. It differs from Type 2 in having a triangular base which is frequently concealed from view. The triangular base is of the greatest importance, since it both eliminates the use of costly cables for anchoring and gives the derrick the mobility needed to erect more than one stack. A log which transects the triangle of the base extends well beyond the apex. When the derrick is in operation this base log is anchored to the ground with a chain and bar and is sometimes loaded with boulders to counterbalance the weight of the loaded fork on the extended boom. Braces reaching from each corner of the triangle support the mast about ten feet above its base.

The authors stacked hay with this type of derrick some three decades ago on their father's ranch at Idaho Falls, Idaho, where it was then used to the near exclusion of other types. It was entirely suitable to the needs of a farm where a moderate amount of alfalfa was produced. It was sturdy enough to support any load of cured alfalfa that the earlier four-tined Jackson fork would carry, but the six-tined Jackson fork, with an increased capacity, easily tipped over the derrick. Construction of more efficient derricks apparently led to the near abandonment of this type, though we are certain that a careful search might bring to light some examples.

Type 4 (Figure 2). Early experiments with derricks capable of being moved led to the use of a rectangular base with the vertical mast supported in its center. Consequently, the mast was six to eight feet away from the stack, and it became necessary to lengthen the boom correspondingly in order to bring the loaded fork over the center of the stack. In derricks of Type 4, the one-directional boom of Type 2d was replaced by a long cross boom suspended on the vertical mast with a log chain to the base of the mast, exactly opposite the center of the stack. When the fork is not loaded it is easy for the teamster, by pulling on the trip rope, to

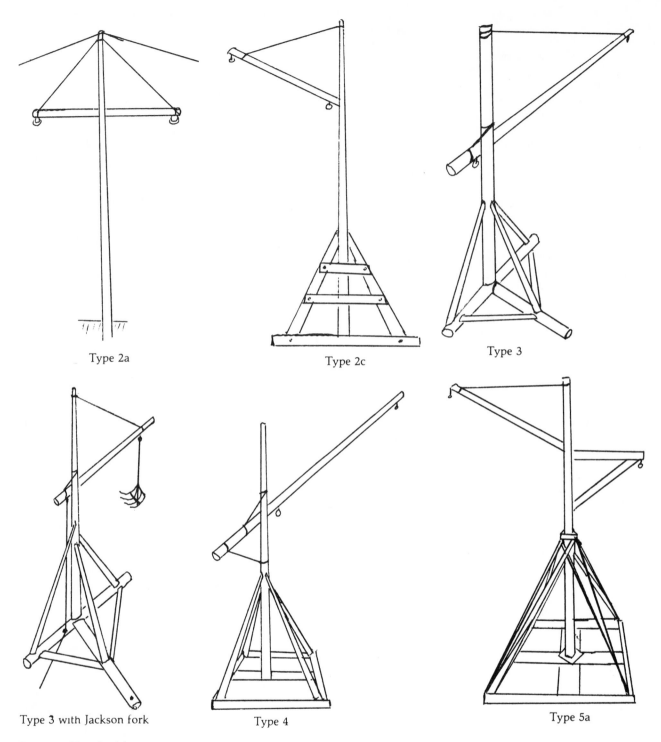

Type 2a

Type 2c

Type 3

Type 3 with Jackson fork

Type 4

Type 5a

Figure 2. Hay derrick types

pull the tip of the boom against the wrapping action of this chain around the mast, back over his loaded hay-rack. But once the fork is loaded, the chain from the diagonal boom to the base of the mast assumes its maximum length, thus pulling the fork to a position over the center of the stack.

We observed a total of 35 derricks of Type 4, all

within the relatively narrow area between Beaver on the south and the Utah Valley on the north. In the valley of Beaver, 41 percent, and in the valley around Nephi, every derrick was of this type.

Type 5 (Figures 2 and 3). Type 5 is a derrick of complex design in which the entire vertical mast and

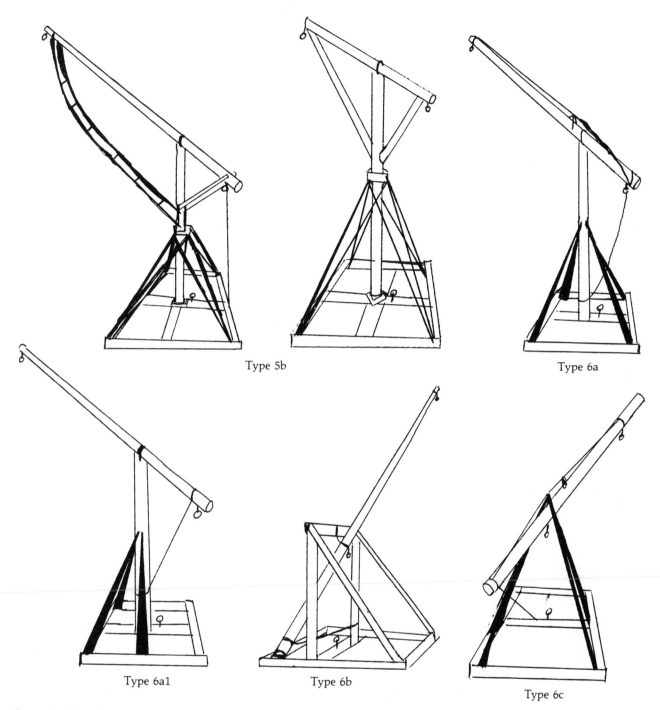

Type 5b

Type 6a

Type 6a1

Type 6b

Type 6c

Figure 3. Hay derrick types

attached booms rotate on the axis formed by the mast. A heavily braced rectangular base is shaped to a pyramidal top which forms or supports a collar in which the mast turns. Subtypes a and b are readily recognizable by the 45° angle boom with counterset triangle, or asymmetrical triangle formed by the booms fixed to the upper portion of the rotating mast.

This derrick requires a minimum of extracommunity materials; the farmer could produce everything but the three pulleys and one cable. It seems clearly to be limited to central Utah, from Parowan to the Utah Valley. Of 153 derricks noted of this type, all but 9 were observed on what appeared to be one large ranch, isolated in the northern part of the Utah Valley. It is also of interest that Subtype b predominated in Millard and Nephi, while 28 of 35 derricks in the Scipio Valley, which lies between Nephi and Millard, were of Subtype a. Only 30 derricks of Subtype a were observed: 2 in Millard, and the others in the one community of Scipio.

Type 6 (Figure 2). The derricks of Type 6 represent the most modern types — the most efficient, the most mobile, and the best suited to the requirements of alfalfa production on a large scale. Like the derricks of Type 4, they have a long diagonal boom supported on a rectangular base.

Subtype a (Figure 3) is characterized by a short, stable, vertical mast with a long diagonal boom balanced upon it. It resembles Type 4 except that the boom is attached directly on top of a short mast instead of being suspended with a log chain halfway up a tall one. In earlier models the diagonal boom was attached to the vertical one by a clevis made from the end of a wagon axle, a bolt, and a U-shaped piece of iron shaped locally. Modern types have a commercially built ball-and-socket joint. The only significant variations in design are symmetrical or counterthrust bracings in the base structure. Derricks of Type 2 from Salt Lake City south usually had a symmetrical base structure. In Cache Valley, in northern Utah, every derrick observed (estimated to be more than a hundred), except one commercial type and one old and deserted stacker of Type 6b, had the counterthrust bracing. Through the upper Snake River Valley as far as Idaho Falls, Type 6a was the most common stacker: the symmetrical-type base seems to be favored there, though some of the stackers have asymmetrical bracing.

Of the 417 derricks observed between Bunkerville, Nevada, and Salt Lake City, 110 — slightly more than 26 percent — were of Type 6a. They appeared with ever-increasing frequency from Parowan, on the south, to Cache Valley (north of Salt Lake), except in the valley of Scipio, where Type 5a was almost universal. In the isolated community of Cove Fort, 4 out of 5 derricks were of this type; in the Salt Lake Valley, 26 out of 36 derricks were of Type 6a.

In function, Subtypes b and c (Figure 3) are quite like Subtype a; in structural design and general appearance they are wholly different. There is no vertical mast. A long diagonal boom is suspended with a log chain from an overhead beam (b), or from the apex of a pyramidal base (c). Subtype b is now almost obsolete, although 7 such subtypes were observed in Bunkerville, Nevada, and one in Franklin, Idaho. Derricks intermediary between Subtypes b and c were observed in the upper Snake River Valley. They consisted of either a truncated pyramidal or a truly pyramidal base with a short horizontal cross beam below its apex.

The distribution of derricks of Type 6 is of interest. Subtype a was observed from Parowan, on the south, to a point about fifty miles north of Idaho Falls, on the north. Hence, its zone seems to coincide entirely with that of derricks of Type 2. Subtype c, on the other hand, seems limited to the upper Snake River Valley

and the Great Basin only as far south as the Utah Valley. Only 5 specimens were observed south of Salt Lake City. However, as one travels north from Salt Lake it becomes more and more common, and, from about fifty miles north of Idaho Falls to West Yellowstone, it seems to be used to the exclusion of all other types.

A COMPARISON OF DERRICK TYPES WITH RESPECT TO ECONOMY OF CONSTRUCTION AND EFFICIENCY OF OPERATION

It seems sage to assume that, by and large, a farmer has been willing to use the simplest and cheapest derrick which adequately meets the requirements of his ranch. At the same time, he has been dependent on the available materials and the traditional derrick types with which he was familiar. If greater hay production forced him to construct a more intricate and more efficient derrick, he knew the added effort meant saving time and toil at haying season.

Hence, derricks of Type 2 continued to serve the needs of all the farmers of the Great Basin and upper Snake River Valley until increased production necessitated the building of more derricks or the development of mobile ones. Derricks of Type 2 require a minimum of two poles, three pulleys, and four cables. In a more sturdy form they require five poles, three pulleys, and three cables. The first experiments in the line of truly mobile derricks must have been the development of Type 3, which requires nine poles, one log chain, three pulleys, and only one cable. Type 4 achieved great sturdiness by the use of a rectangular base, a total of eleven or twelve poles, the usual three pulleys, one cable, and one log chain.

Most attempts to add a base structure to derricks of Type 1, so that they could be moved, were doomed to failure. The tall, fixed mast raised the center of gravity to such a height that the derrick was easily tipped over, especially when the six-tined fork came into use. The triangular base, requiring the location of the mast on one side of the triangle, produced a derrick that would stand alone. Yet this was still so unstable that it had to be anchored to the ground when excessive weight was put on the tip of the boom. The attempt to make derricks of Type 2 stable and mobile with a rectangular base was also doomed to failure because the mast was so far from the stack that even a boom of maximum length could not carry the loaded Jackson fork to the far side.

Stackers of Type 6 solved the problem of mobility by the use of a long diagonal boom. This reached the far side of a stack, even with a rectangular base. At the same time it lowered the center of gravity while the derrick was being moved, since releasing the cable which anchors the butt of the boom to the mast brings its tip to the ground. This development also simplified threading and repair of cables and pulleys.

These modern stackers have achieved the maximum in efficiency of operation and, at the same time, have

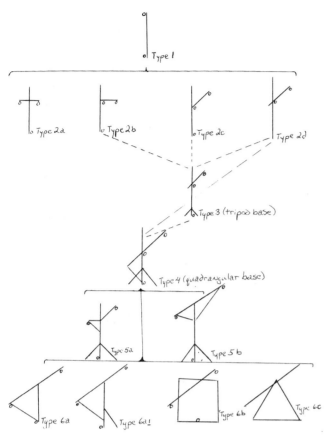

Figure 4. The generic development of hay derrick types of the Great Basin and upper Snake River Valleys.

eliminated the use of costly materials from extracommunity sources. Type 6a requires only a log chain and a commercially built ball-and-socket joint (to join the diagonal boom to the vertical mast) in addition to the usual three pulleys and a cable. Type 6c is even less dependent upon industry, since no ball-and-socket joint is required.

Stackers of Type 5, like those of Type 6, seem to have been developed by a need for mobility. But the problem was solved with such intricate construction — the base structure alone requires up to sixteen poles — that two teams are probably required to drag this sturdy and heavy derrick any distance. This stacker does, however, have two advantages: it requires fewer materials from outside the community than any other derrick — only three pulleys and one cable — and it permits the construction of a tall stack with a very broad base, thus reducing the need for moving the stacker. It should be noted parenthetically that this derrick is used where alfalfa is produced on a relatively small scale.

CONCLUSIONS

The hay derrick is a typical item of the folklore of material culture of the irrigated areas in and on the slopes of the Rocky Mountains. It has a distinct

regional use. There is evidence showing a progressive development of types from a single upright and immobile mast to varied and intricate derricks corresponding to varying types of alfalfa production. The evolution of types seems to have taken place within the area in question and with very little dependency upon methods of folk construction employed in other areas or trades.

Derricks of Type 2 might have continued to satisfy every practical requirement had not the production of hay on a larger scale made it imperative either to build larger stacks or to build stacks in several different places on a given ranch. Faced with this problem, the farmer had either to build more derricks or to redesign his old one to make it mobile. This he accomplished, at first in a somewhat unsatisfactory manner, by mounting it on a triangular base. But this derrick, having so high a center of gravity and a heavy vertical mast, was easily tipped over. Experimentation with a rectangular base produced a more mobile derrick, but its boom did not reach far enough over the stack. Experimentation with longer booms finally developed a long, diagonal cross boom, as in Type 4, which is clearly a transitional form between derricks of Type 2 and those of Types 5 and 6. When a method was discovered to mount the diagonal boom on top of a short mast, Type 6a was created, and there were no subsequent developments in the basic design beyond the replacement of a primitive clevis by a ball-and-socket joint and the innovation of a asymmetrical bracing in counterthrust to the weight of the diagonal boom.

The designers of Type 6b derricks solved the problem of mobility by using an identical rectangular base and suspending the diagonal boom from an overhead beam (Type 6) instead of balancing it upon a vertical mast. However, difficulty was encountered in securing adequate rigidity until the brilliant conception of a pyramidal base was elaborated. The result (Type 6c) is a derrick which is the most effective combination of rugged construction and mobility of any derrick type which has come to our observation. At the same time it requires fewer extracommunity materials than any other widely distributed type.

More difficulties are encountered in explaining the origin of derricks of Type 5. While the concept of a vertical rotating mast is ingenious, it necessitated the development of a base structure so unwieldy that mobility, the very goal of the innovation, was sacrificed. That the practicability of this type is questionable is shown by its limited use.

We may ask to what extent the genesis of the derrick types of the Great Basin and upper Snake River Valley, as summarized above, took place in the area itself. That the early settlers of this area had used hay derricks prior to pioneering the Rocky Mountain West seems doubtful, since the use of any kind of stacker must have awaited the discovery that, in a climate so cold in winter and so dry, hay may be properly stored without a permanent shelter. The existence in the area of der-

ricks ranging from one immobile upright mast capable
of dropping the hay at a single point on the stack to
varying mobile derricks capable of swinging the hay to
any point on a butt of appreciable dimensions suggests
that we have here a folk art created to satisfy the needs
of alfalfa production in the irrigated areas of the north-
western United States. It depended almost wholly upon
the use of native materials and skill and responded to
the changing economic needs of the irrigation farmer,
who had solved his problem so well that the combined
genius of capital and technology have been able to do
no better.

ADDENDUM
Reprinted with permission from Western Folklore,
X (1951): 320–22, "Hay Derricks," by Austin E. Fife.

Interest has persisted in my communication on the
"Hay Derricks of the Great Basin and Upper Snake
River Valley" (*Western Folklore*, VII, 225–39) to the
extent that I have been stimulated to gather further
data, the result of which has been such that in some
particulars I have been able to confirm my hypotheses,
in others, I have been forced to revise them. The Division of Farm Machinery of the United States Department of Agriculture together with the agricultural
engineering departments of several schools of agriculture have all published materials on hay stackers and
even speculated a little upon the origin and dissemination of the various types.[4] A number of patents have
been issued for various hay-stacking devices since as
early as 1858, though, significantly, none of them to inventors residing west of the Mississippi. The in-
vestigator who compiled this data concluded, "Whether
or not any of the machines patented were ever manufactured commercially, or ever came into general use is
unknown."[5]

Some have wondered to what extent the stackers
mentioned in my article are of authentic "folk" development. In order to satisfy myself on this point I have
addressed inquiries to a number of competent agricultural engineers both of the state colleges and of the U.S.
Department of Agriculture.[6] Without exception, I was
advised that these institutions had never undertaken
any developmental work along this line, having limited
their work to the preparation and dissemination of
information on the construction of types already in
common use. They further confirm my belief that the
derricks described in my article have never been designed, manufactured, or sold by nationally known implement companies.

> Perhaps the stacker most frequently mentioned . . . has
> been the so-called "Mormon stacker," or some variation
> thereof. It has been stated that this stacker has been in use
> in some sections over fifty years. This is particularly true
> of Utah, although there they are more apt to be referred to
> as hay derricks, swing derricks, or hay stackers. . . . No

inventor has been named for any of the stackers mentioned by our correspondents, nor has any definite date
for the invention of any of this equipment been given, but
estimates which are considered quite reliable state that
these derricks have been known and used in sections of
Utah over fifty years. . . . One correspondent from northern Utah asserts . . . that actual inventors are unknown
—"knowledge passed from one farm to another."[7]

Actually the term "Mormon derrick" is a misnomer
since it refers not to one particular type, but to a group
of perhaps fifteen stackers which differ essentially from
each other, although all of them have the one point in
common that the hay is hoisted by means of pulleys
and a cable attached to frames of widely differing structure and function.

Data have come to me which make it necessary to
revise significantly the table of generic development.
(See Figure 4 of my original article.) We have observed
an occasional primitive stacker in Utah, Montana, and
near Gilmore, California, which must stand as a kind
of prototype along with the single-pole stacker of our
Type 1. It consists of an A-shaped frame[8] or of two vertical poles with a horizontal pole between them, the
whole anchored by guy wires as was the single-pole
stacker which we originally took to be the point of
departure for all our types. A pulley located in the center of the horizontal pole made it possible to drag hay
up the side of a stack and let it fall at a point directly
under the pulley.

It is also evident that, early in the evolution of the
"Mormon derrick," a tripod stacker was developed
similar to our Type 6c but having no boom. I have not
observed this derrick in the region of my inquiry, but
from descriptions of it in agricultural engineering literature[9] I am convinced that it must still appear in this
region and that formerly it may well have been common. Its absence today could easily be explained by the
fact that a boom was added to the older derricks once
this efficient innovation was discovered.

We also feel obliged to add a statement about the
matter of folk construction and development. While it
is probably true that most of the earlier derricks were
constructed by the farmers themselves, with evolution
to more efficient and somewhat more complicated
types, there has been a tendency to employ the services
of a local craftsman who specializes in the art of derrick
making as a "sideline." This explains the marked uniformity of types in given communities.

Finally, we wish to note the recent intrusion from
other areas of two stacker types into the region of our
investigation: the "beaverslide" and the "overshot."[10]
These types, seemingly of "folk" origin and development also, do not originate in Mormonia, but their efficiency seems to be such that they may in time replace
the "Mormon" family.

Notes

1. The illustrations of the particular derrick types were made by Gordon Tucker, a student at Occidental College, from photographs by the authors.

2. It might be pointed out that our observations were carried out along the principal highways that transect the area of primary Mormon acculturation from its southern to its northern boundaries.

3. Even the best-constructed derricks will swing the hay easily to an area of restricted diameter. A stack of this size is called a *butt*. Some derricks may be moved so that another butt of similar dimensions may be built adjacent to the first one. A stack may consist of from one to several such butts (sometimes called "bents") built end to end and carefully joined together and topped to prevent moisture from getting between them.

4. W. R. Humphries and R. B. Gray, *Partial History of Haying Equipment*, U.S. Department of Agriculture, Agricultural Research Administration, Bureau of Plant Industry, Soils and Agricultural Engineering, Division of Farm Machinery, Information Series No. 74 (Beltsville, Maryland, 1949), pp. 37–45; L. A. Reynoldson, *Hay Stackers and Their Use*, U.S. Department of Agriculture, Farmers Bulletin No. 1615 (Washington, D.C., 1929); and Clyde Walker and Arnold Ebert, *A Boom-Type Stacker*, Oregon State College Extension Circular 480 (Corvallis, 1946). Blueprints of two types of "Mormon stackers" are supplied by the U.S. Department of Agriculture, Bureau of Public Roads, Division of Agricultural

Engineering. Serial No. 2011 of December 31, 1924, and No. 2076 of March 12, 1925.

5. Humphries and Gray, p. 37.

6. Letters to the author as follows: J. B. Rodgers, Head, Agricultural Engineering Department, Oregon State College, Corvallis, Oregon, September 27, 1949. Roy Bainer, Chairman, Division of Agricultural Engineering, University of California, Davis, California, October 25, 1949. B. L. Embry, Assistant Professor in Agricultural Engineering, Utah State Agricultural College, Logan, Utah. O. W. Monson, Head, Agricultural Engineering Department, Montana State College, Bozeman, Montana, October 31, 1949. J. Roberts, Chairman, Agricultural Engineering, the State College of Washington, Pullman, Washington, November 15, 1949. E. M. Dieffenbach, Agricultural Engineer, U.S. Department of Agriculture, Agricultural Research Administration, Beltsville, Maryland, December 2, 1949. J. Clayton Russell, Assistant Extension Agricultural Engineer, State College Station, Fargo, North Dakota.

7. Humphries and Gray, p. 38.

8. Reynolds, p. 38.

9. Ibid., pp. 20–21.

10. The "beaverslide" and "overshot" stackers are described by F. E. Price and W. L. Briebeler in Extension Circulars Nos. 403 and 404 of the Federal Cooperative Extension Service, Oregon State College, Corvallis (Oregon), both of April, 1943.

A Lexical Survey of the Snake River Region

Joan H. Hall

The study of dialects has developed for the most part independently of folklore scholarship, and yet the two are closely related. They share methodology—both use interviews, transcriptions, comparison, and mapping—and they have a common origin in nineteenth-century studies of language and myth: the brothers Grimm are known not only for their collection of folktales but also for the formulation of one of the fundamental laws of language change. In this country, research in dialects has culminated in two monumental projects. One, a geographical analysis of American speech, has produced the Linguistic Atlas of New England *(1939–43) edited by Hans Kurath and other regional atlases. The other, the nearly completed* Dictionary of American Regional English *(or DARE), under the direction of Frederic G. Cassidy, will be an invaluable aid to folklorists interested in regional culture and in the words and phrases that make up folk narrative. Hall's work is the most detailed study to date of Idaho speech.*

Having lived in Ohio, California, Idaho, Georgia, Oregon, Maine, and Wisconsin, Joan Hall has firsthand acquaintance with numerous American dialects. That background is particularly useful in her position as Associate Editor of the Dictionary of American Regional English.

*D*iversity in our language is one thing Westerners seldom fail to notice as we travel in other parts of the country. We are struck by such features as the New Englander's lack of an *r* sound in such words as *fire*, *charge*, *pattern*, or the presence of one in such words as *idea* or *meadow*; we notice that some New Yorkers (and other Northeasterners) make *this thing* sound like *dis ting*; we listen to an eastern Virginian say *about the house* and hear something like *aboot the hoose*; in Wisconsin we're puzzled by phrases such as "Will you borrow me five dollars?"; and in the Southwest we hear people say *arroyo* for what we would call a gully. It feels good to get back home where we understand others and they understand us! But what about visitors to our part of the country? Do they find "strange" words or pronunciations in the speech of the Pacific Northwest? Are people of the Snake River Region recognizable by the way they talk? Two regional language surveys and one nationwide study of regional English are particularly useful in answering these questions.

The first, a lexical survey of the Pacific Northwest, was begun in the late 1940s by Carroll Reed and Henry Person, then both of the University of Washington. The study was designed to trace regional language patterns within the Northwest, and to compare them to those in California and in other parts of the West as other investigations were completed. The second, drawing on the results of the first, was a survey of the Snake River Region (SRR) carried out by my students at The College of Idaho in 1971 and 1973. In writing

about the Pacific Northwest study, Reed had come to several conclusions about usage in the SRR; some of those statements were tested and subsequently corroborated by the SRR survey, and other areas were investigated. The third project, one of vastly greater scope, is the *Dictionary of American Regional English (DARE)*, which has surveyed native speakers in over a thousand communities across the country and provides a larger context into which the other studies fit. Because *DARE* information provides nationwide coverage, it is useful to students of Western speech not only in confirming (or contradicting) results from the smaller studies, but in illustrating the broader patterns which affect the speech of the SRR and to which our region contributes.

Before looking closely at these three projects, it will be useful to take a look at the reasons for language variation and some of the ways in which it is studied.

So far we have talked about "language patterns" or "differences in speech," but have avoided the term *dialect*. The reason for this is simply that, for many people, *dialect* connotes backwoods' hollows, one-room schoolhouses, ungrammatical sentence structure, "funny" words and pronunciation, and just plain "bad" language. For those people it comes as something of a shock to learn that they too—along with everyone else—speak a dialect and that to do so is inevitable and nothing to be ashamed of. For a dialect is simply a particular variety of language, made up of features of pronunciation, vocabulary, grammar, and syntax, that is different in large or small degree from any other variety of the same language. A particular dialect may be spoken by a very large number of people over a wide geographic expanse, or by a relatively small group of people in a restricted geographic area. In addition, dialects within a geographic region can further vary as a result of other factors, such as educational and cultural background, economic or social status, ethnic heritage, or religious background. Such dialects are called social dialects, and often differ greatly in their prestige value within a given region.

While many factors contribute to the development and the maintenance or dissolution of regional speech varieties, some of the most important are: 1) time of settlement of a community or region, and origins of the settlers; 2) physical barriers, such as mountain ranges, vast deserts, and unfordable rivers or swamps that hinder communication with other communities and tend to encourage isolation; 3) political or commercial barriers that prevent easy interchange of goods and ideas; 4) influxes of people from other countries or regions of this country, and the timing of those inmigrations; (conversely, out-migrations of large segments of the population, such as young people seeking greater security or independence elsewhere, also affect the speech of a community). In the United States, all these factors have played parts in the development of our different dialects. The results are particularly noticeable on the East Coast, since settlement occurred there first at a time when physical barriers and technological development hindered communication among early cities. Similar features in the speech of New Englanders and Coastal Southerners, such as the lack of postvocalic r (an r sound following a vowel, as in car, near, door, sermon, mother), can be traced to the fact that early settlers in both of those areas came largely from southern rather than northern England. Early settlers of western Pennsylvania, Maryland, and western Virginia, on the other hand, not only came later, but came in large numbers from Scotland and northern England. They brought with them their home varieties of speech, one feature of which was a distinctly articulated postvocalic r; the result of this difference in origins of settlers remains with us today as one of the most easily recognized differences in American speech. The lack of easy communication among the earliest American cities meant that original differences in speech had the chance to become well established before being affected by competing forms from other settlements. Boston, New York, Philadelphia, and Charleston, for example, developed in relative isolation, having more contact with England than with one another. As time went on, however, and the population grew and commercial and social enterprises contributed to greater interchange among communities, exposure to other speech patterns increased. By about the mid-eighteenth century, when settlements began to expand west of the Blue Ridge, there were even greater opportunities for dialect mixture. As people moved farther from the original population centers, they met other streams of migrants heading in the same directions. Farther west and decades later, in areas such as the Upper Midwest, influxes of German and Scandinavian language speakers further contributed to the diversity. By the mid-nineteenth century, when the Far West began to open up, migration patterns were criss-crossing to the extent that settlers with very different backgrounds were going to the same new communities, all bringing their home speech patterns with them. By the time the first generations of children had grown up in the West, speech patterns had become very mixed. For, rather than speaking as their parents do, children tend to adopt features from the speech of their playmates. Where different dialects come together, no one variety prevails, but unpredictable mixing occurs. The result today is not that Western speech is simply a hodgepodge, but that elements from numerous traditions can be found living side by side, but with different proportions in different subregions.

The two studies of the language of the Pacific Northwest which we will be examining follow in the tradition of dialect study inaugurated in this country in 1930. At that time, a project known as the Linguistic Atlas of the United States and Canada (LAUSC) was begun under the sponsorship of the American Council of Learned Societies and the direction of Hans Kurath.[1] While Americans had long been interested in their own speech (and the American Dialect Society had been formed in 1889 to study it), until 1930 no comprehensive and systematic investigation of American speech had been undertaken. The formidable goal of the Atlas project was to conduct detailed personal interviews with native speakers in communities spread across the country. The information gathered was to provide a framework for understanding regional variation and, if possible, to suggest the locations of major dialect boundaries and indicate where further study would be most profitable. To collect the data, fieldworkers were to use a carefully constructed questionnaire containing hundreds of questions on pronunciation, grammar, and vocabulary. They were to interview people in communities selected to represent the economic and cultural history of the area as well as to reflect general population density. The informants, as the people who were interviewed were called, were all to be natives of their communities and to represent various social and educational groups within their communities. By this method, comparable data would be elicited which would allow nationwide analysis of language variation. Unfortunately, the Depression and World War II played havoc with the master plan, and fieldwork was completed only in New England and most of the Middle and South Atlantic states.[2] That research, however, was meticulously done. And since it covered the primary settlement areas of the country, it provided the data for a basic understanding of the major dialect regions of the country.

What the Atlas research has shown is that there are three basic dialect areas in the eastern United States: 1) the North (comprising New England, New York, northern New Jersey, and the northern third of Pennsylvania); 2) the Midland, which is further divided into the North Midland (the Delaware, Susquehanna, and Upper Ohio river valleys as well as northern West Virginia), and the South Midland (the Upper Potomac and Shenandoah valleys, southern West Virginia, eastern Kentucky, western North Carolina, and eastern Tennessee); and 3) the South (the eastern shores of Delaware, Maryland, and Virginia, the Virginia Piedmont, and coastal North Carolina, South Carolina, and Georgia). Within each of these major regions other smaller regions can be identified,[3] but these three are most important.

While the boundaries of the major regions are most sharply defined along the Atlantic Coast, they can be extended westward with reasonable certainty thanks to other Atlas projects which were completed after the war. Though they were set up as autonomous studies because of lack of funding for the original project, they were associated with the LAUSC and used its methods. The data from the Linguistic Atlas of the North Central States and the Linguistic Atlas of the Upper Midwest[4] have been particularly helpful in tracing the boundary between the North and the Midland. They have shown that, though the "boundary" is not a distinct line but rather a bundle of boundaries or individual isoglosses[5] for specific items, it runs westward from Pennsylvania through the northern thirds of Ohio, Indiana, and Illinois, and veers north slightly to pass through the northern third of Iowa. In South Dakota, several patterns of isoglosses make tracing the boundary a difficult process. The extension of the boundary between the Midland and the South must be posited somewhat more tentatively at this point,[6] but seems to move west through the northern parts of Georgia, Alabama, Mississippi, and Louisiana. Farther west, both in the North and the South, boundaries are difficult to decipher. Isoglosses may be drawn for individual items, but the isogloss "bundles" tend to be dispersed and inconclusive. Rather than talking in terms of dialect boundaries in the Far West, then, linguists prefer to speak of the relative frequencies of terms in a given area: the question becomes not simply whether a Northern rather than a Midland term is used, but how often one is used relative to the other.

Because *DARE* surveyed people throughout the country, its data are useful not only in illustrating Western distributions of terms, but also in providing a larger context by which to understand those distributions. Following in the tradition of Atlas methodology, *DARE* sent trained field-workers to 1,002 communities across the nation.[7] The field-workers located people who had lived in those communities all their lives and and asked them the 1,847 questions in a carefully made questionnaire. Since the questions were asked in exactly the same way in each community, the data are comparable across the country.

The unique feature of the *DARE* project is that all of the responses from the 2,745 informants[8] have been computerized. For any given question a particular response can be called up, and a symbol will appear on a map of the United States showing the locations of all the informants who gave that response to that question. The map used by *DARE* was specially prepared so that one space is allotted for each community in which an interview was done; those communities had been carefully selected both to reflect relative population densities of the states and to include settlements of significant historic importance. As Figure 1 shows, the resulting map is "skewed" so that the heavily populated eastern states are enlarged, while most of the large but sparsely populated western states are diminished in size. The basic geographic outlines of the states have been retained, however, to make them more recognizable. With a little practice and reference to the key map with the states identified, the *DARE* maps can be easily read.

What the *DARE* maps show is that regional usages can be so inclusive as to cover most of the country, or so limited as to comprise only a county, a city, or even

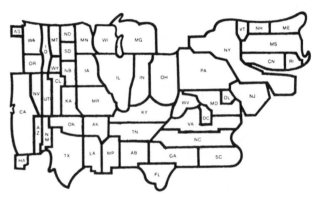

Figure 1.   Usage map designed for the *Dictionary of American Regional English (DARE)* project.

a section of a large city. Figure 2, for example, shows that *roasting ears*, for corn on the cob, is widespread throughout the country except in the Northeast, where it occurs only occasionally. There, the most common term is *sweet corn*. Conversely, in New England the dominant term for poached eggs is *dropped eggs* (Figure 3), a phrase that would rarely be recognized in the rest of the country.

The distribution of a particular word can reflect such factors as migration patterns, ethnic and cultural heritage, topography, and foreign language influences; or, occasionally, a distribution will seem to defy rational explanation. The New England term *angleworm*, for instance, has spread across the North, into the North Midland, and throughout the West (Figure 4)—a direct result of migration patterns of Northeasterners. The set of complementary terms *shivaree, belling, horning*, and *skimmelton* (Figures 5–8), for a serenade of newlyweds, nicely illustrates not just the western concentration of

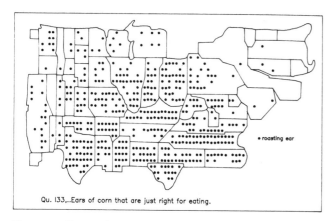

Qu. 133,..Ears of corn that are just right for eating.

Figure 2. Regional usage of "roasting ear."

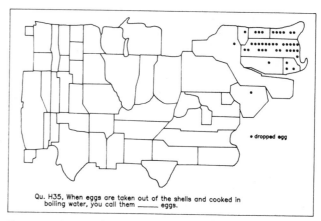

Qu. H35, When eggs are taken out of the shells and cooked in boiling water, you call them _____ eggs.

Figure 3. Regional usage of "dropped eggs."

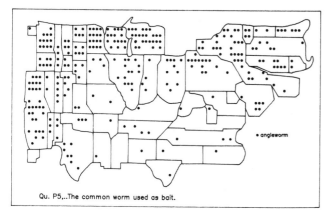

Qu. P5,..The common worm used as bait.

Figure 4. Regional usage of "angleworm."

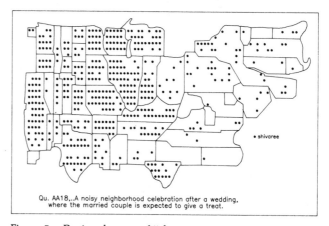

Qu. AA18,..A noisy neighborhood celebration after a wedding, where the married couple is expected to give a treat.

Figure 5. Regional usage of "shivaree."

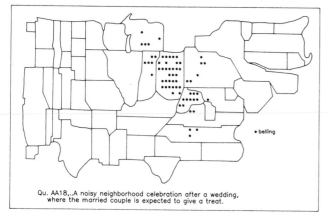

Qu. AA18,..A noisy neighborhood celebration after a wedding, where the married couple is expected to give a treat.

Figure 6. Regional usage of "belling."

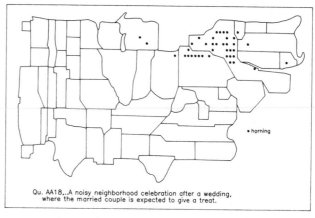

Qu. AA18,..A noisy neighborhood celebration after a wedding, where the married couple is expected to give a treat.

Figure 7. Regional usage of "horning."

shivaree, but also the persistence of local cultural traditions and the retention of folk terms for them. Foreign language influences are obvious in such words as *lagniappe*, in Louisiana, for a gift given by a merchant when a purchase is made, and *Belsnickel*, in Pennsylvania, for a Santa Claus-like figure who both rewards and punishes.

The *DARE* data also generally confirm Kurath's division of the country into Northern, Midland, and South-ern dialect areas. The areas tend to be less clearly defined now, however, than they were fifty years ago. Numerous terms that were then largely restricted to either the North or the South have spread into the Midland as well as to the West. The result is that many terms can now best be described as occurring chiefly in the North and North Midland or in the South and South Midland, with relatively few terms being characteristic of the Midland area only. Figure 9 illustrates the

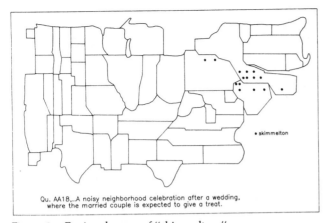

Qu. AA18,..A noisy neighborhood celebration after a wedding, where the married couple is expected to give a treat.

Figure 8.   Regional usage of "skimmelton."

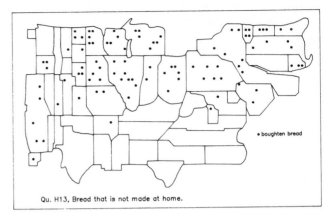

Qu. H13, Bread that is not made at home.

Figure 9.   Regional usage of "boughten bread."

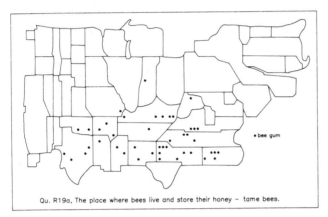

Qu. R19a, The place where bees live and store their honey – tame bees.

Figure 10.   Regional usage of "bee gum."

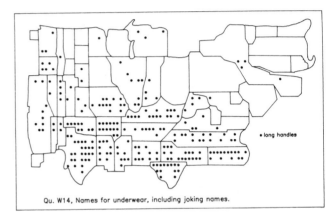

Qu. W14, Names for underwear, including joking names.

Figure 11.   Regional usage of "long handles."

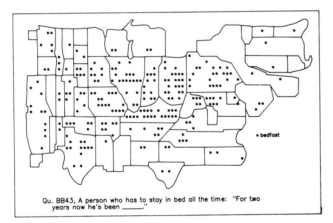

Qu. BB43, A person who has to stay in bed all the time: "For two years now he's been _____."

Figure 12.   Regional usage of "bedfast."

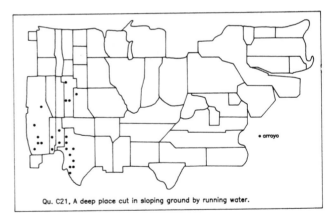

Qu. C21, A deep place cut in sloping ground by running water.

Figure 13.   Regional usage of "arroyo."

basic pattern of North, North Midland distribution, showing the extensions of both regions into the West. In Figure 10, a typical pattern of South, South Midland distribution is shown. Occasionally a term with heavy concentration in the South and South Midland has also spread throughout the West (Figure 11), but this pattern is unusual due to the relatively small part played by Southerners in settling the Far West. A somewhat more common pattern is illustrated by Figure 12, where a

term with basically Midland distribution in the eastern part of the country has very wide currency west of the Mississippi River.

In view of all these contributing influences, one might wonder whether there are any words that are, if not indigenous to the West, at least characteristic of it. Certainly those words adopted into English from Mexican-Spanish and western Indian languages are indigenous to the West. The maps for *arroyo, Santa Ana* and

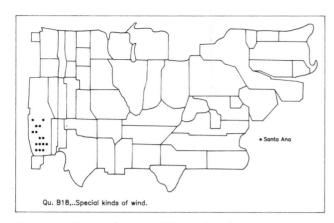

Qu. B18,..Special kinds of wind.

Figure 14. Regional usage of "Santa Ana."

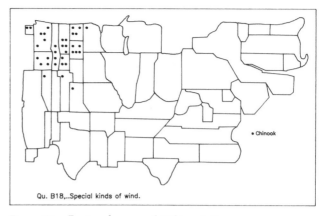

Qu. B18,..Special kinds of wind.

Figure 15. Regional usage of "Chinook."

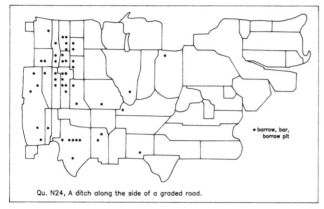

Qu. N24, A ditch along the side of a graded road.

Figure 16. Regional usage of "barrow, bar, borrow pit."

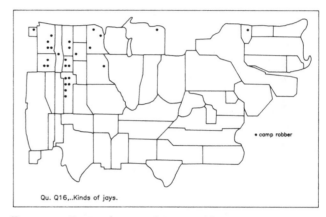

Qu. Q16,..Kinds of jays.

Figure 17. Regional usage of "camp robber."

Chinook (Figures 13–15), for example, illustrate local Western usages based on borrowings. Other terms, such as *bar pit* (or *barrow pit* or *borrow pit*) for a ditch by the side of a graded road, and *camp robber* for a blue jay (Figures 16–17), which occur almost exclusively in the West, have no such obvious explanation. But on the whole, Western speech has relatively few features which are not also characteristic of at least one of the three major dialect areas, the North, the Midland, or the South. It is the ways in which such regional features combine within the regions of the West that provide the focus for studies of Western speech.

What Carroll Reed found after surveying the Pacific Northwest was that while usage was mixed, Idahoans tended to favor Northern terms, while Oregonians favored Midland variants. But within that generalization, Idaho had the highest frequency of some Northern terms, and the lowest frequency of other Northern terms. Similarly, though Oregon had high frequencies of Midland terms in general, it also had highest occurrence of some Northern terms.[9] Within Idaho, Northern terms predominated in the northern part of the state, while Midland terms were more common in the Snake River region. Further, Reed found that strictly Southern terms were rare throughout the Pacific North-

west, and that typically Western terms (such as *corral*) were especially common in eastern Oregon and southern Idaho, and least frequent in Washington.[10]

When the opportunity was provided to study a smaller region within the Pacific Northwest[11]—the Snake River region of southern Idaho and eastern Oregon—Reed's conclusions established the framework within which to investigate further. His statement about the relative distributions of Northern and Midland terms in northern and southern Idaho seemed particularly worth testing. Since geographic, economic, and historical conditions in the SRR had been relatively homogeneous, yet different from those in northern Idaho, statistical differences in lexical usage in the two areas seemed the logical expectation.

Departing from the traditional Atlas method of using only personal interviews for gathering data, but using a technique that had been proven valid as a supplementary measure in the Great Lakes and Upper Midwest,[12] Reed had used a mailed questionnaire to study vocabulary in the Pacific Northwest. More than seven hundred of them representing all parts of Washington, Oregon, and Idaho, provided the basis for his generalizations. In the SRR, it was decided to use a combination of mailed questionnaires and personal field interviews. Before

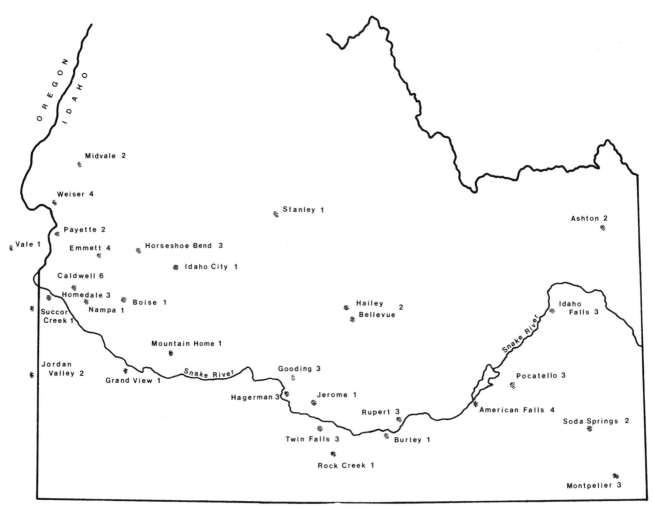

Figure 18.   Communities and numbers of informants used in Snake River Region survey.

doing any data gathering, students in my course in linguistic geography researched the history of the region to determine the network of communities to be investigated. Fifty-eight communities were selected in southern Idaho and eastern Oregon. They were chosen both to represent localities significant in the settlement history of the region and to provide relatively even distribution across the territory. The heavily populated Boise area, however, received closer attention since almost twenty-five percent of the state's residents lived there. Once the communities had been selected, a letter was sent to the local Masonic Lodge explaining that we were doing a language survey and asking that members assist us by finding three native residents who would answer the questions in our questionnaire. Following Atlas procedures, we tried to include informants from three age groups: over sixty,[13] between forty-five and sixty, and younger than forty-five. Response to the request varied from lodge to lodge, but when the mailed questionnaires had been returned and the personal interviews conducted, we had a sample of sixty-eight informants from thirty communities (Figure 18). Their

responses formed the corpus of lexical data on which our conclusions were based.

The questionnaire consisted of one hundred and five items selected in accordance with the guidelines established by A. L. Davis.[14] The items all concern vocabulary and are not affected by attitudes toward "correctness." They have been shown to have variants, but not so many that analysis of their distribution would be impossible, and their range of meaning does not cover so wide an area that several specialized terms might be subsumed. Because it is impossible briefly to describe each item so that all informants offer an appropriate response, several variants are listed after each question, and informants are asked to circle those they normally use. An opportunity is also given for them to write in any which they use but which are not included in the list.

Most of the questions were selected from Hans Kurath's generalized short work sheets, but approximately one-fifth were chosen from other Atlas projects or related Western studies.[15] In addition, questions intended to elicit descriptors or derogatory terms for

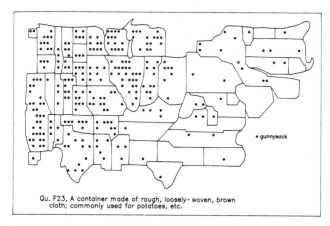

Qu. F23, A container made of rough, loosely-woven, brown cloth; commonly used for potatoes, etc.

Figure 19. Regional usage of "gunnysack."

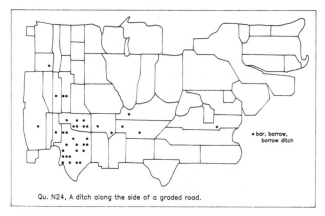

Qu. N24, A ditch along the side of a graded road.

Figure 21. Regional usage of "bar, barrow, borrow ditch."

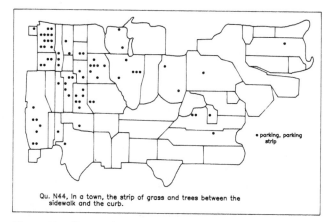

Qu. N44, In a town, the strip of grass and trees between the sidewalk and the curb.

Figure 20. Regional usage of "parking" and "parking strip."

ethnic and social minorities of the region were included. Four questions concerning Basque culture were asked to test the extent to which the terminology of a well-accepted minority has been adopted by the dominant culture. (The questionnaire is appended.)

Unsurprisingly, the results of the SRR survey corroborated several of Reed's generalizations: Midland terms do occur more frequently in the SRR than in northern Idaho; Western terms (e.g., corral, chaps, lariat, lasso, bronco, mustang, cayuse, ranch hand) are also more prevalent in the southern than northern part of the state; Southern terms occur infrequently (though they occurred more often in the SRR survey than in Reed's study). With respect to distributions for particular words, however, the results often vary from Reed's. For example, the words faucet, corn bread, dragonfly, snack, burlap bag/sack, sawbuck, gutters, skillet, and sick at the stomach were found to be significantly[16] more common in the SRR than Reed found them to be in Idaho as a whole; sawhorse, frying pan, and string beans, on the other hand, were significantly less common among SRR informants than among Reed's Idaho informants. All of the preceding words have general distribution throughout the Atlantic states, or occur in at least parts of the North, Mid-

land, and the South. For words of more limited eastern distribution, the SRR survey shows the Northern terms darning needle and devil's darning needle (dragonfly), johnny cake or johnny bread, and sick to the stomach to be significantly less common, and the Northern outhouse to be significantly more common in the SRR than in Idaho as a whole. The Midland terms green bean and hot cake were more common in the SRR than in the rest of Idaho. The regional labels here may be misleading, however, in that Reed's fieldwork was done in the late 1940s and early 1950s, and the SRR survey in the early 1970s. DARE maps show that by the period of 1965–70 sick at the stomach, outhouse, frying pan, green bean, string bean, and hot cake had all become very widespread, so Reed's labels are somewhat dated. The greater use of these words in the SRR probably does not represent migration patterns in the region, but is rather a reflection of generally wider use after the time of Reed's fieldwork.

In addition to the Western words mentioned earlier (corral, mustang, etc.) which deal with specifically Western activities, a number of other SRR terms unrelated to terrain or occupation can be shown to be characteristic of all or a part of the western United States. Delineation of "the West" varies, however, from term to term. For a word like gunnysack (Figure 19) there is a distinct difference in density of occurrence between the region west of a line running from western Ohio to Mississippi, and the area east of that line. While most Westerners would not consider any area that far east to be "the West," respecting the linguistic geography of the country as a whole, this kind of distribution is significant. That the SRR participates fully in this Western pattern is shown by the fact that 49 of the 68 informants used the term; five others used gunny-bag. A more clearly Western distribution can be seen in the map for parking and parking strip (Figure 20), a strip of grass between the sidewalk and the curb. In the SRR these are by far the dominant terms, making up 44 of the 55 responses (some informants had no term for the item). A third kind of Western distribution can be seen when the map for *bar ditch, barrow ditch,* and *borrow ditch* (Figure 21), is compared with that for *bar pit* and variants (Figure 16). While both are distinctly Western terms, they vary regionally by the second element of the phrase: those with *pit* are widespread throughout the West but most frequent in the Rocky Mountains and the Northwest; those with *ditch* are especially frequent in the Southwest. The SRR responses show the same kind of distribution, with 33 instances of *barrow pit,* 17 of *borrow pit,* and 14 of *bar pit,* but only four of *barrow ditch* and two of *borrow ditch.* SRR informants provide welcome confirmation of another regional term, *daveno,* for a davenport or sofa. The *DARE* findings suggest that *daveno* and *daven* occur chiefly in the Northwest, especially Washington; the use of *daveno* by 14 of the SRR respondents both strengthens the use of *Northwest* as a label and also makes it possible to state more precisely that the term occurs chiefly in the Northwest, but especially in Idaho and Washington.

Within the SRR itself, some differences in usage are striking enough to indicate that two minor dialect areas can be posited. The occurrence of one set of terms (*juice harp, mouth harp, downpour,* [*pig*] *sty, fish bait* or *bait worm,* and the series *breakfast, lunch, supper*) almost exclusively in the western half of the region, and of another set (*tules, cherrystone, salamander* [a go-devil or stoneboat], [*devil's*] *darning needle, Jew's harp* [harmonica], *tuckered out, gully washer, tap* [faucet at a sink], *sow belly, prairie* [a desert], *backhouse, rain troughs,* and *daybreak*) almost solely in the eastern half suggests that within the regional dialect, subdialect areas exist. Because the western terms occur as far east as Rock Creek and the eastern terms as far west as Hagerman, a transition area rather than a sharp boundary separates the two. In addition, the occurrence of nine other items (*boonies, reata, windstorm, country bumpkin, midafternoon, miser, civet cat, quarter of,* and variants of *chaps*) almost exclusively in the Boise Valley indicates that Boise may serve as a focal area, with terms spreading from there to outlying areas.[17]

Settlement patterns in the SRR lend support to the notion of eastern and western areas in that there were significant differences in the numbers of migrants from Utah who settled the areas: between 1870 and 1920 Utah was by far the largest contributor to Idaho's population, but the majority of Utahns moved directly north, settling in southeastern Idaho where ties with the home state and the Mormon church were most easily maintained. Since data on Utah lexical patterns are not available, however, the reasons behind the east-west differences within the SRR remain hypothetical. Boise's status as a focal center is probably an accurate reflection of the city's historical importance as a trade and transportation center; its rapid growth in the last decade will probably continue to foster that status. More detailed study will be necessary, though, to confirm that position and to better document the existence of the eastern and western sub-areas within the region.

One section of questions in the SRR questionnaire (questions 82–87) was a departure from other Atlas studies in that it asked informants to supply terms—either neutral or derogatory—for members of ethnic and social minorities of the region. Unsurprisingly, the most easily recognizable minorities received the largest number of appellations. But few of the descriptors commented directly on physical characteristics. *Slant eyes, redskins, red men, butterhead,* and *greaser* derive from observed or imagined physical features, but only those five of the thirty terms used in reference to Japanese, Indians, and Mexicans relied on stereotyped racial characteristics.

Distinctive eating habits were frequently noted in the descriptors used by SRR informants. The connotations of those terms, however, seemed to vary considerably. While *pepper bellies,* for Mexicans, was almost certainly derogatory, the terms *tacos, beanos,* and *chili chompers* may either be derogatory or simply reflect the increasing popularity of Mexican-style fast foods. With reference to Japanese, *fish eaters* might be condescending, but with reference to Catholics both *fish eaters* and *mackerel snappers* could just indicate awareness of the tradition of meatless Fridays. For Mormons, the terms *carrot eaters* and *carrot snappers* hark back to the early difficult years when Mormon pioneers were said to have survived on carrots alone. The emphasis on eating habits is not unique to SRR informants: one study in Chicago[18] elicited *guppy-gobbler, herring-choker* (or *-destroyer*), and *spaghetti-eater* (or *-bender*), and the *DARE* materials provide evidence for *bagel, beaner, frog-eater, herring-choker, kraut-eater, pea-soup*(er), and *spaghetti-bender,* among others. Most such terms occur wherever there are substantial numbers of a particular minority group. Some, however, show regional patterning within that broader generalization. In the *DARE* materials, for instance, all twelve examples of *pepper belly* came from Texas, and all six instances of *beaner, bean,* and *beano* came from California. The occurrence of both terms in the SRR is useful evidence to corroborate wider usage.

Analysis of the ethnic and social descriptors by age of the SRR informants who used them indicates that only two terms can be considered either old-fashioned or obsolescent: *fish eater* and *slant eyes* were used chiefly by informants over sixty. Decreasing use of terms such as *slant eyes* may be a result of increasingly friendly relations with Japan since World War II, though *Jap* persists in all age groups. Like such terms as *colored person* or even *Negro, Jap* may be interpreted as offensive whether it was intended so or not. Analysis of the ethnic descriptors by sex of the informants indicates little difference in usage, whether of neutral terms or those with distinctly negative connotations.

Another section of the questionnaire, questions 88–91, was included in the survey to discover whether selected terms common to Basque culture are being adopted by the dominant culture. The response to question 83 (descriptors for Basque people) substantiates the initial assumption that Basques are well accepted in the Snake River Region. *Basquo (Basco)*, the only frequently used descriptor (twenty-five occurrences), is commonly used by Basques themselves and has no negative connotations. *Sheepherders* is purely descriptive, and *Bass* is probably simply a phonological reduction of *Basque*. The one occurrence of *Dago*, then, is the only evidence of any disharmony between Basques and other SRR inhabitants. The generally amicable relationship does not automatically mean, however, that terms used among Basques are widely known outside their culture. *Bota bag*, a goatskin winebag, was familiar to only ten informants. *Pelota* was used by only six informants (a seventh used *pelotaka*) to describe the game played with a ball and a sickle-shaped basket, although *jai alai* was offered by eleven. The Basque beret was called *chapela* by two informants, and the card game *mus* identified by only five. Such figures emphasize the axiom that acceptance of a minority group is only the first step: sharing in its daily activities is necessary for the adoption of culturally defined lexical items.

To the question posed at the start of this essay, whether other Americans can recognize people from the Pacific Northwest or the Snake River Region by their speech, the answer, for most people, is no. The predominance of Northern and Midland terms means that speakers in the Northwest have most of their vocabulary in common with a very large number of other people, though the combinations of terms may vary from one group to another. To a perceptive listener, clues such as the use of Western outdoors terms and a few shibboleths such as *camp robber*, *bar pit*, and *daveno* can point to a speaker's origins in the Northwest. But on the whole, the region's youth and its heterogeneous makeup mean that the kinds of firmly rooted and easily recognizable differences found in eastern varieties of speech simply have not had a chance to take hold in the Northwest.

Notes

1. For an introduction to the Atlas principles and methods, see Raven I. McDavid, Jr., "The Dialects of American English," in W. Nelson Francis, *The Structure of American English* (New York, 1958), pp. 488–99.

2. The results of this research have been published in several works: Hans Kurath, *The Linguistic Atlas of New England* (Providence, Rhode Island, 1939–43); Kurath, *Handbook of the Linguistic Geography of New England* (2nd ed.; New York, 1973); Kurath and Raven I. McDavid, Jr., *Pronunciation of English in the Atlantic States* (Ann Arbor, 1961); Kurath, *A Word Geography of the Eastern United States* (Ann Arbor, 1949); E. Bagby Atwood, *A Survey of Verb Forms in the Eastern United States* (Ann Arbor, 1953); Raven I. McDavid, Jr., and Raymond K. O'Cain, *The Linguistic Atlas of the Middle and South Atlantic States* (Chicago, 1980), [3 fascicles].

3. See McDavid, op. cit., pp. 580–81 for map and descriptions of smaller regions.

4. The LANCS project was directed by Albert H. Marckwardt, and covered the states of Wisconsin, Michigan, Illinois, Indiana, Kentucky, Ohio, and the southwestern part of Ontario. Fieldwork was done chiefly by Frederic G. Cassidy, Raven I. McDavid, Jr., A. L. Davis, and Harold Allen. The LAUM project, directed by Harold Allen, covered Minnesota, Iowa, North Dakota, South Dakota, and Nebraska. Allen's findings have been published in three volumes as *The Linguistic Atlas of the Upper Midwest* (Minneapolis, 1973–76). Other Atlas projects include *The Linguistic Atlas of the Gulf States*, directed by Lee A. Pederson at Emory University, and the atlases of the Pacific Coast, Oklahoma, and the Rocky Mountains, in various states of readiness.

5. An isogloss is simply a line drawn on a map enclosing all the examples of a particular feature.

6. When *The Linguistic Atlas of the Gulf States* is completed, our knowledge of this boundary will be greatly enhanced.

7. For an introduction to *DARE*, see Frederic G. Cassidy, American Regionalism and the Harmless Drudge, *PMLA*, 82(1967):12–19, and Cassidy, "What's New About *DARE*?" in *Papers in Language Variation* (University of Alabama, 1977).

8. Since answering the questionnaire was very time consuming, in many cases several people in a community completed different sections of a single questionnaire.

9. Carroll E. Reed, *Dialects of American English* (Amherst, Massachusetts, 1977), pp. 61–63.

10. Ibid., p. 63.

11. Located at The College of Idaho in Caldwell, Idaho, the Snake River Regional Studies Center was established in 1970 with a grant from the Hill Family Foundation of St. Paul, Minnesota. The Center serves as a clearinghouse for all information about the Snake River Region, and initiates and supports research, especially in the fields of ecology, economics, and folklife of the region.

12. The mailed questionnaires were used successfully as supplementary information by A. L. Davis, *A Word Atlas of the Great Lakes Region* (University of Michigan dissertation, 1948), and by Harold Allen in *The Linguistic Atlas of the Upper Midwest*.

13. Age 60 was considered the dividing line between "old" and "middle-aged" informants because, in the recently settled West it is often impossible to find enough native residents who are older than 60.

14. Davis, op. cit., pp. 26–28.

15. *A Compilation of the Work Sheets of the Linguistic Atlas of Canada and Associated Projects*, (2nd ed.; Chicago, 1969).

16. In this and the following statements, *significantly* means a difference of at least 15 percent.

17. The possibility of bias in the collecting technique cannot be discounted here, however, since most of the instances of these words were collected in personal interviews rather than the mailed questionnaires.

18. Lee A. Pederson, "Terms of Abuse for Some Chicago Social Groups," *Publication of the American Dialect Society*, 42 (1964): 26–48.

Bibliography

Allen, Harold B., and Gary N. Underwood, eds. *Readings in American Dialectology*. New York: Appleton-Century-Crofts, 1971. A diverse collection of essays on regional and social dialects. They provide a good sampling of studies of major and minor dialect areas, of single features of pronunciation and vocabulary, or sociolinguistic factors, and dialect theory.

Kurath, Hans. "Linguistic Regionalism." In *Regionalism in America*, ed. Merrill Jensen. Madison: University of Wisconsin Press, 1951. An introduction to the dialect regions of the United States by the father of American linguistic geography.

_____. *A Word Geography of the Eastern United States*. Ann Arbor: University of Michigan Press, 1949. A detailed analysis, with maps, of regional variation in the vocabulary of the eastern part of the country, based on *The Linguistic Atlas of New England* and *The Linguistic Atlas of the Middle and South Atlantic States*.

McDavid, Raven I., Jr. "The Dialects of American English." In *The Structure of American English*, by W. Nelson Francis. New York: Ronald Press, 1958. Essential reading for anyone interested in dialect variation in the United States, its causes, and its methods of study.

Reed, Carroll E. *Dialects of American English*. 2nd ed. Amherst: University of Massachusetts Press, 1977. A good introduction to dialect study, including an examination of each of the regional Atlas projects in the United States.

Williamson, Juanita V., and Virginia M. Burke, eds. *A Various Language: Perspectives on American Dialects*. New York: Holt, Rinehart, and Winston, 1971. A wide-ranging collection of studies similar to those in Allen and Underwood, with the addition of essays on literary representations of American English and on studies of urban dialects.

Appendix A

Questionnaire

We would appreciate your giving us the following information about yourself.

Name (optional) _____

Age _____

Race _____

Religion _____

Town you live in (or near) _____

County _____

Birthplace _____

Highest grade reached in school _____

Where did you go to school? _____

Occupation _____

Parents' birthplaces: Mother _____

                        Father _____

Parents' education: Mother _____

                        Father _____

Parents' occupation(s) Mother _____

                        Father _____

Did you know where your grandparents came from?

Mother's parents _____

Father's parents _____

Spouse's age _____

Spouse's race _____

Spouse's religion _____

Spouse's occupation _____

Have you traveled much outside the state? If so, where?

Do you speak any non-English language? If so, what?

VOCABULARY

What term or terms do you use to describe the following items or activities?

1. The time of day when the sun first appears: (sunrise, sunup, dawn, daybreak)

2. The time of day when the sun disappears: (sunset, sundown, dark, nightfall)

3. The time of day around 3 or 4 P.M.: (afternoon, evening)

4. A very heavy rain which doesn't last long: (downpour, cloudburst, squall, flaw, goose drownder, toad-strangler, gully-washer, trash mover, etc.)

5. A rainstorm with thunder and lightning: (electrical storm, electric shower, electric storm, storm, thundershower, thunderstorm, shower, tempest)

6. A dry storm: (dirt storm, dust storm, duster)

7. The room in a home where guests are entertained: (best room, front room, living room, sitting room, parlor, big house)

8. The first thin coating of ice on a lake or pond: (anchor ice, cat ice, first layer, mush ice, scum, shale, shale ice, sheet ice, slush ice, skim, thins)

9. The supports for logs in a fireplace: (andiron, dog irons, dogs, firedogs, fire irons, grate, handirons, log irons)

10. A large, cushioned piece of living room furniture with arms and back: (couch, chesterfield, davenport, daveno, divan lounge, sofa)

11. A window covering which is on a roller at the top of the window: (blinds, curtains, roller shades, shades, window blinds, window shades)

12. To do the housework: (clean house, clean up, do up, straighten up, redd up, ridd up, tidy up)

13. Covered walk between house and other buildings: (arcade, breezeway, walk)

14. Area enclosed by house or by house and other buildings: (court, patio, yard)

15. Devices at edges of roof to carry off rain: (canales, canals, drainpipe, drains, eaves, eaves spouting, eaves spouts, eaves troughs, eave troughs, gutter(s), guttering, rain troughs, spouting, spouts, water gutter)

16. Structural beams of ceiling of roof: (beams, joists, posts, rafters, vigas)

17. Outdoor toilet: (backhouse, john, johnnie, outhouse, privy) Do you use any other terms when speaking of it in a joking manner?

18. Place next to the barn where cows are enclosed: (cow brake, cow lot, cow pen, cow pound, cow yard, cuppin)

19. Shelter and yard for pigs and hogs: (hog boist, hog crawl, hog house, hog lot, hogpen, hog run, pigpen, pigsty, sty)

20. Place where horses are enclosed: (corral, horse lot, lot)

21. Large, open vessel made of wood and used to carry water or milk: (bucket, cedar bucket, cedar pail, pail, well bucket, well pail, wooden bucket, wooden pail)

22. Large, open vessel made of metal and used to carry water or milk: (bucket, milk bucket, milk pail, pail, tin bucket, tin pail, water bucket, water pail)

23. Heavy iron utensil used for frying food on the stove: (creeper, fryer, frying pan, fry pan, skillet, spider)

24. The handle over a sink which you turn to obtain water: (fasset, faucet, hydrant, spicket, spigot, tap)

25. The same sort of handle on a barrel: (fasset, faucet, spicket, spigot, tap, bung)

26. Paper container for groceries: (bag, paper bag, paper sack, poke, sack, toot)

27. Large, loosely woven bag used for carrying grain, potatoes, etc.: (barley sack, burlap bag, burlap sack, croker sack, crocus sack, feed sack, grain sack, grass sack, guano

sack, gunny bag, gunnysack, jute bag, jute sack, sack, seagrass sack, tote sack, tow sack)

28. Small musical instrument which you hold up to your mouth and blow on: (breath harp, French harp, harmonica, harp, Jew's harp, joice harp, juice harp, mouth harp, mouth organ)

29. Small musical instrument made out of metal and held between the teeth and picked: (breath harp, French harp, Jew's harp, juice harp, mouth harp, harp)

30. Thin, circular piece of rubber: (rubber band, rubber binder)

31. Implement used by carpenters for holding boards for sawing: (buck, horse jack, rack, sawbuck, sawhorse, saw jack, trestle, wood buck)

32. Implement for holding firewood for sawing: (buck, horse jack, rack, sawbuck, sawhorse, saw jack, trestle, wood buck)

33. Flat piece of stone used to sharpen knives: (whet, whet rock, whet stone, whetter)

34. Outer working garment: (overalls, overhalls, levis)

35. Leather covering worn to protect trouser legs: (chaps, chaparajos)

36. Swampy ground with small stream running through it: (bayou, bog, draw, marsh, seep, slough, spring, swag, swale, swamp)

37. Level, open space among mountains: (meadow, mountain meadow, basin, cove, flat, hole, hollow, park, rincon, valley, vega)

38. Stretch of bad soil with little vegetation: (alkali flats, allcali, badlands, desert, flats, malpals, mesa, poverty flats, prairie, sandhills)

39. Ditch made by a stream: (arroya, arroyo, barranca, canyon, ditch, draw, dry creek, gorge, gulch, bully, ravine, riverbed, seep, wadi, wash)

40. Grassy strip between the sidewalk and the street: (berm, boulevard, boulevard strip, parking, parking strip, parkway, sidewalk plot)

41. A ditch by the side of a graded road (not an irrigation ditch): (bar ditch, bar pit, barrow ditch, barrow pit, borrow ditch, borrow pit, ditch, grader ditch, gutter)

42. To wait_____someone (e.g., while he is getting ready): (for, on)

43. A game played with horseshoes: (horseshoes, pitch, plates, quakes, quates, quoites, shoes)

44. A wild horse: (bronc, bronco, broomtail, bangtail, cayuse, goblin, mustang, rough one)

45. Bone in the breast of a chicken: (breadbone, wishbone, breastbone, lucky bone, pull bone, pulley bone, pulling bone) Do you know of any traditions or beliefs associated with this bone?

46. A rope with a loop (for catching animals): (lariat, lasso, reata)

47. Bread made of corn meal: (cornbread, corn dodger(s), corn doger, corn pone, hoecake(s), hush puppies, Indian bread, johnny bread, johnny cake, Navajo bread, pone bread, red-horse bread)

48. Round, flat cakes made with white flour and eaten with syrup: (battercakes, flannel cakes, flapjacks, hot cakes, pancakes, slapjacks, wheat cakes, griddle cakes, fritters, flitters)

49. Meat from the sides of a hog, which is salted but not smoked: (bacon, flitch, middlin meat, salt pork, side pork, sour belly, sowbelly, sow bosom)

50. Food eaten between regular meals: (a snack, a bite, a piece, piecemeal, lunch)

51. Small garden which provides enough for family use only: (family garden, garden, garden patch, home garden, kitchen garden, truck garden, vegetable garden)

52. The center of a cherry: (pit, seed, stone, kernel)

53. The center of a peach: (kernel, pit, seed, stone)

54. A peach whose meat sticks to the seed: (cling, cling peach, clingstone, clingstone peach, plum peach, press peach)

55. A peach whose meat separates easily from the seed: (clear seed, clear-seed peach, clear stone, cleave stone, free peach, freestone, freestone peach, open peach, open seed, open stone, open-stone peach)

56. Beans which are eaten in their pods: (green beans, sallet beans, snap beans, snap, string beans)

57. The edible tops of turnips, beets, etc.: (greens, salad, sallet, turnip greens, beet greens)

58. The green, leafy cover of an ear of corn: (husk, shuck, cap)

59. Corn eaten on the cob: (corn on the cob, garden corn, green corn, mutton corn, roasting ears, sugar corn, sweet corn)

60. Small, flat lizard with horns on head and back: (horned toad, horny toad)

61. Bird that pecks holes in trees: (woodpecker, peckerwood)

62. An animal which is black with a white stripe down its back and which smells bad: (skunk, polecat)

63. Worm used for bait in fishing: (angleworm, angledog, bait worm, dew worm, earthworm, fish bait, fishing worm, mudworm, rainworm, red worm, worm)

64. Worms which are especially large and very good for fishing: (night crawler, nightwalker, dew worm, wiggler, town worm, pink worm, grubworm, earthworm)

65. Insect that glows at night: (firefly, firebug, glowworm, june bug, lightning bug, candle fly)

66. The little black insect that curls up when you touch it: (ball bug, doodlebug, pill bug, potato bug, sow bug)

67. An insect which hops and can fly and sometimes destroys crops: (grasshopper, hoppergrass)

68. If a child is very much like his father in physical appearance you might say that the child_____his father. (favors, features, is the image of, is the spittin image of, looks like, takes after, resembles)

69. If a child's behavior is much like his father's, you might say that the child _____his father. (favors, features, resembles, takes after, has ways like)

70. The bumps which appear on a person's body when he is cold: (duck bumps, goose bumps, gooseflesh, goose pimples)

71. If a person from the country came to the city, what might the city people call him behind his back? (backeywoodsman, backwoodsman, clodhopper, country gentleman, country jake, countryman, hayseed, hick, hillbilly, jack pine, jack pine savage, mountain boomer, pump-

kin husker, rail-splitter, redneck, sharecropper, stump farmer, swamp angel, yahoo, yokel)

72. If a person from the city came to the country, what might the country people call him behind his back? (city dude, dude, city slicker, slicker)

73. A person who lives in an undesirable or isolated area might be said to live_____.
(on the other side of the tracks, on the wrong side of the tracks, out in Kansas, in Jimtown, in string town, out in the jim sangs, out in the jim sings, out in the june sangs, out in the sagebrush, out in the skeeta bogs, out in the sticks, out in the toolies, out on the flats)

74. A stingy person: (chintzy, chinchy, tightwad, close, penny pincher)

75. To move a heavy suitcase from one place to another is to _____ it. (carry, pack, lug, tote, hike)

76. A square or park in the center of town: (commons, park, plaza, square, town square)

77. A prankish celebration after a wedding, to tease the bride and groom: (belling, belling-bee, bull banding, bull band, calathump, shivaree, horning, horning-bee, serenade, skimmelton, skimmerton, skimmiton, tin-panning)

78. After eating green apples, a child might be sick_____.
(at his stomach, at the stomach, to the stomach, with his stomach)

79. A person may "become ill" or _____. (be taken sick, get sick, take sick)

80. If a man got extremely angry at another man, you might say that he got_____. (mad, het up, hot, ashy, owly, riled, roiled, ugly, wrathy)

81. After a hard day's work, you might say that you feel _____. (all in, beat out, bushed, fagged out, perished, played out, tuckered, tuckered out, worn-out)

82. Do you know of any terms (used seriously or in a joking or derogatory manner) to describe Japanese people? (These may be terms you have heard but which you do not use yourself.)

83. Terms for Basque people?

84. Terms for Indians?

85. Terms for Mexican people?

86. Terms for Mormons?

87. Terms for Catholics?

88. Do you have a term for a goatskin bag containing wine? _____

89. Do you know a term for a very fast game played with a ball and a sickle-shaped basket which may be strapped to the wrist? The ball is hurled against a wall by one player and caught and hurled again by another._____

90. Do you know a term for the black beret worn by many Basque people?_____

91. Do you have a term for a Basque game similar to poker?_____.

92. What do you call a device used as an aid in stacking and storing hay? (derrick, Mormon derrick)

93. What do you call this time of the day? (a quarter [15 minutes] before five, a quarter of five, a quarter till five, a quarter to five, 4:45)

94. What do you call cooked cereal for breakfast? (mush, porridge, hasty pudding, cereal)

95. What do you call a Prostestant clergyman? (minister, parson, pastor, preacher, reverend)

96. What do you call a farm or ranch employee? (farmhand, hired hand, hired help, hired man, farm help, ranch hand)

97. What do you call an insect with a long, slender body and filmy wings which is often seen around water? (darning needle, dragonfly, devil's darning needle, ear sewer, mosquito hawk, snake doctor, snake weeder)

98. What is a "go-devil"?_____

99. What is a "water dog"?_____

100. A watery place where reeds and cattails grow: (marsh, swamp, bog, slough)

101. A piece of work done regularly: (chore, job, task, duty)

102. Large-leafed plant with edible stems: (pieplant, rhubarb)

103. We fry food in: (lard, grease, shortening, drippings, fat)

104. We call our three regular meals: (1: breakfast, lunch, dinner; 2: breakfast, dinner, supper)

105. We used to call them: (1: breakfast, lunch, dinner; 2: breakfast, dinner, supper)

PRONUNCIATION

1. A penny is one . . . (cent).

2. A dime is . . . (ten cents).

3. If your neighbors moved into their house in 1960, you would say that they have lived there ever . . . (since) 1960.

4. A greeting on December 25th is . . . (Merry) Christmas.

5. A sausage or wiener in a bun is called . . . (hot dog).

6. The parents of Jesus were Joseph and . . . (Mary).

7. Our first president was George . . . (Washington).

8. If a man and a woman want to live together, they go to a preacher and get . . . (married).

9. After the man caught a cold, his voice became very . . . (hoarse).

10. If you want to send a message to someone, you get a pen and a piece of paper and . . . (write) him a letter.

11. On a Sunday afternoon a person might get in his car and go for a . . . (ride).

12. A cowboy rides on a . . . (horse).

13. The parts of a tree that are under the ground are its . . . (roots).

14. You strike a match to start a . . . (fire).

15. The soft, thick black stuff that collects in a chimney is called . . . (soot, sut, smut).

16. Milk comes from a . . . (cow).

17. Years ago, before food items were packaged individually, you could have gone to the grocer and bought such staples as flour and sugar in large quantities. This was called buying food in . . . (bulk).

18. Your parents are your . . . and . . . (father and mother).

19. Robins, blue jays, and sparrows are all . . . (birds).

20. What color is this paper? . . . (white).

21. The common term for a female child . . . (girl).

22. The common term for a male child . . . (boy).

23. A car has four . . . (wheels).

24. Before the man went fishing, he dug some . . . (worms) for bait.

25. If a man isn't rich, then he might be . . . (poor).

26. A girl might keep her coins in a small change . . . (purse).

27. A boy named William might be nicknamed . . . (Billy).

28. In the fairy tale, Little Red Riding Hood met a big, bad . . . (wolf).

29. A farmer plants his corn in a . . . (field).

30. A housewife might plant carrots, lettuce, etc., in a small . . . (garden).

31. The holiday in late November when we eat turkey and dressing is called . . . (Thanksgiving).

32. If a person is in trouble, you try to . . . (help) him.

33. If something isn't wide, then it is . . . (narrow).

34. I'd like to help you, but I just . . . (can't).

35. A shorter name for an automobile is . . . (car).

36. My mother might say to me, "This man is your uncle, and his wife is . . . (your aunt)." Get both words together. If the informant says_____, ask if there is a distinction in usage between_____and_____.

37. Before birds lay their eggs, they must build their . . . (nests).

38. Children used to sit on benches at school, but now they sit at . . . (desks).

39. Before a boy fights, he might clench both of his . . . (fists).

40. A small, flying insect which bothers you in the summertime, and stings and draws blood is a . . . (mosquito).

41. On a clear day you might look up and say, "There's not a . . . (cloud) in the sky."

42. Right now we are sitting inside your . . . (house).

43. If you knew that an animal was getting your chickens at night, but you didn't know exactly what kind of animal it was, what general term could you use to refer to it? . . . (varmint). What animals are included in this term? Would you ever use it to refer to a human being? Under what circumstances?

44. What do you call a small shellfish which is curled in shape and pink or orange in color? It's sometimes served as an appetizer . . . (shrimp).

45. If you don't want a wool sweater to draw up when you wash it, you have to use cool water, because hot water makes wool . . . (shrink).

46. What am I doing? (Hold arm at full length and point.) . . . (pointing).

47. The man who presides over a trial is a . . . (judge).

48. If you want to sue someone, you have to hire a . . . (lawyer).

49. If you don't want your car to get rained on, you put it in the . . . (garage).

50. Another way of saying T.V. is . . . (television).

51. Bread is made out of . . . (flour).

52. If the book belongs to her, it's her book; if the book belongs to us, then it's . . . (our book).

53. Fences nowadays are often made of barbed . . . (wire).

54. One hundred years ago, black people who were not free were called . . . (slaves).

55. The season after winter is called . . . (spring).

56. On Sunday, many people go to . . . (church).

57. If a man wanted to go hunting, he might go and get his .22 . . . (rifle).

58. A furry animal with long ears and a cottontail is a . . . (rabbit).

59. A white grain that is often eaten instead of potatoes and is very common in China is called . . . (rice).

60. At night, you close your eyes and go to . . . (sleep).

61. Sixty minutes makes one . . . (hour).

62. A person who doesn't like to let go of his money might be called a close person or a . . . (stingy) person.

63. The vegetable which makes your eyes water when you cut it is an . . . (onion).

64. If it's not an old suit, then it's a . . . (new) suit.

Ask informant if he will tell you something about the area he lives in, how it has changed in the last fifty (or thirty, depending on his own age) years. Try to find out what he remembers most about the "old" days, what he liked best, etc. If he has any stories, jokes, anecdotes, songs, we'd like to hear them. In any case, try to use the rest of the tape for free conversation.

Appendix B

Responses to the Questionnaire

1. sunrise (48 informants); sunup (22); daybreak (7); dawn (3); break of day (1)

2. sunset (45); sundown (25); dark (4); dusk (1); evening (1)

3. afternoon (59); midafternoon (6); evening (1)

4. cloudburst (34); downpour (20); shower (6); gully-washer (5); squall (4); gutwrencher (2); waterspout (2)

5. thunderstorm (49); electric(al) storm (17); thunder-shower (3); lightning storm (1); thunderbust (1); storm (1)

6. dust storm (54); windstorm (8); dirt storm (4); Mormon rainstorm (3); Idaho rain (shower) (2); bluster (1)

7. living room (49); front room (23); parlor (2); family room (2); sitting room (1)

8. skim (15); sheet ice (15); slush (ice) (10); first layer (3); mush ice (3); skift (3); thin ice (2); skiff (1); thins (1)

9. grate (35); andirons (22); logirons (3); fire irons (2); dog irons (1)

10. davenport (37); couch (17); daveno (14); sofa (7); lounge (1)

11. (window) blinds (43); (window) shades (36); roller shades (1)

12. clean house (42); clean up (13); straighten up (9); tidy up (3); pick up (2); do up (1)

13. breezeway (41); walk(way) (14); patio (2); arcade (1); archway (1); canopy (1)

14. yard (35); patio (29); court (1)

15. gutters (29); (eaves) troughs (19); rain troughs (6); eaves (6); drains (5); drainpipe (3); (eaves) spouts, spouting (2); (eaves) drips (2)

16. rafters (44); joists (21); beams (14); ridge pole (1); braces (1)

17. outhouse (42); privy (16); backhouse (9); john(ny) (house) (8); cranny (3); biffy (3); Chick Sales (3); one-(two-)holer (2); water closet (1); crapping can (1); Martha (1); shanty (1); can (1)

18. corral (28); cow pen (15); cow lot (8); barnyard (4); cow yard (3); barn lot (1); cow shed (1); corral pen (1)

19. (pig)pen (hog) pen (58); (pig)sty (9); hog house (4); (hog)shed (2); hog shelter (1)

20. corral (6); pasture (4); horse barn (2); paddock (1); barnyard (1); stockade (1); field (1)

21. (wooden) bucket (58); (wooden) pail (17); hod (1)

22. (iron, metal, milk, tin, water) bucket (55); (dairy, metal, tin, water) pail (35)

23. skillet (52); frying pan (25); fry pan (4); spider (2)

24. faucet (61); tap (10); spigot (4); spicket (1)

25. spigot (26); spicket (17); tap (11); faucet (10); bung (4)

26. (paper) sack (52); (paper) bag (34)

27. gunnysack gunny-bag (54); burlap sack/bag (22); sack (5); grain sack (4); potato sack (1)

28. harmonica (46); mouth organ (17); mouth harp (13); Jew's harp (4); juice harp (2); French harp (1)

29. Jew's harp (42); juice harp (15); mouth harp (4); harp (1)

30. rubber band (64); elastic band (3); elastic (2); band (1)

31. sawhorse (66); sawbuck (2)

32. sawbuck (27); sawhorse (25); woodbuck (5); buck (1); saw jack (1)

33. whet stone (63); whet (3); whet rock (2); hone (2); oil stone (2); wet stone (1); emery stone (1); carborundum stone (1); grinding stone (1); round stone (1); steel (1)

34. overalls (46); coveralls (12); levis (10); overhauls (5); jumper (2); jeans (1)

35. chaps (64); aprons (6); chinks (3); leggins (1); puttees (1); chinkaderos (1)

36. swamp (24); slough (23); bog (16); marsh (14); swale (3); meadow (3); spring (1); seep (1); tules (1)

37. meadow (26); valley (26); basin (15); mountain meadow (9); flat (3); plain (2); prairie (1); glen (1); hollow (1); park (1)

38. alkali (patch, flat) (31); desert (30); prairie (6); badlands (5); sandhills (3); wasteland (2); flats (1); sagebrush (1)

39. gully (37); wash (16); gulch (12); draw (10); ditch (8); ravine (8); canyon (5); dry creek (2); riverbed (1); arroya (1)

40. parking (27); parking strip (17); sidewalk plot (2); boulevard (1); boulevard strip (1)

41. barrow pit (33); borrow pit (17); bar pit (14); barrow ditch (4); borrow ditch (2)

42. for (57); on (13)

43. horseshoes (68)

44. bronc(o) (40); mustang (25); cayuse (13); wild horse (4); broom tail (3); maverick (1); shitter (1)

45. wishbone (57); breastbone (11); pulley bone (3)

46. lariat (39); lasso (35); reata (3)

47. cornbread (66); johnny cake (bread) (2); corn dodger (1)

48. pancakes (42); hot cakes (41); flapjacks (10); griddle cakes (3); battercakes (1); sinkers (1)

49. salt pork (29); bacon (23); side pork (11); sow belly (8); side meat (3); salt side (1); sour belly (1)

50. snack (58); lunch (5); piece (3); bite (2)

51. garden (44); family garden (13); garden patch (5); vegetable garden (5); garden plot (2); kitchen garden (2); home garden (2); truck garden (1); garden spot (1)

52. (cherry) pit (61); seed (11); stone (3)

53. (peach) pit (32); stone (24); seed (17)

54. clingstone (peach) (52); cling (peach) (26); clinger (2)

55. freestone (peach) (52); clear stone (2); clear seed (1); free peach (1); open-stone peach (1); sweet peach (1)

56. string beans (41); green beans (34); snap beans (2)

57. turnip greens (39); greens (34); turnip tops (1)

58. husks (55); shucks (15); sheaf (1)

59. corn on the cob (45); roasting ears (21); sweet corn (10); ear corn (1); fresh corn (1)

60. horn(ed)(y) toad (62); toad (1)

61. woodpecker (68); flicker (1)

62. skunk (67); civet cat (5); polecat (2)

63. angleworm (58); worm (5); earthworm (5); fish bait (3); bait worm (3); fishing worm (2); fishworm (1); garden tackle (1)

64. night crawler (64); grubworm (1); angleworm (1)

65. firefly (45); lightning bug (18); glowworm (3); firebug (3); june bug (2)

66. sow bug (13); doodlebug (11); potato bug (8); ball bug (5); pill bug (3); roll bug (1); cuddle bug (1); round bug (1)

67. grasshopper (68)

68. resembles (22); looks like (17); favors (15); is the (spitting) image of (11); takes after (8); chip off the old block (2); chip off the old bub (1)

69. takes after (38); has ways like (7); acts like (6); resembles (6); chip off the old block (3); favors (2); features (1)

70. goose pimples (44); goose bumps (29); goose flesh (5); duck bumps (2)

71. hick (21); hayseed (18); hillbilly (17); clodhopper (7); country bumpkin (5); backwoodsman (3); farmer (3); dirt farmer (2); rube (2); yokel (1); yahoo (1); country dude (1); country jake (1)

72. (city) slicker (40); (city) dude (32); greenhorn (2); tenderfoot (2); drugstore cowboy (1)

73a. wrong side of the tracks (24); other side of the tracks (7); across the tracks (4); in the slums (4); below the tracks (1); skid row (1)

73b. out in the sticks (30); out in the tules (11); out in the boondocks (7); (back) (out) in the boonies (3); out in the jim sangs (1); out in the sagebrush (1)

74. tightwad (46); chintzy (9); miser (8); chinchy (6); penny pincher (6); close (3); tight (3); cheapskate (2); skinflint (1); Jew (1); Scotchman (1); Scrooge (1)

75. carry (36); lug (23); pack (13); tote (1)

76. park (42); (town) square (23); plaza (5); city center (1)

77. shivaree (63); serenade (1); belling-bee (1); tin-panning (1)

78. at his (the) stomach (39); to his (the) stomach (21); with his (the) stomach (2); of his (the) stomach (1)

79. get sick (46); be taken sick (11); take sick (1)

80. mad (54); riled (7); het up (6); furious (2); roiled (1); hot (1); owly (1); wrathy (1)

81. all in (25); bushed (20); worn-out (19); tired (out) (13); tuckered (out) (11); beat (out) (4); pooped (out) (4); fagged (out) (3); weary (2); rundown (1)

82. Japs (30); slant eyes (12); gooks, gakes (4); Nips (4); chinks (3); Nipponese (1); fish eaters (1); butterheads (1)

83. Basquos (25); sheepherders (4); Bass (1); dagos (1)

84. redskins (15); bucks (5); red man (4); war whoops (4); squaws (4); Injuns (2); pintos (1); bow and arrows (1); Smokies (1); Siwash (1); chiefs (1)

85. spicks (13); Chicanos (4); pepper bellies (3); greasers (2); tacos (2); chili chompers (1); beanos (1); wetbacks (1); slicks (1)

86. jack Mormons (6); carrot eaters (4); cricket stompers (2); saints (2); carrot snappers (1); crickets (1); sons of Brigham (1)

87. fish eaters (5); red necks (1); papists (1); mackerel snappers (1)

88. bota (bag), botea (10); flask (2)

89. jai alai (11); pelota (5); pelotaka (1)

90. beret (8); tam (3); chapela (2); biretta (1); sash (1); tuque (1)

91. mus (5); barbooth, barbute (2)

92. derrick (56); Mormon derrick (8); hay derrick (5); overshot (2); A-derrick (1); Jackson fork (1); beaver slide (1); harrow bed (1)

93. quarter to (34); quarter till (17); 4:45 (16); quarter of (1); quarter before (1)

94. mush (69); hot cereal (40); porridge (1)

95. minister (46); preacher (25); reverend (8); pastor (4); parson (2)

96. hired man (27); hired hand (19); farmhand (18); ranch hand (11); hired help (4)

97. dragonfly (53); (devil's) darning needle (12); mosquito hawk (2); snake feeder (2); snake doctor (1); water dragon (1)

98. device used for hauling hay (4); stoneboat (3); ditcher (3); sled (2); other responses (8)

99. salamander (7); lizard-like creature (4); other responses (2)

100. slough (31); swamp (25); marsh (16); tules (2); pond (1)

101. chore (54); job (16); duty (2); task (1); stint (1)

102. rhubarb (61); pieplant (14)

103. shortening (39); grease (24); lard (12); fat (7); oil (7); tallow (1)

104. breakfast, dinner, supper (37); breakfast, lunch, dinner (26); breakfast, lunch, supper (7)

105. breakfast, dinner, supper (53); breakfast, lunch, dinner (10); breakfast, lunch, supper (2)

Finnish Log Homestead Buildings in Long Valley

ALICE KOSKELA

Horizontal timber construction captured the attention of folklorists early in the development of American material culture studies. Not only did the log cabin have a romantic, nationalist image, but it also had inspired some of the best European scholarship. One influential article was Sigurd Erixson's "The North-European Technique of Corner Timbering," Folkliv (1937).

Most elements of American log construction derive from German and East European tradition, as described in Henry Glassie and Fred Kniffen, "Building in Wood in the Eastern United States; A Time-Place Perspective," Geographical Review (1966), but in some pockets of recent immigration we may find the very distinctive Scandinavian techniques of corner timbering and log shaping. Alice Koskela's article describes the Finnish method as it was used in Idaho early in the twentieth century by Finnish immigrants in Long Valley.

Koskela is a Finnish-American born in the Finnish community at Long Valley. She has an M.A. degree in English, and she is currently working on a Ph.D. degree in American Studies at Washington State University. Her dissertation is on Finnish-American communities in Idaho. Currently Koskela is a reporter for the Lewiston Morning Tribune.

Although most residents of central Idaho's Long Valley know that the region was once the home of a sizable and active Finnish community, many assume the Finnish church there to be all that remains of the immigrant settlement. The church, located on Farm to Market Road, is the best kept and most accessible Finnish-built structure in the valley. There are other Finnish buildings in Long Valley, however, and although many of these are hard to find and few have been maintained, they too are historically significant. The surviving log homestead cabins, saunas, and farm buildings of this immigrant group are examples of the Finns' extraordinary ability to craft sturdy and weather-resistant structures with a minimum of tools and materials. Some are in amazingly good condition, considering that they have had to withstand the region's harsh winters for, on the average, over seventy years. These buildings are tangible reminders of an important chapter in Long Valley history, and of the late homestead era in Idaho. The structures possess an ethnic heritage, moreover, which has been traced in the United States to 1638, when the first Finns reached the new world and the first log cabins were constructed in America.

Historian and archaeologist C. A. Weslager explains in his book *The Log Cabin in America* that the first colonists to build homes of "horizontally laid logs, both round and hewn," were members of the New Sweden community that established itself on the banks of the Delaware River between 1638 and 1640. According to Weslager, "approximately one-half [of the colonists] were actually Finns," and "the majority of log houses in New Sweden were built by Finns."[1] His conclusion, the result of extensive research into little-known records, suggests that the Finnish contribution to America includes not only the sauna bath and Sibelius' music, but also several methods of building log cabins. Many of the features he notes on the seventeenth-century cabins of New Sweden can be found on Finnish-built homestead structures in Long Valley.

The Finnish settlement of Long Valley was part of a later, major wave of Finnish immigration to the United States. Finns first arrived in the late 1890s, when a group of immigrants from the Pendleton, Oregon, area took up homesteads on the southeast side, near what was once the village of Center.[2] They were followed by others from various places, most notably the Wyoming mining towns of Diamondville, Rock Springs, Carbon, and Hanna. In 1903 a disastrous explosion in Hanna killed 269 miners, 96 of them Finns, and as a result a number of immigrants decided to give up this dangerous occupation for farming in Long Valley.[3] Many descendants of Finnish homesteaders in the area recall that one or more of their relatives lost their lives in the Hanna explosion. Most Finns who came here after 1900 took up land on the northeast side of Long Valley. Of the ninety homestead patents issued to Finnish settlers in Valley County between 1904 and 1925, approximately two-thirds were for quarter sections in Townships 17 and 18 in the north end of the valley, while the remaining thirty granted ownership to farms scattered less densely in the southern Townships 15 and 16. Six of these homesteads are now among the farms under the waters of the Cascade Reservoir.[4]

The highest concentration of Finnish settlers was in an area just southeast of McCall, on either side of Farm to Market Road. A two-room school and teacher's cottage next to the road are the last remaining public buildings of the Finnish community there known as Elo, named for its spiritual leader, Reverend John William Eloheimo. The tiny village, located on Timber Ridge west of the school, once contained a meeting hall, store, and post office, but today Elo's townsite is marked only by a split rail fence which surrounds the five graves of Eloheimo family members. Even the minister's residence, an elaborate Victorian-style home with leaded glass windows, gable returns, and an ornamental tower, was destroyed in a fire.[5] Fortunately a considerable number of the log structures on surrounding Finnish homesteads have not met a similar fate, for about fifty immigrant cabins, saunas, and other farm buildings can be found throughout Long Valley. They suggest a history, recorded almost nowhere else, of the Finnish settlement here, and are examples of a kind of craftsmanship that has all but disappeared: the art and skill of constructing log buildings in the Finnish way.[6]

After inspecting a number of homestead structures in the valley one can usually determine with a glance if a log building is the work of a Finnish craftsman. The distinguishing characteristics of such structures include hewn-log walls (all but one cabin and one sauna are of squared timbers) that fit so tightly together that little or no chinking has been necessary; double, or common-block, full-dovetail, or locked-dovetail corner notches; and inside log partitions notched through outside walls in a way that harmonizes with the building's corners. These features have been noted in descriptions of Finnish homestead sites in both the midwestern United States and British Columbia, where large groups of the immigrants settled.[7]

It is easy to take for granted the smooth hewn-log walls of a homestead cabin, but squaring timbers with a broadax required considerable skill and patience. Although this extra work did not measurably improve a building's strength or durability, it was almost the first step in the Finnish craftsman's procedure. Donovan Clemson, in his study of log buildings on British Columbia homesteads, believes that "hewing was probably practiced so frequently because of the innate desire of the craftsman to do a good job." Clemson observes that "hewed logs looked more professional, removed the building a little from the rawness associated with the standing bush [wilderness] . . . and the house, hopefully, from a distance might even be mistaken for a frame building with dressed sides."[8] Certainly the builder had reason to be proud of his skill with a broadax, with its wide razor-sharp blade. Henry Koski, a second-generation Finn whose family settled in north

Idaho, remembers well the competence of a builder there named Kaarlo Keisala. "Watching Keisala work was something to see," Mr. Koski recalls. "His ability was far superior to anyone else and he could swing that big old ax and take shavings paper thin where needed."[9]

Although nearly all of the Finns' cabins and saunas, and even a number of their farm buildings, were built of carefully hewn logs, the skill of squaring timbers with a broadax is now almost a lost art in Long Valley. A second-generation Finnish craftsman named, appropriately, Bill Ax, is one of the few men left in the valley who knows how to deftly swing "that big old ax." He constructed his first hewed-log cabin in 1914, when he was ten years old, after watching other immigrant farmers in the area erect their homestead houses. Since then he has built scores of log homes, bridges, and other structures in the area and has established a reputation as an expert artisan. He gave a log-hewing demonstration at a Finnish family reunion in McCall in 1977, but otherwise has had little call for this particular kind of work. Unlike the valley's early settlers, people now prefer the rustic look so most of the houses Mr. Ax has built in recent decades are of round logs. The cabin he constructed in 1914, "just for practice" he recalls, still stands on his father's homestead site, a good example of the craft he later perfected.[10]

It is said that "if you can't see daylight through the walls of an old cabin in Long Valley, it was probably built by a Finn," and this standard is one that many log buildings, both round and hewn, can still meet after decades of neglect. Unlike most other homesteaders, the Finns did not leave wide interstices between logs and then chink them later with mud or clay to weatherproof cabin walls. Instead they fit every log snugly on top of the one below it by chopping out a shallow trench in its underside so that it cupped the rounded upper side of the log in the new lower tier. This process was accomplished by the use of a tool called a *vara* (pronounced wah-rah, rolling the "r"), a hand-forged tool about ten inches long with a set of sharp prongs on one end. The width of the prongs can be adjusted by sliding the metal ring around the handle of the tool to the appropriate point along its length: the closer the ring is to the prong-end of the handle the closer the points are, and vice versa (Figure 1).[11] Clemson describes the use of the *vara*, as it was explained to him by a Finnish farmer in British Columbia:

> He told me that the close fit of the logs was achieved by hollowing out the underside of the upper log before setting it down on the upper side of the under log. This involved accurately marking the upper log with a home-forged, caliperslike tool which left a level scratch along the log as a guide to the axman who would hollow it out along the line, using the corner of a double-bitted ax for the job.[12]

When the Finnish craftsman raised another log into position on his cabin wall, he rough-notched it at the corners to determine its approximate placement and

Figure 1.   Settlers in Long Valley used hand-forged *vara* to incise the undersides of logs to guide axmen who then hollowed them out along these lines, insuring a close fit.

Figure 2.   The corner notching on the John S. Johnson (John Sampila) sauna house shows how logs were fitted together lengthwise by hollowing the underside of the timbers.

then adjusted the prongs of the *vara* to accommodate the widest gap between it and the log below. Then he drew the prongs down the length of the logs, inside and out, etching a line in the upper log which corresponded to every bump and curve in the top of the lower one. He next turned the log over, chopped out a trench between the lines he had scribed, and placed some sort of insulation material—usually moss or rags—in the hollow of the timber. Finally he fit the concave underside of the upper log over the slightly convex top of the lower one, and notched the corners securely. On Finnish homestead buildings with block-notched corners one can usually see the trench in the bottom sides of the logs because the timbers extend past the notching (Figure 2). Several of the Finnish homesteaders in Long Valley were accomplished blacksmiths (aside from log building, smithing was a commonly practiced immigrant craft), and both Bill Ax and a Finnish valley resident named Art Johnson own varas forged locally around the turn of the century. These tools, like the broadax, are rarely used for building anymore, but they were once indispensable to the immigrant homesteaders in the region.

In an article on Finnish log buildings in northern Minnesota, Michael Karni and Robert Levin identify the three most commonly found corner notches as the "simple dovetail—in Finnish, *tasanurkka*; the locking dovetail or *lukkonurkka*; and the common block or *pitkanurkka*."[13] These three styles of notching, with a slight variation on the "lukkonurkka," can be seen on Long Valley's Finnish-built log structures. The common block, or double notch (Figure 3), is a more complicated version of the square notch, which required that only the bottom side of each timber be cut away to fit the flat top of the one beneath it.[14] Because a Finnish craftsman molded his logs together lengthwise, a simple square notch was unsuitable because it did not pull the

timbers closely enough at the corners. Thus, he often used the *pitkanurkka*, which worked on the same principle as the dovetail notch except that its outline was rectangular rather than fan shaped. To prevent any slippage the builder extended his timbers several inches beyond the notch itself. Weslager has observed this corner style on eighteenth-century farmhouses in Finland, and Terry Jordan, a scholar of folk architecture, believes that "Finnish immigrants introduced [the double notch] into the North Woods of the upper Midwest in the late nineteenth century."[15] This cornering method can be found on many immigrant homestead structures in Long Valley, such as the John S. Johnson (John Sampila) hewed-log house, built in 1903 by two Finnish craftsmen named Heikki and Abel Niemala.

A notching style found less often on Long Valley's Finnish homesteads is the full dovetail (Figure 4). Because of its configuration, this notch held corners so tightly that they could be cut flush with little danger of slippage. Many of the log buildings in New Sweden exhibited such a notch, and Weslager believes that "full dovetailing and flush corners . . . was clearly a material culture trait" of seventeenth-century Finland and Sweden.[16] The *tasanurkka* notch required considerable skill on the part of the builder, for its angles had to correspond perfectly to those above and below or the corners would not fit. A good example of this notching method in Long Valley can be seen on the John Korvola homestead cabin, now located across the road from the Long Valley Museum in the old Roseberry townsite.

An even more intricate notch, the *lukkonurkka*, required that the builder carve out rectangular teeth on either side of the dovetail fan. A variation of this style, which Finnish folk architecture scholar Matti Kaups has noted on Minnesota sauna houses, has a single tooth on its lower edge.[17] Either style is truly the mark

Figure 3. The double, or common block corner notching of the Gust Laituri cabin rests on a fieldstone foundation.

of an expert artisan; the latter can be found on three valley homestead buildings erected by Herman and Jacob Mahala on their adjoining homesteads (Figure 5).

Karni and Levin note that, in the upper Midwest, "in almost all cases the plan of a Finnish log house can be read from the outside walls,"[18] and this principle applies to structures in Long Valley as well. When a Finnish craftsman erected a building that contained more than one room, he notched the inside partition through the outside walls. If a building had more than one story, the floor joists of the upper rooms were likewise notched into the walls. An excellent example of the extended notching of an interior wall can be found on the Gust Laituri cabin, constructed in 1905. The plan of this large two-room structure can easily be read from the outside. On most Finnish-built log houses the corner notching and method of inside wall extension harmonizes; that is, if full-dovetail, flush corners were used, the inside wall was cut flush to the outside, while if the house corners were double block and extended, the partition was similarly notched and continued.

Few of Long Valley's immigrant homesteads remain intact, but those that do almost always contain a sauna. There are seven homestead saunas in the valley, and one other which has been incorporated into the first floor of the Matt Ilka log home. All correspond to Michael Karni's description of Finnish saunas in Minnesota:

Figure 4. The John Korvola homestead cabin has full-dovetail, flush-cut corner notching.

The steam room contained a wood-burning stove (called a *kiuas*) fitted on the top with a crib in which were placed fist-sized rocks, a barrel-sized container for cold water, another for hot water (the latter usually connected in some way to exploit the heat of the stove), and three ascending tiers of benches (in the manner of bleachers) on which the bathers sat—the most hardy on the top bench where the heat was most intense.[19]

Six of Long Valley's sauna houses contain a hewed-log steam room and a milled-board addition which served as the dressing room (Figure 6), but the John G. Johnson (Rintakangas) sauna is made entirely of round logs hewed at the corners and around the window and door openings (Figure 7). These features give it a more rustic appearance, and since the Rintakangas homestead site is no longer accessible by road and surrounded by low hills, it is easy to stand there, seeing only the seventy-year-old log cabin, barn, and sauna, and imagine what life was like for the early settlers in the region. The Rintakangas sauna stove is connected to a brick chimney, but some other Finnish bathhouses in Long Valley were *savusaunas*, or smoke saunas, so named because smoke was vented through small openings in the walls.[20] The walls of a *savusauna* thus became blackened with soot, and it is said to be proof of Finnish descent if one can bathe in a smoke sauna and come out cleaner than before.

The only Finnish log barn in the valley containing close fit hewed and round logs stands on the Nicholai Wargelin farm. This impressive fifty-foot-wide struc-

Figure 5. The toothed, or keyed notches of the Jacob Mahala homestead cabin use a unique type of North European corner notching.

Figure 6. The Nickolai Wargelin sauna, with a hewn-log steam room and a frame dressing room, is typical of most Long Valley saunas.

Figure 7.   The John G. Johnson (Rintakangas) sauna is the only sauna in Long Valley made entirely of round logs.

ture is built in the style of most Finnish frame barns in the area,[21] but is unique among immigrant log barns here because the timbers have been scribed and notched tightly together. (A similar barn can be found in north Idaho on the O. A. Rainio homestead near Cataldo.) The Wargelin barn, a double-crib structure, has a characteristically steep roof and low walls, made to shed the heavy snow that would accumulate on a less vertical slope. Its interior uprights and cross pieces are hand-hewn timbers joined with wooden pegs in the mortice and tenon style, and the interior log sides of its two cribs, like the partitions in houses, are fit tightly together and notched through the barn's outside walls (Figure 8). Although sawn logs now cover part of the original structure, and have replaced what were probably milled-board gables, the east and west walls remain unaltered, testimony to the skill of the builder.

Perhaps even more indicative of what Clemson called ''the innate desire of the craftsman to do a good job'' is the building identified by the present owner of the Wargelin farm as a ''brooder house.'' This structure, just east of the barn, was probably never intended to be anything but a shelter for farm animals, but its double-notched logs are carefully hewed and scribed so that now, sixty years later, it is as sound and weatherproof as ever. The ridgepole has been purposely placed slightly off-center, creating an unusual pitch to the roof and giving the entire building an interesting geometric form.

Long Valley's Finnish community has, by 1980, become almost entirely absorbed into the larger Anglo-American group which also settled in this region, but its craftsmen left behind a number of remarkable log homestead structures. Many of these buildings are threatened, however, for as the valley assumes the identity and pace of a resort area more farms are subdivided into lots redefined as estates and old structures are destroyed to make way for modern vacation cabins. Certainly some should be preserved, for they are more than simply picturesque. The Finnish log homestead buildings, which have outlived both the culture and the era that produced them, are historians of a way of life now over, tangible record of the skill and craft of the immigrant artisans who settled in Long Valley.

Notes

This study of Long Valley's Finnish homestead structures was begun in the winter of 1978 and sponsored by grants from the Idaho State Historic Preservation Office (funded by the U.S. Department of the Interior).

1. C.A. Weslager, *The Log Cabin in America: From Pioneer Days to the Present* (New Brunswick, N.J.: Rutgers University Press, 1969), pp. 150, 152.

2. S. Ilmonen, *Amerikan Suomalaisten Historia*, Vol. 3

Figure 8.   The Long Valley settlers built gambrel-roofed barns of log or frame construction. This is a view from the northeast of the Nickolai Wargelin barn.

(Hancock, Mich.: Suom.-Lut, Kustannuslikkeen Kirja-painossa, 1926), p. 235.

3. Tyomies Society, *Seventieth Annual Souvenir Journal: 1903–1973* (Superior, Wis.: Tyomies Society, 1973), p. 13.

4. *Index to US Patents: Valley County*, available in the Valley County Courthouse, Cascade, Idaho.

5. Letter from Mrs. Elma (Eloheimo) DeBolt to author, October 7, 1979.

6. There is considerable debate over the question of attributing certain features of American log architecture to particular immigrant groups. This question becomes particularly difficult when attempting to distinguish Finnish from Swedish building methods, as Weslager readily admits (p. 152). The term "Finnish way" in this article is intended to denote those methods of constructing log buildings which have been described elsewhere in articles about Finnish building, and which appear to have been practiced by the immigrants in Long Valley.

7. See Donovan Clemson, "The Scandinavian Way," in *Living with Logs: British Columbia's Log Buildings and Rail Fences* (Saanichton, B.C.: Hancock House, 1974), pp. 60–71; Michael Karni and Robert Levin, "Northwoods Vernacular Architecture: Finnish Log Building in Minnesota," *Northwest Architect*, May–June, 1972, pp. 92–99; and Richard W. E. Perrin, "The Finnish Farmstead," in *The Architecture of Wisconsin* (Madison: The State Historical Society of Wisconsin, 1967), pp. 20–23.

8. Clemson, pp. 30, 32. Today it is difficult to appreciate

the settler's desire to make his log cabin look like a frame house, but this attitude seems to have been prevalent in most pioneer communities. Terry Jordan, in *Texas Log Buildings: A Folk Architecture* (Austin: University of Texas Press, 1978), notes that "log houses became symbols of the frontier, of backwardness, of deprivation. Status could be gained by discarding the log house and replacing it with one of frame, brick, or stone. At the very least, socially upward-mobile folk were expected to conceal the logs with milled siding" (p. 5). Such is the case with the Charles Koski log house south of McCall, an unusually large building erected in 1907 which was later covered with asphalt tiles to make it look "better."

9. Letter from Mr. Henry Koski to author, January 6, 1979.

10. Interview with Mr. Bill Ax of McCall, Idaho, conducted on September 13, 1978.

11. For photos and a description of the use of the *vara* in Minnesota Finnish settlements, see Matti Kaups, "A Finnish Savusauna in Minnesota," *Minnesota History*, Spring 1976, p. 13.

12. Clemson, p. 69.

13. Karni and Levin, p. 97.

14. For an illustration of the "square" or "flat" notch, see Alex W. Bealer, *The Log Cabin: Homes of the North American Wilderness* (Barre, Mass.: Barre Publishing, 1978), p. 41.

15. Jordan, p. 71.

16. Weslager, p. 153.

17. Kaups, pp. 13–14.

18. Karni and Levin, p. 95.

19. Michael Karni, "Honey-heat and Healing Vapors: The Sauna in Finnish Immigrant Life," *Northwest Architect*, March–April, 1973, p. 77.

20. See Kaups, pp. 11–12.

21. For a description of the Finnish frame homestead barns found in Long Valley, see Arthur A. Hart, "Farm and Ranch Buildings East of the Cascades," in *Space, Style and Structure: Building in Northwest America*, ed. Thomas Vaughan (Portland: Oregon Historical Society, 1974), p. 247.

Folk Song Studies in Idaho

Jan Harold Brunvand

Brunvand's survey of folk song studies in Idaho provides both a summary of efforts through 1965 and a discussion of song texts housed in the folklife archives at Utah State University (Fife Folklore Archives), Logan, and the University of Idaho, Moscow. While the University of Idaho collection has not increased its song holdings since Brunvand's departure for the University of Utah in 1965, other regional institutions have either begun new collecting efforts or augmented previous holdings. Interested researchers can find folk song collections from this region at the Idaho Folklore Archives, Idaho State University, Pocatello; The College of Idaho Folklore Archives, Caldwell; and the Nez Perce Music Archives, Washington State University, Pullman.

Jan Harold Brunvand, who received his Ph.D. in folklore at Indiana University, taught at the University of Idaho from 1961 to 1965 and is now professor of English at the University of Utah. He has published in the major folklore journals, and he is the author of The Study of American Folklore: An Introduction *(second edition 1978) and* The Vanishing Hitchhiker: American Urban Legends and Their Meanings *(1981).*

This article is reprinted with permission from Western Folklore, *where it first appeared in vol. 24:4 (1965): 231–48.*

The study of folk songs in Idaho had an auspicious beginning in 1917 when George Morey Miller became head of the Department of English at the University of Idaho. Holding a B.A. from Indiana University (1892), an M.A. from Harvard (1898), and a Ph.D. from the University of Heidelberg (1911), Professor Miller was well trained in "philology," including folklore, as it was studied at the time. His great love, second only to Shakespeare, was British ballads, and he had earlier published a notable contribution to the "communal origins" theory which is credited with influencing F. B. Gummere's ideas in 1907 in *The Popular Ballad.*[1]

As head of the department, until his death in 1937, George Morey Miller was legendary as a colorful figure on the campus and an inspirational teacher. Some of the anecdotes about him still circulate orally—his somewhat eccentric dress and habits, his dramatic flair in the classroom, his ballad singing both in class and out, and his unanimous rating by generations of students as their favorite teacher.[2] Beginning in 1923, when an M.A. in English was first given, six theses that dealt comparatively with British or American ballads were approved under him.[3]

One of Professor Miller's students, Leona Nessly Ball, wrote the only article devoted entirely to Idaho folklore that has appeared in the *Journal of American Folklore*; it described the survival of play parties in north Idaho.[4] Beginning with her professor's statement that "It is possible [that play parties] may still be found in . . . rustic neighborhoods,"[5] Miss Ball published some two dozen Idaho texts, many with tunes. The format was an account of a typical Idaho rural "school

entertainment." She also listed numerous titles of other play parties known in the region.

The most interesting folk song thesis done under George Morey Miller was that of Thomas Edward Cheney, submitted in 1936: "Folk Ballad Characteristics in a Present-Day Collection of Songs." Cheney, an active western folklorist in the English department at Brigham Young University,* wrote that, after having his interest fired by a seminar in 1933, he collected for some two and one-half years in southeastern Idaho. He turned up seventy-one ballads and balladlike pieces which he classified and discussed in relation to their similarity or dissimilarity to the Child canon. Most of his informants were elderly and had never seen the songs they sang in print; no tunes were collected. The songs ranged from a version of a Child ballad (No. 4, "Lady Isabel and the Elf Knight") to British broadsides (e.g., "The Rich Irish Lady"), native ballads, (e.g., "Frankie and Johnny," and "Charles Guiteau") and songs about cowboys, railroad men, and Mormons. Finally, there was a group of miscellaneous, mostly sentimental, "parlor" and music hall songs such as "Do Not Put My Mother's Picture up for Sale" and "You Are Starting, My Boy, on Life's Journey." Two of Cheney's texts are given below, "To Be a Buckaroo," probably a local song, and "In Defense of Polygamy," one on a theme of much local interest.

---

*Cheney is now retired from the Brigham Young University faculty. A portion of his thesis appears in edited form in this volume.–Ed.

TO BE A BUCKAROO

(Cheney thesis No. 26, p. 117. Collected from Cornelius Campbell, Swan Valley, Idaho. "When, where, or how this bit of song came into existence I know not. . . . He said he knew no other names aside from the local insertions.")

To be a buckaroo
I left Victor town
I camped in Pine Creek Canyon;
They called hand me down.

Now Bill says to me
"There's a gray that I own
Corralled in the next canyon
With a sorrel and a roan."

My rope I threw on him;
My saddle I fixed;
He lit into bucking;
I felt rather mixed.

I grabbed for the leather
And "squoze" out its juice,
Or else that gray brute
Would have "shooken" me loose,

Hal Dean was my herder;
Damn little he did
But set there and holler,
"Stay with her, kid."

I stayed with the devil,
The devil I did,
I stayed with the devil
Till I shot over his head.

Now you can brag of your riding
In any old town
But (put) her to practice
And hand me down.

IN DEFENSE OF POLYGAMY

(Cheney thesis No. 37, p. 133. Collected from W. H. Avery, Blackfoot, Idaho.)

There is a bunch of whiskey bloats perluding our fair land;
They are here to see our country laws enforced;
They say that the laws, there ain't enough to punish
    Mormon crime,
And for more, they are always on the yelp.

They say that if the Mormons will polygamy deny,
Like themselves take to houses of ill fame.
They will call them friends and brethren and will take
    them by the hand;
But in this, I think, they'll find they are lame.

Chorus:

Murry holds the reins, the whip belongs to Zane,
Ole Ireland and his aid will go below;
And old Dixon will do well to engage a case in Hell,
For the road he is on will take him there, I know.

They say that the Mormons are a set of low-down
    dragons,
And they're going to rid the land of such a crew,
Or they will build pens large enough to hold Mormon
    men,
And in them they will shove the women, too.

But the Mormons do not fear their threats and always will
    be found
To their God and to their constitution true;
They will support Columbus's cause and defend Colum-
    bus's laws;
Then with righteousness this nation will be blessed.

(A variant of this ballad, "Governor Zane," differs considerably. See Lester A. Hubbard, *Ballads and Songs from Utah* [Salt Lake City, 1961], pp. 456–57.)

Perhaps the greatest long-term benefit that resulted from George Morey Miller's interest in folk songs was to the university library. For the twenty years of his Idaho career, he saw to it that new folklore publications, especially song collections, were acquired, and many of his personal books also went to the library eventually. Since 1937 the subject has been kept up to date, forming a surprisingly complete folklore research collection.

In the years since Professor Miller's death, there has been a trickle of activity in Idaho folk song studies. The WPA Federal Writers' Project volume, *Idaho Lore*, that Vardis Fisher edited in 1939, contained eighteen texts (no tunes). But few have the ring of genuine oral tradition, and no informants are identified.[6] Fisher's editorial criteria for the songs are suggested by a note to the effect that only songs with a distinct Idaho slant were chosen, that profane or lewd songs were rejected, and that some of the printed texts are not known to be traditional.[7] Actually, none of the texts is a verifiable, oral-traditional, folk song; most of them are pseudo-literary in tone, and there are only a few passing references to Idaho in verses which may have had some oral life in the state. The song "Ida-Ho" or "The Girl Named Ida-Ho" compares various states, and it is a piece found elsewhere, at least in manuscripts (see below). "Eagle Rock," using the old name for Idaho Falls, is a rhyme of local boosting, containing such verses as:

It's pleasant to play in Paris
Where gaiety gains renown.
But Oh! when it comes to living,
Give me that dear Idaho town.

"Kamiah Springs" is said to commemorate an Indian battle, in October 1879, presumably near the present town of Kamiah, and it sounds reasonably authentic. Similarly, a verse of "Pioneer Song," which may be a folk song, is given as follows:

My mother and father were very poor people,
They lived by a church which had a high steeple.

They raised apples but sold them so low,
They made no fortune in Idaho.

Finally worth noting is a piece called "The Trail of Idaho," about the unfaithful sweetheart of a wandering cowboy who is off riding on the Idaho trail.

The late Blaine Stubblefield of Weiser, Idaho, who originated the National Old Time Fiddlers' Contest, held there annually in June, was an enthusiastic folk song collector and singer. Alan Lomax recorded his singing of sixteen songs in the Recording Laboratory of the Library of Congress. Mrs. Rae Korson, Head of the Archive of Folk Song, reports that in April 1938, Stubblefield recorded "The Old Chisholm Trail," "The Persian Cat," "She Had a Dark and Roving Eye," "Nine Times a Night," "Nelly at the Wake," "Way Out in Idaho," "The Farmer's Curst Wife," "If He'd Be a Buckaroo," "The Keyhole in the Door," "Brennan on the Moor," and "Devilish Mary," all accompanied by guitar. In January 1939, he recorded "Bryan O'Lynn," and "Poor Miner" unaccompanied and "It's Hard Times, Boys," "Ta-ji-buggeroo," and two versions of "The Lowlands Low" with guitar.[8]

Recently, two western folk song collectors have recorded their versions of songs collected in Idaho. Mrs. Rosalie Sorrels sings twelve songs learned in Idaho on *Folk Songs of Idaho and Utah* (Folkways FH 5343): "Brigham Young," "Death of Kathy Fiscus," "I'll Give You My Story," "Empty Cot in the Bunkhouse Tonight," "The Wreck of the Old Number Nine," and "The Philadelphia Lawyer" (all learned from a fish and game warden in Cascade); and from other informants, "The Lineman's Hymn," "My Last Cigar," "The House Carpenter" (Child No. 243), "The Wild Colonian [sic] Boy," "I Left My Baby," and Blaine Stubblefield's version of "Way Out in Idaho."[9] J. Barre Toelken published five texts from Idaho in an article in *Northwest Review* in 1962:[10] "Sawtooth Peaks" ("Tyin' Knots in the Devil's Tail"), "Judge Duffy," "When I was a Younger Fellow" (an apparent translation from German), "Too Ree Ama" (loggers' brag song), and "Off to Boise City" ("Way Hay Jerusalem"). The last three songs are recorded by Toelken on *A Garland of American Folksongs* (Prestige/International 13023).

A regular undergraduate course in American Folklore (English 174) was initiated at the University of Idaho in summer school, 1963; thereafter, it was scheduled for each spring semester and occasionally in summer school and in extension classes. The number of Idaho folk songs collected either by students or as a result of student leads has been considerable. One of the first collecting ideas that classes responded to was the dissemination of folk song texts in published or written sources. Several clipping files, scrapbooks, notebooks, old record collections, and one songster were found, indicating that folk songs have come into Idaho through every usual medium except broadside printing.[11]

Two newspaper sources of folk songs have reached into Idaho from Spokane, Washington, since the 1920s and 1930s, *The Twice-A-Week Spokesman* (now *The Spokesman-Review*), and *The Idaho Farmer* (one of five regional papers published biweekly by the Northwest Farm Paper Unit). The *Spokesman* no longer carries a song column, but an extension student from Troy, Idaho, turned in a representative group of sixty-seven clippings that can be dated from 1921 to 1923 because of incidental references on the reverse side of some clippings to Harding's presidency. Included were the Child ballads, "Lord Lovel," "Barbara Allen," "Andrew Bardeen," and "The House Carpenter" (Nos. 75, 84, 167, and 243), as well as such English songs as "Froggie Went a Courting," and "Erin's Green Shore," and many American songs, including "The Cumberland Crew," "The Jam at Gerry's Rock," and "Little Sod Shanty on the Claim."

The Idaho Farmer and corresponding newspapers in Washington, Oregon, and Utah continue to publish the column "Songs of Days Gone By," which was announced in the issue of July 2, 1931 (Vol. XLVIII, p. 4), and manuscript files maintained in the editorial offices have proved to be a rich lode of folk songs known in the whole region. In the summer of 1963, Professor and Mrs. Austin E. Fife extracted some 500 cowboy and other western texts from this source, retyping and binding them into three volumes for their massive western folk song archive. During the same summer the Fifes located a personal collection of several thousand newspaper clippings and hand-written texts in Kamiah, Idaho, which are now being classified for eventual addition to their collection.[12]

Recently, this writer spent three days going through the files and extracting all folk song and folk poetry texts, in particular those submitted from Idaho. "Songs of Days Gone By" functions mainly as an informational service for readers who wish to be reminded of the words of old songs they once knew. A reader sends in his request with a title, sample lore, or stanza. The requests are filled from the office file whenever possible; otherwise a query is published. When a response comes in, the original letter is sent to the requesting reader, but a copy of the text is kept. In the past, informants' names or addresses were seldom preserved, but now this information is regularly recorded. All extra copies of texts are filed alphabetically by title in ream-size boxes with variants clipped together, and cross-references inserted when similar songs turn up with different titles. There is no formal index for the collection, nor are there tunes for more than a few of the songs; bits of verse, quotations, recitations, etc. are simply interfiled. Some 450 song texts, in nearly 600 variants, came into the Idaho Folklore Archive from this source alone, to form the nucleus of the classified materials described below.

Except for three general folders marked "Camp Songs," "High School Songs," and "College Songs," the individual folk songs in the Idaho archive have been identified in reference sources and filed according to types and titles. The collection contains some 730 songs in something over 1000 versions. Since materials from *The Idaho Farmer* constitute about two-thirds of this total, there are relatively few tunes recorded—only about 70 at present. (There is also a tape recording of 22 fiddle tunes.) Because of the preponderance of songs from manuscript or printed sources, the folk song collection is less a representative group of traditional Idaho songs than a basis for building such an archive eventually. The newspaper texts are interesting to compare with field-collected songs throughout the circulation area of the Northwest Farm Paper Unit. Therefore, a survey of the archive should be useful to other collectors in the region, and to students of American folk songs generally.

The proportions of print to oral tradition, and texts to tunes, in the folder of Child ballads, is typical of other sections of the file. The archive contains 49 versions (36 printed or manuscript, 13 oral) of 19 different Child ballads; only 5 with tunes. The ballads represented are Child numbers 2, 3, 4, 12, 18, 46 (frag.), 73, 75, 79, 84, 85, 167, 209, 243, 274, 277, 278, 286, and 289.

Using the two Laws indexes,* we have identified 57 Native American ballads in 83 versions, and 41 British broadsides in 71 texts. The ballads represented are as follows:

Native American:
 A. War (5, 8, 14, 15, 18)
 B. Cowboy and Pioneer (1, 2, 3, 4, 6, 9, 10, 11, 14, 18, 24, 27, 41)
 C. Lumberjack (1, 13, 14, 17, 25)
 D. Sailors and the Sea (4, 27)
 E. Outlaws (1, 3, 4, 5, 11)
 F. Murder (1, 2, 5, 13, 16, 20, 28, 31)
 G. Tragedies (1, 2, 14, 16, 17, 22, 26, 30, 51)
 H. Various Topics (1, 4, 6, 7, 8, 15, 23, 26, 31)
 I. Negro (16)

British Broadside:
 J. War (none)
 K. Sailors and the Sea (10, 12, 13, 28, 36)
 L. Crime and Criminals (16B, 20)
 M. Family Opposition to Lovers (4, 25, 32)
 N. Lovers' Disguises and Tricks (7, 20, 35, 38, 39, 42, 43)
 O. Faithful Lovers (3, 4, 32, 36)
 P. Unfaithful Lovers (1A, 1B, 9, 14, 17, 21, 24, 27, 35)
 Q. Humorous and Miscellaneous (1, 3, 4, 14, 15, 17, 20, 26, 27, 32, 34)

*Refers to G. Malcolm Laws *Native American Balladry* (1950) and *American Balladry From British Broadsides* (1957).–Ed.

Immediately following the two groups in Laws ballad-folders are one folder each of other American and other British ballads, either positively identified as such, or classified tentatively by internal evidence. The titles of these items are as follows:

OTHER AMERICAN BALLADS

Archie Brown
Billy Richardson's Last Ride
Bobtail Cannonball
Chicago Fire
Death of Albert Johnson
Death of Ellsworth
Death of John Dillinger
Dingy Miner's Cabin
Fate of the Fleagle Gang
George Nidiver (The California Hunter)
Haunted Woods (or The Haunted River)
Huntsville Jail
James Rogers (Murder of Mr. Swanton)
John Kelley (Kelley's Lament)
Judge Duffy (Old Judge Duffy)
Morro Castle Disaster
My Good-Looking Man
Oklahoma Charlie
Old Blue the Outlaw

Panhandle Jack
Preacher and the Bear
Prison Fire
Remember the Maine
Richmond on the James
Roame County
Salmon River Diggin's
Sinking of the Submarine S 4
Sinking of the Submarine S 51
Sucker Flat
Tune the Old Cow Died On
When Sherman Marched down to the Sea
Willie Moore
Wreck of the No. 52
Wreck of the Prairie Bell
Wreck of the 1256
Wreck of the Virginia Train No. 3
You'd Better Quit Kickin' My Dog Around (Ole Jim Dawg)
Yuba Dam

OTHER BRITISH BALLADS

Bonaparte (The Isle of St. Helena)
Butter and Cheese and All
Darby Ram
Donnelly and Cooper
Frog's Courtship
Grace Darling

Mush Mush
Off to Philadelphia
Rosy
Three English Blades
Three Jolly Welshman (The Fox Hunt)
Willie Ray

The remaining texts are filed in seventeen subject folders, and one marked (inevitably) "Miscellaneous." Categories have been borrowed from major printed collections or invented as needed. All texts are arranged alphabetically within these groups:

Courtship Songs
"I Wouldn't Marry" and "Wish I was Single" Songs
Nursery and Children's Songs
General Western Songs Parodies of "Beulah Land"
Songs about Idaho
Cowboy Songs
Loggers' Songs

Farmers' Songs
Songs of Gamblers, Drinkers, Ramblers
Nonsense Songs
Song Parodies
Comic Dialect Songs
Mnemonic Songs
Play Party and Dance Songs
Folk Lyrics
Sentimental Balladlike Pieces

Among the miscellaneous ballads and songs are the following items which seem particularly interesting:

Bingen on the Rhine
Cat Came Back
Coast Artillery Song
Daddy's Whiskers
Ella Ree
Four Thousand Years Ago

Hard Times
Johnny Kerbeck
Let's All Go Around to Mary Ann's
Life is But a Game
Name Song (Longest Name Song

Old Tobacco Box   Union Prisoners from
Puttin' On the Style   Dixie's Sunny Land
Quaker Down in Quaker   Whistling Rufus
   Town

The question that ultimately arises when a regional
archive is established is, "Which of these items has a
genuine local origin, or at least shows some local
influence?" The answer for folk songs, of course, is
usually "Mighty few." Still there are a fair number of
texts that, clearly enough, must have originated or
have been significantly modified in Idaho; not all of
these, however, have had oral circulation, or at least
they are on file now only in versions from the farm
newspapers.

The northwest folk song "collector's dilemma"
appears from this archive to be about as Toelken has
described it: "While the region is exceptionally rich in
folklore of all kinds that originated elsewhere, one finds
very few ballads of local origin."[13] The most familiar
ones in Toelken's article occur here with few significant
variations; "Acres of Clams," for instance, was sent in
by one Oregon and two Washington readers with little
more deviation from the original text than what Toelken found, except that two further descriptive verses
are preserved. Likewise, the ballad "Judge Duffy"
which Toelken heard attributed to the old mining town
of Florence, Idaho, was sent to *The Farmer* by four
Washington and Oregon readers whose texts differ only
in particulars. They establish nothing further about the
song's origin. Printed circulation is strongly suggested
for this ballad, especially when one correspondent
wrote, "This song was found in a collection of old
songs and ballads a while back." (No name or date was
recorded.) The following text of "Judge Duffy" came in
from Bremerton, Washington, and only nine of its sixteen lines vary at all from Toelken's; the changed words
are italicized (underlined).

OLD JUDGE DUFFY

Old John Martin Duffy was judge *in* a court,
In a small *rising* town in the west;
Although he knew nothing 'bout rules of the law,
For Judge he was one of the best.

One night in the winter a murder occurred,
And the blacksmith accused of the crime.
They caught him red-handed and though he'd two trials,
The verdict was guilty each time.

Now he was the only good blacksmith we had,
And we wanted to spare him his life,
So Duffy *rose* up in the court like a lord,
And with these words ended the strife.

"I move we *discharge* him; *We need him* in town,"
And he spoke out the words that have gained him renown,
"We have two Chinese laundrymen, everyone knows;
Why not save the poor blacksmith and hang one of those?"

Several interesting items that one would like to call
"northwest traditional ballads" were sent to *The Farmer*,
but a strong measure of faith is required to accept them as
such; in fact, some of these must be judged probably
neither "northwest," "traditional," nor even "ballads." A
piece called "Out in the Great Northwest," for instance,
begins:

I'm going way out west
To where the buffalo used to roam;
I'm going to try to settle down,
And build myself a home,
   Out in the great Northwest,
   Way out in the great Northwest.

The song continues for twelve verses of commentary —
some of it somewhat inappropriate to the region — and a
second version differs only in language. Both of them are
anonymous carbon copies.

Another song called "Oregon Mist" is, at least, more
accurate in details, beginning:

It's raining again, or maybe it's yet,
And all the wide world seems eternally wet.
It showers at night and it rains in the morning,
The sun starts to shine, then it pours without warning.

However, this song tells no coherent story, and the
three coastal webfoots who sent it in wrote nothing further that would establish its oral life.

Songs submitted in only single versions may be intriguing, especially one like "The Salmon River
Diggins'," in which the tone is folksy and the place
names (southwest Oregon, northern California in the
Siskiyou mountains) are accurate; this came from a
reader in Paisley, Oregon. Another, in Rainier,
Oregon, sent an equally fascinating piece — seemingly a
true outlaw ballad that deserves to be fully printed in
hopes of locating parallels:

ARCHIE BROWN

I am a bold highwayman,
My name is Archie Brown.
I've robbed in every country,
Both city and in town.
I've robbed the rich and poor alike,
As you may understand,
'Twas down in California
I was captain of a band.

I came to Portland City,
To see that lively place.
I purchased there some blankets
Which proved my great disgrace.
I instantly did pay for them,
And that without delay,
Unto a noble broker
Whose name was Walter Shay.

As he was counting out my change,
I, with my glancing eye,
Stood looking through the showcase,
Some jewelry I did spy.

From underneath my coat sleeve
Cold iron I did haul,
Three raps I gave him on the head
Which made him quickly fall.

As Walter lay upon the floor,
All bleeding in a gore,
I robbed him of his jewelry,
But still I wanted more.
I hunted for his money
But didn't have long to stay,
But five gold watches I did take
To tell my time of day.

Swartz, myself, and Johnson,
As we were all the same,
Swartz being young and cowardly,
He failed to play the game.
'Twas off to California
Poor Johnson ran away,
But soon was overtaken
To become the hangman's prey.

And now we are three prisoners,
All in the county jail,
All loaded down with iron
Our sorrows to bewail.
Farewell, my loyal heroes,
'Tis you I still adore.
I'm of the strong opinion
That I shall rob no more.

Farewell, my loving mother
To you these lines I write.
I'm almost broken-hearted;
I write by candle light.
When you receive these deadly lines,
The tears you can't forbear,
As you peruse them over
You'll find my tearstains there.

Farewell, my loving comrades,
The time is drawing nigh,
When you look upon the scaffold
Your captain you will spy.
'Twill cause you all to sigh, my lads,
But it's little you'll have to say.
I'll sing you Old Tom Rogers
Upon that fatal day.

Farewell, my loving brother
Relations, too, likewise,
When you receive this letter
It may you all surprise.
My work is done, my race is run
My robbing days are o'er.
One prayer, my loving brother,
Poor Archie is no more.

Certainly the woes of herding sheep make an appropriate folk song topic, but when two individual readers, one in Washington and one in Oregon, send in almost identical twelve-stanza texts of "The Sheep-

herder's Lament," the effect of printed, rather than oral, circulation is felt. The song begins:

I have summered in the tropics,
With the yellow fever chill;
I have been down with the scurvy,
I've had every ache and ill.

I have wintered in the Arctic,
Frostbitten to the bone;
I've been in a Chinese dungeon,
Where I spent a year alone.

I've been shanghaied on a whaler,
And was stranded on the deep,
But I never knew what misery was
Till I started herding sheep.

A song on the same theme that begins "There's a pretty spot near Boise/ Where the sage and saltgrass grow," exists in the file only in one anonymous carbon copy; it too laments the life of the sheepherder with such pathetic lines as:

A tear runs down his wind-tanned cheek,
And a sob that shakes his frame,
For he's just a poor sheepherder
And has sheep on his brain.

Another common topic among the regionally inclined songs is parody of Chinese language and culture; four of these pseudo-Chinese dialect songs, in ten versions, are on file, three from the memories of living Idaho informants. The most popular seems to be one in which a poor, lonesome Chinaman leaves Chinatown and serenades a white lady he admires, only to suffer either having her throw things at him from her window, or this treatment:

The ladies of the very next town,
Came up the hill to roll him down;
From top to bottom they all began,
To toss and tumble this Chinaman.

Although this would seem to be humor of an earlier generation, one Idahoan wrote, "My mother used to sing this song to us as long ago as I can remember. I sang it to my children when they were little, and now I am singing it to my grandchildren."[14]

A search for purely Idaho folk songs is almost unrewarded. Sister M. Alfreda for her two-volume *Pioneer Days in Idaho County* searched as hard as anyone ever has in one part of Idaho for authentic local traditions. The only folk composer she heard of whose works bore the hallmarks of familiarity with oral tradition was "Seven Devil's Johnson," credited with composing songs such as "Seven Devil Song" which begins with these stanzas:

Come all ye bold adventurers
And listen to my song,
About the Seven Devil mines,
I will not keep you long:
Those mines of wealth that's lately found

Display the ore bright,
And millions yet beneath the ground
Is bound to see the light

Chorus

Then dig boys, dig let us the ore find,
And open up in handsome style the Seven Devil
      mines.
And when you pack your old cayuse,
And start to make a raise,
And stop upon a grassy plot
To let the equine graze,
You're liable at any time
To meet the rattle bug.
Then don't forget the snake bite cure,
Corked up in the brown jug.[15]

Whether anyone ever has sung this can only be guessed, but one could sing it to several familiar ballad tunes without straining text or tune.

Another doubtful but interesting item is "Lost River Desert," a six-stanza parody of "Red River Valley" describing an Idaho scene. Two readers sent it in, and the texts differ only in that the one from Mackay says a "cowboy who welcomed you there," and the one from Spencer says "a ranger."

Parodies of "Beulah Land" are ubiquitous beyond the hundredth meridian, and the archive has them in abundance for Dakota-land, Kansas, Nebraska, Oregon (a wet version), desert-land, and for Idaho, one positive and one negative version. Since the typical text is about "the land of wind and heat/Where nothing grows for man to eat," here, for variety, is a local boosting version sent in by a reader from Caldwell:

GRAND IDAHO

Kind Providence our lot may cast,
And yet we have to choose at last.
If you're inquiring where to go,
Come down to southern Idaho.

Chorus:

Oh, Idaho, grand Idaho,
It's just the place for you to go,
With climate fair and sunny skies,
Where mountains rich in grandeur rise,
Where fruit in great abundance grows,
Down here in southern Idaho.

The farmers here may be at ease
And work amid fruit-laden trees;
Whate'er he plants is sure to grow,
And make a crop in Idaho.

For genial showers you need not wait,
You only have to hoist the gate
And let the waters ever flow,
O'er valleys rich in Idaho.

Now you who would contentment gain,
Help build the state with brawn and brain,
To mine the hills, or reap or sow,
You're welcome here in Idaho.

An abundance of copies of sentimental songs and poems about the state sent to *The Idaho Farmer* prove only that this, like most other states, has plenty of homespun poets with lots of local pride. These are not folk songs, and there is no point in doing more than listing titles:

Grand Idaho
Idaho ("nestled among the lofty mountains")
Idaho Jack (about a rodeo cowboy)
Idaho Magic
Idaho, Oh Idaho
My Idaho, My Idaho
Our Idaho
Our Own Home State
Pal Pinto and Ida-Ho

Finally, three songs survive the panning process to remain as possible golden bits of Idaho folk song.

1). Three separate residents sent in three varying texts of a song about a "Girl Named Ida-Ho"; all of these only generally match the one Fisher printed in *Idaho Lore*. While their tone and style suggest popular songs, their variations make some oral tradition at least a possibility.

2). The fragment of "A Prospector's Song," collected by a student in 1963, from a seventy-eight-year-old resident of Lewiston, Idaho, is described as a folk song by the informant, a retired sawmill worker and farmer. It contains, in its chorus, echoes of the song "Salmon River Diggin's" already mentioned:

A PROSPECTOR'S SONG

I looked to the east,
I looked to the west;
I saw a John Chinaman a-coming,
With a big sack of rice,
And a rocker on his back,
Trudging his way to the Salmon.

Chorus:

Save your money boys
To pay your way through
If you don't like the Salmon,
You can go to Caribou.
Don't get hasty and get the "golden fever,"
We'll all make a fortune
When we get to Salmon River.

Which of several Salmon Rivers in the West is being referred to here is by no means clear.

3). In the last analysis, it is probably only "Way Out in Idaho" that remains a well-attested original Idaho ballad. Blaine Stubblefield's version (as sung by Rosalie Sorrels)[16] is a first-person narrative song developing into a complaint about bad working conditions on a railroad job; it has the chorus:

Way out in Idaho, way out in Idaho,
A-workin' on the narrow gauge, way out in Idaho.

Only the ending of this ballad — where the suffering laborer promises to return to marry his Mexican sweetheart — is echoed in this undated version sent to *The Idaho Farmer*:

Remember what I promised you,
As we sat side by side,
Beneath the big persimmon tree;
I said I'd be your bride.

Chorus:

Way out in Idyho,
We're coming to Idyho,
With a four-horse team we'll soon be seen,
Way out in Idyho.

Farewell, it's mother and child,
I'm off to stay for a while;
So won't you kiss me before I go,
And call me your darling child?

An even simpler version was collected by a student in
1964 from his eighty-five-year-old grandmother in
Boise:

Way out in Idaho,
Way out in Idaho.
To Idaho we're bound to go,
Way out in Idaho.

We're going to Idaho,
We're going to Idaho.
A four-horse team will soon be seen,
Way out in Idaho.

But in at least one American version of "The Twa
Brothers" (Child 49) the line is nothing more than a
kenning for "far, far away":

"O, what shall I tell your true love, John,
If she inquires for you?"
"O, tell her I'm dead and lying in my grave,
Way out in Idaho."[17]

One would hope that this example will not typify the
straying of Idaho pioneer songs and ballads from their
original vitality to a point of no return, lost amid the
profusion of imported folklore. Certainly this Idaho
collection of folk songs, as it now stands, suggests this
disconcerting possibility, although the presence of so
many other recognizable folk songs is at the same time
a compensation. If nothing else, the Idaho collection
should encourage some long-overdue systematic fieldwork throughout the state; perhaps in the process more
regional ballads and songs will be discovered.

Notes

1. "The Dramatic Element in the Popular Ballad," *University Studies of the University of Cincinnati*, Ser. II, Vol. I, No. 1 (Jan.–Feb., 1905). See D. K. Wilgus, *Anglo-American Folksong Scholarship Since 1898* (New Brunswick, N.J., 1959), pp. 11, 44.

2. See Rafe Gibbs, *Beacon for Mountain and Plain* (Moscow, Idaho: University of Idaho Press, 1962).

3. Evlyn Rosenberger Clark, "The Conception of the Family as Shown in the Simple Ballads" (1923); Dorothy Carolyn Hall, "A Comparative Study of Popular Ballads of England and America" (1923); Lillian Olga White, "The Folksongs of the American Negro and their Value Today" (1925); Pauline Lamar, "The Function of Incremental Repetition in the English and Scottish Popular Ballads and in the Literary Ballads" (1930); Bethel Packenham Poulton, "The Epic Elements in the Robin Hood Ballads" (1932); and Thomas E. Cheney's thesis, which is discussed below. Three songs from Cheney's current personal collection are given in Richard M. Dorson, ed., *Buying the Wind* (Chicago, 1964), pp. 527–30 and 532–35.

4. "The Play Party in Idaho," *Journal of American Folklore* 44 (1931): 1–26.

5. Miller, "Dramatic Element," p. 31.

6. (Caldwell, Idaho, 1939), pp. 217–37.

7. *Idaho Lore*, p. 217.

8. The index numbers for the 1938 session run from 1633 A1 through 1636 B2; for the 1939 session they are 1848 A and B, and 2505 B1 through 2506 B. An excerpt of "Brennan on the Moor" appears on IC record L 49, *The Ballad Hunter*. A copy of the Stubblefield tapes is in the Idaho Folklife Archives of the Idaho State Historical Society.–Ed.

9. Mrs. Sorrel's singing of "The Lineman's Hymn" is also included on the Folkways recording *The Unfortunate Rake* (FS 3805).

10. "Northwest Traditional Ballads: A Collector's Dilemma," *Northwest Review*, V (1962): 9–18.

11. Seven scrapbooks of printed and written songs have been found by students in their family's possession. The collectors have described the books in detail, listing titles and copying sample texts from each. Dates run from the 1890s to the 1930s; the contents range from a dozen songs to several hundred. Most of the books were old composition books or scrapbooks, while others were ledgers or printed books with blank sheets and clippings pasted in. The songster is a tabloid format newsprint collection of tunes and texts; the paper is extremely yellowed and margins are badly torn. There is no date, but the address of a New York City publisher is given. Folk songs included are "Old Dan Tucker," "The Wabash Cannon Ball," "Little Joe the Wrangler," "The Dreary Black Hills," "The Days of 49," and "Utah Carroll." Bill Sutton of Midvale, Idaho, a folklore student in spring 1964, brought in part of a collection of Edison 78 rpm discs which he acquired from a neighbor, and I made taped copies of such items as Ernest V. Stoneman's "Wreck of the C & O" and "Sinking of the Titanic" (51823), Vernon Dalhart's "The Wreck of Number Nine" and "The Mississippi Flood" (52088), "Fiddlin' Powers," "Sourwood Mountains," and "Cripple Creek" (51789), and Frank Luther and His Pards' "Barbara Allen" and "Butcher's Boy" (52377).

In confirmation of Brunvand's assertion that song archives and scrapbooks provide useful leads, it is proper to note that Polly Stewart's article in this volume is based on research beginning with a visit to the University of Idaho Folklore Collection.–Ed.

12. This material is mentioned on pp. 41 and 43 of an article by the Fifes in *The Folklore and Folk Music Archivist,* VII (Spring, 1964).

Both the *Idaho Farmer* collection and the Kamiah texts are presently housed at the Fife Folklore Archives at Utah State University. The latter collection is titled the "Stella M. Hendren Collection" in honor of its compiler.–Ed.

13. Toelken, "Northwest Traditional Ballads," p. 9.

14. See Hubbard, *Ballads and Songs from Utah,* pp. 170–71 for two similar anti-Chinese songs from the West.

15. Vol. II (Caldwell, 1951), 309.

16. See Kenneth Goldstein's comments on her text in notes with the Folkways recording described above.

17. Louise Pound, "Traditional Ballads in Nebraska," JAF, XXVI (1913), 351–66; "Brought to Nebraska from Nodoway County, Missouri, by its contributor" (p. 353). Reprinted in Louise Pound, *American Ballads and Songs* (New York, 1922), pp. 45–46 and MacEdward Leach, *The Ballad Book* (New York, 1955), pp. 166–67.

The Montgomery House: Adobe in Idaho's Folk Architecture

JENNIFER EASTMAN ATTEBERY, KENNETH J. SWANSON, JOE TOLUSE AND
FREDERICK L. WALTERS

The folklife researcher interested in Idaho architecture and the diffusion of architectural features is faced with a confusing array of data. One reason for this diversity is the number of cultural streams that converged in the state. In addition, regional styles are affected by climate, geography, and the occupations of the people who settled here.

The following article is an illustration of the painstaking research necessary to document a single building and to account for its particular construction elements. Detailed studies of single buildings provide the data needed to formulate regional patterns. This study is complicated by its focus on a structure that not only incorporates two unusual building techniques—adobe infill and vertical post construction—but also may have functioned both as a dwelling and as a commercial establishment. The authors' analysis shows that the Montgomery House reflects the many cultural currents that traversed early southern Idaho.

Although there is no single comprehensive work that attempts to treat the broad national patterns of American folk architecture, individual studies are listed in Howard Wight Marshall's American Folk Architecture: A Selected Bibliography *(1981).*

Jennifer Eastman Attebery is State Architectural Historian, Kenneth J. Swanson is Curator of Collections, and Joe Toluse is Curator for the Idaho State Historical Society, Boise. Attebery is a Ph.D. candidate at Indiana University, Bloomington. Swanson is completing his M.A. in anthropology with an archaeology emphasis at Idaho State University, Pocatello. Frederick L. Walters works as a historic preservation consultant for the architectural firm of Ronald Thurber and Associates, Boise. He specializes in the technology of early building material and construction.

The houses of nineteenth-century Idaho were usually constructed of wood—horizontal logs, board and batten, or framed studs with clapboard or shiplap siding. Wood was used whether the settler was a trapper erecting a temporary shelter in the central Idaho mountains or a businessman hiring a contractor to work from the finest house plan available in an established town—brick being the choice for only the most pretentious buildings. Obtained locally or freighted in, wood played a substantial part in the history of building technology in Idaho.

As important as wood was to Idaho's settlement, though, there was a concurrent tradition that influenced the construction of the state's early buildings: the use of adobe. Adobe materials and techniques, or the incorporation of those techniques and materials into a building constructed of wood, can be found throughout southern Idaho. In this article we will describe one such case in detail—the Montgomery house in Middleton— and we will suggest parallel examples of the influence of adobe construction on other southern Idaho buildings.

Most early settlers in the lower valley of the Boise River built log houses before the Oregon Short Line Railroad came through the valley in 1883. The few buildings already documented have all been log. The Johnston brothers' cabin, the Young cabin, and the McKenzie cabin, all near present-day Caldwell, were built of hewn or round log timbers stacked one upon another and joined at their corners with V and half-dovetail notching.[1]

We were surprised, therefore, to discover the Montgomery house, an adobe-influenced structure built near the Boise River sometime between 1865 and 1870 (Figure 1). In local memory the house was associated with William Montgomery, who platted the first Middleton townsite. Its essential features included hewn cottonwood studs[2] with adobe brick infill, a hall and parlor floor plan, a roof with rafters laid on continuous one-by-twelve-inch plates and bearing on the wall studs, and a cellar and foundation with squared basalt quoins and coursed cobblestone walls laid in a herringbone pattern with adobe mortar.

Montgomery's house was donated in the fall of 1979 to the Idaho State Historical Society, and a team of

Figure 1.   The Montgomery House seen from the northeast, 1979. In the foreground curators Kenneth J. Swanson and Joe Toluse uncover a rock-lined well.

field-workers in folklore, preservation technology, and archeology recorded and dismantled the house for later reconstruction. Our investigations uncovered not only the house's unusual construction but also the historical context of its construction: Montgomery's attempt to establish the town of Middleton.

The passage of the Homestead Act in 1862, the discovery of gold in Boise Basin in August of that year, and the establishment of Fort Boise as a military out-post on July 4, 1863, precipitated a change in the Boise Valley: whereas settlers heading west along the Oregon Trail had previously passed through the valley, many now stayed to try the soil near the wooded river and to supply the Boise Basin and Owyhee mining com-munities. William Montgomery was among them. Born in either Pennsylvania or Illinois, Montgomery first appears in Idaho records in July of 1863. On July 23, according to the plat he filed with Boise County, Ter-ritory of Idaho, Montgomery chose and named the townsite of Middleton just north of the Boise River and about twenty-two miles west of Boise City. In January 1865, a townsite was surveyed, resembling many other "paper towns"[3] platted alongside rivers throughout the Midwest and West: eight blocks—one of them a public

square—with 136-foot-square lots and 100-foot-wide streets. The town's two named streets were called Montgomery and Payette.

Montgomery and his partner V. R. Fuller opened a store in about 1865.[4] By this time Montgomery was married to Nancy Caroline, born in Illinois, and their first child, Ora L., had been born. His property is men-tioned in several 1860s documents. In 1865 the Ada County commissioners used the Montgomery house as a reference point for a public road between the Payette River and the Oregon Trail. The commission minutes and a very rough sketch map locate the house "where the Payette Road leaves the Boise City Road."[5] The minutes also record the use of Montgomery's house as an election place; by 1866 Montgomery was a county commissioner.[6] Accounts of soldiers traveling along the Oregon Trail in 1866 mention stopping at a place called Montgomery's while en route to Fort Walla Walla, Washington Territory,[7] and a United States land survey in August and September of 1867 shows the Montgom-ery store, the Munday Store, and three houses within Montgomery's Middleton plat. None of these buildings were located at the present Montgomery house site, but it is possible that the surveyor did not record the house, which stood in the center of a section. The surveyor's map does locate Montgomery's store on the alternate branch of the Oregon Trail as it passed through the Middleton plat north of the Boise River. The Montgomery store site, as given on the 1867 map, was a quarter mile from the Payette–Boise City Road junction; the Montgomery house site of 1979 was three-quarters mile from the junction.

By 1868 Middleton had two stores, a blacksmith shop, a wagon shop, a butcher shop, and a flour mill.[8] In 1869 it was estimated that ten thousand acres of land were under cultivation in the Boise Valley.[9] Montgomery, however, was in trouble. One source written decades later states that Montgomery's store failed in 1866,[10] but Internal Revenue assessors did collect from Montgomery and Company for liquor and tobacco sales during 1867 and 1869.[11] Certainly, by 1869 Montgomery and Company was in trouble, as sheriffs' deeds show the company in arrears to C. Jacobs and Company. Boise City merchant Cyrus Jacobs obtained some of Montgomery's land in and around the Middleton townsite through a sheriff's auction in the fall of 1871.

The Boise *Capital Chronicle* of 1870 reported a Middleton hotel, a Farmers' Club, a dance hall at the Eggleston place, and a blacksmith shop run by Perry Munday (who had a long-term lease from Montgomery). Montgomery appeared three times in the 1870 *Chronicle*: once experimenting with pea cultivation, once as a delegate to the Democratic county convention, and once as the host of a Middleton picnic.[12] By the 1870 census, Montgomery, listed as a farmer, owned real estate worth fifteen hundred dollars and a personal estate of one thousand dollars. With Montgomery, aged thirty-three, his wife, aged twenty-eight, and their two children, lived an Irish-born hired hand. Their neighbors were still few: Middleton boasted five households and twenty-two residents. Among them were only a few clerks and craftsmen, including one carpenter. The majority of these people were born in Missouri, Tennessee, Kentucky, and Illinois. The Montgomerys were, demographically, an average family for the Middleton vicinity in 1870.

The Montgomerys appear in few records extant from the 1870s and 1880s, aside from an 1874 land patent for the house site. In 1878 Montgomery patented the land immediately north of the house. By the 1880 census the Montgomerys, now with four children, had two boarders. William was still a farmer, and Middleton was not much larger than before, having twelve households and forty-four people.

It must have seemed evident by 1880 that Montgomery's Middleton venture was not a great success. He may have platted his town expecting his fortune to grow with its growth, but the 1865 version of Middleton was replaced by 1886 with a new plat farther north of the Boise River, a better location for avoiding annual spring floods. The construction of the Middleton mill ditch, started in 1864, diverted population north of the flood-prone site of Montgomery's town.

In 1888 two judgments brought against Montgomery in favor of Jacobs and Company showed Montgomery to be deeply in debt. In public auctions he lost most of his land, and he sold the land with the house to S. S. Foote, a Middleton miller, in 1888. Jacobs obtained the remainder. In 1889 Montgomery made a legal record in Boise City of his two patents. S. S. Foote sold the land with the Montgomery house to Peter A. Watkins, father of the house's fourth and last private owner.

The Montgomery house, then, may be tentatively dated between 1865, when a Montgomery house is mentioned in the Ada County commissioners' minutes, and 1870, when Montgomery had lost part of his estate to Jacobs, was no longer operating a store in Middleton, and was farming. Montgomery's house, like his town plat, was an ambitious idea, but like the townsite it had flaws, underwent reconstruction, and was unfinished in some details. In 1979 it appeared to us as a puzzling and anomalous part of the cultural landscape until we had documented its construction and compared it with other southwest Idaho buildings.

The Montgomery house had long ceased to be a dwelling when our investigation of it began. The owner used the building to store grain and other feed for his livestock, and it had not been maintained for many years. As a result, the house was in an advanced state of deterioration.

We decided that the structure was too fragile and unstable to move from its site, as originally intended, and that the only way to preserve the technology of the building was to dismantle it and document its construction. The remaining adobe infill, weathered wooden framework and sheathing, and rusting nails and spikes were severely deteriorated. The house's location on uneven ground made a move difficult, and the very nature of its construction would have endangered the building in a move. The fireplace and chimney, for example, had a separate foundation that provided a firm bearing for the rest of the house by reducing settling, racking, and twisting. The adobe infill that remained in the walls was heavy enough to render the entire building unstable, and the studs had little horizontal bracing, no diagonal bracing, and very little vertical stability. In addition, the framing beneath the floor was constructed so that the floor joists, foundation timbers, and support timbers were on several different planes.

These structural problems appeared as intriguing examples of pioneer technology once the decision had been made not to relocate the structure but rather to document it. As we disassembled, measured, and photographed the house, we discovered a number of surprises in its plan and construction.

As it stood in 1979 the Montgomery house was a two-room structure with a hall and parlor floor plan measuring fifteen feet ten inches by twenty-two feet six inches. The front door opened onto the main room of the house, where there was a fireplace. A secondary room was set off by a partition. Although it was a small structure, the building accommodated five windows and four doors.

The foundation of the house consisted of seven stone pillars made of random-laid lava rock mortared with adobe. There was a pillar at each corner. Three additional pillars, one each on the north, east, and south sides, were built as part of the cellar, which was under the east end of the building (Figure 2). The cellar was entered from the outside on the east end through a doorway formed by two of the pillars with a lava-rock sill between. The doorway had cobblestone retaining walls leading into the five-foot-deep cellar. The walls of the cellar between the lava-rock pillars were constructed of oblong river rock laid horizontally in a herringbone pattern to form a tightly coursed twelve-inch-wide wall that broadened to twenty-four inches at the base. The rocks of the cellar wall were amazingly uniform in size and length, indicating considerable effort on the part of the builder in his selection of materials. An analysis of the mortar showed that the builder used mud without any trace of lime to harden the mixture.

The proximity of the building to the Boise River may have influenced the nature of its foundation. Built before the Boise River had any flood controls, the house must have been subject to periodic spring flooding. In fact, the 1867 survey showed the two sections around the Middleton townsite as marshy land. The elevation of the house on lava-rock piers was probably a practical solution by a builder who may have had experience constructing buildings on bottomland.

The floor of the Montgomery house was framed with three main longitudinal bearing beams, the two exterior beams rough-sawn (milled coarsely through a circular saw) and the center one hand hewn. Across these beams lay nine cottonwood floor joists ranging from six to twelve inches in diameter and hewn on top and bottom to a four-inch thickness. Some of the joists still had their bark. Again, the two end members were rough sawn while those on the interior were hand hewn. Only the corners of the rough-sawn sills were secured with nails; elsewhere lap joints were used. It is not surprising to have found rough-sawn beams in the structure. Boise Valley settlers set up small lumber mills as early as the 1860s.[13]

Several of the hand-hewn beams used in the subfloor had notches and drill holes with no apparent relationship to the construction of the Montgomery house. These beams quite possibly were reused from another structure. All the cross beams and end sills were mortised to accept the wall studs. Two layers of one-by-six-inch flooring covered the beams, both layers running along the length of the building.

During the dismantling of the building a row of mortise holes was found beneath the first layer of flooring and centered along the length of the building. The major partition that the holes indicate, which had been removed, would have created a floor plan quite different from that of 1979. The installation of the second layer of floor boards around the hearth, the condition of the roof around the chimney, and the condition of

Figure 2. The east exposure of the Montgomery House reveals the remains of the foundation's stone quoins, the stud and infill construction of the walls, and the clapboard siding. The area between the foundation stones was once filled with a cobblestone foundation wall.

the floor framing members around the fireplace suggested that alterations also were made to accommodate the fireplace. Apparently the partition was partially or completely removed when the fireplace was installed. It is possible, too, that the Montgomery house was originally the Montgomery store as located on the 1867 survey map. The lateral partition would make more sense in a commercial building than in a dwelling, and moving and remodeling the store into a house might have called for the addition of a fireplace. Two stovepipe holes of an uncertain date were discovered under repairs to the roof in the northeast and southwest quadrants of the building.

As mentioned earlier, the fireplace and chimney constituted a separate structure with its own lava-rock foundation. On either side of the fireplace were cupboards built of planed lumber and with paneled doors, probably installed when the fireplace and chimney were built. There was a good-sized flue. The firebox, also large, had a floor of mud built up approximately eighteen inches thick on top of the lava-rock foundation. Under the fired-brick surface of the fireplace and

Figure 3. A view out of one of the Montgomery House's southern doors shows stud and infill construction. Between sections of infill are nogging boards. The door probably was not original to the building, as the stud above it was cut to make the doorway. In the door sill the mortise for the stud can be seen.

firebox was an adobe-brick infill. In the exposed portion above the roof, fired brick and adobe mortar were used. The chimney may have been replaced with fired brick above the roofline because an original chimney of adobe was rapidly deteriorating. The lack of lime in the mortar for both the adobe and the fired-brick sections of the chimney and fireplace suggests that the floor plan was altered and the chimney and fireplace added at an early date. A good local lime source was not discovered until 1870, but an earlier one of inferior quality was located somewhere along Willow Creek, which passes close to the house site.[14]

The walls of the building were framed of approximately four-by-four-inch cottonwood studs tenoned into each floor beam. These studs were partially hewn. On the inner wall the studs still had their bark, making the type of wood identifiable. On the east and west walls the studs were positioned accurately at twenty-four inches on center. On the longer north and south facades, stud locations varied between twenty-five and forty inches on center. The exterior of the walls was covered with one-by-eleven-inch milled shiplap (one-half inch lap) with simple butt joint corners.

Immediately inside the shiplap layer and between the studs was the most interesting feature of the house—coursed adobe-brick infill (Figure 3). This infill consisted of unfired adobe brick approximately two and one-half by four by eight inches in size, laid up with adobe mortar. The bricks showed some evidence of charring—perhaps the builder's attempt to fire the brick, an attempt that had little or no effect. Evidently the infill was placed in the building after it was sided, as the adobe mortar had been pushed up against the shiplap siding and conformed to the inside surface of the shiplap. As the adobe bricks and mortar were laid between the studs from floor to ceiling, a series of nogging-pieces one by four inches in size were placed horizontally between the studs at varying intervals. These boards were installed simply by placing them on top of a level of infill and then toe-nailing them into the studs. The nogging-pieces stabilized the infill, allowing it to extend the full height of the wall, and it minimized the shrinkage of the adobe by separating the infill into small areas. On the interior the wall surface was covered with cheesecloth stretched between the studs and covered with wallpaper. The interior surfaces of the studs showed no other evidence of finishing materials.

The roof framing of the Montgomery house was not typical of truss roofs on frame buildings. A top plate of rough-sawn two-by-fours existed only along the east and west walls. This plate lay on top of the wall studs and extended outward eight inches on each end. A similar two-by-four-inch sawn member tied across each pair of studs on a north-to-south axis. These tie members extended outward eight inches beyond the studs in a fashion similar to the end plates. On top of the ends of the plates and stud tie pieces, a twenty-three-foot one-by-twelve ran continuously along the length of the north and south walls. The roof rafters lay directly on top of this board. The rafters on the ends of the roof were rough-sawn four-by-four-inch pieces, while the rafters of the central roof area were split from cottonwood poles with a radius of from four to six inches. The rafters were nailed to a one-by-four-inch ridgeboard and toe-nailed to the one-by-twelve plate at the top of the wall. The roof structure had no collar ties or braces, nor was there any evidence of there having been any. Over the rafters was a sheathing of one-by-ten-inch rough-sawn boards covered with sixteen-inch sawn cedar shingles with a five-inch exposure. The shingles were not original; in 1979 the owner could remember that the building had been reroofed during his lifetime.

Little of the building's original window glazing was extant, but most of the window openings seemed to fit a typical double-hung sash frame. The only exceptions were two fixed six-pane windows on the south elevation. The house's doors were made of one-inch boards nailed together and secured with Z-bracing.

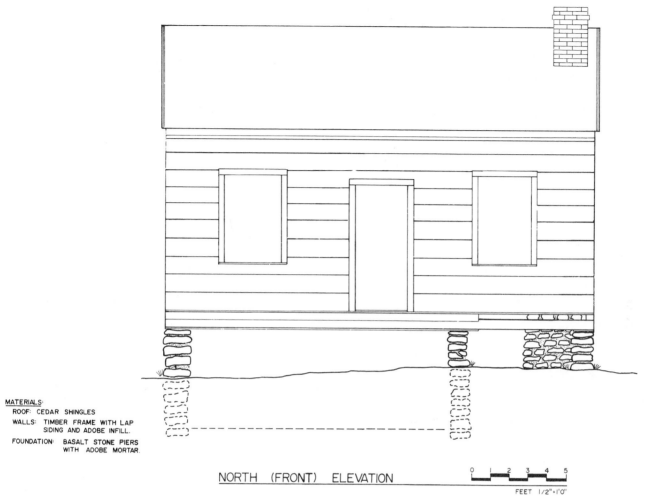

MATERIALS:
ROOF: CEDAR SHINGLES
WALLS: TIMBER FRAME WITH LAP
SIDING AND ADOBE INFILL.
FOUNDATION: BASALT STONE PIERS
WITH ADOBE MORTAR.

NORTH (FRONT) ELEVATION

0 1 2 3 4 5
FEET 1/2"=1'0'

Figure 4. Montgomery House, Middleton, Idaho, 1979. North elevation.

This was the Montgomery house as we discovered and dismantled it. The earliest form of the house, however, probably had a double-pile floor plan without the fireplace and with a central wall along the row of mortises revealed when the floor was dismantled. There was evidence, too, that the building had had a rear addition or porch below the level of the fixed southern windows.

The unusual construction and plan of the Montgomery house initially made it appear to us as an oddity of folk architectural history. The house did not fit the folk house types or structural systems typical of the vicinity, but further investigations did reveal parallels for many of its individual features. Some of the parallels are geographically remote and, therefore, may have no historical connection with the Montgomery house; some of them are closer at hand and may be part of the regional traditions that the builder of the Montgomery house drew upon. [15]

The original double-pile floor plan, for example, does not fit the typical English and Anglo-American house types in which main partitions are set parallel to the gable walls. It is not a plan that the authors have observed elsewhere in Idaho. The plan is instead suggestive of French houses of the late eighteenth and early nineteenth centuries in Illinois and Missouri and farther south along the Mississippi Valley. The French settlers built houses divided in half laterally and then subdivided into smaller rooms along each half. [16] The removal of the central dividing wall in the Montgomery house and the installation of the fireplace and a second layer of flooring gave the building an Anglo-American character. The substitute floor plan, which fits the hall and parlor house type, is a plan that has been found in Idaho dating from the last half of the nineteenth century; it has clear antecedents in the eastern and midwestern United States [17] and in Utah (Figures 4–7).

While buildings with all-adobe walls are not uncommon in Idaho, the use of adobe infill is relatively undocumented in the state. In the eastern United States, however, infill has a long tradition. Both the English and the French colonists used adobe infill. The English used this method, often called half-timbering, in timber frame buildings early in their settlement of the east

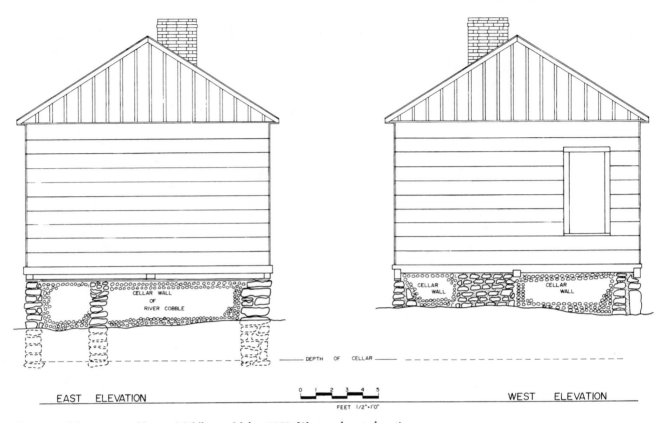

EAST   ELEVATION   0 1 2 3 4 5   WEST   ELEVATION
                                     FEET 1/2"=1'0"

Figure 5.   Montgomery House, Middleton, Idaho, 1979. West and east elevations.

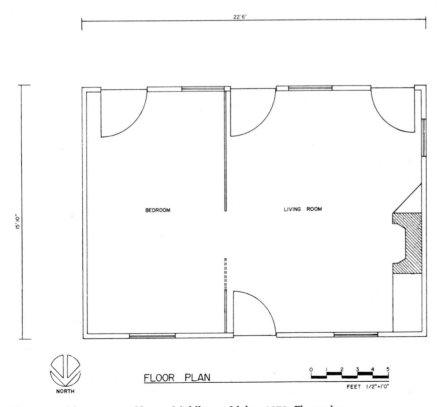

FLOOR   PLAN   0 1 2 3 4 5
NORTH   FEET 1/2"=1'0"

Figure 6.   Montgomery House, Middleton, Idaho, 1979. Floor plan.

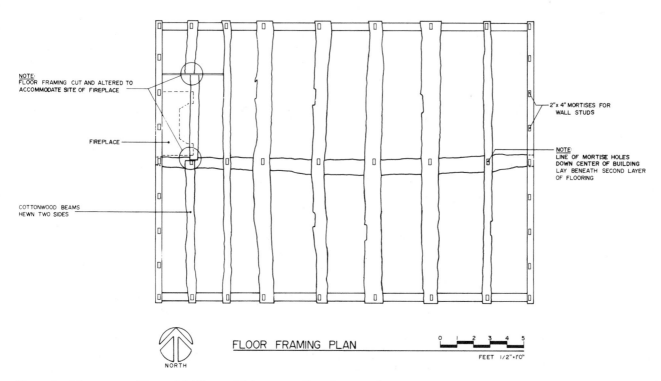

NOTE:
FLOOR FRAMING CUT AND ALTERED TO
ACCOMMODATE SITE OF FIREPLACE

FIREPLACE

COTTONWOOD BEAMS
HEWN TWO SIDES

2"x 4" MORTISES FOR
WALL STUDS

NOTE:
LINE OF MORTISE HOLES
DOWN CENTER OF BUILDING
LAY BENEATH SECOND LAYER
OF FLOORING

NORTH

FLOOR FRAMING PLAN

0 1 2 3 4 5
FEET 1/2"=1'0"

Figure 7. Montgomery House, Middleton, Idaho, 1979. Floor framing plan.

coast during the seventeenth century. The French settlers of Canada and, in the eighteenth and nineteenth centuries, the Mississippi Valley used a form of building called *maison de poteaux sur solle* or *colombage pierrotee*, a system incorporating thick uprights with an infill of stone, fired brick, or adobe. Related forms were used to build the Northwest fur trading posts, including an 1809 Idaho example, and German settlers built timber-frame structures with adobe or fired-brick infill into the nineteenth century. All these examples of the use of infill involve framing with heavy wooden timbers, whereas the Montgomery house's construction is in some respects closer to balloon frame. Kniffen and Glassie consider such marginal cases to represent the vestigial survival of half-timbering.[18]

The tradition of adobe, stone, or fired-brick infill, then, has so many sources that it is difficult to attribute the Montgomery house's construction to any one influence. But the house is not our only example of adobe infill in an Idaho building. In Idaho and Utah, adobe was used as infill between studs in balloon-frame and timber-frame buildings, although we cannot say how common this was. The Spalding mission at Lapwai (1836–1847), for example, had among its buildings some with braced frame construction and adobe-brick infill.[19] We have observed at least one balloon-frame dwelling in Paris with adobe infill that appears not to have been shaped into bricks, and another in Hailey has adobe-brick infill identical to that of the Montgomery house.

Many other Idaho buildings from the 1860s and later

may have infill in their walls. In a thesis on nineteenth-century folk housing in the Mormon culture region, an area that includes southeast Idaho, Pitman maintains that "the pioneers who built wood frame houses quite frequently placed adobes between vertical studding behind the clapboards for the purpose of insulating and adding strength to the house."[20] One of Pitman's informants in Duchesne County, in northern Utah, explained to him that after the house was framed and roofed,

> the next job was to make adobes to line the house, so . . .
> I began carrying adobes to lay them out in the sun to
> dry. . . . The adobes dried quickly so by late summer we
> were anxious to get them into the walls. . . . I . . . lay the
> adobes up between the 2x4's in the walls so we could have
> our home livable before winter set in. . . . When three
> layers had been laid, . . . I would drive a spike nail in the
> two-by-four on each side then bend them down so the
> adobes would be held in place good and solid. . . . We
> kept warm that winter.[21]

Although Pitman argues that the Mormon tradition of using adobe developed out of the early experience of the Mormon pioneers with Spanish adobe construction in the Southwest, he does not discuss the derivation of its use as infill. Pitman maintains that the use of adobe was relatively unknown in the former Mormon settlements of the upper Mississippi Valley. He does not consider whether any French or German influences may have been carried to the new settlements of the West.

The roof structure of the Montgomery house, unusual for a frame house, is almost identical to that of early adobe and masonry buildings found in Idaho. At present-day Walter's Ferry an adobe building erected in about 1864 has a roof framing system that is identical to that of the Montgomery house roof from the wall plate upward. In Hailey another adobe building similar in wall construction to the Walter's Ferry building has a roof system very close in detail to the Montgomery house roof. And the 1873 brewery in Challis, a stone building laid up with adobe mortar, has an identical wooden plate that sits on top of the stone wall to provide a base for the roof. The roof framing of the Challis building is different from the Montgomery house roof only in its use of dimensional lumber rather than split poles.

It may be merely coincidence that Perry Munday moved from Middleton to Walter's Ferry in 1874, but in any event the two communities, which lay on stage routes from Boise, were in contact when Montgomery's house was built. Walter's Ferry is only about thirty miles from Middleton. Whether or not the builder of the Montgomery house adapted its roof from local sources, he apparently approached its construction as if he were placing a wooden roof atop a masonry or adobe wall. The walls and studs were fastened at the top with cross members and probably raised into place in a fashion similar to raising wall sections in a barn raising, each section a discrete unit hoisted intact and fastened to the other sections once raised. Atop the lateral walls the builder placed oversized plates, plates identical to those used to tie a masonry or adobe wall to a wooden roof. And atop those plates was the rafter system.

When the members of this study team first observed the unbraced walls and untied rafters of the Montgomery house, we knew that the house was outside our previous fieldwork experience. But the conclusion that the Montgomery house is unusual is at best only a fraction of its story. The house is an example of the changes that folk artifacts undergo as settlers come into a new region. In its combination of traditions—perhaps half-learned ones—from a variety of sources, the house reflects the diverse origins of the settlers of Idaho. The Montgomery house represents a combination of techniques not usually found together, making it an obvious case of technologies gotten from separate sources. It is possible that less obvious examples exist, too. Perhaps the log houses that stood near the Montgomery house in the lower Boise Valley bear a similar relationship to their eastern and western culture sources, a complex relationship that deserves re-evaluation.

Notes

1. Unless otherwise specified, conclusions in this article are based on records at the Idaho State Historic Preservation Office, Boise, Idaho; at the Canyon County Courthouse, Caldwell, Idaho; at the Bureau of Land Management, Boise, Idaho; and in the United States censuses for 1870 and 1880. The authors are indebted to Jennie Cornell of Middleton, the dedicated local historian who discovered and drew our attention to the Montgomery house; to the staff of the Idaho State Historical Society for their assistance; and to the U.S. Interior Department's Historic Preservation Fund for partial funding of this project.

2. A number of construction terms are used throughout this article. *Studs* are uprights that form a framework for a building's walls. Usually of wood, they are smaller and more closely spaced than the heavy timbers of timber framing. The two-room *hall and parlor* house type has one square room set beside a narrower room. The plan is one room deep. *Double-pile* floor plans are two rooms deep. *Quoins* are stone blocks appearing at the corner of a stone wall; often they are distinguished from the wall material through texture and large size. *Mortise and tenon joints* are formed by fitting a projecting member (tenon) into a slot (mortise) on another timber. *Lap joints* are formed by halving timbers at their ends and overlapping the halved sections. *Joists* are the horizontal members that support a floor or ceiling. A *plate* is a horizontal member on top of a wall that provides a platform for the roof structure.

3. See John W. Reps' discussion of paper towns in *Cities of the American West: A History of Frontier Urban Planning* (Princeton, New Jersey: Princeton University Press, 1979), p. 345.

4. Autobiography of Junius B. Wright, MS 334, Idaho State Historical Society, Boise, Idaho.

5. Minutes of the [Ada] County Commissioners, 1865–1868, AR 202, Idaho State Historical Society, Boise, Idaho, p. 91. The only history that mentions Montgomery is Morris Foote's *One Hundred Years in Middleton* (Middleton: Boise Valley Herald, 1963), in which Foote notes that Montgomery drew up the first town plat and had a ranch and a retail store that failed, pp. 14–17.

6. Minutes of the [Ada] County Commissioners, 1865–1868, AR 202, Idaho State Historical Society, Boise, Idaho, pp. 7, 10, 18–19, 20, 91, 166, 265; and Minutes of the [Ada] County Commissioners, 1877–1888, AR 202, Idaho State Historical Society, Boise, Idaho, p. 38.

7. Herbert B. Nelson and Preston E. Onstad, eds., *A Webfoot Volunteer: The Diary of William M. Hilleary, 1864–1866* (Corvallis: Oregon State University Press, 1965), pp. 146, 157–58.

8. *Boise Democrat*, 29 February 1968, p. 2.

9. (Boise) *Capital Chronicle*, 1 December 1869, p. 4.

10. Autobiography of Junius B. Wright.

11. *Internal Revenue Assessment Lists for the Territory of Idaho; 1865–1866* (Washington, D.C.: National Archives Microfilm Publications, 1968), No. 763, Roll 1, Record Group 58.

12. (Boise) *Capital Chronicle*, 26 January, p. 1; 12 February, p. 4; 16 March, p. 2; 13 April, p. 4; 16 April, p. 3; 11 May, p. 3; 21 May, p. 2; 25 May, p. 1; 20 July, p. 3; and 30 July, p. 1; 1870.

13. Arthur Hart, "Farm and Ranch Buildings East of the Cascades," in *Space, Style and Structure; Building in Northwest America*, ed. Thomas Vaughan and Virginia Guest Ferriday (Portland: Oregon Historical Society, 1974), p. 245.

14. (Boise) *Idaho Tri-weekly Statesman*, 22 February 1870, p. 3.

15. It is possible, too, that Montgomery drew on a published description of regional construction techniques, like C. P. Dwyer's *The Immigrant Builder* (Philadelphia: Claxton, Remsen, and Haffelfinger, 1872). Every technique used in the Montgomery house is described by Dwyer, although not put together in one building.

16. Henry Glassie, *Pattern in the Material Folk Culture of the Eastern United States* (Philadelphia: University of Pennsylvania Press, 1968), pp. 117–24.

17. Ibid., pp. 80–81.

18. Fred Kniffen and Henry Glassie, "Building in Wood in the Eastern United States; A Time–Place Perspective, *Geographical Review* 56:1 (January 1966): 40–66. Descriptions of the use of adobe infill may be found in Hubert G. H. Wilhelm and Michael Miller, "Half-Timber Construction: A Relic Building Method in Ohio," *Pioneer America* 6:2 (July 1974): 43–51; Hubert G. H. Wilhelm, "German Settlement and Folk Building Practices in the Hill Country of Texas," *Pioneer America* 3:2 (July 1971): 15–24; A. J. H. Richardson, "A Comparative Historical Study of Timber Building in Canada," *APT Bulletin* 5:3 (1973): 77–102; and Hugh Morrison, *Early American Architecture* (New York: Oxford University Press, 1952), p. 30.

19. Arthur H. Hart, "Fur Trade Posts and Early Missions," in *Space, Style and Structure; Building in Northwest America*, ed. Thomas Vaughan and Virginia Guest Ferriday (Portland: Oregon Historical Society, 1974), pp. 39–40.

20. Leon Sidney Pitman, "A Survey of Nineteenth-century Folk Housing in the Mormon Culture Region" (Ph.D. diss., Louisiana State University and Agricultural and Mechanical College, 1973), p. 38.

21. Ibid., pp. 38–39.

Folklife and Group Identity

The Paradox of Mormon Folklore
WILLIAM A. WILSON

New Sweden Pioneer Day
HAL CANNON

Orofino Lumberjack Days
CHARLENE JAMES-DUGUID

Basque Celebrations in Eastern Oregon and Boise
SARAH BAKER MUNRO

"Prairie Chickens Dancing . . .": Ecology's Myth
ALAN G. MARSHALL

The Paradox of Mormon Folklore

WILLIAM A. WILSON

A theme to which William A. "Bert" Wilson frequently refers in essays and lectures is the value of folklore not merely as an enrichment to the study of such disciplines as history, literature, and psychology but as a discipline of merit in its own right. Folklore, he argues, has its own structure, its own esthetic, and its own way of presenting truth.

In this essay he says that psychological truth may be at variance with ledger-book facts but that this truth gives a clearer view of the ethos of a people than can be gained in any other way. Although he focuses upon Mormon folklore, the implications of his essay extend beyond religious, ethnic, or national considerations and apply to human communities everywhere.

Among the subjects discussed in this essay are the Nephites, often the Three Nephites, said to appear at critical or opportune times in the lives of those requiring assistance. Three is, of course, a recurring motif: tithes of mint, anise, and cumin; gifts of gold, myrrh, and frankincense; in Mormon cosmology celestial, telestial, and terrestrial heavens and therefore three glories.

Those who are concerned with folklore as another way of understanding the nature of truth should read Professor Wilson's "Folklore and History: Fact Amid the Legends," in Readings in American Folklore *by Jan Brunvand (1979). For further discussion of the Nephites and other Mormon lore, see Austin and Alta Fife's* Saints of Sage and Saddle: Folklore Among the Mormons *(1956).*

William A. Wilson is a professor of English and history and Director of the Folklore Program at Utah State University, Logan.

This essay was first published in Essays in the American West, 1974–75 *(Provo: Brigham Young University Press, 1976) and permission for its reprinting has been granted by the Charles Redd Center for Western Studies.*

As I began work on this paper, I asked a number of friends what they would like to know about Mormon folklore. The responses were at such cross purposes the task ahead seemed hopeless. Finally a colleague solved my problem by confessing that he knew next to nothing about the subject. "I would like to know," he said, "what Mormon folklore is and what you fellows do with it." I should like to answer these questions. I shall tell you what I, at least, consider Mormon folklore to be; I shall try to demonstrate what those of us who study it do with it; and I shall try to persuade you that what we do is worth doing, providing significant insight into our culture that we cannot always get in other ways.

In the 130 years since the word "folklore" was coined,[1] folklorists have been trying unsuccessfully to decide what the word means. I shall not solve the problem here. Yet if we are to do business with each other, we must come to some common understanding of terms. Briefly, I consider folklore to be the unofficial part of our culture. When a Sunday School teacher reads to his class from an approved lesson manual, he is giving them what the Correlation Committee at least would call official religion; but when he illustrates the lesson with an account of the Three Nephites which he learned from his mother, he is giving them unofficial religion.[2] Folklore, then, is that part of our culture that is passed through time and space by the process of oral transmission (by hearing and repeating) rather than by institutionalized means of learning or by the mass media.

Not everything, of course, that we transmit orally is folklore. We distinguish folklore from other forms of verbal communication by clearly discernable structure. We are all familiar with the "Once upon a time" that signals the beginning of a fairy tale and the "And they lived happily ever after" that marks its end. The markers that set off other forms of folklore are often more subtle, but they are nevertheless there, and when we hear the initial signal, most of us know immediately that conversation is going to be interrupted by the telling of a tale. Further, not only is folklore in general set off from regular conversation by its structure, but the different forms of folklore (for example, ballad, folktale, legend) are also separated from each other by the distinctive ordering of their parts. Thus a Nephite story, reduced to its basic elements, is quite a different creature, structurally, from a story about J. Golden Kimball.[3] It is because of this structural patterning, among other things, that we are justified in considering folklore to be literature. Another reason, as we shall see, is that through these narrative patterns we come to terms with some of our most significant Mormon experience.

To suggest that folklore is literature is to suggest that it is fiction; to suggest that it is fiction is to suggest also that it is not true, that it does not recount history accurately. This suggestion will not trouble many when we apply it to folk songs or to humorous anecdotes, which we really don't consider factual; but when we apply it to stories of the Three Nephites or to accounts of visits to or from the spirit world or to divine help in genealogical research, then eyebrows arch all over the place. And this brings me once again to my colleague's question: "If we have three accounts of something Joseph Smith did, does that mean it's folklore?"

The answer to that question depends on the antecedent of the pronoun *it*. If the pronoun refers to the actual event that started the stories, the answer is clearly no. The event is whatever the event was, and the folklorist will leave to the historian the task of deciphering it. But if the pronoun refers not to the event but to the account of it circulating orally, the answer is yes. The account is, or is on the way to becoming, folklore.

Folklore comes into being through a process we call communal re-creation. In general the materials of Mormon folklore come from three places: they are borrowed from others and then adapted to fit the contours of our culture; they sometimes originate, as Joseph Fielding Smith said, speaking of Nephite stories, from the vivid imaginations of some of our people;[4] and they develop from actual happenings. But whatever the source, the stories become folklore when they are taken over by the people and are reshaped as they are passed from person to person.

This communal re-creation occurs in two ways. First, the stories are reshaped to fit the structural patterns available to the narrators. My mother, a devout Mormon not easily given to criticism, complained the other day that all the talks of returned missionaries sounded the same. What she had perceived was that the returning home address is a traditional form into which the missionary must fit his personal experiences, altering them, or at least carefully selecting them, to fit the pattern. The process is similar to the one followed when a writer attempts to develop his personal experiences into a short story. To be successful, he must alter the experience to make it fit the structural requirements of the form.

Consider, for example, the stories of the Three Nephites. The basic structure of these stories seems to be this: someone has a problem; a stranger appears; the stranger solves the problem; the stranger miraculously disappears. A story may have more to it than this, but

it must have these features. Any account that is taken into the Nephite cycle will be adjusted (probably unconsciously) to fit the pattern. The remarkable disappearance is particularly interesting. I see no compelling reasons why the Nephites must disappear. In Book of Mormon times they were thrown into prison, into dens of wild beasts, and into furnaces, and in none of these instances did they solve their problems by disappearing. But in the modern stories they vanish from the back seats of speeding cars; they vaporize before one's eyes; or they walk away and someone later tracing the footsteps in the snow finds that they abruptly end. The Nephites disappear, I believe, because the story requires it. The disappearance is the climax toward which the narrative builds, overshadowing in many instances the kindly deeds the Nephites came to perform in the first place.

The second way in which communal re-creation occurs is that the stories are reshaped (again probably unconsciously) to reflect the attitudes, values, and concerns of the people telling the stories. In 1962, a student in an anthropology class at Brigham Young University (BYU) collected the following item from one of her teachers:

> Brother James Rencher was a very devout man, who, in all of his spare time, read and reread the Book of Mormon. However, no matter how many times he pored over the book, there remained ten questions concerning it which he could not answer. Every year during the fall, the Renchers moved down into town to escape the harsh winter. One day in October 1898, Brother Rencher was moving some furniture and provisions down the mountain, when it began to snow. All of a sudden, a strange man appeared several yards in front of him and asked for a ride. The stranger climbed into the wagon, and immediately began talking about the Book of Mormon. During the next few minutes he answered all of Brother Rencher's questions about the book. Then he jumped out of the wagon and started to walk away. Being concerned that the stranger would freeze in the cold snow, Brother Rencher went after him. He traced the man's footprints to the top of the mountain; there they suddenly disappeared.[5]

I have several accounts of this story quite similar to this one, except that in some not even the Mormon General Authorities[6] could answer Rencher's questions and in some Rencher was from Pine Valley while in others he was from Heber City or from Idaho. In two versions of the story published by Austin Fife in 1940, Rencher picked up an old hitchhiker who explained political and religious matters "to his satisfaction just perfectly."[7] These accounts suggest that the story once had a double theme—politics and religion. A story collected just last year emphasizes the politics:

> Brother Rencher was closing up a campground and left to go home. After he had been driving in the mountains for a way, he came across a man who seemed to appear from nowhere. They were out in an area where there was no one living and very few people passed that way. Brother Rencher in order to start conversation asked the man what he thought of the political parties. The man who turned

out to be one of the three Nephites answered: "They are both as corrupt as hell."

What we see here then is that different people, or groups of people, perceive the important "message" of an item differently, and that as they continue to tell the story they drop or add details to strengthen what they consider to be important in the story. [8]

Another example of the shifting shape of folklore lies closer to home. Most of us will remember the turbulent period in late 1969 and early 1970 when BYU athletic teams and the marching Cougarettes met violent demonstrations in neighboring schools, when a spate of stories was circulating about busloads of Black Panthers making their way to the state to blow up Mountain Dell Reservoir and to invade Temple Square, and when some people feared to travel beyond the state's boundaries because they had heard gory stories of people with Utah license plates being stopped and beaten up by blacks. Emotions were intensified by the revival and rapid circulation of the apocryphal Horse Shoe Prophecy attributed to John Taylor. This prophecy was first written down in 1951 by Edward Lunt, who said that in 1903 or 1904 he had learned it from his mother, who said that she had received it from President Taylor in 1885.) [9] In Lunt's account, President Taylor supposed he saw a day of great trouble and warfare striking the Saints, with "blood running down the gutters of Salt Lake City as though it were water." As versions of the prophecy began to multiply during the violence of 1969 and 1970, a new motif was added to it —the notion that the blood would run in the gutters because of racial warfare. For example, an employee of Seminaries and Institutes [10] stated:

> that it was common knowledge among teachers in the Church educational system that a confrontation with Black Panthers was going to take place in the streets of Salt Lake City and that this would be a fulfillment of the prophecy that blacks would wreak havoc in the streets of Zion. He said that this prophecy was given to President Taylor. It was common knowledge from reliable sources [he said] that blacks and hippies were arming themselves in the canyons east of the city and that the FBI had uncovered plans by revolutionaries to hit Salt Lake City with a violence campaign.

Another individual, a stockbroker who claimed he did not believe the part about Negroes, stated:

> John Taylor is supposed to have said that the Negroes will march to the west and that they will tear down the gates to the temple, ravage the women therein, and destroy and desecrate the temple. Then the Mormon boys will pick up their deer rifles and destroy the Negroes, and that's when the blood will run down the street.

On 30 March 1970, the First Presidency, [11] concerned by the growing emotionalism, released a statement in which they denounced the Horse Shoe Prophecy and urged members to school their feelings. [12] In their statement, the First Presidency quoted a memorandum from the Church Historian's office which pointed out that of the five copies of the prophecy on file in that office no two were identical in wording, and that the statement about Negroes was in one of the copies but not in the others, "particularly" not in the version signed by Lunt. What the First Presidency actually did was conduct a small-scale folklore study. They discovered, as we have discovered with the James Rencher stories, that as stories are passed from person to person they are "adjusted" to reflect the concerns and to fit the predispositions of the people.

What I am saying, then, is that while folklore may be factually false, it is psychologically true. Students of Mormon culture turn to it not to discover the ledgerbook truths of history but to fathom the truths of the human heart and mind. The truths that we find may not always please us, but if we really want to understand ourselves I know of no better place to turn than to folklore.

I say this with some hesitation because I am well aware that Mormon literature, *belles lettres*, gives us good insight into the Mormon ethos. But I am convinced that Mormon folklore gives us a still clearer view. My reason for believing this is simple: the works of Mormon *belles lettres* are the creative products of individuals; the works of Mormon folk literature are the creative products of the people, constantly being reshaped, as we have seen above, to mirror contemporary values, anxieties, and social practices. The Mormon poet or short-story writer, however much he draws on his Mormon background and however much he discusses his works in process with his Mormon friends, still gives us his own *individual* interpretation of our culture, an interpretation, I might add, that is elitist in approach. On the other hand, an item of Mormon folklore, to have become folklore, must have moved from the individual expression of its originator to the communal expression of those who preserve it, losing, through the process of communal re-creation described above, the marks of individual invention and assuming in time a form that reflects the consensus of the group.

In a recent BYU address, N. Scott Momaday made this point far more eloquently than I when, speaking of a Kiowa Indian tale, he said: "As many times as that story has been told it was always but one generation removed from extinction." [13] As soon as any story, Kiowa or not, ceases to appeal to its hearers, then, it dies or it is changed to reflect a new reality. No two tellers, of course, will ever relate the same story the same way; but if that story is to live, they cannot, in the telling of it, depart too far from the value center of the audience whose approval they seek.

I have been dealing thus far with the revelatory nature of Mormon folklore and have ignored its functional role. That is, I have been discussing what folk stories mean to the student of Mormon culture, but I have said nothing yet about what they mean to the people who tell them and listen to them, nothing about the force of folklore in the lives of human beings. In the remainder of this paper, I should like to discuss the influence of Mormon folklore on church members, as it functions to reinforce church dogma and practice, to sanction approved forms of behavior, and to give people a sense of stability in an unstable world.

In 1694 the Puritan divines, Increase and Cotton Mather and the Fellows of Harvard College, instructed the New England clergy to record the remarkable providences that would show the hand of God in their lives. "The things to be esteemed *memorable*," they said, "are especially *all unusual accidents*, in the heaven or earth, or water: all wonderful *deliverances* of the distressed: Mercies to the godly; *judgments* on the wicked; and more glorious fulfillments of either the *promises* or the *threatenings* in the Scriptures of truth with *apparitions*, *possessions*, *inchantments*, and all extraordinary things wherein the existence and agency of the *invisible world* is more sensibly demonstrated."[14] This passage seems not unlike instructions on how to keep a Book of Remembrance.[15] And indeed we Mormons, like the Puritans, seem eager to seek evidence of the invisible world, not simply because we like sensational stories but because, as Richard Cracroft and Neal Lambert point out, "the Mormon world is a God-made, man-centered world" and because "each Latter-day Saint in his personal life is challenged to bring forth evidence that supports this belief."[16] But in the stories we tell, we are seeking not just evidence that God lives but also that his programs are inspired and that he expects us to follow them. Stories about genealogical research and temple work illustrate this point well.

We are all familiar with the plethora of stories genealogy workers tell to encourage others to keep up the pursuit of their dead ancestors. For example, two Latter-day Saint (LDS) men driving to a conference pick up a man (later thought to be a Nephite) who urges them to do their genealogy work and then disappears from the backseat of the car. On another occasion, a lady who has trouble tracing her genealogical line prays for help. While she is out of the room where her typewriter is located, she hears its keys clicking. Investigating, she finds the missing information typed in the proper places on her pedigree chart.[17] And so the stories go: A stranger appears to a man in the temple and warns him to get busy on his genealogy because the time is short. A Nephite brings to the temple genealogical sheets that a couple had left home on the table. A man is instructed by a stranger to visit a graveyard, where he finds his missing family names. A man is instructed to go to a pawnshop, where he finds his genealogical data in a Bible. In exchange for a meal, a Nephite gives a lady a book containing information which she needs to extend her family genealogy. And a woman finds the missing names she has been searching for in a newspaper left mysteriously in her car. All of these stories make two main points: first, genealogical research must be important because the Lord helps people complete it, and, second, if one keeps struggling

faithfully ahead, not getting discouraged, he will eventually succeed.

If genealogical research is important, so, of course, is temple work, both for oneself and for one's ancestors. And once again circulating oral narratives stress the importance of this work. For example, couples who have not been sealed in the temple are visited by mysterious strangers (usually Nephites) who warn them to make haste in getting their work done. Couples who have been to the temple pick up old men along the highways who urge them to attend the temple often because time is short, warn them that otherwise they will not be ready when the Savior comes, and then disappear. Stories are legion about temple workers missing one of the names on a list and then having this mistake made known in a miraculous way. But the most widely circulated story today is probably the following:

> A lady in Salt Lake City, Utah, was desirous of going to the temple but was afraid to leave her children at home alone. She hadn't been able to locate a suitable baby-sitter but finally she did. She went to the temple a little apprehensive and about halfway through the session she felt so uneasy that she got up to leave. As she got to the back of the room, a temple worker stopped her to find out what the matter was. She, the lady, said she felt like she was urgently needed at home. The temple worker promised her that if she would return to her seat and finish the session everything would be fine. So she did. After the session was over she hurried home, and sure enough, there were fire engines and police cars all around her house. As she was running to her house, a neighbor lady stopped her and explained that her daughter had fallen into the ditch and couldn't be found. As the lady came to the house, there was her daughter soaking wet and crying. Her mother grabbed her and hugged her. After, the little girl gave her mother a note and explained that the lady who'd pulled her out of the ditch had given it to her. There on the note was the name of the lady for whom this woman had gone through the temple that day.

In some versions of this story it is the new baby-sitter herself who pulls the child from the water. In these instances the sitter then disappears and the mother later recalls that the person whose work she had done in the temple that day had the same name as the baby-sitter.[18] In one version the mother, and her husband, though faithful in other duties, have not been attending the temple and finally decide to go only after their bishop makes a personal request. In another version the couple actually call home, learn that their child is missing, but, after praying and getting a feeling that all will be well, remain and complete the session. But whatever form the story takes, it serves always, as one informant said, "as a testimony to the truthfulness of temple work."

These stories, then, not only mirror our concern with genealogical research and temple work, they also reinforce our belief that these pursuits are of God and thus persuade us to participate more eagerly in them.

In one of the most common stories of the Three Nephites, one of the old men visits a home, asks for nourishment, is given it, and then blesses the home with health and prosperity. But in one instance the lady of the house hasn't "time to bother" with her visitor; as a result she loses some of her children to the flu. In another, a lady who turns a beggar away has her lawn overrun with Bermuda grass. Stories like these are what Cotton Mather called "judgments on the wicked." They teach us to do right by showing us what happens to us when we don't. Many of them have to do with blasphemy and graphically demonstrate, in the words of one informant, that "the Lord will not be mocked." For example, in 1962 two priests from California decided to baptize a goat; they were struck dumb and haven't talked yet. In Idaho, the wayward son of a stake president consecrated a glass of beer; he passed out immediately, fell into a coma, and died a few days later. Two boys were in a chapel on Saturday without permission; they put bread on the sacrament trays and were running up and down the aisles; one of them looked down and discovered the bread had turned black. In 1860 Brigham Young dedicated "Salem pond," a new irrigation project, and promised that no one would die in the pond if the people refrained from swimming on Sunday; the eight people who have since drowned there were all swimming on Sunday. In southern Utah, a young man refused a mission call; about a month later he died in an automobile crash. In Springville not long ago three boys took a ouija board to the cemetery on Halloween night and asked it when they would die; within three years, in accordance with the ouija board's answer, all three were dead, one from suicide and the other two from accidents.

In no place do these stories flourish as abundantly as they do in the mission field. They are told over and over again to impress on the missionaries the sacredness of their callings and to demonstrate that the power of the priesthood is not to be tampered with. According to one story, a photograph taken of an elder in swimming, against mission rules, showed an evil-looking form hovering over his head. A story from Brazil tells of a missionary who refused to sleep in his garments at night because of the hot, humid weather: "When his companion woke in the morning he found the errant elder pressed into the wall so hard that he could hardly pull him off. The elder was obviously dead from being thus mashed into the wall." One of the most widely known stories, recounted in practically every mission, tells of elders who, as in the following account, are struck dead for testing their priesthood power by attempting to ordain a post or a Coke bottle or an animal: "Two missionaries were messing around, and they decided to confer the priesthood on a dog which they saw on the street. Before they could complete the ordinance, a bolt of lightning came and struck the dog and the two elders, and it *zapped* them."

One of the most frightening cycles of stories is that which tells of missionaries who seek a testimony by going through the back door—that is, by seeking first a testimony of the devil. The following story is typical:

I heard from one of my companions about a particular individual that decided that he would gain his testimony by finding out about the adversary. And so he decided that he would pray to the devil and pray for a manifestation or a vision of some type . . . As he proceeded to pray, hour after hour, his companion had gone to bed and left him in the middle of the room on his knees, praying for a manifestation, or waiting to see the devil in person. And so, as the story goes, he finally reached the point where he woke, or he made enough noise so his companion woke and went to the window and saw a black figure on a black horse coming down the road towards their apartment. And they were up at least two stories, and this particular individual, as the story goes, jumped out of the window.

Another version of the same story ends a little differently:

He (the companion) looks over to the bed where his companion has gone to bed finally, and he's completely white and obviously dead from his appearance, and there's a black figure on a white horse in the room, who is laughing. And then it just kind of fades away, until there's nothing. And the companion's dead.

In many versions, the nonpraying companion summons the mission president for help. Usually when they enter the room by breaking down the door they find the praying elder suspended in the air, his hair sometimes as white as an old man's. In one account, when they opened the door, the suspended elder's body is slammed against the wall, instant death the result. In another they find the bed pinned to the ceiling with the missionary dead between bed and ceiling. In still another the elder is in bed, burned from one end to the other.

These stories do not make pleasant reading, nor telling. Anyone who doubts their evocative power need only sit in his office late at night, as I have done, listening to them on tape. I think I can say with some assurance that a group of missionaries sitting up telling the stories would not lightly dishonor their priesthood for some time to come. From them, unpleasant though they may be, we find a good example of how folklore controls behavior, moulding it, in this instance through tales of horror, to fit the accepted norms of the group.

Most Mormon folklore is not so dark and gloomy as these devil stories. Much of it, indeed, suggests that God is in his heaven and that all is right with the world—or, at least, that all will be right with the world. Committed to a Messianic view of life, most of us are convinced that if we will only endure to the end we will win at the end. Yet, as turmoil and unrest swirl around us, it is difficult at times not to feel, with Matthew Arnold, that

. . . we are here as on a darkling plain
Swept with confused alarms of struggle and flight,
Where ignorant armies clash by night.[19]

But our folklore persuades us otherwise. It teaches us that there is, after all, order in the universe and that if things get too much out of hand, God will step in and set them right.

Consider, for example, the following story:

There was war between the Arabs and the Jews and the Jews were out-numbered by hundreds, thousands. They had one cannon and they had like about ten men, and the Arabs had stuff from Russia, artillery and all sorts of stuff. And the Jews were banging on cans and moving the cannon over here and they'd shoot it and then they'd move it back and shoot it so the Arabs would think they had lots of men. And they were only fooled for a little while.

And then when the Jews had just about run out of all their ammo and they were ready to surrender, then the Arabs, they all threw down their weapons and came walking and waving the white flag and everything, surrendering to these Jews. And the Jews walk out and there's ten of them. And the Arab guy who was spokesman for the group said: "Where are those thousands of troops that were just across the hill with the man in white leading them? This man was dressed in white and he was leading all these thousands of men and he had a long beard."

In some accounts *three* men with white flowing beards appear to the Arab generals and warn them to surrender or to face annihilation. The story, one of the most popular Nephite accounts to develop in recent years,[20] has been attached to all the Arab-Israeli wars: the 1948 War, the 1956 War, the 1967 War, and the recent war that brought about the oil crisis. It persuades those who believe it that God's plans for the Jews will not be thwarted and that he will not allow the wrong side to win in the Middle East.

On a less grand, but no less significant, scale, we hear stories which convince us that the missionary system will succeed in taking the gospel to the world. For example, a recent story tells of a missionary in the Language Training Mission[21] who had gotten up one hot night to take a shower:

He took his shower and returned or began to return to his room. Halfway down the hall he stopped because he heard a noise and wheeled around. Upon doing so he saw before each door an armed guard. Each one was a full six-feet-six-inches-tall, and regally dressed as one might expect a Nephite army to be dressed. One sees many such pictures of Moroni.[22] Each one was standing at attention, and the ones at the end of the hall behind him were changing guard, therefore the noise.

From the mission fields come numerous accounts of these guardian warriors being put to good service. Missionaries are saved from storms, rescued from violent mobs, and pulled from flaming wrecks on the freeway. In one instance, two lady missionaries, who run out of gasoline in the middle of a New Mexico desert, fortuitously discover a service station, fill up, and proceed on their journey; on their next trip over the same road they learn that no station has ever existed at the place where they filled their car with gas. After being badly treated on one street in Taiwan, the missionaries shake dust from their feet and the entire street burns down. In South America the elders dust their feet and a town is destroyed by wind. Two elders leave their garments at a laundry, and when the proprietor holds them up for ridicule, both he and the laundry burn, the fire so hot, in one instance, that it melts the bricks.

With the monstrous Texas murders fresh in our minds and with other stories of opposition to the missionary program familiar to us all, we take comfort in stories that testify that the missionary system, and with it the gospel, will prevail and that our righteous sons and daughters will be protected from harm.[23] The stories thus provide their listeners a sense of security and equilibrium in an unsure world.

In discussing the contribution of myth and ritual to the stability of a society, the anthropologist A. R. Radcliffe-Brown has argued that members of society share a "system of sentiments" (about right and wrong and about the order of the universe) and that it is the continuance of these collective sentiments that makes the survival of society possible. The function of folklore, he says, is, through "regular and adequate expression," to keep these sentiments alive in the minds of the people.[24] All the examples I have given above fit Radcliffe-Brown's formula rather neatly. They reinforce our belief in church dogma and practice; they persuade us to follow accepted standards of behavior by showing what will happen to us if we do and, particularly, what will happen to us if we don't; and they give rest to our souls by showing that there is order and purpose in the universe. But in all the examples I have given, I have left out one very important person—J. Golden Kimball.

How do we deal with J. Golden Kimball? More important, how do we deal with the fact that thirty-seven years after his death Mormons still tell more anecdotes about him than about any other figure in church history? At first blush, the stories told about him certainly seem not to fit Radcliffe-Brown's model. They often make fun of church practice. They do not give one a particularly strong feeling for the cosmic order of things. And they inspire correct behavior only in the sense that those who tell the stories fear they may be struck dead for doing so.

To answer this question about the J. Golden Kimball stories, let us look briefly at a missionary tale. By far the best known and most popular story my colleague John B. Harris and I have collected in our study of missionary folklore tells of a pair of enterprising elders who, deciding to take an unauthorized trip, make their weekly activity reports out three months in advance, leave them with their landlady with instructions to send one in each week to the mission office, and then leave on an unearned vacation. A few weeks before their return, the landlady mixes up the reports, sends one in out of sequence, and they are caught. The place of the unauthorized trip (New York, The Riviera, Cairo, Moscow, the Easter Islands, the bush country of Australia) varies greatly; otherwise, the details of the story, known in virtually every mission, are the same. One could argue that, since the wayward elders are always caught, the story serves as a warning to obey mission rules. Perhaps it does. But most missionaries enjoy the story because they find it amusing. One returned missionary who had served as assistant to the mission president, told me: "You would always like to do something like that yourself, and you kinda admire someone who has the guts to do it." In other words the hero in this story does for the missionary what he is not allowed to do himself—travel five kilometers beyond the boundaries of his assigned city.

Folklorists have long been intrigued by the problem we face here: Why do characters in traditional narratives commit acts that the tellers of the tales cannot, or would not, commit themselves? The answer seems to be, as the comment of my returned-missionary friend suggests, that folklore as a mirror for culture reveals not only outward behavior but also inner desires, not only what we can do but also what we might like to do if society did not decree otherwise.

Speaking to this issue, Roger Abrahams has argued that hero stories project cultural values in two ways: "as a guide for future action in real life and as an expression of dream-life, of wish-fulfillment." Of this second kind of projection, he says:

> In many groups there is a trickster hero who expends much of his energy in antisocial or antiauthoritarian activity. Even when this results in benefits to the group, his actions cannot be interpreted as providing a model for future conduct. He is a projection of desires generally thwarted by society. His celebrated deeds function as an approved steam valve for the group; he is allowed to perform in this basically childish way so that the group may vicariously live his adventures without actually acting on his impulses. To encourage such action would be to place the existence of the group in jeopardy.[25]

Applied to the J. Golden Kimball cycle, Abrahams's dictum means that the stories provide us the pleasure of sin without the need of suffering its consequences. More seriously, they contribute to the social cohesion Radcliffe-Brown talks about by making it easier for us to live with societal pressures that inhibit our natural inclinations and might otherwise be the undoing of both ourselves and our society.

In this connection, we should remember that the J. Golden Kimball stories are, in the final analysis, no longer about J. Golden Kimball at all. They are about us. We are the ones who keep them alive by continual retelling and by continual reshaping. We should be concerned, I believe, not so much with trying to characterize Kimball but rather with trying to understand ourselves—trying to understand why we have created the kind of character who lives in the legend, and trying to discover what need the telling of the stories fills in our own lives.

I believe it is a need to assert one's own personality and to resist, or at least to deflate, those who exercise authority over us. One of my friends, for instance, says he takes delight in the J. Golden Kimball stories because J. Golden is always putting down the revered.

Those who would like to censor the stories because of their colorful language have really missed their best argument. If the stories are dangerous, they are so not because of their language but because of their expressed disrespect for authority. In joke after joke, J. Golden is juxtaposed alongside a higher, more sour and dour authority. In almost every instance he lets the air out of this authority and gets away with it. For example, "J. Golden was talking with one of the Quorum members[26] one time and the 'brother' said to him: 'Brother Kimball, I don't see how you can swear so much. Why I'd rather commit adultery than swear so much.' J. Golden answered: 'Wouldn't we all, brother? Wouldn't we all?'" Another story states: "This happened in St. George. J. Golden was down there with an Apostle for stake conference.[27] J. Golden fell asleep while the Apostle was talking and fell off his chair right at the feet of the Apostle. The Apostle looked rather strongly at Brother Kimball, who responded: "Well, you shouldn't be so damn boring."" Most of us know the story of how President Grant insisted on writing J. Golden's conference address because he had lost confidence in the crusty old man's ability to speak without swearing. J. Golden took the talk as he walked toward the podium, stared at President Grant's handwriting, then screeched over the microphone: "Good hell, Hebe, I can't read a damn word of this."[28] There is humor, of course, in the swearing and in the thwarting of President Grant's plan, but the real laughter is evoked by the word "Hebe." Prophet, seer, and relevator—yes. But never Hebe. Therein lies the sacrilege.

Though the J. Golden Kimball accounts are best known, they are by no means the only stories that put down authority figures. A large number of "Mormon Bishop" jokes also serve this end. The following story, which has also been told for years about Protestant ministers, Catholic priests, and Jewish rabbis, is typical:

> The bishop lost his bicycle and suspected that it was stolen, so he talked with his counselors about it and asked them to help him find out who stole it. The bishop decided to give a little talk in church about the ten commandments, and when he came to the commandment about 'Thou shalt not steal," he would slow down and pause so that his counselors could see who squirmed and find out who it was that stole his bicycle. Well, the bishop got up in church and started preaching about the ten commandments, but when he came to the commandment about stealing he didn't even slow down. He just rattled right on and didn't even pause at all. Afterwards his counselors asked him why he didn't slow down so they could see who squirmed when he talked about stealing. The bishop said, "Well, when I came to the commandment 'Thou shalt not commit adultery' I remembered where I left my bicycle."[29]

(It is interesting to note that not only is the bishop in this joke made to look ridiculous; he is made so by violation of the very law that bishops are usually most diligent to enforce among their charges.) Even among our children the tendency to rebel against authority by using folklore is sometimes evident. Fed a diet of saccharine-sweet songs by solicitous Primary and Sunday School teachers, youngsters often respond with parodies like the following:

I have five little fingers on one little hand;
I have six little fingers on my other hand.
During all the long hours till daylight is through,
I have one little finger with nothing to do.

Some of the jokes project not just a resistance to authority but also a concern with certain church practices. For example:

One day Saint Peter was repairing the Gates of Heaven and a Catholic priest who had just died came to get in.

"It'll be a few minutes before you can enter," Saint Peter said. "The gates are broken. You can go over there and have a cup of coffee while you wait."

The priest calmly began drinking his coffee and Saint Peter returned to his work. Not long after, a Protestant minister who had just died approached Saint Peter to enter heaven.

"You'll have to wait while I fix these gates," Saint Peter said. "Just go over there and have some coffee."

The minister joined the priest. Soon a Mormon bishop who had just died came up to Saint Peter and wanted to get into heaven.

Saint Peter said, "You'll have to go to hell; I don't have time to make hot chocolate."

A joke which made the rounds a few months ago tells that

President Kimball sent out messages for all members of the church to meet on Temple Square for an important message. The Tabernacle, the Assembly Hall, and the Salt Palace were full, and people were all over. President Kimball got up and said: "Saints, I've got some good news and some bad news. First the good news. We have just received a telegram from Western Union; the Millennium is here. Christ arrives in two days. Now for the bad news. We're all supposed to meet at the Vatican."[30]

Some Mormons are offended by this story because we haven't the necessary psychic distance to tell jokes about a living head of the church the way we can tell them, for instance, about Brigham Young. But the story itself is relatively innocent, spoofing the belief that only Mormons will make it to heaven. Other jokes are more serious. For example, an anecdote collected recently but first heard by the informant in the 1930s tells that when Heber J. Grant was president of the church and Rudger Clawson, who was a year younger than Brother Grant, was president of the Quorum of the Twelve, Brother Clawson was trying "with all his strength" to "outlive Heber." At a later date, the same story was attached to David O. McKay and Joseph Fielding Smith, who also were close in age and were president of the church and the Quorum of the Twelve respectively:

Before President McKay died, Jessie Evans Smith used to get her husband out of bed each morning and say: "All right, Joseph, it's time for our exercises. Ready. One, two, three. Outlive David O.; outlive David O."

I am quite sure that neither of these anecdotes has any basis in actual fact, but they both have a basis in the psychological fact discussed earlier—that is, both reflect a real concern of some Mormons that ascendancy to the presidency seems to result from longevity rather than from revelation and that we are forever destined to be led by men long past their prime. I personally cannot hear the anecdotes with pleasure—I have been taught too long and too well to honor the prophet. But they exist, and if we wish really to understand varying Mormon attitudes, they cannot be ignored.

The stories we have been considering here suggest that however willingly we live under our authoritarian system we do not always do so easily. If the jokes trouble us, we should remember the point made by Abrahams: jokes like these do not provide models for conduct; they provide instead a means of easing the pressures developed by the system we live under (and no matter what system we live under there will be pressures). We should also remember that the people who tell these jokes are not out to overthrow the system. They are simply finding release from their frustrations through laughter. Next Sunday will find most of them in church faithfully attending their duties. The fact that they are there may indeed be a result of their saving sense of humor. These stories, then, like the stories of divine intervention in the affairs of men, contribute to the stability of both the church and its members. And herein lies the paradox of Mormon folklore: On the one hand, it persuades members to accept and support church dogma and practice; on the other hand, it provides them with the means of coming to terms with the tensions such support at times imposes upon them.

In conclusion, and in answer again to the introductory questions: Mormon folklore is Mormon literature, folk literature. The materials of this literature are not some sort of fossilized artifacts surviving from an earlier period and valuable only to the curious collecting antiquarian. They are instead a body of living traditions constantly renewed and constantly re-created as Mormons react to the circumstances of their contemporary environment. This material is valuable to the student of Mormon culture because it gives him keen insight into the Mormon mind and a better understanding of Mormon behavior. It is valuable to the people themselves because it reaffirms their conviction in the truthfulness of the gospel; it inspires them to conform to accepted patterns of behavior; it persuades them that God is on their side and in times of trouble will come to their aid; and, finally, when the burdens of their religion at times weigh too heavily upon them, it provides them with the means to ease the pressure by laughing at both themselves and the system and thus to face the new day with equanimity.

Notes

1. The term *folklore* was coined by William John Thoms in a letter to *The Athenaeum*, No. 982, 22 August 1846, pp. 862–63. Thoms, writing under the name Ambrose Merton (the names of two Oxford colleges), suggested that this "good Saxon compound" replace the *popular antiquities* then in vogue. For definitions of folklore given by twenty-one twentieth-century scholars, see *Funk & Wagnalls Standard Dictionary of Folklore, Mythology and Legend*, ed. Maria Leach, 2 vols. (New York, 1949), 1:398–403. For a recent appraisal of folklore study, see *Toward New Perspectives in Folklore*, ed. Richard Bauman, special issue of *Journal of American Folklore*, 84, (1971).

2. The Correlation Committee is a central church committee which reviews and approves materials, including instructional manuals, for publication. According to the Book of Mormon, a colony of Israelites left Jerusalem some 600 years before Christ and made their way to the new world. Following his resurrection in Jerusalem, Christ visited the remnant of these people, called Nephites, established his church among them, and chose from them twelve apostles. Three of these apostles, the Three Nephites, chose, as John the Beloved had done in the old world, to "tarry in the flesh" until the second coming of Christ. Mormon lore is replete with accounts of these ancient wanderers appearing to contemporary Mormons in time of need, helping them out of difficulty, and then disappearing.

3. J. Golden Kimball was a church leader renowned for his salty sermons. During his youth he learned the rough language of the frontier and, when he later became a church leader, did not entirely put this language behind him. A spate of trickster stories about Kimball still circulate among Mormons today.

4. Joseph Fielding Smith to Hector Lee, 15 December 1941, as cited in Lecture "The Three Nephites: The Substance and Significance of the Legend in Folklore," (Ph.D. diss., University of New Mexico, 1947), p. 217.

5. Unless otherwise noted, all items of Mormon folklore discussed in this paper as well as comments of informants, are located in the Brigham Young University Folklore Archives, c/o English Department.

6. Local Mormon congregations are presided over by lay leaders, who hold their leadership positions on a rotating basis. The entire church is presided over by General Authorities, who in most cases hold their positions for life.

7. Austin E. Fife, "The Legend of the Three Nephites among the Mormons," *Journal of American Folklore*, 53 (1940): 27–29.

8. The same individual will often tell the same story quite differently, depending upon his reasons for telling it and upon his audience. For example, I have two versions of the James Rencher story told by the same informant, one with the political theme and one without it. In the first instance, the informant focuses on politics because he wants to persuade the students in his religion class that the General Authorities have the right to speak out on political issues.

9. Brigham Young University, Harold B. Lee Library, Special Collections, Manuscript Collection, M884.

10. Seminaries and Institutes is the organization responsible for Mormon religious instruction in secondary schools and in the universities—released time instruction in secondary schools and extracurricular instruction in universities.

11. The first presidency is comprised of the president (or prophet) of the church and of his two counselors. These three men form the highest governing body in the church.

12. The first presidency first addressed the issue in a letter (30 March 1970) mailed to stake presidents, mission presidents, and bishops. The letter was reprinted in the *Church News*, 4 April 1970.

13. N. Scott Momaday, "The Man Made of Words," Brigham Young University Forum Address, 14 January 1975.

14. Cotton Mather, *Magnalia Christi Americana: Or, The Ecclesiastical History of New England* (1702), 2 vols. (Hartford, Conn.: S. Andrus & Son, 1853), 2:362.

15. Every Mormon is encouraged to keep a Book of Remembrance—an account of his or her spiritual sojourn through life, richly illustrated with faith promoting stories.

16. Richard H. Cracroft and Neal Lambert, *A Believing People: Literature of the Latter-day Saints* (Provo: Brigham Young University Press, 1974), p. 3.

17. Every Mormon is encouraged to seek the names of his or her deceased ancestors through genealogical research and then to have saving gospel ordinances vicariously performed for them in a Mormon temple. A pedigree chart lists these ancestors in a direct line from oneself as far back in time as one is able to go.

18. For a brief discussion of this version of the story, see Jan Harold Brunvand, "Modern Legends of Mormondom, or, Supernaturalism Is Alive and Well in Salt Lake City," in *American Folk Legend: A Symposium*, ed. Wayland D. Hand (Berkeley, Los Angeles, and London: University of California Press, 1971), p. 200.

19. Matthew Arnold, "Dover Beach," in *The Poems of Matthew Arnold, 1840–1867* (London: Oxford University Press, 1926), p. 402.

20. This story seems to have entered the Nephite tradition from printed sources. A somewhat different version from the one given here was cited by Joseph Fielding Smith in *The Signs of the Times* (Salt Lake City: Deseret News Press, 1952), pp. 227–29. Two years later LeGrand Richards printed the same story in *Israel! Do You Know?* (Salt Lake City: Deseret Book, 1954), pp. 229–33. Both President Smith and Elder Richards cited as their source an article in *The Jewish Hope* by Arthur U. Michelson. Neither of them argued that the men in the story were Nephites but merely suggested that they might have been.

21. The Language Training Mission was the instructional center in Provo, Utah, where newly called Mormon missionaries received language training before entering the field. The name has now been changed to Missionary Training Center.

22. According to the Book of Mormon, Moroni was a famous warrior and last survivor of the Nephite people (see n. 2). Mormons believe that it was Moroni, now an angel, who delivered to Joseph Smith the plates from which Smith translated the Book of Mormon.

23. The reference here is to a murder in Texas in which a deranged individual killed two young missionaries and mutilated their bodies.

24. A. R. Radcliffe-Brown, "The Interpretation of Andamanese Customs and Beliefs: Myths and Legends," in *The Andaman Islanders* (Cambridge: Oxford University Press, 1922), pp. 376–405.

25. Roger D. Abrahams, "Some Varieties of Heroes in America," *Journal of the Folklore Institute*, 3 (1966): 341–42.

26. The Quorum of Twelve Apostles, after the first presidency the leading governing body in the church, is often referred to simply as "the quorum"; apostles are referred to as quorum members.

27. A "stake" is a geographical administrative unit, the equivalent of a diocese. Twice a year each stake holds a conference for all members living within the stake's boundaries.

28. "Hebe" was the nickname for church president Heber J. Grant. Mormons are taught from childhood to revere church leaders. Referring to the president of the church by his nickname would be a sign of disrespect.

29. Many stories like this one are Mormon not by birth but by adoption. They come originally from the large body of anticlerical stories known throughout the world. The central character, in the above instance a Mormon bishop, is a rabbi, a priest, or a minister, depending upon the religious affiliation of the people telling the jokes. The popularity of such stories throughout the Judeo-Christian world suggests that religious subjects everywhere have enjoyed deflating those who exercise authority over them.

30. This is a widely traveled story, told by Catholics, Mormons, and Reorganized Mormons alike. The pope in the Catholic version and the church president in the RLDS version both advise their people that the gathering place is to be Salt Lake City. Occasionally Mormons tell of the pope sending his followers to Salt Lake City, the geographical setting varying according to whether the teller is making fun of his own religion or someone else's.

New Sweden Pioneer Day

Hal Cannon

Reunions, festivals, and celebrations are among the most vital and viable expressions of contemporary ethnic and local cultures. They are also among the oldest forms of human expression and have in fact been reported and described at least since Herodotus.

The question Hal Cannon asks is, why do people continue to meet in these ways and at traditional times? Although a reunion is a group event, Cannon's point of view is always that of a real individual — a central performer like Dave Sealander, an anonymous participant, or the questioning outsider. This approach to New Sweden's Pioneer Day reveals the reunion's complex meanings by portraying and analyzing personal rituals, low key gestures, understatement, and private appraisal. In accordance with more conventional scholarship, Cannon also presents the historical development of New Sweden Pioneer Day (diachronic analysis) and the reunion as it is today (synchronic analysis). He finally goes beyond both kinds of analysis to portray the timelessness that is a sensory and philosophical theme of the reunion itself.

For other attempts to understand the festival as folk expression see Robert J. Smith, The Art of the Festival *(1975), "Festivals and Celebrations" in Richard M. Dorson's* Folklore and Folklife: An Introduction *(1972), and Bruce Giuliano's* Sacra O Profano? A Consideration of Four Italian-Canadian Religious Festivals *(1976).*

Hal Cannon is Folk Arts Coordinator for the Utah Arts Council. He has authored and edited numerous articles, books, and media presentations on folklife of the Great Basin.

REUNION AND CELEBRATION

We take delight in watching familiar faces grow old with us. We go through life making a festive occasion out of gathering back the old and once well known and making an attempt at refamiliarization. This is the kind of celebration we call a reunion. We reunite with family, old friends, community, schoolmates, to name a few. The only thing that separates a reunion from any other gathering is that it is shared, in the main, between people who do not ordinarily have everyday union and desire reunity.

In this article I will look at a specific reunion and make some general observations about human nature, about ethnicity, about the nature of communities, about Idaho, a place in Idaho called New Sweden, and a family from New Sweden called the Sealanders.

Why do we need to turn inward, look back to our past? Why do we find comfort in old and rather normal relations? I must admit that as a cynical person who rarely enjoys groups of more than four people, these questions are of true concern to me.

A fascinating pursuit, at a reunion, is to view the complex ways in which people reunite and reestablish intimacy with each other. What we find is that the ways in which people come to intimacy follow finite yet creative patterns which are generally traditional. Most of this interaction is private, though if you are an insider, and know the individuals and their pasts, you will undoubtedly see a great deal more going on at a reunion than an outsider would. For an outsider, documenting a reunion, except in the most general terms, is nearly an impossible task. One can take pictures of people having a good time, and one can record interviews and document any formal program which is presented to the group, but the meat of the event is private. Recently I was a guest at a family reunion where I was photographing the event. One of the uncles approached me with a tattered and fat wallet in his hand. One by one he pulled out faded and torn photographs of family members which he had been carrying around for years. For each photograph he took me to the subject of the old photo and had me photograph the person holding the picture of himself in a younger state. His desire brought me head on with his private mechanism to accommodate the past and the present with his own extended family. Each pose demanded a private and individualized interchange before I was allowed the photograph. Not only was this gesture a symbol of bringing the past and present together, but it was the old uncle's way of showing his relatives that he cared for them by contiually carrying their images with him at all times. The wallet was not just brought out for the family reunion, but it was also carried into the coal mines each day throughout the years. In a sense, the collection of photographs formed a portable altar. That brings out the second underlying purpose for a reunion, and that is for people who share a legacy to show consistency for that legacy in spite of the distance of time and space.

These private elements are varied and creatively individualized. It is generally neighbors and relatives who compare recipes, talk about the quality of animal judging at the fair, exchange prankster stories from school days, gossip about a third party, or exchange dirty jokes. These examples and countless other interchanges tell us much about individuals, family, and community relationships.

These private elements are of interest to psychologists and sociologists. The event, both private and public, is of interest to the anthropologist. And those traditional items which are used by people to link themselves together are the domain of folklorists. In my examples of conversations at a reunion, the tradition of sharing private photographs, accounts of animal raising and competition, recipes, prankster stories, gossip, and even dirty jokes are all items of folklore. To this folklore we apply disciplines of other human sciences, such as psychology, sociology, anthropology, and history, in our attempt to understand the significance of traditional elements in the everyday lives of ourselves, the people around us, and people unlike us whom we want to understand and therefore bring closer to us.

The reunion is just one kind of celebration. To understand the function of a reunion, it is valuable to consider the more general issue of the celebration. Also, it is important to keep in mind that "reunion" is an aspect of many celebrations, particularly as they become less public in nature. There is very little written on the reunion, whereas the celebration has been studied by an array of social scientists in the past decade with fascinating observations and contributions to the ethnographic data bank. Richard Dorson points out, "The term celebration can encompass festivals, rituals, ceremonies, spectacles, fetes, holidays, extravaganzas, and partakes of all these elements."[1]

The word itself is derived from the Latin "celeber" which means "numerous and much frequented." Victor Turner explains this term with assistance of the French sociologist Durkheim as "effervescence—generated by a crowd of people with shared purpose and common values."[2] By the root of the word celebration, it seems the spirit or feeling of the event is at the core of meaning. This "effervescence," "spirit," or, as Turner calls it, "communitatas," is a phenomenon which has been interpreted in numerous ways. An existential explanation is forwarded by Grimes when he defines a public celebration as "a rope bridge of knotted symbol strung across an abyss. We make our crossings hoping the chasm will echo our festive sounds for a moment, as the bridge begins to sway from the rhythms of our dance."[3] Again, Victor Turner accounts for the celebration in psychological terms: "Celebration may be said to bring about a temporary reconciliation among con-

flicting members of a single community. Conflict is held at abeyance during the period of ritualized action. Perhaps the euphoria associated with the stimulation of 'right-hemisphere' capabilities and functions leads to the perception of shared emotional states I have called 'communitatas!' This might involve a de-emphasizing of 'left-hemisphere' control over logical, linear, and classifying functions associated with social structuring and conflicts arising from structural opposition."[4]

In "The Language of Festivals," Roger Abrahams talks about celebrations in more organic terms, tying them to the passage of seasons in a year. "In spite of the growth of our cities and the technological sense of control over nature this entails, we continue to maintain our connection with the year's passage through festive engagements that still speak out in behalf of fertility."[5]

Dorson feels that criteria of celebration "should fall at fixed periods and should involve sacred and symbolic elements." He laments the quality of these sacred and symbolic functions when he observes a "deplorable lack of festive occasions in the United States."[6] There is no doubt that we find celebrations of foreign, tribal, and ancestral people more dramatic than our own. Generally, we seek the dramatic festivity full of material accoutrements such as handcrafted masks and idols, and sacred ritual and dance. These elements seem to hold the mystery of effervescence.

Is the yearly New Sweden Pioneer Day "effervescent?" Is there, actually, a deplorable lack of festive occasions in twentieth-century America? Is the problem that we do not accept our own contemporary culture and simply are blind to the drama of our own celebrations? Certainly, elements such as ritual, craft, and dance are present at today's celebrations, but they may seem transparent. We tend to look at the old forms of folklore romantically and in an idealized fashion. New forms go unnoticed. We are unwilling to see the new and creative and fit it into the rubric of folklore. Stephen Stern has generalized that there have been shifts in ethnicity which we can extend to all of folk activity "from the old to the new, from the longer to the shorter, from complex to simple, from sacred to secular, from supernatural to realistic, from communal to individualistic."[7] If we are able to accept these shifts while examining the components of contemporary celebration, we too can find "effervescence" in New Sweden Pioneer Day. The dearth of celebrations may be apparent rather than real.

NEW SWEDEN AND ITS PIONEER DAY

Occupations and their inherent folklore comprise worlds of knowledge, ritual, behavior, and rites of passage. The more independence and survival play in making a living, the more intricate the folklore of the occupation. Farming is such an occupation. People who are involved in the occupation itself rarely know the honor which is paid to someone who is considered a

Figure 1.   1980 Harvest Dance handbill.

By hand and team, they made each stream, to quench this
thirsty soil.[8]

New Sweden—indeed all the land in the Snake River
Valley—was thought to be a desert waste having no
practical potential. In a memorandum from Captain
Wilson Price Hunt to Washington Irving, the region
was described in the following excerpt:

> A dreary desert of sand and gravel extends from Snake
> River almost to the Columbia. Here and there is a thin
> pasturage for horses or buffalo. Indeed, these treeless
> wastes present vast desert tracts that must ever defy civili-
> zation and interpose dreary and dirty wilds between the
> habitations of man in traversing which the wanderer will
> often be in danger of perishing.[9]

Eagle Rock was the first permanent town on the river
and was primarily founded as a river crossing and supply point for travelers on their way to and from the
gold-rich mountains to the north. In 1891 the town of
Eagle Rock changed its name to Idaho Falls. It was at
this time in Idaho's history that a potential for this land
was realized. Within fifty years, two-thirds of the now
famous Idaho spuds were being grown in the irrigated
valleys around Idaho Falls. New Sweden itself was the
brainchild of Chicago investors who successfully peti-
tioned for water diversion from the Snake. Through the
Great Western and Porter canals which they dug, four
Swedish-Americans organized in 1894 as the great
Western Land Company. It was not long before advertisements appeared in all the Swedish language papers
around the country advertising the good land of New
Sweden. The ads made particular note of twenty acres
donated by the company where a Swedish church
would be built where men could worship God in their
native tongue. Land was cleared of sagebrush and a
model farm was set up. The house on it was called
"Swede Land Company," and it not only housed Mr.
and Mrs. J. A. Johnson, but it generally provided the
first night's lodging for visitors who came on the train
to inspect the new land. At this time there were 11,524
acres of land available from the company. The following year, crops were planted by the founding families
who had come west from homes primarily in Nebraska.

The first twenty-five years of settlement were particularly full of hardship. After just two or three years
all of the new farmers were not only in debt to the
point of foreclosure, but they were not producing successful crops, being inexperienced and clumsy with
their new role with the scarce water. Mormons like to
claim their position as the developers of the science of
irrigation, yet in the early days of Idaho, irrigation was
little more than guesswork in this high land which was
deceptively level land. These two problems, irrigation
and capital, nearly doomed the new farming community to failure. It was only through the settlers' refusal to
continue their mortgage payments to the land company
in Chicago until they could renegotiate contracts that
the first problem was diminished. The Chicago-based

good farmer. A part of being good is based on the
degree of participation in the folklore. This observation, of course, is not just limited to farming, for this
serious devotion is true to countless occupations where
the criterion of being good is a lifetime quest.

In New Sweden, men are judged by how well they
farm. Being a good farmer entails year after year of
back-breaking work, and in the upper Snake River
region of Idaho, it requires a man to cleverly
manipulate the limited amount of Snake River water
which he has to work with. The social history of this
entire region of Idaho is read from the heart of the
region, the Snake, through its main arteries, the
primary canals, down to its capillaries, each furrow
and ditch on every farm. It is impossible to know what
importance water has to this place unless you visit a
social gathering such as the annual New Sweden
Pioneer Picnic where water is a primary topic of
conversation.

> Water! Precious Water! What a glorious destiny,
> The blood of the earth, of priceless worth, in this capacity
> Was brought by dauntless pioneer, who worked with
>   ceaseless toil;

company sent J. H. Stevens to report on the uprising in New Sweden. He reports in part:

> The cause of their holding back in their payments on their lands is attributable wholly to their belief that they were buncoed by the Swede Company who induced them to buy at prices so much greater than equally good and contiguous lands could have been bought. I cannot discover that there exists any difference in the values of lands on the east and west sides of the river. The prices on the east side are and have been $8.50 to $10.00 and $12.00 per acre, the character of the soil and convenience to market, and in everything it is fully the equal of these lands on the west side, for which your settlers, as they are termed, have agreed to pay all prices from $16.00 per acre to as high, I believe, as $22.00 per acre.[10]

Through this report and the help of Judge G. E. McCutcheon, the contracts were renegotiated, and eventually the settlers bought the water rights from Great Western and became Idaho's first self-run irrigation district. These victories alone gave the pioneers of New Sweden an increased sense of community. Added to this was the practical necessity of families banding together to help clear the sagebrush and help in the building of dams and ditches. Every family has stories of dams being washed away and the neighbors coming to the rescue repairing the damage. A spirit of cooperation in this relatively isolated ethnic enclave continued to be nurtured not only through the building of a community church and school, but in an everyday manner, learning to harness and cooperate with water. The isolation itself contributed to homogeneity in the community. The Swedes were literally surrounded by Mormon settlers in those early days. The Mormons were a much more diverse group who considered themselves Americans even if they were newly in the country. After all, they belonged to the new American church. Though relations were friendly and neighborly between New Sweden and the surrounding Mormon communities, there was a small undercurrent of tension. The Mormons were a zealous lot who were concertedly building a kingdom of God on earth which seemed exclusive. They looked upon the Swedes as foreigners, in more than one sense of the word. The Swedes, on the other hand, were ambitious as well, but held different priorities. For example, it was the practice of Swedes to build a big, beautiful barn before a nice house was built. The care of animals came almost before the care of the family. Many times the Swedes would grumble about the way Mormons used and abused their animals. Over the years these differences have dissipated so that now the outward appearance of material culture of the past is the only thing which distinguishes any of these communities on the river.

The year 1919 brought a realization to the community of New Sweden. The land was cleared. A system of irrigation had been worked out which was programmed and reliable. Dams and reservoirs had been built which assured the water supply for crops. New people were moving into the area who were not part of

Figure 2. Residents of New Sweden reunite at annual picnic.

that drama which took place in the last quarter century. The children of New Sweden were growing up as Americans with lesser skill in the native tongue. The crops were good and people were, for the first time, prospering. These new circumstances prompted a group of pioneers to gather on the evening of June 1 to form the New Sweden Pioneer Association. At this meeting they decided there needed to be an annual event which would bring the community together "to keep alive the old memories of pioneers days in New Sweden from the very first days when this settlement was reclaimed from the desert, and through hard labor and numerous hardships by the pioneers was made to be a beauty spot in the Snake River Valley."[11] It was decided that the first annual pioneer picnic would be held later in the summer and that those settlers who had arrived before 1904 would be considered members of the association.

Since this first picnic over sixty years ago, there has been a gathering each year in July to celebrate the memory of the pioneers of New Sweden. Though there is no drama that will equal that of those first years of settlement, there is a saga told in the minutes of all

Figure 3.   Picnickers line up for dinner.

those picnics which is not a formal history. It is, however, a story of a community responding to the pressures of the world. One hardly realizes the incredible consistency of tradition by attending a current picnic. We are deceived by a veneer of style. We see a bucket of Kentucky Fried Chicken on the picnic table rather than ornate Swedish sugar cakes, and kids in cut-off jeans and men in shiny feed store caps rather than an array of dark suits and parasols. Each year a secretary is elected who keeps minutes of the picnic. Each year a secretary looks back at her predecessor's report and fits this real live event into the same literary form she has inherited. On the surface this literature seems mundane, but through it there are glimpses of the life and progress of this community.

> I think that here lies the sense of literary creation: to portray ordinary objects as they will be reflected in the kindly mirrors of future times: to find in the objects around us the fragrant tenderness that only posterity will discern and appreciate in the far-off times when every trifle of our plain everyday life will become exquisite and festive in its own right: the times when a man who might put on the ordinary jacket of today will be dressed up for an elegant masquerade.[12]

The picnic is remarkably consistent. Every year you could plan on arriving at the picnic and seeing a gigantic and sumptuous feast of potluck dishes set in neat rows. There is always a program which includes speeches, music, and a variety of entertainment. Games are played, usually baseball and volleyball, and the association provides ice cream, cake, coffee and lemonade, every year without fail. One thing which has changed over the years is the location of the picnic. For the first few years it was held at Carlson's Grove. Then for years it was held at the New Sweden Irrigation Company ranch, and then at the New Sweden School. In 1954 it was moved to a park which Clause Sealander had created in a grove of trees on the edge of the expansive lava fields which border the family farm. During the first years of the picnic, attendance fluctuated between one and two hundred people. During World War II attendance and enthusiasm started to slip. At one picnic a motion was entered to discontinue the picnic, but a counter motion was passed which asked that the picnic be continued for another fifteen years to see how it was going. It was at this point that a committee was formed to write a history of the first fifty years of settlement. In this publication's conclusion the struggle to keep community spirit was stated:

> In the horse and buggy days, the neighbors would be together for Sunday dinner after church and a close neighborhood spirit prevailed as all were ready at any time to do anything possible to help anyone in trouble or adversity. Now, in this modern age, we hardly know our neighbor. Sunday afternoon will find us visiting, not our neighbor, but some place 100 to 500 miles away. The farmer, his boys, and the hired man, each has a car, and of course those cars are made to be used. . . . Yes, the world has made progress, tremendous progress, in fifty years; and our community, starting from "scratch" fifty years ago has made progress.[13]

In 1967 the last of the original pioneers died at the age of 93. In these years since the original pioneers are gone, the picnics have steadily grown in popularity. The civil rights movement in the sixties ushered in an age when many people have found a need to reassess their place in a family, ethnic, and community heritage. In turn, this need has brought a new generation into the involvement of New Swedishness. These are the grandchildren of those original settlers. These people, too, are coping with a new kind of progress which threatens their community. Today New Sweden is an outlying suburb of Idaho Falls. Some of the best farmland has been divided into five-acre ranchettes. Land prices have looked better to many of the families than the toil and insecurity of farming. The New Sweden School was closed in a move to consolidate in 1978. Notwithstanding these diluting forces, there is a spirit that resides with a core of young who have stayed and with a large number of old people who choose to reside in the valley in their retiring years.

The annual picnic today is very much as it has

Figure 4. David Sealander playing on 1982 Pioneer Day program.

always been. People start showing up at about noon. They carry a covered plate of food with them. Fifty years old seems to be the mean age at the picnic though there are many young families with small children. Many of the older people seem to be having the most fun as they hurry to set up their chairs in the shade on the edge of the activity. These people know what this affair is all about, and they are totally animated in earnest reunion with old acquaintances. The young people generally mill around looking more concerned with the long wait for dinner than anything else. I overheard one conversation where an old fellow shook his head to his contemporary and said, "You know, when I walk through town I don't know anyone anymore. I recognize a lot more people in the cemetery now days." Another scene found two people proudly greeting each other in Swedish, passing the pleasantries in a halting anglicized dialect. The only other thing which was Swedish about this picnic, on the surface, that is, was the cure prescribed when one old gentleman complained of a bad cough to his friend who said, "By golly, you ought to go over and have a cup of that good coffee."

The social context of coffee in Scandinavian life cannot be overstated. It is often said that Danish Mormons kept coffee on the stove just for the smell of hospitality in the home long after they quit drinking it, as dictated by the church's "Word of Wisdom."

About 1:30, when almost everyone has arrived, an officer of the association climbs the three steps to the cement and lava-rock stage and announces dinner, and

then a blessing is given on the food. An old wagon running gear has been converted into the legs of a twenty-foot-long serving table where lines form on either side. Paper plates are available, though most people have their own china and utensils. The plates of food are varied. Occasionally there is a dish prepared from old-country recipes, but fried chicken, casseroles, potato salads and the like are predominant at this feast. After dinner, the old folks reposition their chairs in rows in front of the stage. The minutes of the year's previous picnic are read and business is transacted. Usually the only business pertains to the finances of the organization, election of officers, and the state of affairs of the cemetery. The program begins with a local bluegrass or fiddle group. Then there might be a recitation or speech. In years past, these were sometimes humorous renditions done in Swedish dialect. Mr. and Mrs. Phillip Swenson occasionally sing a couple of religious songs accompanied by a zither from the old country. Then there is always Swedish accordion music played by the Sealander men. It was a special year at 1982's picnic because just one month earlier Clause Sealander had passed away. Though there was nothing said officially, the picnic this year seemed to be a memorial to this man who had started playing his accordion at the picnics as a boy in the early twenties and had played at most gatherings over the years. He had created this park for his community to use and had been the driving force behind a much-treasured stone memorial to the pioneers of New Sweden which stands at the cemetery. In fact, in 1975 the picnic day was

Figure 5.   Rolling barbecue used at Sealander Park and made by one of Clause Sealander's best friends, "Hank" Henry Malcom, who was an extremely talented blacksmith from Shelley, Idaho.

designated Clause Sealander Day in recognition of his craftsmanship in the erection of the memorial. Mrs. Sealander and her five children were present this year. I heard many people approach the Sealanders and say, "Well, I wasn't planning to come this year, but I just got to thinking about Clause and wanted to come and see how you were doing." The program featured performances by David Sealander playing a few old Swedish dance tunes on the accordion, and David's brother, Robert, singing a couple of folk songs accompanying himself on the guitar.

In years past, the programs were varied. For many years the program began by the congregation singing the state song, "Here We Have Idaho." Also, for years there was a speech given by a member of the local clergy on some aspect of the pioneering. In 1948 Mrs. Alfred Kress displayed chalk drawings as she sang "Red Sails in the Sunset." In 1952 Shirley and Sharron Enell played electrical guitar numbers. The Erickson family have sung in different combinations all through the years. In 1960 the Ruffles and Russets square dance group performed. And in 1976 the program was primarily patriotic with a lengthy flag ceremony that displayed flags through U.S. history. After the program, through all these years, fresh coffee is made and cakes and ice cream are served, then there is more

socializing and game playing. The crowd trickles away and all go home to their normal lives for another year until the next picnic.[14]

Obviously, this reunion, this picnic, this celebration comprises only a few hours out of people's lives in New Sweden, once a year. Through this one small ritual we can learn about the people who make up a community. We see the values and tastes of the people throughout the years. We see how the pressures of the ever-changing world are reflected in a time once a year which is constant, continuous, and traditional.

Heritage has not always meant the same thing to all people. Today's heritage is weighted toward ethnic pride, but ethnic pride has not always been popular. During World War II, for instance, there was anti-Swedish sentiment in this country because of Sweden's neutrality and sympathy for the German cause. At this point in the history of New Sweden, it is impossible to generalize about the state of ethnicity in the community as a whole. Perhaps in 1920 it would have been easier to say something about this place when it was more homogeneous, but this matter of ethnicity in America today is complicated. There is a vast array of issues, of which only some are discussed in this article.

ETHNICITY AND INDIVIDUALS

The most obvious celebrations of ethnicity in America are public revivals which promote, as Larry Danielson terms it, "ethnic-historic identification."[15] These celebrations are held in most cities and many towns across the nation. Their popularity has increased immensely over the last two decades with a rise in ethnic pride. This type of celebration is often a studied attempt to create an idealized representation of a culture rather than a celebration that draws on aspects of local life which still survive from the mother culture. A good example of this kind of festival is "Scandinavian Days," which has been held the last few years in Ephraim, Utah, a Mormon community made up of mostly third- and fourth-generation Danes. Through the efforts of people who work for a small state junior college, one day each spring the local arts council sponsors a festival aimed at being an educational and tourist attraction. Costumes and flags representing the old country and its provinces are displayed. School children are taught folk dances which they perform during the festival. A few old-world foods are prepared and sold, though the sales are predominantly of local crafts, few of which have bases in Scandinavian tradition. This kind of cultural revival not only is widespread, but is important to communities of people who, as Danielson points out in his study, *The Ethnic Festival and Cultural Revivalism in a Small Midwestern Town*, need to find public symbols to demonstrate their uniqueness.[16] Ethnicity in recent years has become an acceptable way of distinguishing individuals and communities. Again, it must be remembered that this movement is a rather recent phenomenon in America where the norm in the past was towards an American melting pot rather than a nation of ethnic enclaves.

Scandinavian Days in a small Mormon community is interestingly contrasted with New Sweden Pioneer Day, which takes place in a similar physical and cultural geography. Both communities are proud of their Scandinavian heritage and of their progenitors who pioneered the land. The differences in the way that this heritage is celebrated speaks of each community's differing background. Besides Scandinavian Days, Ephraim holds a yearly celebration, as do all Mormon communities, which celebrates a day in 1847 when Brigham Young and his followers entered the Salt Lake Valley. This day, July 24, is called Pioneer Day. Pioneer Day is really quite similar to New Sweden's picnic, much more so than Scandinavian Day in these respects. Scandinavian Day is designed for the outsider. It is truly a public event, whereas New Sweden's day is primarily an insider's picnic. Nearly everyone who attends has a family tie to the area. Showing Scandinavianness is only an occasional element in New Sweden. There are some basic differences in these towns which might explain how ethnicity is viewed by both groups of people.

It is hard to measure at the subliminal level how much influence generations of tastes and values have on people. We all grow up with our parents cooking things which they like, planting gardens like those their parents planted, and choosing clothing which has certain design and color qualities. How much all of this is affected by older ethnic influences defies generalization. It is, however, discernible how much outside influence affects a people. In Mormon cultural history, the pressure has always been on assimilation into American life, which in many cases means subscribing to popular style. Native language was always discouraged, though in places like Ephraim, Danish language services were held through the 1920s. Also, when people join a religion like the Mormon faith, they symbolically leave their old lives behind. In the nineteenth century, Europeans joining the Mormon church were often ostracized from family and friends when they joined the new American faith. When they left Europe, they had already made a conscious choice which gave up some sense of ethnicity. At recent Pioneer Day picnics in New Sweden, there have generally been visitors in attendance from the old country who are reestablishing their ties with their American relatives. This exchange is reciprocal and not only represents an age in which it is easy and fairly inexpensive to travel abroad, but also shows a real emphasis on individuals' finding and knowing their own roots. These renewed ties add a new dimension to ethnic folklore. Seeing a relative from the old country would be rare at Ephraim's holiday. The final difference between these two communities is that there are still several people living in New Sweden who were born in the old country, whereas I know of only one Dane still living in Sanpete Valley. New Sweden was settled a generation later than Ephraim, and each generation away from the ethnic source has great impact on a group.

Studying the ethnic folklore is complicated by the fact that the folklore discipline was conceived in the documentation of European peasant culture. It has been difficult for scholars to give up notions of the "old lore." We need to accept the idea, as Linda Degh has, that "the ethnic group is an open system of social interaction and strings of cultural traditions manifested in dynamic processes of growth and decay."[17] The fact is, that to varying degrees, live for second-, third-, and fourth-generation ethnics is not particularly affected by old-world ethnicity. In our study of contemporary American ethnics, we must reevaluate our notions about tradition. It seems, as Stephen Stern points out, "that on a personal level ethnicity is only one factor in the folklore of an individual."[18] It should be stressed that the key to ethnicity is through the individual, then the family, and then less intimately through the community. For all we know, the people of Ephraim may take off their old-world costumes and flags when the clock strikes midnight after "Scandinavian Days," and they may not do another thing that is outwardly ethnic for the next year. But in Ephraim it doesn't stop there. It is the mother who makes sweet soup for her family as an occasional treat, or the retired man who plans a trip to the place in Denmark described in his grandfather's journal, which are at the heart of ethnicity.

It is these more intimate and personal things which define ethnicity in New Sweden. A greeting between two old friends in Swedish or the offering of coffee in a certain way — these are the social contexts of ethnicity.

THREE GENERATIONS OF SEALANDERS IN NEW SWEDEN

July 1982. If there is a single person whose costume betrays the fashion of the picnic each year, it is David Sealander. He is dressed in dark trousers, an old European-style wool vest, and a string tie. With a beard and long hair, he looks the part of a thirty-five-year-old original settler. As he hoists his heavy accordion straps over his shoulder, he bows his eyes to the stage in one last gesture of a natural shyness, then gently pulls the bellows. His right hand introduces the melody of an ancient Swedish *polska* as his left hand beats a driving dance rhythm and an intricate chordal accompaniment. It builds as all stop their conversation and look toward the orchestra of sound.

David sang his first Swedish song," Å Jänta Å Ja," at the picnic when he was four years old. A neighbor lady wrote the words phonetically from an old 78 rpm record so Mrs. Sealander could teach the words to David. In the subsequent years David has played on the program in various combinations with his father and brothers. This is the first year that his father has not been at the picnic to share the assumed obligation of music for the picnic. David, unlike his two older

Figure 6.   David Sealander playing accordion for dog and grandfather's scultpure, called ''Old Hitler.''

brothers, Jan and Robert, never stopped playing the accordion. They both were fine players in their youth but gave up playing as did many young aspiring accordion players when the accordion started losing popular appeal in the late fifties and sixties. David has always been undaunted by style and is steadfast in his convictions, not only in his dress and accordion music but in matters of conservation, land use, and alternative energy. He describes himself as the black sheep of the family, and he is told that he has many characteristics of his grandfather, who is sometimes referred to as ''a little tyrant'' by family members who remember him as stridently unyielding. David stands in awe of his father's abilities on the accordion and has spent most of his life learning music. David is unmarried and lives in his parents' home unless he is off working on short-term jobs as a pipe fitter helper in the oil fields of Wyoming, clearing brush on a tree farm on Bainbridge Island, or playing popular and show tunes for the winter months at the Sun Valley Ski Resort. His real love in music is the old Swedish dance music. Six years ago when I met him, he was unaware that there was a tremendous ethnic revival going on and that young musicians all over the country were energetically learning the old styles of dance and music. Later that year he was invited to play at an innovative festival called the Northern Rockies Folk Festival. There he not only met other young people who were learning Scandinavian music, but he became friends with some of the guiding lights in music and dance from the old country who were on the festival's faculty. Since then David has spent a good deal of time in the Seattle area, learning and sharing his talents with a well-organized and active Scandinavian revival. Much of the music David brings to the picnic each year is so old it would have been out of style at the first picnic sixty years ago. He is intensely interested in expanding his knowledge of music and that has lately been a process of looking back. I've heard him say that ''as the world gets smaller, we have to grow.''[19] To everyone's benefit he shares that quest. David has been active as a past president of the Pioneer Association. He loves farming but has made little money from it. For eight years he has grown crops of organic grain varieties, alfalfa, and carrots. He also runs a cereal milling business, supplying local stores with flour and cereal products. His mother and younger sister, Alisa, run this business while David is away from home. He and the rest of his family are ardent environmentalists who scorn the new farmers in the area who only take from the soil rather than rotate crops and put back manure and organic nutrients to feed the soil. They feel that subsidizing the soil year after year with chemicals is horribly shortsighted. The hundred acres of tilled land on the family farm and dairy are now rented out to a neighboring dairy farmer.

July 1979. A slight and agile older man moves around to his neighbors, greeting them. Each interchange contains a laugh with which he infects each person greeted. Between greetings he efficiently gathers an empty can, moves a bench, and rolls a welded, wheeled barbeque out of the way. After the formal program the old neighbors call for Clause Sealander to play a few numbers. He says, "I never pick up the damn thing anymore." As he picks it up, the glistening black Excelsior professional model looks as if it has outgrown him. He teeters a bit from the weight of the ungainly instrument then breaks into "Sweet Georgia Brown." It is obvious that he is uncomfortable with the instrument, but a lifetime of music overcomes a few missed notes. The audience doesn't notice, particularly the older folks, and there could never be another accordion player like Clause. His repertoire contains standards, popular music from the last half century, a few square dance tunes, and a wealth of old Scandinavian tunes which he learned primarily from ordered records. His style is energetic and reminds me of pop and jazz accordion playing with many sweeping runs and flourishes. Even the old Swedish numbers have an undercurrent of popular styling. David's style, on the other hand, is a little more classically based with a good deal of counter melody and variation in his themes. This style reflects David's formal training, whereas Clause always played by ear.

When Clause started school he spoke no English; Swedish was always spoken in the home. As English and the influences of American life swept him away from the traditions of home, he developed a fascination with what he considered the old Swedishness. He and his neighbor, best friend Noble Lundblade, would sit out with the "old Swede" hired hands just to hear them talk. He said, "Whenever we heard something that was twisted up, goofy, or had some slant of humor to it, we'd really hash it over."[20] One of their favorites was the three old Swede rail workers who asked for their pay in this way, "Vee are Svedish boy alle trey. Vee vant our money right avay, vee vork on da himlaties, for half past dollar every day."[21]

Clause also loved to hear the old songs and music.

Clause spoke, jokingly, of a neighbor named old Dan Backlund who "would sing songs so long that his friends would go do their chores and get back in time for the last verse."[22]

When Clause was four years old his father sent away to Montgomery Ward for an eight-dollar button accordion. During these childhood years both Clause and his friend Noble had button accordions and showed interest in music. At age sixteen Noble was sent to live with his uncle in Minneapolis to study piano at a conservatory. By the time he had returned, Clause had traded in his button accordion for a piano model and was playing regularly for assemblies and local parties. Noble got a piano accordion and soon was practicing diligently with Clause.

On Christmas Eve, Noble and Clause were asked to play on a request program on the new radio station in Idaho Falls, KID. The boys were in a pretty good mood and decided to do their whole program fooling around in Swedish slang, playing only Swedish melodies. At one point Clause said, "We've been playing up here for a couple of hours. It's funny that nobody can't send up a little snoose (snuff) for us Swedes to have."[23] Immediately, a neighbor named Russ Burkman called up Western Union and had a big roll of Copenhagen Snuff sent up to the station. From that time until Noble moved away in 1946 they were known as the Copenhagen Twins. Over the years the two traveled all over southeastern Idaho playing music for dances, and after high school becoming active on their fathers' farms, as well.

In November 1931 Ruth Johannessen introduced her sister Edith to Clause. After two and one-half years of courtship the Johannessen sisters married the Copenhagen Twins. So Noble and Clause progressed from best friends, to twins, and finally to brothers-in-law. After Clause and Edith were married they lived for a time in Idaho Falls managing a hotel which Clause's father owned, The Elenore Hotel. They then moved back to the family farm into the original lava-rock house which sits behind the big farm house. During these first years of marriage and raising a family, there was plenty of work playing music. At one time the Copenhagan Twins had opportunities to join the Frank-Mark vaudeville circuit and were asked to play on a passenger ship bound for the Orient. Unfortunately, both Noble and Clause were needed by their fathers on the farm and had to decline. One of Clause's real regrets in life was that he did not have the choice to stay on the farm or not. He resolved that he would never put any pressure on his children to continue the farm. In fact, he hoped that they could all do something of their own choice. Of the five, all have pursued other things than the life of farmer, though the three older boys, particularly David, have a love for farming and would like to return to the farm. Another regret for Clause was that the close community which he had grown up with had disintegrated. He talks with emotion of the old barn dances which would last until five

Figure 7. Copenhagen Twins, Clause Sealander (right) and Noble Lundblade.

in the morning. He said, however, that it finally got so just anybody would come out from Idaho Falls. "They had no respect for the community, they didn't bring food, they threw cigarettes around, so the Swedes just quit."[24]

In the early forties Clause began to create a place of beauty on the farm for friendly gatherings. He had always loved a low-lying alcove in the lava fields which border the farm to the west. This bottomland was basically a swamp when Clause started filling parts of it and planting trees around his ponds. Whenever he had some free time he could be found landscaping his park. It wasn't long before the family met there to relax and eat a picnic meal. People from the community discovered the park and started asking if they could gather there. Clause decided that he wanted to share his private Shangril-La with others so he made it known that his park would be available on a reservation basis. Today it is reserved every day from spring to fall by as many as three groups at a time. The family likes to describe the advent of the park as "growing like topsy."

The Sealanders are people of action. It is remarkable that Clause could be a successful farmer, a well-respected community leader, a family man, and a hot musician. As well, Clause belonged for many years to the Idaho Falls Astronomical Society, and there have

been many late nights when Clause and his scientist friends would sit out in the dark late summer evenings at the farm and speculate on the heavens.

July 1939. A group of men sit around a table, all with steaming cups of coffee. The pitch of their conversation is high as they argue about politics. Among them is a little man with intense eyes who is convincingly arguing about America's involvement in the war in Europe. Not only does he give practical reasons, but he launches into his feelings about the uselessness of war in general. He quotes passionately from Fitzgerald's *War, What For.* After too much picnic feast and owing to the heat of the day, the argument dissolves into a state of reverie, each man looking into his cup of glistening black coffee. Later there is music and Carl Sealander is called on to make up a song. He stands briefly getting into a poetic mode and begins. His face takes on a totally different look from that of the arguing pacifist. His rhymes, his allusions, the tune and the quality of his Swedish are masterful and delightful. When he is done, someone asks if he will play a tune on the button accordion. He says, "No, I don't play that." The requester recounts the time he played tunes all evening at a barn dance. Carl retorts, "Get that one and only son of mine up here. He's the musician in our family."

Carl Sealander was born in Hinnryd, Sweden, in western Småland. He came to America as a young man and worked for several years in the mines of Utah and Colorado. Though he had no formal education, he was a voracious reader who became convinced of a need for socialism. Even in the old country he was politically minded. He and over a million Swedes left the old country primarily for economic reasons. For Carl it was also to avoid being drafted into the Swedish army. It was at this time he picked up a new popular instrument, the button accordion. It was an instrument that the old-timers decried as capable of ruining good music, but Carl loved the idea of a portable instrument that had great volume and which could not only play melody but had chords that would accompany, and because of the diachronic nature of the instrument, held a natural rhythm in its pushing and pulling. It is interesting that just thirty years later Carl felt that the saxophone was doing the same disservice to music. Each time Clause would put a jazz record on his father would scream, "There's another dog caught in the fence."[25] In 1902 Carl came to New Sweden and picked out a hundred acres of land. His first job was to clear seven acres of land and plant oats. After several disasters with breaking levees and crops being washed out by cloudbursts, he learned some hard lessons about farming. By 1920 he had a successful farm with hired hands and a large barn and a big house being built. His home was the envy of the community. It had beveled, leaded-glass windows, ornate woodwork and fireplace, and muraled walls painted by a Norwegian named Mr. Borg. It was in this home and the original one-room

Figure 8. Carl Sealander dressed as a preacher with a group of friends.

rock home that Clause was raised and that Clause raised his five. For fifty years Carl Sealander managed a strict and successful farm. He owned and ran The Elenore Hotel in Idaho Falls until it burned in 1941. He read continually and was considered a self-taught intellectual. He was never active in religion, though he belonged to the local Lutheran church. He was critical of Mormon farmers, but gave five hundred dollars for the Woodville Mormon church to be built. In the mid-fifties both he and his wife passed on. Clause and his family remodeled the old house, lowering the ceilings and removing the original woodwork and old-fashioned murals. They have lived in the old house since. In 1970 Clause retired from farming, renting out his land and dairy. In 1982 Clause died while he and Edith were visiting in Arizona where they spent recent winters. Edith and five children continue the Sealander legacy.

CONCLUSION

To the Sealander family of New Sweden the celebration of Pioneer Day is not merely a memorial statement of "lest we forget." Rather, it embraces the present-tense meaning of pioneer. It is a celebration of exploring the unknown, looking to the future. Through three generations, this pioneering spirit has been rekindled in a myriad of pursuits, many of which are shared with a sympathetic community. People like the Sealanders act as the catalyst for that spirit which is at the root of celebration, "effervescence." They do this in the way that they reorganize their farm into the landscape of a park. Not only do they contribute the space, but they also fill the space with musical sound. These two elements alone tremendously affect everyone's perception of Pioneer Day. And over fifty years this degree of involvement affects the community's sense of itself.

Anyone who has successful social interaction may use ethnicity to form bonds. After all, ethnicity is not just "old-country roots" but means more. Being an American, a westerner, an Idahoan, a Lutheran or Mormon, all delineate groups based on ethnicity. In this brief study these identifiable groupings of people all come into play in the lives of New Swedeners. Beyond Swedishness there is a New Swedishness which has been developed in this outpost of ethnicity in Idaho. It is exhibited in the most ordinary of interchange, the simplest covered dish of food, or in the repertoire of an accordion player. These things are the art and stimulus for the common feeling of celebration. Every ethnic group has its artists. The ethnic artist bases creation on the ingredients of tradition. And every artistic creation is a pioneering experience.[26]

Notes

1. Richard M. Dorson, "Material Components in Celebrations," *Celebration: Studies in Festivity and Ritual*, ed. Victor Turner (Washington, D.C.: Smithsonian Institution Press, 1982), p. 33.

2. Victor Turner, Introduction, *Celebration*, p. 6.

3. Ronald L. Grimes, "The Lifeblood of Public Ritual: Fiestas and Public Exploration Projects," *Celebration*, p. 282.

4. Victor Turner, Introduction, *Celebration*, p. 20. By left and right hemisphere, Turner is making use of psychological theory which delineates function of the two sides of the brain. This theory is currently being oversimplified in all the human sciences.

5. Roger D. Abrahams, "The Language of Festivals: Celebrating the Economy," *Celebration*, p. 282.

6. Richard M. Dorson, *Celebration*, p. 33.

7. Stephen Stern, "Ethnic Folklore and the Folklore of Ethnicity," *Western Folklore*, Vol. 36:1 (Jan. 1977), p. 20.

8. Rose Ward Scoresby, "Water," *Pioneer Irrigation, Upper Snake River Valley*. ed. Kate Carter (Salt Lake City: Daughters of Utah Pioneers, 1955), p. 66.

9. Captain Wilson Price Hunt, from M. D. Beal, *A History of Southeastern Idaho* (Caldwell, Caxton Printers, 1942), p. 141. Quoted from Washington Irving's *Astoria* (Norman: University of Oklahoma Press, 1964).

10. J. H. Stephens, "The New Sweden Irrigation Canal System, After Fifty Years," *Pioneer Irrigation*, p. 111.

11. From the minutes of the New Sweden Pioneer Association, June 1, 1919.

12. Vladimir Nabokov, "The Streetcar," *Details of a Sunset and Other Stories* (New York: McGraw Hill, 1976), p. 94.

13. Chas. E. Anderson, Irene Welsch Grissom, Grover Jensen, Axel B. Anderson, S. A. Johnson, *After Fifty Years* (Idaho Falls, 1941).

14. Minutes of New Sweden Pioneer Association Picnic, 1919–1982.

15. Larry W. Danielson, *The Ethnic Festival and Cultural Revivalism in a Small Midwestern Town*, Dist. Indiana University, 1972, p. 23.

16. Larry W. Danielson, *The Ethnic Festival and Cultural Revivalism in a Small Midwestern Town*.

17. Linda Degh, prepared comments by Linda Degh to Richard M. Dorson's "Is There a Folk in the City?" *The Urban Experience and Folk Tradition*, ed. Americo Paredes and Ellen Stekert (Austin, 1971), pp. 54, 55.

18. Stephen Stern, "Ethnic Folklore," p. 31.

19. David Sealander in a taped interview, July 16, 1979, New Sweden, Idaho.

20–25. Clause Sealander in a taped interview, July 16, 1979, New Sweden, Idaho.

26. The author wishes to thank the Utah Folklife Center, the Utah Arts Council, the Idaho Commission on the Arts, and the Institute of the American West for encouraging and assisting in the fieldwork and research presented here. Thanks also to Edith and David Sealander for their help in compiling information for this article. The work here is dedicated to the memory of Clause Sealander.

Orofino Lumberjack Days

CHARLENE JAMES-DUGUID

Throughout Idaho and most of the United States, small towns typically hold annual celebrations that may be viewed as statements of community identity and values. These festivals are usually based on elements of the town's history or economy that set it apart from similar communities. In addition to the north Idaho festivals James-Duguid mentions, Payette has its Boomerang Days, Shelley its Potato Festival, Emmett its Cherry Blossom Festival, and Weiser its Oldtime Fiddlers' Contest.

Although these contests are not purely folk events, unlike their much older and more complex European counterparts, folklorists are devoting increasing attention to them as expressions of attitudes and as forums for performances that are derived from folk tradition. We are beginning to recognize in them an impulse that goes beyond local boosterism. James-Duguid's description of the Orofino Lumberjack Days points out both the conscious manipulation of tradition and the genuine function the events play within the context of life in Orofino.

Descriptive essays such as this will provide the groundwork for further studies comparing and interpreting regional American festivals. Recent essays on the nature of the festival are brought together in Victor Turner, ed., Celebration: Studies in Festivity and Ritual *(Washington, D.C., 1982).*

Charlene James-Duguid is with the National Associates Program of the Smithsonian Institution.

Orofino, Idaho, may not be a unique community in the lumbering region of the Inland Empire, yet an elaborately organized group in the town asserts its preoccupation with the timber economy every year in an annual celebration. For the past thirty-four years, Orofino Celebrations Inc., (O.C.I.) has sponsored Lumberjack Days in conjunction with the Clearwater County Fair. Traditionally held on the third weekend in September. With "booster" vigor, the organization has institutionalized the festival into the cyclical calendar and the social conscience of the community.

Orofino (population 3,711) is located in the Idaho panhandle. This essay focuses on its Lumberjack Days Festival to probe the dynamic qualities of this logging region. The daily values of the community concerning the forests, the interplay between loggers and nonloggers, and O.C.I.'s desire to plan a celebration which conveys to the young a sense of the time before mechanized logging practices replaced the rugged axe-wielding woodsman, are intensified during this weekend. Most important, O.C.I., a legally organized group, embodies the dedication of the community in perpetuating the values and occupational folk tradition of the area. O.C.I. is not always able to please all segments of the population, or provide the logging community with what it believes to be a true picture of itself, but it has been an instrument by which the logging industry of

Orofino, modified by time and technology, has retained its visibility while bringing the community together in celebration.

Many of the members of O.C.I., though not loggers themselves, have been involved in planning the lumbering celebration and bringing professional and local loggers together in competition for many years. They work on the parade as official judges and as timekeepers and promoters of the events to outsiders. Working their way up the ranks in O.C.I. from committee to committee, the local planners eventually become officials and directors. Names of the principals reappear year after year; among them are Johnson, Ponozzo, Barnett, Burnham, McLaughlin, Bessent, and Reece. In many cases entire families, both male and females representing several generations, are involved in organizing the events.

During two visits to Orofino in 1980 and 1982, I participated in the celebration and photographed each activity. Interviews with community leaders, members of O.C.I., loggers, contestants, and people who had a stake in the lumbering industry, complemented the gaps in observation. A midyear trip to Orofino in May 1982, allowed me to visit the town when it was not festive. This visit also offered the opportunity to observe the selection of the queen and the initial preparations for the September celebration.

Figure 1.   Two-Jack sawing contest in 1950s. "Boss" Snook, the official timer (with whistle) was one of the founders of Lumberjack Days.

Personal experiences were reinforced by contemporary journalism, primarily the supplements of the *Clearwater Tribune*, which provided a rich source for the history of O.C.I. Newspaper accounts and archival photographs gave a vivid picture of the persistence of the celebration in community life. Other historical sources provided general background on the area and O.C.I. but were less helpful in clarifying the way O.C.I. functions as a means of transmitting folklore.

Changes in the logging process have been pronounced in the past forty years, and descriptions of the logging camps in the early days provided a backdrop for viewing Lumberjack Days. Knowledge of extinct logging methods added to an understanding of some of the skills demonstrated in the contests, but in general, my concern was less with the techniques of either manual or power logging than with the attitudes toward logging in the image of the hardworking, determined logger as he continues to exist as a part of a folk tradition regardless of the tools of his trade.

The beginnings of O.C.I. were, in part, a reaction to changes in the logging industry. Several enthusiastic, civic-minded residents met in an unlikely site, the home economics cottage of Orofino High School. Jake Arf-

sten and Vernon Butler spawned the idea for a community festival and began generating interest for it among the civic and service organizations of Orofino. The "Days," planned to supplement the county fair, were originally proposed as Paul Bunyan Days. Instead, the name of the fabricated woodsman was dropped for a more universal title, simply, "Lumberjack Days." To this day, discussions still rage among O.C.I. and independent loggers as to the proper way to portray accurately the work of the woods.

The group was incorporated, adopted a constitution and bylaws, and elected officers. Their objectives were firm: to call attention to the importance of lumbering, to create an atmosphere of entertainment before winter, and to use the proceeds of the events for community service while putting aside a reserve for the activities the following year. The writers of the constitution called attention to the need for continuity, for festive nonwork behavior, and for an appreciation of the local way of life. The celebration, ritualized year after year, reinforced to the community the overpowering importance of lumbering, its customs and patterns. Nostalgia is played out by performing activities which require skills no longer used in the woods. At the same time, local individuals and companies are brought into the limelight as they demonstrate their role in continuing the logging tradition.

Early in O.C.I.'s history, the local business community, both loggers and nonloggers, made material and service donations, though never direct financial contributions to the events. Since they wanted to retain the noncommercial attitude and family atmosphere of the occasion, national tobacco and alcoholic beverage companies are not considered proper sponsors of the events.

Even through adversity, O.C.I. continued Lumberjack Days. When the Clearwater River flooded the exhibition buildings and the arena, the officials would not hear of canceling the events. Two of the early supporters of the Fair and Lumberjack Days, Bob Oud and Melvin "Boss" Snook were quoted as saying, "We'll have it if just the two of us are there. If we give it up this year, chances are we'll never get it started again."[1] With this determination, typical of O.C.I.'s attitude, the show that year was a great success. In the 1950s the events drew about four thousand spectators. Today, as many as ten thousand people visit Orofino for the weekend. When the founders of O.C.I. proposed to do "big things" for the city, they were not idle talkers but dynamic promoters of the celebration.

Snook suggested the log donation and sale, which were instituted when financial difficulties hit the celebration. This technique has been used to subsidize the events ever since. To show his support, Snook's operation alone was known to have donated three of the five loads of logs shown one year. Typical of the way local loggers react to praise, he shared the glory with the men who actually did the work and prepared the logs. (Figure 1).

The pieces of the festival come together during the spring and summer prior to the celebration. O.C.I. gears up to promote the events. Communities outside the valley are informed of Lumberjack Days with a glossy, four-color brochure, distributed through the Chamber of Commerce. Words could not describe the events better than the pictures in the flyer. It is replete with action: photographs of the floats coming down the street, horse pulling contests, and young girls falling from the birling log. The stereotypic lumberjack teetering on a plank in the obstacle pole sawing contest is a compelling image for the celebration.

Clearwater County maintains a master calendar of fall festivals. Each neighboring community stresses an important element of its locale. For example, while Orofino emphasizes lumbering, Lewiston demonstrates the ranching aspect of its tradition with its Roundup, and Pierce, the oldest settlement in the area, gains recognition through its Pioneer Days. The interdependence and willingness of communities to participate with each other is demonstrated when the queens and marching bands from their respective communities appear in the Orofino parade. In return the Orofino royalty and musical groups travel to other communities for their celebrations. The young royalty learn quickly that the role may look glamorous, but in reality it is hard work. They are expected to commit themselves totally to their privileged position. Private and personal lives must wait until after they give up their crowns.

It is critical for O.C.I. to attract the citizens of Orofino to attend as well. During the week before the Fair and Lumberjack Days, local logging companies and town businesses assist O.C.I. by placing prominent advertisements in the newspaper. Their compelling messages say less about the merchandise and services available than about the importance of supporting the celebration: "Your neighbors are going . . . Why don't you, to the Clearwater County Fair and Lumberjack Days Celebration at Orofino,"[2] or "Lumbering and Logging is part of the Living History of Clearwater County. Join the Celebration of our Heritage and Its Meaning for TODAY." (Riverside Lumber Company)[3] (Figure 2). The list of sponsors for the celebration includes not only the service organizations represented on the O.C.I. committee, but also most of the businesses in town. The electrical contractor, cable television station, beauty shop, banks, grocery, variety stores, bars and restaurants, logging companies, and automobile dealers are all boosters of the events.

Year after year, the schedule of O.C.I. Lumberjack Days has remained essentially the same. Some events less related to the logging industry, like a fiddlers' contest and dog show, have been eliminated, while the events which highlight the skills of the lumbermen have been retained. The events take place in sequence, no two major activities occurring simultaneously. Spectators do not have to choose, but can share in the full extent of all the festivities. For example, it is not until the last load of logs has finished its journey down the parade route that the exhibition building opens and the parade watchers are able to see the prize-winning projects.

On Thursday and Friday the events concentrate on the agricultural projects of the Clearwater County Fair. The 4-H livestock, home economics, and culinary project judgings take place. The culmination of these competitions is the awarding of prizes and the display of the blue, red, and white ribbons in the exhibition building. The fair committee continues to seek ways to enhance the image of the fair during the O.C.I. celebrations. The fair's history dates back to 1913, nearly thirty-three years before Lumberjack Days began, yet the lure of the lumbering events has always drawn more attention than those devoted to agriculture.

Of all the activities planned during the weekend, the events most important to understanding the role of Lumberjack Days to Orofino are the Children's Parade on Friday at noon, the Celebrations Parade on Saturday at 10:30 A.M., the Log, Lumber, and Miscellaneous Product Auction on Saturday at 1:00 P.M., and the Free Logging Show featuring old and modern logging skills on Sunday at 1:00 P.M. Equally important but attract-

OROFINO LUMBERJACK DAYS

AND CLEARWATER COUNTY FAIR

September 16, 17, 18, 19

1982

At Orofino, Idaho

Free Admission
To Fair Exhibits
Logging Shows
Auctions

*1982 Theme:
"Tomorrow
And Forever"*

*1982 Royalty
Queen Leann Harrell
Center
Princess Caren Cantrell
Left
Princess Theresa Brown
Right*

★ *2 Dances - Friday And Saturday*
★ *Old Timers Social*
★ *Lumberjack Breakfast*
★ *Lumberjack Run For Fun*
★ *Fair Exhibits*
★ *Carnival*
★ *Two Big Logging Shows*
★ *Horse Pulling Truck & Skidder Driving*
★ *Two Big Parades*
★ *Friday Lumberjack Luncheon IOOF Hall*
★ *Two Auctions*

The "Super Logger" Legend Lives "Tomorrow & Forever" At Orofino

Figure 2.   The front page of the *Clearwater Tribune Supplement*, September 9, 1982, advertises the events, introduces the royalty, and calls attention to the theme of the celebration, "Tomorrow and Forever."

ing a smaller audience are the Truck Driver and Skidder Operator Contests on Sunday at 7:00 A.M. and the Logging Show Preliminaries, held to determine the finalists in the Logging Show. These last two events are significant because of the presence of local contestants in contrast to the predominance of internationally known professionals in the Logging Show.

By the morning of the Children's Parade, red jackets and shirts, the badges that identify supporters of O.C.I., begin to dapple the town. Mothers prepare their young for the parade with cardboard signs, crepe paper streamers, and balloons. There is no need for costumes purchased at the store. The children's everyday clothing can be modified easily to fit the theme of the parade. The mothers, dressed in discarded cocktail dresses, shabby socks, tennis shoes, and roller skates—themselves caught up in the lighthearted spirit of the occasion—precede the tots, as the main street floods with children.

Classes are suspended on Friday so that the young children can participate in the parade as older children help in the preparations. The youngsters, some on horseback, others on bicycles or roller skates, in their mothers' arms or kept in tow by older siblings, wear

signs which live out the theme of the weekend. For example, "Happiness is . . ." was demonstrated by "standing up on your own two feet," "being seven and having a 10-speed bicycle," and "being a lumberjack's wife." The 1982 theme, "Tomorrow and Forever," brought forth several attempts to emphasize that the community revolved around lumber and would always do so. A squad of hearty, pint-sized loggers paraded in hard hats, carried axes, and led their pet dogs (Figure 3). A touching sight was a couple of three-year-old girls in high heels, long beads, velvet dresses and picture hats with signs on their backs: "Mothers of Tomorrow, On the go, Forever." The event lasts less than a half hour, yet it is the Children's Parade that is given premiere importance as an opening to the festivities.

Throughout the weekend, a child, generally an infant carried by the father, will occasionally become the focus of attention. The child will be expected to "give grandpaw the prize-winning kiss," or the parent asked to show "how big the little critter has grown." At no time are children restricted from the weekend's activities. They participate and observe without being expected to learn or question exactly what is going on. It is through the sense of festivity and close proximity to the celebration that the child experiences the tools and the skills of logging. It is not unusual to see youngsters in the arena after the contests, rolling away the remains of logs as they help in the cleanup operation. Even though many of these children will never become loggers, the events socialize them to appreciate the importance of the industry to their community.

Not long after the sun comes up on Saturday morning, the officials and timekeepers for the preliminaries arrive at the arena to prepare the logs for the sawing and chopping competitions. Anticipation is stimulated by newspaper accounts of local entries in the competition. Only six of the thirty entries in the preliminaries will make the finals. One senses that although the inevitable will happen, that is, a traveling professional will win the sawing contest, perhaps some magic will occur and an old-time logger will come out of retirement, get past the preliminaries, and upset the professionals at the Logging Show. More than any other events, the preliminaries of the power sawing contest and the Driver and Skidder Operator Races demonstrate the participation of local loggers.

In 1980, hopes were riding high on Jake Altmiller. He became a folk hero as the Orofino contestant remembered for his skill in the 1950s. Could this man, now refusing to give his age, compete with the "chrome set?" He had placed first in the power contest in 1976 with a cut of 13.4 seconds, but could he repeat this triumph four years later? He claimed he could still cut through a tamarack log three times in seven seconds. From his memories, published in the *Clearwater Tribune*, sprang a reawakened appreciation of the past. He recounted the close quarters of the logging camps, the snoose and spittoons, as well as the spirit of competition which pervaded the camps. Hard work was the

Figure 3.   Two young boys and their dog join in the children's parade typifying the importance of the lumbering industry as it is transmitted from generation to generation.

essence of his stories. He remembered men coming in with lather where suspenders might have been, and looking as if they had been wearing horse harnesses. Jake did not win the 1980 competition but he was there, sawing with the professionals, a local man, a real man of the woods.

Just as in the past when the axman sharpened his own ax, today the competitors sharpen their own chains for the chain saw competition. Men share their theories as to the best way to complete this sophisticated operation during the chain saw preliminaries. All the contestants use the same saw: in 1982 a 410 Homelite with a 4.2 cubic inch engine. The saw has a 28" sprocket tip bar with a ⅜" pitch. Contestants furnish their own 91 drive link chain which they carry sometimes reverently wrapped in a terry cloth towel. The feat is to saw through a 24" larch log, entering it within a 4" mark on the the opposite side, cutting up, severing the top without pulling the saw bar out, then down through the log to complete the cut.

The preliminaries continue throughout the day, and the winning contestants are entered in the Sunday Logging Show. Since many of the other events—the Two-Jack and Two-Jill Sawing, the Obstacle Pole Sawing, and the Ax Throwing—do not draw as many contestants, it is not necessary to hold preliminaries. These events are dominated by the professionals who arrive in Orofino from throughout the Pacific Northwest. It is Saturday morning, though, during the chain saw preliminaries, that the community's hopes rise. The local sawyers, their families and friends wait for the results.

It is not unusual to see a man and his son competing against each other in the power sawing contests. Several professional families generally enter, but in 1982 so also did a local sawyer and his elderly father. The young man's cuts were even, thin, and skilled. His father and mother collected them as souvenirs. When the father's turn came to saw, the son helped him start the motor of the Homelite. The father was steady, equally skilled, and knew the sawyer's craft. An observing official mentioned that had the father more strength to lift the saw in the cut, he would have had a

Figure 4.   A load of blue-ribbon logs on parade during 1982 Orofino Lumberjack Days and Clearwater County Fair.

time good enough for the finals. Strength and time were against him, but the ability of a sawyer had not left the man in his advanced age.

The Celebration Days Parade, which takes place on Saturday morning before the auction, is another way of demonstrating the attitudes and values of the community. The floats entered by service organizations interpret the theme. Political candidates use the parade as an opportunity to become more visible. Local businesses show their support for the celebration and the logging tradition by displaying their contributions to the auction.

Since the marching bands are in competition, they stop at the reviewing stand and present a precision drill for the judges. Donations to the auction—a wood-burning stove, plumbing supplies, and firewood—come down the street. The National Guard has provided trucks to carry wood, and a small girl with tousled blonde hair stares out of the camouflage-colored truck which her father drives down the parade route. The Shriners ride past on their minicars. A towing company from Lewiston adds comedy to the parade with a burly male masquerading as a buxom, overblown caricature

of Dolly Parton on a bucking bronco. Each entry, in its own way, tries to depict the theme of the year.

The most memorable themes are those which allow the entries to show creatively their feelings about the community. For example, the O.C.I. secretary feels that the best themes included "Best Little Town by a Dam Site" (referring to the Dworshak Dam and Reservoir), "Living the History of Clearwater County," "Grow with Idaho," "Happiness Is . . .," and "Community Dreams" (Figure 4).

As the finale of the parade, the trucks bearing the beribboned prize-winning loads of logs come down the street. A sight this fine is rarely seen in the woods or coming down the highway today. These exact loads, perfectly aligned on the truck, are reserved for the once-a-year celebration. It is difficult to find prize trees in the forest today, so from the outset of the process contemporary loggers are at a disadvantage when their task is compared to that of their predecessors. Yet the loggers feel it is important for their reputations to enter the parade.

Early on the morning of the parade, over coffee, a proud, long-standing member of the Orofino logging community offered to answer the question of what makes a prize-winning load of logs.[4] He stated that it should be made up of good-looking logs, with no limbs or knots. The cut should be smooth with no burn or "cat face" on the surface. The bark of the tree should be blemish free. Generally, these logs are longer than those normally loaded and they are placed flush on the truck. The section of the log chosen for the parade would come from the second cut of the tree. Each of the logs on the truck would come from a separate tree, instead of from the same tree, as would be the case on most logging trucks normally seen on the roads.

Preparing the load would take a crew of four men — the boss, skidder operator, sawyer, and truck driver — a full day. The trees might be chosen from a stand reserved all year especially for the parade. Yellow pine, the best choice for prime lumber, is very difficult to find, but on occasion, the Forest Service will sell that stumpage for the O.C.I. celebration. White pine, fir, or cedar are other choices. In cutting, the crew would use a new bar and chain on their saw, trying to cut each log to exactly the same length. Because the logs must be free of grapple marks, they would be loaded with straps instead of hooks or chains. The approximate cost of the stumpage, crew, and machinery for the parade load would be about $1,000. And what accolade does the logging company receive for all the effort? The prize is a ribbon and a traveling trophy that the winner relinquishes the following year to the next winner.

Although a donation is not mandatory, the logging companies have the privilege of donating their entries to the auction. This is a mixed blessing. If the prize winner submits the load for auction, the only way the winning company can capitalize on the honor of the show load is to buy it back. This contribution, essentially a double donation of logs and the money bid, is a common occurrence in the redistribution of wealth in the community. The winning company then advertises the load for sale as the blue ribbon logs at the Orofino Celebrations Lumberjack Days. Their purchase price becomes part of the funding to perpetuate the events.

Why do the lumber companies go through the effort and expense of entering logs? The informant suggested several answers. The load shows two things. First, the ability of a company to choose good logs counts for about 60 percent toward the prize. The other 40 percent shows that the crew know their job, they have excellent skills in logging techniques, their equipment is first-rate, and they appreciate lumber of the highest quality. Having dispensed with the company's self-serving reason for showing logs, he added, "We want to try to remind people that there are still good-looking logs around."

The auction during Lumberjack Days becomes a community performance in which the people of Orofino go on display for themselves and to an audience. Instead of a musical, dramatic, or dance form, the auctioneer uses knowledge of the community as a source for his spontaneous patter. His use of in-group jokes

and transgressions of local norms becomes a show in itself. The auctioneer's insights into personalities, their traditional bidding habits, and Achilles' heels serve to raise the bids.

The Sunday morning events usher in the performance of contemporary logging skills. By 6:00 A.M. an official of O.C.I. is at the parking lot of a logging company about a mile outside Orofino. In one area, stakes are being set for a truck driving obstacle course, while uneven, difficult to handle logs are dumped on the adjacent skidder course. These two contests have been incorporated especially for the local loggers, who, instead of competing for national acclaim and cash awards, perform on the course intended to simulate their work in the woods. They compete with their reputations on the line, observed by their families and friends. Put to the test in public view are both the skills generally masked in the dense woods as well as the inadequacies that can be hidden in remote work sites.

A truck driver mounts to his cab. He is carrying a full load of logs and knows that within five minutes he must navigate the course, back into two areas marked by flimsy, flagged stakes, and return to the starting point. All his actions will be timed and the errors recorded by a complex set of point reductions. The prize money is modest and the spectators are few, yet local contestants become tense when their time arrives to take the course. These performed skills are necessary in today's logging industry but are demonstrated publicly only once a year. In 1982 seventeen drivers tried the course; their scores varied from a high point of 450 to a low of 85. The winner stepped forward grinning shyly in a blue tee shirt which read, "If you lead a good life, say your prayers and go to church, when you die, you'll go to IDAHO."

During the Skidder Contest, one operator charging the course in his Caterpillar, maneuvered his machine skillfully, sped to the logs, set the choker, pulled the logs around the course, released them and jumped down from the cab. Then he ran over to a group of young boys who were watching the competition. He lifted one of them, his son, into the air, swung him around into a hug, paused to ask the official his time, and kissed the boy when he heard that his score was the best run so far.

The planners of Lumberjack Days look upon the Logging Show as the most important event of the weekend. All activities preceding it are intended to build excitement. But if we look at the program of the show, we see that this performance is dominated by national entries. The local flavor and demonstration of the community's perception of itself, which are evident in the parades, preliminaries and Truck Driver and Skidder Operator Contest, lessens. Auckland, New Zealand; Deming, Washington; Eagle, Idaho; Cowichan, British Columbia; Cascade, Oregon; and Avon, Montana, are the hometowns of the Sunday afternoon contestants.

The gap between the performers and the spectators is more pronounced. The audience, still in a festival

Figure 5.   An annual highlight of every year's lumberjack competition is the appearance of the "hot saws," run with cycle engines on nitroglycerine.

mood, is presented with a rendition of logging which may not conform to the local loggers' version of their world. The events focus toward finding the best all-around lumberjack from among strangers, typical of the region, but not of the community. Rules of the Worldwide Association of Timber Sports are followed, and the contestants gather points to be applied to national and international ratings. Winners go to the Homelite Tournament of Kings held in Charlotte, North Carolina, where the stakes are high. First prize alone is six thousand dollars.

In order to reintroduce the community spirit, O.C.I. has incorporated competitions for local logging companies in the show. The five-man relay tag teams and the tug-of-war teams are composed of local men. They are spotlighted in competitions which redirect their efforts in activities rarely performed in the woods but used today to symbolize their work. The feats they perform such as ax throwing, pole throwing, and horizontal chopping, demonstrate the determination and teamwork of the independent companies. The relay races pit logging companies against one another, creating a festive and neighborly atmosphere.

On occasion, the Orofino tug-of-war team, drawn from the strongest of all the local loggers, competes against a champion team from the state. According to a newspaper interview with their coach, "There's more to fielding a champion tug-of-war than simply securing ten behemoths to a rope. Weight is important but technique is just as critical and being downright ornery might just give you the edge. There will be close to three ton of human flesh pulling in opposite directions. The champion team averages two hundred ninety pounds. It's all for fun but we're damn serious about it. The team pulls for prize money but the purse is small compared to the side bet greenery that changes hands."[5]

Birling, requiring the ability to remain upright while rolling a log in water, takes place in the afternoon. It is a skill no longer necessary in an industry that transports logs by truck. Yet, the birling pond is central to the Logging Show arena and, by tradition, the graduating class of Orofino High School is expected to clean the pond before the events. Birling could be removed from the schedule without losing a significant event, yet it seems to have been retained as a reminder of the days when logging and the waterways of Idaho were closely connected. It also provides a place for the traditional, affectionate dunking of royalty or officialdom.

Though the spirit of the past remains, some events reflecting the work in the logging camps and log drives were eliminated because it is difficult to find men with these traditional skills. The use of a peavy and canthook are not presented because O.C.I. officials feel that these skills are far too dangerous to be attempted by the logger who casually tries to recreate them in performance. Even the pole climb now draws only a few daring young local contestants and a high school teacher turned professional high pole climber. He is the major attraction in this event, dressing like a clown and performing the daring feat of climbing the pole, then fastening his harness to the guy wire and plummeting to the ground.

The Logging Show closes with a demonstration of "hot saws," an impractical and improbable entry into the future technology of logging (Figure 5). Carried to Orofino in trucks and generally covered with a quilt or soft fabric sheet, the saws are laid out casually in the area behind the arena with no real deference to their cost, design, or power. The contest, though not a part of the point competiton for the best all-around lumberjack, is the highlight of the afternoon. Powered by a motorcycle engine, each saw has its own individualized muffler, a long, sometimes curved attachment which protrudes into the air. The saws run on nitroglycerine and are known to guzzle oil. They have no cutoff or break and will stop only when the nitro is exhausted.

There is a sense of danger when, wearing chaps and hard hats, the professional sawyers come into the arena with their saws. The timekeeper seems to want the event finished as soon as possible. He senses the threat of a flying chain or exploding motor so near the con-

Figure 6.   Two-Jill sawyers carrying on a family tradition in the 1982 competition. Their saw is reversed while they concentrate on an even cut and await the official timer's whistle.

clusion of a flawless afternoon. Their cuts are almost instantaneous. Local sawyers do not compete with the hot saws nor are preliminaries held for the contest because this is an added attraction, more a brush with danger than a contest which demonstrates specific logging skills. The audience enjoys the chances the professionals take, perhaps in a small way reliving vicariously the dangers which lumbermen encounter every day. The technology is impractical for the woods and restricted to the fairgrounds and the Lumberjack Days Logging Show.

The pattern of the show is always the same—the pledge to the flag, local contests, chopping and sawing of several types, birling demonstrations, the pole-climbing clown, and finally the two-saw competition. Interestingly, though the events during the show have a formal beginning and an announced sequence, they end abruptly after the hot-saw competition. The audience filters out of the bleachers and down to the amusements. The O.C.I. officials have noted, to their dismay, that they have never been able to find closure to the performance. The trophies, cash prizes, and ribbons are still to be given out and yet the audience does not perceive these as a critical part of the show. The spectators have had their experience, and now they are ready to leave before the awards ceremony.

Throughout the entire weekend, the festival functions to promote and perpetuate folklore. The young and uninitiated have been exposed to logging. The

old-timers have been honored. The boundaries of questionable behavior have been extended so that the otherwise controlled community will relax its regulations and enjoy the fun before the onset of winter. The audience appreciates and recognizes that the events are based on the existence and continuation of the logging industry and the values which it stimulates in the community. Stability of any group depends on its ability to find and use tactics which illustrate and reinforce the accepted values of the culture. In Orofino, O.C.I. is that vehicle. Its stated intent is to stress pride in occupational roles, the natural resources, and the logging economy, but we learn that it also supports the underlying attitudes which keep the community alive. Over the years, Lumberjack Days has become a rallying point, a vital celebration in the community's attempt to be and remain Orofino.

The values placed upon a good life and strong family ties prevalent year round in Orofino are demonstrated during the celebration events. The parade, floats, and banners repeat these values: pride in home, community, work, and environment. The stress on family life is seen in the competitions in which husbands and wives compete in the Jack and Jill sawing (Figure 6). Daughters compete in the Two-Jill contests and sons in the Two-Jack competitions. Young girls have taken over the birling pond, and sometimes sisters compete against each other. Both professional and local fathers and sons compete in the preliminaries, and O.C.I.

history is filled with family names for several generations.

The skidder may have supplanted the team of draft horses, and the Homelite chain saw may have replaced the bulging muscles of a crosscut sawyer, but Lumberjack Days still thrives in a community described by a Mrs. McNichols in the *Clearwater Tribune*:

We have no limos but plenty of teenagers with learner's permits. Our kids do not go to Fat Farms, they have big frames, or bad glands or will grow out of it. We have no diaper service, instead, [we] fold [diapers] while watching TV. We have no cocaine or jet set parties; instead sophistication means you don't have to BYOB and there is more than one kind of chip dip.[6]

Notes

1. Supplement, *Clearwater Tribune*, Orofino, Idaho, September 1976, p. 3.

2. Ibid., p. 11.

3. Ibid.

4. Interview on May 15, 1982, at Ponderosa Lounge and Restaurant, Orofino.

5. Supplement, *Clearwater Tribune*, Orofino, Idaho, September 1978, p. 22.

6. *Clearwater Tribune*, September 1980, p. 12.

Basque Celebrations in Eastern Oregon and Boise

Sarah Baker Munro

In the Intermountain West, two urban areas serve as focal points for the Basque population: Reno, Nevada, and Boise, Idaho. In close proximity to Boise, the outlying communities of Mountain Home, Idaho, and Jordan Valley and Ontario, Oregon, form a regional network of rural Basque population centers. The celebrations observed in this area unify the Basques by emphasizing their common ethnic backgrounds and kinship ties. Munro's study indicates that rural celebrations of the past combined pre-Christian agricultural rites with an overlay of Catholic festivals. In the absence of a regulatory parish priest, the celebrations ceased. Present-day rural celebrations, such as picnics and anniversaries, are performed to intensify kinship ties. Somewhat conversely, the major urban celebration observed in Boise focuses on San Ignacio, the patron saint of the Basques, but includes peripheral traditional activities, such as athletic competition and dancing, strengthening various aspects of Basque heritage simultaneously.

Further readings about the Basque people in America can be located through a bibliography by William A. Douglass and Richard W. Etulain, Basque Americans: A Guide to Information Sources *(1981).*

Sarah Munro has an M.A. in folklore from the University of California, Berkeley. With Rachael Griffin, she co-edited Timberline Lodge *(1978).*

The most richly traditional activities of the southern Idaho and eastern Oregon Basque communities are the picnics and balls that are held each year in Boise and Ontario. At these events, a number of Basque customs, which include a variety of genres of folklore, are consciously recreated. In outlying rural areas like Jordan Valley, on the other hand, exclusively Basque celebrations are not held, although celebrations of family rites of passage include traditional Basque elements. The significance of the family celebrations in Jordan Valley today is that they reflect the obligations felt by former Jordan Valley residents to their relatives and family who still live there. At one time, seasonal and religious holidays in Jordan Valley included Basque elements, but few of these remain. While Basque folklore in Jordan Valley must be collected in small isolated remnants, various genres of Basque folklore are displayed each year in picnics and dances by the ethnic-conscious Basque communities in Boise and Ontario.

Celebrations in Jordan Valley can be divided into those which occurred in the past and those which take place at present (see Table 1). Within each of these categories, celebrations are religious, seasonal, rite of passage, or political in purpose, although these subdivisions are somewhat arbitrary. St. John's Day is, as an example, more a celebration of the growing season than it is a commemoration of St. John. The distinction between religious and seasonal celebrations can be made between those which include a Catholic service or commemorate a Catholic saint and those which do not.

To aid in the description of these celebrations which were observed by the author (0) or described by informants to the author (1) in fieldwork during 1970–71, the celebrations are broken down into their component parts, or segments. A segment[1] is a unit which is recognized as a separate entity by the culture in which it occurs and can be analyzed in terms of its relation to other segments and variation from one ceremony to another. The segments which were described in the Basque celebrations of the West include (1) religious services, (2) drinking, (3) eating, (4) singing—either casual or ritualized, (5) dancing, and (6) games—both competitions and demonstrations.

The list of celebrations in Table 1 is not exhaustive, nor is the description of each contemporary celebration tempered by observation of it over several years. It is a working table, included here because it condenses and organizes elements of those celebrations with which the author came into contact.

JORDAN VALLEY—CELEBRATIONS OF THE PAST

The celebration of religious holidays in Jordan Valley was left up to the people of the area because its Catholic church, St. Bernard, was a mission from 1914

Table 1

CELEBRATIONS

Kind of Celebration			Religious Service	Drinking	Eating	Singing Casual	Singing Ritual	Dancing Public	Dancing Demonstration	Games
Jordan Valley	Past	Religious								
		Three Kings' Day (Jan. 6)	I(1)	I(2)				I(3)		
		Santa Agueda (Feb. 5)		I(2)	I(2)		I(1)	I(3)		
		San Juan (Jun. 23)					I(1)	I(1)		
		Christmas (Dec. 24)	I(2)	I(1)			I(2)	I(1)		
		Seasonal								
		New Year's (Jan. 1)		I(2)			I(1)			
	Contemporary	Rite of Passage								
		50th Wedding Anniversary	I(1)	O(2)	O(2)					
		Political								
		Memorial Day (May 30)								
		(Rodeo)		I(1)	I(1)					I(1)
Ontario-Boise	Contemporary	Religious								
		San Ignacio (Ca. Jul. 31)	I(1)	O(2–6)	O(2 & 5)	O(4)		O(6)	O(3)	O(3)
		Seasonal								
		Sheepherder's Ball (Ca. Dec. 20)		O(1–4)		O(4)		O(2)	O(3)	O(3)

Key

I = Informant's Account
O = Observation by Author
Numbers indicate order in which segments took place.

until 1958 (with brief intervening years during which it had a resident priest). The priest visited Jordan Valley about once a month, and not usually on holidays. The Basque community set up celebrations of religious and seasonal holidays within the boarding houses. Christmas, New Year's, and Three Kings' Day (January 6) were held at one of the three local boarding houses. Christmas took place at Marquina's boarding house, New Year's at Madariaga's, and Three Kings' at Elorriaga's. Generally, people gathered together after dinner to drink and dance. *Chorizos* were often served as snacks, but no formal dinners were prepared.

On some Christmases, a priest offered Mass in the Jordan Valley church. On these occasions, the dance broke up before midnight and everyone went to the church to celebrate the *misa degayo* (midnight Mass). Nights were bitterly cold and many had been drinking for some hours, but everyone attended the Mass. Presents were not exchanged in those early years. Another custom was widespread: wives usually baked a loaf of bread which was kept in the cupboard for a year. At the end of the year each member of the family ate part of it to insure his or her health for the following year.

New Year's was a seasonal rather than a religious holiday and it was celebrated with a singing ritual that distinguished it from the celebration of Christmas and Three Kings' Day. On New Year's Day, men would trek from house to house and sing a ditty. In return, they expected to be given a drink. If they were denied, one of a number of obscene or slanderous verses could be added to the traditional ones. This custom still takes place at present, although somewhat irregularly. The traditional verses are:

1. Uŕte baŕi kaŕi
   Year new bring

   Txaŕi belaŕi
   Pig ear

   Dakonak   estakonaŕi
   Someone who has to someone who doesn't have

   Emotia Saŕi
   Give reward

   Nik   ezdekot
   I don't have it

   Eta zuk
   And you

   Emoizu niŕe
   Give it to me

2. Uŕte zar
   Year old

   Joanda
   Is gone

   Baŕi etoŕi
   New came

   Eman   gatoz   lau
   We are coming here four

   Kampa Jotzale bi
   Ring bell   two (Two bell-players)

   Emoizu   limosnia
   (You) give us a handout

   Jaungoikoa gaitnik[2]
   God's name for

Uŕte baŕi kaŕi was always a drinking game among men in Jordan Valley, but it is based on an Old World children's custom. On New Year's in the Basque provinces, children walked from house to house singing this ditty in exchange for which they were given small coins. The practice may have started among men in Jordan Valley in the days when most Basques in the area were single herders. Adapted to the predominantly young male population in the early days, *uŕte baŕi kaŕi* remained a men's drinking game after the sex ratio was equalized and the number of children increased. At present, non-Basque men as well as second generation Basque-Americans follow the custom when it takes place. *Uŕte baŕi kaŕi* was not observed or described as one of the Basque customs in Boise or Ontario.

The New Year's celebration in Jordan Valley had two parts which occurred in order: singing and, as a consequence or reward, drinking. When boarding houses were being operated in Jordan Valley, a dance was also held. Dancing was apparently auxiliary to the primary activity of drinking, and it is this latter segment that longest remained part of Jordan Valley's New Year's celebration.

A procession from house to house was part of the celebration of Zanta Agueda's name day (February 5), both in the Basque provinces and in Jordan Valley. In the Basque province of Vizcaya, children would mask their faces and march from house to house singing a song to Zanta Agueda which was punctuated by pounding a stick in time to the song. They collected bacon and sausages at the homes they visited and skewered the meat to the end of the stick they carried.[3] In Boise, Basques sometimes celebrated Zanta Agueda's Day by marching from house to house with a stick which had a candle tied to the end of it. Jordan Valley Basques followed a similar custom. At each house they visited, they collected food to make up a large feast. When enough food had been collected, the group, which had also been increasing in size, gathered at one of the boarding houses to eat and dance. The processional song had many verses, but best known were the first four:

1. Zanta Agueda Agueda
   Saint Agatha Agatha

   Biar   da Zanta Agueda
   Tomorrow is Saint Agatha's

   Biar   da Zanta Agueda's eta
   Tomorrow is Saint Agatha's and

2. Bedeinkatau izan deidala
   Sanctified to be we wish

   Etxe onetako gentia
   House of this people

   Pobre eta humilde
   Poor and humble

   Dabilzanentzat
   People (who want to be through with life)

   Badanke   borondatia
   They have good will (charity)

3. Zanta Martinik maitea
   Saint martyr   beloved

   Dago erukis   betia
   She has compassion plenty (of)

   Arek emondaidela
   She will give

   Ozazuna eta
   Health   and

   Bakia
   Peace (to everyone)

4. Zanta Agueda Agueda
   Saint Agatha Agatha

   Gure martin maitea
   Our martyr beloved

Arek emondaidozu
She will give (to you as an individual)

Zoriona   eta pakia[4]
Happiness and peace

Caro Baroja has noted that Zanta Agueda's Day was one of the few Basque celebrations of a saint's day that was not based on a pastoral or seasonal event.[5] More common were celebrations of San Anton (January 17) which was a day to bless the beasts, San Blas (February 3) which was associated with practices to cure and preserve men and beasts, and San Marcos (April 25) which fell near the time when corn and beans were sown. Christianity was, Caro Baroja concluded, an overlay on these basically pre-Christian agricultural rituals.

San Juan (June 23) fell on the longest day of the year and was traditionally celebrated by rural peasants who set small bonfires in their fields and danced around them singing. It was a time one could sing about the witches without being accused of associating with witchcraft. The purpose of the ritual was, according to Caro Baroja, to insure preservation from such illnesses as mange, to cure those illnesses, to expel the elements that caused such diseases to other regions, to insure preservation from destructive animals, to insure preservation from accidents, and to guarantee an upcoming marriage.

A third-generation Basque-American girl raised on a ranch north of McDermitt, Nevada, remembers that on San Juan's Eve her Vizcayan grandmother took her, her sister, and her cousin into the garden and led them through a dance around a fire, singing a song about driving the witches away. She remembers only the first two lines of the song:

Done Juan, Done Juan,
Saint John, Saint John,

Gaur, bijar,   Done Juan.
Today, tomorrow, Saint John.

None of the other Basques whom the author interviewed remembered the celebration of San Juan's Eve. No one remembered celebrating San Anton's Day, San Marcos' Day, or San Blas' Day in the Jordan Valley area.

After immigration of Basques to the American West, a great many traditional celebrations seem to have been dropped almost upon arrival. Others were continued without the guidance of a Basque parish priest. As a result, some celebrations became standardized. Christmas, New Year's, and Three Kings' Day were celebrated by a dance at one of the boarding houses, for example. The celebrations were somewhat distinguished one from another, Christmas sometimes by the *misa degayo* and New Year's usually by *urte bari kari*. The more distinctive celebrations of Zanta Agueda's Day and San Juan's Day were less widespread in the American West and took place more irregularly where they did occur.

JORDAN VALLEY — CONTEMPORARY CELEBRATIONS

Contemporary celebrations among Basque families in Jordan Valley are not Basque in focus but rather family oriented. Two immigrant couples who had lived for a long time in Jordan Valley celebrated their fiftieth wedding anniversaries during the period of this study. One celebration was held in Jordan Valley and the other in western Oregon where the couple has lived for about twenty years. In both cases there was a religious service attended by the couple and their children and in-laws, which was followed by a reception, attended by friends and relatives, and usually sponsored by one or more of the children. The couple who held their reception in Jordan Valley held it at the Catholic hall. Wine and a buffet dinner, parts of which were brought by members of the family, were served at both receptions. The fiftieth wedding anniversary was a significant enough occasion to draw family and friends from Jordan Valley to western Oregon in one case, or from a number of towns in Idaho and Oregon to Jordan Valley in the other.

A second celebration in contemporary Jordan Valley is Memorial Day. Each year on the Sunday closest to Memorial Day, a committee in Jordan Valley sponsors a rodeo. The rodeo committee, a group of six men (only one of whom is of Basque descent), puts up the money to sponsor the rodeo and collects the profits (if any accrue). The rodeo is a two-day affair and includes a number of cattle competitions, stagecoach rides, and a town parade. On Memorial Day many former Jordan Valley residents visit the area to eat dinner with their relatives who still live there and to visit the graves of those who are buried there. The Basque families as well as non-Basque families celebrate Memorial Day in this fashion. The two most organized celebrations in contemporary Jordan Valley are final rites of passage of surviving grandparents and memorials to deceased family members. An interest in Basque culture plays no part in their enactment. Consequently no Basque songs, dances, or games were observed at these celebrations.

ONTARIO — BOISE — CONTEMPORARY CELEBRATIONS

Picnics. In contrast, an interest in Basque culture plays an important role in the celebrations of picnics and dances sponsored by the Boise and Ontario Basque societies. The picnic on San Ignacio's Day (July 31) is perhaps the most traditional of these. One Basque immigrant remembers attending a Basque picnic at the Riverside Pavilion in Boise in 1933. He thought that this may have been the first such picnic held in honor of San Ignacio, patron saint of the Basques and founder of the Jesuit Order. Traditionally, San Ignacio's name day was celebrated by a pilgrimage to the monastery dedicated to him near Azpetitia in Guipuzcoa. In the American West, Basques from hundreds of miles around Boise gather at Boise's Municipal Park on the

Figure 1. *Jasotales*. Weight lifters hoisting 225-pound cylindrical weight.

Figure 2. Weight lifters carrying 105-pound bell-shaped steel weights as long as they can.

Sunday falling nearest July 31. The picnic is attended by as many as fifteen hundred to two thousand people and has increased in popularity in recent years. In the last ten years a number of similar smaller picnics have been initiated, sponsored by Basque families in other towns in Idaho, Nevada, and Oregon—Mountain Home, Elko, Winnemucca, and Ontario, among others.

The picnics in each of these other towns are scheduled for different Sundays so that people can attend a number of them throughout the summer. The sequence of events seems to be similar to those of the Boise picnic. Each family prepared and brought most of its own food. Drinks and ice cream were obtained at the picnic grounds. In Mountain Home, although every family prepared several dishes, which were all put at a large buffet table, the meat (lamb) was brought by a Basque restaurant owner. Traditional foods include: *chorizos*—sausages, made commercially by two companies in Boise, although a number of families still make their own; *bacalao*—dried cod, fried; *tripacallos*—tripe, cooked in tomato sauce; *lengua*—tongue, fried; lamb, roasted; *paella*—rice, fried with chicken, *chorizos*, or other meat; *omlettas potatas*—potato omelets.

For the Boise picnic, some families arrived early enough in the morning to attend Mass at St. John's Cathedral in Boise; others arrived at the park about noon to eat. The afternoon was filled with games, dances, and singing.

The games at the annual Basque picnics began about 2:00 P.M., after a large picnic lunch. The first games at the Boise picnic in 1970 were simple running games, gunnysack races, and egg-throwing contests between girls and boys of different ages. The most popular games followed these races and featured as participants young men, many of them herders on contract from the Basque provinces. All of these field events are still played on festive occasions in the Basque country. Outstanding participants are known through the Basque-American community, as well as in the Old World.

At the Boise Basque picnic, the field events began with weight lifting. Weight lifters (*jasotales*)[6] hoisted to their shoulders a 225-pound cylindrical weight made especially for the Basque games (Figure 1). Only two men competed in this event at the Boise picnic: Ignacio Mendiola lifted the weight twelve times in five minutes; Jose Luis Arrieta twenty-two times in the same time span. Arrieta, known for several years as the Basque strong man, succeeded Benito Goitiandia who earlier achieved fame throughout the Basque community.[7]

The most popular weight-lifting event required that each participant carry two 105-pound bell-shaped steel weights from one end of the game field to the other until he dropped them (Figure 2). At the Mountain Home picnic, one of the same bell-shaped weights was held between the legs and thrown as far as possible (Figure 3).

Men also threw the javelin (*palanka*) from between the legs at the Mountain Home picnic (Figure 4). Gallop

Figure 3.   One of the bell-shaped weights was held between the legs and thrown as far as possible.

Figure 4.   The *palanka* (javelin) is thrown from between the legs.

stated that *isterpe* or *anke-pa* was one of four positions from which the Basques threw the *palanka*, which weighed between ten and twenty-five pounds.[8] In 1913, Gallop reported, Gabino Lizarre of Berastegui threw the *palanka isterpe* one hundred feet. At the Mountain Home picnic the farthest throw was about fifty-five feet. *Bularrez*, an over-the-shoulder throw familiar in American track events; *biraka*, in which the throw is preceded by a half-turn; and *zazpi-bira*, meaning seven turns, in which a three-quarter turn precedes the throw, are three other ways that the *palanka* is thrown. The throws preceded by a turn have been outlawed in the United States, since they are considered dangerous.

At both the Mountain Home and Boise picnics, log-chopping contests were held (Figure 5). The *aizkolaris* (log choppers) were four in number: two on each of two teams. With one member of a team chopping at a time, each team was to chop through two logs, and the first team finished won. The men chopped on each side of the log, working toward the core.

Before attending the Mountain Home picnic, the author had been told that a sheep-herding contest might be held, in which the herder whose dog most quickly corralled a flock of sheep won. Perhaps due to the complications of providing adequate space, this contest did not take place. The author found no mention of this contest in Old World Basque literature, and it seems likely that the game became popular in the New World, inspired by the herding occupation.

A number of other games which were described to the author as traditional Basque games likewise did not take place: women carrying buckets of water on their heads, stone-boring (*arrizulatzales*), goose games or hen games. The Basque women in Boise, according to Roesch,[9] used to compete in water-carrying contests, but the game seems to have died out in the last fifteen years.

After the competitions and demonstrations in the afternoon, singing groups formed at some of the picnic tables. Songs were initiated by priests or older immigrant women. The choices of songs included the well-known Basque anthem, *Guernika'ko Arbola*, which is familiar to most Basques.

1.   Guernika'ko arbola   da bedeinkatua,
     Of Guernica the tree is blessed,

     Euskaldunen artian guztiz maitatua.
     The Basque   among much loved.

Figure 5. Log-chopping contests are held.

Eman ta zabal zazu munduan frutua;
You gave wide around the world fruit (benefit);

Adoratzen zaitugu, arbola santua.
We adore you, tree sanctified.

2. Milla erte inguru da esaten dutela,
  A thousand years about they say that is,

Jainkoak jarri zuela Guernika'ko arbola.
God who brought you (to us) of Guernica the tree

Zaude, bada, zutikan orain ta denbora,
Be you, yes, standing now and always,

Eroitzen ba'zera erras galdu gera.
If you die surely we will perish.

3. Ez zera eroriko arbola maitea,
  You will not die tree beloved.

Baldin portazen ba'da Bizkai'ko Juntea.
With justice if performing of Bizcaya the congress.

Laurok artuko degu zurekin partea,
The tour of a will take with your part,

Pakean bizi dedin euskaldun jentea.
In peace can live (so) the Basque people.

These songs were familiar in part to second- and third-generation Basque-Americans. Immigrant women and priests knew the most verses to each of these songs. Second- and third-generation Basque-Americans are learning the songs through the Oinkari dance troupe of Boise and similar dance groups in the West. Some of these songs are mimeographed and taught to the children. The teachers of these songs are few, and children learn one or two verses. Consequently many of the verses are being forgotten by the Basque community. Because children are taught by a few individuals, standardization in the Basque music is taking place. The only similar project initiated in Jordan Valley was a Basque hymn which was taught to the parish by a non-Basque priest for Christmas in 1967.

Dances. Traditional Basque dances are performed by the Oinkari dance group, of Boise, and other similar smaller dance groups from other towns, such as Mountain Home, Winnemucca, and Elko. The Oinkaris are perhaps the largest and best known of the groups.

During the 1950s, Basque dances were taught to small children by Jay Hormaechea.[10] In 1960, a group of young Basque-Americans from Boise visited Spain. While they were in San Sebastian, they met the Oinkari dancers of Spain and learned some of their dances. Back in Boise, the group adopted the name of "Oinkari" which means "those who foot it fast."[11]

When the Oinkaris were invited to dance for the Seattle World's Fair in 1962, the Basque and non-Basque community of Boise contributed to the preparation for this trip. The success at Seattle brought subsequent invitations to appear elsewhere in the country. Financing the trip to the New York World's Fair in 1964 called for widespread cooperation from the Boise community.

Today, the Oinkari group includes between forty and fifty dancers: twelve boys and the rest girls, ranging between fourteen and twenty-two years of age. Younger children, between five and fourteen, are taught Basque dances as well, but when they reach fourteen, they must audition for the Oinkaris. In order for a dancer to qualify for the Oinkaris, at least one parent must belong to the Boise Basque Society, all of whose members are of Basque descent.

For most dances, girls wear full red cotton skirts with two or three dark bands several inches above the hemline, black bodices over white blouses, black-laced *espadrilles* over white stockings, and white kerchiefs tied in a three-corner knot at the back of the head. The boys wear white shirts and trousers, red berets and sashes, *espadrilles*, and occasionally, pads just below the knees.[12]

Their repertoire of about twenty dances is most often performed to the accompaniment of Jimmy Jausoro's Basque Orchestra of Boise—a three-piece group including an accordion and drums. The *txistu*, a three-holed flute held in the left hand, is played with a drum which the *txistulari* hooks over his left arm and beats with his right hand. The *txistu* is no longer played publicly in Boise,[13] although it was used to accompany the Oinkaris when they were first organized.

Figure 6.   The final figure in the *ezpatadantza* was the *brokeldantza*—small hoop dance.

The Oinkaris fuse traditional with modern forms which they feel appeal to the widest range of audience.[14] Among their repertoire is the *jota*, long considered the traditional Basque dance in Boise, Ontario, and Jordan Valley.[15] The popular *porrosalda* that Jay Hormaechea taught Basque children in Boise is a form of the *jota*. Traditionally danced with tiny jumping steps, the Oinkari have slowed the steps and expanded the jumps which appeal to audiences farther away from the performers and can be danced to the accompaniment of an accordion more easily.

The *ezpatadantza* (sword dance) is considered to be of pagan origin.[16] The *ezpatadantza* in Vizcaya was preceded with the *ikurnia*, a processional. Once the dancers were on stage, they performed the *arkuak*—hoop dance. The *makil tchikiak*—little stick—figure followed the *arkuak*. The *makil anndiak*—big stick—figure followed the *makil tchikiak*. The *ezpatadantza*, after which the entire sequence is named, was performed fourth. The dancers were all boys, each of whom carried a sword in both hands, the hilt covered with a handkerchief. Unlike the earlier figures in which dancers tap each other's hoops and sticks, the dancers did not touch each other in this dance. The dance culminated in the symbolic sacrifice of a victim who was carried off on the shoulders of the other dancers. The final figure in the *ezpatadantza* was the *brokeldantza*—small hoop dance (Figure 6).

Although traditionally the *ezpatadantza* was performed only by boys, the Oinkaris have included girls in a number of figures. Figures from the *ezpatadantza*

were performed but not in any special order. As performed in Boise, August 1970, the Oinkaris danced a twirling dance with female dancers forming three rings; a *laukodantza*—hoop dance performed only by girls; a *jota* in which boys and girls danced as partners; the *ezpatadantza* figure, performed only by boys; the *manodantza*—hand dance performed by boys and girls; and the *arkodantza*, danced with both boys and girls.

The addition of twirls and kicks in the *jota*, the variation in traditional order of figures in the *ezpatadantza* and the addition of girls in the *ezpatadantza*, have been made by the Oinkaris. Oinkaris have inspired the formation of similar although smaller dance groups in other towns in Idaho and Nevada (Figures 7–8). The alterations that Oinkaris have made to traditional Basque dances are paralleled in these groups. In the group at Mountain Home, for example, some girls are dressed as boys to compensate for the lack of male dancers.

In the Basque provinces, alterations have also taken place. The traditional Basque ritual and recreational dances are no longer performed in towns by local townspeople but professionally by such dance troups as the Olaeta.[17] In the Basque provinces as well as in the United States, traditional names and forms have been retained although meanings have been forgotten. The forms have been altered to please the tastes of an audience looking for entertainment not ritual, and forms are not considered to have religious meaning.

At a dance observed by the author, after the Oinkaris presented a demonstration of some Basque dances,

Figure 7. Basque dancers.

Figure 8. Basque dancers.

competitions for *jotas* were opened to the public. Most of the participants were young, and many of them were also Oinkaris. Each couple was to dance a *jota* for several minutes to the accompaniment of the Basque orchestra, while judges determined how well the dancers performed together. The dance was then turned into a public street dance in front of the Basque Center. It was crowded, and many *jotas* were danced by people of all ages. Older people left by midnight, earlier if they had to drive home a long distance. Other people stayed until later.

Sheepherders' Ball.   The annual Sheepherders' Ball held in Boise, was initiated by John Achabal, "Basque Sheep King," until his death in 1945.[18] The ball is still held as a charity function. It is less traditional than the New Year's celebration, since it was unprecedented in the Old World and was begun here by a single individual. Many more non-Basques participate in the dance in a major way. The dance is generally held at the Riverside Pavilion in Boise. In 1971, it began at 9:00 P.M. People purchased drinks and danced to the accompaniment of Jimmy Jausoro's Basque Orchestra. Part way through the evening there was a demonstration of Basque dances by the Oinkari dancers and a solo by a Basque girl from Bayonne. A lamb and sheepskin were auctioned off, the money to be used for the construction of a new Basque center. There were no more than three or four *jotas* played to which the public could dance. Basque elements of the Sheepherders' Ball are few and self-conscious.

In summary, the Basque celebrations that were held

in Jordan Valley at Christmas, New Year's, and Three Kings' Day were traditional but simplified ceremonies due to the absence of a parish priest who could annually lead religious services. The individuating features of the *misa degayo*, *uŕte baŕi kaŕi*, the Zanta Agueda procession, and the San Juan ritual dance have broken down to a large extent in contemporary times. The present family celebrations organized by Jordan Valley Basques and their descendants show few Basque features and emphasize the obligations that former Jordan Valley residents feel toward their friends and relatives (deceased and alive).

The Basque celebrations, dances, and picnics that are held elsewhere in Idaho, Nevada, and Oregon are unparalleled in Jordan Valley. These ethnic-conscious celebrations are becoming increasingly standardized. The religious element of San Ignacio's day is purely secondary to the social function of gathering together many people of common descent to revive traditional customs. The pattern of celebration varies little from one to another of these picnics and, since most of the dances and songs are taught to Basque descendants by a few troupe leaders, simplification and standardization of the genres of folklore have resulted.

Notes

1. Katherine Story French, "Culture Segments and Variation in Contemporary Social Ceremonialism on the Warm Springs Reservation, Oregon," (Ph.D. dissertation, Columbia University, 1955).

2. A.A., C.D., K.C., interviews, Jordan Valley and Ontario, November 1970 and March 1971.

3. Rodney Gallop, *Book of the Basques* (Reno: University of Nevada Press, 1970), 130.

4. J.Y., K.C., interview, March 1971.

5. Julio Cara Baroja, *Los Vascos: Etnologia* (San Sebastian: Biblioteca Vascongada de los Amigos del Pais, 1949), 433–36.

6. Gallop, *The Book of the Basques*, 248.

7. Robert Laxalt, "Lonely Sentinels of the America West: Basque Sheepherders," *National Geographic* 129 (June 1966): 870–88.

8. Gallop, *The Book of the Basques.*

9. Ethel A. Roesch observed Boise women carrying buckets of water on their heads at a picnic, in "Basques of the Sawtooth Range," *Frontier Times* (1957): 18.

10. J.H., interview, Boise, August 1970.

11. (Al Erquiaga), "General History of Oinkari Basque Dancers," *Viltis* 21 (June–September 1966): 5.

12. Gallop stated that knee pads are uniquely Viscayan in *The Book of the Basques*, 188.

13. Grant McCall, "Txistulan," *Viltis* 27 (January-February, 1969), 4–7.

14. David Eiguren, President of Oinkari Dance Troup, interview, Boise, August 1970.

15. The *jota* was first observed among Basques in the Old Country in 1870 (Gallop, *The Book of the Basques*, 181). A *fandango*, the *jota* is thought to have originated in Aragon rather than the Basque provinces.

16. Ibid., 184. Gallop divided traditional Basque dances into ritual and recreational dances. The *ezpatadantza* he classified as a ritual dance since it had ritual meaning in pagan times. The *aurresku* is also danced by dance troups in the United States. The author witnessed it danced by Mountain Home dancers. Gallop classified it as a recreational dance because it was performed with both men and women and never had religious overtones. See also Violet Alford, "Ceremonial Dances of the Spanish Basques," *Musical Quarterly* 18 (July 1932): 471–82.

17. Olaeta Dancers performed in Boise, 2 November 1970.

18. Utahna Hall, "Basques Getting Americanized," *The Oregon Journal*, Pacific Magazine (27 January 1946), 27.

"Prairie Chickens Dancing . . .": Ecology's Myth

ALAN G. MARSHALL

To anthropologists, literary scholars, cultural historians, students of folklife, and comparative religionists, the words myth *and* mythology *are not used to indicate a false belief but to identify a class of stories that embody a culture's beliefs about its origins and about its place in the world. In this essay, the reader may see something of the intricate belief system in which the wholeness of the created order is made explicit in and through a myth-ritual that reflects a Nez Perce ecological theory.*

Twenty or more years ago it would have been difficult for the Euro-American reader to accommodate a world view that looks upon all creation as interrelated and interdependent, each part vital to the whole and all working together for the good of the whole. Such a view, however, has long been held by Native Americans, and the post-sixties ecological sensibility finds the Indian view no longer quaint but profound, responsible, and even scientifically sound.

The myth-ritual examined here focuses upon certain relationships among various life forms — prairie chickens, elk, and other animals — and the earth and the spirit energy or power which pulses in all and through all. The disruption of the prairie chicken's dancing disrupts the entire order, and serious consequences follow, among them a reduction in the number of elk and other game animals that people depend upon for food.

Herbert Spinden's The Nez Perce Indians *(1908) and Deward Walker's* American Indians of Idaho *(1973) are studies to which the reader may turn for additional knowledge of the Nez Perce people.*

Marshall teaches anthropology at Lewis-Clark State College, Lewiston, Idaho. He is, as this essay suggests, vitally interested in ecological anthropology and Native American Studies.

One major problem faced by folklorists and anthropologists is deciphering the oftentimes cryptic statements of people with whom they work. These comments are cryptic because they refer to knowledge, attitudes, or "paradigms" which are assumed to be self-evident and yet are not. Such commonplaces are probably the most difficult aspect of human life to understand and explain. Yet they are of equal importance with myth for understanding culture and folklore. If anthropologists and folklorists are to get beyond the illumination of arcana or the cataloging of daily details, connections between the two must be made because everyday life is the way people illuminate their myths, while myth gives everyday life meaning. One cannot exist, or be understood, without the other.

It is this point that I wish to make in the context of Nez Perce Indian life. I will do so by taking a cryptic, everyday statement of Nez Perce natural history and developing its mythic dimensions. Two other significant related issues will also be discussed: (1) the problem of translating myth from one sociocultural setting to another and (2) the sociopolitical significance of correct translation. I will illustrate these issues from my fieldwork with Nez Perce people in northern Idaho.[1] The purpose of this research was to discover relationships between Nez Perce social groups and their environment. As I explained my project to them, I was given a great deal of "irrelevant" information: myths, legends, and statements about Nez Perce "religion." My reaction was similar to that of many other non-Indians in dealing with Nez Perce: I wanted to know more about ecology. What I found later was that I was learning about a theory of ecology, something that few people would credit to nonscientists.

Three caveats about my information are necessary. First, what I am dealing with is a Nez Perce ecological theory. Like Euro-American ecological theories, there are many variations on basic themes in the way Nez Perces understand their relationship to the environment.[2] Equally, the theories themselves are objects of contention, though there are basic agreements among people who concern themselves with such things. This

dialogue in itself is one of the problems of myth translation: the nonrecognition by outside observers of the
variability of myth and its political importance.

Second, my information was gained almost entirely
in English, though I do not believe this fact vitiates my
work. Instead, it adds an intriguing dimension to translation. The natural assumption is that one culture's
English is the same as any English. Such correspondence is not the case, as is apparent in many seemingly
nonsense statements made by people with whom I
spoke. That is, inferences that could be made ordinarily
from utterances of English speakers could not be made
from similar statements of Nez Perce English speakers.
The reasons for this translation difficulty is that the
referential world of these Nez Perces was different from
that of most English speakers. Still, because many Nez
Perces speak English only, recognition of "myth" is
difficult.

A third caveat is that these explanations are still being developed. That is, because the people with whom I
collaborated are often thought of as acculturated, some
observers may conclude that their knowledge is somehow adulterated, or not Nez Perce, but Euro-American.
Again, I would argue that such is not the case. If the
objective of study is how people live and how they
assimilate and explain things, rather than some antiquarian purpose, information such as presented here is
valid. In fact, the mythical world of Nez Perces is quite
lively. It is as ever present as the mythical world of
anyone else. Further, it is not the same world as that of
non-Indian people. The problem comes in identifying
that world and recognizing it for what it is. Nez Perces,
like many other Native American groups, have not
disappeared. They have changed along with their circumstances. Changed circumstances demand new
myths.

It is worth comparing Nez Perces with other ethnic
groups which also work at a social disadvantage. The
basic disadvantage is that they are forced to accommodate to a dominant group on, and in, the latter's
terms. Deviation from the majority's terms, linguis-
tically and behaviorally, leads to negative sanctions.
Hence, boundaries are maintained. In some settings,
the dominant group's terms are evident; in others, the
ethnic group's terms are used.[3] The involutions of this
situation are obvious. One that I have noted among the
Nez Perces is a rephrasing of myth which successfully
camouflages their referential world, allowing it to persist covertly despite overt agreement with the referential world of the dominant group.

The entailed problems in translation are not immediately apparent. The case considered here is one I
encountered in my fieldwork. It does not deal directly
with a myth text, but rather with the everyday natural
historical context of a myth.

After two years of research on the relationship of
social groups with the environment, I was reasonably
well versed in talking about the environment with some
people. A persistent topic of conversation was the lack
of game animals, particularly elk, in northern Idaho.
Much of the blame for low game population was directed at "whites." In one conversation I agreed, pointing out that increased human population, increased
road-building in the mountains, increased logging, and
increased habitat destruction in the mountains was the
cause. My teacher said, "No. The reason that there is
no more game in the mountains is that prairie chickens
don't dance on the prairie anymore."[4]

The question of why prairie chicken is so important
came immediately to mind. My teacher, upon further
questioning, merely restated that no prairie chickens
dancing meant few elk would be found. He cited no
myths. Nor was the answer immediately apparent in
the myths that had been collected.

Prairie chicken is not an important figure in Nez
Perce mythology, if the number of myths in which it
appears is taken as the measure. In fact, the only myth
in which prairie chicken appears as a central figure is
one concerning the length of days. Roughly, the myth,
obtained in English, is this:

> The animals had all gathered near Mission Creek. They
> were trying to decide how long the days and nights were
> going to be. The chief among the birds was prairie
> chicken. Prairie chicken spoke for them. He said, "There
> should be a night for each day." Grizzly bear was very
> fierce—he led the furred animals. He growled that a night
> should last for five years at a stretch. The other animals
> were afraid of him so they went along. Prairie chicken
> spoke for the birds, "But if night is five years long, how
> will we survive? We can't eat at night." Grizzly bear didn't
> care. So they all went to war, the birds on one side, the
> furred animals on the other. Bat didn't want to be injured,
> so he flew back and forth, first fighting on one side, then
> on the other, depending on who was winning. He egged
> them on. The battle went back and forth. Many were
> killed.
>   The little furred animals got together. They said, "We
> will all be killed if this goes on. Besides, we can't live like
> grizzly bear and the other fierce ones. They all hunt at
> night." The chipmunk was the first to go over to the other
> side. Grizzly bear saw this and tried to grab him. His claws
> scratched chipmunk's back, and its stripes are the scars.
> Pretty soon, all the little animals had gone over. Only
> grizzly bear, black bear, bobcat, lynx, and mountain lion
> were left. They were defeated. So, each day is part light
> and part dark. That's all."[5]

The lack of an apparent explanation led me to find
out more about prairie chickens. By looking at their
natural history, perhaps I could establish some basis for
understanding the statement and the myth. Before massive non-Indian intrusion, the upland prairie regions of
Nez Perce country harbored fairly large populations of
the "prairie chickens." Gathering in spring, the male
prairie chickens stake out large areas for nuptial
display, referred to in English as "leks" or, in the vernacular, "booming grounds." The leks are kept clean
by the male birds, and the grass grows little higher than
two to three inches while the lek is in use. The male
birds begin every morning singing, booming, and danc-

ing. This activity goes on for several hours over a period of several weeks. The females, meanwhile, wait around the edges of the lek, observing the action, frequently presenting themselves for copulation with the dominant males. The latter, indeed, gather harems.

The natural history includes two significant points. First, the observations of prairie chicken behavior is similar for both non-Indians and Native Americans. Second, the Nez Perces manifested a different attitude towards it. One jokingly saw mating as the important aspect, comparing it to Nez Perce dances. But the specific parallels were drawn when the lek, or "booming grounds" in Nez Perce English, were named in the Nez Perce tongue. The word used is /weye·s/, and it includes two morphemes whose meanings are crucial in Nez Perce thought.

The first morpheme is /wey/. Not easily translatable, it refers to spirit power. It is found in other word forms: /weyekin/, "spirit power"; /weyiknin/, "a person with spirit power"; /weyikwecet/, "spirit dance"; /weyikwanipt/, "spirit song"; and others. The concept of the spirit power includes many key ideas. One of these is that the spirit powers are akin to natural phenomena or, perhaps better, are embodied in natural phenomena. There are many /weyekin/; they may be water animals, land animals, weather phenomena, celestial phenomena, or inanimate objects such as rock.[6] Some other phenomena, for example, shadow or ghost or /qawxqawx/, a boy-sized being, are also /weyekin/. These powers exist separately from humans. It is these powers which populated the earth before humans came. When humans appeared, these powers assumed their present shapes; but, they occasionally still appear as humans, and humans can embody them. I suppose that /weyekin/ marry, have children, eat, war with one another, and so forth.

A second basic idea is that the /weyekin/ act in accordance with their nature. Grizzly bear, as in the myth given above, is always fierce, always demanding his own way. Grizzly can be mollified by food or sex, but is otherwise always fierce. Chipmunk, on the other hand, is daring—he was the first to break away from the furred animals. Chipmunk can afford to be daring, though, because he is also an escape artist. Suffice it to say that all /weyekin/ act in accordance with their nature.

A third important idea is that not all /weyekin/ are equally powerful, even those of a single kind. Simply, some chipmunk powers are better at escaping than others. Obviously, there must be many individual powers in existence at once. That is, a single, monolithic "chipmunkness," which all chipmunks exhibit does not exist. Rather, they display the attributes of being chipmunk, and some do it better than others.

Fourth, although grizzly bear is fierce and powerful, grizzly bear power might not be more powerful than a given chipmunk. Grizzly bear gives only a certain kind of power and will dominate only in certain kinds of situations. Thus, the powers are context specific. It is

rather like the game of scissors, stones, and paper—depending on the shape others assume, one might win, lose, or draw.

The second form in the term /weye·s/ is /é·s/. This form refers to a place to live. It is found also in the terms of /tewyenike·s/, "village"; /wise·s/, "places to live while traveling"; /wispeyke·s/, "a place to live while traveling"; and others. The term /weye·s/ refers to a place where the spirit powers congregate. They are invisible, for the most part, though people say that their presence can be felt and that intruders may be injured by the powers.

The only spirit powers that congregate at a /weye·s/ are those who possess, and are possessed by, a human being who embodies them.[7] Other spirit powers are found elsewhere. Further, a spirit power is found at the /weye·s/ used by its human counterpart. The Nez Perce theory of spirit power is still more complex, but suffice it to say that they are primarily manifested overtly when the human and the human's /weyekin/ dance on the /weye·s/.

As far as I know, only two kinds of beings build a /weye·s/: prairie chickens and humans. Furthermore, only two kinds of beings dance on the /weye·s/: prairie chickens and humans. Other parallels also exist—for example, prairie chickens, like humans, produce a drumming sound while dancing and both cry out as they dance. In summary, prairie chickens are outstanding among the birds for the relationship with the /weyekin/. This connection is fairly explicit for some Nez Perce. Until a few years ago, there was a /weye·s/ on Lapwai Creek in Idaho—the English term for it was "the booming grounds."

Prairie chickens and humans are thus unique in their connection with the natural world. The nexus of their connection is dance. The power of the natural world is concentrated on the /weye·s/. The dancers, in a sense, weave their way through the world in dance. A dancer dances in a manner peculiar to the dancer's power. In this way, the /weyekin/ are physically manifested on the dance floor. The entire use of the spirit dance floor expresses the proper relationship between things. Thus, there is no more game in the mountains because the prairie chickens don't dance on the prairie anymore. The relationship between things is upset because the dancing has stopped, and the prairie chicken's integral role is no longer played. But is it true that prairie chickens influence elk populations?

The region that Nez Perces are part of encompasses many kinds of natural communities. These areas are sensitive to the great elevational differences in northern Idaho, southeastern Washington, and northeastern Oregon, the region in which Nez Perces still retain aboriginal rights to hunt and fish. Elevations range from roughly 700 feet to over 10,000 feet above sea level. Many of these communities have been vastly altered by Euro-American farming patterns. I will first briefly describe the prefarming natural communities, pointing out how elk depended upon them. The changes made by Euro-Americans will be pointed out, showing that certain areas critical to elk have been reduced in extent. At the same time, the prairie chicken's place will be noted, as will be the Nez Perce use of the region.

Briefly, there are four broad environmental zones relevant to Nez Perces. Formerly, Nez Perces had a very fine-grained categorization of specific habitats that were exploited in various ways before their economy was overwhelmed by that of Euro-Americans. At the time of my study, four regions were recognized. "Along the river" and "in the canyons" differentiate two different economic patterns: spring-summer fishing and winter hunting. "The prairie" differentiates a region in which summer root crops are occasionally gathered. "The mountains" distinguishes yet another region, where summer-fall berry-gathering and hunting occur.

The reason for detailing these zones should be apparent from the previous section. The myth puts animals in specific regions. Indeed, the behavior of the animals cannot be understood apart from their ecological niche. The accurate translation of the myth apart from words and phrases must include these because they are implicit in the myth.

The canyon zone is comprised of rivers deeply incised into the country rock. Small sidestreams drop precipitously into the river from intracanyon springs or from the surrounding prairies and mountains. The canyon walls are thus a complex of steep ridges, rather than sheer cliffs. Minimum canyon depth is 1900 feet. The zone's deepest section, in Hell's Canyon of the Snake River, is over 8000 feet from river surface to the top of the Seven Devil's massif. Slopes exposed to the sun are grassy and, in the spring, vegetable resources are found there. Unexposed slopes are covered with conifers and shrubs. In winter, elk spend their days in the forest, their nights grazing on the grassy slopes at elevations less than 2500 feet. Prairie chickens also wintered in the canyons, and roosted in the streamside deciduous trees where they ate buds. People also spend the winter in the canyons — the canyons are relatively mild in winter, very hot and dry during summer.

The prairies are rolling hills, up to 150 feet high, which are found on plateaus between 1900 and 2500 feet in elevation. The area is moderate in size, including perhaps 5000 square miles. Streams are bordered by deciduous trees. The exposed slopes are grassy, but brush occurs on wet spots. Protected slopes are covered by conifers. In mild winters, elk graze the prairie and resort to the trees for daytime cover. Prairie chickens also lived there. Some winter hunting occurs, but Nez Perces use the zone most intensively during summer.

The montane zone lies between 2500 feet and 10,000 feet or more. The area ia large — over 20,000 square miles in extent. Many streams have eroded this area into a complex of steep ridges. A wide variety of coniferous trees and shrubs cover most slopes. Some slopes, however, are grassy as a result of little effective precipitation. Elk graze these slopes, and escape from the daytime heat in the surrounding forest. Prairie chickens were never found in this zone. Nez Perces begin hunting there in summer, and hunt the highest places in September through October. Berries are collected at the same time. Some fishing of spawning salmon also occurs.

The yearly cycle of nature and traditional[8] Nez Perce economy is governed by temperature-moisture relationships and elevation. Because of the great elevational differences, winter is very short and often mild in the canyons, especially at the lowest elevations. In some portions of the Nez Perce canyon region, 50 percent of the plants are photosynthetically active through the winter. Summer, on the other hand, is the period of quiescence: fewer than 10 percent of the plant species are active through the summer. The situation is completely reversed in the montane region. Summers are very short there: the snow may not melt completely on north-facing slopes of the montane zone. Early snows begin in September or October.

The rhythm of life is strongly affected by this relationship. Elk stay in the area just below snow line. Thus, during summer they live at high altitudes in the montane zone; as snow begins to accumulate, they move to lower elevations. During winter, they live below 2500 feet or so. Elk herds will move into the canyons if the winter snow accumulation is great. The herds disperse in spring, traveling back into the mountains as grazing areas begin to produce food. Prairie chickens lived between 1900 and 2500 feet throughout the year. But when snowfall was great, or temperatures were very low, they went into the canyons where they roosted in tall streamside trees. The Nez Perces, too, are affected by this seasonal change, their activities being constrained by the location and productivity of their traditional resources.

Low elk populations constitute a major game management problem in northern Idaho from the standpoints of hunting and habitat improvement. Elk hunting is a popular pastime for many people — resident and nonresident licenses for elk are now limited in order to reduce hunting pressure. Kill rates are low, meaning that people are hunting despite the considerable chance of not getting an animal. Poached elk is a favorite northern Idaho meal. Again, despite the large fine for illegal elk hunting, many individuals engage in it. Some people derive income from market hunting. Thus, the elk populations suffer from great hunting pressure. At the same time, hunters demand higher elk populations.

Habitat management also poses a problem, and it is linked with hunting pressure. Elk have a relatively rapid reproductive rate, but it is dependent upon how much good food and cover is available. Under the best conditions, a female elk will bear twins. Female elk will not reproduce under the poorest survival conditions. In other words, the elk population is almost always near the limit that its food supplies can allow and the cover protect. The excess population dies of starvation and exposure during winter. Thus, in an improving elk habitat, elk populations can be enlarged, and the hunters have better opportunities — more hunters will buy licenses, game department revenues will increase, and political pressures will decrease. Habitat management thus provides the key to the problem of low elk populations.

There are competing interests, however. The energy, agricultural, and timber industries all affect the elk population. The region's deep canyons still have enormous potential for hydroelectric power. Dworshak Dam on the North Fork of the Clearwater River became operational in 1971. Its pool destroyed one of the most important wintering grounds for elk. There was no other area suitable to supporting the population dependent on it.

Agriculture also affects elk populations. Capital-intensive farming, based on wheat and peas, literally blankets the region's prairies. Since monocropping is most economically productive, vegetation covers most of the land during spring and early summer. At other times, the land is bare. Large farm machinery makes large fields necessary and aids in bringing marginal land under the plow. Some of this land was formerly forested. Since the land bank was discontinued, most arable land is now cultivated. Major elk wintering grounds were destroyed through agriculture.

The timber industry has mixed effects on elk habitat. On the one hand, extensive clear-cutting of timbered areas has led to some increase in the availability of spring and summer grazing. On the other hand, increased roads and access into the montane zone has led to more human use. Also, the broad policy of timber management has had negative effects. Fire suppression, in particular, is a factor in the decline of the elk herds.[9]

Forest management is aimed primarily at monocropping. The same problems in the relationship between elk and agriculture may arise in the forests, as well.

Generally speaking, the effort to increase elk populations is perceived by many people as a problem confined to the forests. Nongame management people commonly blame the Department of Fish and Game, believing that mismanagement is the problem. Game managers generally focus on the problems of forest management and especially fire policy. The point here is that Euro-American ecology, too, is a myth. There are social aspects to consider. First, Idaho society is stratified. Thus, there are conflicting assessments of the problem and, generally speaking, the differences are found between people with a college education including ecology and game management and those without it. Their conflicting constructions of reality are played out in the political arena.

However, some basic kinds of agreement in the political arena are found. Unlike Nez Perces, who view ecological relations as what we might call a religious category, non-Indians view them economically. For example, the metaphors used by ecologists are heavily laced with economic terms, such as energy budget,

food supply, and gross productivity. The basic model used by ecologists was developed by Malthus. Hence, the most important factor in population control is the limiting factor (in this case, winter-grazing). Further, game management people now try to quantify the value of wildlife. Still others attempt to place economic value on wilderness areas. Both undertakings are notoriously difficult.

Finally, the efforts to increase elk populations are often perceived by many people as a problem confined to the forests, perhaps because it is the only management they can affect. Thus, the management of game is powerfully influenced in practice by the economic infrastructure of United States society.

What this has to do with prairie chickens dancing by now should be apparent. Prairie chickens, in fact, are a key indicator species for the number of elk. They are especially sensitive to disruption by agriculture. In order to survive as a population, prairie chickens must remain undisturbed on their leks. Farming destroys the lek and disturbs prairie chickens. But for farming to be extensive enough in this region to destroy the leks, it must also be extensive enough to destroy winter grazing of elk herds. For this reason, my teacher was correct — there is no more game in the mountains because the prairie chickens don't dance on the prairie anymore.

But what about the Nez Perce myth? How are we to understand that? I think that three points are important. First, prairie chickens' ascendency over many of the land animals is related to the fact of dancing. Dancing is an expression of power to influence others. The dances themselves are important because they are the physical manifestation of relationships between things. The relationships between beings in the myth are an expression of postulated relationships between things in the world. Furthermore, the text concerned just with prairie chicken deals only with a specific instance, one limited by time and space. The significance of this is that the "myth" cited above is only part of a larger cycle, of which each substantive member locates a variety of animals in time and space. The locations, in fact, are those locations where one goes to find both the animals and the powers represented in myth.

Second, in order to understand the myth, one must know how the subjects of the myth live their lives. That is, a myth remains only a myth as long as it is not brought to earth. While myths may only properly be told in certain contexts, they are constantly *used* in a wider variety of contexts. The text cited above is an excellent example. It, and others, were recited only in fall and winter, a common pattern. But references to them are made constantly in discussions of particular events, as when I was told why elk populations were low. Stories about particular powers were often triggered by particular events that were in one way or another significant. The significance is found in the life patterns of the organisms involved. Thus, one must know the natural history of the region in which people live in order to understand and translate their myths.

The third important point is that knowledge about how Nez Perces practice their lives is crucial as well. Myths are informed through experiences. A person must observe in order to learn the natural history of a region, but the observations themselves take on meaning only in a practical sense. In this case, how do people gain a living in their environment? Where are they? What do they do there? In other words, people's activities in the world have effects. These effects, in turn, buttress what it is that people believe.

I am arguing here for what Geertz terms "thick description."[10] Geertz, too, sees some parallels between ethnography and folklore. He regarded the best of both as being interpretive approaches. At their worst, the interpretations of both ". . . tend to drift off into logical dreams, academic bemusements with formal symmetry."[11] In order to avoid this tendency, Geertz keeps as close to concrete forms as possible rather than appealing to the "darker sciences." Geertz is aiming towards a semiotic understanding of culture.

Yet another writer has approached the problem of translation and interpretation in a similar way. Bourdieu is concerned with a theory of practice.[12] In his work, he directly links practice with symbols. In particular, he asserts that the meaning of symbols is found in practice. He denies that symbols are subject to laws apart from practical considerations. Through the manipulation of symbols, he suggests, people build social capital, gaining influence over their environment. Again, the plethora of symbols and the situationally unique ways in which individuals use them require thick description.

The point of this is an old one: contextualization is the key element in the interpretation of cultural life, of which myth is a part. Symbols are invested with meaning through action, and minute description of practice is necessary for understanding the meaning of symbols. The juxtaposition, opposition, and disjunction of things in practice are reflected by the similar attributes of symbols in myth. In a sense, then, people lead lives that are mythical and enchanting.

It is the enchantment of life that hides myth from people living out a practical pattern.[13] As praxis changes, reality becomes a myth, in its ordinarily accepted definition. By implication, individuals of two different practical traditions recognize the other's models of reality as myth, and their lives as impractical. This well-recognized reaction, ethnocentrism, grinds the second edge on translation's sword: the translator must be aware of his or her own myth.

Hsu points out a problem that vitiates much of the work done by anthropolgists.[14] The problem is the lack of comparative material from "Western" societies. Bluntly, in the enchantment of their lives, anthropologists and folklorists lack awareness of their own myths. This lack of awareness, according to Hsu, results in incorrect interpretation even though the translator/interpreter is a perfect speaker and actor in her or his own language and culture.[15] In other words, the

model of the relationship between individuals and culture developed by anthropologists applies to themselves.

The task of myth translation becomes monumental in this approach: the problems lie not only in finding appropriate word and grammatical forms in shifting from one language to another or even one of strictly interlinear forms of translation. Myths have a practical dimension as well. Thus, in the instance referred to here, individuals using the same word forms and grammar may come to different conclusions and live differently practical lives. Herein lies the urgency of correct myth translation.

Currently in northern Idaho, a confrontation between the Nez Perce and state authorities is under way. The confrontation is over the correct way for people to relate with their environment. On the one hand, Idaho officials wish to have complete authority over the time and place of fish and game resource use. They also want to determine what will be used and how much will be used. This control, they feel, is necessary for a number of reasons: ease of law enforcement, higher revenues accruing to the state through licensing, more control over game populations, and so forth. It is often expressed in terms of protecting resources from overexploitation. The issue is also stated as one of practical economics.

This view of the problem is one that Nez Perces characterize as "greedy." The practicality of many, though not all, Nez Perce lives is that they need the fish and game resources. There are a number of reasons for this need. Among them are the following: (1) these resources provide some of the highest quality food the Nez Perces eat, (2) for active hunters and fishermen, it is an important route to social approval, (3) for some, it demonstrates their interdependent relationship with the natural world, (4) for some, the activities are a spiritual act of great importance, and (5) the pattern of hunting and fishing demonstrates their personal identity as distinct from the engulfing non-Indian population.

These practical considerations all support the Nez Perce "myth." If these important aspects of the "myth" are not accounted for in translating Nez Perce reality-models into English, then incorrect understanding of the Nez Perce "myth" will result with very real effects. For example, can "myth" be used by courts of law as evidence in deciding points of law? Or, in an example directly related to the problem in the paper, should Nez Perces remain exempt from the fish and game laws that the state of Idaho devises? Obviously, deeper constitutional questions are involved as well. Accuracy in such a context is obviously necessary.

It is clear that anthropology and folklore share not only data, but also the problem of translation. An ethnographer uses oral history and reports, as well as direct observation, in constructing images of an alien community. This technique yields egocentric views of events. Such views necessarily represent an individual's self-presentation.[16] Insofar as the representations reflect the agreed-upon goals and practice of life in a community, they are also ethnocentric and reflect "culture." In making such representations understandable, people rely on the ultimate standards of their society, which are practically phrased and exemplified in myth. Thus, anthropology and folklore have a great deal in common.

Yet another common aspect of anthropology and folklore is continued criticism by members of Native American communities. There are several bases for these criticisms. Many point out that the anthropologists come to the community for only three months, then return to their comfortable, well-paying academic posts, whence they issue pronouncements on the way things were. Still others point to the distortions that appear through poor interpretation, poor translation and, in some instances, sloppy scholarship. All these can be identified by members of the communities in which we work.[17]

In the end, I do not wish that anthropology, at least, should return to the breast-beating and self-condemnation of the 1960s.[18] Although this period generated much heat, little light was shed on the problem of translation or, for example, the adequate reflection of how individuals of other cultural traditions relate to their social and natural environment. Evidence for lack

of change in academia is found in continued critiques of anthropology and folklore by the people with whom we work. It also appears sporadically within anthropology from "non-Western" members.[19] Criticisms by Native Americans are valid. In particular, objections founded upon the lack of long-term involvement by nongroup members seem especially appropriate, even when criticisms of translated myths are made.

Correct myth translation is an urgent problem, for it affects the practical daily lives of both Native Americans and non-Indians. The problems of myth translation include the way that we understand what myths are. I have briefly analyzed a statement about reality made by a Nez Perce in English, showing that by understanding the statement, a clearer understanding of a myth is gained. Incidentally, I have reiterated some old and new ideas about myth. The first is that myths are reality-models or, better yet, constitute the human way of understanding themselves and the nature of the world. I have alluded to the political process in social groups that is concerned with settling upon which model will be accepted. Second, I have shown that myths conform with the practice of life. Third, I have addressed the ethical problems of myth translation and the responsibility of translators. Finally, we can see that there is no more game in the mountains because prairie chickens don't dance on the prairie anymore.

Notes

1. Mr. Samuel Watters and Mr. Cyrus Red-Elk spent many hours tutoring me on Nez Perce natural history. The Nez Perce Tribal Executive Committee graciously approved my study efforts. Financial support was provided by the Smithsonian Institution Program in Urgent Anthropology and the Ford Foundation Dissertation Fellowships in Ethnic Studies Program. The cooperation and support by these people and organizations made my work possible.

2. Paul Radin, *Primitive Man as Philosopher* (New York: Dover Publications, Inc., 1957).

3. Fredrik Barth, *Ethnic Groups and Boundaries: The Social Organization of Culture Difference* (London: George Allen and Union, 1969).

4. Mr. Red-Elk was *not* referring to what Euro-Americans call "prairie chicken" (*Tympanicus* spp.), but rather to sharp-tailed grouse (*Pediocetes phasianellus*). The Nez Perce language word for this bird is *gaxno*. Following Nez Perce usage, I will translate *gaxno* as "prairie chicken."

5. Interview with Samuel M. Watters in Lapwai, Idaho, 1971.

6. Deward E. Walker, Jr., "Nez Perce Sorcery," *Ethnology* 6 (1967): 66–96.

7. Verne F. Ray, "The Bluejay Character in the Plateau Spirit Dance," *American Anthropologist* 37 (1937): 593–601.

8. I describe these resources as "traditional" for lack of a better term. Traditional foods are more than symbolically important. Not only are they served on important social occasions, but they are preferred foods at other times as well, especially game and fish. For many family groups, these

resources are crucial to their economic survival. These are the reasons why myth is important today.

9. Thomas A. Leege, "Prescribed Burning for Elk in Northern Idaho," *Proceedings American Tall Timbers Fire Ecology Conference*, No. 8 (1968), 235–53.

10. Clifford Geertz, *The Interpretation of Cultures* (New York: Basic Books, 1973).

11. Ibid., p. 24.

12. Pierre Bourdieu, *Outline of a Theory of Practice*, trans. Richard Nice (New York: Cambridge University Press, 1977).

13. Mircea Eliade, *Myth and Reality*, trans. Willard R. Trask (New York: Harper & Row, 1963).

14. Francis L. K. Hsu, "The Cultural Problem of the Cultural Anthropologist," *American Anthropologist* 81 (1979): 517–22.

15. Ibid., pp. 524–28.

16. Erving Goffman, *The Presentation of Self in Everyday Life* (Garden City: Doubleday and Co., Inc., 1959).

17. For example, see Vine Deloria, Jr., *Custer Died for Your Sins* (New York: Macmillan Co., 1969).

18. For example, see Dell Hymes, ed., *Reinventing Anthropology* (New York: Random House, Inc., 1969).

19. Two examples are Maxwell Owusu, "Ethnography of Africa: The Usefulness of the Useless," *American Anthropologist* 80 (1978): 318–34. Francis L. K. Hsu, "The Cultural Problem of the Cultural Anthropologist," *American Anthropologist* 81 (1979): 517–22.

Folklife and Individual Style

Retention and Change in the Singing Tradition
of a Northern Idaho Family
POLLY STEWART

Len Henry: North Idaho Münchausen
JAN HAROLD BRUNVAND

A Contextual Survey of Selected Homestead Sites
in Washington County
LOUIE W. ATTEBERY

Retention and Change in the Singing Tradition of a Northern Idaho Family

POLLY STEWART

The principal object of this essay is an analysis of the singing tradition of an Idaho family. Secondarily but equally interesting is what Alan Dundes has called "metafolklore," the folklore about folklore. Stewart perceptively includes in her study not only the songs and the contexts in which they were sung, but also the metafolkloric comments made by the singers about both. She also includes a description of the process by which a folklorist can unintentionally modify a tradition. Two similar studies of folk singers and their repertoires are Henry Glassie, et al., Folksongs and Their Makers *(1971) and Roger Abrahams, editor,* A Singer and her Songs: Almeda Riddle *(1971).*

One of the song texts included here is "Rissity Rassity," which can be compared with other variants of "The Wife Wrapped in Wetherskin," (Child 277), in Bertrand Harris Bronson, The Traditional Tunes of the Child Ballads *(1959).*

Polly Stewart, who teaches folklore and literature at Salisbury (Maryland) State College, was born in Utah and schooled in Utah and Oregon. She has done folklife research and made presentations in Idaho, Utah, and the Delmarva Peninsula east of the Chesapeake Bay.

What do folklorists look for when they do field research? There is no law that mandates the criteria, but most of us would probably say something like the following: We want performance that can be documented with photographs and tape recordings. We want data that are suitable for comparison with data collected elsewhere to show that the texts are indeed in a folk tradition. We want a well-defined group within which the traditions are performed. We want evidence of continuity of tradition over time and space, along with artistic dynamism in performance. And we want the highest possible quality of performance. Many a folklorist's dream is to discover all these valued qualities within a single family.

Such discoveries do not occur often. But in 1979 I found myself in northern Idaho looking for folk artists to present at a teachers' conference in Sun Valley. As a virtual stranger to the area I had few leads, so one of my first stops was at the folklore archives of the University of Idaho in Moscow. There, among student reports of regional lore and history — of loggers, farmers, immigrants — was a 1961 collection of several dozen family songs. A large number of the items in this collection were readily identifiable as folk songs — "The State of Arkansas," "Whistle, Daughter, Whistle," "Wish I Was Single Again," "Little Brown Jug," "Old Dan Tucker," "I Bought Me a Cat," and others. If these songs had truly been orally transmitted, they were valuable indeed. The collection itself was interesting to look at, for its lyrics and musical notations were metic-ulously done by hand. Evidently all the pages had been prepared by the same person and numbered as though for a handmade book, then photocopied and submitted to the archives with additional information by the student, whose name was Helen Bundy. Several other Bundy names were given in this collection — Adell Showalter Bundy, Bryan B. Bundy, Iris Bundy Anderson, Wilson W. Bundy — and some of their addresses were practically next door, over in Nez Perce County. My interest heightened; surely this was worth following up. But the collection was eighteen years old. Could any members of this Bundy family still be living? Would any of them still be in Nez Perce? They could and they would, as I discovered by opening up the Lewiston telephone directory and looking under B.

So began a most friendly and rewarding association with the Bundy family. It was my pleasure to present Iris Bundy Anderson and her daughter, Jeannine Anderson Lemm, at the Sun Valley conference that summer, and to rerecord the family's folk song repertoire for another project two years later, this time including the singing of Bryan Bundy. Recently Bryan has sent me a tape of his own making. I have also briefly met Wilson Bundy, compiler of the archived songbook, who has taught elementary school music in Alaska and Washington and has used the songbook in his work; Helen Bundy is his wife. The mother of Bryan and Iris and Wilson was Adell Showalter Bundy, and she was the source of all but one of the folk songs presented in this paper.

BEARERS OF THE BUNDY FAMILY SINGING TRADITION

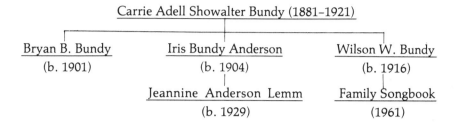

Carrie Adell Showalter Bundy (1881–1921)

Bryan B. Bundy (b. 1901)   Iris Bundy Anderson (b. 1904)   Wilson W. Bundy (b. 1916)

Jeannine Anderson Lemm (b. 1929)   Family Songbook (1961)

The songs in the Showalter legacy are important, a valuable body of data, because they demonstrate the viability of a folk song tradition not merely over geographical distance but also over generations within a single family. However, no intrinsic value is guaranteed a folk song text by itself. This is a point worth stressing: the words of a song are only that — words. Sweet words they may be, rare words, words to warm the dusty heart of the comparativist; but unless we consider who sings them, and when, and to whom, and why, and what artistic merit is accorded them by singer and audience alike, we are getting nowhere beyond pedantry. Most folklorists understand they cannot get along without texts, but texts are only the beginning of a greater study whose goal it is to appreciate the text as it lives in performance and in the hearts of those who perform it. For that reason, while this paper will certainly provide song texts, indicate where variations occur among family members, and furnish cross-references in other published sources, the focus of interest will be on matters that go well beyond the texts themselves.

It would be improper to leave the impression that folk songs were the only songs the Bundy family had Mrs. Bundy was a woman of broad musical tastes, in whose home were phonograph recordings of Nellie Melba, John McCormack, Enrico Caruso, Jascha Heifetz, selections from *The Mikado*. She also sang popular songs of her day and she sang in a church choir. That some of the songs in her repertoire are folk songs must not blind us to the wider range of her musical interests. The same may be said of her descendants: Bryan and Iris learned both popular and semi-classical songs (such as ''Trees'') from their mother, and their friends in the neighborhood shared many songs with them during their growing-up years in the first quarter of the century. As a young man, Bryan learned a number of comic and popular songs while away at college and at military camp; he has also studied music formally, and his wife Ethel is an accomplished musician who has taught him a great deal about music. Iris's daughter Jeannine learned many songs at home, including hymns and semiclassical pieces, but much of her popular song and folk song repertoire and all of her country-western repertoire came only after her marriage and departure from her parents' home. And

Wilson, the music teacher, has been greatly interested in the American urban folk song revival that spanned the three decades starting in the 1940s; his repertoire reflects that interest, for in his book he included, besides the family folk songs, a number of urban revival folk songs — ''The Cat Came Back,'' ''A Bonnie Wee Lassie,'' and others. (In the spirit of folk song study, Wilson omitted from the book those family songs he could tell were popular, not folk.) To my knowledge, all members of the family have participated in church singing.

It should be clear, then, that this gifted and inquiring family is neither narrow nor uninformed in its musical tastes. Even so, for purposes of the discussion at hand I intend to focus almost wholly upon those songs that were introduced into the family by Adell Showalter Bundy, and further to limit most of the discussion to the handful of songs common to the current repertoires of Bryan, Iris and Jeannine — the three family members I have had the privilege of documenting.[1]

Carrie Adell (Dell) Showalter Bundy was about ten years old when her family migrated to Moscow, Idaho, from Cherry Creek, Kansas. The family brought with it a tradition of folk singing that was shared by other people in the Central Plains region.[2] In January 1898 Dell married William H. Bundy, a rancher, and they moved from Moscow to Nez Perce County, settling near Lapwai. Dell had just turned eighteen. In the following quarter-century she worked hard to make a pioneer ranch home. She bore seven children, five of whom lived. And she sang a great deal. Her son Wilson speculated that in those days Dell may have suffered from loneliness — ''My mother was pretty well locked at home'' — and that this is why ''many of these songs are on the sad side.''[3] On the other hand, Dell had a streak of jollity and a streak of spunk. Wilson and Iris have reminisced about the April Fool's pranks their mother used to pull, and Iris has more than once remarked fondly that her mother ''was just so full of the dickens.''

Will Bundy, his children report, was not musical in the slightest. Both Bryan and Wilson have said that their father ''couldn't carry a tune in a bucket,'' and Wilson amplified: ''We always said he was a half a tone low and a half a note slow.'' Despite his lack of musical aptitude, Will loved music, furnishing the Victrola on which the family's classical phonograph records were

played. He was also a vigorous man who applied his
education, civic pride, and penchant for hard work to
the development and betterment of his community.
Besides doing the difficult job of running a pioneer
ranch, he worked toward establishing a school district
and a church, and he participated with his wife in many
community activities. They complemented each other
as a couple; while Dell was vivacious and had "a
twinkle in her eye" (as Iris says), Will was sobersided,
patriarchal. Iris put it this way: "Mother brought the
fun into our lives; he brought the authority." Though
he admired his wife's singing ability, he might not
always have approved of the content of her songs.
There may well have been something of that "twinkle
in her eye" when Dell sang the two following songs,
both of them are about men named Bill. When Iris sings
these songs today, she too has a bit of a twinkle in her
eye.

BEAUTIFUL BILL

Beautiful Bill was a beautiful beau,
Beautiful Bill who bothered me so.
Sweetest of Williams, adorable Bill,
Beautiful, beautiful, beautiful Bill.

'Twas at a ball I met my Bill,
He made the neatest bow.
He squeezed my hand in a quadrille
And we danced on anyhow.

Beautiful Bill was a beautiful beau,
Beautiful Bill who bothered me so.
Sweetest of Williams, adorable Bill,
Beautiful, beautiful, beautiful Bill.[4]

Though only the one verse and the chorus remain in
either Iris's or Bryan's memory, Iris says that the rest of
the song tells how Bill turns out to be married to someone else; this suggests that their mother may have sung
it all the way through at an earlier time. Iris almost
always follows "Beautiful Bill" with this one:

COMMON BILL

I will tell you of a fellow, of a fellow I have seen
Who is neither ripe nor mellow, but he's altogether green.
His name it is not charming, for it's only common Bill
Yet he urges me to wed him, but I hardly think I will.

Last night he came to see me and he made so long a stay
I began to think that blockhead never meant to go away.
At first I learned to hate him and I know I hate him still
Yet he urges me to wed him, but I hardly think I will.

I should, I should not choose him, but the very deuce is in
    it:
He says if I don't wed him that he cannot live a minute.
And you know the blessed Bible plainly says, Thou shalt
    not kill
So I've thought the matter over and I think I'll marry Bill.[5]

These two songs are active in Bryan's repertoire, but he
does not sing them in tandem as Iris does; that is, in
Iris's mind they go together, but in Bryan's they do not.
Why would this be? Possibly for Iris the two songs

serve an artistic need that Bryan does not have. Folklorist Charles Perdue has observed that folklore is "a
way of talking about things without talking about
things."[6] What he means is that people are often able to
express their feelings through the structured community
artistic medium called folklore even when they do not
have the internal resources to do so. Dell and Iris
served successively as homemakers under Will's sometimes stern authority. The songs may have given both
of them a way of registering veiled protest—poking fun
by means of the two fictive Bills, each so charmingly
and ironically different from the real-life Will.

Family stories have grown up around the pious Will
Bundy and his distress over the lyrics of some of his
wife's songs. Both Bryan and Iris have reminisced about
certain of the words in "Old Dan Tucker." In the
Bundy version the second verse goes, "Old Dan
Tucker, he got drunk / He fell in the fire and he kicked
up a chunk / A red-hot coal got in his shoe / And you
bet a nickel [cookie] that his shirt-tail flew." Bryan
says, "Kind of an interesting thing about that shirt-tail.
For some reason our father took exception to it. . . .
And so when he was around, we sang it, 'And you bet a
cookie that the ashes flew'." Iris says, "My dad thought
that wasn't very dignified, him getting drunk and his
shirt-tail flying [laughter]." But Dell was not always so
compliant to her husband's wishes. I once asked Iris if
her father approved of "Wish I Was Single Again"—a
song which, though not ribald, has some raucous lines
in it—and she replied, "Oh, he didn't, he was awful
strait-laced. . . . But anyway, she'd have gone on and
just sang it, and he'd have to put up with it [laughter]."
And in "The State of Arkansas," there is a verse in
which the speaker says that on the day he left Arkansas, "I staggered into a saloon and called for whiskey
raw." Will didn't like that line. Iris says, "He didn't
want her to put that line in, and she said, 'Well how in
the world would I sing the song and not put *that* in?'
[laughter]."

Tragically, Dell died of cancer in 1921 at the age of
forty-one. Bryan, the eldest child, was by that time an
adult and on his own. Iris, the next, was only seventeen, yet it fell upon her to help her father bring up the
three smaller siblings, the youngest of whom was only
two. Taking on her role as a substitute mother, Iris
sang to the younger children in the same way Dell had
done. This included singing during household chores
and singing to lull the children to sleep. Two songs in
particular served as lullabies. Although neither has
words that seem especially suitable for a lullaby, the
first has indeed served as a lullaby in the larger folk
singing tradition, outside the Bundy family. It is known
generally as "Rocking the Little Baby to Sleep."

HI LO, BYE LO

I have a little wife, she is just twenty-five,
Just ten years younger than I.
She's full of enjoyment, likes plenty of fun,
But she likes to go out on the sly.

Cho: O it's hi lo, bye lo, rockabye baby
Toss up that baby ever so high
O it's hi lo, bye lo, rockabye baby
Mama will come by and by.

One night as I was rocking this baby to sleep
I chanced for to glance on the street.
There before my eyes to my greatest surprise
Was my wife with a soldier six feet. [7]

Cho:

That the song is fragmentary in the Bundy tradition does not seem to have bothered the young children in the least, nor does the nature of the words. All the present-day singers have commented on these words. Bryan said, "Why they'd put this kind of a story in a baby's lullaby beats me," and on another occasion Jeannine observed, "That sure doesn't make good listening, does it." However, as Iris remarked, "That's [a] tear-jerker. But the kids didn't seem to see it that way." Sadly, Iris also recalled that when she sang it to her younger siblings, they would cry at the line, "Mama will come by and by," knowing that their own mother would not be coming back.

The other song that served as a Bundy lullaby is found in other traditions not as a song but as a children's dialogue game, with the lines spoken instead of sung. [8] This is one song that Bryan has never sung for me, either during the sessions I have recorded or during the one he recorded himself. Yet both Iris and Jeannine almost always sing it together with "Hi Lo, Bye Lo." I was puzzled by this and thought that Bryan's mother might not have known the song when he was a child of lullaby age, or that Bryan had dropped it from his repertoire for artistic or personal reasons. The answer to the puzzle came from Iris: "I have been unable to remember who taught me 'Babylon.' It wasn't Mother." But the song, however it came into Iris's repertoire, has had such a profound effect on the children she sang it to, including her younger siblings and her children, grandchildren and great-grandchildren, that it is worth presenting here even though Dell herself did not sing it.

HOW MANY MILES TO BABYLON

How many miles to Babylon?
Four score and ten.
Can you get there by candlelight?
Yes, and back again.

Open the door and let me through.
Toll first you pay.   [Iris sings "Told"]
I have no gold, what shall I do?
Turn and go away.

The content, again, does not seem lullaby material, but as Iris said, "That's the one the babies liked too. And I sang it to Jeannine when she was little and she never forgot it." Asked if the song seemed sad to her, she replied obliquely: "Well, they all just loved it—they'd go to sleep." My own feeling is that these lullabies were among the songs that Wilson was thinking of when he

said that some of his mother's songs were "on the sad side." I have seen Iris get tears in her eyes while singing these lullabies. Maybe it's that way for her too.

Today, members of the Bundy family make use of the songs in different ways. Iris says that her youngest brother Gordon and his wife Myrtle, who enjoy square dancing, have presented comic dramatizations of "Rissity Rassity" at square-dance conventions "every place from Denver to Seattle." As mentioned above, Wilson uses the songs in his teaching. When Jeannine's children were young, she involved them in singing the songs at numerous church and school performances. For years she thought her now-adult children were not interested in the songs, but has learned that this is not so; she recently wrote, "It seems they all know them." Jeannine still sings them to her grandchildren and nieces and nephews. I sat in her kitchen on a summer day in 1979 and listened to her and her ten-year-old grand-daughter Tracie sing song after song. The degree of exposure each family member has had to the songs does seem to affect whether the tradition gets passed on. Iris mentioned once that her daughter Sandy "never really taught her girls the old songs; Sandy doesn't know as many. I guess I was getting so much to do by the time I got her." My guess is that while a family member like Sandy probably *knows* many of the songs, she would defer to another member, such as her older sister Jeannine, if asked to perform them.

Public performance has always played a role in the family's singing tradition, but the greater application has been private, at home among family members. Whatever the audience, each performer makes artistic decisions as to how the songs will be sung. If the singing tradition is to continue, it must be made aesthetically worthwhile to its bearers. How this is done will depend on the tastes and aesthetic needs of each person. Bryan, Iris, and Jeannine have gone their separate ways in this respect. Of all of them, Iris's manner of performance remains closest to the Anglo-American traditional style; it is unaccompanied and understated, and she does not use eye contact. Bryan, who also sings unaccompanied, performs with more dynamics than Iris, as though he were treating the material more as art song than as folk song. Jeannine, whose favorite kind of music is country-western, sings in the country-western style. She has a contralto voice that is perfect for country singing—it is throaty and capable of glides and glottal shocks. She learned how to play the guitar after she got married; to my knowledge she never sings without guitar accompaniment, even though she learned the family songs unaccompanied from her mother. Jeannine has therefore made an important change in the performance style of the family songs, without which she might not be interested in singing them at all.

We can learn much about individual taste in performance by seeing how the singers treat the five family songs that are common in their repertoires. These are "In Kansas," "The State of Arkansas," "Rissity

Rassity," "The Hunter / The Cuckoo Song," and "A Game of Cards."

In my first perusal of Wilson's songbook in the archives, I was rather surprised to find the comic song which is here called "In Kansas." This song is in an old tradition which denigrates people from a particular geographical region by describing their habits and habitat in ironic terms.[9] "In Kansas" is a spoof of Kansans, yet Dell, a Kansan, passed it along to her children and apparently sang it with amusement, if her descendants' way of singing it is any indication.

IN KANSAS

> Oh, they chew tobacco thin in Kansas
> They chew tobacco thin in Kansas
> They chew tobacco thin
> And the juice runs down their chin
> And they lick it up again in Kansas.
>
> Oh, we eat a cherry pie in Kansas
> We eat a cherry pie in Kansas
> We eat a cherry pie
> Every bite you get a fly
> Makes you sick enough to die in Kansas.

In the first verse, when it comes to "lick it up again," Iris lolls her head and tongue, lingering on the "l" sound, her eyes twinkling all the while. Bryan does the same when he sings it. The second verse gives equal pleasure; again, here is a song that makes fun of Kansans, yet Kansas was Dell's home state.

Wilson's book had just the two verses above, but I knew there were other verses in the larger tradition. Unsure whether any might have been omitted from the book, at my first meeting with the Bundys I asked if they had any verses besides the two. I was thinking specifically of one that goes in a similar song, "Over There":

> Oh potatoes they grow small over there
> Oh potatoes they grow small over there
> Oh potatoes they grow small
> 'Cause they plants them in the fall
> Then they eat them tops and all over
>   there.[10]

I sang this verse to them on the chance that it might remind them of one they knew. They had not known of it before, but they liked the verse and picked it up immediately, amid a discussion of its merits. Bryan's wife Ethel said she had heard that one cannot eat potato tops without being poisoned. Then, too, there was the futility of planting potatoes out of season. Everyone could see that this new verse was appropriate to the tone and content of the other two verses. When I came back to rerecord the family two years later, I found that all the singers—Bryan, Iris, Jeannine—had incorporated the new verse, having rearranged the words to fit the format of their song:

> Oh, they grow potatoes small in Kansas
> They grow potatoes small in Kansas
> They grow potatoes small
> 'Cause they plant them in the fall
> Then they eat them tops and all in Kansas.

This verse was placed between the other two, so the succession was tobacco, potatoes, cherry pie. In my effort to discover the extent of the family's singing tradition I had inadvertently modified the tradition.

In addition, this apparently minor augmentation of the words tapped a veritable reservoir of possibilities for creating new verses. When I recorded Bryan on the second trip he sang the three verses, and added a new one of his own composition just before the "cherry pie" verse:

> They grow corn tall in Kansas
> They grow corn tall in Kansas
> They grow corn tall
> Have to pick it from a wall
> Oh, they grow corn tall in Kansas.

Two days later when I visited Jeannine, she sang me three new verses of her own. She had composed them quite independently of Bryan:

> Bugs are mighty big in Kansas
> Bugs are mighty big in Kansas
> Bugs are mighty big
> So you feed them to your pig
> And you watch them dance a jig in Kansas.
>
> Men are mighty fine in Kansas
> Men are mighty fine in Kansas
> Men are mighty fine
> So stay away from mine
> So stay away from mine in Kansas.
>
> Land is awful flat in Kansas
> Land is awful flat in Kansas
> Land is awful flat
> And I guess it's tit for tat
> I'm staying where I'm at in Kansas.

Two observations about this experience are warranted. One is happy and has to do with serendipity: "In Kansas" was a closed artistic entity until an outsider—for reasons that became irrelevant—opened it up by the introduction of new material, which occasioned a remarkable creative output by the bearers of the tradition. The other observation is more serious. We must take this story as an illustration of the flexibility—under other conditions we would say fragility—of folk traditions. The speed with which the Bundys picked up material from outside their immediate tradition, transformed it, and amplified it is little short of astonishing. In the present case the results were pleasing, but I must point out that change induced by outsiders is not necessarily always beneficial. I consider it lucky that I did not do damage. All outsiders run this risk when they work in traditional communities.

Another song that Dell brought with her from Kansas is one that enjoyed a wide popularity in the last quarter of the nineteenth century, particularly in the Ozarks and Great Plains. Like "In Kansas," this is a comic song that disparages a certain region of the country. In the Bundy family it is called "The Arkansas Traveler," but to avoid confusion with another song of that title I will use the title by which it is generally known—"The State of Arkansas."

It was eighteen hundred and seventy-six in the merry month
    of June
When I landed in Van Buren on a sultry afternoon
Up walked a living skeleton with a long and lantern jaw
And invited me down to his hotel in the State of Arkansas.

I followed up that big old bloke unto his dwelling place
Where poverty was written on his melancholy face
His hair it hung in rattails o'er his long and lantern jaw
He was the photograph of all the chaps in the State of
    Arkansas.

I told him to call me early to meet the morning train
Says he to me, You'd better stay; I have some land to drain
I'll give you fifty cents a rod, your board and washing all
You'll find yourself a different man when you leave Arkansas.

I stayed a month with this old bloke, Jess Harold was his
    name
He was six feet seven in his socks and slim as any crane
He fed me on corn dodger and his meat I couldn't chaw
Said he, You'd better stay awhile in the State of Arkansas.

He fed me on corn dodger as hard as any rock
Till my teeth began to loosen and my knees began to knock
I got so thin on sassafras I could hide behind a straw
You bet I was a different man when I left Arkansas.

I remember the day I left there, I dread the memory still
I shook the boots clean off my feet with a bloody blasted chill
I staggered into a saloon and called for whiskey raw
Indeed I was a different man when I left Arkansas.

Farewell to those swamp angels, their canebrakes and their
    chills
Farewell likewise to sassafras and those corn dodger pills
If ever I see this land again I'll give to you my paw
For it'll be through a telescope when I see Arkansas.[11]

This song is in a minor key, and the melody and tempo can only be described as lugubrious. The end of the third line in each stanza plunges sepulchrally. The vocal range is wider than usual for a folk song—an octave plus three. These factors when added together fairly cry for a histrionic performance. The Bundys' performance is in keeping with that of others who sing the song traditionally; the mock melancholy is oddly both appropriate and ironic with respect to the words.

Another favorite of the family is one they call "Rissity Rassity."[12] It too is a comic song, but it has a bite—it instructs by horrible example. Other songs in this vein are the British ballads known as "The Farmer's Curst Wife" and "The Wife Wrapt in Wether's Skin."[13] In all of them a woman is shown doing things that are inappropriate for her to do; the underlying message for girls and women in the audience is to take heed and not act like the woman in the song.

RISSITY RASSITY

I married my wife in the month of June
    Rissity rassity now now now
I took her home by the light of the moon.
    Rissity rassity hage and daffity
    Willity wallity rustic in quality
    Naggity naggity now now now

She combed her hair just once a year
And every time it brought a tear.

She swept the floor just twice a year
She said that brooms were very dear.

She churned the butter in her dad's old boot
And for a dasher she used her foot.

The butter turned out all grizzaly gray
The cheese took legs and ran away.

The saddle and bridle hang up on the shelf
If you want any more song, go sing it yourself.

As I mentioned earlier, Jeannine's general style of performing differs greatly from that of Bryan or Iris. "Rissity Rassity" provides a good illustration of the difference. The elder singers perform it in a moderate 6/8 tempo that remains the same throughout the song, excepting necessary pauses for breath in the long part of the refrain. Jeannine, on the other hand, sings the two lines of the verse and the first line of the refrain rubato, almost contemplatively, with a range of vocal and emotional dynamics appropriate to the words. For instance, "She combed her hair just once a year / And every time it brought a tear" is often followed by mock sobbing. Then in the long part of the refrain Jeannine switches to a distinct and percussive 4/4 beat, ending with delayed timing on the last "now now now." In the final verse, Jeannine speaks rather than sings the line, "If you want any more song, go sing it yourself." The difference in effect between these two approaches to performance is so remarkable that when I presented Jeannine and Iris at the Sun Valley conference I asked them to alternate their versions of the song.

It is worth repeating that a singing tradition will stay alive only so long as the bearers of it are allowed to make performance choices that meet their own aesthetic needs. Jeannine says that her attitude toward music and her approach to musical performance owe a great deal to her father's—the Anderson—side of her family. Her talented paternal grandfather and aunts all played wholly by ear, and she also vividly remembers her father Andy singing Anderson songs to her when she was a child. To a large extent, then, Jeannine's aesthetics and her performance style have developed in a way not shared by relatives on the Bundy side of the family, which explains in part their artistic differences. Moreover, Jeannine has told me that she really doesn't care for the sameness of presentation that characterizes traditional American singing; the many verses, the same tune repeated over and over, are just not appealing to her—frankly, she finds such music boring, and she assumed her young household audience would find it boring too. So she jazzes things up. If she did not feel comfortable doing this she would probably quit singing the songs.

The next song was popular in Kansas, Nebraska, and Missouri in the last quarter of the nineteenth century; according to Louise Pound, it was composed and marketed as sheet music in the Northeast some fifty years earlier, then migrated west. Pound gives a version of the song in her 1915 collection of Nebraska folk songs.

THE HUNTER (THE CUCKOO SONG)

A little boy went to hunt one day
He carried his arrow and bow
For guns are dangerous things for play
In the hands of little children, you know.
     A little bird sat in a cherry tree
     And whistled and sang, You can't shoot me

Cho: Cuckoo, cuckoo, cuckoo, cuckoo, cuckoo

Just wait, said the boy, 'til I get near enough
And see if I don't shoot you through.
Do you think, said the bird, I'd be silly enough
To sit here and be shot at by you?
     Indeed, you're very kind, sir
     But an arrow is not in my mind, sir

The little boy raised his bow to his eye
And aimed it quite well for a while
The little bird laughed and away she did fly
Saying, A miss is as good as a mile.
     The little boy threw down his arrow and cried
     The little bird laughed 'til she nearly died

Take warning, young man, before you aim,
To court a young lady so sly.
Before letting her know what you are about
Away she may surely fly.
     She'll leave you alone with a broken heart
     Not letting you know what has caused her to part[14]

When Jeannine entertains youngsters at home, she often personalizes this song for them by projecting them into the song; she will sing, "Oh Shaney went out to hunt one day," and so forth. Jeannine is probably the most creative user of the family song tradition, but then she does similar things with popular and country songs—to the tune of the well-known popular song of the 1930s, "Oh, Johnny, Oh," she will sing, "Oh, Toni, oh, Toni, how you can love"—again, for the amusement of the little ones.

The last of the songs in this presentation is known in the family as "A Game of Cards." Playing-cards have been important in the image-stock of folk poets for centuries, and the figure shows up everywhere from Middle English poems to country-western songs. Here the four suits serve to represent what the poet saw as important parts of human experience—fortune, love, war, death.

A GAME OF CARDS

This life is but a game of cards which each one has to learn
Each shuffles, cuts and deals the pack, and each a trump doth turn.

When diamonds chance to crown the pack, 'tis then men stake their gold
Large sums have oft been won and lost by gamblers young and old.

When hearts are trump we play for love, and pleasure rules the hour
Two hearts have ofttimes been made one while in a rosy bower.

When clubs are trump, look out for war, on ocean and on land
For many a bloody deed's been done while the club was in the hand.

And then at last is he turned up by the busy hand of time
'Tis he who endeth every age in every land and clime.

For no matter how much a man may win, nor how much a man may save
We find the spade turns up at last to dig each gambler's grave.[15]

Both Bryan and Jeannine capitalize on the obvious dramatic possibilities of this song, presenting each suit in some way that is appropriate to the content. This is especially clear in the "clubs" verse. There Bryan sings with much greater force, and Jeannine during that verse plays her guitar in a slightly menacing way as though to suggest war drums. Iris, by contrast, sings it in the understated way that characterizes all her singing, but this does not mean she is not emotionally involved in the song. Once during a recording session she wept at the "spades" verse. Later in the same session, she remarked that as you get older "you think back on the songs" and understand them in a way you couldn't before.

Because of Adell Showalter Bundy's untimely death, her three youngest children—Wilson among them—learned most of the family songs from Iris. And because Bryan had already left home and was unlikely

Figure 1.   Bryan B. Bundy and his sister, Iris Bundy Anderson, laughing (they have just discovered that they sing their family songs differently, even though they both learned them from their mother).

to be present when Iris sang to the children, Wilson's later compilation of the songs reflects Iris's repertoire, not Bryan's. Bryan is only three years older than Iris, but three years among children constitute a large gap. Too, Bryan first heard his mother's songs at an earlier stage in her artistic development; they would be impressed in his memory that way, regardless of changes she may have made later on. As years went by, Bryan's own versions would also have evolved. It is therefore not surprising that a number of the songs in Wilson's book differ, sometimes quite noticeably, from the way Bryan remembers them.

Wilson's book complicates matters even with regard to Iris. Though she collaborated with Wilson on it, I have seen Iris falter in her singing because she was confronted with words in Wilson's book that differed from those in her own memory. In the taping of one song, with Wilson's text in front of her, she made a false start and later stopped in the middle, saying, "I don't think that's right." It could be that this was not one of the songs on which she collaborated with Wilson back in the early 1960s, but it is equally possible that Iris's private version of it has evolved in the intervening years.

All of this invites comment about the nature of folk-song texts, and about the role Wilson's texts play in the Bundy family singing tradition. Everyone acquainted

with folklore is aware that oral texts exist in variation, that we need not think of an "original" or "correct" version. Even if a song's authorship can be identified, such information is far less important to a folklorist than the changes that the author's original text may have undergone in oral circulation. Similarly, questions of correctness or authenticity are not interesting to most folklorists, except possibly in the legal sphere. There were some raised eyebrows, for example, when members of professional folksinging groups such as The Kingston Trio, Peter, Paul and Mary, and The New Christy Minstrels modified folk songs and copyrighted them under their own names, thereby earning large amounts of money for themselves. Earlier, the Appalachian folksinger John Jacob Niles had copyrighted traditional songs that he had reworked, and he used to sue other singers who tried to perform his material commercially. Before that there was a famous court battle over copyright ownership of "The Wreck of the Old 97," a battle that did not end until a folklorist showed that the song had existed orally prior to the publication date of the disputed text. But these text-fixing attempts are aberrations. We normally anticipate and welcome folk song text variation and assume that it occurs because of artistic changes wrought by individual traditional performers.

However, most traditional singers legitimately carry

in their minds versions of their own that they regard as correct. When they sing a certain song, they will try to perform that version faithfully and will develop a commitment to it even though it may evolve considerably over time. Folklorist Barre Toelken says he once collected versions of a particular folk song from two elderly Ozark singers; they were sisters and had learned the song from their father when they were children. The two versions were decidedly different in mode, tune, tempo, and words, yet each sister stoutly defended her version as the exact one their father had taught them.[16] Within the Bundy family the textual differences are less glaring, but the same principle applies—each bearer of this family's singing tradition retains a preferred version of each song, yet it is not difficult to imagine that changes can have occurred over the years, both before and after Wilson gathered the songs in his book.

A book of folk songs is an odd thing. While it preserves the songs in black and white, thereby saving them from the threat of oblivion, it simultaneously fixes them in a way that is not represented in actual oral performance within a living community. A book is concrete, solid, a document that can be referred to— but by this very attribute it defies the tradition out of which it comes. When Wilson put his book together, he gave copies to members of the family: official, unchanging, it was a monument to the state of the family art as of 1961. In 1979, when I first recorded the family, it became clear almost at once that Bryan and Iris had difficulty taping the songs. So loyal were they to Wilson's book that, unless I specifically asked them not to,

they almost always referred to it while singing. Yet when they did so they were torn between their own versions and the competing authority of the written word. The result was hesitation, on-the-spot editing, artistic gear-shifting. Recording sessions were therefore often marked by discomfort on everyone's part. I suspect that by being there at all I was setting up an area of artistic conflict within the family that may never have been openly identified before.

Even in the absence of the book, the differences that had evolved were apparent. I once asked Bryan and Iris to sing "Hi Lo, Bye Lo" together on tape. They found they were in agreement about the tune in the first and third lines, but not in the second and fourth. After several attempts at reconciling the tune, there was nothing to do but accept the differences and burst out laughing.

It need not seem curious that a family with a common body of folk songs could develop artistic differences like these. Though kin, the Bundys are individuals whose aesthetic lives are independent of each other and have been so for some time. They do not, as I early discovered, make a habit of singing together; I believe the general session I set up in 1979 marked the first time in years—perhaps ever—that Bryan, Iris, and Jeannine had assembled for the purpose of singing the family songs. For this reason I have refrained from referring to them as a singing family. They are, rather, a family with a singing tradition. Each bearer of that tradition has used its materials in ways that suit his or her particular aesthetic.

Notes

1. Though I met Wilson once, briefly, at Iris's home while he was visiting from Alaska, I did not have an opportunity to document his repertoire. The other two siblings are Gordon G. Bundy (b. 1917) and Doris Dell Bundy (b. 1919). I did not meet either of them, but Bryan tells me that Gordon and his wife Myrtle were instrumental in assembling the family songbook.

2. For discussions of the Central Plains folk song tradition, see Louise Pound, *Folk-Songs of Nebraska and the Central West: A Syllabus* (Lincoln: Nebraska Academy of Sciences, 1915); and Samuel J. Sackett and William E. Koch, *Kansas Folklore* (Lincoln: University of Nebraska Press, 1961).

3. All quotations by family members are drawn from interview tapes made in 1979 and 1981, and from letters sent to me in 1982. Iris and Bryan have vigorously corrected Wilson's perception that their mother was "locked at home"; they stress that Dell was very outgoing and that both she and her husband were leaders in the community.

4. The song texts in this article are drawn from the 1979 and 1981 taping sessions. Because folk songs will vary slightly from one performance to another, the texts presented here are not fixed; each represents just one performance. For two other versions of "Beautiful Bill," see Vance Randolph, ed., *Ozark Folksongs*, 4 vols., rev. ed. (Columbia and London: University of Missouri Press, 1980), 3:81.

5. "Common Bill." See Emelyn Elizabeth Gardner and Geraldine Jencks Chickering, eds., *Ballads and Songs of Southern Michigan* (Hatboro, Pa.: Folklore Associates, 1967), pp. 430-31; John A. Lomax and Alan Lomax, eds., *American Ballads and Songs* (New York: Macmillan, 1934), pp. 325-26; and Louise Pound, ed., *American Ballads and Songs* (New York: Charles Scribner's Sons, 1922), pp. 214-15, 255.

6. Professor Perdue made this remark informally in 1982 at a meeting of the Middle Atlantic Folklife Association, but the idea behind it is a standard principle of folklore study. See, for example, William R. Bascom, "Four Functions of Folklore," *Journal of American Folklore*, 67 (1954), 333-49; rpt. in *The Study of Folklore*, ed. Alan Dundes (Englewood Cliffs, N.J.: Prentice-Hall, 1965), pp. 279-98.

7. "Hi Lo, Bye Lo." See Randolph, 3:117-19, and Lester A. Hubbard, ed., *Ballads and Songs from Utah* (Salt Lake City: University of Utah Press, 1961), pp. 232-33.

8. Paul G. Brewster cites numerous versions of the game in *The Frank C. Brown Collection of North Carolina Folklore*, Vol. 1 (Durham, N.C.: Duke University Press, 1952), 74-78; rpt. as *Children's Games and Rhymes* (New York: Arno Press, 1976); and in his *American Nonsinging Games* (Norman: University of Oklahoma Press, 1953), pp. 52-53.

9. "In Kansas." See Randolph, 3:17-19.

10. As a child I learned "Over There" from the popular *Fireside Book of Favorite American Songs*, ed. Margaret Bradford Boni (New York: Simon & Schuster, 1952), p. 293. According to Sigmund Spaeth, "Over There" was first published as sheet music in New York City in 1844 (*Read 'Em and Weep*, 1945, pp. 30–31).

11. "The State of Arkansas" is so widely represented in the American folksinging tradition that Malcolm G. Laws, Jr. has assigned it a standard number (H 1) in his reference work, *Native American Balladry*, rev. ed. (Philadelphia: American Folklore Society, 1964), p. 230. In his discussion of the song, Laws cites versions collected in West Virginia, Indiana, Missouri, North Carolina, and elsewhere.

12. Under the title "Risselty, Rosselty, Now, Now, Now," this song may be found in Randolph, 3:190–91. See also Louise Pound, *American Ballads and Songs*, pp. 236–37 and 257; and Sackett and Koch, *Kansas Folklore*, pp. 168–69.

13. These two songs are Nos. 278 and 277 in Francis James Child's collection, *The English and Scottish Popular Ballads*, 5. vols. (1898); rpt. New York: Cooper Square Publishers, Inc., 1965, 5:104–8.

14. Louise Pound, *Folk-Song of Nebraska*, p. 72.

15. "A Game of Cards." A search of standard folk song reference works and of regional folk song collections reveals no parallel to this text. However, a folk tradition of expounding religious and philosophical ideas by means of the "deck of cards" metaphor is well documented. See, for instance, D. K. Wilgus and Bruce A. Rosenberg, "A Modern Medieval Story: 'The Soldier's Deck of Cards'," in *Medieval Literature and Folklore Studies: Essays in Honor of Francis Lee Utley*, ed. Jerome Mandel and Bruce A. Rosenberg (New Brunswick, N.J.: Rutgers University Press, 1970), pp. 291–303.

16. Professor Toelken tells this story in his folklore classes, then demonstrates the two versions, which anyone can tell are markedly different. In his textbook, *The Dynamics of Folklore* (Boston: Houghton Mifflin, 1979) he alludes to the story as follows: "When a singer says she is singing a ballad exactly as her father sang it, she may be referring to a fidelity to plot and symbol, not to an exact replication of a memorized text" (p. 35).

Bibliography

Bascom, William R. "Four Functions of Folklore." *Journal of American Folklore* 67 (1954) 333–49; rpt. in *The Study of Folklore*, ed. Alan Dundes. Englewood Cliffs, N.J.: Prentice-Hall, Inc., 1965, pp. 279–98.

Boni, Margaret Bradford, ed. *The Fireside Book of Favorite American Songs*. New York: Simon & Schuster, 1952.

Brewster, Paul G., ed. *American Nonsinging Games*. Norman: University of Oklahoma Press, 1953.

_____. *The Frank C. Brown Collection of North Carolina Folklore*, Vol. 1. Durham, N. C.: Duke University Press, 1952. Rpt. as *Children's Games and Rhymes*. New York: Arno Press, 1976.

Child, Francis James, ed. *The English and Scottish Popular Ballads*. 5 vols. (1898). Rpt. New York: Cooper Square Publishers, 1965.

Gardner, Emelyn Elizabeth, and Chickering, Geraldine Jencks, eds. *Ballads and Songs of Southern Michigan*. Hatboro, Pa.: Folklore Associates, 1967.

Hubbard, Lester A., ed. *Ballads and Songs from Utah*. Salt Lake City: University of Utah Press, 1961.

Laws, Malcolm G., Jr. *Native American Balladry*. Rev. ed. Philadelphia, Pa.: American Folklore Society, 1964.

Lomax, John A., and Lomax, Alan, eds. *American Ballads and Songs*. New York: Macmillan & Co., 1934.

Pound, Louise, ed. *American Ballads and Songs*. New York: Charles Scribner's Sons, 1922.

_____. *Folk-Song of Nebraska and the Central West: A Syllabus*. Lincoln: Nebraska Academy of Sciences, 1915.

Randolph, Vance, ed. *Ozark Folksongs*. 4 vols. Rev. ed. Columbia and London: University of Missouri Press, 1980.

Sackett, Samuel J., and Koch, William E. *Kansas Folklore*. Lincoln: University of Nebraska Press, 1961.

Spaeth, Sigmund. *Read 'Em and Weep*. Rev. ed. New York: Arco Publishing Co., 1945.

Toelken, Barre. *The Dynamics of Folklore*. Boston: Houghton Mifflin Co., 1979.

Wilgus, D. K. and Rosenberg, Bruce A. "A Modern Medieval Story: 'The Soldier's Deck of Cards'." In *Medieval Literature and Folklore Studies: Essays in Honor of Francis Lee Utley*, ed. Jerome Mandel and Bruce A. Rosenberg, 291–303. New Brunswick, N. J.: Rutgers University Press, 1970.

*L*en Henry: North Idaho Münchausen

JAN HAROLD BRUNVAND

In this significant contribution to scholarship in the genre of the tall tale, the author calls attention to the fact that fakelore (defined in the text) has too often overshadowed authentic materials dealing with hero tales: "Unlike the fakelore heroes who only embody giant size and brute strength, ... regional Münchausens embody some of the most characteristic traits of native American folk tradition." Len Henry was such a regional narrator.

An interesting publication history accompanies this study by one of the nation's well-known folklorists. This article first appeared in Northwest Folklore *in the summer of 1965. Professor Brunvand's revised and updated version was published in a Romanian translation as "Ruputatia, Repertoriul şi Stilul Unui Münchausen American," in* Revista de Etnografie şi Folclor *(1971) in Bucharest. The title means "Reputation, Repertoire, and Style of an American Münchausen." In 1972 the English version was reproduced mimeographically in a collection of Brunvand essays titled "Studies in Western Folklore and Fiction" for class use at the University of Utah, a collection unfortunately unavailable now. This revision integrates the texts into the discussion, frames the study with observations pertinent to regional folklore, and provides a glossary for certain dialect terms. Len Henry is also the subject of a chapter in Richard M. Dorson's posthumous book,* Man and Beast in American Comic Legend *(1982).*

Professor Jan Brunvand teaches English and folklore at the University of Utah.

This article is reprinted with permission from Northwest Folklore, *where it appeared in volume 1:1 (Summer, 1965): 11–19.*

A striking phenomenon of modern American culture, mass produced and mass consumed though it is for the most part, is the high value assigned to elements that are supposedly drawn from native folk tradition. Perhaps as a reaction against the merchants of mass culture who operate via phonograph records, television, movies, etcetera, Americans seem to need some kind of lore from a bygone era that was anonymously conceived, orally transmitted, simple, romantic, and rural. This need manifests itself in fads for folksinging, storytelling, square dancing, bread baking at home, weaving, communal living experiments, astrology, and the like.

Ironically, the very examples of supposed folk tradition that most Americans know the best and regard as the most typical were themselves put into circulation by commercial interests and are really "fakelore" not folklore. Major instances of the "cult of the folksy," as one writer has called it, are ersatz folk heroes, such as the giant lumberjack Paul Bunyan or the superhuman cowboy Pecos Bill.[1] Numerous books, for adults as well as children, have been devoted to tales of such figures. Descriptions of these two and many other such manufactured folk heroes appear in every popular survey of American folklore. Yet they were all first described by professional writers, not folklorists, and the forces of advertising, journalism, juvenile literature, and mass entertainment

have long since smothered whatever shallow folk roots these "heroes" ever had.

An authentic strain of American hero legends does exist, however, in stories by and about local characters who specialize in telling big lies. The American Münchausens like their European prototype were spinners of tall tales who cast themselves in a hero's role and gained a reputation as storytellers and sometimes also as pranksters. While they never became known to a wide public, their local fame developed so strongly that people still may not venture to retell a tall tale except "the way old man so-and-so used to tell it." Unlike the fakelore heroes who only exemplify giant size and brute strength, these regional Münchausens embody some of the most characteristic traits of native American folk tradition such as broad humor, exaggeration, an eccentric personality type, dialect, ingenuity, wit, audacity, and self-confidence. The repertoires of these characters blend European motifs with New World settings and themes, while their modes of narration transmute age-old plots into a regional vernacular style. Functionally, such narratives provided their communities with a sense of pride in the achievements—if only imaginary—of a commonplace figure from their midst. The stories constituted an oral literature of humorous boasting associated with a skilled narrator of the region. Men competed among their neighbors for the reputation of a master liar. Nowadays, in memory, these story-tellers and their tales represent a link of fantastic humor to an earlier period of daring pioneering and real challenge that seems very remote from the tame contemporary age of affluence and mechanization.

In the 1940s a scattered trio of regional tall tale tellers was first brought to light—John Darling in New York; Gib Morgan, "minstrel of the oil fields"; and "Lying Abe" Smith of southern Indiana and Illinois.[2] Although all of the subjects themselves were dead by that time, their legends remain; indeed, new examples of such characters and stories are still being discovered.[3] My purpose here is to present another outstanding folk liar in Len Henry, a north Idaho Münchausen.

Len Henry was the last survivor of the pioneer squawmen[4] on the Nez Perce reservation at Lapwai, Idaho. He had moved there with his Indian wife about 1889 while the government land was being allotted, and he died on March 14, 1946, near the site of his original cabin. A photograph of Len Henry taken two months before his death showed him as a tall, erect old man with long light hair and mustache, wearing baggy trousers, a vest, and a floppy hat, standing with one hand on his hip and his eyes look-ing directly into the camera lens with a serious air. He had just told the photographer that he was going on 105 years old, but it seems clear that he was following the habit of a lifetime and stretching the truth—this time by about eleven years. It is said that people had commented *then*, "That's the last lie that old Len Henry will ever tell."

The few printed accounts of Len Henry that appeared during the year following his death mentioned his tale-telling abilities, and our printed tales, only one short paragraph each, were published in a popular book of local history.[5] But in 1959 the standard *History of Idaho*[6] merely named Len Henry in a list of other squawmen, and neither of the publishers that had printed photographs of him in 1946 and '47 was able to locate copies. The last of the Nez Perce squawmen, once a noted oral storyteller, seemingly had faded quietly out of history.

That is, *printed* history. Len Henry and his stories are still vividly held in the memories of many old-timers in the vicinity of Lapwai and across the Snake River from Lewiston in Asotin County, Washington, where he had settled earlier. With the aid of University of Idaho students, and newspaper publicity, I collected one hundred sixteen versions of sixty-seven distinct Len Henry stories; I drew on twenty-eight informants.

Little is recorded about the early life of Len Henry. He said he was born in Kansas City, Kansas, in 1841— probably it was more like 1852. A biographical sketch of his older brother Noble ("Nobe") states that the Henrys originated from Pennsylvania-Dutch stock and migrated through several plains states before coming to the northwest in the 1860s.[7] Nobe Henry was appar-ently the most prominent figure in the family by 1930

when this was published, for the rest of the clan were merely enumerated, and on the list we find "Lorenzo, residing near Lapwai." Nobe and Len were partners in Asotin County in various farming, stock raising, and freighting enterprises before the turn of the century. Sources differ on the year Len moved to Idaho: his obituary says 1895, but a reliable informant remembered meeting him there in 1891, "after he had been living on the reservation for two years." His cabin was built about two miles south of where the settlement of Sweetwater formed, just west of the present U.S. Highway 95.

Len Henry was known as a yarn-spinner before he came to Idaho. Charley J. Knight, who lives on his own family's 1870 homestead near Cloverland, Washington, was well acquainted with the Henrys when they worked at rounding up wild horses in Asotin County. He recalled, "You could depend on anything Nobe told you to be the truth, but when Len told you something, you could never depend on it. When I was a kid I used to get scared to death from some of the stories I heard Len telling my father."

William Jones of Clarkston, Washington, took time out from his 87th birthday celebration February 1964 to give me his memories of Len Henry from 1882:

> Him and his brother worked for a crew that was survey-ing a road through our place, and they boarded at our place, for about two weeks. . . . He must have been a man of about thirty at that time. [This jibes exactly with the best estimate of Len Henry's age.] He was the only one that I knew of that would make up stories and tell them like that. . . . He was working there, and in the front room in the evening he'd tell them.

Sweetwater, Idaho, an unincorporated village, today consists of a grain elevator and a grocery store bracketing the highway, and a cluster of houses off on the east side of it. Bert Ankney, age 70 (in 1964, the year for which all subsequent ages are given), has lived there all his life, and heard Len Henry tell stories as far back as he can remember. Mr. and Mrs. Ankney com-mented:

> Wherever you met that man he was telling stories. The man could set for hours at a time and tell one after another, and it was so odd that anyone could think up stories constantly like that. . . . He always had something, no matter what you brought up. . . . He could tell one, and later on he'd tell the same story exactly the same way.

The store at Sweetwater was opened in 1929 by Phil Crawford, now retired at 81 and living in Clarkston, who said Len Henry could tell stories "anytime, anyplace, anywhere." He said Len liked to come to the store where he could gather a knot of five or six men around him, sit cross-legged on the floor, and cut loose with the tall tales. Phil thought that Len had said he helped with the camp outfit for Alice Fletcher when she came out from Washington, D.C., for the land allot-ment, but nothing in the records shows this.[8] In 1944

Dick Alfrey acquired the Sweetwater store, and he observed Len Henry in action there during the last two years of his life. He remembered Len Henry getting up from his cross-legged position without touching his hands to the floor until two weeks before he died. He said that as many as fifteen or twenty men would cluster around when he started talking — either before the stove inside, or at a bench in front on sunny days, and "people got a kick out of his stories and would try to start him off telling them." Len chewed tobacco and spit towards the stove when he talked, and Alfrey remembered that when he got through he always had to mop up after him.

Barney McGovern, age 74, was a freight-wagon driver in Idaho until World War I; he lived across the road from Len Henry from 1929 to 1934, married a granddaughter of Nobe Henry's, and they now live in Lewiston. The first thing he told me about Len Henry was this: "I used to get so damn mad at those stories; they'd go on from morning to night . . . but Len never hurt anyone with his stories." McGovern described the circumstances when he heard the stories in this way:

> The bunch went over to Yakima country, hop picking, you see, and they took all the grub and everything else. By golly, he'd come over to our place, you know. And he ate over there. You see my wife is his grandniece . . .
> J.B.: And he told stories?
> B.M.: Oh — told stories! I tell you boy, he was a good one . . . yeah. Something would come up, you know, and he'd have a story all whittled[9] out for it. Didn't make any difference what it was.

B. E. Eller, now of Arlee, Montana, married a cousin of Len Henry's in Lapwai, where his father barbered, and he lived there until the Depression. He wrote me this:

> Len Henry was a nice old man. He never done anyone any harm. He used to believe his own stories. He was always serious when he use to tell the stories. He would tell stories and never slow down only to wipe the chewing tobacco from his chin. . . . I used to walk four miles to listen to Len Henry stories.

It was men mostly who heard the Len Henry stories and who remembered them; few women had opportunities to hear him, and not many were interested in such stuff. Even one of Len's daughters, Lydia, who kept house for him for some twenty years after her mother died, could recall none, although she did remember hearing tales being told to her husband and other men while she was working in the kitchen. Lydia Henry Switzler died of the complications of diabetes only one week after I interviewed her in October 1963; she had furnished some biographical facts on her father, but no tales. Two other women, however, turned up as good informants.

Mrs. Esther Sweeney, now living in Lewiston, wrote:

> I remember Mr. Len Henry very well, but was too young and of the wrong sex to be allowed around the big stove in the old Sweetwater store. My knowledge of these stories came from my father who spent some time there.
>
> Our homestead was about a mile up on a hill above where Mr. Henry and family lived. As a very small child I remember him walking over his pastures caring for horses or fixing fence. As my brother and I reached school age we walked about a mile and a half to and from school and passed through Mr. Henry's pastures and very near his home. He often talked to us and we were thrilled. . . . We considered him very famous as our father always repeated the stories he heard, and we had many a good laugh in the evenings at home.

The single best informant interviewed was Mylie Lawyer of Lapwai, daughter of the prominent Nez Perce Indian, Corbett Lawyer. Miss Lawyer's sister collected from her for my folklore class, and later I visited her to record this description of the unique circumstances in which she heard Len Henry narrate:

> I graduated high school in 1929, and two or three years prior to that time I had to write English themes every school day for the English teacher. And I run out of material, so that's how I began to go up there in a mixed group, and sometimes there'd be more white kids than there would be Indians. But they'd be just whoever I happened to be with. We'd go up there and listen to his stories. We always sat out on the porch, and he knew I was taking these for class . . .
> J.B.: Did the other students use his stories?
> M.L.: No, nobody.

Len Henry's general characteristics as a raconteur can be reconstructed from the informants' comments. On the whole his reputation resembles those of the other regional Münchausens, who were also credited with having apparently limitless repertoires, a story for any occasion, and the ability to repeat long narratives verbatim. He was willing to swap tales; he would often speak up last to cap a session of others' tall yarns with a superior one of his own. His fame as a high-powered liar was well established in the small area of his residence: one informant said that Len Henry was first pointed out to him as "the biggest liar in seven states." He is remembered by all of his acquaintances as a kind, friendly, and likable man, inclined constantly to draw the long bow, but never shooting any barbed arrows.

Nearly any social situation would set Len Henry off telling tales. Several people spoke of asking him a question or telling him an experience in order to, as Bert Ankney put it, "get him lined out." Barney McGovern described how Len Henry would veer off from discussing a business deal to tell a tall story, or how he would slip a lie into an otherwise factual conversation. Dick Alfrey said that people deliberately tried to draw out his tallest lies, but then they usually let on to believe them. But sometimes the listeners were not quite sure; Frank McIntyre, age 85, said:

> There was a story he told down in Colorado or something, but he described that country just like it was. . . . He'd tell it, and you was pretty sure he was lyin', but he described places there that he didn't know of, you

see, he said he lived there. And we don't know whether he did or not. Have no way of tellin'.

One informant doubted that Len Henry had ever been across the Continental Divide, and several seemed to think he had been born in the northwest. One said that Len was a half-breed Nez Perce, and another gave his name as "Glen" Henry.

The Sweetwater store was regarded as Len's storytelling headquarters, but several men said he was at his best by a campfire on a hunting or freighting trip through the mountains. Both Mylie Lawyer and her neighbor in Lapwai, James Maxwell, another Nez Perce who knew him, said that Len Henry was also known to have told stories in the Indian sweathouses.

Although the informants for these stories ranged from those who were superb storytellers in their own right to others who could give only a skeletonized outline of a tale, we learn much about Len Henry's oral style from their descriptions and examples. Informants are unanimous in saying that he maintained a dry and serious manner when narrating, and this is consistent with the American tall tale tradition of delivering a lie with a straight face. In this way the lying story becomes a kind of practical joke or prank in which the unwary listeners or perhaps a newcomer are fooled into partial belief until the utter absurdity of the plot becomes obvious.[10] Sometimes this device is carried to the degree of creating a "catch tale" ending for a story (Type 2200, Motif Z13.2.), or as one informant described it:

> Sometimes he'd, you know, have an afterthought, like . . . a little something at the end after he'd get all through. I like that one about where we'd have to wait and then we'd say, "Well, what happened?" And he'd tell you what.

All of the texts of narratives collected were either tape recorded, written out by informants, or taken by dictation (the latter usually by the students). As desirable as tape recordings are for such studies, it was found that every collecting method preserved useful data, as an example of each illustrates.

First, here is a direct transcription from a field tape; it begins with a mention of the occasion for the tale, and the setting, then illustrates Len Henry's adroit manipulation of a stranger's unfamiliarity with his lying. The story plot itself turns out to be a catch tale, doubtless told for the benefit of the local audience who enjoyed seeing an outsider fooled.

> One time there was[11] a fellow came there to our place to buy a cow. And Len was up. You see the original place was up on Asotin Creek; Nobe had a place up there. And he was tellin' about one time he pulled in there and he said they want some fish. "Well," he says,[12] "in the fall of the year—fish hadn't gone down yet, so" he said, "there was about six or eight inches of snow on the ground. Well," he says, "I just went and kicked around and I got a couple of dozen grasshoppers, and I went out," he says, and I used

them grasshoppers, and in no time," he says,"why I had ten–twelve fish in just a few minutes. And I went back, kicked around and I got another dozen or fifteen grasshoppers . . ." Just about that time he happened to think, you know, that grasshoppers when snow's on, there's no such thing, you know. He says, "That was the damndest year for grasshoppers I ever seen!"

The wit in such a story as this lies in the use of what magicians call "misdirection"; that is, listeners are deluded into thinking that buying a cow, or catching fish, or the exact depth of snow or the number of grasshoppers is the point of the story. When the illogic of the weather conditions and the presence of insects becomes clear, and the listener asks a question, the real point is compressed in the punchline "That was the damndest year for grasshoppers . . . ."

Second, here is a text written from dictation by an informant to a folklore student. Though reduced to only three sentences (either by or for the benefit of the amateur collector) the traces of oral style are still preserved in the direct quotation, in the emphasis on the word "box," and in the expressions "well," "slow on the think," and "old Len says." In the very simple form, this story too is a catch tale, because Len Henry leads the storekeeper into the trap of trying to correct his order for two shells. The story is typical of anecdotes about Len Henry's quick wit which helped to sustain his reputation as a noted liar:

> Well, Len came into Heckner and Carlson's store in Lapwai, and he said, "I want two 30-30 shells." Old Heckner was kinda slow on the think, said he should buy a box of 'em. Then old Len says, "I only need two; your damned game laws only allow me one deer and one elk."

What is implied in Len's response here is not only the suggestion that he was an expert marksman, but also that he had the old mountain man's loathing for formal hunting regulations. Both themes, incidentally, are central to James Fenimore Cooper's characterization of the frontiersman in his "Leatherstocking" novels.

Third, here is a text given exactly as written by an informant. By way of introduction, we have a capsule description of his narrative style, then an attempt to render an exact first-person version of the story. The phrases "devil of a time," "do you know," and "golly" all suggest authenticity:

> Mr. Henry was not a talkative man. Very droll and slow of speech. He didn't tell these good stories often but would listen to the other men spin yarns, then he could always tell one better. Here is one of the stories I remember best.
> "In the early days I was driving a six-horse team with two wagons up a very steep, narrow, and crooked trail. During rainy weather the wagons had cut deep ruts in the road. I came to a very sharp turn and had a devil of a time getting all those horses and both wagons around it. It took some doing, but I made it. After a bit I missed my dog so I thought I better see about him, and do you know, I walked back a piece and golly if he wasn't cramped in that turn."

Variants of this story, which was collected in ten texts, illustrate the variety of details Len Henry could supply to develop a given theme. Each informant claimed he was telling the story as nearly as possible in the way he heard it, yet there is great variation. Three specific locations were given; some said Len was driving up, some said down the hill. In most versions he drove a mule-drawn freight wagon with twelve to twenty-four mules hitched up, but others said it was two wagons pulled by four or six horses. One said Len was driving a pack train and no wagons at all. Some versions are very specific about where the dog (or dogs) ran, either behind or under the wagon (or wagons). When the dog gets stuck, sometimes it howls, and other times Len simply misses it. Some versions end here, while others continue with the claim that Len snapped the dog by the tail to straighten it out. One informant said Len ended by saying that the dog lived twenty-four years longer, but never got the kink out of its back. The specific figures given are typical of American tall tales in which the technique of juxtaposing a lie with exact measurements is often used.

The relationship of all tales collected to known traditional plots in oral circulation elsewhere helps to establish Len Henry's personal repertoire and style. Of the sixty-seven types, nineteen tales (fifty-two variants) match *specific* well-known oral ones; eighteen tales (thirty variants) make use of *general* motifs known in other versions.[13] Seventeen tales (twenty-one variants) employ no motif with a close parallel known in tradition; thirteen tales (thirteen variants) are anecdotes *about* Len Henry or his family. Roughly one-half of the repertoire, then, in terms of *story types* is well-established traditional material. The other half seems to have been generated by Len Henry's creative imagination and out of his reputation as a trickster. But more than two-thirds of the *actual variant texts* of the tales that were told belong to widespread rather than local tradition. Thus, the material that Len Henry seems to have used the most and that which he is best remembered for is also from widespread tradition. We can see here that the reputation Len Henry enjoyed for making up new tales is contradicted by his actual personal repertoire which is predominately that of American tall storytellers in general.

Of the nineteen stories directly drawn from folk tradition, only one is a clear Aarne-Thompson tale type, and, as might be expected, it is *The Wonderful Hunt* (Type 1890).[14] The following text, taken from a tape recording, begins as a paraphrase and concludes in first person. At the point in the story when the fish first begins to bite, the informant spoke more and more rapidly:

> He said that one time he was going out hunting to get meat for the winter. So he took his gun and his dog and his fish pole and he came to the riverbank and threw in his line. He put his gun beside him and his dog on the other side. All at once a fish got on his hook, and right away another fish came and grabbed its tail and another fish. He

pulled it out and saw that there were three fish, and he hit his gun and it shot and killed a buck deer. And, he said, over on the other side was a blue grouse got so scared it fainted, and, he said, "My dog went and got it for me, and so I had my fish and meat both."

Len Henry also told such other familiar stories from the Baron Münchausen cycle as the one about falling from a balloon and sinking into rock up to his hips (X1731.2.), the giant log-sized snake (X1321.1.2.), the horse tied to a church steeple (X1653.1.), and the sprouting buggy whip (X1470). The following tape-recorded text, interrupted with the informant's repeated attempts to clarify it, is based on motif X1755.1.:

> That was supposed to be down here in this river—the Clearwater. He said that—that was before the highway was there—and he said there was this real steep bank and he went fishing and he threw his—in high water—he threw his hook in the water, and as he bent over why his pocket—his watch fell out of his vest pocket. He didn't know what to do, so he took off his clothes and he dove in there looking for it, and he couldn't find it. So he gave up and he went home, and three years later he went back there to find it and he said—it was low water—and he said, "I found it, and it was still running." [A listener to this version then commented, "That was the time, I think, he mentioned the fact that he had a good watch and it didn't lose any time."]

Better narrated is this text, really consisting of two variants of one tale, from a tape recording, and embellished with oral stylistic qualities that are indicated in brackets. It belongs to Motif X1623.2.1.

> There was one about the echo, you know, was frozen. He was going along in a canyon and he camped overnight, and he knew that there was an echo there. And he hollered, "How are you" [Slow and drawn out] And no answer, 'cause it was real cold. So he banked up his fire and he lay down and he went to sleep. Then he got up the next morning and he listened, and no echo. So he left. And he said in the summertime he'd come back to the same place and he fixed his campfire, and just as he started to eat his supper somebody said, "I'm fine." [Imitating the style of the original call]
>
> And then there was another echo story. He said one time he was going down into this deep, deep canyon. And it had cliffs on each side, and he was travelin' a long, long ways, and he knew he had to get up early in the morning. So he fixed his fire again, and he lay down and then he thought, "Well, how am I goin' to get up early in the morning?" So he got up by the fire and he stood there, and he said, "Wake me up at sunrise!" And he said it three times before he laid back down. He had a good night's sleep, and pretty soon somebody said, "Wake up! Wake up! Wake up!" So he got up and he said the sun was juuuust [word spoken in a long high-pitched tone] coming up over that cliff.

The most often repeated story employing a specific folk motif is this one, based on Motif X1741.2.:

> One day he was goin' someplace a horseback, and he come to a crik. Crik wasn't so awful wide, but it was deep,

and he was afraid to swim it, 'cause he'd get so wet, see; so he got back and took a run and jumped his horse across. Wasn't too wide. Just before he got there he looked over on the ground—there was a great big rattlesnake a-layin' there, see? So he just turned around in midair and went back.

In this recorded text the abbreviations and sentence fragments retain the oral style effectively, even though the informant's sly facial expressions are lost. In other versions the reasons for the return trip vary from Indians, a rattlesnake, no place to land, to "just saw that I couldn't make it."

The eighteen tales that employ only generalized motifs of folk tradition include stories about Len Henry as a remarkable rider (X1004), roper (X1003), blacksmith (X982), thresher (X1001), or even a spitter (X934). His riding feats, for instance, include jumping a horse down a sheer cliff, riding a bronco that bucked so hard that a hunting knife was driven out of its scabbard and into solid rock, and riding fast enough to overtake and bulldog a deer. A favorite tale, heard from eight informants, and also one of the few printed previously, is this one, given in a version dictated to a student collector:

On one occasion the Indians were chasing Len on horseback and were getting so close he was sure to be overtaken. Right in the midst of the danger he came to a big washout in the trail. There wasn't time to turn back: the banks were too steep to go either up or down, and it seemed they were doomed. But being Len Henry, he at once saw a way out. There was a ledge of rock immediately above the wash over the trail, so he threw his lasso rope over the crag, backed his horse a few steps, half-hitched the rope over the saddle horn, got his knife in readiness, then threw the spurs to his horse. The rope held and swung the horse to the other side. Len cut the rope and the horse landed on his feet on the other side safely.

Here the language has been somewhat formalized into a pseudo literary style with terms such as "occasion," "overtaken," "doomed," and "readiness." Still oral traces remain in the terms "washout," "half-hitched," and "threw the spurs." This informant was also one of the few who resisted the tendency to imitate Len Henry's first-person delivery.

Two further texts from the same group also illustrate the storyteller's ability to spin a well-constructed tale from a basically simple motif of mere exaggeration. The first is based on the uninspired idea of big trees (X1471), but it effectively disguises this point until the last moment:

It was getting that time of year when Len always moved his cattle across the Clearwater to his summer grazing; well this one year the spring thaw came a little early and the Clearwater was near capacity when Len got to it. He found his old fording place impossible to cross, so he spent the morning hunting for a crossing. About noon he found a tree laying across the river, so he started driving his cattle across. And when he got them about half way the cattle

took off into all directions, and it took him 'till the next day to round up his cattle from off them branches.

The second text is more oral in style, though also taken by dictation by a student. It is related to Motif X1235.1., *Large Cow*:

Once Len was talking to me about my grandfather's cattle. My grandfather had quite a herd of Red Angus. As most people know, Angus cattle are natural muleys.[15] Len said, "Boy, them Red Anglers[16] are sure good cows. I bought one of them steers offin your grandad. Had horns six feet long, it did. And grow! Why, when I sold that steer I got one hundred dollars for it, and beef was only three cents a pound that year."

Again here, as illustrated earlier, the wild exaggeration is offset by specific figures, "one hundred dollars" and "three cents a pound." In effect the listener is required to do some mathematical figuring before the joke is clear to him.

The group of seventeen stories that contain no specific motif or close parallel from tradition must include tales that Len Henry made up at the spur of the moment. A neighbor introduced him once to some teachers who were on a tour of historic sites and Len Henry blandly informed them that he had been teaching school himself when Lewis and Clark arrived. He told another neighbor a sad story about a good grey team of horses he had once, but his brother Noble mentioned later that Len had never owned a team of greys in his life. Once Len Henry was watching someone fix a car, and he got hold of a spark plug wire while the engine was running and jerked sharply back. "Did it shock you, Len?" they asked. "Nope," he replied, "I was too quick for it." One witty tale from this group is based on the well-known cowboy weapon, the six-shooter. The text is given as written by the informant:

He said he was camping on top of the Swallow's Nest.[17] He said there was a level place up there for a camp. One day he was riding a bucking horse. It started to buck toward the cliff; he figured he would go over with the horse and be killed, so he reached down and unfastened the cinch and rolled off with the saddle, just as the horse went over, leaving him and saddle on top of the cliff. He didn't like to see the horse fall all the way down and suffer, so he pulled his six-shooter and shot him seven times before he hit the ground.

To assure that his reader would understand the point of the story, the informant added, "He must have loaded pretty fast to shoot him seven times."

All of Len Henry's Indian stories are either based on non-traditional motifs or are in fact in the fourth category—anecdotes *about* Len Henry. He claimed that he had killed the squaw that scalped General George Custer and then escaped Indian capture by riding an elk over the mountains. He told the Nez Perce Indians a comic tale involving one of their most serious religious beliefs, and the anecdote is still a favorite one in Lapwai. He told them that he went to the mountains to fast so that he could acquire a guardian spirit like the Indians have; but when a big grey wolf finally appeared to him in a vision, he said he asked it to wait until he could go back to town and have lunch. The Indians also say that Len Henry once got up to dance in the longhouse and he sang a translation into the Nez Perce language of a Christian hymn instead of some appropriate native song.

Most anecdotes about Len Henry make him out to be the trickster in real life he was in his stories. For instance, people say he sold three ganders once to a man who wanted to start raising geese. He is supposed to have run into a mountain cabin full of greenhorn hunters chased by a bear and to have shouted at them, "You skin this one and I'll go get another!" (Actually, this is a traditional folktale which was probably part of Len Henry's repertoire, but it became attached to him as an incident of his life.)

It is not surprising that people in the area of Len Henry's fame (a radius of about twenty or thirty miles around Lapwai) regard the stories as the original creations of their neighbor. The texts are rich in details of real life there. They deal with hunting, fishing, camping, freighting, raising cattle, Indians, fording streams, shooting accurately, threshing, farming, roping, and so forth. They contain local place names or are connected to known local characters, sometimes relatives of of storytellers and audiences. Only a few informants were aware that the same stories with differing details are told elsewhere in the United States, and none mentioned European prototypes for the big liar.

The plots of the stories are simple and their situations are topical, further connecting them to the local scene. Something came up in conversation or daily life, and an appropriate tale was introduced about it. Usually the tales contain only one episode based on a single crisis or problem that is resolved by an unlikely or impossible act of the hero's. For instance, the beginning situation may introduce some situation of tension or unrest (a dog is missing, a watch is lost in the river, a horse will suffer if it falls) and the hero resolves this (the dog is found to be stuck on a turn, the watch is found three years later, the horse is shot before it lands). His actions go beyond reality into the unbelievable (a team and wagon had been driven where the dog got stuck, the watch is still keeping good time, the horse is shot seven times with a six-shooter). Although the nature of the incident is often a simple exaggeration of reality (cold weather is made colder, a big tree is made bigger, etc.) more commonly, impossibilities and contradictions *per se* occur (insects in the snow, echo frozen, jumping back from mid air, etc.). Of the texts collected, only *The Wonderful Hunt* is an exception to these principles with its threefold patterning, serial development, and basis in pure good luck rather than skill or ability. The other stories all lack the elaborated format of the full-scale traditional tale type; they depend on one (or at most two) traditional motifs

about which new variants may be easily developed.

The distinctive style in which all such oral tales are traditionally delivered is characterized by subtlety and understatement. The joke is over or has been implied before the listener is fully aware of it, and the storyteller never belabors or underscores his point, but instead disguises or implies it.

The Paul Bunyan or Pecos Bill stories, in contrast, are far removed from such oral tales. In them instead of the sly casual style of a local raconteur who playfully *pretends* to be the hero of outrageous adventures, we hear a voice, heavy with a contrived "folksy" dialect, of a sophisticated professional writer trying too hard to seem natural as he describes labored plots of his own invention in which a giant figure really does perform marvelous feats. (Sometimes these writers are hopelessly self-conscious; one even compared himself to Homer reworking native legends into a national epic!) The giant, superhuman fake heroes undeniably do great deeds in their stories, but they do them with no sense of humor and little ingenuity. Paul Bunyan drags his peavey[18] behind him and thus digs the Grand Canyon, but this is really too witless and inane an act to be memorable. There is no suspense or even sense of anticipation in a lie like that, nor in ninety percent of the other Paul Bunyan stories. Since Bunyan is a giant, naturally he can do gigantic feats, and having accepted that premise the saga practically writes itself. People have never told such lying tales *orally*, yet every published volume of Bunyan stories reports them as coming from folk tradition. The contrast with traditions about Len Henry is profound when we recall, by way of example, his rapid response when the spark-plug wire shocked him: "Nope, I was too quick for it."

Yet what both the regional Münchausen and the fakelore hero share is an alignment with the past — essentially the pioneer period. No American who reads Paul Bunyan stories believes that lumberjacks still tell them, but the stories are thought to refer to the old days (up to the late nineteenth century) of ax logging in the East and Midwest. Similarly, the youth of northern Idaho may hear their parents or grandparents tell Len Henry stories, but they do not themselves adopt them into their own oral lore, and so eventually the stories will die out. Undoubtedly, then, the writer's pen and the folklorist's tape recorder are keeping alive a little longer than is natural tales that are no longer functional either in folk or popular tradition. A bragging, clownish, trickster persona is alien to the spirit of contemporary America, however well it fit the taste of a past epoch. The modern humorous folk narrative in the United States tends to be more verbal than practical, urban rather than rural, more aggressive and tense than these tall tales, less placid and genial. By way of example, here are two of the first oral jokes I heard in northern Idaho when I moved to Moscow (site of the state university) in 1961, two years before anyone told me about Len Henry:

You know, the state of Idaho has three capitals—Boise, Spokane, and Salt Lake City.

Do you know why Boise has the state prison and Moscow has the university? (Boise had first choice.)

Both of these jokes are mere verbal quips—riddles or riddle-jokes rather than narratives. They have nothing of the leisurely pace of a well-told tale. Both are rather negative and melancholy in contrast to the buoyant frontier optimism of Len Henry's tales. The first one recognizes the economic domination of northern Idaho by the largest city in eastern Washington and the general cultural influence of the religious authorities of the Latter-day Saint church in Utah whose first campus religious center was established at the University of Idaho. The second joke reflects the galling fact of southern Idaho's general domination over the geographically isolated north. Boise is located in the more accessible part of the state, along good east-west routes, while Moscow in the remote north has the prestige of an educational center by way of compensation. In the fantasy of the joke, the crafty Boiseans preferred the prison to a university, but now, ironically, they have both, for the city college of Boise has enjoyed such growth in recent years that it has become the fastest expanding educational institution in the state. And Boise also has, by virtue of large representation in the state government, "first choice" over Moscow.

Such comments should not be taken to mean that there is no humor in modern jokes but only resignation and dismay. In fact, an important function of such quips is to render laughable the facts of life—to take things with a grain of salt and a sense of humor. In any case, it is certainly no longer the humor of a regional Münchausen like Len Henry, however collectable his legend may still be for a few more years.

Notes

1. These and other American folk heroes are thoroughly discussed in Richard M. Dorson's *American Folklore* (Chicago, 1959), especially Chapter Six, pages 199–243. Dorson also coined the apt term "fakelore."

2. Dorson discusses regional Münchausens on pages 226–31 and cites the relevant bibliography.

3. See Susan Mullin, "Oregon's Huckleberry Finn: A Münchausen Enters Tradition," *Northwest Folklore*, 2 (1967), 19–25; and C. Richard K. Lunt, "Jones Tracy: Tall-Tale Hero from Mount Desert Island," *NEF*, 10 (1968), 1–75.

4. "Squawman" was a demeaning term used for a white man who married or lived with an Indian woman.

5. The obituary in the *Lewiston Idaho Morning Tribune* (March 15, 1946) reported, "He was known in the reservation as a great story-teller and when surrounded by his progeny was at his best." C. T. Stranahan, former Indian Agent and a long-time friend of Len Henry's, published an interview with Len in the *Tribune* on May 5, 1946, without alluding to the tall tales, but in the 1947 edition of R. G. Bailey's *River of No Return* (Lewiston), pp. 106 and 585, a resume of these two newspaper articles closed with this interesting statement plus four examples:

Len Henry . . . was an inveterate story teller. His were always "true" stories, and he was invariably the hero. Whenever he was in a reminiscent mood, which was when he could get a bunch of listeners together, he could ramble on seemingly without end.

Two photographs of Len Henry taken by a *Tribune* photographer on January 26, 1946, were printed with the newspaper articles, and one was reprinted in *River of No Return*, p. 106. Stranahan reprinted his article without pictures in *Pioneer Stories* (Idaho Writers' League: Lewiston, 1947), p. 2. My own article in the *Lewiston Morning Tribune*, "Spinner of Tall Tales," appeared on January 5, 1964, and contained a description of collecting that had been done.

6. Merrill D. Beal and Merle W. Wells, 3 vols. (New York, 1959), I:201.

7. "Noble Henry," in *An Illustrated History of North Idaho* (Western Historical Publishing Company, 1903), pp. 182–83.

8. There is no mention of Len Henry in Kate C. McBeth, *The Nez Perces Since Lewis and Clark* (New York [1908?]) where a good account of Miss Fletcher's work is given by one of the first missionaries to the Lapwai area; nor is there anything about Len Henry in a historical article based on the detailed letters of her companion: Allen C. and Eleanor D. Morrill, "The Measuring Woman and the Cook," *Idaho Yesterdays*, 8 (Fall, 1963), 2–15.

9. To "whittle," of course, is to carve aimlessly on a stick of wood with a pocket knife. Generally a man or boy who is whittling is not making anything except shavings. Whittling is a popular way for old country people, including storytellers, to pass the time. The implication is that Len Henry, although he seemed to be an idle daydreamer, always had a clever new invention ready for display.

10. The Ozark collector Vance Randolph catches the spirit of this technique in the title of his tall tale anthology *We Always Lie to Strangers* (New York, 1951).

11. "One time there was" is an opening formula as familiar in American tall tales as "Once upon a time" is in British fairy-tales. This speaker also uses the phrase "one time" to get back from his digression to the tale itself.

12. Typically this narrator uses "well," "he says," and "he said" as phrasing devices in the story. In reality, then, the tale is mostly a quotation of Len Henry's words.

13. All assertions about motif distributions are based on Stith Thompson's *Motif-Index of Folk Literature* (Bloomington, Ind., and Copenhagen, Denmark, 1955–58).

14. This is the most frequently collected tale of exaggeration in the United States. It was first printed in *The Farmer's Almanac* of 1809, but was undoubtedly popular much earlier.

15. A "muley" is a cow without horns. A "natural muley" breed would be one that never has horns.

16. Deliberate comic mispronunciation of the proper name for the breed.

17. A steep and inaccessible cliff overlooking the Snake River near Clarkston, Washington.

18. A lumberjack's heavy tool for prodding logs as they float in a river or millpond.

A Contextual Survey of Selected Homestead Sites in Washington County*

Louie W. Attebery

In this comprehensive description of homestead sites in Washington County, Idaho, Louie Attebery uses a definition of "context" that is broader than that used by such contextualists as Richard Bauman and Roger Abrahams, who refer only to social context. Attebery's context is the geographical and historical context in which homesteads were established, thrived, or did not thrive. The model for this kind of study is the cultural geographical school of folklore developed by European scholars and represented in journals like Folkliv *and* Ethnographia Scandinavia. *In this school of folklore scholarship every aspect of folklife—agricultural processes, foodways, art, narrative, housing, and so forth—is collected and mapped, eventually resulting in folklife atlases. In the United States such comprehensive studies of rural life are beginning to appear in journals like* Pioneer America.

Louie Attebery is Acting Vice-president of Academic Affairs and professor of English at The College of Idaho.

Those who reflect upon homesteading at all are likely to have two fairly distinct images of the homesteader and his lot. Both images are tied closely to the still prevailing American success ethic. In the one instance, there is the homesteader who made good. He proved up on his claim, but the real measure of his success lay in the extent of his expansion. Indeed, success ultimately meant expanding beyond the acres of the original patent. The other image is that of the defeated homesteader and the abandoned farm. For whatever causes—weather, grasshoppers, depressed prices, inaccessibility of markets, sharking money lenders—it is true that many homesteads were abandoned, some going to enlarge the holdings of the first category, the successful ones.

But in the course of defining the rationale upon which this study rests, a third image presented itself in the form of a question that became a hypothesis significant to the scope of the project: Isn't there a reality lying somewhere between the two however real popular images? Were there no homesteaders who stayed small, none who somehow were able to make a go of it . . . just barely . . . but in the process discovered and articulated certain values?

Since this is not a mystery story, the question may be answered at once. Indeed there was a third category, certainly small but nevertheless real, and this was the subsistence homesteader. What this study establishes, then, is the context for viewing twentieth-century homesteads in Washington County and a survey of three representative sites.

THE FRIEND A. MOORE HOMESTEAD

In March of 1910, as soon after the birth of their daughter as they could travel, Friend A. and Carmeta Cole Moore and their infant daughter Helena moved into a tent on the western slopes of Cuddy Mountain near a small stream called Starveout Creek. Now owned and occupied by Helena Moore Schmidt, it is still the original 110-acre homestead. Although the place is in Washington County, it is accessible by road through Council, some forty-six miles distant, the seat of Adams County.

Today the place seems remote, even though the county maintains most of the road, and a pickup can make the trip in and out without too much difficulty. But remoteness is as much a cultural thing as it is a fact of space and time. Outsiders visiting an old mining camp or a contemporary ranch many miles from any town often reveal their values and lack of awareness of history by asking, "Why would people want to live 'way out here?" or "How did they end up so far from any place?" Aside from the obvious responses that

---

* The original study from which this essay derives was undertaken through the Idaho State Historic Preservation Office. Ed. note.

Figure 1.   The cabin built by Friend Moore.

that's where the mineral was or that's where the range-land was, there is another way to look at the matter. What did remoteness mean, one might ask, before there were settlements of any consequences and before there were railroads or, more recently, highways? Viewed this way, much of the West in an earlier time was remote. Town, or more likely, the store, was where you had to go to get what you could not supply for yourself; it was not the object of any aesthetic or cultural quest. The authentic business and processes of living were back on the ranch, to which you hurried as soon as your business of a less important nature was transacted. Trails, freight, and stagecoach routes traversed areas that seem remote by today's standards. It is unlikely that self-sufficient people at whatever great distance from town would think of themselves as remote.

The Friend A. Moore place is about halfway up the side of Cuddy Mountain, whose summit is well above 7,000 feet. The county road follows Wildhorse River, which one leaves to reach the Moore place by taking a steep, narrow road with many switchbacks for about three miles. This road, which is privately maintained by Mrs. Schmidt, is a recent addition to the cultural landscape, dating from 1962. At the end of this road sits a handsome one-and-a-half-story log house, with several outbuildings, sheds, and a large barn. The man-made structures and a small field are situated on a bench of the mountain quite level and a pleasant relief from the imposing steepness. It is the house that commands the attention of the infrequent visitor.

Made of hefty pine logs perhaps twelve inches

through, the house is well constructed and shows little sign of its age. Larger than many log structures, the Moore cabin is thirty feet long and twenty-four feet wide with eight-foot ceilings. The exterior of the logs is not shaped; corners are v-notched by ax and adze. The roof is galvanized sheet iron; chinking may be of lime or lime-cement.

The floor plan is simple. A twenty-four by fifteen living room extends east and west along the northern part of the house; the southeast corner is a twelve by fifteen kitchen, and the southwest corner is a twelve by fifteen bedroom. A stairway with a homemade bannister of pine sapling handrail and birch supporting posts leads from the southwest corner of the living room to the two upstairs bedrooms.

The logs of which the house is built came from a timbered place above the dwelling called the Pot Hole. Mr. Moore tried to avoid commercial lumber in building the house since, in the absence of a road, boards had to be dragged up the hill by horse. In order to protect such boards as had to be used, he set aside one piece which he then used as a primitive runner, fastening other boards to it.

On the interior, the logs were hewed flat, and over a layer of cheesecloth a quarter of an inch of deadening felt was pasted on, over which two thicknesses of building paper and composition wallboard were added. The flooring is described by Helena Schmidt as two floors with a layer of paper insulation between. The upstairs was insulated by Mr. and Mrs. Schmidt with mica pour-on insulation and rock wool.

Abutting the house along the south wall is a fourteen

by twenty-two utility room added about 1964 or '65 by Mr. Schmidt. Extending the length of the east side is a roofed but open porch.

Certainly Mr. Moore's woodworking skills are revealed in the integrity of the enduring log cabin on Starveout Creek, a place name which helps provide an entree into the context of life there.

According to tradition, two families moved into the area in the early days, the Myers (spelling uncertain) and the Emerys. By agreement, one family was to stay and look after things, and the other family was to bring in supplies. For reasons not included by tradition, the supplies did not arrive, and the family starved out and left.

The Moores produced most of what went on their table: garden vegetables including potatoes, such fruit as strawberries and raspberries, and from their orchard pears, cherries, apricots, plums, and several varieties of apples—delicious, yellow banana, Jonathan, snow, and black Ben. Both fruit and vegetables were canned and dried. They slaughtered beef and pork, preserving ham and bacon with salt and liquid smoke before deciding to use green alder to flavor the pork in a traditional manner. Chickens were important for both eggs and meat. The Moores made their own butter always and cottage and hard cheese from time to time. Venison and grouse were easily obtained. For only a few items did they look to the outside world: flour, sugar, coffee, salt, and similar commercial products.

Just about the only product of the place that might be considered a cash crop was cattle. The increase of the small herd beyond the number required for replacement could be sold, but an equally reliable source of income from their herd was the two five-gallon cans of cream sold each week after an arduous trip by packhorse to Brownlee, Oregon, where a store and post office were located. What wheat was grown was cut and stacked as straw to which the chickens could run.

There were few circumstances that took the Moores away from their place. One was the elementary education of Helena which took place in Cambridge, Idaho. Mr. Moore practiced his trade of carpentry in and around the new town and the older community of Salubria nearby. Then when Helena was ready for high school, the Moores moved to LaGrande, Oregon, where Mr. Moore was employed as a millwright. In addition, whenever circumstances required his skills, he would take occasional jobs in the forest or as a carpenter for brief periods of time.

Helena attended normal school at Bellingham, Washington, and returned to teach the elementary grades at the Brownlee Creek school in Idaho. She married Henry Schmidt in 1937, and together they built a fairly large and successful cattle operation, owning several places including No Business Basin. While she and her husband lived down in the canyon of Wildhorse River, her parents continued to live up the mountain on the Starveout Creek place. After the death of her parents, she and her husband moved into the homestead cabin. Her husband is now deceased, and Helena, with a hired

couple, lives a kind of life not too different from that which was her birthright.

There is no electricity at Starveout Ranch, although there is a telephone. The house is heated by a wood-burning heater and a wood-burning cookstove. Cooking is done on either the woodburner or on a propane range. Propane and kerosene are both used for lighting. Much farm work is done with horses. All in all, the place is still quite self-sufficient. The difficulty of negotiating nearly fifty miles of winter roads and the price of gasoline have helped convince Mrs. Schmidt that the patterns of life she has absorbed since childhood are sane and wholesome alternatives to a consumption economy.

That the place is productive through generations-old subsistence techniques (the day of the site visitation food was drying in the sun between two screens to keep the flies off) is suggested by a conversation Mrs. Schmidt had with the proprietor of what used to be the area's outstanding harness shop. When she asked about buying a horse collar, he asked if she wanted to put a mirror in it, for a form of folk art consists of decorated horse collars used as frames for mirrors. She replied, "No, I want to put a mare in it."

In the building processes utilizing native wood, in the hand work with axes and adzes and pitchforks, in the use of horses, in the production and preservation of food—in all these things tradition survives. Whether beautiful or not, small works.

THE CARTTER HILLIARD PLACE

In reference to the composition of Idaho's population, it has been observed that Missouri captured the state without firing a shot. Dialect studies done by students of The College of Idaho support the census records in validation of the wry folk observation. Cartter Hilliard helped swell the number of Missouri emigrants, arriving by train from a small place near St. Louis in 1911 and settling near Weiser. He was then too young to file a homestead claim, but in 1914 he found a site on Sheep Creek, and since he was then old enough, he filed on the place he only recently sold but still lives on.

Mr. Hilliard did expand beyond the limits of his original claim, but he nevertheless qualifies for this study, for the crops produced on his total acreage—even after expansion—netted little profit. It was the supplemental income from working out, milking cows, raising chickens and selling eggs that paid the taxes and bought the necessities. And it was the homegrown, the making and repair of equipment, and the constant recycling of materials that kept the list of necessities short.

In response to questions about why he left Missouri, Mr. Hilliard spoke of higher wages and homestead opportunities in Idaho that he had heard about from an aunt and uncle living in Midvale. Then, too, he wanted to go somewhere where he could raise cattle, and Idaho seemed a good place to begin. As to how or why he chose his homestead site, he merely says that Tom Hopper helped him choose it. The spot chosen is about

Figure 2.   A hand-forged hinge made by Cartter Hilliard.

nine miles north of Weiser on Sheep Creek on the
Jenkins Creek Road. (The outsider should not be surprised to learn that he takes this road to reach Sheep
Creek, upper Monroe Creek, Scott Creek, Big Rock
Creek, Little Rock Creek, and Jenkins Creek.) There is
no physical evidence remaining of his original homestead shack, for it has long since been dismembered and
recycled into other buildings. In 1919, having proved
up on his claim, he bought the adjoining Tom Hopper
homestead, and in May he and Anna Gleim were married. They moved into the house where they still live, a
house built by Tom Hopper in 1915 which Mr. Hilliard
has been working over for sixty years. During the fall
of 1979 when he gave a series of interviews for this
study, he added awnings to the west windows.

Mr. Hilliard points out that in 1914–15 thirty-nine
homesteaders used the Jenkins Creek Road that passes
by the foot of the hill on which his house and outbuildings stand. From that time until the Depression, the
Hilliard house was a kind of way station for the homesteaders, who usually did not stay in the back country
during the winter. Each fall and each spring as soon as
the roads had been worked, the families with their
teams, wagons, and milk cows would stop overnight.
Sometimes the house would be full of families and the
barnyard would be full of livestock. Only the Hilliards
have lived on the Jenkins Creek Road since 1969 when
William Wavrick died and Mrs. Wavrick moved into
Weiser.

When asked how he made a go of it while other
homesteaders were losing their land, Mr. Hilliard sets
forth a recipe for survival involving unceasing work,
thrift, the use and reuse of homemade articles, and
making every aspect of the farm venture produce at
least something. The car he drives, a fifty-one-year-old
Model A, is an appropriate symbol of the kind of
human endeavor required to persist as a small home-

steader, embodying as it does simplicity, dependability,
efficiency, and a kind of indefinable integrity.

First there is the matter of work. Hilliard's place is in
dry land country at an elevation of 3500 feet. There
were rocks to move, brush to grub out, fences to build
and maintain. One of the most commonly abused
expressions in American journalism and advertising
(where, granted, one doesn't expect much) is the term
"way of life." Rightly used, it may very well apply only
to those who farm or are engaged in animal husbandry.
Of all the workers of the Western world, only they find
that their work is never done, that vacations are for
other people, that they live amidst their work. That
was true of Cartter Hilliard, who, until he recently sold
his place, could say, "The sun never caught me in bed."
His working day usually began at four-thirty in the
morning. If his task that day was building fence, he
would begin driving posts as soon as he could see (having done the barnyard chores by lantern light), swinging an eighteen-pound maul. Working alone, he could
put up over a half mile of fence a day. At dusk it was
time to do the barnyard chores again. When asked
what he did for recreation, whether, for instance, he
went to country dances, he said he had no time for anything but work, adding, "And I'm still working."

Each season had its own fairly specific activity: hauling manure to the fields in the spring, spring plowing if
spring grain was to be sowed, driving posts for fences
when the snow was just about gone and the ground was
soft, branding, castrating, and vaccinating calves, and
shearing sheep. Then in early summer, around the first
of June, there was the first cutting of hay. When it was
put up, the fences needed further attention; then it was
time for grain harvest. That finished, it was time for
second cutting. When that was done, it was time for
fall plowing. And fence fixing. And hauling the winter's
supply of wood from the mountains. Then came winter
with nothing to do but feed the livestock twice a day,
break a new horse or two, butcher and process the
meat and fat, repair harness, repair any other items
requiring attention, and perhaps complete or begin
construction of a building. And all the time this
seasonal work was going on, there was the daily
work—feeding the pigs, milking, separating.

But work meant more than this, for from all these
activities together there was no guarantee of sufficient
money to buy groceries or pay taxes. Cash was
required and to get it, the small farmer who did not
want to lose his place worked out at whatever job he
could find. Cartter worked for a neighbor, Mrs. Roseborough, helping put up hay, working her cattle,
building a dam. At other times he ran a threshing
machine, making enough on that occasion to pay the
mortgage and save his place. He was also a ditch rider
for the Crane Creek project.

Every structure on the place (Figure 2) except the
house was built by Mr. Hilliard. Many of the building
components were fashioned by him. He designed and
forged the hinges; he made the fastenings for most of

the doors. When asked where he got the idea for the pattern, he replies, "Oh, I just made it." Much of the lumber in the buildings other than the barn was reclaimed from other homestead buildings and shacks as they were abandoned. The barn is quite a different matter.

The full context of Cartter Hilliard's life and work must allow room for other aspects of his role as tradition bearer. He butchered his own meat—sheep, beef, hogs—and salted and smoked the pork, using alder from the nearby creek. He stacked long hay with a derrick and a Jackson fork. He is well attuned to folk beliefs. Coyotes, for example, predict the weather. When they howl a great deal, a storm is coming. The third of December is supposed to rule the winter; that is, the kind of weather that prevails on that day is the kind of weather that will prevail all winter.

In addition to all this, Mr. Hilliard is a water witch. And that, too, figures in the context within which a homestead site exists, for often wells were put down, pipes laid, and houses built in relation to witched sources of water. Abundant literature exists on water witching, so it is hardly necessary to detail the process here. Yet one aspect of it does bear a closer look because it is often ignored. That is the means by which it is determined how far below the surface the water may be found.

To find water, Mr. Hilliard uses two metal rods about twenty inches long with about six inches bent at right angles and enclosed loosely in metal sleeves, permitting the rods to swing. With one of these rods in each hand just about chest high and tipped slightly down so they will have to turn against gravity, Mr. Hilliard walks forward (Figure 3). If there is underground water, the rods begin to swing toward each other in their sleeves. When they cross, he stops, for that is the place to put down the well. The next step in the process tells how deep to dig. Substituting a rod perhaps four and a half feet long, Mr. Hilliard sits down, holding the rod in front of him so that the tip is resting on the spot where the shorter rods swung toward one another and crossed. Then he lifts the end of the rod perhaps five or six inches from the ground, and since the rod is thin and flexible it begins to bob up and down. The number of times the rod taps the ground is the number of feet to water. His method has never failed, and at the time of this study he was putting down another well, the third one on the place, with the assistance of ten sticks of dynamite.

Most of Hilliard's buildings represent a kind of traditional eclecticism. In erecting them he accomplished two things. He met, first of all, the various needs imposed upon him by the circumstances of his homestead—a granary, a sheep fold, a woodshed, a chicken house, a smokehouse, a shop, a garage, feed bunks. In the second place, he put to good use lumber already used. This was essential to his sense of thrift. Why should those homestead structures be left to weather and decay after they were abandoned by the numerous

Figure 3. Cartter Hilliard witching water.

homesteaders who left? So the buildings were either dismantled and their wood incorporated into a new structure or dragged intact to the Hilliard place and incorporated into a structure or left fairly intact and added onto. But with the barn, Mr. Hilliard's creative impulse came into play.

Much of the value of a site survey resides in the fact that what is surveyed is found to be typical. This or that structure is representative of its time and place and therefore incorporates and expresses the esthetic and economic values of the community of which its builders were a part. Thus sites surveyed may be presumed to provide a kind of cultural index. The Hilliard barn is atypical. An artifact on the cultural landscape, it is also an index of Mr. Hilliard's character. And that is important, too (Figure 4).

Figure 4.   Three-level barn built by Cartter Hilliard in the 1930s. The board and batten structure measures 40 by 70 feet. Gable ends are on an east-west axis with the long slope of the roof to the south. Hay door and hood over it are still unfinished (fall, 1979).

Built of new lumber over a three-year period and mostly by himself, the barn cost only slightly over $800 —$475 for lumber and $350 for the twenty-eight gauge galvanized iron for the roof. The figures do not include compensation for Mr. Hilliard's time. He suspects it would cost $10,000 today; he is probably underestimating its value as subsistence farmers are apt to do when they guess yield of grain or weight of animals they send to market.

Mr. Hilliard says he had an idea in mind for a different kind of barn, but this one took shape as it did because of a layer of basalt he had not anticipated. In digging where the north foundation would be, he struck a layer of impenetrable basalt fairly near the surface, and that became the foundation of that side. But the formation dipped abruptly, and the foundation for the other three sides is made of rocks hauled for that purpose. Consequently, the barn roof has an abrupt slant to the north but a long slant to the south, giving the barn the appearance of a great shed. The gable ends are on an east-west axis.

The barn has three levels, a fact partly determined by the basalt on the north side. The top level of the barn is a hay mow that is reached from the north side, not through the hay doors in the gable ends on the east and west. In times past the mow has held 1400 bales.

On the level immediately below the hay mow are stalls for six horses and mangers and stanchions for six cows. These are ranged along the north wall. Double doors on either end of the barn will accommodate a team of horses, and a wagon can be driven through the central driveway. Since the ceiling of this part of the barn is the floor of the hay mow, it must bear or be capable of bearing great weight. It is supported on the south side of the driveway by thirteen posts about ten inches in diameter, eight of the same size along the north side of the driveway, and ten such posts at the ends of the stalls and mangers against the north wall. Cross members resting on the posts and undergirding the ceiling-floor consist of twenty-eight posts (actually small logs) of about the same size. In addition, many long bolts salvaged from siphons and flumes that burned on the Crane Creek project reinforce the structure.

The lowest level is another area for cattle, and it may be reached by a stairway inside or through outside doors at ground level on either end. A particularly interesting feature of this level, which is on the southern side of the barn, is the row of ten windows, nine panes to each window, which cannot be opened. There are five doors interspersed with and the same size as the windows that can be lowered. There is also a door of standard size placed just west of the center of this wall. The light from the south and the light coming through the open double doors at the ends of the central driveway on the next level up give the barn a bright and airy spaciousness. But there is also the impression of sturdy durability because of the substantial uprights and cross members.

Another good example of resourcefulness in the use of available materials was the telephone. In 1914 some of Mr. Hilliard's neighbors developed a telephone circuit that was conducted along a barbwire fence. Then in 1922 a single telephone wire was substituted, and this new circuit went through central downtown. There were sixteen neighbors for this one line which included people on Sheep Creek, Monroe Creek, and Mann's Creek.

THE WILLIAM H. WAVRICK HOMESTEAD

In 1929 William Henry Wavrick bought a Model T Ford, the first and only car he ever owned. The next year he moved his family to the place about nineteen miles north of Weiser that he had homesteaded in 1913, there to live the rest of his life. He had a section of land, and when he died in 1969 the place was smaller by the two hundred acres he had sold. An account of the life of the Wavrick family on upper Monroe Creek reads like an essay in survival; that is, survival in the folkloric sense.

William Wavrick was born in Pittsburgh, Pennsylvania, in 1885, to Mr. and Mrs. John Wavrick, who had emigrated from Bohemia. Later the family moved to DeQueen, Arkansas, where William met Velma Hargis, his future wife. Still restless and now attracted by prospects of homesteading in the West, John Wavrick in 1903 took his family to Poverty Flat west of Weiser, Idaho. Here the Wavrick family settled.

As was customary in those times, the Wavrick men obtained the wood for the family stoves by taking teams and wagons to the fir and pine forests north of Weiser. On one such trip William discovered the Upper Monroe Creek Valley, and it pleased him. He decided that that was where he should homestead. Selecting a spot up a draw with a good spring, perhaps a quarter of a mile from the creek itself, William built a log cabin. While living in it, laying out his fields, burning and grubbing out the sagebrush, and building fences, he found time to build two more houses nearer the creek, a board and batten structure and a log cabin just a few feet from it. These will be described in detail later. In 1920 he and Velma Hargis, the girl from Arkansas who used to attend dances where William played the violin, began a married life that was to endure forty-nine years.

Initially it appeared that the William Wavricks, like many of the other thirty-nine homesteaders of that general area—Monroe Creek, Big and Little Rock Creeks, Scott Creek, Jenkins Creek, and Sheep Creek—would use their place on upper Monroe Creek in a manner suggestive of the shielings of Scandinavia and Scotland. There it was customary for women to move the cattle to higher pastures in the summer and make butter and cheese, returning with the cattle at the end of summer or early in the fall. And the dairy business during this general period of time was flourishing. Figures from the 1935 *Idaho Digest and Blue Book* (p. 536) indicate that farmers on both a large and small scale relied on milking cows to help make a living, for in 1902 there were 50,000 milk cows valued at $35 per head; in 1930, 118,000 at $80 per head; and in 1933, 200,000 at $31 per head.

But in 1930, the Wavricks went up to their mountain place and stayed. Their shieling became their permanent home.

As is observed elsewhere in this study, isolation is both a cultural phenomenon and a function of time and space. The William Wavrick homestead was between nineteen and twenty miles north of Weiser, and in that distance the elevation increases from about 2100 to about 5200 feet. Until 1929 the Wavricks relied upon a team and wagon. That meant every summer trip to town was a three-day trip for Mr. Wavrick—a day to get to town, a day to sell cream, buy supplies, and attend to business, and a day to return. It also meant that Mrs. Wavrick and the girls did a lot of milking and separating. And even after the purchase of the Model T, roads were often impassable by car, so a team and wagon would have to be used. Today the road still requires fording Monroe Creek three times, and a shower makes the 'dobe difficult and unsafe to drive upon. It was here that William and Velma Wavrick reared Della Hope, born on the Weiser Flat in 1921; Wilma, or Billie, who was born in the second log cabin in 1923; and Anna Marie, the youngest girl, born in Weiser in 1930.

A look at the survival of patterns that can best be called folkloric or traditional will establish the context within which the Wavrick site may be studied.

The first cabin on the homestead was built of logs with strips of wood nailed over the cracks. The roof was made of shakes that Mr. Wavrick rived out with a froe, to use a verb Mrs. Wavrick employed. It is a one-room cabin with two windows and no loft. The cornering is v-notched.

In 1914–15, Mr. Wavrick, with the assistance of his brothers and father, built two houses near the banks of Monroe Creek, placing their gables on a north-south axis with three and a half feet between them. The northernmost house is of board and batten with a tar paper roof. If the sod shanty was the prototypal homestead structure for the Great Plains, the board and batten tar paper shack was the common structure for much Western twentieth-century homesteading where

Figure 5.   The Wavrick house with the board and batten kitchen in good repair but the log bedroom in a collapsed state.

timber was not close by. In this house was a woodburn-
ing range with warming ovens, and this was where the
family ate. The floor was covered with linoleum, and
there were built-in shelves. Referred to as the living
room or the kitchen, it has two double hung sash windows, one on the east and one on the north. The room
was papered several times.

Separated from the kitchen by a breezeway was the
log house, an arrangement Billie Wavrick Waldrop
(Mrs. James C. Waldrop) believes to have derived from
her grandfather's memory of similarly placed houses
and outbuildings in Austria designed to minimize
discomfort and snow problems in areas with severe
winters. The logs were surfaced for the inside of the
house but are in their natural round on the outside.
Corners are v-notched, and the chinking is of local
adobe with straw intermixed. The notching was apparently done with an ax. The shingles were of red
fir — the roof collapsed under last winter's snow — that
Mr. Wavrick rived out with a froe. There were three
windows on the first level and a window and door in
the north gable end of the upper half story. It was
through this door that the girls reached their bedroom
in the loft after climbing up an exterior ladder. The
building was heated by a wood-burning stove on the
main floor.

After these two dwellings were finished in the summer of 1914 or 1915, Mr. Waverick did an oil painting
of them, with their border of hollyhocks, and sent it to
Velma. Following their marriage in 1920, the young
couple put up additional structures as circumstances required. The remains of a garage, a barn, a chicken
house, a spare "dormitory" for guests, a shop, a
smokehouse and separator room, and sheds of various
kinds give the place the appearance of a well-planned
farmstead, even in their ruinous condition.

Blacksmithing was another of Mr. Wavrick's skills.
He had a forge and anvil, and Billie remembers that her
father knew the exact color or shade of color required
to heat metal for a particular purpose and whether or
just how long the metal should be immersed in water
for the temper desired. Many of the hinges for the
building were home forged. Some, however, were
made of leather as a convenient and thrifty way to use
otherwise wasted material, perhaps a boot top or hame
strap broken beyond repair.

Another aspect of the make-it-yourself-or-do-with-
out building tradition within which Mr. Wavrick
worked is related to equipment necessary to run the
farm. The walking plow was, of course, of commercial
manufacture, although he sharpened the share himself.
Instead of working the plowed ground with disk and

harrow, he used a drag made from logs to break up the clods and level the ground. Ladders were homemade as were his various sleds. Used not only in winter but as stoneboats or slips, these contrivances were convenient ways of transporting small loads of hay, grain, or rocks from a field, or anything that needed to be moved. One sled shows ingenuity in the addition of wooden strips to the runners. These strips of wood absorbed the wear and tear, could easily be replaced, and thus spared the runners themselves. In addition he made knives from worn-out saws and files (for handles he used hickory from broken ax handles), the kitchen table and chairs, and the cupboards with their doors, hinges, and shelves. For his shop, he made screwdrivers and awls. What wagon iron he needed, he forged himself out of scrap iron. His self-sufficiency extended to using native thorn wood for his forge instead of coke or coal. Even skis were homemade.

Provisioning processes were important for several reasons. Good health required good nutrition so what was preserved had to be well put up. Expenses could be kept down by utilizing everything that could be produced at home rather than procured from town. Finally, since the family did not leave after the first snows, for the road was not maintained and snow up to twelve feet in depth prohibited any travel except by snowshoe or ski, provisions had to be abundant. There was, of course, considerable guesswork as to when they would be snowed in, so supplies had to be laid in early. Once snowed in, the family stayed in until perhaps April. To assure an adequate diet, at least the following supplies were obtained and stored: ten fifty-pound sacks of flour stored in large tin cans, one hundred pounds of white and one hundred pounds of brown sugar, one hundred pounds of rice, five gallons of honey, some sorghum, five or ten pounds of baking powder, fifteen gallons of kerosene.

They raised chickens both for eggs and for cooking. Fruit and vegetables were canned or dried. Chokecherries and currants were usually abundant and excellent for jams, jellies, and syrup. Vegetables were traded to their neighbors, the Hilliards, for some of Cartter's homegrown and processed honey. Various kinds of pickles were made, and sauerkraut put up by the gallon. This latter food was cut very fine with a knife, for Mrs. Wavrick had no kraut cutter. Adding one tablespoon of salt to each gallon of cut cabbage, she filled a ten-gallon stone crock and some five-gallon wooden kegs. After fermenting ten to fifteen days, the kraut was ready for storage in the cellar.

Butchering time was important because from the two hogs slaughtered the Wavricks gained both meat and lard and from the lard, soap. Their manner of preserving pork was generally similar to other well-known procedures. After dry curing the meat by salting it down in a wooden box, alternating layers of bacon with layers of salt and splitting the hams to add salt to the interiors, then covering the bacon and hams with a layer of salt—a process that might take up to five weeks—the hams and bacon slabs were taken out of the box, cleaned off, and smoked with green alder. Mrs. Wavrick made soap of lard rendered from pork fat, willow ashes, and water. It was used for all purposes except personal cleanliness. For that, Mr. Wavrick insisted upon Ivory soap.

Two important structures associated with provisioning processes were the smokehouse and the cellar. In the former, pork was hung above a smoldering fire of green or wet alder chips until the meat had absorbed the proper amount of smoke. Whether the smoke actually helped preserve the meat is a question on which opinion is divided, but it is certain that alder imparts a pleasant smoky flavor. The tree is native to the area. The cellar was important the year around. In the summer it kept food cool and fresh, especially the cream, which will be discussed later, and in winter it kept fresh vegetables, fruits, and home-canned foods, including meat, from freezing. It was an excavation dug into the side of the hill just east of the houses and roofed over with logs which were then covered with dirt. Fixed like a room with shelves and bins, the cellar was equipped with an outer door, a space, then an inner door to the cellar proper. It was an effective arrangement which assured that the stored Jonathan, Ben Davis, and winesap apples would keep.

If self-sufficiency was important to the Wavrick family, so was simplicity. Thoreau would have approved. Nowhere are these two characteristics more clearly apparent than in the traditional farming practiced by Wavrick. It has already been noted that he plowed his fields with a walking plow, the old "footburner," and worked the soil with a homemade drag. By standards usually applied to dry farming which required a large area to compensate for scanty yields expected in a dry country (for Washington County is not the Palouse) his fields were small, from forty to eighty acres. Even so, the yield per acre was fairly consistently high, an indication that the annual spring manuring of his fields and his refusal to leave one field in production too long were beneficial traditional practices. Moreover, he never grazed more cattle than his pastures could accommodate.

The grain was sowed broadcast from a bag suspended from a shoulder strap fashioned by Mr. Wavrick. Taught this age-old technique by his father, Mr. Wavrick passed the skill along to his daughters, dipping the hand into the bag of seed for just the right amount, releasing the seed evenly from the hand which moves in a circular motion, singing as they worked. Favorite varieties of wheat included turkey red, federation, and Lemhi. Oats, rye, and barley were also planted in this traditional manner.

After the early homestead boom, which was tapering off about the beginning of the Depression and finished by that national spiritual and economic spasm, Mr. Wavrick and his family harvested the grain by hand. Earlier, he, Cartter Hilliard, and Jim Stover jointly owned and used a threshing machine, but changing cir-

Figure 6.   A bundle of grass, hand-tied with a grass band by Velma Wavrick.

cumstances, including the decline in custom work because of dwindling numbers of homesteaders, caused the thresher to be abandoned. So Mr. Wavrick cut his grain with scythe and cradle, and Mrs. Wavrick and the girls gathered it into bundles with Mrs. Wavrick, usually, tying them by hand.

This activity merits closer analysis, for it illustrates clearly the transmission, utilization, and survival of skills and processes centuries old. Like many of the skills possessed by Mr. Wavrick, he learned this from his father, although the use of cradles was not unknown on the Weiser Flat. When the grain was ready, usually early in September, Mr. Wavrick began cutting it, swinging his scythe with attached cradle in a fluid, easy motion, Billie recalls. The implement, which she alone of the three daughters did not find difficult to master, weighed not over twenty pounds, and she did not find the weight oppressive. With each stroke, he tipped the cradle, depositing the cut grain in little piles which the girls gathered into small bundles. Mrs. Wavrick followed them with ties made of cut grain that had been soaked in water. She wrapped a tie around each bundle, "scotching" the tie at just the right point so as to be able to twist the tie firmly under itself so that the ends would not "swarm," a dialect word referring to

what could happen if the ends were not properly secured and came loose. Her bundles could be tossed around severely without coming undone. After the grain was bundled, it had to be shocked—bundles placed together, butts down, heads leaning together—in groups of ten bundles to a shock until the grain got dryer at which point twenty bundles made up a shock. This was a convenient way of counting the harvest.

After the grain had dried sufficiently, it was time to thresh. The girls would bring the bundles to where Mr. and Mrs. Wavrick had spread a large (at least nine by eleven) canvas. Each bundle would be broken apart with the heads of the grain pointing in toward the center of the canvas; Mr. Wavrick would hammer the heads with his homemade threshing clubs, turning up the corners of the canvas as necessary to keep the grain confined. After the grain had been separated from the heads, it was necessary to separate the kernels from the chaff; this operation was accomplished by scooping up grain and chaff from the pile in the center of the canvas and pouring it into a large tub. They were always grateful for a breeze that would blow the chaff away. The grain would then be sacked and taken from the field where the threshing took place into one of the outbuildings for storage. Most of the wheat was ground by a hand mill into flour of varying fineness, depending on what the baking requirements were, as a change from commercially milled flour, or into cereal for the breakfast table. Oats, barley, rye or wheat would be ground or cracked for hog feed. Sometimes Mr. Wavrick would sell ten or twelve sacks in town, receiving ten cents a sack more than the going price since this grain was free from weed seed and thus desirable as seed.

To solve the problem of rodent destruction of growing and unharvested grain, the Wavricks relied upon the hunting and maternal instincts of cats. Using two mother cats for each grain field, the Wavricks constructed little houses for them, taking out food and water as necessary. It was then a matter of the mother cats hunting to satisfy the increasing appetites of the growing kittens. After harvest the cats were returned home to keep the storage areas free of rodents. Many of the kittens must have turned feral, for they were seldom seen after they reached maturity. They were usually not around when their mothers were returned home.

Even though the Wavricks produced much of what they consumed and made many of the articles their living required—all their clothes except overalls were made from yard goods—a subsistence economy still required a certain amount of currency. The sale of cream, as has been noted, was an important source of income, no matter how small. It should be noted that they used a cream separator, a form of centrifuge, rather than a fleeter, a hand skimmer like a shallow scoop with holes for the milk to drain through. That the cream could stay sweet for as long as two weeks is testimony both to the cleanliness of the family and to the quality of the cellar. An improperly washed, unscalded separator

Figure 7. Two threshing clubs, about 22 inches long, used by William Wavrick.

Figure 8. Frames for stretching coyote hides, handmade by William Wavrick.

would turn cream unspeakably bad very quickly. When presented with such stuff, the men at the creamery would either dump it into the waste gutter or, more likely, send it back. But even a clean producer of cream had to stir it every day lest it develop a thick, hard surface, and for this Mrs. Wavrick used a peeled thornbush stick. As hardwood, it would not impart an offensive odor or taste to the cream. Lids were kept on the cans of cream in the cellar with an added covering of cloth atop the lids. Wet gunnysacks helped keep the cans cool on the long trip into town.

Hogs, too, were an important source of cash, and the Wavricks raised from ten to fifteen each year, permitting them to graze out on berries and roots or bulbs in the early spring and fall. They had to be confined, of course, during late spring, summer, and early fall when vegetables were growing. Potatoes, rutabagas, turnips, pumpkins, head lettuce, radishes, corn — all these served as cash crops for sale to Weiser stores. In addition, Mr. Wavrick did what so many struggling farmers had to do: in winter he would split posts to sell. Not only did winter provide relatively free time to do this chore, but there was also a widely held conviction that posts cut in winter lasted longer because the sap, it was believed, was in the roots of the tree from which posts

were made. Mr. Wavrick also trapped coyotes and other fur-bearing animals, stretching the pelts over his homemade frames. Chickens were sold as fryers, bringing in a little cash.

And they made it. They were unlike many farmers of the homestead boom years who, after proving up on their land, borrowed from the Federal Land Bank, putting up their patents as security and subsequently losing them. But even the Wavricks had to borrow from this bank to buy cows, and twelve years were required to pay off the loan. Many of those years were spent in labor from four in the morning until they could not see at night; often they would not go to bed until eleven. Under these conditions the care of small children was a problem. It was solved when the elder Wavricks built a small topless wooden box into which they would put the children when it was time to milk. Thus they could have the children in the milking corral with them, and the children would be out from under foot and not get mixed up with cranky milk cows.

If the study up to this point indicates that the Wavricks worked hard and were thrifty, the record is accurate. But it must also be noted that there was time for recreation, for entertainment, and for formal school-work for the youngsters. Of the three girls, only the two older ones went to public school . . . for one year. The rest of their education, including their theological training, was completed as circumstances dictated on the homestead.

During fall, winter, and spring the Wavrick household was also a part-time school. Mrs. Wavrick had taught two or three years in Arkansas, and Mr. Wavrick had finished through the eleventh grade, being awarded the high school diploma after taking the appropriate tests. Why couldn't they educate their children, especially in view of the fact that there was no alternative? So they obtained texts from the nearest public school, District #26, and I recall quite clearly one fall when Mr. Wavrick, dressed in what I remember as a black broadcloth suit with a string tie and a big Western hat, face wreathed in smile, knocked at our schoolhouse door to borrow books for the coming year. The memory may be inaccurate in its particulars, but it is a fact. The Wavrick girls studied the same subjects the eight students at District #26 worried over: reading, history, geography, grammar, civics, physiology, arithmetic. And art and music. For pleasure reading they had such books as *The Keeper of the Bees, The Trail of the Lonesome Pine, The Rim of the World, The Winning of Barbara Worth,* and *The Calling of Dan Matthews.*

One year Sheriff Frank Kennedy appeared at the Wavrick homestead with an affidavit sworn by people Billie describes as "do-gooders" claiming the Wavrick children were growing up deprived. As a result the girls were taken to the Washington County courthouse and given achievement tests. The results indicated that the girls were doing fine, and the county superintendent suggested that they could provide an example to other scholars in the county schools. Each spring thereafter the county superintendent would travel up to the Wavrick place to administer achievement tests, and each year the girls compared favorably with their contemporaries.

Part of their education was art, and Mr. Wavrick, whose 1914 or 1915 oil painting of the two houses has been referred to, shared with the youngsters his understanding of how to mix colors to create the illusion of distance, of composition, and of other artistic matters. He stimulated an interest in art in all the girls, and it is still vigorous in the two older ones, Billie's paintings exhibiting qualities found in American limners.

Besides painting and sketching, at least one of the Wavrick girls — Billie — showed some skill in sculpture, working with native clay to create works ranging from a half-life-size bust of a neighbor to utilitarian objects like pipe racks.

Music, too, was encouraged by Mr. and Mrs. Wavrick, who somehow managed to get the girls harmonicas, violins, guitars, and a small accordion. But the interest in music is not surprising, for southern musicality is frequently observed and remarked upon from George Pullen Jackson's *White Spirituals of the Southern Uplands* to Grand Ol' Opry and Hee Haw. Mr.

Wavrick's progenitors were Bohemian, and his people had been musicians and instrument makers in Europe where a grandfather had conducted a popular orchestra. Mr. Wavrick, as noted earlier, played the violin for dances in Arkansas, playing tunes his father had taught him. He passed on to his daughters such tunes as "Bohemian Girl" and "Blue Danube." Before their musical education was complete, the girls could play the accordion and harmonica by ear, the guitar and violin by note, and the fiddle by ear. "Fiddle" and "violin" is a distinction Billie makes to refer to playing the traditional fiddle tunes her father used to play for dances — "Old Joe Clark" and the "Peekaboo Waltz" — as opposed to playing music by notation.

Music, then, was both something to be studied and something to be enjoyed. By comparison, our musical education at Pleasant View School, District #26, left a great deal to be desired. In other respects, however, the Wavrick school and the district school were quite comparable, as far as results are concerned. One calendar custom the Wavrick and the district children shared was the observation of Christmas. Certainly the Christmas season was the time that was joyful and elaborate for all of us, though the celebration took different forms as dictated by circumstances. A brief description of a Wavrick Christmas helps establish the context within which the subsistence economy of the homesteader exercised its harsh demands.

The season began for the Wavricks about a week before Christmas when Mr. Wavrick and the girls would select the tree from evergreens growing on their place. Once in place, the tree was decorated from the hoard of tinfoil carefully saved from candy and chewing gum wrappers during the months since last Christmas. Obviously there were no lights for the tree. Nor did the family string popcorn or cranberries; instead they used wild rose hips. Santa Claus was real for a long time, and he was expected Christmas Eve, leaving presents that were opened Christmas morning. Even the appearance of a lot of homemade gifts did not disillusion the girls about St. Nick. Wooden spools, for example, recognized as wooden spools, were transformed into excellent spinning tops without causing disbelief.

Following the opening of presents, preparations continued for the big Christmas dinner to which Cartter and Anna Hilliard could be expected to come, roads permitting. Mrs. Hilliard, who had a reputation as an excellent cook, could be counted on to bring mince pies and a chicken roasted with her special oyster stuffing, a dish that Billie Waldrop still prepares following Anna's recipe. In addition, the Wavricks would supply fruitcakes, pumpkin pies, candied squash (rather than sweet potatoes, which the Wavricks could not grow), roast pork, and always nuts and candies. Billie, reflecting upon their life back then, remembers that their father always had candy appropriate to the season and marvels how he did it: Christmas candy at Christmas, heart candy for Valentine's Day, Easter egg candy for Easter.

After dinner, the Wavrick girls played their instruments and sang.

In spite of their physical isolation, which was quite literal after the first snows (in advance of which most of the milk cows would be taken down to winter with some of the relatives, usually Mr. Wavrick's father), the family were neither intellectually nor culturally removed from the world, for Mr. Wavrick, who was a well-read man, had progressed from wet battery radios to the most recent dry cell receiver while experimenting with crystal sets. It is difficult to describe the pellucid clarity with which those early battery radios, miles from any interference from electrical sources except, perhaps, the northern lights, received stations far and near, especially at night. And as might be expected, the Wavricks used radio as an audial aid to education as well as a source of entertainment. Because batteries were expensive and the only way to charge them was by putting them in the Ford and idling it, radio time was strictly managed: news of the world, including Mussolini's campaign in Ethiopia, local news, music, certain programs with cultural or educational thrust, a few programs like Uncle Billy's children's request program from KIDO, Boise, the Arizona Wranglers, Amos 'n Andy, Myrt and Marge, Shafter Parker and the In-Laws, Frank Watanabe and the Honorable Archie, Burns and Allen. Radio was a resource that gave the Wavricks a knowledge of the world which they were in but not of and helped prepare the girls for life away from Monroe Creek.

A final aspect of their education had to do with the religious instruction the children received, for the Wavricks were devout Catholics, and it was impossible for them to get to town for catechism. This Mr. Wavrick took charge of, using books he had obtained for this purpose.

An important aspect of the framework within which the Wavricks lived requires a brief comment before concluding this portion of the study. It is appropriately considered because it, too, is part of what the places would say if they could talk and reflects the tenuousness and vulnerability of lives lived in the remoteness of Washington County.

After the early thirties the neighbors of the Wavricks were four: nine miles south lived the Hilliards; five miles east lived the Noah McGinnis family, but they used their homestead principally as a shieling, returning to the lower country near town in the fall; the Anderson Bloomer place, two or three miles north, was another shieling where Cora and Bess Bloomer milked and separated and other family members came up to pick up the cream and take it to town; Oscar Fallers, a bachelor, lived perhaps ten miles west on the head of Rock Creek, or, more accurately, between the headwaters of Rock Creek and Wolf Creek. Really, then, the Wavricks had for neighbors Cartter and Anna Hilliard and Oscar Fallers when, in about 1934 or 1935, there was a smallpox visitation.

In October Mr. Fallers had gone to town for some supplies, probably not for the entire winter, which would not be likely to set in for a couple of months. From someone whom he saw in Weiser, perhaps, or through some other exposure he encountered smallpox virus. After returning to his isolated cabin — he nearly always traveled horseback — and undergoing the appropriate incubation period, he came down with it. He was very ill; before long his supplies gave out completely. He could just make it to the door of his cabin to shoot a grouse or sagehen or a rabbit, whatever small game came near to eat the thorn berries. Then he would boil the meat and eat it and the broth.

When he had recovered some strength, he saddled Old Major and rode to the Waverick place. He yelled from a distance that he had smallpox and was out of food; could Mrs. Wavrick fix him a sack of supplies, maybe a small can of milk and things he could fix soup of. He did not wish to touch a thing, did not want to come near. Mrs. Wavrick fixed some things he could put in his saddlebags, and she also prepared some things that she put in a gunnysack that he could tie behind his saddle. He told Mrs. Wavrick to leave them out in the field and then to get clear away. He rode some distance off, Mrs. Wavrick placed the supplies where he could get them and went back to the cabin. He could barely get off his horse, tie the supplies on, and get back on. He was asked to stay but said "Nothin' doin' " and rode off. He survived.

Even with these precautions, however, smallpox struck the family, and in about two weeks Della Hope and Billie came down with it. Billie recalls that she had it very severely. As was customary in those times, the girls had to be sat up with. With no neighbors to share the burden, the total responsibility fell to the parents who took turns sitting up with the girls all night long. After the girls had partially recovered, the parents and the youngest daughter fell ill, although their cases were comparatively light.

Billie remembers that they had just about all the usual diseases of childhood and other sickness, but they survived . . . even Billie's eating of wild geraniums when she was a toddler. In this case, a dose of ipecac induced vomiting which eliminated the danger of poisoning.

In concluding this portion of the study it is difficult to suppress the conviction that the Wavricks attempted (and perhaps succeeded in the attempt) to make a fine art of living. Always the folklorist is faced with the danger of sentimentalizing his subjects, and that temptation is here. A balanced treatment, however, must accommodate the beauty and small triumphs of such lives as have been set forth here as well as the hard work, the pain and illness. Assuredly Mr. Wavrick knew them all, and even in his last summer — he died of cancer in 1969 in the house he had built on the place he had homesteaded — he neither complained of pain nor bemoaned his lot. When the end came, Mrs. Wavrick walked the nine miles to Cartter Hilliard's place to telephone Billie.

Billie remembers: "Daddy taught us to see the beauty of life and nature: 'Take time to look up at the stars at night, watch the moon rise, watch the sun set, watch the buds open in the spring, watch for the first flower and listen for the first bird.' And to this day I still do."

CONCLUSION

Washington County has many examples of major agricultural and livestock operations whose core is a nineteenth- or early twentieth-century homestead. These deserve study in their own right, for in many respects they reflect the American dream of upward mobility. The formula can be expressed as "homestead plus hard work plus thrift equals expansion or success." On the way to success, these entrepreneurs swallowed up small and unsuccessful homesteads, often eliminating fences, homestead shacks, orchards, and other visual evidence of the integrity of the original claim. But of the other kind of homestead—the small-scale operation that stayed intact—there are few examples.

To one sort of mind that scarcity poses no problem because the small subsistence operation does not square with the two popular images of homesteading. But to the student of culture who wishes to get beyond the stereotype, however real it is, this third category poses challenges of all sorts.

These twentieth-century homesteaders came to Washington County for a variety of reasons, but most of them can be subsumed under the general heading "Opportunity." Appearing on the scene somewhat late, they were obliged to take unclaimed land, although this is not to say that it was from their perspective undesirable. Whereas most homesteaders of this period used their land as shielings*, the sites identified in this study were not used in this fashion, becoming, instead, permanent homes. In all three cases the first structures on the homesteads were houses—the Moore log cabin, the Tom Hopper house which Cartter Hilliard has continued to rework, and the first Wavrick cabin built up the draw from the permanent home site. This is not surprising since a domicile was required by the homestead law. What is a bit unusual is the integrity of the Moore cabin, for here the original became the permanent.

The eventual configuration of a climax homestead, to borrow a term from ecology to refer to the type of homestead with which this study is concerned, may be described as a clustering of structures around the permanent dwelling, built as needed. For the Moore homestead, the configuration includes a small log cabin behind the dwelling, used for storage, an addition to

---

*In 1916 Congress passed the National Grazing Homestead Act, providing grazing lands in quantities of 320 acres. In the same year the Federal Farm Loan Act made money available for the development of agriculture. Although these laws were not mentioned by my informants, Congress may nevertheless have helped influence homesteaders to view their mountain lands as shielings.

the dwelling itself, a machine shed, and a fairly recent (1940s) barn. The pattern is similar at the Hilliard place, although even to the casual eye it must appear that Mr. Hilliard has a very great many buildings, among them the many times modified house, chicken house, storage sheds, a loafing shed, well house, shop, garage, hay barn, machine shed, and the newest structure, a large and interesting barn. The Wavrick place is different from the other two in several respects. In the first place, the two 1914–15 dwellings retained their integrity; they were not modified structurally nor added onto. There is only one board and batten-tar paper roof structure; all the others are framed with logs or poles and covered with shakes of red fir. The Wavrick buildings cluster together more closely than do those on the other two sites and are also on a smaller scale. The Moore and Hilliard places have recent large barns; there is no comparable element in the configuration of the Wavrick homestead where the barn and enclosure for horses are both small.

In and around some of these structures repose various artifacts associated with climax homesteading. For example, in the first Wavrick log cabin are stored some homemade frames for stretching coyote skins. A homemade ladder leans against the cabin. Around the later dwellings the following home-shaped items may be seen: a tall pole which was part of Mr. Wavrick's radio antenna, a trough made from a small log, several slips (or "sleds" or "stoneboats"), a ski, the remains of some harness, the wooden box in which the Wavrick girls were placed to keep them safe while their parents milked the cows, scraps of iron left over from Mr. Wavrick's blacksmithing, including a hand-forged branding iron. It is appropriate to point out here that the day after Mr. Wavrick's death when Mrs. Wavrick had moved to Weiser, vandalism and theft began, crimes unfortunately still in progress. On the Hilliard homestead one sees "rock corners" (or rock jacks, means of bracing fences on rocky ground), mangers, a shelter for salt, a wheelbarrow, and a trailer—all homemade. Mr. Hilliard's forge is still there, and he uses an extraordinarily well-equipped machine shop.

If these homesteads are indeed the surviving examples of their type in Washington County, then they may be considered typical of such climax homesteads in southwestern Idaho. Never numerous, they may also be considered an increasingly endangered species.

Subsistence farming as practiced by homesteaders whose operations either by choice or necessity remained small made great demands. Some of those demands were met by traditional skills and provisioning processes that were an essential part of the context within which they lived. My father may have spoken for generations of such people when he said, "I didn't mind starving as long as I could be my own boss." No evidence exists that the homesteaders treated in this study ever approached the poverty level, for their various capabilities banished the proverbial wolf. But he might have been heard to howl once or twice.

Folklife and Change

Early Dairy Barns of Buhl
MADELINE BUCKENDORF

Medical Care in Latah County, 1870–1930
KEITH PETERSEN

Folk Ballad Characteristics in a Present-Day
Collection of Songs
THOMAS EDWARD CHENEY

Motorcycles, Guitars and Bucking Broncs:
Twentieth-Century Gravestones in
Southeastern Idaho
CAROL EDISON

Early Dairy Barns of Buhl

Madeline Buckendorf

The settlement of irrigated farmlands along the Snake River in south central Idaho co-incided with a rapid development of agricultural technology and increase in popular instruc-tion in progressive farming techniques. Farmers responded to these changes in their agricultural practices, their choices of machinery, and their construction of barns and other outbuildings. In the following article, Buckendorf focuses on the dairy barns built by a group of settlers near Buhl. In tracing the development of barn styles, roof framing, and other ar-chitectural elements, she illustrates how farmers and builders chose among old and new technologies. One important conclusion implicit in Buckendorf's analysis is that folk patterns are not automatically dropped in the presence of a new industrial alternative. Further, in many examples an intermixing of traditions occurs: builders used what they perceived to be the best of different traditions. The resulting cultural complex is a hybrid one, with the presence of both old and new elements, and with the promise of new alterations to fit the changing environment.

Madeline Buckendorf is a graduate of The College of Idaho in Caldwell. As Coordinator of the Idaho Oral History Center, a program of the Idaho State Historical Society, she has worked closely with the historic sites survey program of the State Historic Preservation Office. Buckendorf currently directs an NEH-funded project, "Working Together: A Regional Approach to Community Traditions and History in Idaho."

*E*ast of Buhl, along a four-mile stretch of country road running north and south, stand monuments to the beginnings of the dairy industry in southwest Idaho. These monuments are the barns, the "business build-ings" of dairy farmsteads. "The barn builds the house" is an expression heard often from long-time farmers of the area, underscoring the importance of the barn to their livelihood. A well-built barn was vital to the dairy farmer: "It must house valuable animals and keep them healthy, be clean and sanitary, provide comfortable conditions for workers and adequate storage conditions for milk and feed."[1]

Research into the history of these barns has un-covered the history of a small dairying community that was initially settled by farmers from Tillamook, Ore-gon, between 1910 and 1912. Other farmers from other regions soon settled in the neighborhood and also became involved in dairying. The time period of settle-ment was also a time of great change nationwide in agricultural practices, especially in barn construction and the development of the new dairy industry. This article will describe the early history of this small dairy community, the design of two styles of its barns, and the various factors that influenced the form, style, and construction of these structures.

FROM TILLAMOOK TO BUHL

By the 1900s Tillamook County, on the Oregon coast west of Portland, had been settled for forty years. Its population was made up primarily of Swedes, Swiss,

and Irish; the main occupation was dairy farming.[2] The owner of one of those dairy farms was Gustave Kunze, a German-American who had moved to Tillamook in 1891 from McKeesport, Pennsylvania. Kunze was no stranger to dairy farming; he had owned a dairy farm in McKeesport, and his family had owned a small dairy herd in Allegheny, Pennsylvania.[3] When Kunze moved to Tillamook, he bought a farm that had a house and a low, one-story barn with sheds on each side of it. Kunze built and operated a small cheese factory on his farm. He enlisted the help of Arnold Tannler, a cheesemaker originally from Switzerland. Neighbors sold their milk to Kunze; he, in turn, would make it into cheese.[4] Some of the neighbors who brought milk to Kunze's factory were the families of Riley Maxwell and Alfred Carlson.[5] Carlson owned a transverse-crib style of barn[6] and Maxwell a long, low shed with pens on both sides. These families, with two other families from the Tillamook area (T. P. Bowlby and A. A. Stauffacher), would eventually make the move to Buhl.

Lured by the promotional advertising distributed by the Buhl Commercial Club, Gustave Kunze visited Buhl in 1910. Great tracts of land were being developed under the Carey Act, a law passed by Congress in 1894 to reclaim the desert under public domain for agricul-ture by privately funded development. Milner Dam and an accompanying canal system had been finished in 1905, providing water to the arid acres. The land was cheap and water plentiful. Kunze was also at-tracted to the area by the fact that alfalfa could be grown in great quantities; grain and hay had to be freighted into Tillamook.[7] He purchased a section of uncleared land in 1910, and by the early part of 1912 he had erected a barn, a home, and a cheese factory. He brought Arnold Tannler, who eventually married Kunze's daughter Lenora, to make the cheese.

The dedication of the Cloverleaf Cheese Factory in April of 1912 was a major event in the area; the newspaper gave it full coverage on the front page. Kunze's "immense" dairy barn is discussed in the article: "[it] is said to be the largest dairy barn in the state. This barn has a capacity for over 100 head of stock . . . and has a hay capacity of 200 tons in the loft."[8] The names of Bowlby, Maxwell, Carlson, and Stauffacher are also mentioned in the article, described as "rich dairymen from Tillamook" who moved to Buhl because of climatic conditions.[9] They all settled on property within a one-mile radius of one another, and only three miles from Kunze's place. Three of these farmers followed Kunze's example and built large new dairy barns. All of them brought milk to the Cloverleaf Cheese Factory.[10]

Gustave Kunze's own children also became involved in his dairy business. His son Rudolf helped run the cheese factory and managed a small dairy herd of his own. His daughter Frieda married Art Maxwell (no relation to Riley Maxwell), who worked for Kunze. They settled close by, started a dairy operation, and brought milk to the cheese factory. Other farmers in the neighborhood became interested in the dairy business; for example, Max Dau, who lived close by, had a dairy barn built on his place in 1913.[11]

Another person who played an important role in the development of the Buhl dairy community was Henry Schick. Schick was a Russian-German immigrant who had lived in Chicago before coming to Idaho in the early 1900s.[12] A farmhand and a builder, he helped in the construction of Kunze's barn and cheese factory and is reputed to have built the barns of Alfred Carlson, T. P. Bowlby, Max Dau, and Art Maxwell.[13] Schick had particular competence in cement work and iron work, which he learned from working with his brother, a building contractor in Chicago, and from employment in an iron-works factory there.[14] Schick eventually became interested in the dairy business, bought a parcel of land from Gustave Kunze,[15] and erected his own large dairy barn. Schick brought milk to Kunze's cheese factory and continued to do some building as well.

By 1915, the dairy industry was in full swing in the Buhl area. Gustave Kunze became president of the State Dairy Association and received a medal for his cheese products at the Panama/Pacific International Exposition in San Francisco.[16] Kunze and Schick were written up as successful farmers in newspapers and promotional literature. Kunze decided to retire from farming and sold his place in 1918 to E. T. Sandmeyer. Sandmeyer ran the cheese factory four to five years, then leased it to the dairy farmers of the area, who ran it as a cooperative.[17] The Sego Milk Company, in turn,

leased the factory from the farmers in the mid-twenties in order to test the area's milk production for building a milk factory in Buhl.[18] When the milk factory eventually opened, many farmers then started to take milk to it rather than to the cheese factory, and the Cloverleaf Cheese Factory ceased operation. In later years, dairying took a lesser role in comparison to raising beef cattle and growing row crops such as beets, beans, and potatoes. Many farmers kept a few cows and sold milk to the factory in Buhl, but few dairies the size of Kunze's operation still existed. The large dairy barns became outdated structures when hay began to be baled and stored outside and cows were no longer kept indoors. Yet the dairy barns still stand, reminders of the beginnings of the dairy industry in Buhl.

THE BUHL DAIRY BARNS

Gustave Kunze, T. P. Bowlby, and Alfred Carlson chose to build a new style of barn that was far different from the style of barns they had owned previously (Figure 1).[19] The gambrel-roofed dairy barn had come into vogue in the early 1900s and was advertised in agricultural bulletins and building plan books. This new style of barn was just beginning to be built in Tillamook around 1910.[20] The use of concrete as a building material was also promoted at that time; Kunze and Schick had experience in working with it. Kunze chose to build his new barn in Buhl using these new building features; Bowlby and Carlson followed suit. Others in the area who built later also used the idea of a gambrel roof and concrete walls, but the type of construction methods used began to change. Two types of gambrel roofs emerged in the dairy community of Buhl. Changes in the methods of putting up hay also occurred, as did variations in the barns' floor plans. The following descriptions of the barns, in the order they were built, will point out some of these changes.

The Gustave Kunze Barn. It is highly likely that barn forms of all kinds, including gambrel-roof barns, existed in the region before the coming of Gustave Kunze to the Buhl area. However, his barn was the first in Buhl that was built specifically for dairying; most other barns were multipurpose structures used to store crops and house cattle, hogs, and sheep.

The Kunze barn was a specialized structure, completely devoted to the new "science" of dairy farming. Its mammoth proportions—120 feet long, 70 feet wide, 45 feet tall—reflect the fact it was built to house and feed a hundred dairy cattle. Concrete was used in the floor and ten-foot walls of the barn. A huge gambrel roof with slightly flared eaves capped the second-floor hay-storage loft. A large cupola and dormers in the roof and double-sashed windows in the side walls were used for ventilation. Two large cement silos were built close to the barn.

The floor plan of the first floor is a relatively simple one (Figure 2). Four rows of stanchions run the entire length of the barn. The rows are in two sets, with the

Figure 1. The Gustave Kunze barn. The extension on the right-hand side of the photo is the horse barn added on in 1917.

cows facing inwardly towards each other in each set. The cows enter the barn from the south end; passages for the cattle flank each set of mangers, forming a large central passage in the middle of the barn. Feed alleys run up the center of each set of mangers. A milk room is located on the northwest corner of the barn, with water running through a trough in it to keep the milk cans cool. Calf pens are placed under the ramps that run up to the second story on the east and west sides of the barn.

These ramps to the second story were used for the unloading of hay into the loft of the barn. The hay wagon was driven up the east ramp into the middle of the barn, where the sling in which the hay was loaded was attached to a rope which was suspended from tracks running on the interior slopes of the roof.[21] A load of hay could be dropped anywhere along this length. The empty wagon was driven out of the west side of the barn. Hay and grain were then provided to the cattle through holes cut in the loft floor above the wagon drives. Eight years after the barn's construction, cows were fed out of doors instead of in the mangers in front of the stanchions.[22]

The superstructure of the roof shows a very early type of support given to a gambrel roof. The upper rafters run from the roof ridge to the break in the slope, supported by three pieces of wood nailed together. This is called a secondary plate. The secondary plate is supported by twelve 25-foot posts, six to a side, extending through the loft to the bottom floor. The lower rafters run from the secondary plate to the edge of the loft floor. These lower rafters connect to the floor joists,

which function as tie beams across the building.[23] The actual tie beam has been moved up toward the ridge, allowing the hay carrier to move freely through the center of the loft. The upper and lower rafters are braced to each other by a diagonal framing. Originally, there was no braced framing used to support the rafters. E. T. Sandmeyer added the diagonal framing in 1928 because he was concerned about the roof caving in under a heavy snow.[24] Sandmeyer may have been influenced by other barns built later in the area which used diagonal bracing to frame their roofs (Figure 3).

An addition markedly different from the original barn but similar to ones built later in the area was built in 1917 to house the horses separately from the cows. It was made necessary by governmental regulations concerning the sanitary conditions in which milking occurred.[25] The sides of the walls of the addition extend five feet above the loft floor. There was also a change with this addition in the method of putting up hay. Hay was unloaded from the outside of the barn, rather than from the inside. The hay carrier track extended over the gable end of the barn and was protected by a square hay hood.

The T. P. Bowlby Barn. Built soon after the Gustave Kunze barn (in 1912), the T. P. Bowlby barn is strikingly similar to it on the exterior (Figure 4). Its proportions are much the same: 70 feet wide, 110 feet long, and approximately 45 feet tall. The gambrel roof extends downward to the 13½-foot concrete walls, which are a foot higher than the first floor. As with the Kunze barn, the secondary plate of the roof is secured

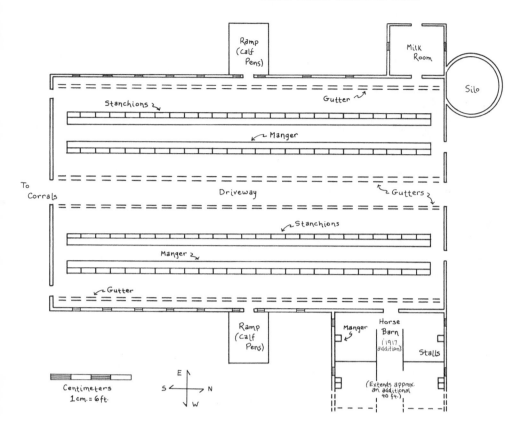

Figure 2. Floor plan of the first floor, Gustave Kunze barn.

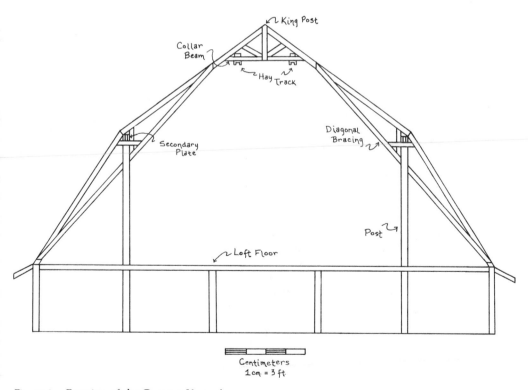

Figure 3. Framing of the Gustave Kunze barn.

Figure 4. The T. P. Bowlby barn.

with huge posts; however, the posts in the Bowlby barn run only to the loft floor and do not run all the way to the bottom floor. The framing of the Bowlby barn is similar to the Kunze barn, with the collar beam up out of the way of the hay carrier. Here diagonal framing is again used to brace the upper and lower rafters; whether this is part of the original construction or added on later is not known. A slight variation in construction occurs: the concrete walls extend above the loft floor one foot. The weight of the roof bears down on the wall, rather than on the crossties of the loft floor.

The floor plan of the Bowlby barn is quite different from the Kunze barn. Only a small portion of the barn is utilized for milking cows. It was built more on the lines of a multipurpose or general farm barn, with a large portion of the barn consisting of stock pens with dirt floors. Twenty stanchions are put in the southeast corner of the barn on a cement floor, with the milk room right beside them. The cows face inwardly with an alleyway for feeding them in front of the manger. Stalls for ten horses were built on the northwest corner, far away from the milking area. The method of putting up hay also differs from the Kunze barn. The wagon is driven into the barn, but through the side of the first floor at the northeast end of the barn. The hay is again in slings and was lifted up to the second floor by a rope and pulley.[26] The hay is moved along the track suspended from the collar beam of the roof frame. Feed for

the milk cows, horses, and other stock is delivered through holes in the floor above their stalls. Grain is stored in bins above the horse stalls, with chutes running to both the exterior of the barn and interior of the first floor. The animals are also fed silage from a wooden silo 32 feet high located at the west end of the barn.

A variety of "filler" was used in the cement walls of the Bowlby barn. Large chunks of lava rock, barbed wire, and sections of small steel pipe were used for reinforcement. Sections of stove pipe were also placed vertically in the cement for ventilation from the first floor of the barn to the outside. The boards used to build the forms for pouring the concrete were later used in the floor joists for the loft, and portions of the cement can still be seen clinging to them.

The Alfred Carlson Barn. Parallel exterior and structural systems mark the Bowlby, Kunze, and Carlson barns, though the Carlson barn is smaller in proportion (Figure 5). The Carlson barn was built close to the same time as the Bowlby barn; in fact, local long-time residents say the two were competing to see who built the bigger barn. Bowlby won; the Carlson barn is 84½ feet long, 56½ feet wide, and 45 feet high. However, Carlson milked more cows, and there were sixty stanchions on the interior of the barn. The floor plan is altogether different from the other two barns (Figure 6). The feed alley is placed off-center, running the length

Figure 5. The Alfred Carlson barn. Note the matching gambrel-roofed cupola.

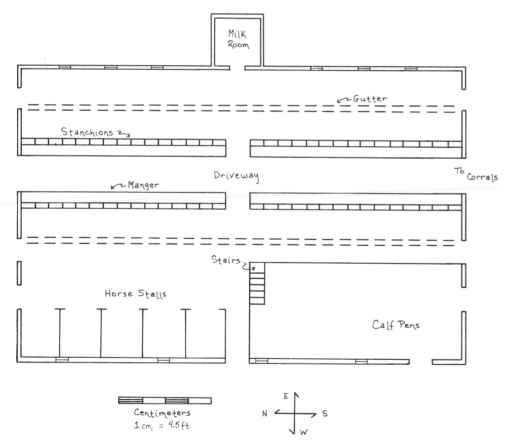

Figure 6. Floor plan of Alfred Carlson barn.

Figure 7.   The Max Dau barn.

of the barn. The stanchions face inward, and the cows enter through two doors in the south end of the barn. Four or five horse stalls are located in the northwest corner of the barn; the southwest corner was presumably used for calf or stock pens. The concrete walls of the first floor are eleven feet high; enclosed in the walls are stove pipes for ventilation. The floor of the barn is also concrete. The milk room is a lean-to on the east side of the barn.

The roof structure is similar to both Kunze's and Bowlby's roofs. Carlson's barn follows the pattern of Kunze's barn in that the lower rafters connect to the first-floor joists. However, the posts that support the secondary plate do not go all the way through to the floor, but rest on the loft floor as in the Bowlby barn.

Hay is unloaded in an entirely different way in the Carlson barn. The wagon pulled up outside of the barn, where a pulley extended on a track over the gable end of the barn. The track and hay door openings are protected by a square hay hood. Hay is unloaded from the wagon, possibly with the use of slings again. The hay is moved along the length of the track, and deposited on the loft floor. It is then fed to the cattle through trap doors in the loft floor. Unloading the hay from the outside of the barn, rather than from the inside, was the practice most commonly used by the farmers who came later to the Buhl area.

Four more dairy barns appeared in the neighborhood east of Buhl in the period from 1913 to 1915. These barns were smaller than the first three built; however, their dimensions created a striking appearance. The newer barns were narrower, and the height of the loft area was increased significantly. These barns mark a transition into a second type of gambrel-roofed dairy barn.

The Max Dau Barn. Built in 1913, the Dau barn (Figure 7) housed a rather small dairy operation. The barn measures 52 feet in length, 31½ feet in width, and 34 feet in height. Iron stanchions for only twenty cows were built inside. A narrow passageway and two gutters run down the middle of the barn. The cows face outward on both sides of the barn with a feed alley in front of them. There is a milk room in the northwest corner of the barn, and a small area in the southwest corner may have been used for calf pens (Figure 8). The walls of the first floor were 8½ feet high and made of concrete. The floor is also concrete.

Hay is unloaded from the outside of the barn through a bottom-hinged hay door in the gable end of the barn. The track is protected by a pointed hay hood rather than a square one. The loft floor has holes cut on each side of it, so hay could be dropped down in the feed alleys. An interesting ventilation system is used: large ducts run from the bottom of the south end wall of the barn. They join together in the loft and form one duct leading to a ventilator on the roof.

The framing of the barn is quite similar to that of the

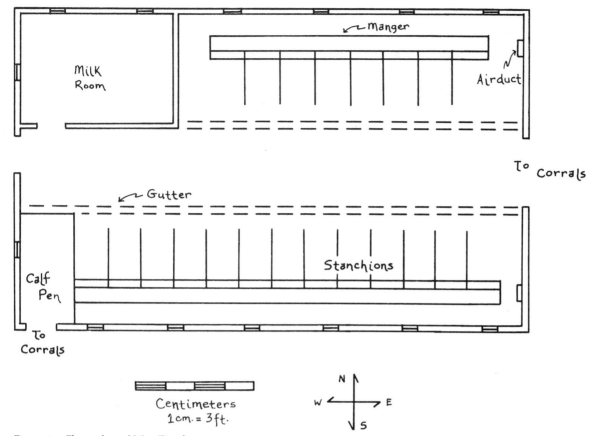

Figure 8. Floor plan of Max Dau barn.

first barns discussed. Six posts run from the secondary plate to the floor with a diagonal brace between the upper and lower rafters. However, the wall extends up beyond the loft floor four to five feet; the roof structure bears on this wall (See Figure 9). The strong curve of the gambrel roof is carried to the outside of the wall by an "outrigger" attached to the lower rafter and resting on the top of the wall, reinforced with a second piece underneath it. This style of framing is somewhat similar to the framing on the mansard roof of a house.[27]

The Henry Schick Barn. Henry Schick, who was involved in the building of the four barns previously mentioned, built his own barn in 1913 and 1914 along the lines of the Max Dau barn, only larger (Figure 10). The dimensions are 68½ feet long by 36 feet wide and 38 feet tall. The framing of the roof structure is almost the same as that of the Dau barn: posts support the secondary plate, and side walls extend five feet above the loft floor. Schick used leftover curved pieces of wood from the forms used to pour the cement silo as the outriggers supporting his flared gambrel roof.[28] Schick did not use any type of diagonal bracing between the upper and lower rafters, as was the case on other barns he helped build. Instead, the lower rafter, outrigger, and side wall form a brace for support.

Though the dimensions of Schick's barn are larger

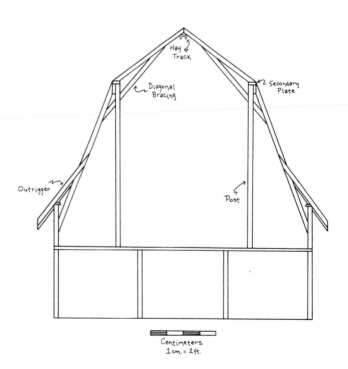

Figure 9. Framing of Max Dau barn.

Figure 10.   The Henry Schick barn. Large cement and wood lean-tos flank each side of the barn.

than those of Dau's, Schick utilized his first-floor space quite differently (Figure 11). Only ten cement stalls are built on the west side of the barn, with the cows facing toward the wall. The cows enter from a door on the west side. A large alleyway and gutter run down the middle of the barn. The east side of the barn consists of five pens with cement floors, used to hold calving cows or cows with their calves. Concrete walls 9 feet high enclose the first floor of the barn. The milk room is built on the west side of the barn, around the cement silo. Large concrete lean-tos are added on to the west side of the milk room and on the east side of the barn. They are enclosed on the top and side to shelter the cattle when they were out of doors.

Schick added many special touches to his barn that made it a "deluxe" dairy barn, though some longtime farmers of the area considered it impractical. Instead of using stanchions, a large sliding pole is set into the cement manger. Large leather straps are attached to the pole; these straps could be fastened around the cows' necks. Thus, the cows have some freedom of head movement. Individual drinking fountains were put into each stall and two in each calf pen. In the northwest corner of the barn is a bathroom with a sink and toilet and tub. (Schick's own house had no running water.) Hand-forged iron gates enclosed each interior cow pen, and hand-forged iron latches fastened each door. A huge ventilator shaft runs from the bottom floor of the

barn to the onion-domed cupola; a matching onion dome capped his cement silo.

Again, hay is unloaded on the outside of the barn by use of slings and a pulley system.[29] A square hay hood covers the tracks for the pulley on the outside of the barn; hay is pulled along the track through the bottom-hinged hay door by a winch. Hay is then pushed from the loft to the bottom floor through two chutes built onto the sides of the barn. There is a special chute from the loft for grain.

The Rudolf Kunze Barn. Prior to the latter part of 1912, the barns of the Buhl dairy community (the ones previously described) were constructed by using a combination of the new "balloon" framing and a diminished form of post-and-lintel construction. This combination utilized light wooden members for framing, but the roof load was supported by a secondary plate and a series of posts. An important step in the design of barn roofs was the development of a framing system which eliminated the posts and secondary plate. This system would allow for the creation of a single unobstructed loft space.

From 1913 to 1914, carpenters in the Buhl area began to utilize this new style of loft construction. The Rudolf Kunze barn (Figure 12) is an example of this style. A series of diagonal bracing was used along the loft side walls and rafters, allowing for the removal of the

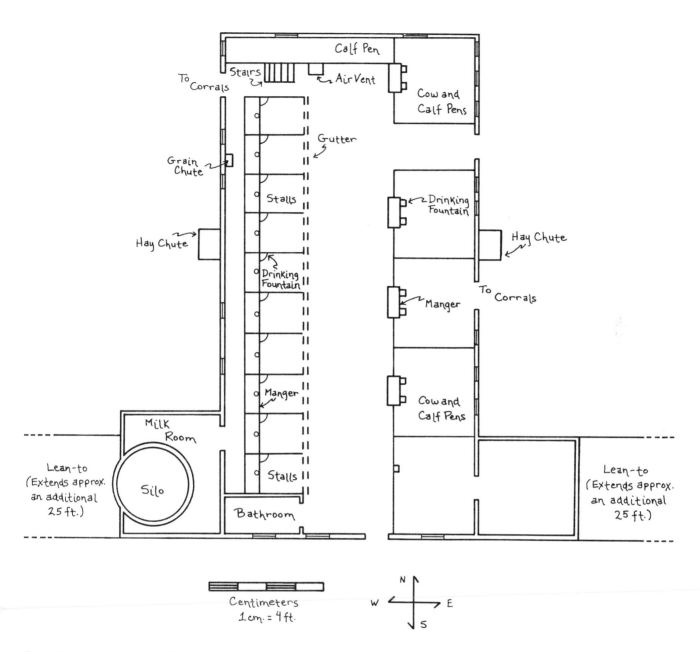

Figure 11. Floor plan of the Henry Schick barn.

secondary plate and posts (Figure 13). There was also more room created for hay storage with this type of framing, because the posts were no longer in the way.

Here, too, hay is unloaded on the outside of the barn and taken into the barn through a bottom-hinged hay door. No hay hood protects the opening. Two openings in the loft floor are located on both sides of the barn above the pens and manger.

The bottom-floor plan of Rudolf Kunze's barn is a simple one. Wooden stanchions and mangers for twelve cows are arranged so that cows face the wall on the west side of the barn. There is a feed alley between the stanchions and mangers and the outside wall. A

concrete passageway and gutter run laterally through the middle of the barn. The milk room is enclosed in the southwest corner; horse stalls are located in the southeast corner. Calf pens are placed on the east side of the barn. The walls of the first floor are of wood framing, rather than cement. Later, cement was poured between the studs on the interior of the walls. This barn is leaning quite a bit, so the cement may have been poured later to help prevent further leaning. The dimensions of the barn are 36 feet wide, 57 feet long, and 36 feet high.

Henry Schick was supposedly not involved in the building of the Rudolf Kunze barn. He is given credit

Figure 12.   The Rudolf Kunze barn.

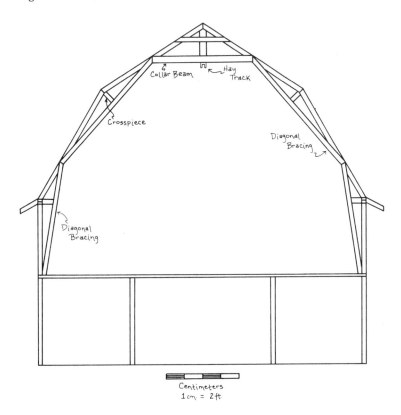

Figure 13.   Framing of the Rudolph Kunze barn.

Figure 14.   The Art Maxwell barn. Large dormers allow light into the loft, which was utilized for many a party and dance.

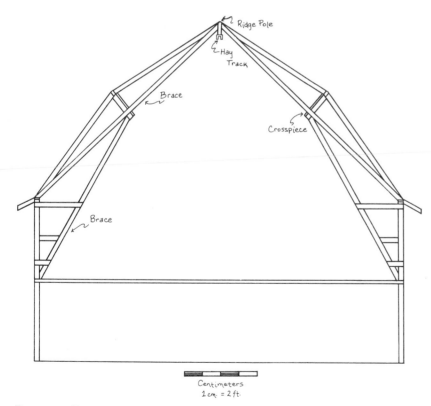

Figure 15.   Framing of the Art Maxwell barn.

for building another barn at about the same time as the construction of Rudolf Kunze's barn: the Art Maxwell barn.

The Art Maxwell Barn. When Frieda Kunze married Art Maxwell, her father Gustave had Henry Schick build a barn for them in about 1915 (Figure 14).[30] The framing of the Maxwell barn roof marks a change from Schick's previous method of framing roofs, as it creates a more complex truss system of framing (Figure 15). The collar beam has been completely eliminated; a truss rafter assembly runs from a vertical ridge pole to the top of the side wall plate extending five feet above the loft floor. This method of bracing allows more room for hay storage than Schick's previous method of framing on other barns.

Hay is unloaded from the outside of the barn into the loft by a track and pulley system; a pointed hay hood covers the outside track. Another style of hay door is seen on the Maxwell barn—sliding, rather than bottom-hinged.[31] It is difficult to determine the original floor plan of the barn, since it has been altered over the years. The stalls for the cattle run from side to side in the barn, rather than lengthwise. This barn is a little more square than the previous barns (62 feet long, 40 feet wide, and 36 feet high), so this may have been part of the original floor plan. However, there are stanchions now for only ten cows; Maxwell reportedly milked twenty cows. A new milk room has been built where the other stanchions probably stood. The stanchions are in two rows, with mangers facing outward. A calf pen is in the northeast corner of the barn, and the original milk room was in the northwest corner. Cows entered the barn through a central passage in the middle of the east side of the barn. A partition was built along the entire south end of the barn to separate the horse stalls from the milking area. Approximately five double stalls are included in this area. The floor of the barn is concrete, as well as the walls, which are approximately nine feet high and enclose the entire first floor.

THE BARNS: INFLUENCES ON CONSTRUCTION

Three major changes in the design, construction, and use of dairy barns took place in the period when these barns were built. One is in the dimensions and framing of the barn. There was a move away from using large posts to support the roof on a wide expanse of barn to the use of a balloon truss system to support the roof on a smaller, narrower barn. Second, there was a change in the method of putting up hay into the barn. In the first two barns, hay was unloaded on the inside; in the rest of the barns, hay was unloaded on the outside. Third, while floor plans vary quite a bit among all the barns described, there seems to be a move to have all the cows face outward, rather than inward.

These changes were influenced by several factors— factors that influenced the building of all barns during this time period. The major factors were the technology

of the time, the barn owners' experience with other barns, climates, and building materials, and the barn builders' particular expertness.

Well before Gustave Kunze's move to Buhl in 1910, several advances in technology affected the way barns were built. The availability of precut lumber and the rapid growth of lumber companies led to a move away from traditional methods of building, such as hand-hewn framing and heavy timber post-and-lintel construction. The concept of feeding cows in separate stalls, rather than in stock pens, was also introduced. Barns became more specialized structures; certain barns were categorized as "dairy" barns with the introduction of the milk separator in the 1890s.[32]

Another invention changed the way barns were constructed. The use of a track-and-pulley system to load hay into the loft began with the introduction of the mechanical hayfork in 1860. Such a system called for a barn with a full second story. The Western style of barn, a barn type found in the Tillamook area, had this increased volume and complete separation of the second story from the first floor. Hay could be loaded onto the fork in two ways. The wagon could be driven into the barn on a high central drive and unloaded there, or the hay could be unloaded on the outside of the barn by a fork on a track extending beyond the exterior wall of the barn. The exterior portions of the track and the hay door were usually protected by a hay hood. Outside unloading of hay and the use of hay hoods were common characteristics of Western barns.[33] At the barns near Buhl, slings, rather than forks, were used on the track system to unload the hay. This method was an alternate way of unloading hay, and was also one of the methods used with hay derricks of the area.[34]

Storing hay by a track and pulley system in the loft called for the interior space of the barn loft to be open. Crossties and crossbeams needed to be eliminated. The development of the gambrel roof came from such a need. The engineering techniques used on the gambrel roof evolved slowly: the first ones did use crossbeams for support,[35] but later roofs were a balloon truss system. The latter system was called "balloon" framing or "plank" framing in some barn plan books. The techniques of such roof styles and framing ideas were contained in standardized barn building plans, which could be found in many contemporary widely circulated publications. *Modern Engineering Practice*, first published in 1902, shows one of the early methods of framing a gambrel roof.[36] The 1906 edition of *Barn Plans and Outbuildings* discusses the revolutionary "plank" framing.[37] *Radford's Combined House and Barn Plan Book* of 1908 shows a "balloon-roofed" barn with the comment that such a roof "makes it possible to store a great deal of feed overhead. Roofs like this are comparatively new. . . ."[38]

Other building features were discussed in the barn books; among them were the use of cement as a building material, ventilation and lighting systems, and placement of the cows in the barn. Double-sashed windows, dormers, and cupolas with vents running from them to the bottom floor are recommended under various barn plans in Radford's 1906 edition. In the same edition, concrete is endorsed as a building material for walls: "In some parts of the country stone is plentiful and farmers prefer to lay up a stone wall, but generally speaking a concrete wall is cheaper and better. The materials may be put together in the ground and dumped into the trenches with unskilled labor. . . ." Concrete floors were also recommended.[39]

Radford's book also discussed the way cows should be placed in the barn: "A good many dairymen prefer to have the cows face outward. This is a matter of individual preference. Probably nine stables out of ten are made to face the cows in, but there is no dead open and shut reason why this stable should be built that way."[40] Under a barn plan showing the balloon roof, cows are shown facing outward: "This arrangement makes it easier to remove the manure. . . ."[41] The books mentioned previously are by no means the only barn plan books that were available to farmers. It would be difficult, if not impossible, to trace what barn plans were used by the early dairy farmers of Buhl. It is clear that the barns built in Buhl parallel barn styles presented in early agricultural literature, but one cannot find a direct correlation between existing barn plan books and the floor plans and framing system of the Buhl dairy barns. Other factors, besides technology and standardized barn plans, enter in.

The individual owner and the builder had a great influence on the design of the barn. For example, plans for utilizing the truss system were printed in popular literature before Gustave Kunze had a plan to build his barn. However, an older method of framing his wide expanse of roof was used — a portion of the post-and-lintel construction method. Concessions were made to new technology by moving the crossbeam up out of the way of the operating hay fork. Whether the roof framing was part of a barn plan he obtained, his own idea, or his builders' idea is hard to say. It may have been that the owner wanted to have the new style of gambrel-roofed barn with a hay fork, but the builders had not yet gained the knowledge of how to frame such a barn. The builders may have adapted the method of construction they were familiar with (post-and-lintel construction) to build this new style of barn.

Even though Radford's book makes it sound as if anyone could mix and pour concrete, a certain amount of experience was needed to work it as a building material. Both Gustave Kunze and one of his builders, Henry Schick, had previous experience in working with concrete, so they could put it to use in the construction of the Kunze barn.

Two other dairy farmers newly arrived in Buhl, T. P. Bowlby and Alfred Carlson, chose to imitate Kunze's style of barn. Yet each farmer elected to use a different floor plan and different method of putting up hay. Their individual experiences, plus information shared

with other farmers, probably shaped the choices they made.

The barn owners' experiences with other climates also affected the way they chose to build their barns. When Gustave Kunze, Alfred Carlson, and T. P. Bowlby moved to Buhl, they found a very different climate from that of Tillamook. Because it rained a lot in western Oregon, hay had to be stored inside to prevent it from rotting. Hay hoods of various kinds were often constructed to protect the hay in the unloading process. Cows also needed to be protected from the rain. This protection was included either in the design of the interior of the barn or in the design of enclosed loafing sheds around the sides of the barn. The cows were usually fed inside the barn.

The Buhl area, in contrast, has a dry climate. The rainfall was far less, eliminating the need for long-term indoor stabling of cattle. Cows were eventually fed outside in corrals. The indoor storage of hay eventually disappeared. However, when Kunze and Bowlby first began dairying in Buhl, they kept their cows indoors with only a small barbed-wire enclosure on the outside. The lofts on their barns were large enough for long-term storage of hay, and hay was unloaded on the inside for protection against the elements. Alfred Carlson did unload his hay on the outside of his barn; however, there is a large square hay hood on the end of his barn for protection against the elements.[42]

Topography was also an influence on barn styles. The terrain in Tillamook was quite hilly; several barns make use of a natural slope or bank for access to the second floor of the barn. This style existed before 1880 in eastern and midwestern states. The banked barn also had earlier antecedents in Alpine Europe.[43]

The terrain of Buhl is quite flat in comparison to Tillamook. Banked barns were an unusual feature in the Buhl area, since there were few hills on which to build them. However, Gustave Kunze created an artificial bank, or ramp, to the second floor of his barn. Although he did not own a barn with a ramp in Tillamook, he may have been influenced by his association with the banked barn style in Tillamook and Pennsylvania.

The next four barn owners, though they were associated with Kunze, Bowlby, and Carlson through business or family, chose to build a new type of barn — one smaller and narrower. This barn type had already been introduced to the neighborhood by the owner of a general farm barn, George Watt, in the latter part of 1912.[44] The Watt barn was framed by the new braced framing or truss system. The barns of Max Dau and Henry Schick are similar in appearance to the Watt barn, but have interior framing similar to the earlier barns. Since Schick was involved in the framing of the first three barns and built the next two, one can see in these barns the barn builder's adaptation to a new type of barn. Schick knew how to build a barn using the post system, eventually supplementing that system with a diagonal brace. He may have also had the experience of creating flared eaves while building houses in Chicago. He copied the exterior of the new barn in the neighborhood (Watt's), using framing methods he was familiar with on the interior of the barn.

The last two dairy farmers to build barns in the neighborhood—Rudolf Kunze and Art Maxwell—also chose the smaller, narrower barn type. Kunze had someone other than Schick build his barn, someone who was familiar with the truss system of building. Schick built the Maxwell barn, but an interesting shift occurred in his framing methods. He adapted the new form of truss assembly, perhaps indicating he had been influenced by other builders' methods or by new designs in barn plan and engineering books.

All four of the later dairy farmers—Dau, Schick, Rudolf Kunze, and Maxwell—picked barn plans in which hay was unloaded from the outside. They all used the same methods to unload hay. That the hay hoods on their barns vary from square to pointed to none at all suggests a choice made by the farmer, rather than any particular climatic need.

Each of these last four farmers also chose a different floor plan, probably based on which particular plan best suited his needs. There seems to have been a move toward having the cows face outward, rather than inward. Why this change occurred is hard to say, except that the barns were easier to clean that way. Again, technology could have been an influence: a manure spreader could be loaded easily from a wide central passage through the barn.

CONCLUSION

In their move from Tillamook to Buhl, the dairy farmers left behind a more traditional barn type and built a new style of barn, one widely advertised in farm literature. During the period of the establishment of the Cloverleaf Cheese Factory and associated dairies, the barns built in the Buhl neighborhood gradually changed in design, construction, and use. These changes were brought about by several factors, none of which can stand alone as an influence on the design of these particular dairy barns. The availability of new technology played a large part, but its influence was tempered by the barn owner's wishes and the barn builder's particular competence. Other barns built in the neighborhood, and the different methods used to construct those barns, also had an effect. These influences are intertwined and cannot be looked at singly when studying the evolution of barn types.

Little study has been done on the development and use of barns in the early twentieth century, perhaps because of the difficulty in tracing their roots in traditional and popular culture. The Buhl barns suggest some trends, but further research is needed in order to place the study of these few dairy barns into a broader cultural context. Investigation into national trends in the dairy industry over the last century would help create this broader context. Other local studies, including interviews with longtime farmers and barn builders and documentation of dairy barns and other types of barns would help our understanding of the progression of barn building types. If these studies were done, perhaps further understanding could be gained about the evolutionary steps from traditional barn building to the plan book barns of the twentieth century.

Notes

A debt of thanks is owed to Sanford Rikoon, Fred Walters, and Judith Austin for their advice on this project and the article. The U.S. Department of Interior's Historic Preservation Fund and the Idaho State Historic Preservation Office are also acknowledged for their partial funding of the project. Photographs are from the Idaho State Historical Society. Drawings were done by Belinda Davis of the Idaho State Historical Society.

1. Loren W. Neubauer and Harry B. Walker, *Farm Building Design* (Englewood Cliffs, N.J.: Prentice Hall, 1961), p. 50.

2. United States Census Office, *Twelfth Census of the United States, Taken in the Year 1900: Population*, Part 1 (Washington: United States Census Office, 1901) p. 778.

3. Phyllis Tannler Kessler, Portland, Oregon, letter to the author, August 15, 1982, p. 1. Mrs. Kessler is the granddaughter of Arnold Tannler and Lenora Kunze Tannler (daughter of Gustave Kunze).

4. "The Future of the Buhl Country as a Dairying Locality," *Buhl Herald*, January 1, 1911, p. 1.

5. Joe Maxwell, interview with the author, Tillamook, Oregon, August 10, 1982, field notes and tape on file at Idaho Oral History Center, Idaho State Historical Society, Boise, Idaho (hereafter IOHC).

6. For an example, see Henry Glassie, *Patterns in the Material Folk Culture of the Eastern United States* (Philadelphia: University of Pennsylvania Press, 1968), pp. 88–92.

7. "The Future of the Buhl Country as a Dairying Locality," *Buhl Herald*, January 1, 1911, p. 1.

8. "Dedication of the Cloverleaf Cheese Factory," *Buhl Herald*, April 1, 1912, p. 1.

9. Ibid.

10. Ted Sandmeyer, second interview with the author, June 28, 1979, pp. 10–12, on file at the Idaho State Historical Society Library, Boise, Idaho (hereafter ISHS). The Sandmeyer family have lived in the Buhl area since 1906; they purchased the farm of Gustave Kunze in 1918.

11. "Activity in the Building Line," *Buhl Herald*, September 18, 1913, p. 1.

12. Eleanor Schick Byglund, Boron, California, letter to the author, July 27, 1982. Ms. Byglund is the daughter of Henry Schick.

13. Ibid., Sandmeyer interview, June 28, 1979, pp. 10–12. Several other longtime residents mentioned Schick's name in relation to these barns.

14. Ibid., p. 5. See also Ted Sandmeyer, interview with the author, July 1, 1982, tape on file at IOHC.

15. Agricultural Department, Union Pacific System, *Dairying in Idaho* (Omaha, Nebraska, 1925), p. 13.

16. "Kunze is Congratulated by Governor," *Buhl Herald*, January 15, 1914, p. 1. See also, September 2, 1915, p. 1.

17. Ted Sandmeyer, fourth interview with the author, November 20, 1982, tape on file at IOHC.

18. Ibid.

19. Riley Maxwell built a small, one-story frame barn and A. A. Stauffacher built a transverse-crib style of barn. Since their barns are types other than gambrel-roofed dairy barns, which are the norm in the Buhl country, they are not discussed in this article.

20. Maxwell interview.

21. Sandmeyer interview, November 20, 1982.

22. Ibid.

23. For a further explanation of this, see Frank W. Gunsaulus, ed., *Modern Engineering Practice*, Volume XII; *Ventilating, Heating, Plumbing, Carpentry Index* (Chicago: Robert O. Law, 1906), p. 400.

24. Field notes based on unrecorded interview by author with Ted Sandmeyer, February 10, 1983, IOHC.

25. Ted Sandmeyer, first interview with the author, December 8, 1978, p. 15, transcript on file at ISHS.

26. Field notes based on unrecorded interview with Orvin Freeman, Buhl, Idaho, November 21, 1982, IOHC. Mr. Freeman is the present owner of the Bowlby barn.

27. For an example of mansard roof framing, see Gunsaulus, *Ventilating*, p. 401.

28. Eldor Schaefer, interview with the author, November 19, 1982, tape on file at the IOHC. Mr. Schaefer has rented Schick's property since 1942; he was also a neighbor of Schick's.

29. Ibid.

30. Sandmeyer interview, November 20, 1982.

31. Another barn in the same neighborhood—the George Watt barn—has a sliding hay door. It was a general farm barn, rather than a dairy barn, and was built in 1912 and 1913.

32. Phillip Dole, "Farm Houses and Barns of the Willamette Valley," *Space, Style and Structure: Building in Northwest America*, Thomas Vaughn and Virginia Ferriday, ed. (Portland, Oregon: Oregon Historical Society, 1974), p. 213.

33. Dole, "Farm Houses," p. 220.

34. Sandmeyer interview, November 20, 1982, and Schaefer interview, November 29, 1982.

35. See Gunsaulus, *Ventilating*, p. 400.

36. Ibid.

37. *Barn Plans and Outbuildings* (New York: Orange Judd Co., 1906), p. 16.

38. William A. Radford, ed., *Radford's Combined House and Barn Plan Book* (New York: The Radford Architectural Co., 1908), p. 132.

39. Ibid., pp. 117, 118.

40. Ibid., p. 122.

41. Ibid., p. 132.

42. Square hay hoods provide protection for the track, the hay as it comes up the pulley, and the opened hay door. A pointed hay hood would protect only the track.

43. Robert Esminger, "The Search for the Pennsylvania Barn," *Pennsylvania Folklife* 30 (Winter 1980–81); pp. 51, 60.

44. Bill Watt, interview with the author, November 20, 1982, on file at IOHC, Boise, Idaho.

Medical Care in Latah County, 1870–1930

Keith Petersen

The following article by Keith Petersen shows how Idaho folk culture responds dynamically to changes in technology and academic practice. In this regard his essay complements Buckendorf's study of Buhl dairy barns. Petersen focuses on folk medical practices during the transitional period when institutional medicine was just beginning in Idaho and when doctors may or may not have had adequate academic training. He finds folk medical practices existing contemporaneously with popular and scientific practices. Demarcations among the three practices are blurred and overlapping.

The study of folk medicine has lagged behind research into some of the more glamorous genres, especially songs, narratives, and material culture. Medical practices normally occur in the privacy of family life and require the tact of a good collector for documentation. In this study Petersen relies on materials culled from over 200 oral history interviews of the Latah County and Whitman County historical societies. By including whole excerpts from his interviews, Petersen demonstrates the importance of collecting belief narratives — a form of medical exemplum — that support folk medical practice and the importance of discerning the attitudes that practitioners hold toward various folk customs. For further reading on folk medicine, consult Wayland D. Hand, American Folk Medicine: A Symposium *(1976) and Harry M. Hyatt,* Folklore from Adams County, Illinois *(1935).*

Petersen is a historical consultant living in Pullman, Washington. He was director of the Latah County Historical Society in Moscow from 1977 to 1981 and is now working on a research project on the development of six communities in the Palouse with historian Mary Reed.

Settlers moved into northern Nez Perce County — the part later known as Latah County — in the late 1860s and early 1870s. Latah is locally called the place where "the prairie and the pines meet," with the southern and western parts consisting of rolling grasslands and the northern and eastern sections being largely forested. The first inhabitants located in the grasslands, near present-day Genesee and Moscow, becoming farmers and cattle ranchers. As this prime property was settled, later emigrants took homesteads in the timber. Eventually sawmills developed, and with the formation of the Potlatch Lumber Company in the early 1900s the timberlands began to be heavily logged. New towns and lumber camps came into existence.[1]

Latah County settlers came from a variety of places, many being first-generation immigrants, particularly from Scandinavian countries and Germany, although Chinese, Greeks, Italians, and other nationalities were included. Emigrants from within the United States came from both the West and the East, with the Midwest particularly well represented after the incursion of the Potlatch Lumber Company, which was largely owned by Minnesota logging interests.[2] Regardless of where they came from or where they settled, early county residents faced a shortage of doctors and hospitals, an abundance of unsanitary conditions, and problems with illness, injury, and disease.

Such health care deficiencies were not unique to Latah County, however. Rapid westward expansion in the nineteenth century, combined with the absence of professional and legal standards, gave free rein to medical commercialism. No fewer than four hundred American schools awarded medical diplomas to virtually every student attending. Even elite institutions found it difficult to maintain standards. In 1870 the Harvard Medical School did not administer written examinations because students could not write well enough to complete the tests. On the other hand, even dedicated students in the late nineteenth and early twentieth centuries found themselves unprepared to deal with many health problems. Although Joseph Lister introduced antiseptic surgery in 1867, appreciation of sanitation and cleanliness was slow in coming, and in many places not until late in the nineteenth century were cigar-smoking doctors replaced in operating rooms by surgeons practicing Listerian methods. The Pure Food and Drug Act was passed in 1906, but even at that late point a doctor's medical bag looked similar to a home medicine cabinet as the surge in modern drugs was still years away. The nation's first full-time county health officer was not appointed until 1912 in North Carolina. As Dr. Willard J. Hawkins stated about his practice of the 1890s in Carol Ryrie Brink's novel of Moscow, *Buffalo Coat,* "You have to use your wits here because you'll come across things that aren't in the medical journals."[3]

The quality of doctors was a major concern, but even with medical schools turning out "doctors" in assembly-line fashion, quantity was an equally serious problem in isolated rural areas. The vast majority of people in these areas relied on home remedies and family doctoring. Scientific medicine, with hospital care from birth to death, was as yet unknown. Rural Western health care in the 1920s oftentimes bore more resemblance to the medical practices of the 1870s than it did to that of the 1970s. In 1946, Madge Pickard and R. Carlyle Buley dedicated their book on early Midwestern health care "To the Pioneer Doctor who boldly faced the wilderness; and to the Pioneer who bravely faced the Doctor."[4]

In recent years researchers have increasingly studied the folk medical practices of people around the world. For this paper, "folk" medicine is defined as the set of cultural attitudes, practices, and values relating to health care that are normally transmitted by oral instruction and imitation within groups. These groups, or communities, are usually defined by family, occupation, ethnic origins, or other shared characteristics. "Scientific" medicine, for purposes of this essay, denotes medical practices learned in formal contexts and relies on the printed word for transmission. Folk medicine is usually practiced in domestic situations whereas scientific medicine relies on official institutions constructed especially for medical treatment. These distinctions are thus descriptive of distinct cultural processes, and do not denote any inherent gradation of benefit or sociocultural ownership.

Folklorists typically divide folk medical cures into two broad categories—practical and magico-religious. A practical folk cure is one that provides a curing application *directly* to a disease; for example, the drinking of herbal teas for stomach indigestion because the tea is believed to contain ingredients that work directly on the ailment. Magico-religious cures require a medium, such as an amulet or religious faith, that works between the curing agent and the disease. The recitation of prayers during a time of illness, in the belief that God (the medium) will cure the illness, is an example of a magico-religious cure. Many folk medicine practitioners rely on both types of cures.[5]

The recent scholarly work of anthropologists and folklorists has largely focused on cataloging illnesses and their various folk cures, with a particular interest shown in magico-religious folk medicine. Historians have largely ignored the field of pioneer health care, except to chronicle the stories of frontier doctors and the development of scientific medicine.[6] But to truly understand the westward experience we must understand the health care of the time, which involves more than cataloging cures or knowing when the first doctors arrived in a region. This paper will examine some of the medical practices of Latah County residents in the first sixty years of the county's development. This was a time of transition in medical history. Scientific medicine during much of the period was not far advanced above home medical treatments. Furthermore, throughout this time, many Latah County residents lived in isolated areas largely inaccessible to doctors, and without hospitals. Doctors were asked to make house calls only on the most serious occasions, and hospitals were places where only the sickest people went.

This essay is an attempt to understand the total range of health care, including folk medicine, available to residents of one Western county during its developmental stage. Although the paper is a beginning overview, it will serve as an invitation to scholars to look more seriously at health care as an aspect of social history. In one small Western county over a sixty-year period there were magico-religious curers, medical inventors, widespread use of local and exotic plant cures, and a general concern about health care availability uncharacteristic of more recent times. There is little reason to believe that Latah County was unique, and yet we know little about this fascinating aspect of our past.

The primary source of information for this article comes from interviews conducted in the 1970s with over 200 Latah County residents as part of the Latah County Historical Society's oral history project. To the extent possible I have tried to tell the story in their words.[7]

Latah County's first doctor arrived in Moscow in 1878 when the three-year-old town had a population of under 200 people. By the turn of the century, doctors were working in Kendrick and Genesee as well, and in the early 1900s hospitals were established in Bovill and Potlatch to supplement Moscow's two institutions. Scientific medical care became progressively more available to county residents, but long distances, geographical barriers, and impassable roads made such assistance inaccessible to many, as Michael Bubuly, a logger born in 1896 recalled:

> I've seen guys drivin' a team of horses . . . [with] a string of logs, and they come to a curve, and this log that the horses was hooked to, that he was . . . walking along side of . . . caught someplace back there, . . . hooked onto something, and it lifted the front log and drove that against his leg. Shoved this bone clear out here. . . . he bled to death before they got him to the hospital. . . . And that wasn't a very pretty sight to see, either. . . . Thirty miles away from a hospital or anything. . . . Takes you a long time to get a man out.[8]

The inhabitants of Moscow, Bovill, and Potlatch in the early 1900s were more fortunate than other country residents in that they had hospitals. Still, scientific health care was far behind modern standards. There were many times when no doctor was present in Bovill, for example, and the hospital's nurse was expected to "know as much as a doctor. And if you didn't know as much as a doctor you just weren't very smart," recalled nurse Lucille Denevan.[9] Even when the town did have a doctor, its isolation often caused him to resort to drastic measures, as Joseph Holland reminisced:

> There was only one doctor there, didn't matter what it was, he had to do it. . . . He certainly wasn't stingy with the knife. . . . They'd drag somebody in there, my gosh, . . . you got to try and save his life. And if cuttin' his leg off would do it, well that's what you do. I imagine that he cut off many legs that nowadays wouldn't have to be done.[10]

Many Latah County residents were even more sequestered than those in Bovill, and as a result doctored themselves for all but the most serious illnesses. "We never thought of a doctor," remembered Frances Fry who was born near Kendrick in 1893. "You had to do what there was. If you thought you was doing right, that was it. It's very seldom that we ever went to a doctor."[11] Or as Oscar Olson, a logger born in Deary in 1906 pronounced when asked if he ever saw a doctor when growing up, "No way! . . . We didn't have no doctors, never took no shots or nothing."[12] Though such families were highly self-sufficient medically, serious illness was a time of neighborliness. "The neighbors come and helped you take care if there was anybody sick at your house," stated Mamie Munden, born in 1906. "And if there was anyone sick at the neighbors' house you went to the neighbors' house and took care of them."[13]

Regardless of whether neighbors assisted or families cured themselves, Latah County residents relied on a wide variety of remedies. Indicative of this transitional period in the history of modern medicine, some cures called for remedies passed down from earlier generations, while other home cures took advantage of modern technological innovations.

Throughout this period people used plant cures consisting of native and garden plants, as well as imported medicinal plants, the most remembered of the latter being asafetida.[14] Asafetida hung from the neck in a small bag—some people insisted it be made of red flannel— and was used to "ward off diseases and colds and croup and all kinds of bad things." Its strong, unpleasant odor was, as Lola Clyde remembered, probably its biggest asset. "It kept people away who had colds, and you didn't catch it from them."[15] Included among medicines made from native plants were teas from tansy and yarrow and laxatives from shinnebark and dandelions. Cattails could be made into a poultice to treat burns, and mullein leaves mixed with water and sugar provided a cough syrup. Nez Perce Indians introduced some medicinal plants to the settlers, as Edward Groseclose, born near Juliaetta in 1893, remembered:

> There's a little plant . . . up here in the hill that the Indians showed. . . . You take them leaves and rub 'em this way and they'll divide, and where they divide you take that juicy side and put that on a sore. . . .
> There was a little girl that had a sore on her leg and they never could heal it. . . . And there was an old Indian

woman brought this to 'em and showed 'em, said, "You put that on there, pretty soon she go hop-skip like any little girl." And it healed it up. They had no medicine that'd heal it up.[16]

Among the garden-variety plant cures, onion poultices and mustard plasters seemed to be the most widely used. Both controlled colds and congestion, being heated and applied to the chest, although hot plasters were also occasionally utilized for sprains and bruises.[17]

These generations of Latah County residents also took advantage of substances unavailable to their ancestors when concocting their home remedies. Kerosene was a widely used cure-all, a few drops often being combined with sugar to make a throat syrup. Although not new, turpentine was employed in a similar fashion, as well as for treating small cuts and burns.[18] Families used carbolic acid for severe injuries and, like many home remedies, some considered it to have preventive capabilities. "I remember there was a smallpox scare at one time," commented Lola Clyde. "My father put some carbolic acid in a pan of water and he got a little whisk broom and he went about sprinkling everybody in all the house with that carbolic acid water. It's a wonder he didn't burn some of our skin off, but he thought that the carbolic acid . . . would disinfect the air and disinfect us kids."[19] Listerine was being used as an antiseptic in the early 1900s, and by then Vaporub had replaced chest plasters in some homes.[20]

A fascination with changing technology also brought about experimentation with electricity as a cure-all. In 1912 Marcellus McGary, proprietor of a sanitarium in Helmer, patented an electric treatment machine which would bring "perfect health"—for $25.00. "It was electric shock treatments," recollected Nona Lawrence, who lived in the town.

> You'd hang onto electrodes. . . . he had a belt that you'd put around your body and then you wet them electrodes and put 'em on, and then you sleep in that and it would blister, you know, if you turned it on too high. . . . And then you could take your shock treatments through the day. . . . And then he even give treatments. Other people'd come here—several come here and he treated 'em for maybe three weeks or something like that. Them days you didn't have to have a license.[21]

Actually, McGary invented several electrical cure-alls. The Electro-King sent a current through the body and was primarily used to alleviate rheumatic pains. He also invented the electric belt to cure while people slept, and an electric comb that would restore youthful color and make hair grow on bald heads.[22]

The widespread use of purchased, ready-made medicines also indicates that this was a transitional period. Some of these remedies were pure hoax, while others had beneficial qualities. Some were old, while others became popular by appearing to incorporate the latest in scientific knowledge. Although not new, one of the most pervasive ready-made remedies in any home health kit was alcohol. Elva Bennett, born in 1891 in Colfax, Washington, a few miles from Latah County, recalled that her father "didn't smoke or drink — that was out of the question. We would keep a little whiskey though, and when we'd have a cold momma'd make us a whiskey toddy."[23] Helen McGreevy, born in nearby Pullman, Washington in 1901 had a similar remembrance: "The only time we ever had hard liquor at our place . . . excepting Thanksgiving and Christmas time . . . [was] when we were children and we got a bad cold . . . or be running a temperature. Mother would fix a hot drink for us."[24] Lora Albright recalled that if her grandmother "had alcohol and camphor[25] she could cure everything from a toothache to malaria fever."[26]

Not all bottled medicines were as palatable as alcohol. Lola Clyde remembered that when her family went to town after a store-bought remedy "it was generally cod liver oil,"[27] while Martha Long, born in 1903, wryly commented, "There was always castor oil. And you didn't try to show you had a little stomachache, because if you got it, you got a dose of castor oil."[28] Families also relied on Carter's Little Liver Pills to to treat various symptoms. Lora Albright remembered that "dysentery" was rampant: "Now, I know that some of that dysentery probably was infectious hepatitis and a few other things that we learned later. But in those days, they had what they called liver pills, which was a glorified laxative really, and they would clean out those poor little kids' systems. . . . and I'm really surprised that they didn't lose more than they did."[29] Such little-known substances as Oregon Blood Purifier and Tonic Vermifuge, as well as better-known medications like Ex-lax, epsom salts and Mentholatum, regularly made their way to family medical shelves. "My uncle said when he come out here from Illinois," remarked Mary Lynd, born in 1895, " 'Why people out here, if they'd break the wagon tongue they'd put Mentholatum on it!' "[30]

Although medical practices were becoming more sophisticated and some people had more faith in new medicines and doctors, technology was only gradually changing medical practices. But if doctors often relied on the same cures as lay people, a doctor's presence could sometimes instill more confidence than a home medicine cabinet. Henry Smith, born in neighboring Whitman County, Washington in 1898 looked back upon the day that

> Old Ernest come in. He had to have some medicine. So the doctor mix up some stuff, but didn't tell him it was salts. He put a little sweetenin' in it, put a little pink colorin' in it. It was the best medicine he'd ever seen! This old doctor . . . doctored everything out of the same bunch of pills. He had a big can of them there.[31]

Latah County residents in this period seemed willing to give doctors and scientific medicine a chance, but there was still a great reliance on the old remedies. For example, "folk" cures persisted even among people growing up late in the period. Madeline Gorman, born in 1913, explained how to cure an earache:

> You take a tiny bit of garlic about the size of the head of a common pin . . . and you put it in cotton. And I take the oil and I just . . . dump the bottle over so there's just a little bit of oil on my hand. And I rub that in there, make a kind of a little ball-like and stuff it in the ear. That's all you have to do. . . . And I know it works because I've had earaches upon earaches.[32]

And while people were more willing to put their trust in doctors and science, some took comfort in knowing that often their cures were better than the doctors'. There are many stories in the Latah County Historical Society's collection relating how home remedies succeeded where doctors failed. Dixie Groseclose, born in 1900, recalled a friend who had a nosebleed so bad "you couldn't hardly stop it. . . . They had the doctor up there several times. . . . And so the doctor was there one day and told 'em . . . 'Ed won't be here in the morning.' . . . 'Cause he was so low, you know, and they was having trouble with his nosebleeds." Somebody told him to sniff powdered alum, which he did, stopping the nosebleed. "The next morning they called the doctor, and of course, he figured they'd called him, I guess, something about telling Ed was gone, but they called him and told him that he was still there and he said, 'I can't believe it.' But he come out of it and lived to be what? Eighty-one years old, wasn't it?"[33]

Unfortunately, not every illness had such a happy ending. Whether treated by doctors or by the family, death from disease — particularly among children — was accepted as an unfortunate product of the times. "My folks had four boys and four girls and they only raised one boy to be grown," related Ada Schoeffler, born in 1901. "That was quite common."[34] Lola Clyde recollected that "Many of the families would say 'Well, we had fourteen children and we raised seven of 'em.' And that was a good average."[35] "They had to have so many spares because there was so many died off," observed John Eikum, born in 1888. "Now, our neighbors, they lost six, six children with the croup."[36]

People especially feared epidemics which, in days before widespread use of vaccines or knowledge of the importance of sanitation, often spread quickly through the country. Diphtheria hit especially hard in the Moscow area in the late 1870s. "In the very early days before we had any kind of toxins, antitoxins, so on and so on, . . . kids died with diphtheria here," remarked Lola Clyde. "There's lots of tiny headstones out in the Moscow cemetery that date back to the great diphtheria epidemics of 1877 and 1878. And there wasn't anything they could do. They didn't have the means of it. . . . And at one time some of the early histories report that half the children in the town of Moscow died with black diphtheria."[37] Dora Fleener was born in 1894 and lived in rural Moscow. Even that late she remembered that her father worried about the disease:

It was that age when there was so much of that around. Looked down our throat and if he saw any white patches down our throat, why he'd blow sulphur in our throats. Make a funnel out of a paper and put the small end and then he'd blow it down the throat. We breathed in a lot of it . . . in our lungs. If any of 'em were drawing in their breath at that time, why, wasn't very comfortable.[38]

Such treatments had marginal effectiveness against a serious illness. Bernadine Adair Cornelison, whose father was one of Moscow's early doctors, was born in 1897 and remembered that not even medical experts had sophisticated means of preventing the dreaded disease:

Flora [my sister] got diphtheria. . . . Daddy was so terrified that the rest of us would get it. Worried about quarantine. And I was about three then. I still can remember this house and he hung wet sheets up over each door. That was one way of hoping that the rest of us didn't get what she had, and we didn't. Now whether he had some antiseptic on those or not, I don't know, but I can remember those sheets. . . .

She got over the diphtheria, they thought that's what it was then, but we think it was probably a form of polio, because she got over the diphtheria part, but she was paralyzed and died shortly after. She was about nine years older than I.[39]

Typhoid struck the county with alarming frequency. "One disease never seen around here any more is typhoid," wrote Kendrick's Dr. Douglas Christensen in 1982. Christensen arrived in Latah County in 1931 and recalled that even that late "I had several cases. . . . There was no specific treatment. All one could do was to maintain hydration and nutrition as well as possible until the body overcame the infection. One very important thing was to prevent the spread of the disease to others. This required special nursing care with regard to the handling of bowel discharges."[40]

By the 1930s the connection between typhoid and unsanitary conditions was understood. But in the 1890s Moscow's fictional Dr. Hawkins was resigned to the belief, after several years of regularly combating the illness, that "typhoid's a summer sickness, like diarrhea and cholery morbus. I've been a physician for a quarter of a century, and, by George, I've never yet had a full-fledged vacation when I wanted to take it!" Doc Hawkins made his patients boil milk, but did not undertake any other preventive measures. When confronted by an upstart new doctor concerning the inadequacy of Moscow's overworked cesspools, Hawkins could see no connection between them and typhoid. "Dr. Allerton doesn't like the odor of our cesspools. . . . He doesn't like the taste of our clear mountain water that comes rushing down from God's high summits. . . . Allerton is all for pumping our water up from the infernal regions." But the townspeople, fearful of continued epidemics, voted to improve the town's water and sewer systems, against the advice of Doc Hawkins.[41]

In some of the outlying areas, however, it took longer for Latah County residents to recognize the connection between typhoid and unsanitary conditions, and the disease was long a menace. Ada Schoeffler had a brother who died of typhoid:

There used to be lots of typhoid fever, but you hardly ever hear of that any more. It was unsanitary conditions and the water supply and all that. And then, of course, they had the outside houses and flies and all that sort of stuff. There used to be a lot of typhoid fever. I know I had a sister that had it. . . . She had it when she was 17. . . . I had an uncle that died of it, too. He was in his thirties, close to 40.[42]

Other epidemics such as scarlet fever and smallpox hit the county occasionally. The most common action taken to prevent the spread of such diseases was to quarantine homes or place people in pest houses. "They quarantined the homes in those days when people had scarlet fever or diphtheria or smallpox," commented Clarice Sampson, born in Moscow in 1894. "And there would be a sign put up by the front door—'Quarantined'—and the name of the disease. And us children, of course, if we'd ever see that on somebody's front door, we'd cover our mouths with our handkerchiefs and just run by as fast as we could, so we wouldn't get that germ.[43]

By far the most infamous epidemic among Latah County informants was the flu of 1918 and 1919. People in small towns and rural areas remembered this as a time when schools closed, neighbors helped ailing families with chores, and social functions were canceled. Lucille Denevan, the Bovill nurse, recalled that seven young lumberjacks from nearby logging camps died with the flu. Edward Groseclose told about treatment in the outlying areas:

They used to take aspirin to keep your fever down and take something to keep your bowels well open. . . . You had to keep yourself cleaned out and keep your temperature down. And we got to doing that, why they didn't lose many patients after that. But doctors didn't know what to do on the start and they lost a lot of people.[44]

In Moscow, the county's main population center, the flu was even more severe. Conditions were especially difficult there because many young men were in town as part of the war effort. "In the Army in World War I, I was sent to the University as possible officer material," recollected Abe Goff.

I was quartered in a temporary wooden barracks and mess hall back of the Administration Building. We went to classes, usually in the morning and then drilled in the afternoon. Now these people that weren't alive here in Moscow can't really realize what a tragedy it was for the nation and the whole world. It reached Moscow in the fall of 1918 and continued through October and early November. Twenty million people in the United States were stricken by the Spanish Influenza. . . . It was a very serious disease. It started as a cold. People went to bed—they had a high fever. Most of the casualties came when they were better and got up and went out. They'd often die within a day or two after they went out. They didn't realize that long bed confinement was necessary before it was safe to go out. Local doctors, nurses, and volunteer nurses worked day and night. They could prescribe no remedies but aspirin, hot soup and bed rest, although various . . . lay cures were advanced. In Moscow volunteers manned soup kitchens. Every place was pressed into service for hospitals. There was the old Gritman Hospital . . . and the downtown hospital of Dr. Carithers. But buildings were taken over for hospitals nearly any place. Everybody wore a simple "flu mask" of gauze, covering the nose and mouth. Movie houses were closed and public meetings called off.[45]

As in rural Latah County, the flu epidemic ushered in a time of neighborly assistance in Moscow. Clarice Sampson helped organize some of the relief groups:

When that flu epidemic came . . . they asked me to do the calling for the Red Cross in our neighborhood, and I went from door to door and got blankets and pillows, and the people were all asked to mark them so they could get them back. Because they had boys in the gymnasium, even in one of the livery stables here and the Elks Temple—sick boys. . . . And one of the big homes here in Moscow . . . they used as a kitchen, and women went in to prepare the soup and so on. They transported it—'course we had cars by then—around to these places where the sick boys were. But so many died. It was a terrible thing.[46]

The flu, of course, was not selective and occurred all over town, not just in the barracks, as Lola Clyde recalled:

I was in high school, and they closed the high school down. And our superintendent . . . died with it. And many, many people just died. There was just nothing—there was just no remedy for it. . . . And our school must have been closed for three months here in Moscow because the flu was just everywhere. There was nobody to go and nobody to teach. They were all down with the flu.[47]

The only real remedy Lola remembered was "just go to bed. That was about all they did."[48] Still, the town's few doctors were kept extraordinarily busy. "Dad went day and night," Ione Adair remarked about her father, Dr. William Adair. "And I'd get in—when I'd leave work and come home and he'd have someplace out here in the country and he'd tell me to go to a certain place, like out here at Joel, and he said, 'I'll tell you from there.' And he'd go to sleep and I'd drive the horses until we'd get to Joel, and then he'd tell me which way I was to go from there."[49] "I know Mr. Gritman was on his feet sometimes 24 hours a day. And . . . in making these country calls, he had a driver and he would sleep until they would get to the place where the sick person was," remembered Pearl Machlied, a nurse at Gritman Hospital at the time.[50]

Even in this relatively recent period, however, doctors often did not know much more about treating flu patients than lay people, as is indicated in a reminiscence of Bovill's Madeleine Gorman, who explained a method of sweating, a popular home remedy for the flu and many other ailments:

The doctor had seen Daddy and he had told Mother that Dad was very sick and to be sure and keep the medicine going the way it's supposed to. So Mother said, "Yes," And this fellow came down to see Dad, and he looked at Dad and he looked at Mama, and he said, "Juliet, have you got blankets?" "Yes." He says, "Go get me all the blankets you can get. I want hot, boiling water." And Mother says, "I have that." And he says, "Do you have lemons in the house?" And Mother said, "Yes." He said, "All right, I want three lemons." And he told Mother to get a container that could stand hot, boiling water without breaking. . . . And I remember him . . . juicing the lemons. And he put this lemon in the bowl, put a tiny bit of, I don't know whether it was honey or sugar, but a little bit of sweetener. . . . And he reached in back of his—pulled out a bottle [of alcohol] and took the cork off and dumped the whole bottle in it and then poured a certain amount of hot water and stirred it up. And he went back in and he says, "Tom, you're a sick man. I want you to drink this. I want you to drink all of it. It's gonna be hot." . . . And so he helped Dad up . . . to a sitting position, more dead than alive. And Dad drink the whole thing. . . . And I remember Daddy being extremely white and then all of a sudden . . . he started getting kinda red. And then I noticed that Daddy was beginning, you know, the beads of perspiration. And then I remember him telling Mom, he says, "All right. Now Juliet, start packing the blankets on. . . ."
I remember there was an awful stench in the house of sweat—like you wouldn't believe! I have never smelt that odor before or since, but the stench was horrible. . . . All during this time they were changing Daddy and changing the bed and what-not. . . . And then the next morning when the doctor come in, he saw Dad and he said, "Tom, what did you do?" Daddy says, "Nothing." . . . And he said, "Like hell you didn't, you did something." And he says, "I want to know what you did. Because it isn't my medicine that did this." . . . So Dad told him. And he says, "Well, I don't mind telling you, Tom, I've got your death warrant here. . . . I was ready to sign it." And that's how close Dad was. The doctor had given up hope.[51]

Perhaps the greatest change in preventive medicine in this period came with the gradual realization that unsanitary conditions contributed to a wide variety of health problems. Grace Wicks, born in Genesee in 1906, recalled that

Dr. [W.C.] Cox was a deeply respected person as a family physician. However, as time went by he moved to Everett, Washington to practice, and it was there that his wife died. And the cruelest blow of all, she died of puerperal fever, which means somewhere in her care there was someone or something that was not sterilized. They didn't know. Pasteur had not discovered germs at that time. And doctors, midwives and nurses were not always careful to wash their hands because they didn't know that it did any particular harm for a physician to go to one person to another.[52]

If the importance of sanitation escaped doctors, it can easily be understood why lumberjacks failed to see the significance of remaining clean. Albert Justice was a head cook for lumber camps between the two world wars, sometimes supervising meals for over 350 men. He explained that he was at times considered a "slave driver" because he insisted upon a certain level of cleanliness:

> We say now we'll go to the bathroom, but in them days it was on the side of a hill, you know. Well, I hate to see a man, or anybody, go to the toilet — we'll be plain about it — and come back and start right to work without washing his hands. I had many and many an argument about that. And I made enemies, I know I did, about a little thing like that. . . . There was always a certain amount of those guys that I used to keep an eye on. They'd come back and they'd put on their apron and go right to work. Well, I could not help but mention that to a man.[53]

Hershiel Tribble was born near Princeton in 1896 and remembered the interior of a bunk car at one of the lumber camps:

> There were no electric lights. There was . . . cold water, but no hot water. . . . And these people, most of them never took a bath. There was no place for them to bathe unless they went in an ice cold creek. Once in awhile, some that was a little bit neater, they'd get a little five gallon can, punch a few small holes in the bottom of it, hang it in a tree, and jump in under it right quick, fill it with water and . . . try to take a shower from that.
>
> But anyway, of a night, there were socks. They had these big old heavy wool socks on, and they'd be wet from sweat. If they weren't wet from the snow and water, they'd be wet from sweat. They'd hang these on wires above the stove to dry. Some of 'em used tobacco, chewed tobacco, and they'd spit at this sand around the stove, and a lot of 'em wasn't very good shots. They might either aim too low or too high, and hit the stove or the floor. And then with these socks a-stewin' up above the stove, you can think that there must have been a little odor in there. In fact, if you wasn't used to that, and didn't have a cast steel stomach, I don't know if you'd ever make it full-length of that car and save your last meal that you'd ate or not. I tell ya, that was wicked.[54]

Lumberjacks typically carried their own bedrolls from job to job and camp to camp. They seldom bathed, and even less did they launder. There were numerous health problems associated with these unsanitary conditions, but one of the most common was more of an inconvenience than a threat. Because of the unclean conditions, bedbugs and body lice were rampant, as Byers Sanderson, born in 1896, attested:

> Oh, they were terrible! I've gone in — I was railroading at the time — I've gone in and we'd pull in at one, two o'clock at night from bringing the logs in, putting 'em on the sidings — and I've gone in to lay down and I felt something crawling on me, and I turned my flashlight on, and I bet I coulda counted a hundred and fifty bedbugs crawling over. . . . And you take their pillows — I've seen their pillows just dotted all over with blood where they'd smashed those bedbugs. Stink! . . . I'm right here to tell you, the lice and bedbugs were *terrible*! You couldn't stay there, but what you'd get lousier than a pet coon.[55]

Eventually, under pressure from the Industrial Workers of the World, the Potlatch Lumber Company controlled the insects by providing bedding and laundering sheets and blankets once a week. Prior to that, however, lumberjacks experimented with a number of cures to remedy the situation. Elmer Flodin, born in 1899, remembered that his father used powders, quicksilver and a salve that was smeared on the body to control lice and bedbugs.[56] Hershiel Tribble heard a tall tale describing a unique method of eliminating them:

> I heard a fella tell how to ger rid a' them things. He said you put a lot of salt on your clothes. And he said, them greybacks 'd eat it. And he said, you go down close to the water, jerk your clothes, lay 'em down, and he said, the greybacks will all run for a drink. And he says, then you grab your clothes and run, while they were down gettin' a drink. He said you could get rid of them every time that way.[57]

Considering the general level of medical knowledge during this period, the inaccessibility of doctors and hospitals, and the lack of understanding about the need for sanitation, the residents of Latah County in many areas had an admirable record of successful home health care. Perhaps no better example exists than in childbirth, which was almost universally a home event, seldom with a doctor present. "Most of them," asserted Lola Clyde, "thought that it was just ridiculous bothering about doctors, as having a baby was the most normal thing in the world. And your next-door neighbor came in and delivered the baby and severed the cord, and wrapped him and brought down hot soup and chicken dinners for them and doctored them up."[58]

In most neighborhoods one or two experienced women who attended most home births attained a reputation of being midwives. As with other forms of health care, this was also a time of neighborliness, as Kate Grannis explained:

> There was generally some lady in the neighborhood who was just a good hand at waiting and they were considered just welcome to come and help. But . . . the neighbors did help each other if there was a child born . . . I know that's the way it was at our house and there was two different ladies in our neighborhood who were considered just good midwives. And one or the other of 'em would come, go to a place where a child was being born and help them.[59]

Later in the period doctors more frequently attended, but births — particularly outside of the few towns with hospitals — still took place at home. "Had all my children born at home but the last one," stated Mamie Munden, born herself in 1906. "And I said if I have to have another one I'll go on up to the barn myself. I'm not going to the hospital. I think I would, too!"[60]

There were occasional problems with childbirth because of the primitive nature of medical knowledge.[61] But perhaps the biggest health problem was that women were expected to have too many babies. Although women did get long periods of rest after childbirth, often as much as two weeks in bed — "That's the only rest they ever got"[62] — having many children in rapid succession took its toll on all but the strongest. Grace Wicks recalled that her mother had serious health problems, many of them brought on by childbirth:

She'd had her babies fast and without a great deal of care. So Mother was never well. . . . She said . . . that a female animal before giving birth, or even before conception, was given a little time to rest and be ready for her inner chores, but a woman had her children when she was depleted physically and conceived most easily. . . . I think . . . she understood it as the fact that she seemed to conceive when she was, in her words, "run down." When she was tired and least physically fit to handle the business of having a child, then was when she conceived. And she had her first three children in about five years, less than five years. Then there was a space of three and then there was a space of four. . . . Of course, in those days of no restrictions of any kind on reproduction, a woman just lived as best she could. [63]

Most health care in the first sixty years of Latah County's history relied on natural remedies and existing scientific knowledge. However, there were some who also placed their faith in magico-religious cures. Lola Clyde remembered that "there was great hocus-pocus about what to do to have healthy babies. And the granny women would tell about 'don't look at the full moon or the new moon,' you know. And 'don't let the moon shine on the baby's face' after the baby was born. And there was much talk about cats would come in the room and suck the baby's breath. Keep all the cats away, otherwise the cats would come and jump right up on the crib and suck the baby's breath and kill it." [64]

Late in this period Frank Bruce Robinson moved to Moscow and began Psychiana, a non-Christian, positive thinking movement which in the 1930s grew to be the largest mail-order religion in the world. Robinson developed a reputation among his followers throughout the world as a faith healer, but, believing his religion was controversial enough anyway, refused to allow Latah County residents to become students, so his healing powers were not generally available to local residents. [65] However, there were Latah County residents who did treat local patients with cures which could be described as magico-religious.

Swen Ringsage, who lived near Park in the southeast part of the county, developed a reputation as a healer in the early 1900s. He healed by "magnetism," and his daughter-in-law, Jean Ringsage, remembered how the cures worked:

Here's a person that feels he has this electric or magnetic power—he called it magnetism. You are the object and he visualized—he was visualizing that healing power flowing from himself into that body. And particularly the part that was hurting the most; he diagnosed the ailment. It was a case of mental visualization.

Ringsage isolated himself in a bedroom, visualizing the illness. At the same time, the patient was in another bedroom. Ringsage "could be in the next room or he could be a hundred miles [away]." The patient would "go in a room; quiet, separate from everyone else. Lie down on top of the bed, not in between the covers; loosen your clothes if there is anything tight or confining and take off your shoes; close your eyes; and then start relaxing as much as possible within you. And think good thoughts. Think loving thoughts. Don't have any animosity or hatred in your heart towards anyone."

At one time Ringsage's sister was very ill. The family was skeptical of Swen's healing capabilities, [66] but asked him to come and help if he could. "He didn't touch her. He worked—he just held his hands, he just sort of cupped 'em just like this; up and down, never touching her. And he says, 'Now you rest, and I'll get up and give you another treatment after I've rested.' . . . And when he got up at 11:00 she was walking. And he gave her a few more treatments, just like that. She got well."

A neighbor woman once had a lump on her side which a doctor diagnosed as possibly malignant. After a month of treatment from Ringsage the lump disappeared. His healing powers were even effective on animals. A neighbor's stallion once was badly cut on a barbed-wire fence. Ringsage "made a pass or two over [the wound] with his hands and that was it. Stopped the bleeding." [67]

Robert Foster was a contemporary of Ringsage and practiced in nearby Juliaetta. Foster combined magico-religious curing capabilities with scientific knowledge to develop a wide reputation. In fact, one of the primary factors in the early growth of Juliaetta was Foster's School of Healing, which attracted patients from throughout the Northwest. With them came a great increase in business activity.

Foster first learned he had a natural gift to help sick people when, as a young man, he wrapped his arms around a sick baby and transferred its high temperature to his own body. Seeking to refine his skills, he attended numerous medical schools. Like Ringsage, he, too, believed his healing power was magnetic and his curing ability came from intuition, telepathy, and suggestion. He encouraged patients to be assertive, to believe in self-help and to eat natural foods. However, Foster also included science in his practice, and was most renowned for his ability to cure skin cancer through his own "burner" method. This treatment consisted of applying a paste to the affected area and allowing the paste to burn the cancer from the skin. Over 50 local people were cured by Foster while he was in Juliaetta. He later moved to nearby Clarkston, Washington, where his fame became even more widespread. The Mayo Clinic recognized the importance of his work, and actress Mary Pickford once requested his assistance in curing her mother. [68]

Even though people like Robinson, Ringsage, and Foster did bring a certain magico-religious element to Latah County medicine, throughout this period most health care by most people consisted of dispensing a variety of medicines, herbs, and plants which were kept handy in the family medicine cabinet.

Irwin Press, writing in 1978, noted that "rural communities in developing . . . areas . . . are notoriously unhealthy places. . . . Illness is a common state for most individuals.''[69] That statement is certainly applicable to Latah County during its developmental phase. People had insufficient knowledge of the importance of a balanced diet and of the necessity for sanitary conditions. Pests, diseases with no cures, and a lack of safety precautions which led to numerous accidents, all caused an illness and death rate high by modern standards.

The type of health care one received depended greatly upon when and where a person was living during this period. Clarice Sampson, born in Moscow in 1894, was vaccinated for smallpox as a small child—a preventive remedy not available to most rural families. Sophia Delegans, born in 1914 and raised in nearby Colfax, Washington, which had a hospital, felt that she ''didn't grow up in very primitive days,'' and remembered the use of no home remedies, having always been under a doctor's care.[70]

On the other hand, scientific medicine was for some people either inaccessible or too expensive to use except in the most extreme cases. ''That was terrible if you had to pay a doctor $1.50 or something or other,'' lamented Thelma VanTine, born in 1908. ''Hi had to have his teeth extracted and he cut cords of wood, he butchered a hog, I dressed I don't know how many chickens that paid for that tooth situation. The bill for that was $35.00. It took whole dressed hogs and everything to pay for it because a whole dressed hog brought about $3.00.''[71] Thus Glen Gilder, born in 1901, remembered that a friend's father amputated his own toe because of a painful corn, while William Stowell, born in 1903, recalled that lumberjacks regularly purchased syringes,

had friends write prescriptions, and attempted to treat venereal disease themselves. Marie Clark had a young sister who died of meningitis in 1923 because it took several days to get proper medication to Elk River.[72]

This period in Latah County history might best be described as a time of eclectic health care—a period when scientific medicine was only gradually becoming more sophisticated than home doctoring. While a town the size of Moscow had dentists and other medical specialists as early as the 1880s, Perry Cram, born in 1894, remembered that his family relied heavily on ''oxydonor,'' a short piece of copper tubing which, when put with a crock of extremely cold water—gathered from a snowfield whenever possible—would cure nearly everything.[73] While some people placed their confidence in medical doctors, others relied solely on natural cures and home remedies, and some sought the assistance of magico-religious healers. Most people of the period, however, used a variety of treatments, which was indicative of this period of transition in medical history.

A few informants looked back upon this period with fondness. ''Some of those old remedies were just as good as a doctor anyway,'' reminisced Agnes Gilder. ''Anyway it worked. And I'm still around.''[74] ''We were always healthy, so I guess it worked,'' seconded Martha Long. ''We never died, either.''[75] More typical, however, was the viewpoint of Lola Clyde:

I hold no grief for any of those old medicines. I just never have. . . . We've come a long way and I don't enjoy those good old days half as much as some people do. I just like to think about some good toxins, antitoxins, some good immunization for the children.[76]

Notes

1. Latah is the only county in the United States formed by an act of Congress, being separated from Nez Perce County in 1888. For background on the early development of the county see *An Illustrated History of North Idaho* (Chicago: Western Publishing Company, 1903), and Lawrence Ray Harker, ''A History of Latah County to 1900,'' unpublished MA Thesis, University of Idaho, 1941. For the important role of the Potlatch Lumber Company in the history of the county see Ralph W. Hidy, Frank Ernest Hill and Alan Nevins, *Timber and Men: The Weyerhaeuser Story* (New York: The Macmillan Company, 1963, and Keith Petersen, ''Life in a Company Town: Potlatch, Idaho,'' *Latah Legacy, the Quarterly Journal of the Latah County Historical Society,* Spring 1981, pp. 1–13.

2. A detailed study of migration patterns into Latah County has yet to be undertaken. Kenneth O. Bjork, *West of the Great Divide: Norwegian Migration to the Pacific Coast, 1847–1893* (Northfield, Minn.: Norwegian-American Historical Association, 1958), pp. 463–70, 491–99, 625–26, contains some excellent material on Norwegians in the Genesee area. Richard D. Scheuerman and Clifford E. Trafzer, *The Volga*

Germans: Pioneers of the Northwest (Moscow: University Press of Idaho, 1980), deal briefly with this group in Latah County, while Scheuerman's ''European Immigrant Settlement in the Palouse Country, 1880–1930,'' unpublished historical report from the University of Idaho Museum, in the Latah County Historical Society Library, is a helpful beginning for selected groups.

3. For the number and inferior quality of medical schools see Erwin H. Ackerknecht, *A Short History of Medicine* (New York: The Ronald Press Co., rev. ed., 1968), pp. 224–27; and Bruno Gebhard, ''The Interrelationship of Scientific and Folk Medicine in the United States of America Since 1850,'' in Wayland D. Hand, ed., *American Folk Medicine: A Symposium* (Berkeley: University of California Press, 1976), pp. 87–98. For an introduction to the relatively recent development of scientific medicine see Ackerknecht, *Short History of Medicine*; and Robert F. Karolevitz, *Doctors of the Old West: A Pictorial History of Medicine on the Frontier* (Seattle: Superior Publishing Co., 1967), especially pp. 65–79. The quotation is from Brink, *Buffalo Coat* (New York: Macmillan Company, 1945; reprint, Moscow: Latah County Historical

Society, 1980), p. 31. Brink was born in Moscow and *Buffalo Coat* is one of several novels for children and adults based on her childhood experiences. Dr. Hawkins is patterned after her grandfather, Dr. William W. Watkins, one of Moscow's first doctors, who was killed in 1901 in the town's most celebrated murder.

4. Pickard and Buley, *The Midwest Pioneer: His Ills, Cures & Doctors* (New York: Henry Schuman, 1946).

5. For some folk medicine definitions see Irwin Press, "Urban Folk Medicine: A Functional Overview," in *American Anthropologist*, March 1978, p. 78; Gebhard, "Interrelationship of Scientific and Folk Medicine," p. 90; and Don Yoder, "Folk Medicine," in Richard M. Dorson, ed., *Folklore and Folklife: An Introduction* (Chicago: University of Chicago Press, 1972), pp. 191–215. Yoder clearly distinguishes between practical and magico-religious folk medicine, as do Carl Lindahl, J. Sanford Rikoon, and Elaine Lawless, *A Basic Guide to Fieldwork for Beginning Folklore Students* (Bloomington, Ind.: Folklore Publications Group, Indiana University, 1979), p. 24.

6. For some of the better examples of recent research into American folk medicine by folklorists and anthropologists see Wayland D. Hand, *Popular Beliefs and Superstitions from North Carolina: The Frank C. Brown Collection of North Carolina Folklore* (Durham: Duke University Press, 1961, 1964), vols. 6 and 7; Clarence Meyer, *American Folk Medicine* (New York: Crowell, 1973); M. Estellie Smith, "Folk Medicine Among the Sicilian-Americans of Buffalo, New York," *Urban Anthropology*, Spring 1972, pp. 87–106; and various articles in Hand, ed., *American Folk Medicine*. Very little has been done on folk medicine in Idaho. The following, however, serve as an introduction to the subject: Louie W. Attebery, "Folklore of the Lower Snake River Valley: Home Remedies and Superstitions," in Grace E. Jordan, ed., *Idaho Reader* (Boise: Syms-York, 1963), pp. 92–100; Janice S. Jones, "Folk Beliefs Popular in the Lower Snake River Valley," *Northwest Folklore*, Winter 1978, pp. 12–15; Konni Bowlby, "Cures: A Collection," 10 Dec. 1971; and Peggy Voltolini, "A Collection of Cures," 28 April 1972, both in the Idaho Folklore Collection, University of Idaho Special Collections Library. For two of the better histories dealing with American medical practices see Richard Harrison Shyrock, *Medicine and Society in America, 1660–1860* (New York: New York University Press, 1960); and Pickard and Buley, *The Midwest Pioneer*. Few other medical historians have dealt with the social impact of medical practices in this country.

7. The Latah County Historical Society oral history collection is housed at the University of Idaho Special Collections Library. Approximately three-fourths of the 600-hour collection has been transcribed, and all transcripts are also available at the research library of the Historical Society. In addition, selected tapes and transcripts are available at the Idaho State Historical Library in Boise. For access to the collection see Sam Schrager, ed., *A Guide to the Latah County, Idaho Oral History Collection* (Moscow: Latah County Historical Society, 1977). In order to simplify citations in this paper, reference to the collection will be cited only by the name of the interviewee, the date of the interview, and the page of the transcript. Unless otherwise noted, all interviews were conducted by Schrager.

8. Michael Bubuly, 14 Aug. 1974, p. 9. For a brief introduction to the coming of doctors and hospitals to Latah County see Lillian W. Otness, *Early Health Care in Latah*

County (Moscow: Latah County Historical Society, exhibit brochure, 1980).

9. Lucille Denevan, 11 Nov. 1975, p. 13.

10. Joseph Holland, 23 Aug. 1974, pp. 25–26. Karolevitz, *Doctors of Old West*, p. 52, states, "As for surgery, the frontier physician did what he could under the circumstances. Amputations—with or without anesthesia—were extremely common, partly because of the battlefield training of many of the doctors in the Civil War and partly because they didn't know of any other way to save a patient from more disastrous effects."

11. Frances Fry, 3 Aug. 1976, p. 22.

12. Oscar Olson, 16 June 1976, p. 12.

13. Mamie Munden, 24 June 1975, p. 28.

14. Asafetida is a gum resin obtained from the roots of genus *Ferula* plants native to Asia.

15. Lola Clyde, 3 July 1975, p. 8. Also see Edward Walters, interviewed by Margot Knight, Dec. 1977, pp. 27–28; and Chauncey Kennedy, interviewed by Kay Turner, 27 March 1978, p. 31, both in the Whitman County Historical Society oral history collection. Whitman lies adjacent to Latah County in Washington. [Hereafter reference to the Whitman County Historical Society oral history collection will be abbreviated as "WCHS Collection."]

16. Edward Groseclose, 1 June 1976, pp. 21–22. See Lora Albright, 25 May 1976, pp. 21–24; Mabel Spencer, 29 Jan. 1975, p. 45; and Madeleine Gorman, interviewed by Laura Schrager, 21 Aug. 1974, pp. 12–13 for other native medicinal plants.

17. Many informants spoke of onion poultices and mustard plasters. See, for example, Glen and Agnes Gilder, 29 July 1975, pp. 41–42; Lola Clyde, 3 July 1975, pp. 4–8; and Helen McGreevy, interviewed by Margot Knight, 13 June 1978, WCHS Collection.

18. See Dora Fleener, 16 Dec. 1974, p. 25; Martha Long, 25 Oct. 1976, p. 28; and Mamie Wurman, 24 June 1975, p. 31. Minnie Brandon, who was born in Tekoa, Washington, near the Latah County line in 1883, remembered, "I got a cousin around here . . . who had the diphtheria and they gave that boy turpentine every day and pulled him through the diphtheria." Interviewed by Margot Knight, 22 March 1978, p. 19, WCHS Collection.

19. Lola Clyde, 2 July 1975, pp. 8–9. Joseph Lister found carbolic acid to be an effective surgical antiseptic in combating bacteria. His results, which he started publishing in 1867, were astonishing. Although it took some time for the entire medical community to see the significance of carbolic acid, eventually it was accepted and gradually made its way into use as a home cure. See Ackerknecht, *Short History of Medicine*, pp. 190–91.

20. See, for example, Glen and Agnes Gilder, 29 July 1975, p. 41; and Martha Long, 25 Oct. 1976, p. 28.

21. Nona Lawrence, 27 Jan. 1976, pp. 23–24, 27. An advertisement concerning McGary's "remarkable discovery" can be found in the Deary, Idaho *Enterprise*, 3 Oct. 1913. Electricity, in various forms, was considered a curing device by many throughout the country. See, for example, Gebhard, "Interrelationship of Scientific and Folk Medicine," p. 96.

22. For more information on McGary see Anna Marie Oslund, "Marcellus McGary," 1964, unpublished paper in the

Idaho Folklore Collection, University of Idaho Special Collections Library.

23. Elva Bennett, interviewed by Margot Knight, 9 March 1978, p. 19, WCHS Collection.

24. Helen McGreevy, interviewed by Margot Knight, 9 June 1978, p. 22, WCHS Collection.

25. Camphor is a gummy crystalline compound obtained from the wood of camphor trees.

26. Lora Albright, 25 May 1976, p. 25.

27. Lola Clyde, 3 July 1975, p. 5.

28. Martha Long, 25 Oct. 1976, p. 28.

29. Lora Albright, 25 May 1976, p. 21.

30. Mary Lynd, 24 June 1975, p. 32. Also see Henry Smith, interviewed by Kay Turner, 3 Oct. 1978, pp. 37–38, WCHS Collection.

31. Henry Smith, p. 38.

32. Madeleine Gorman, interviewed by Laura Schrager, 21 Aug. 1974, p. 13.

33. Dixie Groseclose, 21 July 1976, p. 63.

34. Ada Schoeffler, interviewed by Karen Purtee, 7 Feb. 1976, p. 21.

35. Lola Clyde, 3 July 1975, p. 3.

36. John Eikum, 8 Dec. 1975, p. 8.

37. Lola Clyde, 3 July 1975, p. 3; 12 Oct. 1976, p. 4. For more on the diphtheria epidemics of the late 1870s see Alma Taylor-Lauder Keeling, *The Un-Covered Wagon: A Glimpse of Pioneer Days in Moscow, Idaho* (Moscow: Alma Taylor-Lauder Keeling, 1975), p. 5.

38. Dora Fleener, 16 Dec. 1974, pp. 25–26.

39. Bernadine Cornelison, 16 Nov. 1976, pp. 13–14.

40. Douglas A. Christensen, *The Life and Times of a Country Doctor* (Kendrick, Id.: Douglas A. Christensen, 1982), p. 41.

41. Brink, *Buffalo Coat*, pp. 264–76.

42. Ada Schoeffler, interviewed by Karen Purtee, 7 Feb. 1976, p. 20.

43. Clarice Sampson, interviewed by Laura Schrager, 13 Nov. 1974, p. 7.

44. Edward Groseclose, 21 July 1976, p. 61. For more on the flu epidemic in rural Latah County see Lucille Denevan, 11 Nov. 1975, p. 35; Frances Fry, 3 Aug. 1976, pp. 25–26; Oscar and Hazel Olson, 16 June 1976, p. 11.

45. Abe Goff to the author, 2 Sept. 1982. Also see Goff oral history, 13 Nov. 1974, pp. 7–8. In nearby Pullman, Washington, also a campus town, home of Washington State College, the experience was similar. Over 600 soldiers were housed in the town. By the end of the epidemic, over 40 had died of the flu. See Harold E. Helton, ''WAZZU at War: Washington State College During the Great War,'' *The Bunchgrass Historian*, Fall 1982, pp. 3–21.

46. Clarice Sampson, interviewed by Laura Schrager, 13 Nov. 1974, p. 25.

47. Lola Clyde, 3 July 1975, p. 6.

48. Ibid.

49. Ione Adair, 16 Nov. 1976, p. 44. While automobiles were in use at this time, doctors often still used horses for house calls into the country—especially during wet weather.

50. Pauline Machlied, interviewed by Rachel Foxman, 1 May 1978, p. 44.

51. Madeleine Gorman, interviewed by Laura Schrager, 21 Aug. 1974, pp. 41–43.

52. Grace Wicks, 8 Oct. 1974, p. 73.

53. Albert Justice, 23 Aug. 1974, p. 36.

54. Hershiel Tribble, 23 July 1973, pp. 23–24.

55. Byers Sanderson, 13 Nov. 1975, pp. 17–18.

56. Elmer Flodin, 25 June 1974, pp. 13–14.

57. Hershiel Tribble, 23 July 1973, p. 25.

58. Lola Clyde, 3 July 1975, pp. 6–7.

59. Kate Grannis, 24 Feb. 1976, p. 26.

60. Mamie Munden, 24 June 1975, p. 29.

61. See for example, Lora Albright, 25 May 1976, pp. 37–39, who lost her first child to uremic poisoning.

62. Lucille Denevan, 11 Nov. 1975, p. 45.

63. Grace Wicks, 8 Oct. 1974, pp. 11–12.

64. Lola Clyde, 3 July 1975, p. 7.

65. For more information on Robinson and Psychiana see Keith Petersen, ''Frank Bruce Robinson and Psychiana,'' *Idaho Yesterdays, the Quarterly Journal of the Idaho State Historical Society*, Fall 1979, pp. 9–15, ff.

66. Ringsage did not know he had healing power until he was about 40.

67. Information on Ringsage comes in two interviews with his son and daughter-in-law. See Jean and Stiner Ringsage, 5 Oct. 1976, pp. 61–68; 19 Oct. 1976, pp. 26–30.

68. For background on Foster see Carolyn Gravelle, ''Juliaetta's Forgotten Humanitarian: Robert Foster, Sr., 1868–1934,'' *Latah Legacy, the Quarterly Journal of the Latah County Historical Society*, Spring 1980, pp. 1–10. Also see Ruth Leland, 25 May 1976, pp. 1–3; and Catherine Mahon, 27 Sept. 1976, pp. 65–69.

69. Press, ''Urban Folk Medicine,'' p. 73.

70. Sophia Delegans, interviewed by Kay Turner, 6 Feb. 1978, p. 28, WCHS Collection; Clarice Sampson, interviewed by Laura Schrager, 13 Nov. 1974, p. 7.

71. Thelma VanTine, interviewed by Kay Turner, 17 Jan. 1978, p. 5, WCHS Collection.

72. Glen Gilder, 17 June 1975, p. 32; William Stowell, 28 Sept. 1976, pp. 26–28; Marie Clark, 9 July 1976, p. 5.

73. Perry Cram, interviewed by Kay Turner, 6 Feb. 1978, p. 1, WCHS Collection.

74. Agnes Gilder, 29 July 1975, p. 42.

75. Martha Long, 25 Oct. 1976, p. 29.

76. Lola Clyde, 3 July 1975, p. 5.

Folk Ballad Characteristics in a Present-Day Collection of Songs

Thomas Edward Cheney

A preoccupation of early ballad scholarship was the problem of ballad origins. Cheney, writing in 1936, was influenced by F. B. Gummere and G. L. Kittredge, who held that ballads originated in group dancing and composition sessions, the verses composed by individuals and the refrains sung by everyone in the group. This theory, outlined in Gummere's The Beginnings of Poetry *(1901), inspired great controversy among ballad scholars, receiving criticism from Louise Pound in* Poetic Origins and the Ballad *(1921), and thoughtful reinterpretation by Phillips Barry in his theory of "communal re-creation" and by G. H. Gerould in* The Ballad of Tradition *(1932), a classic of folk song scholarship. Working out of this theoretical base, Cheney joined many other early twentieth-century ballad scholars in the hunt for examples of the Child ballads (ballads recognized by American ballad scholar Francis James Child as the oldest and best of the traditional English ballads) and native American ballads, and he was one of the few to make his search in Idaho. Cheney's study is of interest today as an inventory of traditional songs in southeast Idaho of 1933–36 and as an early attempt to discern the influences of the West on American song traditions. At the end of the article is a list of the song titles, texts of which are included in Cheney's master's thesis at the University of Idaho.*

Cheney is a retired professor of English and folklore at Brigham Young University, Provo, Utah.

Having heard fragments of folk songs of American origin from my mother and childhood associates, I began at every opportune time to collect old songs. As my collection grew, my interest increased, for I found the work most fascinating. From 1933 to 1936, I assembled seventy-one songs, which are presented as an appendix to my master's thesis on file at the University of Idaho. Twenty-one texts have subject matter and construction of or comparable to the Child ballads (Nos. 1–21), fifteen are typically American ballads with less resemblance to the Child group (Nos. 22–36), twelve are folk lyrics true to the lyric type (Nos. 37–48), and twenty-three songs have no relation to Child ballads (Nos. 49–71).

Although some of the latter group may not be recognized as folk songs, they came to me in folk-song manner. They were not taken from the printed page but from oral circulation, from older people who learned them in their youth. Within the short time since I began the collection, two of the contributors have died—Mr. William H. Avery of Blackfoot, Idaho, and Mrs. Eliza Jane Avery of Burley, Idaho. Others are feeble with age. With few exceptions, contributors were over sixty years of age and had never seen in writing the songs they contributed.

I began my research in the hope of finding versions of Child ballads. One and only one did I find—a version of "Lady Isabel and the Elf Knight" is my lone wolf. Had other interests than the primary one not arisen, I should perhaps have tired of the near-vain search, but in the ballads contributed I observed a resemblance to the medieval English and Scottish popular ballads, and this similarity sustained my interest.

A true folk ballad is a unique union of epic, lyric, and dramatic elements into a single musical identity. In its earlier stages it was a two-line stanza with a refrain. It deals with a limited number of people in instinctive situations of family life, such as lover and truelove, life and death, and supernatural circumstances. It is possessed of a strong dramatic element as evidenced by impersonality of the author, spirited and lively action, and dialogue. It is the property of the folk either by having come into existence through communal authorship or having evolved after its individual authorship through members of the society who considered it their own. It contains varying amounts of repetition in the various types of refrain and parallelism. These are the characteristics of the simple folk ballad, in accordance with which I shall measure the specimens I have collected.

Little has been done toward collecting English ballad survivals in the West. In my brief search for ballads in southeastern Idaho, I have found only one of the Child ballads, "Lady Isabel and the Elf Knight" (Child 4). Mrs. Elizabeth Curtis of Victor, Idaho, told me of an old song she had known, the story of which she related; it was "Bonny Barbara Allen" (Child 84). That many of these songs exist in the Western states may be safely assumed.

Other ballads than the Child texts, however, exist. Sharp classified eighteen songs as ballads of English and Scottish origin which are not Child ballads. Cox in *Folk-Songs of the South* classified thirty-four as ballads that are of American origin. Much has been adapted to local conditions. As I proceed in this study, I shall attempt to show to what extent some of the mass of present–day folk song approaches the ballad type, as described above.

There is no other ballad which has had and still has the cosmopolitan and broad local circulation of "Lady Isabel and the Elf Knight." It is nearly as well known in southern as in northern Europe. It has wide circulation in Poland, Germany, and Scandinavia. Child, in his detailed introduction to the ballad, briefly relates the story as told in German, Polish, Bohemian, French, Dutch, Flemish, Danish, Norwegian, Swedish, and Icelandic. In English it is still in circulation. In America nearly every collector has found it. Arthur Kyle Davis in *Traditional Ballads of Virginia* gives nineteen variations; Barry, Eckstorm, and Smyth in *British Ballads from Maine* give nine variations; Campbell and Sharp in *Folk Songs of the Appalachians* give five variations; Reed Smith in *South Carolina Ballads* gives two versions; and Mackenzie in *Ballads and Sea Songs from Nova Scotia* gives one. This ballad has been found everywhere in America where anyone has made even a partial search.

The story contained in Child's E version, from Herd's MS. (1776), most nearly approaches the version I present. In the first stanza the story is told in first person, an outlandish knight "came a wooing me." Neither girl nor man is named. She is asked to get some of her father's gold and mother's fee and two of her father's best horses. She obeys. The couple mount and ride to the seaside in the northland, arriving three hours before day. She is commanded to dismount and give the milk-white steed she rides to the robber, for she is to be drowned there where six pretty maids have preceded her. In turn she is commanded to remove her silken gown, the silken stays, and the Holland smock, for they are too precious to rot in the salt sea. She cleverly requests as she removes the last of her clothing that he turn his back unto her, "For it is not fitting that such a ruffian a naked woman should see." He grants her the favor, but, as his back is turned, she tumbles him into the stream. He scrambles to the side asking her to give him a helping hand. She refuses, mounts her horse, leads the dapple gray he rode, and returns to her father's abode. The parrot in the window hears her return and questions her. Fearing the parrot will tell tales, she promises a new cage made of glittering gold. The king in his chamber above awakes to question the

parrot as to why she talked, but is given no information other than that the cat has come to the window and she is afraid. The girl commends the parrot on the "well-turned" story and promises again a glittering gold cage, this time with an ivory door.

The name given to me for the ballad I collected was "Pretty Polly," a name used for the girl in nearly half of the forty American versions current in West Virginia, Maine, South Carolina, and Nova Scotia. The story told in this variation is very much the same as the Child version just told. It differs by beginning with the American ballad introduction, "I'll tell you." The man in the story, still unnamed, becomes a rich young man; she is merely a fair lady. An added enticement of an offer of marriage is given the lady; he rides a brown pony instead of a dapply gray; he offers a bribe for her help, as he struggles in the water, of "ten thousand." The only allusion to her being a king's daughter is in his statement: "For it's six king's daughters I've drounded [sic] here, and you the seventh shall be." Rather than a glittering gold cage Polly offers the parrot a cage lined with gold and locked with a silver key. The parrot when questioned offers a more plausible lie in saying that she called Polly to scare the cat away. The following version was collected from William H. Avery, of Victor, Idaho, in the autumn of 1933.

> I'll tell you of a rich young man
> Who came courting a fair lady;
> He came into her father's house
> Her life for to betray.
>
> "Hand down, hand down your father's gold
> Likewise your mother's fee,
> And I'll take you to the north country,
> And there I'll marry thee."
>
> She handed down her father's gold,
> Likewise her mother's fee,
> And she took the best horses in her father's barn,
> And there stood thirty-three.
>
> She mounted on her milk-white steed,
> And he on the brown pony,
> And they rode till they came to the north country;
> 'Twas on a summer's day.
>
> "Alight, alight, my pretty Polly,
> Alight, I say unto thee,
> For it's six king's daughters I've drowned here,
> And you the seventh shall be.
>
> Take off, take off that fine clothing,
> Take it off, I say unto thee,
> For it is too fine and too costly
> To rot in the deep, deep sea."
>
> 'Then turn your face toward the west
> Toward the willow tree,
> For 'tis not fit for any young man
> A lady's figure to see."

He turned his face toward the west
Toward the willow tree.
And she clasped her arms around his waist
And threw him into the sea.

"Hand down, hand down that lily-white hand,
Hand it down I say unto thee;
For it's many a bargain I have made with thee,
And I will ten thousand give."

"Lie there, lie there, you false young man,
Lie there I say unto thee,
For it's six king's daughters you've drownded there,
Go keep them company."

She mounted on her milk-white steed
And led the brown pony,
And she rode 'til she came to her father's house,
'Twas just before it was day.

And then up spoke the pretty parrot
That in the cage did stay,
Saying, "Where have you been, my pretty Polly,
This long sweet summer's day?"

"Hush up, hush up, my pretty parrot,
Tell no tales on me,
And your cage will be lined with pure shining gold
And locked with a silver key."

And then up spoke her own father
Who in his bed did lie,
"What is the matter, my pretty parrot?
You speak before it is day."

"The cat was at my own cage door
My life for to betray,
And I called upon my pretty Polly
To drive the cat away."

The changes in subject matter between Child's broadside (C) and my American version are minor—chiefly a falling off of allusion to knighthood and royalty, a more believable lie, and more conservative reference to lavish riches. My version gives one stanza to the removal of fine clothing, does not name any one article of clothing, and Polly's promise to the parrot is a gold-lined cage and silver key, compared with a glittering gold cage and an ivory door. The phrase "A naked woman to see" is changed to "A lady's figure to see."

The ballad *The Old Shoe* is an example of a type, extant in America, which is not an actual version of a Child ballad, yet contains in its gist ballad situations and incidents. Songs of this group are in reality modern versions of old ballads so sophisticated as to be almost completely disguised. The following discussion will illustrate my point.

The story of *The Old Shoe* runs thus: A beautiful young lady, unencumbered by her father's riches, was courted by a young man. To prove the young man, she told him she would not be his bride, at which he im-

pulsively swore in her presence he would marry the first woman he saw. Shrewishly, the girl ordered her servants to delay the young man while she put away her rich jewels and clothing and dressed as a beggar. When her hands and face were besmeared with soot and she looked like a beggar, even to the old shoes, she ran down the road like a witch to be first to meet him. True to his self-imposed oath, he proposed marriage to the supposedly despicable creature and received an affirmative answer at once. Being fearful of taking her to his proud parents, he left her at a neighbor's, but promised to return when the wedding was planned. The parents, informed of the vow the son had made, advised him to bring the lady home and marry her; and with new clothing she would do very well. The wedding was announced, and guests were invited to the feast. The servants attempted to dress the bride, but she refused to wear other than her old clothes. At the wedding feast the beggar bride clawed out the meat with her hands, burned them in the hot pudding, then wiped them on her old rags. His friends laughed, some much pleased, others much grieved. The bride took a candle to light her way to the chamber. As she went from the room, she informed her husband he might come when her old shoe went "clung" on the floor. At the signal, he went to the chamber where he retired without the aid of a light, his back to the bride. She rolled, tumbled, and turned until he asked "what the devil" was the matter. Her shins were sore; she must have a light to dress them. By the light of the candle he saw his old bride clothed in the finest of things and fairer than pictures of gold. He voiced his surprise by the expression, "Is it you? Is it you?" Here is the text as it was sung to me by Eliza Jane Avery in Burley, Idaho, August 1933.

'Tis of an old man in Plymouth did dwell
And he had a daughter, a beautiful girl;
A young man, he courted her to be his bride;
This plentiful fortune encumbered her pride,
      Encumbered her pride.

He courted her long and gained her love,
But still she intended this young man to prove;
One day he said to her, and thus she replied,
She told him right there she would ne'er be his bride,
      She would ne'er be his bride.

Then hearing those sad words from his dear;
'Twas with a sad oath, oh then, he did swear
That he'd have the first woman that e'er he did see,
If she was mean as a beggar could be,
      As a beggar could be.

She ordered her servants this young man to delay
While she her rich jewels had all put away;
Then she dressed herself up in the worst she could find;
She looked like old Cheepi, before and behind,
      Before and behind.

She rubbed her hands on the chimney jam,
She rubbed her face from corner to chin,
And down the road she ran like a witch

With her petticoat hoisted all on a half hitch,
    All on a half hitch.

Then as he came riding, and thus he did see her;
It was for his sad oath, oh then, he did fear,
With her old shoe heel jammed down to ascrew,
He soon overtook her and says, "Who are you?"
    And says, "Who are you?"
"I'm a woman."

This answer, it struck him as well as a dead man,
He stumbled, he staggered, he hardly could stand.
"Oh, how can I fear for to have you?" said he.
And then he soon asked her, saying: "Will you have me?"
    Saying: "Will you have me?"
"Yes, I will."

This answer, it suited as well as the rest,
But lay very heavy and sore on his breast,
'Twas for his oath's sake he must make her his bride,
And then soon asked her behind him to ride,
    Behind him to ride.
"Your horse will throw me; I know it will."

"Oh, no! Oh, no! My horse, it will not."
She mustered around and behind him she got.
"My heart it doth fail me, I dare not go home,
My parents will say I'm forever undone,
    I'm forever undone."

He took her to neighbors, with whom he was great;
'Twas of his sad story he dare not relate.
"It's here with my neighbors a while you will tarry,
And in a short time I with you will marry,
    I with you will marry."
"You won't! I know you won't!"

He told her he would, and home he did go;
He told his father and mother also,
And of his sad case and how he had sworn.
"All's well," said his parents, and they did not mourn,
    And they did not mourn.

"Son, break not your vows, but bring home your girl,
And we'll fix her up so she'll do very well."
So published they were, and invited the guests,
And they intended the bride for to dress,
    The bride for to dress.
"I'll wear my old clothes as I used to."

Then he invited his old spark to come;
Her servants replied, "She is not at home."
He ordered his servants to wait on her there,
And then for the wedding they all did prepare,
    They all did prepare.

And when they were married and sat down to eat,
With her fingers she clawed out the cabbage and meat,
And in the hot pudding she burned them to fags;
She licked them and wiped them all on her old rags,
    All on her old rags.

Then faster endeavor, she at it again,
They all laughed in private 'til their sides ached with pain;
Then while they were stopped some called her his bride,

Saying, "Go, you love, do and sit down by his side,
    Sit down by his side."
"I'll sit in the corner as I used to."

Some, they were tickled and very much pleased,
While others were sorry and very much grieved;
They gave her a candle, what could she ask more?
And showed her the way to her chamber door,
    To her chamber door.
*"Husband, when you hear my old shoe go, 'clung,' then,
    you can come."*

Upstairs she went and kept stepping about;
His mother says, "Son, what think you the row?"
"Oh, Mother! Dear Mother, don't say one word,
For no more comfort may this world me afford,
    May this world me afford."

And by and by the old shoe it went, "clung";
They gave him a candle and bade him go along.
"I choose for to go in the dark," then he said,
"For I very well know the way to my bed,
    The way to my bed."

He jumped in his bed with his back to his bride,
She rolled, and she tumbled from pillow to side,
And as she turned over, the bed it did squeak.
"What the devil's the matter? Why don't you lay still?
    Why don't you lay still?"
"My shins are sore, I want a candle to dress them by."

He called for a candle to dress his wife's shins,
And found she was clothed in the finest of things;
And as she turned over, her face to behold,
He found she was fairer than pictures of gold,
    Than pictures of gold.

"Is it you? Is it you?" with his arms around her waist.
The answer was "Yes," and they all came in haste;
They looked like two pictures that pleased the eye,
And through many a fair glass we wish them much joy.
    We wish them much joy.

Although this ballad has no exact counterpart in Child, it is a typical ballad story. In the first place it has to do with a private personal affair. It deals with a love story, a subject of more than one-third of the Child ballads. If we include sex crimes as a violent and illicit perversion of love, 152 of the 305 come under this classification. An element of relationship is seen to "Gil Brenton" (Child 5) who marries without knowing the girl is the victim of his earlier lust. In "The Old Shoe" the man married a girl he does not know to be his earlier sweetheart.

The story of "The Old Shoe" so closely resembles some versions of "The Knight and the Shepherd's Daughter" (Child 110) as to be considered its direct offspring. Briefly, the story of version E runs as follows: Earl Richard meets a beautiful lady "with towers of gold upon her head" who so enthralls him that he at once proposes marriage (in a crude way), afterward offering lavish gifts which she freely refuses until,

He caught her by the milk-white hand,
And by the grass-green sleeve,
And there has taken his will of her
Wholly without her leave.

After this casually treated rape, the lady insisted on being told his name. He gave the Latin for Richard which, to his surprise, she promptly interpreted. As he rode away, she followed persistently and at the castle put her case before the queen, who promptly promised to force marriage. The maid identified Earl Richard, the queen's brother, as the man. Richard married the lady most reluctantly, for she told outlandish stories how her mother and she were both loathsome beggars. Not only did she tell such stories but demonstrated in her actions what she pretended to be. When in bed,

He turned his face unto the stock,
And she hers to the stone,
And cold and dreary was the love
That was these two between.

There was great mirth in the kitchen and hall but,

He (Earl Richard) wept till he fell fast asleep,
Then slept till light was come,

And he heard the gentlemen in the outer hall say the union was a very fine match between the girl, the king of Scotland's daughter, and the queen of England's brother.

"The Wife of Bath's Tale," which Chaucer is supposed to have taken from a current tale of Sir Gawain, is also related. "The Wife of Bath's Tale" differs from the story just told in that the case is taken to King Arthur who allows the knight the alternative of death or marriage to the girl. The marriage is so distasteful to him that one would not be surprised to see the knight choose death.

"The Marriage of Sir Gawain" (Child 31) has much in common with "The Old Shoe." King Arthur encountered in the woods a bold baron who gave Arthur his choice of fighting or returning before New Year's Day with an answer to the question, What do women most desire? Arthur puts the qustion everywere and collects many answers in which he has little confidence. As he rides to meet the baron, he meets a frightfully ugly woman; she intimates she can help him. Arthur promises her Gawain in marriage if she will, and she gives him the right answer. Arthur finds the baron, and, after presenting the answers he had gathered elsewhere, all to be contemptuously rejected, he gives the answer the woman on the moor gave: that a woman would have her will. This answer is right. Now Arthur must keep his promise. He assembles his knights, and they ride to meet the lady. All but Gawain detest her sight and decline the match in vehement terms. Somehow Gawain overlooks "a little foul sight and misliking." She is bedded in all her repulsiveness and turns during the night to a beautiful young woman. To try Gawain further she asks him if he will have her fair by night or

by day. Manfully, Gawain gives her her choice. This is all that is needed to make her permanently beautiful, for she has been bewitched by a stepmother to dwell on the moor as a fiend until some knight would give her all her own way.

In the stories of "The Knight and the Shepherd's Daughter" (Child 110), "The Marriage of Sir Gawain" (Child 31), and "The Old Shoe" a beautiful lady of high rank is thought by a lover to be most distasteful but is transformed while in bed to her true self.

The first outstanding difference between "The Shepherd's Daughter" and "The Old Shoe" is the removal in the latter of the sex story. This change we would expect in present-day lore, when even the most humble of folk have been trained in sex taboo for several generations. Not only is it eliminated because of taboo, but present-day society will not tolerate rape, a sin which was looked upon, if interpreted in the spirit of the ballad, most casually. It is, then, a fact that if a song is to be sung to present-day society, stories of rape must be kept out.

The most noticeable difference between "The Marriage of Sir Gawain" and "The Old Shoe" is the fact that the supernatural occurs in "The Marriage of Sir Gawain" but does not in "The Old Shoe." The idea of a person being under the power of a stepmother witch to the extent of being a fiend is preposterous to modern society. To be popular with folk today, the old pagan superstitions must be removed and the story placed in a new setting.[1]

I have given ample evidence that the song "The Old Shoe" is a ballad which deals with the perplexing problem of love common to many ballads. It deals with a domestic problem in a single incident affecting only two main characters. Evidence has also been given that the story has been changed, having a rearrangement of characters, setting, plot, and narrative to make a plausible story adapted to present-day life. The change is, first, elimination of the crude sex story; second, eradication of all superstition. Evidence would lead one to believe, and with sufficient foundation to be no guesswork, that society will not tolerate, to an extent of its becoming popular tradition, the two themes cited.

"The Old Shoe" starts in the objective narrative, third person, past tense. The introductory phrase, "'Tis of," is particularly American. The objective narrative is carried pretty much throughout, although the dramatic method enters appreciably. The introduction is dramatically abrupt, the two main characters being introduced in the second and third lines of the first stanza and the plot suggested in the fourth line. The movement of the plot is lively. Several descriptive sentences enter —"She looked like old Cheepi before and behind," "With her shoe heel jammed down to ascrew," "She was fairer than pictures of gold," and "like two pictures that pleased the eye." These are not features of true ballad structure, but, it will be observed, they are short and trite, the only type of descriptive phrase acceptable in a ballad. Exposition enters in such brief phrases

as—"plentiful fortune encumbered her pride," "She
intended this young man to prove," and "'Twas of his
sad story he dare not relate." Although exposition has
no part in the ballad, the presence of these brief expressions does not seriously affect the dramatic
presentation.

The feeble lady, Mrs. Eliza Jane Avery, now
deceased, who sang this song to me in 1933, sang the
entire song in rather lilting rhythm, except the extra
speeches tacked on the end of many of the stanzas.
These she gave in her talking voice in a dramatic
fashion—gruffly, of course, imitating the beggar maid.
The lady explained when questioned as to the manner
of rendition that in her youth a group at a quilting bee,
or some such gathering, when tired of work often
stopped to sing songs. Some individual would sing this
song, the extra speeches following the normal stanza
being supplied by the audience. For example, stanza ten
would be sung by the entertainer through the first and
second, "I with you will marry." The audience, in
speech rather than song would say, "You won't; I know
you won't." This expression would vary in wording
according to individuality of the group. The singer
would then continue with the next stanza. "He told her
he would"—etc. When the group did not know the
song, Mrs. Avery said she often sang the stanza and her
husband characterized the beggar maid in the extra
speeches.

This explanation, coming from the lips of the one
who preserved the song in tradition, establishes it as a
folk ballad, both through its dramatic presentation and
its folk transmission and variation.

The story of "The Old Shoe" begins in objective narrative; and, in fact, it is, for the main part, an objective
narrative story. Dialogue, however, is introduced in
the sixth of the twenty-one stanzas, and from that point
to the end only two stanzas are without dialogue. Some
have but one line of dialogue; others, four. In proportion nearly twenty percent is dialogue.

Repetition is less prominent than dialogue, but
nevertheless present in ballad type. The last phrase of
each stanza is repeated. As previously discussed, a
rebuttal follows the stanza irregularly. This phenomenon is not characteristic of ballads, but when considered in the light of the manner of rendition described
above it is ballad-like in spirit if not in form.

The verse form of "The Old Shoe" compares favorably with that of "Lord Randal." "Lord Randal" (Child
12) is not as one would suppose in typical ballad verse.
The diagram following shows for comparative purposes the resemblance in verse form in accented and
unaccented syllables of both songs.

Lord Randal

$$\_ \; ' \; \_ \; \_ \; ' \; \_ \qquad ' \; \_ \; \_ \qquad '$$
$$\_ \; ' \; \_ \; \_ \; ' \; \_ \qquad ' \; \_ \; \_ \qquad '$$
$$\_ \; ' \; \_ \; \_ \; ' \; \_ \; \_ \; ' \; \_ \; \_ \qquad '$$
$$\_ \; \_ \; ' \; \_ \; \_ \; ' \; \_ \; \_ \; ' \; \_ \; \_ \qquad '$$

The Old Shoe

$$\_ \; ' \; \_ \; \_ \; ' \; \_ \qquad ' \; \_ \; \_ \qquad '$$
$$\_ \; ' \; \_ \; \_ \; ' \; \_ \qquad ' \; \_ \; \_ \; ' \qquad '$$
$$\_ \; ' \; \_ \; \_ \; ' \; \_ \qquad ' \; \_ \; \_ \qquad '$$
$$\_ \; ' \; \_ \; \_ \; ' \; \_ \; \_ \qquad ' \; \_ \; \_ \qquad '$$
$$\qquad \_ \qquad ' \; \_ \; \_ \qquad '$$

Like men, no two folk ballads are identical.
Although there are thousands of them, no two are
exactly alike at the time they are taken from oral tradition. The ballad I have just considered, "The Old
Shoe," has no counterpart to my knowledge, yet its
similarity in subject matter to the Child ballads is clear.
It is a ballad story with the objectionable sex story,
reference to classes of people, and superstition
eliminated. In structure, society has made the verse
form more elaborate, increased the objective narrative
at the expense of dialogue, and decreased the amount
of repetition. In all of these respects there remains, as
has been shown, an appreciable quantity of the old.

"Frankie and Johnny" is representative of a great
many ballads of comparatively recent origin. It is not a
carry-over of an old idea, orally current for centuries,
but an entirely newborn creature of separate identity
which, as I shall show, maintains the characteristics of
the species. Unlike ballads of earlier birth, it came into
existence in a somewhat civilized, literate society as did
many of its kind now in circulation. Here is the version
collected from John Crossman in Victor, Idaho, in
1933.

> Frankie and Johnny were lovers,
> And, oh, how they could love,
> Tried to be true to each other,
> Just as true as the stars up above;
> He was her man; he wouldn't do her no wrong.
>
> Frankie went down to the corner,
> Just after a bottle of beer,
> Frankie said, "Mr. Bar-tender,
> Has my lover, Johnny, been here?
> He's my man, and he wouldn't do me no harm."
>
> "I don't want to cause you no trouble;
> I don't want to tell you no lies,
> But I saw your lover just half hour ago
> Making love to Mary Bries;
> He is your man; and he's doing you wrong."
>
> Frankie crawled up to the transom,
> And there, to her great surprise,
> There on a couch sat Johnny
> Making love to Mary Bries;
> He was her man, and he's doing her wrong.
>
> Frankie drew back her kimona
> Drew out her little forty-four;
> Root, toot, toot, three times she shot
> Right through the hardwood door;
> She shot her man; because he done her wrong.

"Roll me over easy;
Roll me over slow;
Roll me over on my left side
Because the Devil's got my soul;
I was her man, and I done her wrong."

Frankie went to the warden
And said, "What am I going to do?"
The warden said, "Frankie,
It's the electric chair for you;
You killed your man, because he done you wrong."

My text of "Frankie and Johnny" contains the brief story in seven stanzas. It is indeed brief compared with the longest versions of more than sixty stanzas. Frankie speaks half of the second stanza; the fourth stanza is narrative; the fifth is narrative; the sixth is spoken in its entirety by Johnny; the seventh is one and one-half lines narrative, one line Frankie's speech, and two and one-half lines the warden's. The song is forty-five percent dialogue. The remaining fifty-five percent is so dramatic as to be almost visible to the listener. The greatest of dramatists could add no more realism and action to a written stanza than:

Frankie drew back her kimona,
Drew out her little forty-four;
Root, toot, toot, three times she shot
Right through the hardwood door;
She shot her man, because he done her wrong.

In only the last clause is the dramatic narrative method, at its height, withdrawn. The movement is speeded up by decisiveness so clear as to make Frankie live and act before us.

The song has repetition; the type is incremental with no refrain. The movement of the song is so swift that one would not be chagrined if it were delayed enough to allow a refrain, unless the last line of each stanza be called a refrain. The objectivity is so complete that the intrusion of a subjective refrain would detract from the song's approach to perfection. The bulk of repetition appears in a fifth line of each stanza, having its mate in every other stanza. In my text the repetition of the fifth line is not exact in any two stanzas, being true incremental. The total song is one-fifth repetition.

One cannot say that "Frankie and Johnny" is in good ballad meter. It would approach the ballad form more nearly if stanzas had four lines instead of five. Considering the fifth line a refrain and counting out irregularities of meter, relationship in verse form to older ballads is observable.

"Frankie and Johnny" is an example of a folk ballad (it deserves that name), born and nurtured in America in recent times under conditions of literacy. As a fighting bulldog holds his prey in his teeth, the folk hold on to material which has from the beginning appealed to the people, primarily material in which instinctive interest lies. "Frankie and Johnny," a child of the folk of today, holds entirely to the type of subject matter used by man in former ages. The story is essentially a ballad story. In adaptation to present-day life Frankie uses a forty-four instead of a wee pen knife; her story has its setting in a saloon and hotel, not a bower and a greenwood; and Frankie surrenders herself to the law instead of to Johnny's relatives. In my text she is promised punishment in the relatively modern implement of torture, the electric chair. The song is in transmission a folk ballad. Although transmission in this day is influenced by the art of writing—some copies being made by folk, publishers printing and influencing the script—this song, "Frankie and Johnny," has consistently passed from mouth to mouth. The copying of the song has contributed to speedy and widespread transmission, in that respect adding to its value as folk literature. Granting that the printing press has influenced the song under discussion does not concede its being a product of the written art. It has partaken of the influences of great literary men. "Frankie and Johnny" demonstrates the very pinnacle of dramatic presentation. Every word is an addition to its action. Even the explanatory phrase, "He was her man, and he's doing her wrong," adds to dramatic form because of its answering the vital question—Why?— and because of its being repeated at dramatic intervals with slight variation adding zest to an already tense performance.

I have now discussed three types of songs found in my collection: (1) A Child ballad preserved in oral tradition, "Pretty Polly"; (2) A ballad related in subject matter so closely as to be a direct descendant of Child ballads, "The Old Shoe"; and (3) A specimen of recent American origin drawing its story from contemporary American life, but showing relationship to Child ballads in material and structure, "Frankie and Johnny."

In my collection are twenty-one ballads showing similar close relationshp to Child ballads. Time and space will not permit my dealing with each separately. In this part I propose to discuss them as a group. The subject matter of the following material is summarized in the individual analysis of each ballad of this division at the end of this section. The intervening discussion gives some explanation regarding my analogies.

The songs "Florella," "The Rich Irish Lady," "The Lawyer Outwitted," "Warren and Fuller," "The Rovin' Gambler," "The Dark Eyed Sailor," "If You Will Marry Me," "The Dying Hobo," "Little Mary Pigan," "Dick Turpin," "Billy Boy," and "At The Matinee" all contain subject matter very closely related to Child ballads.

The "Florella" story is another jealous lover tale. Edward, the lover, invited his sweetheart to accompany him to the meadow. Having wandered until the fatigued girl asked to be taken home, the heartless man informed her she must die. Disregarding her plea for mercy, he plunged the gleaming knife into her bosom. As her life ebbed away she reassured her murderer that she was innocent of deceiving him, and, in Christlike manner, she forgave him. Deep remorse follows, as he realizes he has "killed his own Florella as true as the rising sun."

This story so closely resembles the Child ballads in subject matter as to be one of them. The jealousy, the leading of the victim out into the woods, the cruel murder with the knife, the forgiving spirit of the girl after she has received the fatal wound, and the remorse of the murderer are all oft-repeated ballad situations. Young Johnston, the villain of Child 88, kills his true love because of jealousy. The injured girl of "Jellon Grame" (Child 90) is a similar story. Grame sends his foot page just before dawn to Lillie Flower's bower-door to bid her come to the wildwood. She obeyed, rode three miles and arrived at an open grave. Grame, emerging from the trees, informed her she was to die. She pleads for life, presenting as a reason why he should spare her:

> Your bairn, that stirs between my sides,
> Moun shortly see the light;
> But to see it weltring in my blude
> Would be a piteous sight.

He took no pity on the lady but pierced her body, presumably with a knife. To this point the story is nearly parallel to "Florella," but the story does not end here. The murderer rescues the baby weltering in its mother's blood, and takes it to "nurses nine," who care for the boy until he is a man. The young man, now grown, questions his recreant father about his mother, in answer to which the father recounts the story of the murder in a most casual way. The story is not received so lightly, for the grim youth bends his strong bow and sends a well-aimed arrow through Jellon Grame.

Remorse does not occur after the murder in either of the ballads cited. It is, nevertheless, a commonplace in Child, there being no fewer than six ballads of the collection containing it.

"The Rich Irish Lady" story begins with the lady's refusing advances of a young squire, until she becomes tangled in love; then she calls for him. He is too proud to accept her in her condition. She dies; whether by his hand, her own, or by childbirth we do not know.

The tale as I received it is quite corrupted. In fact, without a knowledge of the ballads one might wonder what it was all about. Sophistication has attempted to remove sex from a story based entirely on it. You will find in reading the song that it is the story of a sex entanglement which a girl sought to cover by appealing to a man whom she had considered beneath her standing. Instead of his marrying her at once to hide her shame, he informs her he is proud, too, and that his birth is noteworthy. To gratify his revengeful spirit he kills her. This story can be closely compared with Child ballads too numerous to name.

"The Lawyer Outwitted" fails to present a blood-and-thunder incident analogous to ballads I have discussed. It presents a delightful story of a squire's only son who won a fair lady, the daughter of a lawyer, through a clever ruse. Although the subject is approached differently, the situation of young lovers winning the parents' consent to marriage is as prevalent in the ballads as any other family situation. In its present form "The Lawyer Outwitted" is comparable with "Hind Etin" (Child 41), a story of a young man who ran away with a daughter who later was reunited with a hostile father.

Both Warren and Fuller, in the song by that name, love the same girl. Fuller killed Warren then surrendered himself to the law. A similar situation occurs in Child 66, when two brothers who love the same woman kill each other. A killing for jealousy, as before cited, is common to the ballads.

In "The Rovin' Gambler" a young lady lost her heart to a transient man, contrary to the desire of her mother, and eloped with the gambling "Don Juan." This has its near parallel in "Dugall Quin" (Child 294) in which a mother or a father objects to the daughter's union with a questionable character.

The cardinal point of the "The Dark Eyed Sailor" lies in the test of devotion placed upon a true love of being told, by the sailor who had been away, that her lover was dead. The sailor being assured of her faithfulness reveals his identity; he is the absent lover. My text of this number resembles a copy of "Fair Phoebe and Her Dark Eyed Sailor" published by Gray in *Songs and Ballads of the Maine Lumberjack* and listed as a common broadside current in England and Scotland. He also gives a much corrupted copy of "The Dark Eyed Sailor." W. Roy Mackenzie in *Ballads and Sea Songs from Nova Scotia* (p. 64) gives an alternative with a comment that copies of it appeared in both England and America in printed form as early as 1869.

Similar tests of love as that wished upon Phoebe occur frequently in Child. One, "The Baliff's Daughter of Islington" (105), differs only in the test being given the man by the girl rather than to the girl by the man. A closer parallel of situation between "The Dark Eyed Sailor" and Child ballads lies in the sailor's proving his identity by producing half of a ring, the counterpart of which Phoebe had. A ring is halved at parting by husband and wife in many ballad stories. Child (Part 1, p. 195) cites a Flemish broadside of "Hind Horn" (17) in which a ring is halved at parting. Seven years pass; the wife is to be married again. On the wedding day Hind Horn, her husband, returns. He places his half of the ring in a cup of wine, which reaches his queen and identifies him as her lost husband. Again halving of a ring has a part in the ballad story of Young Beichan (53), Version E (2), and in "John Thompson and the Turk" (266).

"If You Will Marry Me" is a trivial story of a lover offering a girl, as an incentive to marry him — in turn a paper of pins, key to his heart, a little black dog, a coach and eight, and key to his chest. The story lacks the tragedy of most ballads, yet it is no more insignificant than "The Wee Wee Man" (Child 38) or "Get Up and Bar the Door" (Child 275). In fact, the battle of wits in the latter number has its relationship to "If You Will Marry Me." The modern ballad is likewise much the same type of story as the many riddle ballads, such as Nos. 1, 31, 46, 47. "If You Will Marry Me" presents a young man trying to guess the offering he must make to win the lady. The refusal to accept the lady after making the right offer and receiving her consent is a surprise as modern as O. Henry.

"The Dying Hobo" has relationship to Child more in phrasing than in story. A mother's offering consolation, as she does here, to a daughter who has lost a lover appears frequently.

"Little Mary Pigan" combines melodrama of today with gruesome savagery. It is in the murder only that this story is related to former-day oral literature.

The kinship of "Dick Turpin" to the Robin Hood cycle and other famous robber ballads cannot be questioned. The notorious highwayman Dick Turpin plied his trade on the roads of England during the few years previous to his death. He was hanged April 10, 1739. At least five ballads dealing with episodes in Turpin's life were current in the eighteenth century. The ballad of "Dick Turpin and the Lawyer" has had wide popularity in England. Mackenzie gives a copy found in Nova Scotia differing noticeably in subject matter and arrangements from mine. [2]

Like Robin Hood, [3] Dick Turpin of this ballad is an outlaw, courteous and free, who lives by robbery from the higher orders—knights, lawyers, etc.—but harms no husbandman and is friendly to the unfortunates. His cleverness, good nature, liberality, manliness, and boldness, with ready wit and general refinement, make him akin to Robin Hood.

When I think of "Billy Boy" I always think of Lord Randal (Child 12). The relationship, I know, is vague, but the questions asked of Billy Boy—Where have you been? Did she bid you come in? Did she bid you a chair? Did she give you something to eat?, etc., are not different from the "Lord Randal" questions—Where ha you been? Who met ye there? What did she give you? "Billy Boy" is only a parody to "Lord Randal," having none of the tragic story. In fact, "Billy Boy" is a humorous take-off on the undesirable wife.

In the song "At the Matinee" a young sheik makes a confession of how he was dupe to a girl. The flirtation ends abruptly after the girl introduces her husband. The husband, different from the representative ballad character, is not at all jealous of his "darling little wife," or the "nice young man." The turn from the old in this ballad to eliminate the sex-murder story is most optimistic.

"Tia Juana I Come," "Corduroy," "The Old Bachelor," "The Drunkard's Dream," "The Poor Little Soldier's Boy," and "Fair Charlotte" have less pronounced relationships to Child ballads than songs previously discussed, yet in various details I could point out resemblance in subject matter should space permit.

The analysis of these twenty-one ballads shows that twelve have marked evidence of folk influence, and the remaining nine have evidence less marked. By folk influence I mean communal composition or transmission orally with consequent variation. Seven of the twenty-one ballads have typical ballad meter—one line four foot, iambic, alternating with one line three foot, iambic. Thirteen are in various kinds of meter used in the ballads. Only one is in meter entirely foreign to Child ballads. Only three of the group are entirely in dialogue. Seventeen begin with objective narrative and go into dialogue. One has dialogue but begins subjectively. Five of the group have repetition of one kind or another in true ballad style. Seven others have incremental repetition. Nine have very little repetition. In author relationship nearly all these ballads are true ballads—nineteen of the twenty-one show the author is entirely impersonal, in one he is somewhat impersonal, and in one personal.

The following table helps clarify the matter. For each of the six ballad characteristics— (1) ballad story, (2) dialogue, (3) objectivity of narrator, (4) "folk influence" (i.e., variation), (5) repetition, and (6) meter—a judgment is made as to each ballad's degree of conformity, ranging from (a) high degree of conformity, to (b) some correspondence, to (c) little or no connection with ballad characteristics. This table is provided only for this first group since they are closest to the ballad model.

Pretty Polly—1a, 2a, 3b, 4a, 5b, 6a
The Old Shoe—1a, 2a, 3b, 4a, 5b, 6b
Florella—1a, 2a, 3b, 4a, 5b, 6b
The Rich Irish Lady—1a, 2a, 3b, 4a, 5b, 6b
The Lawyer Outwitted—1a, 2a, 3b, 4a, 5c, 6a
Warren and Fuller—1a, 2a, 3b, 4b, 5c, 6b
The Rovin' Gambler—1a, 2a, 3b, 4a, 5b, 6a
The Dark Eyed Sailor—1a, 2a, 3b, 4b, 5c, 6b
Frankie and Johnny—1a, 2a, 3b, 4a, 5a, 6c
If You Will Marry Me—1b, 2a, 3b, 4a, 5a, 6b
The Dying Hobo—1a, 2a, 3b, 4a, 5b, 6a
Little Mary Pigan—1a, 2a, 3b, 4b, 5c, 6b
Dick Turpin—1a, 2a, 3b, 4b, 5a, 6a
Billy Boy—1b, 2a, 3a, 4a, 5a, 6b
At the Matinee—1b, 2c, 3b, 4b, 5b, 6a
Tia Juana, I Come—1b, 2a, 3b, 4a, 5c, 6b
Corduroy—1c, 2a, 3b, 4b, 5a, 6b
Old Bachelor—1c, 2a, 3b, 4a, 5c, 6b
The Drunkard's Dream—1c, 2a, 3a, 4b, 5c, 6b
A Poor Little Soldier's Boy—1c, 2b, 3b, 4b, 5b, 6b
Fair Charlotte—1c, 2a, 3b, 4b, 5c, 6a

The foregoing brief discussion establishes definite relationships of these songs in subject matter. Some few which have little relationship in subject matter are closely related in structure and form. Contrasts and analogies other than those recorded here could be given, but sufficient has been given to establish definite relationship and to show persistence of the old ballad type.

Next in my collection is a group I call cowboy and related songs (22–36). The individual analysis of each of these songs reveals that as to type of story, meter, dialogue, repetition, and author relationship, they are far removed from the Child type. In nearly every one the story is not a ballad situation. The dramatic, epic, narrative form becomes subjective narrative told in the first person. In one way only are they like Child ballads — they are property of the folk.

The songs were, no doubt, written by a single author. As subject matter he used material and composed a song about an event known and talked about by the camp. If his composition told the story well, in the eyes of the group, it lived. On the other hand, if it proved in the least out of tune with the current thinking, it was doomed for destruction, or for violent revisions by a more gifted composer. It had to bear the criticism and alteration of the group if it were to live. In this sense any such composition would be communal property. Passing from camp to camp, from mouth to ear, every man became its literary critic. Like water passing from vessel to vessel fitting itself to its container, the song adapts itself to its environment. The existence of many divergent versions affirms this fact.

"The Cowboy's Lament" is characteristic of the group. It is a pathetic story of a cowboy's death told in the first person. The dying cowboy himself launches the story and tells it consistently, until the second line of the last stanza when the death occurs. The singer, no longer able to tell of the passing of his own soul, changes from the dying cowboy to narrator. None of the dialogue which characterizes most Child ballads appears here. Yet in its stead stands the dramatic monologue, and one could find no better substitute for dialogue than that. The first person usage functions to dramatize the story, and the type of subject matter presented could make no nearer approach to the dramatic form than in its present arrangement.

Mackenzie in *Ballads and Sea Songs of Nova Scotia* says this song is sometimes called "The Dying Cowboy." Of it he states:

> It is an American song derived, apparently, in some fashion from the English broadside song, "The Unfortunate Rake" or "The Unfortunate Lad."[4]

This adaptation of former English broadsides to American life affirms my position that it has definite relationship to the old.

I shall take time to call attention to one relationship to former ballads. The dying cowboy asks:

> Bury beside me my knife and six-shooter,
> My spurs on my heels, and my rifle by my side.

It is possible that an American cowboy should take some consolation in knowing his old weapons would be buried with him, but it is more likely that the idea of making such a dying request is a carry-over from the day when superstition ruled. The burial of war gear of various types appears in "The Two Brothers" (Child 49), version D.

> Ye'll lay my arrows at my head,
> My bent bow at my feet,

> My sword and buckler at my side —
> As I was wont to sleep.

Again in Robin Hood's Death (Child 120), version B.

> And set my bright sword at my head,
> Mine arrows to my feet
> And lay my yew-bow by my side
> My met-yard wi. . . .

As was suggested before, these songs contain no ballad dialogue. Its substitute is the dramatic monologue. If the author must be personal and inject his sentiment into the story as he does in this type, and if the story is to be an object for character teaching, and this type is, then no nearer approach can be made to the previously used dramatic form than the dramatic monologue used in cowboy and related songs.

As an example of the foregoing appears "Bad Companions," a didactic story having for its main incident the dagger murder of a fair young maiden by the hand of her drunken lover. In incident it is a ballad situation, but the treatment is positively opposed to ballad method. The concentration of interest is not on the killing but on the killer, who tells the story himself, using his disgrace as a means to teach the lessons — take heed of mother's advice; stay away from bad company; and avoid drinking. The author is not only personal, he is the one and only actor. This style is the dramatic monologue. The story may be a Calvinistic adaptation of an old ballad.

The song "Charles A. Guiteau," dealing with the assassination of James A. Garfield, parallels "Bad Companions." Characteristic of both songs is the repentant heart and Russian spirit of resignation to fate of the murderer. Immediate remorse of this type common in Child was previously discussed.

The three songs of Indian life — "Billy Venero," "Bright Amanda," and "The Sioux Indian" — are somewhat impersonal as regards the author. "Bright Amanda" has a ballad type of dialogue. The John Smith/Pocahontas story, somewhat reversed, contained therein, in many respects has relevancy to stories of heroism in Child. Even so, there is noncompliance in detail, the fathers of which are elaboration in description, figures of speech, and exposition.

The next group of folk songs (37–48) I have classed as folk lyrics. There is no exact line of demarcation between ballads and lyrics as they now exist. I am aware that some of the group approach the American ballad type. Nearest is "The Rustic Beauty," which plainly is a parody on the Child type of ballad and is perhaps the work of a conscious artist, as the Library of Congress reports. "I Wish I Was Single Again" tells a story covering several years' time. Instead of its being a dramatic presentation of dialogue pattern, it is the dramatic monologue. The personal feelings of the author color the entire song. We laugh because the singer is happy. Yet, approaching the ballad type, it has no elaboration or sophistication.

Dramatic monologue songs herewith, comparing closely with "I Wish I Was Single Again," are "A Sleigh Ride," "Give Him One More As He Goes," and "The Lazy Club." Another close approach, "Why Didn't You Say So Before," is a monologue with reported dialogue. Others of this list are in the main good folk lyrics, were it not for the fact that collectors have made many of them a part of the written art and some, according to the Library of Congress, are the work of composers.

The various types of refrain and repetition in this group witness affinity with traditional song — inarticulate refrain in 'The Lazy Club" and "A Sleigh Ride"; ballad type of related refrain in "Give Him One More As He Goes," "The Ship That Never Returned," "Why Didn't You Say So Before," "Poor Old Maids," and "Bald Head End of the Broom." The latter and "I Wish I Was Single Again" are more than seventy-five percent repetition.

The group called cowboy and related songs (22–36) are songs of American folk origin unlike Child ballads in type of story, meter, and form. They are for the main part the dramatic monologue, a substitute for the dramatic form of Child ballads, which lends itself readily to the sentimental, didactic form of these songs. This change in song type is the resulting influence of America's Puritanic ancestors. Notwithstanding this big change we still find a persistence of an occasional old ballad situation.

The folk songs called folk lyrics (37–48) are, on the whole, dramatic monologues accompanied by true folk-song repetition and refrains. A few are probably work of the conscious artist. "I Wish I Was Single Again" is listed in the Library of Congress as the composition of J. F. Drennan. His song differs in wording and melody from my version. For that reason I list this version as a folk song.

To analyze and compare the next group of songs (49–71) is a monstrous task. For that reason I shall make only a few generalizations, which, I admit, will be of doubtful value, since generalizations are proverbially unscientific. It is in hope that these observations will be of value to the reader that I go forward.

Alone, I collected these songs from oral tradition. At least in its last gesture every song in the collection herewith is a folk ballad. The people from whom they came declare they learned them from oral tradition, yet they are very near to original form insofar as I can judge. The people from whom they came were not illiterate, nor were they as a group those who belong to the lower strata of society. The contributor of the most songs, W. H. Avery, now deceased, was a man of intelligence and ability. In occupation he was a sheepman. The latter part of his life he held the position of superintendent of a large sheep company, Austin Brothers, of Salt Lake City, Utah.

The grouping of the songs is in terms of folk influence as indicated by construction and comparison with other copies. The first of the list is "Do Not Put My Mother's Picture Up For Sale," which, although too

carefully planned to be much tampered with by the folk, shows evidence of folk influence in transmission. With all of its literary power it cannot equal the last of the list, "After the Ball," in arrangement. I do not contend that any one of this group of songs came into being in the communal way. They had individual authorship. Yet for a time most, if not all, have been property of the folk and suffered slight changes. Different from the groups previously discussed, these numbers changed relatively little. The reason may be because of a short oral existence. I have been able to find copies of only six of the group elsewhere. Although the Library of Congress, Department of Music, lists authors for another half dozen, four of the six, numbered 68 to 71, have the author's name attached: "The Fatal Wedding Night," "My Mother Was a Lady," "Hello, Central, Give Me Heaven," and "After the Ball." My copies of two of the four have suffered very noticeable changes from the copies recorded by Spaeth[5] and Elizabeth Greenleaf.[6] Not only are these four songs skillful pieces of work showing little change in transmission, but numbers 61 to 67 appear to be as constant with one exception, "The Letter Edged in Black." A version so different appears in *American Mountain Songs*[7] as to make one believe that oral tradition has placed a permanent earmark on the number. The Library of Congress lists Hattie Nevada as the author; yet I think if she could collect copies of the song now, she would scarcely be able to recognize her production.

Whatever the origin of these numbers may be, the evidence exists in the songs themselves that as a group they are not the work of literary masters nor of ignorant people. For the main part they are the work of insignificant versifiers. They were created within the lifetime of many people still alive. Their salaam was made among a heterogeneous people, the majority of whom read and write and, consequently, depend upon the eye more than the ear. Despite all these handicaps, the songs have been transplanted from person to person enough to have lost some of the harness marks of the printing press.

Songs numbered 49 to 71 have little of the life and death, murder and bloodshed, and blush-raising sex episodes of the Child ballads. Death is not uncommon, but instead of the murder the deaths pictured are mostly from accident or material causes. The dying for the main part is not the paramount incident, but the lament that follows. Nearly all are bristling with melodrama. Sentimentality howls its wail like a hungry wolf on the ice fields of the north. It seems that the motto of the society which accepted them and preserved them was, "Let us weep again." They are the irritations of sadness, the Al Jolson type, which promise to bring tears to the driest eye. They never fail to make the most of an angry word, filial ingratitude and death. Only four of the songs fail to have this characteristic — "The Battle Ship Maine" and "Just as the Sun Went Down," two patriotic numbers, and "Jack and Joe" and "Down to the Club," two mildly humorous numbers.

Such a thorough break occurs from Child in the subject matter of these songs that one might conclude that the pendulum has swung to its other extreme. Stories of filial gratitude or ingratitude are unpictured in Child. The objectivity of the Child ballad made pulling on the heart strings to whet the pathos of an uncomfortable situation impossible. In ballads like "Lord Randal" (12) one can scarcely realize the man is to die of poison until he is dead; then the story is over. One could not imagine the mother, who asks calmly during the son's last moments what disposition he would have made of the property, fitting into any of the melodrama of these tales. This elaboration of circumstances is a literary corruption of oral art.

Like Amos searching for the word of God from east to west and north to south and not finding it, one might search in vain for ballad form in these songs. They seem to be completely denuded of it. A thread of resemblance appears very rarely in dialogue, in refrain, in repetition, and in verse form, but like Gratiano's words, "You search all day ere you find them, and when you do they are not worth the search."

The first twenty-one of my group are worthy of the name of folk ballad because of nearness of approach to the traditional type. Another group (22–36) are different in a number of ways, but are typical American folk-song ballads. Numbers 37 to 48 are not ballads but folk lyrics of American origin. No apologies need be made when we call them folk lyrics. Numbers 49 to 71 are rather a heterogeneous group of songs of questionable standing. In the light of these findings, I conclude that old songs preserved in southeastern Idaho are about two percent true Child ballads altered in adaptation to local conditions. About fifteen percent are alterations of the traditional ballads which have changed in subject matter to eliminate superstition, the sex story, and reference to royalty and lavish riches. Another fifteen percent are ballads of recent origin, comparing favorably in form and structure with the true ballad. Twenty percent are songs of American origin such as the cowboy group which are unlike early traditional ballads, yet are a species standing alone. About ten percent are folk lyrics with some ballad characteristics. The remaining thirty-eight percent of old songs in oral circulation cannot be called folk songs at all. The entire collection differs from Child ballads in phrasing. In this way a ballad suffers its first alteration.

Notes

1. A miracle story exists in the ballads of a special spell cast over a person being removed by three kisses from a knight or lover. Sometimes the creature is capable of changing forms from snake to lizard, to frog, or some such situation. The three kisses are efficacious in transforming the creature into a normal beautiful woman.

2. William Roy Mackenzie, *Ballads and Sea Songs from Nova Scotia* (Cambridge: Harvard University Press, 1928), p. 311.

3. See Child, Part V, p. 42.

4. Mackenzie is quoting from John H. Cox, *Folk-Songs of the South* (Cambridge: Harvard University Press, 1925).

5. Elisabeth Bristol Greenleaf, *Ballads and Sea Songs of Newfoundland* (Cambridge: Harvard University Press, 1933), p. 368.

6. Sigmund Gottfried Spaeth, *Read 'Em and Weep, The Songs You Forgot to Remember* (Garden City, N.Y.: Doubleday, Page, 1926), p. 172.

7. Ethel Park Richardson, *American Mountain Songs* (New York: Greenburg, 1927), p. 170.

Index of Songs

1. Pretty Polly
2. The Old Shoe
3. Florella
4. The Rich Irish Lady
5. The Lawyer Outwitted
6. Warren and Fuller
7. The Rovin' Gambler
8. The Dark Eyed Sailor
9. Frankie and Johnny
10. If You Will Marry Me
11. The Dying Hobo
12. Little Mary Pigan
13. Dick Turpin
14. Billy Boy
15. Tia Juana, I Come
16. At the Matinee
17. Corduroy
18. The Old Bachelor
19. The Drunkard's Dream
20. Fair Charlotte
21. A Poor Little Soldier's Boy
22. The Cowboy's Lament
23. The Last Round-up
24. The Cowboy's Dream
25. When the Work's All Done This Fall
26. To Be a Buckaroo
27. Bad Companions
28. Charles A. Guiteau
29. Billy Venero
30. Bright Amanda

31. The Sioux Indians
32. The Miner's Lone Grave
33. The Dream of a Miner's Child
34. The Wreck of the 1256
35. The Wreck of Number Nine
36. I Ain't Got No Use for the Women
37. In Defense of Polygamy
38. The Rustic Beauty
39. A Sleigh Ride
40. I Wish I Was Single Again
41. Give Him One More As He Goes
42. The Lazy Club
43. Poor Old Maids
44. The Farmyard
45. The Bald Head End of the Broom
46. Kickin' Mule
47. Why Didn't You Say So Before
48. The Ship That Never Returned
49. Do Not Put My Mother's Picture Up for Sale
50. The Auction Sale
51. Poor Little Bessie

52. The Drunkard's Lone Child
53. It's Not the House that Makes the Home
54. Sliding Down Our Cellar Door
55. Down to the Club
56. Jack and Joe
57. You Are Starting, My Boy, On Life's Journey
58. Just As the Sun Went Down
59. Battle Ship Maine
60. The Gypsie's Warning
61. Don't Be Angry With Me, Dad
62. The Three Wishes
63. The Mistletoe Bough
64. Two Little Boys
65. Stay in Your Own Back Yard
66. The Letter Edged In Black
67. I Love Her Just the Same
68. The Fatal Wedding Night
69. My Mother Was a Lady
70. Hello, Central, Give Me Heaven
71. After the Ball

Motorcycles, Guitars, and Bucking Broncs: Twentieth-Century Gravestones in Southeastern Idaho

Carol Edison

Gravestones traditionally record names, dates, and family relationships and hence are a valuable resource for historians. In addition to that information, however, many gravestones are ornamented with memorial verses and symbolic images: a weeping willow, a cross, or something more elaborate. Folklorists and cultural historians have extracted a wealth of information about Puritan beliefs and values from New England churchyards; three important studies are James Deetz's In Small Things Forgotten *(1977), Allan Ludwig's* Graven Images: New England Stonecarving and Its Symbols *(1975), and Dickran and Ann Tashjian's* Memorials for the Children of Change: The Art of New England Stonecarving *(1974).*

Carol Edison describes a set of gravestones that may prove equally revealing to the attitudes of twentieth-century Idahoans. Changes in gravestone images reflect advances in stoneworking technology, important historical movements, and a general shift in values from spiritual considerations to more earthly experiences.

Edison is a folklorist for the Utah Arts Commission.

*I*n the field of folklore "material culture" is the term often used to categorize those individual or community expressions that are essentially nonverbal or nonperformance in format, i.e. tangible objects or artifacts.[1] Yale University art historian Jules David Prown defines the study of material culture as "the study through artifacts of the beliefs . . . values, ideas, attitudes and assumptions . . . of a particular community or society."[2] Certainly gravestones, through their multiple role of marking the burial site, symbolizing life's final rite of passage, and memorializing an individual's life in a manner that is both acceptable and understandable by the community as a whole, should provide a history of community values and attitudes that is both rich and accurate. By charting the evolution of southeastern Idaho gravestones and their symbols, much can be learned about the culture of the region, contributing to a more complete definition of Idaho's folklife.

The earliest grave markers made of stone that are found in southeastern Idaho were carved in the last half of the nineteenth century by regional artisans. Using first local materials and later marble imported from Eastern quarries, these craftsmen fashioned gravestones that exhibited graceful script and beautiful design. By the end of the century, Idaho's demand for gravestones had increased to the degree that local and regional stonecutters often supplemented their own production with monuments carved in New England. After the arrival of these precut monuments by rail,

local carvers skillfully added the deceased's name and dates.

Whether produced in the West or imported from Eastern quarries, nineteenth-century Idaho gravestones, like those throughout America, exhibited the symbolism of Judaic-Christian Western intellectual tradition. Representative symbols included the dove, the lamb, flowers, and the human hand. The commonly used dove represented the soul, which in death leaves the body and flies to heaven. Additionally, as the bearer of good tidings in the story of Noah or as the embodiment of the Holy Spirit (God's messenger and companion to man), the dove was seen as a symbol of God's promise of an afterlife. Another biblical symbol, the lamb, represented both Christ and his followers, and symbolized qualities of purity and innocence. Lambs were most often used on the graves of children or on those of the pure and innocent, who believed with "childlike faith."

Flowers, whether roses symbolizing love and perfection or the lily representing the resurrection, were popular nineteenth-century gravestone symbols. Broken-stemmed roses indicating a life had been "nipped in the bud" were frequently used on the grave of young girls.

The image of the human hand, which appeared on nineteenth-century gravestones in a variety of postures, generally represented the physical body. Often used in combination with other symbols, for example the hand holding a bouquet of flowers or the hand with forefinger pointing toward heaven, the message was generally one of belief in ongoing life for the spirit if not a resurrection and reuniting with the body. The clasped hands symbolized the reunion with God or spouse of the deceased after death. The reunion with God beyond the veil between heaven and earth was indicated by cuffs of similar design, while the reunion of husband and wife was suggested by representations of their respective clothing.

These traditional images were familiar to the men and women of nineteenth-century Idaho and were part of a body of knowledge that was commonly gained through family, religious, and even academic training. As Austin Fife suggests in *Forms Upon the Frontier*, "The stones that mark the place of man's eternal rest bear the usual symbols of a society's most enduring beliefs. . . ."[3] Certainly, the symbols of doves, lambs, flowers, and hands chosen by these Idahoans reflect their Judaic-Christian beliefs in an afterlife, resurrection of the body and reunion with God and loved ones. They decorated their graves with symbols rich in both tradition and meaning, and reflective of the attitudes and values of both American society as a whole and their own specific society.

With the twentieth century came a new era in gravestone carving—an era originating in the earlier industrial revolution and shaped by subsequent technological advances and sociological developments. New ideas about cemetery maintenance, the use of new materials and stonecarving techniques, as well as the eventual development of a new, highly personalized gravestone symbology, characterize this era.

One element of great change was in the method of gravestone and cemetery maintenance. As the century progressed, the population grew and people became increasingly mobile. The responsibility for burial plot maintenance gradually shifted from the family, where it had traditionally been, to various governmental units and private corporations. Delineations between family plots were obliterated as enclosures of wood or metal and landscaped vegetation were replaced by more easily cared for lawns. The introduction of smaller, rectangular gravestones, often installed at ground level, was in part a response to the need to facilitate cemetery maintenance by allowing for mechanized grass cutting.

Another factor in this shift from the upright, marble gravestones of the nineteenth century was the increasing availability of stronger, denser stone, such as granite, and the development of new tools and processes with the capability of incising images into such materials. During the 1920s, the development of pneumatic or air-powered chisels allowed the gravestone ter to virtually hand cut images into stone that was too hard to incise with the traditional chisel and wooden mallet. But, by the end of the 1940s, the use of pneumatic chisels had effectively been replaced by a newer, more powerful incising process known as sandblasting.

Sandblasting represents a logical progression beyond its predecessors, hand carving and pneumatic chiseling. Just as pneumatic carving eliminated the use of a mallet by providing the chisel with its own power, sandblasting eliminated the chisel, replacing it with a stream of fine silica directed and controlled, not manually, but through the use of a latex stencil. Stones are incised by scouring away those areas that are exposed while leaving intact those surfaces covered by the stencil.

Ultimately, the process of sandblasting had more significance in the changing nature of twentieth-century gravestones than simply its ability to incise images into hard, dense granite. Sandblasting allowed an unprecedented expansion in gravestone imagery by shifting not only the designing process but also the actual creation of the image to a changeable surface—paper.

Earlier stonecutters working with mallet and chisel often used templates of their own creation to transfer designs onto the stone. When precut monuments from Eastern quarries became available, designs and images were commonly borrowed from these imported stones or from commercially available pattern books. The pneumatic cutters who followed, with their more powerful, harder to control chisels, used a similar process of design and transfer. As is evidenced by the gravestones from the 1920s, 1930s, and 1940s, these craftsmen soon found their tools to be particularly well suited to the creation of elaborate lettering and intricate, nonrepresentational designs. In both of these technologies, even though the design was completed before being transferred onto the stone, the stonecutter incising with wooden mallet or air-powered chisel was still permanently handcrafting each individual image in a painstaking, time-consuming manner, on an unchangeable surface. Logically, these processes, both of which relied heavily on the use of traditional templates and commercially available designs from pattern books, contributed to the repetition and maintenance of mastered images and design elements on nineteenth- and early twentieth-century gravestones.

Conversely, the succeeding generation of stonecutters who used sandblasting to incise stone, created completed images on paper, and then, through a stencil, virtually duplicated the image on stone. Variations from one use of a specific stencil to the next became nonexistent. Suddenly, as a result of this transfer from design to execution, the modern gravestone carver was not limited to perfecting a finite number of mastered images. Rather, by using sandblasting, a stonecutter had at his disposal an unending array of potential symbols because any image could be duplicated intact on the stone. This technological development was instrumental in preparing the way for the unprecedented explosion of twentieth-century gravestone imagery that occurred after midcentury.

Yet in spite of its importance, technological development cannot solely explain the significant changes in funerary symbolism evidenced in Idaho cemeteries. Rather one must also look at the sociological developments in twentieth-century America precipitated by

Figure 1. Gravestone of Darrell Taylor. The importance of the western landscape, that awesome space, is indicated in this double gravestone from the late 1970s. When it becomes necessary, a portable sandblasting unit will be used to incise the name and dates of the spouse. (Pocatello; photo by C. Edison)

Figure 2. Gravestone of Thomas V. Daniels, Sr. Gravestone images of ranching or cowboying reflect both the personal and occupational significance of geography and climate to modern Idahoans. (Malad; photo by C. Edison)

such historical factors as the migration westward, the industrial revolution, the world wars, and the nuclear age. Such events have altered both society and man's view of himself within that society. These changes cannot be discounted when analyzing the new gravestone symbology.

In a 1978 essay, noted folklorists Austin and Alta Fife suggested that gravestone art is conservative and unchanging unless two conditions simultaneously exist. First, traditional images must lose some of their symbolic power, possibly through disuse or through lack of relevance. And second, alternative images stemming from significant new life experiences must develop to replace the old images.[4] Considering these possibilities in southeastern Idaho yields some interesting explanations.

The culture in Idaho is, in large part, a product of both its natural landscape and its relatively recent immigration and settlement. The experience of westward migration and the process of homesteading a sparsely inhabited, rather hostile environment are, for many, still within first- or second-generation memory. Additionally, in spite of settlement and urbanization, the landscape itself, that awesome space of range, desert, and mountains, remains a pervasive element that significantly affects not only economic life but lifestyle and outlook.[5]

As well, Idahoans share with the world in general the experience of the twentieth century in which technology has changed the fabric of life. This new world is one in which population expands geometrically, ideas are communicated almost instantaneously, and the threat of extinction remains ever present. Certainly, such developments have altered man's view of the world as well as his view of himself within the world. The need to stand apart and be recognized as an individual, not as a number in a computer, is a common complaint for twentieth-century man.

The underlying conditions deemed necessary by the Fifes for a change in gravestone symbolism do exist in contemporary Idaho. Traditional images have indeed lost some of their power, both through their gradual disuse that began in the late 1920s with pneumatic carving's emphasis on lettering and decorative design, and through their lack of relevance to modern life. No longer does the average person learn the meaning of or respond to images such as the clasped hands or the solitary dove. Such knowledge, although perpetuated through some of society's institutions, is only one symbology in a world in which communication has increased the awareness of many. Additionally, powerful images that more accurately reflect the experience of living in twentieth-century western America have gained popularity. These new symbols, which are more specific and personal in nature, are both relevant and understandable to twentieth-century Idahoans and consequently have gained acceptance and ever-growing use.

Images of the out-of-doors, the most pervasive and ever-present aspect of Western life, are among the most common symbols found on modern Idaho gravestones. Through their use as gravestone symbols, representations of the landscape, cactus-covered deserts, pine-covered mountains or rows of plowed fields emphasize the significance of geography and climate in people's lives. Images of sports, those that have grown out of the land, such as hunting and fishing, as well as team or individual sports, are becoming increasingly popular. Everything from baseball players and skiers to motorcycle riders, skateboard riders, and skydivers are becoming appropriate gravestone symbols.

Images of the Western experience—cowboys, horses, cattle, sheep, horseshoes, and log cabins—suggest that Western activities such as cowboying, ranching, and rodeoing not only have economic significance to the region, but also greatly influence interests and life-

Figure 3. Gravestone of Paul Myron Jones. Representations of hobbies and interests on the graves of adolescents function like occupational images on the graves of adults. (Malad; photo by C. Edison)

Figure 4. Gravestone of Donald Lee Davis. Oftentimes modern gravestone images both reflect personal interests or activities and suggest an accidental death. (Pocatello; photo by C. Edison)

style. As might be expected, traditional Western symbols of death, such as the riderless horse or the empty boots and hat, are also quite common.

A number of occupational gravestone images are also found in Idaho cemeteries. Images include work-related machinery such as buses or semitrailers, and the tools of a specific trade or professional symbols, each commemorating the occupational contribution to society by a particular individual. Although occupational symbols are not a new phenomenon, their use and acceptance are undoubtedly growing.

Just as occupational symbols are often used to memorialize an adult through his or her career, images representative of a variety of hobbies and other special interests are currently being used to memorialize individuals who, because of sex or age, are without publicly recognized professions. For example, representations of various sewing implements—knitting needles, needles and spools of thread or sewing bags—are beginning to appear in place of the traditional rose on the gravestones of homemakers. Similarly, musical instruments, renderings of personalized vehicles, pets, and sports symbols are often used on the graves of adolescents.

Although nineteenth-century gravestones sometimes displayed symbols or designs indicating membership in social or fraternal organizations, such as the Elks, Lions, or Masons, or affiliation with one of the armed services, the use of these images has proliferated on gravestones. Symbols of religious beliefs and affiliations including Catholic crosses, praying hands and Mormon temples are also plentiful and provide extremely appropriate gravestone imagery. The representation of a Mormon temple, the holy place where members of the Church of Jesus Christ of Latter-day Saints are married and "sealed" to family members for eternity, symbolizes the reunion of the family after death in the same way the clasped hands of the nine-

teenth century symbolized reunion for earlier Mormons. Owing to the number of Mormons in southeastern Idaho, one finds many gravestones displaying the silhouette of either the Idaho Falls or Logan, Utah, temples.

The practice of including a likeness of the deceased on the gravestone, a tradition most likely of Eastern and Southern origin, is becoming a more common phenomenon. The Greeks and Slovenians who came to the country around the turn of the century commonly placed photographs under the protection of glass or sliding metal coverings. While these photos often fell prey to vandals, modern gravestone photographs are now protected by a convex covering of plastic, which should add to their longevity. Other methods of preserving the likeness involve the use of line-drawn portraits and even sandblasting reproductions of the deceased's signature.

The common thread in this new gravestone imagery is its emphasis on earthly existence through the use of specific images representing twentieth-century experiences and life-styles. By memorializing the life of an individual through accomplishments, events, interests, and affiliations rather than through abstract character attributes or representations of the afterlife, the new markers emphasize the individual life and create a more personalized statement than that provided by the common nineteenth-century gravestone vita name and dates.

The phenomenon of personalized objects is not limited to the gravestone genre. Rather, it can be found in a variety of twentieth-century artifacts. The bumper stickers, T-shirts, custom car or truck paint jobs, and vanity license plates of the 1980s can be seen as popular manifestations of this same phenomenon. Even in traditional realms of expression dictated by custom and convention, such as wedding announcements and public notices of death, evidence of the trend toward per-

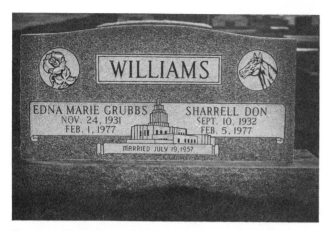

Figure 5.   Gravestone of Edna Marie Grubbs Williams and Sharrell Don Williams. This typical Mormon headstone reflects not only personal interests and religious affiliations, but also affirms the family's belief in reunion after death. The temple marriage date indicates the husband and wife have been ''sealed'' together for eternity, as have their children, who were all born after that date, hence, ''under the covenant.'' (Malad; photo by C. Edison)

Figure 6.   The back of the Williams headstone. (Malad; photo by C. Edison)

sonalization can be found. Interestingly, the same images as those found on gravestones often appear in these forms. Many contemporary wedding announcements include a photograph of the bride and groom pictured out-of-doors, in sports clothing or with a church or temple in the background. Obituaries, once matter-of-factly written by members of newspaper staffs, are now more frequently provided by family members. These new obituaries include more specific information about personal or private interests and events, hobbies, sports or personality traits, in addition to the expected listing of public affiliations and accomplishments.

Personalization of publicly visible materials, whether it be exhibited on T-shirts, wedding invitations or gravestones, is interestingly a by-product of the same technological advances through which the need for identity and reaffirmation of individualness was born. The technology which has shaped our modern world has, in one sense, allowed for the homogenization and depersonalization of the individual. Yet simultaneously, this same capacity for efficient mass production provides the means for personalization. Essentially technology has perfected mass production to the degree that variations on the basic product can be easily, skillfully, and most important, inexpensively made. Just as modern photographic processes make it simple to include a young couple's portrait on a wedding reception invitation, modern sandblasting processes make the duplication of a person's signature on a gravestone an everyday matter. By providing the means, technology plays an active role in encouraging all forms of personalization.

The personalization of objects, including the trend to personalize modern gravestones, functions not only as

a means whereby an individual can maintain recognition and individual identity, but also as a means of communication. Personalized objects communicate specific, personal information. Whether dealing with political, religious, or social matters, the attitudes, interests, affiliations and beliefs of the T-shirt wearer or invitation sender are being proudly advertised and publicly affirmed. Similarly, gravestones that display personalized images are not simply functioning as signs to mark the site of burial, but are also communicating information about an individual that is considered important enough to be incised into a permanent stone memorial. And as evidenced by the growing trend to utilize gravestones that communicate personal information about a loved one, this specific information is both understandable and acceptable to the community as a whole.

Archaeologist James Deetz states in *In Small Things Forgotten*, ''Material culture . . . is not culture but its product. Culture is socially transmitted rules for behavior, ways of thinking and doing things . . . whether it is the language we speak, the religious beliefs that we subscribe to, or the laws that govern our society. All such behavior is reflected in subtle and important ways in the manner in which we shape our physical world.''[6] By studying the gravestones in southeastern Idaho's cemeteries and by analyzing the evolution of gravestone imagery, much can be learned about the culture of southeastern Idaho. Certainly images that are elevated to the level of life symbols through use on gravestones provide a partial definition of what is significant to individuals. In turn, any image or category of images used with consistency indicates a larger acceptance and understanding that suggests a community expression of values.

In Idaho's graveyards since the turn of the century, the traditional symbols of Judaic-Christian origin have in large part been replaced by contemporary images of ''western migration . . . the out-of-doors and sports.''[7] The hand-chiseled marble lambs, doves, and flowers

Figure 7.   Gravestone of Russell Troy Buck. Man's affinity with nature, his joy and pleasure with the out-of-doors as well as a tragic story of youthful death are all found on this contemporary gravestone. (Pocatello; photo by C. Edison)

Figure 8.   The back of the Russell Buck headstone. (Pocatello; photo by C. Edison)

that comforted earlier generations stand in contrast to sandblasted granite motorcycles, guitars, and bucking broncos. Yet these new symbols not only communicate specific personalized information about deceased in-

dividuals, but also provide a wealth of information about the living community. Through the images by which southeastern Idahoans wish themselves and their loved ones to be remembered, the values, attitudes, concerns, and beliefs of these twentieth-century folk can be discovered.

Notes

1.   The author wishes to thank the Utah Folklore Center and the Folk Arts Program of the Utah Arts Council for encouraging and assisting in the fieldwork and research presented here. Portions of this article were presented in a paper on gravestone symbolism at the 1982 American Folklore Society meeting in Minneapolis, Minnesota.

2.   Jules David Prown, "Mind in Matter: An Introduction to Material Culture Theory and Method," *Winterthur Portfolio*, No. 1 (1982), p. 1–20.

3.   Austin Fife, "Merrill Art Gallery and Special Collections Library, Utah State University, July–August, 1968, in *Forms Upon the Frontier*, ed. Austin and Alta Fife and Henry H. Glassie (Logan: Utah State University Press, 1960), p. 18.

4.   Austin and Alta Fife, "Gravestone Imagery," in *Utah Folk Art: A Catalog of Material Culture*, ed. Hal Cannon (Provo: Brigham Young University Press, 1980), p. 141.

5.   E. Richard Hart, ed., *That Awesome Space: Human Interaction with the Intermountain Landscape* (Salt Lake City: Westwater Press, 1981).

6.   James Deetz, *In Small Things Forgotten: The Architecture of Early American Life* (Garden City: Anchor Press/Doubleday, 1977), p. 24.

7.   Austin and Alta Fife, *Utah Folk Art: A Catalog of Material Culture*, p. 145.

Folklife and Folk History

The Story of Molly B'Dam: A Regional Expression
of American Ideology
DENNIS C. SHAW

The Narrative of "Chief Bigfoot":
A Study in Folklore, History, and World View
J. SANFORD RIKOON

Folklore in Regional Literature: Carol Brink's *Buffalo Coat*
MARY E. REED

Land Use Attitudes and Ethics in Idaho Folklore
BRIAN ATTEBERY

The Story of Molly B'Dam: A Regional Expression of American Ideology

DENNIS C. SHAW

To a folklorist, a legend is a traditional story believed by its tellers, whether it is about flying saucers, spiders in beehive hairdos, or actual people and verifiable events. The legends about Molly B'Dam, a local character in Murray, Idaho, show the effects of repeated oral transmission in the way the events of her life are arranged into orderly patterns. Dennis Shaw uses the method pioneered by anthropologist Claude Lévi-Strauss to interpret the traditional structure of the Molly B'Dam legend and in doing so draws conclusions about the collective values and attitudes of the storytellers and their community. Lévi-Strauss's analytical method stimulated structuralist reevaluations within many disciplines in the United States during the 1960s and 1970s; for other examples of folklorists' use of the idea, see the collection edited by Pierre Maranda and Elli Kongas Maranda, Structural Analysis of Oral Literature *(1971).*

Dennis Shaw is an anthropologist currently teaching at Lower Columbia College in Longview, Washington.

The fine line which distinguishes history from myth has been blurred in recent years.[1] The traditional distinction between the validity of history and the spurious qualities of oral tradition has been challenged by a set of new understandings. Today, historians are beginning to recognize the historical merits of oral accounts of past events and are utilizing oral histories to supplement their traditional sources of written documents. Indeed, there has been a move on the part of historians toward the promotion of the recovery and preservation of these oral accounts of the past.

At the same time, social scientists have begun to question the authenticity of historical truth. The traditional view of history as the objective chronicle of historical events has given way to a new understanding. A major force in the reevaluation of the status of history is the structuralist movement led by Claude Lévi-Strauss. In his response to Jean-Paul Sartre's claim that history should be our ultimate standard of validity, Lévi-Strauss presents a view of the "history" of the historians as a selective representation or model of the events of the past which strives to make this set of events intelligible.[2] From this new perspective, historical facts are granted no greater empirical validity than any other model or representation. Historical facts are an abstraction which is a product of the selective process of the historian who is an active participant in their formulation. A truly total history would cancel itself out. "What makes history possible, Lévi-Strauss argues, "is that a sub-set of events is found . . . to have approximately the same significance for a contingent of individuals who have

not necessarily experienced the events. . . . History is therefore never history, but history for."[3]

Thus, the ultimate merit or value of a "history" lies not in its chronicling of the events of the past, but in the meaning or significance which historians attach to these events. The historian through the selection of certain events over others weaves a web of significance which makes the past intelligible to the present. "History" is a semiological system. "History" not only represents the past to the present; it also represents the present in the past. "History" is a narrative structure which reveals through the representation of the events of the past the values and attitudes of the present. "History" is modern society's *myth.*

The recognition of the historical value of oral tradition and the recognition of the mythical qualities of history have led to the replacement of the absolute contrast between history and myth with the realization that we have a spectrum of narrative forms. The spectrum runs from the near-complete chronicling of historical events with no more formal structuring than the use of chronology to the representation of events with little reference to actual occurrence. In between these two extremes lies a range of forms. Here we find myths which aspire to history and histories which realize myths.[4]

It is in this realm of blurred categories that the object of this analysis falls. The story of Molly B'Dam is based upon events which are believed to be true. Indeed, the recorders—although their sources are primarily accounts from oral tradition—attest to the validity of their renditions. Whether accurate or not, the authors of the versions of this story aspire toward the writing of history. Yet, what emerges is not so much a history as a myth, and therefore, is subject to the same type of formal analysis that has proven successful in furthering our understanding of other narrative forms.[5] Such formal analysis reveals the unconscious selective forces which went into the construction of the narrative structure. The structural analysis of the story of Molly B'Dam reveals a formal structure which highlights certain fundamental features of American ideology, and thus, makes explicit the implicit significance that this story has for a people of a specific region. It is a regional expression of a number of the major tenets of American culture.

I first came into contact with the story of Molly B'Dam while doing research in the Coeur d'Alene Mountains of northern Idaho. While collecting oral histories for the Bureau of Land Management, I discovered that one story, the story of Molly B'Dam, carried a special significance for the people of the area. Not only was the story recorded in most of the popular accounts of the history and the lore of the area, but also, Molly B'Dam herself held a special meaning for the people of the area. Thus, when the Bureau of Land Management sought to restore an old cemetery, it was the marker on Molly B'Dam's grave which the local community wanted preserved, and when a bridge was to be built in the area, Molly B'Dam was promoted as a possible name for the bridge.

When placed within the overall context of the history of the region, the emphasis placed upon the story of Molly B'Dam by the local communities seems exaggerated. The gold-rush era of Murray, of which Molly's story is only a small part, was of short duration and was quickly overshadowed by the growth of industrial mining and the major labor wars of the Wallace/Kellogg region which carried far greater historical significance for the development of the Coeur d'Alene Mountain region. Indeed, Molly's story has little historical value; rather its value lies in its realization of the ethos of the community. By singling out the story of Molly B'Dam from the hundreds of possible stories of the region, the community was unconsciously realizing certain conflicts in the American experience.

Working in a different context, Robert Bellah has defined some of the basic conflicts in American ideology.[6] In an examination of the ideological conflict evident in the political turmoil of the 1960s, he defines the two major ideological forces prevalent in American thought. Bellah argues that the two forces have always been present in American thought, and although at odds with each other, they have generally complemented each other and prevented the extremism of either view to prevail. He labels the two underlying interpretations of American reality as the "Biblical tradition" and "Utilitarian individualism."[7]

The Biblical tradition, as the name implies, draws its inspiration from the religious sector. It finds its secular expression in the tenets of American civil religion and professes a view of American society as a strong moral order with an emphasis upon self-sacrifice and moral responsibilities.[8] Central to its theme is an understanding of individual motivation through conscience and a strong sense of community.

Utilitarian individualism, on the other hand, draws its inspiration from the philosophy of Hobbes and Locke with a strong emphasis on utility, productivity, and self-interest. To quote Bellah: "The Biblical understanding of national life was based on the notion of community with charity for all the members, a community supported by public and private virtue. The utilitarian tradition believed in a neutral state in which individuals would be allowed to pursue the maximization of their self-interest, and the product would be public and private prosperity."[9]

Although formalized by political philosophers, the conflict between these two philosophies transcends the esoteric realm of political philosophy and permeates all aspects of American life. The struggle between these two ideological forces is endemic to the American experience. It is in this arena of ideas that the story of Molly B'Dam gains its significance.

There are several variations of the story of Molly B'Dam which appear in print. Each varies in length and each claims to be the true story. The stories appear in collections of stories from the early history of the area and in personal accounts of the early years of the Coeur d'Alene region by local figures.[10]

The version used in this presentation draws heavily upon the Bankson and Harrison version because of its completeness.[11] However, it should be recognized that all the elements of the story appear throughout the other versions. To emphasize the Bankson and Harrison version is not to grant it a greater validity. Indeed, it should be recognized that the reenactment of the story in this presentation draws from all the versions and is told in my own words. Those readers who are more empirically minded may find the lack of emphasis on "original" texts in this presentation objectionable. Although the decision to present the story in a version which—although consistent with the facts of the Bankson and Harrison version—has never existed and is a product of my own creation in response to stylistic criteria, this decision is consistent with the tenets of structural analysis and reflects the structuralist's perspective on myth.

From a structuralist's perspective, the recorded versions of oral tradition are merely artificial preservations of segments of a continuous conversation which remains alive as long as the stories continue to be passed from teller to teller. The "true" version of the myth lies not in any one version of the story but in the living dialogue of the community. "We define the myth," Lévi-Strauss argues, "as consisting of all its versions; or to put it otherwise, a myth remains the same as long as it is felt as such."[12] Recorded versions exist in relationship to the actual myth in much the same way that a fossil exists in relationship to a living organism. From it we can gain an understanding of its structural arrangement and gain an appreciation of its attributes and qualities, and yet we must recognize that it is only an artificial remnant of the whole. By reciting my own version of the story of Molly B'Dam, I am essentially inserting myself into the dialogue. Indeed, this analysis in itself may be viewed as a continuation on a highly formal level of the dialogue. It would not be wrong — as Lévi-Strauss has said about his own work — to consider this analysis a myth.[13] I have chosen to relate the story of Molly B'Dam in five episodes and reveal the structural arrangement of each episode. The structural relationship among the five episodes then reveals the overall structural arrangement of the story.

Episode 1: The first episode depicts Molly's humble beginnings and her immigration to America. Despite the wishes of her family and the traditional teachings of the church, Maggie Hall (Molly's name at birth) chose to disregard the traditional forms of authority and come to America. Upon arriving in New York City, Maggie quickly found acceptance and work in the Irish-American community. She found a job as a barmaid and became the favorite of the clientele, who were highly protective of her beauty, and no man was allowed to lay a hand on her.

The major struggle depicted in the first episode is Maggie's refusal to yield to traditional authority. The two major elements of the episode are Maggie and her family which are presented in stark contrast. The family represents the ties of affection and loyalty. It stands for the forces of tradition and community. In contrast, Maggie represents the antithesis of these traditional forces. She manifests emerging individualism and is willing to break with the forces of the past and move to America. In the language of Bellah, the two antagonists of this episode represent the forces of the Biblical tradition and utilitarian individualism.

Out of the struggle of this episode emerges a new order. Maggie emerges from this episode displaying the traditional components of love and compassion, and her new community becomes a realization of the inversion of individualism which led to its conception; that is, the patrons of the tavern create an environment of love and protection. This can be represented by the following formula:

$$\text{Episode 1: Family}_a/\text{Molly}_b \; \overset{\sim}{=} \; \text{Molly}_a b^{-1}$$

By way of the above formula we see that the first episode consists of the contrast (/) between two elements (Molly and her family) each of which manifests a particular symbolic function (a, b). Functions a and b stand respectively for the qualities of the Biblical tradition and utilitarian individualism. The outcome of the episode is Molly displaying the function of a and the inversion of the function b (b^{-1}) and it becomes an element, that is, the emergence of a new social order out of the forces of individualism based on a sense of community and conscience.

Episode 2: The second episode involves the downfall of Molly and the emergence of a new cynicism. As the story goes, there comes into the tavern one night a man dressed in fine clothes and jewelry. With time, he and Maggie (Molly) fall in love, and he asks her to marry him. He is the son of a prominent New York family, and he insists that she make some major changes in her life. He insists that she quit working and leave the tavern. Against her protests, he refuses to be married by a priest and chooses a civil ceremony. Moreover, he expresses displeasure with the name Maggie and demands that she change her name to Molly.

The newly married couple move into a luxurious apartment and begin a life of luxury. With time, the husband's family learns of his marriage to Molly and feels that he has brought disgrace upon the family name by marrying a simple barmaid of unacceptable ethnic background. In response to the marriage, they disown the husband and cut off his monthly support. The newly married couple become more and more destitute, and the husband becomes extremely distraught over his first experience with poverty and begins to drink and gamble. These activities only increase their debts, and finally one night Molly's husband asks her to eliminate a gambling debt by having sexual intercourse with a creditor.

Molly agrees to her husband's request and thus begins her fall. She continues to pay off his debts in this fashion and her marriage fails. At the same time, the church refuses to forgive her persistence in "sin" and, in turn, she abandons her faith. She leaves New York and seeks her fortune as a prostitute in the communities of the West. Working her way from gold stampede to gold stampede, she is quite successful at her new profession.

This episode can be represented by the following formula:

$$\text{Episode 2: Husband}_b/\text{Molly}_a \; \overset{\sim}{=} \; \text{Molly}_b a^{-1}$$

By way of the above formula, we see that the second episode consists of the contrast (/) between two elements (Molly and her husband) each of which manifests a particular symbolic function (a, b). As with the formula of the first episode, functions a and b stand respectively for the forces of tradition and individualism. He is the modern man who rejects the teachings of religion and the mandates of family responsibility. He makes Molly turn her back on her religion and makes her give up the name given by her family. His ultimate request clearly reflects his emphasis on utility over traditional morality. In contrast, Molly's actions are motivated by the traditional definitions of wifely responsibility. She yields to her husband's wishes, and her fulfillment of her husband's ultimate request is represented as being a sacrifice for the greater good.

The outcome of the episode is Molly's acquiring her husband's values and becoming the cynic who is motivated by function and utility rather than conscience. Thus, Molly acquires the function of b. Function a is inverted and it becomes an element; that is,

Molly enters into a new social order which is dominated by individual interests and questions of utility.

This transformation is clearly indicated in a story which is a supplement to this episode. On the train to the Idaho Territory, Molly came in contact with the notorious Calamity Jane. In their conversation, it was quickly acknowledged that they were both heading to the same community and for the same purpose. Rather than entering into a pact of cooperation, they viewed each other as potential competitors and Calamity Jane chose to go elsewhere. Thus, as revealed in this story, the social context in which Molly had entered did not involve a sense of community or comradeship, but rather, was one of extreme individualism and competitiveness.

Episode 3: The third episode is a transitional episode. It marks the transition in the story from those episodes which take place prior to Molly's arrival in Murray and those episodes which occur in Murray. Appropriately, the episode takes place in the mountain pass between Montana and Murray, Idaho. More important, the third episode marks a transition in Molly's character which is highly significant in the development of the myth.

Crossing the mountain pass between Thompson Falls in the Montana Territory and Murray was not an easy task. As late as March, there was still plenty of snow in the pass, and snow storms were quite common. Only the most fortunate could afford the price of a horse, and many had to make the journey by foot. As Molly and her fellow travelers began to make the difficult trek, a blizzard began, and those on foot fell behind those on horseback.

As the trip grew more difficult, Molly, who was one of the fortunate ones with a horse, stopped and shared her mount with a woman and her child who were on foot. Upon reaching a lean-to constructed on the side of the trail by some prior travelers, Molly stopped and helped the woman and her child into the shelter. There she shed her fur coat and wrapped it around the woman and her child. Recognizing that the woman and child could not travel any farther in the storm, Molly stayed behind with them as the rest of the travelers moved on.

By next day, the entire community of Murray had learned of Molly's heroic deed from those who had finished the journey, and much of the town was waiting for her arrival. Molly arrived with the woman and child and instructed the townspeople to give the woman a cabin and some food at Molly's expense. Thus, Molly became an instant celebrity in her new home.

The structural arrangement of this episode can be represented in the following formula:

Episode 3: $\mathrm{Woman}_a/\mathrm{Molly}_b \rightleftharpoons \mathrm{Molly}_a b^{-1}$

By way of the above formula we see that the third episode consists of the contrast (/) between two elements (the woman and Molly) each of which is characterized by a particular symbolic function (a, b). Although the woman's qualities are not clearly defined in this episode, Molly's characteristics have been clearly developed in the prior episode. Molly, the prostitute, represents the qualities of cynical pragmatism characteristic of utilitarian individualism (b). Motherhood, in contrast, with its high moral and altruistic qualities, reflects the qualities of conscience and community (a).[14]

Through the development of this episode, Molly demonstrates that even the cynical prostitute is capable of expressing the virtuous qualities of altruism and compassion. Thus, the outcome of the episode is Molly taking on the symbolic function of a, and the community who welcomes her arrival recognizes these qualities. Also, the function of b becomes inverted and becomes an element; that is, Molly enters into a community in which there is a sense of appreciation of social and moral responsibility.

This representation of the community of Murray is in itself interesting. The mining communities of the West were far from virtuous. They were not established by men and women who were interested in forming a new social order, but by individuals motivated primarily by the search for wealth and adventure. If any ideological force dominated the formation of these settlements, it was the self-interest and pragmatism of utilitarian individualism. Yet, what emerges in the oral accounts of these communities is the theme that although these men and women were motivated by self-interest, there existed at the core of their nature a sense of moral responsibility and community. Nowhere is this better represented than in the characterization of the prostitute with a "heart of gold."

It is also interesting to note that the episode in which Molly's "true" qualities reemerge concludes with her acquiring a new name. As we have seen, Molly's rejection of her traditional values and her assumption of a cynical exterior coincided with a name change. Likewise, episode three ends with an anecdote about how she became known as Molly B'Dam. Among the welcomers was an Irishman by the name of Phil O'Rourke. Upon hearing that her name was Molly Burdan, he interpreted it for the crowd as Molly B'Dam, and the name stuck. The name lends a touch of irony to the story in that she was by traditional religious standards indeed damned, and yet, it is her virtuous qualities for which she is remembered.

Episode 4: The fourth and fifth episodes are more anecdotal and less biographical in nature. They are given by the chroniclers to illustrate the character of Molly's life in Murray. We are assured that there are countless other examples which would demonstrate the same qualities. They differ from the prior episodes in that Molly's symbolic function in these episodes does not change, but remains constant. They stand as testimonials to her humane nature.

Episode four tells the story of a miner known as

Lightnin' and his dealings with Molly B'Dam. The hills surrounding Murray were dotted with isolated mines which were worked by one or two miners. The miners would spend many months in isolation working for their fortunes, and when they had collected a large amount of gold, they would come into Murray seeking a good time. Lightnin' was such a miner, and when he arrived in Murray with his heavy poke, which contained a year's earnings in gold, he went directly to Gold Street (the center of prostitution in Murray). He spent the entire day going from saloon to saloon drinking and generally having a good time. He finally fell asleep in the cabin of one of the prostitutes.

Upon waking in the morning, he discovered that his poke was missing. In a rage, he went directly to Molly's cabin, (where) he burst through the door, and began to accuse her of taking his hard year's earnings. Unshaken by the interruption, Molly informed him that she was not responsible for what happened when he was alone in one of the cabins and that he had brought his troubles on himself by the way he acted the night before. As Lightnin's head began to clear, he realized that Molly was right, and yet, he was out a year's earnings and didn't have enough money for a stake for the upcoming year. Molly offered to find another source for the money. Finding another grubstake, Lightnin' returned to the mountains and the incident was forgotten.

Three months later, Lightnin's partner came into Murray and reported that Lightnin' was dying of "mountain fever" (typhoid). Hearing of Lightnin's illness, Molly had several pack mules loaded with food and medical supplies and forced Lightnin's partner to take her to Lightnin'. Molly nursed Lightnin' for several days, and the fever finally broke. Waking up, Lightnin' was shocked at seeing Molly in his cabin and asked her what she was doing there. She told him that she had stopped by to bring him something, and she handed him his poke with all of his gold.

The structural arrangement of this episode can be represented by the following formula:

$$\text{Episode 4: } Molly_a/Lightnin'_b \eqsim Lightnin'_a b-1$$

The two antagonists in this episode are Molly and Lightnin'. Molly treats Lightnin' with care and compassion. Even though he brought the problem on himself, Molly recovers his stolen gold, and although he treats her as a common prostitute, she is the one who comes to his aid when he is sick. Lightnin', on the other hand, shows little concern for Molly's feelings and even refuses to accept her offer of a grubstake. Thus, Molly displays the spirit of generosity and charity characteristic of the Biblical tradition (a), and Lightnin's scorn for Molly and his refusal to accept her help is symptomatic of utilitarian individualism (b).

The outcome of this episode is that Lightnin' gains a new respect for Molly, and he takes on some of her compassion thus acquiring the symbolic function of a. Also, the spirit of utilitarian individualism becomes inverted (Molly the prostitute becomes Molly the nurse) and becomes an element; that is, one is left at the end of the episode with the general lesson that compassion and altruism win out over self-interest and utility.

Episode 5: The fifth episode takes on a structural arrangement similar to the fourth episode. Indeed, the two are interchangeable in message and content. In April of 1886, a stranger rode into Murray, burning with fever. He went into the local saloon and began to drink. Shortly, he fell over dead, and the people in the crowded saloon quickly realized that he had brought smallpox to Murray. Within two weeks, a smallpox epidemic swept through the community. Men and women were dying everywhere, and those who did not have the disease were afraid to help the sick. Townspeople locked themselves in their cabins, and the sick went unattended.

Molly became outraged and sent Phil O'Rourke out to call a mass meeting on Main Street. Addressing the crowd, she told them that the only way to beat the epidemic was to come together and help those that were ill. The crowd resisted and she got more angry. "You poor, miserable fools!" she lashed out. "You don't lick anything by running away from it, or hiding your heads under your pillows! You hole up in your homes or rooms, thinking maybe this won't find you, while your friends and neighbors are dying off alone, unattended."[15] She instructed the crowd to empty the hotels and turn them into sick wards for the ill.

Reluctantly, volunteers came forward, and the town banded together to fight the disease. For three weeks, the town with Molly as their inspiration fought to break the disease. Many died, but the community as a whole survived. Molly worked day and night caring for the ill until the disease was defeated.

The structural arrangement of this episode can be represented in the following formula:

$$\text{Episode 5: } Molly_a/Murray_b \eqsim Murray_a b-1$$

The two antagonists in this episode are Molly and the town of Murray. Molly takes on the symbolic function of altruism and compassion (a). Even when facing the danger of catching this dread disease, she did not waver in her responsibility to her community and fellow humans. The townspeople of Murray, on the other hand, initially allowed fear and the urge of self-preservation to stand in the way of their meeting their responsibility. They clearly represent the forces of self-interest and utility (b). The outcome of the episode is that the town assumes more human compassion and unites to fight the disease. Thus, utilitarian individualism is inverted and spirits of compassion and community emerge.

This quality of compassion and community are clearly evident in the accounts of Molly's death and funeral. Late in the fall of 1887, Molly became tired and listless. By November, she no longer had the energy to get out of bed. The town began to care for Molly. Church women organized the care and someone was always with her. The townspeople would gather every morning to hear how she was doing. On January 17, 1888, the report came that Molly had died. The next day, the town newspaper was bordered in black, and much of the front page was devoted to stories about her life. On the day of her funeral, all the stores were closed, and everyone attended the services. Clearly, the forces of altruism, compassion, and community had been fostered by her life in Murray.

Now that we have examined each episode and revealed its structural arrangement, it is time to look at the story as a whole. The story divides into two major components which counterbalance each other respecting the message which they express. The first component consists of episodes one and two, and the second component consists of episodes four and five. The major distinction between the two components is that the first component involves aspects of Molly's life prior to her move to Murray, and the second component gives a sample of Molly's life in Murray. The third episode serves as a transition between the two components. As noted above, it is only appropriate that the events which take place in the third episode should occur in the mountain pass which served as the geographical link between Murray and the East.

More specifically, the events in the first component take place in the East and outline Molly's fall. The outcome of the first component is that Molly becomes a prostitute and enters into a social order marked by the inversion of the spirit of community and cooperation (b^{-1}). The second component draws examples from her life in Murray (the West), and the outcome is that the spirit of utilitarian individualism which motivated men and women (including Molly) to settle in Murray is inverted (1^{-1}). Thus, the total configuration of the story of Molly B'Dam can be represented in the following formula:

$$East : West :: a^{-1} : b^{-1}$$

For those who settled the West, the eastern part of America had somehow failed. Although its first settlement was motivated by higher ideals (at least as this settlement has been represented in the lore of American civil religion[16]), it somehow inverted these ideals. The forces of utilitarian individualism with its emphasis upon utility, self-interest, and profit as the prime motivators became the dominant factor. It became what the German sociologist Ferdinand Tönnies called a *Gesellschaft* society.[17] Lost were the expressions of community, altruism, and cooperation.

The West, on the other hand, had been founded by people who were seeking their fortune and who were motivated by far from lofty ideals. Yet, these people through their common struggles were able to transcend the motivations of self-interest and utility and develop a sense of community and cooperation. The communities of the West became what Tönnies called *Gemeinschaft* societies.[18] Regained was a spirit of com-

munity and cooperation. Such representations of the decadence of the East and the settlement of the West are not meant to be accurate historical representations, but reflect the views of these events as expressed in the popularization of this history.

Yet, the story of Molly B'Dam is about more than just regional chauvinism. It strikes at the core of the struggle in the American value system. Lévi-Strauss has argued that myths serve as the unconscious mechanism by which the human intellect seeks to resolve some of the basic contradictions in the human condition. If these contradictions are truly unresolvable, then the intellect will continue to grapple with the problem until it plays itself out. This, Lévi-Strauss argues, is the major reason myths tend toward repetition of events and structures.[19]

We have seen throughout this analysis the repetition of the themes of utilitarian individualism and the Biblical tradition. The juxtapositioning of these two antithetical ideological forces within the American value system represents a major ideological contradiction which is truly unresolvable. The motivational network developed around the qualities of brotherhood, community, and self-sacrifice is in direct confrontation with the motivational network developed around the qualities of utility, pragmatism, and self-interest. Stories such as the story of Molly B'Dam allow us to recognize that both motivational systems can be operative within the same person. Such acknowledgement does not eliminate the contradiction, but rather, makes it more intelligible. One need not sacrifice the more desirable qualities of community and self-sacrifice to pursue self-fulfillment. This is the ultimate message revealed in the story of Molly B'Dam.

We began this exercise by looking at the nature of history, and it would be only appropriate to conclude with some comments on the meaning of history. Throughout the communities of Idaho, there are individuals who either collectively or individually are seeking to record the local histories of their communities. Unlike the academic historian, they are not involved in trying to solve the great intellectual questions of the how and why of the human condition. Rather, they are seeking to preserve the common thread of events which brought their communities into existence and to build a body of tradition around which the spirit of community can persist. In times of mass communication (with its effect of increased homogenization), alienation of the masses, and the deterioration of American civil religion, the spirit of community and the sense of place in American society are seriously threatened. Local histories with their tendency to emphasize the human side of life's struggle can serve the same function for the local community that the stories of the founding of America once did for the nation as a whole. In this respect, the value of local histories may lie more in the meanings they communicate than in their intrinsic value as history.

Notes

1. An earlier version of this paper was presented at the Thirty-Third Annual Meeting of the Northwest Anthropological Conference under the title, "Towards a Non-Historical Approach to Oral History."

2. Claude Lévi-Strauss, *The Savage Mind*, trans., George Weidenfeld and Nicolson, Ltd. (Chicago: University of Chicago Press, 1966), pp. 245–69.

3. Ibid., p. 257.

4. See Claude Lévi-Strauss, *Myth and Meaning* (New York: Schocken Books, 1979), pp. 34–43.

5. For a more fully developed explanation of the structural method of the analysis of folklore see Claude Lévi-Strauss, *Structural Anthropology*, trans., Claire Jacobson and Brooke Grundfest (Garden City: Doubleday and Company, Inc., 1963), pp. 202–28.

6. Robert N. Bellah, "New Religious Consciousness and the Crisis in Modernity," in Charles Y. Glock and Robert N. Bellah, eds., *The New Religious Consciousness* (Berkeley: University of California Press, 1976), pp. 333–52.

7. Ibid., pp. 334–36.

8. For a further elaboration of the concept of American civil religion, see Robert N. Bellah, *Beyond Belief: Essays on Religion in a Post-Traditional World* (New York: Harper & Row, Publishers, 1970), pp. 168–89.

9. Bellah, "New Religious Consciousness and the Crisis in Modernity," p. 335.

10. E.g., Jim Estes, *Tales of the Coeur d'Alenes* (Spokane, WA: Steptoe Publications, 1971); George C. Hobson, *Gems of Thought and History of Shoshone County* (Kellogg, ID: Kellogg Evening News Press, 1940), pp. 69–70; Russell A. Bankson, Lester S. Harrison, *Beneath These Mountains* (New York: Vantage Press, Inc., 1966), pp. 61–79.

11. Russell A. Bankson and Lester S. Harrison, *Beneath These Mountains*, pp. 61–79.

12. Claude Lévi-Strauss, *Structural Anthropology*, p. 213.

13. Claude Lévi-Strauss, *The Raw and the Cooked: Introduction to a Science of Mythology, Volume I*, trans., John and Doreen Weightman (Harper & Row, Publishers, 1969), p. 12.

14. For a more detailed analysis of the symbolic meaning of mothering see Nancy Chodorow, *The Reproduction of Mothering: Psychoanalysis and the Sociology of Gender* (Berkeley: University of California Press, 1978), pp. 3–10.

15. Russell A. Bankson and Lester S. Harrison, *Beneath These Mountains*, p. 75.

16. cf. Robert N. Bellah, *The Broken Covenant* (New York: Seabury Press, 1975).

17. Ferdinand Tönnies, *Community and Society, (Gemeinshaft and Gesellschaft)* trans. and ed. Charles A. Loomis (East Lansing, MI: Michigan State University, 1957).

18. Ibid.

19. Claude Lévi-Strauss, *Structural Anthropology*, p. 226.

Recommended Readings

Bellah, Robert N. *The Broken Covenant*. New York: Seabury Press, 1975. An excellent analysis of symbolic meaning of American history as viewed in the context of American civil religion.

Bellah, Robert N. "New Religious Consciousness and the Crisis in Modernity." In *The New Religious Consciousness*, edited by Charles Y. Glock and Robert N. Bellah. Berkeley: University of California Press, 1976. An incisive analysis of the conflict of American ideology and its relationship to the political turmoil of the 1960s.

Claus, Peter J. "A Structural Appreciation of Star Trek." In *American Dimensions*, edited by W. Arens Susan Montague. New York: The Alfred Publishing Co., Inc., 1976. An entertaining analysis of the popular television show which offers a good illustration of the structuralist's method of analysis.

Leach, Edmund. *Genesis as Myth and Other Essays*. London: Jonathan Cape, 1969. An often cited structural analysis of the stories of the Bible by a leading British anthropologist.

Lévi-Strauss, Claude. *Structural Anthropology*. Translated by Claire Jacobson and Brooke Grundfest. Garden City: Doubleday and Company, Inc., 1963. Lévi-Strauss's work continues to be the best example of the structuralist method, and this classic in the anthropological literature offers many of the major papers on the development of structural anthropology.

Lévi-Strauss, Claude. *Structural Anthropology II*. Translated by Monique Layton. New York: Basic Books, Inc., 1976. A further collection of Lévi-Strauss's structural approach to anthropology with his very incisive analysis of "The Story of Asdiwal" which stands as one of the best examples of the structural analysis of the Native-American myth.

Wright, Will. *Sixguns and Society: A Structural Study of the Western*. Berkeley: University of California Press, 1975. A good illustration of the use of the structural method in the analysis of a genre of American film.

The Narrative of "Chief Bigfoot":
A Study in Folklore, History, and World View

J. Sanford Rikoon

In 1965 Idaho historian Merle Wells called for cooperation between the members of his discipline and folklorists in the evaluation of historical source materials. Regretfully, this plea has received little response from historians and only periodic efforts from folklorists. Rikoon's article focuses on a complex of legends about an Indian in southwest Idaho who has become the central character in several narratives reflecting Native American/Anglo-American hostilities of the early settlement period. As is true of many local characters, Chief Bigfoot has entered into the world view of the area in the form of historical writings, popular culture, and folk narrative. The author's effort is not so much to verify the content of particular stories, though that is also an important research area, but to probe the reasons for their popularity and search for their significance within their cultural context.

The spokesman for the union of history and folklore is Richard M. Dorson, whose essays on this topic were collected in American Folklore and the Historian *(1971). Among the best case studies are William Montell,* The Saga of Coe Ridge: A Study in Oral History *(1970); Gladys Marie Fry,* Night-Riders in Black Folk History *(1976); and Edward I. Ives,* Joe Scott: The Woodsman-Songster *(1980).*

Rikoon was formerly Director of the Idaho Folklife Center at the Idaho State Historical Society, Boise.

On November 14, 1878, the Boise *Idaho Tri-Weekly Statesman* presented its readers with the first of two narratives on "THE BIGFOOTED FIEND. A Thrilling Account of the Career of the Notorious Indian Bigfoot and the hand to hand conflict between him and his slayer, J. W. Wheeler."[1] Penned by "An eye-witness to the scene," William T. Anderson, the inaugural article detailed various exploits, depredations, and superhuman escapes attributed to Bigfoot, "Who, like a gigantic monster, as he truly was, roamed over the plains and mountains of Idaho." The initial piece ends with Anderson trapped in a rocky pass in Owyhee County, fearing for his life as Bigfoot and two braves approach from one direction and the Boise City-Silver City stage from another. The concluding installment, on November 16, describes the providential appearance of Wheeler and his ambush slaying of Bigfoot.[2] Before the Indian dies, Wheeler and Anderson are privy to Bigfoot's "Last Confession," a startling autobiographical narrative of his half-breed heritage and early years in Oklahoma, a trip west that included an unrequited love affair with a white woman, and Bigfoot's revenges against whites as a result of that event and other personal injustices. The date of Bigfoot's last fight is given as "late July, 1868." (See Appendix for full texts.)

Six years after the *Statesman* articles, H. N. Eliot became the first of many authors who, over the past century, have printed some variant of the Bigfoot story.[3] In his preface, Eliot touches on the question of

the historical accuracy of the narrative, concluding that "the story has all the marks of strict truthfulness." Debates over the trustworthiness of Bigfoot accounts have not diminished since 1884; meanwhile, the narrative complex has attained a solid position within academic, popular, and folk traditions. The story is considered important enough to Idaho history to warrant some variant of it an appearance in virtually every local, state, and regional history focusing on southwest Idaho or early adventures along the Oregon Trail. Most of these written accounts appearing in historical treatises are pirated directly from the original articles or Eliot's version. Other authors, writing mainly for such popular culture magazines as *Real West* and *True, The Man's Magazine*, take greater liberties with the written tradition in their preparation of sensational Bigfoot articles for the mass media. Finally, there is an oral narrative tradition of Bigfoot legends continuing today, particularly in southwest Idaho. In many cases there is obvious interchange among the written, popular, and folk traditions.

In this essay I will address two questions reflecting a folklorist's perspective on the Bigfoot complex, especially the debate over historical truth. First, I want to probe the original narrative to examine the hypothesis that it should be regarded less as a historical report and more as a tall tale. Second, I believe that the *raison d' etre* for the story (and its persistent popularity) is not so much to retell a specific event but rather to express continuing cultural concerns and perceptions relating to settlement conditions, difficulties with hostile (to whites) Native Americans, and the eventual subjugation of both the land and its pre-white inhabitants to Euro-American methods and ideals. In this sense, the stories are analyzed to reveal certain cultural truths and attitudes that transcend, perhaps, standard historical questions.

An astonishing aspect of the accumulated discussion of the Bigfoot story is that no researcher takes a hard look at the "author" of the *Statesman* series. While many historians and other scholars correctly question the authenticity of the story's contents, none suspect that close examination of the source of the account may provide valuable clues about the narrative itself. Who was William T. Anderson and why did he choose to enlighten *Statesman* readers about an infamous Indian's death more than ten years after it supposedly occurred? In the 1878 accounts the audience is asked to believe that Anderson was sworn to secrecy about the event by Wheeler. As a prerequisite to Bigfoot revealing his life story, Wheeler promises the dying man that "we should not send him nor take him to Boise City after he died; but to drag him in among the willows and pile some rocks upon him and to lay his old gun by his side. . . . Wheeler made me promise to say nothing about the affair, as he had given his word to Bigfoot, and was resolved not to break the promise he had made."[4] The author apparently held to this pact until 1878.

Anderson's by-line lists Fisherman's Cove, Humboldt County [California], as his home at that time. There is, however, no written evidence that a W. T. Anderson lived in Humboldt County at this (or any) period. The name does not appear in the 1880 census for Humboldt County, nor have local researchers uncovered any records (property assessments, death notice, and so on) that point to his existence in the area.[5] In the 1878 narrative, Anderson claims that he worked as a carpenter in Silver City until that fateful July date with Wheeler and Bigfoot. Again, though, a search of Owyhee County records and the *Owyhee Avalanche* (Silver City) for any trace of Anderson proves fruitless. In summary, we have no evidence that places a W. T. Anderson in Humboldt County at the time of the Bigfoot series printing, nor do we have any proof of his residence in southwest Idaho at the time of the depicted events. These findings suggest, then, that the "William T. Anderson, Fisherman's Cove, Humboldt County" by-line is a literary ruse.

It is my contention that the author of these articles is none other than John F. Wheeler himself. This conclusion is based on three sources of evidence: documentation of Wheeler's experiences in Idaho, Oregon, and California; accounts of Wheeler's habits and personality; and the resemblance of the text to parallel trends of popular Western novels, tall tales, and personal anecdotes.

John Wheeler's story is difficult to piece together because the notoriety attached to his name and ac-

tivities over the past century has fueled a variety of sensationalistic accounts of his life. Depending on the motivations of the writer or raconteur, Wheeler is generally presented as either a hardened stage robber and glib-talking murderer, a reluctant thief whose criminal activities were justified by unfair treatment at the hands of the legal system, or a hard-luck character who could never manage to settle down. There is no doubt, however, that Wheeler spent most of his last twelve years, 1868–80, either planning or committing robberies, or behind bars in state and federal prisons. On August 30, 1868, he was arrested in Boise and charged with planning and participating in a series of stage robberies in the Blue Mountains of Oregon.[6] Wheeler was also suspected of murdering a man named Welch during a robbery on the Wood River.[7] Although he temporarily escaped his captors on the way to trial in Portland, Wheeler was recaptured on September 5 near LaGrande and eventually sentenced to ten years' imprisonment in San Quentin. Wheeler's actual term at the California institution ran almost eight years, from April 1, 1869, to February 17, 1877.[8] While at San Quentin, he seems to have learned the practice of dentistry, for upon his release Wheeler moved to San Rafael to practice that trade. In the summer of 1878 he left for Mendocino City and there opened up a practice as doctor of dentistry and medicine, acquiring the name of "Doc, the Dentist."[9] Wheeler's medical career was short-lived, though, for in October 1879 he was arrested and charged with masterminding a robbery scheme that resulted in the death of an innocent man near Mendocino City. Wheeler again escaped captivity for a short time but was recaptured. On May 14, 1880, he was convicted and sentenced to death by hanging. Wheeler eluded a public execution one day later by committing suicide through ingesting an overdose of chloral hydrate.[10]

The events noted above place Wheeler in a position both to author the *Statesman* articles and to be well-informed about Euro-American–Native American hostilities in southwest Idaho during the turbulent 1860s. Prior to his first arrest, Wheeler lived in the Boise area for at least three years. During the mid-1860s, Native American forays against the settlers and miners were at their peak, and Wheeler was no doubt familiar with the newspaper reports and rumors.[11] A portion of the Indian hostilities were attributed to Howluck, a large man known as the "Ogre of the Owyhees" (even though he was based in the Weiser area). As I shall note later, Howluck's activities provided a believable context into which Wheeler placed Bigfoot's exploits. Further, it is likely Wheeler was aware of the cessation of troubles in June 1868 and the removal of most Native Americans, including Howluck, to reservations in Idaho and Oregon. Wheeler's trial in Portland and the eight years in San Quentin approximate the span between the *Statesman* articles and the date given for Bigfoot's death. It would have been very difficult for Wheeler, from his jail cell in California, to write letters to Boise newspapers before the summer of 1877. Finally, we are presented with his move to Mendocino County only months before the article appeared. Humboldt County is the next county north of Mendocino County along the California coast. If Wheeler wrote under the name of Anderson, he would likely not have used his true place of residence, yet at the same time the by-line could not identify either an Idaho location or major population area easily verifiable by newspaper editors or other interested persons. Based on the lack of examination of the by-line quoted by dozens of researchers since that time, one would have to admit that Wheeler chose very well.

Other known facts about Wheeler's life support the hypothesis that he acted as his own publicity agent. We know that Wheeler was an intelligent person who, for example, acquired a good deal of medical knowledge in prison at a time before penal reform was an established objective. Wheeler arrived in Mendocino County "highly recommended in his profession. He became acquainted with, and was well-liked by the people of Mendocino."[12] Wheeler also acted as his own lawyer during the California trials during which he managed to draw out the jury-selecting process to almost two full days. Other reliable sources note that Wheeler carried on a large amount of correspondence while not incarcerated.[13] In California he displayed his literary abilities through many letters to Mendocino papers, friends, and family. A search of the jail cell in which the suicide occurred yielded a fairly incredible collection of sentimental essays and letters. Included in these writings is the following passage from a piece titled "Wheeler's Sentiments":

> A child, though the most innocent thing on earth, has no conscience until it has understanding, and knows what is called right and wrong; therefore it appears to me that the soul, the understanding, and the conscience are one and the same thing, and are governed by raising and hereditary laws and surrounding circumstances.[14]

In addition to his literary propensities, Wheeler appears to have been something of a boaster, raconteur, and actor. While in Mendocino he claimed to have worked with General Custer and Buffalo Bill as an Indian scout.[15] We have no way of knowing the truth of these claims, although considering Wheeler's 1865 arrival in Boise, it would have been difficult for Wheeler to have fought the Indians alongside Custer. We also have evidence that Wheeler was born in 1843; thus his scouting days must have indeed been at a tender age.[16] There are further inconsistencies between Wheeler's account of his involvement in the Blue Mountain stage robberies and that reported by eyewitnesses and undercover agents.[17] Reports of Wheeler's activities confirm that he was extremely clever in his manipulations. During the period of the Oregon crimes, he managed to move freely throughout the area by representing himself as a Deputy U.S. Marshal from Boise City.[18] In both Boise City and Mendocino City he

joined committees and posses formed to capture the same outlaw gangs in which Wheeler himself either participated or led. Keller reports that in California Wheeler had the daring both to "make a speech advising against following the men" and to be appointed to a select committee organized to plan the pursuit.[19] Less than twenty-four hours later, Wheeler was arrested.

Wheeler appears to have used his own life and early experiences as a model for developing Bigfoot's origins in Oklahoma and the trip west. Independent sources note that he was part Indian and, further, that his Native American parentage was Cherokee (the same as ascribed to Bigfoot)[20]. Wheeler, like his literary creation, grew up in the Oklahoma Territory inhabited by many mixed-blood Cherokees and traveled across the plains with a wagon train. These experiences seem to account for the camaraderie he shows Bigfoot in the promise to keep the halfbreed's burial place a secret: "I guess I will [keep the promise], as I am from the Cherokee nation myself, and have a little Cherokee blood in my veins, I will not refuse to grant your dying request."[21]

The preceding discussion demonstrates that John F. Wheeler and not William T. Anderson is the likely author of the 1878 Bigfoot accounts. It also seems reasonable to suggest that Wheeler wrote the Statesman articles as an exaggerated adventure story to boost his own reputation. The articles, then, are clearly not historical reports, but are more closely aligned with the folklorist's concepts of the tall tale. To view the Anderson-Wheeler text as a tall tale is not to deny either that it contains kernels of real historical circumstances or that the narrative is written with the intention that the audience believe in the narrative content. The "tall tale" label is most appropriate because the account is given in tall tale style, it contains many standard motifs common to "exaggeration narratives," and the episodes are localized through the use of specific names, locations, and events. Tall tales are not a uniquely American phenomenon, but they were very widespread in this county in both folk and popular literatures during the second half of the nineteenth century.[22] These tales thrived in the shifting frontier and settlement areas of the American West because here were found the marvels and extremes of the natural elements and the dangers and excitement of an uncivilized society. As Dick d'Easum notes, early Idaho newspapers sometimes included local tall tales for the readership's entertainment.[23] These narratives contained many floating folklore motifs, including mosquitoes that killed and ate fish, and bears that devoured dynamite. During this period, also, a receptive audience for popular media texts could be found "back East" and in the growing population areas around the country. The Bigfoot stories, for example, were printed in the St. Louis Globe–Democrat soon after their Idaho presentation. Adding to this fertile climate for tall tales was the growth of the Western dime novel and story genres as popular entertainment. During the 1870s, such publishers as Beadle and Adams printed by the thousands formulaic Western tales, set mainly in the Plains and Rocky Mountain regions. These stories were often serialized in newspapers, journals, and magazines, and they served to perpetuate an idealized and desirable, albeit errant and racist, view of the American frontier and its native inhabitants.

Tall tales are generally identifiable by their presentation of exaggeration and amazing coincidence in a matter-of-fact style.[24] The exaggerations normally surround everyday events, persons, or phenomena that have some special characteristics. In the Anderson-Wheeler texts, these qualities include Bigfoot's size, speed, and strength. In the narrative the identifying characteristics are exaggerated to the point of incredulity. Later Bigfoot texts continue to portray the largest Indian possible or to augment his speed and strength. We find Bigfoot able to bend guns into metal pretzels or swim back-and-forth across the Snake River at its most difficult portions. Above all there is Bigfoot's size, with the Anderson-Wheeler description representative of only the median statistics offered in oral texts: "Around the chest, 59 inches; height 6 feet 8½ inches, length of foot 17½ inches; around the ball of the foot 18 inches, around the widest part of the hand 18 inches . . . [and] weighed at least three hundred pounds, and all bone and sinew, not a pound of surplus flesh about him."[25]

The entire Anderson-Wheeler story is told in a sober fashion; Wheeler fulfills our expectation for understatement from the tall tale hero who "talked the whole affair over as unconcernedly as though nothing unusual had happened." Three days later "Anderson" meets Wheeler in Boise City. The writer notes the hero's characteristic humble and modest behavior:

> The day I left Boise City I saw Wheeler very neatly dressed, sitting and conversing quietly with some gentlemen. He did not appear at all like the man who, three days before, had met and killed in combat two of the most desperate of all the braves of Idaho, and a deed which would have been proudly boasted of by almost any other man, was kept a secret from the world by the singular but brave Wheeler.[26]

It is rather uncommon for a tall tale raconteur to place himself in the third-person form during an oral rendition in which he is the hero; most storytellers prefer to present themselves in the first person. The "eyewitness" device used here reflects the special circumstances of the author's background and his need to establish credibility for a story in which the hero's actions run counter to the audience's knowledge of his previous activities. The Anderson-Wheeler text appeared only ten years after Wheeler's stage-robbing conviction. His 1868 arrest, escape, and recapture were covered in detail by the *Statesman*. If Wheeler had used a first-person form, it is probable that either the editors would not have printed the articles or the audience would have placed little credence in the narrative content.

John Wheeler's articles to the *Statesman* likely did not constitute his first attempts to portray himself as the slayer of Bigfoot. As noted previously, this crafty fellow had a propensity for telling boastful and fantastic tales about his own life and experiences. Further, we have evidence that Wheeler told stories about this affair to members of his family and visitors to his jail cell in California.[27] During his imprisonment and short periods of freedom, the raconteur had ample opportunity to experiment with various episodes, refine the content, and lengthen the account. The oral narratives told before and after the *Statesman* articles probably were in the form of personal experience stories—told in the first person and bare of the literary conventions contained in the newspaper texts. These devices, such as the "Last Confession," relate more to popular literature presentation than folk narrative performance. The 1878 account is also much longer and less focused than most oral tall tales and personal narratives; a careful reading of the text reveals that it includes at least two independent stories—the initial chase scene and the death fight. The written presentation also necessitated the use of filler to introduce various contexts, characters, and events, and to construct a patina of belief around the depicted activities.

Wheeler-Anderson's ability to localize floating folklore motifs and to provide kernels of historical events increases the narrative's believability as a historical report. As noted, for example, Bigfoot is patterned after a real figure, Howluck, and Wheeler was well aware of the hostilities between Native Americans and Euro-Americans. The author manages to weave a variety of unsolved depredations into Bigfoot's "Confessions" thereby increasing the credibility of both this account and the threat posed by the terrorizing Indian. The most noteworthy of these incidents are the fall 1867 murders of Sergeant Denoille and his wife near Camp Lyon and Mrs. Scott and her husband on the Burnt River.[28] Both of these cases were unsolved, although Indians were blamed for each, until Bigfoot admitted his responsibility for them in the 1878 recounting. It is of interest to note that some authors since that time have furthered Bigfoot's reputation by attributing even more unexplained devastations to his work. Perhaps the most spectacular implication is Gregg's claim that Bigfoot led the war party responsible for the Ward Massacre in 1852.[29]

Localization also takes place through the use of persons familiar to the southwest Idaho audience. For example, the author names well-known figures including Charlie Barnes, Judge Rosenborough, and Mrs. Record as riding the stage that passed the spot of the final encounter between active moments of the struggle. Their presence, albeit at the time the major participants were all hiding behind rocks, provides nonverifiable proof and elements of believability. Other instances of this stylistic device include Bigfoot's association with Joe Lewis, a renegade white killed before 1868, and the opening chase scene of Bigfoot by Wheeler, Frank Johnson, and a man named Cook, the latter two persons long disappeared (if they ever existed at all) by 1878.

Anderson-Wheeler's expertise in establishing credence in his main character is partially responsible for the myriad of oral traditions that continue to circulate today. It would be difficult, if not impossible, to unravel these narratives in the hope of establishing prototypes or discovering dissemination routes. We also do not have enough texts to establish local ecotypes. Yet, a few observations concerning oral accounts can be made. First, verbal texts are typically distinguishable from their written counterparts by the former's lack of literary conventions and the use of an informal style. Oral narratives about Bigfoot are generally short, monoepisodic, and follow no set form. Second, the tall tale first-person character of the Anderson-Wheeler text has been replaced by legendary traits. Bigfoot stories are usually told now as local historical legends relating to actual regional historical developments. The context in these narratives is, however, long before the lives of present-day narrators. Establishing credibility thus becomes a matter of the raconteur's ability to associate himself with reputable sources or cite documentary proof.[30] In some cases the stories are not, perhaps, fully believed by the narrator, yet the narratives are told as true. The introduction of a Bigfoot narrative into conversation may be the stimulant of some debate over historical veracity, but in all instances the legends are told on the side of positive proof. Third, the entry of Bigfoot motifs into oral tradition results in a great deal of variation between texts and the introduction of elements not found in the relatively unchanging written tradition. These changes are due to a variety of factors, including substitutions of motifs from other stories or regional lore,[31] the need to localize texts, independent invention and innovation, and rationalization of various actions and activities.

One winter, Bigfoot and other renegades were stealing cattle in the west end of Canyon County, near Marsing. Abner Calloway, then a U.S. Marshal, and some of the others trailed Bigfoot. They were closing upon him and he decided to hide behind a snowdrift. He raised his head over the snowdrift to see if his pursuers had left. Calloway and some men saw, shot, and killed him on the spot.[32]

Chief Bigfoot Nampa they claim was half Shoshone and half Negro. And he was a big man over three hundred pounds and probably six foot four inches tall and his feet were about sixteen inches long. He was so strong he could run for thirty or forty miles at a stretch and of course he was a road agent and he killed people. When they finally got him, it was just up the [Snake] river from the place here [five miles from Marsing], where the ford was. And the stage had just forded the river and he was waiting to waylay it and this guy was waiting for him. He shot him but he didn't kill him. He downed him and so he asked him not to mutilate his body. So in return for the gold that he had, the guy promised not to tell anyone where he was buried so that no one could get his big feet. There was a lot of people who would have liked to get them and use them to get money because of their big size.[33]

Bigfoot stories in folk, popular, and academic processes are as prevalent today as they appear to have been one hundred years ago following the *Statesman* accounts.[34] Given this tenacity, scholars of Idaho culture and the American West have been forced to evaluate the significance of the Bigfoot complex. In almost every case, however, one finds these commentaries devoid of any comprehensive treatment of the oral texts and full of skepticism toward written narratives. The popularity of Bigfoot stories among Idaho citizens is matched, in these discussions, only by the strength of the scholarly rejection of the possible value of Bigfoot tales.

Historians have been saddled with the major burden of coming to grips with this legendary figure. Most academicians tend to dismiss Bigfoot stories as fantastic tales containing, at best, only shreds of historical accuracy. The majority of these writers base their judgment on the lack of written historical evidence about a half-breed Indian born in Oklahoma. They believe that the character is based on the previously mentioned Howluck who led a group of hostile (to whites) Northern Piute and Shoshone.[35] Based in the Weiser Valley, the group was largely dispersed during the Crook military campaigns of 1867–68. Howluck was captured in eastern Oregon "by a military force and an independent party of Willow Creek miners in June, 1868."[36] Before the end of these conflicts, however, supposed sightings of Howluck (or Oulouck, Oulux or Howlark) were reported from a number of locales in western and central Idaho. The newspapers in Boise City and Silver City, unaware (like most whites) of Native American names, began calling him Bigfoot in 1867 because of the large footprints found by whites at locations of supposed Native American hostilities.[37]

Once the historical validity of the depicted events is questioned, oral or written accounts are presented, if at all, as bits of "local color" intended to enliven generally dry chronological listings or discussions. One recent author, before presenting slices of the Anderson-Wheeler text, cautions his readers that "since the style and authenticity are more Wild West genre than factual history, it is noted here only as a piece of folklore that incorporated many of the tall tales of the day, lightly salted with facts."[38] This type of attitude toward folk culture is unfortunate and misleading in regard to the potential significance of active folk traditions. Historians have a legitimate interest in discovering "what really happened" (the truth), yet people's perceptions and acceptance of what they consider their own history to be (the truth) can offer researchers a proven barometer of central values, attitudes, beliefs, and world view. It is precisely these aspects of human life that are often missing from the historical record and sources. Further, if one wanted to probe the impact of previous historical events on any group, it would be most important to isolate how those events were interpreted by individuals within that group. For example, we have ample evidence that Euro-American relations with Native Americans, and government policies in the West, were guided more by ideological and sentimental images than by any real knowledge of historical events or resident peoples.[39] It seems clear, then, that folk culture can be important because it not only provides us with a window into central cultural concerns but also plays a large role in shaping the behaviors that create historical events.

The focus of all narratives is, of course, the Bigfoot character. In some texts dating from after 1917 he is called Nampa(h) or Chief Nampa(h) because of place name legends concerning the name of the town of Nampa. According to these legends, first begun as a promotional scheme by town businessmen and promoters, the Shoshone terms "namb" (which can be translated as "foot") and "puh" (which can be translated as "footprint") were used by settlers to name the town in honor of Bigfoot.[40] In virtually every text, regardless of the Indian's name, the man is most identifiable by his large size, physical prowess, and antipathies toward Euro-American settlers.

The unchanging nature of the Bigfoot character clearly represents concerns relating to overt difficulties of the settlement period and covert attitudes of whites toward the Native American inhabitants. Euro-American expansion into southwest Idaho was not without occasional difficulties with local Piute, Bannock, and Shoshone groups, though the level of violence certainly does not approach that which Hollywood and the general media would like the (general) public to believe. The worst years, especially for southern Idaho Native Americans who generally lost twenty people to every white killed, were between 1863 and 1868.[41] By this latter date, the overwhelming majority of Native Americans had either been killed or agreed to move to reservations at Fort Hall or elsewhere. During the time of heightened hostilities, most whites had one basic policy toward Native American protesters — death by whatever means possible. On January 1, 1866, the *Owyhee Avalanche* (Silver City) offered this plan to its readers:

> We are informed that ten Indians recently made their appearance on Catherine Creek, where Isaac Jennings is wintering his stock, and told him that they would make peace if the whites would agree to give them all the food and clothing they want, and would, also, return a portion of the stock stolen last summer; but if the settlers refused, they would drive off everything they found. Mr. Jennings promised them to see the Governor immediately and have some arrangements made. Now, if some Christian gentleman will consent to furnish a few bales of blankets from some smallpox hospital, well innoculated with that disease, we will act as distributing agent, and will see to it that not an Indian is without a blanket. This kind of peace will probably prove more lasting than all the regular treaties that could be made.[42]

Euro-American–Native American hostilities were settled primarily by the arrival and campaigns of General George Crook and the establishment of military outposts in Boise, Camp Lyon, and other places throughout the region.[43] Local citizens and newspapers cheered every army victory and promoted "Indian hunting." In a typical article of that period, the *Statesman* offered praise for one departing soldier: "[Lieutenant George] McTaylor has clearly proven himself an efficient subordinate during his stay at Camp Three Forks, having participated in three Indian hunts and secured his game every time — the first time three, the second eight, the third and last thirteen."[44] Meanwhile, civilians were called upon to do their own part in ridding the area of the "Io," as the *Statesman* editor called those Indians not willing to immediately move to a reservation. The citizens of Silver City formed a committee in 1866 to promote "Indian hunting" and advertised that "for every buck scalp be paid one hundred dollars, and for every squaw scalp fifty dollars, and twenty-five dollars for everything in the shape of an Indian under ten years of age."[45]

Early Euro-American inhabitants made few distinctions between Native American groups or individuals. Thus, when an especially large Indian was identified as a leader of the hostile "Snakes,"[46] he became a symbol to which gravitated all of the worst sentiments of the Indian-haters. Throughout the 1860s Euro-Americans were never sure of the man's name or his whereabouts. He was blamed, nevertheless, for a variety of depredations. Reports of Bigfoot's death in a battle with General Crook near Steen's Mountain in December 1866 proved premature.[47] A correspondent writing under the ominous name of "Henry Rifle" in the *Owyhee Avalanche* of April 14, 1867, reported Bigfoot very much alive. The article reflected local feelings: "For ten years [Bigfoot] has been quite a terror in this country — rapid in movements, striking where least expected . . . His career will one of these days be at an end, as the whole community have vowed him vengeance and are watching him closely."[48]

The Bigfoot of written and oral traditions symbolizes two of the worst fears of the white settlers — the marauding Indian and the half-breed whose allegiance and character, while belonging to neither race, are overly influenced by the dark (in this case Indian) stock. The transformation of Bigfoot from his half-breed origins to white-hating Native American, confirms the perceived dangers and sinful nature of miscegenation and is an important element of the Bigfoot complex. A common element in texts detailing Bigfoot's early adult years is that he was a threatening, though not vengeful, character until his love for a white woman went unrequited. When a white competitor for the woman's affections insults Bigfoot, in some narratives calling him a "Nigger,"[49] Bigfoot kills the man and thus begins his notorious career. Implicit in this episode is the nonacceptance of half-breeds by whites and the fate of these individuals to inhabit the fringes of society. In one text this marginality is made quite overt and neurosis-forming.

According to our legend, our local Bigfoot was a psychopathic Indian who lived in Owyhee County killing whites and Indians alike in the middle 1880s. He got his size and temper from the circumstances of his ancestry. His mother was half Cherokee and half Negro; his father was white. He was much lazier than either parent or any of his playmates and, as a result, was treated unmercifully. He wasn't accepted by Cherokee, Negro, or white due to the other bloodlines in him.

Later a white girl turned him down in his marriage proposal. All the persecution of his life came to a climax and he experienced a mental disorder. He became an insane murderer, killing all the people he found, other than occasional renegades he rode with sometimes. One of his methods of killing was to walk straight up to the man firing at him, take away the gun, twist it into a pretzel, then strangle the man.

It's not known how many people he killed. Undoubtedly many deaths were falsely attributed to Bigfoot. On the other hand, he was supposed to have killed lone travelers and prospectors whose deaths were never known. Eventually, he was ambushed and shot to death.[50]

The half-breed's reactions, if not always so dramatically presented as in the above text, are certainly one of a move toward disorder, the urge to create chaos, and the desire to inflict instant revenge on the perceived source of pain. These behaviors are attributed to a transcendence of the Indian, non-Christian portions of Bigfoot's background and support notions of the childlike behavior of Native Americans. In a larger context, Bigfoot's reactions support Euro-American attitudes that the impulsive Indian was unable to deal in a civilized manner with white norms, mores, and institutions.

The transcendence of the savage heritage is often portrayed graphically in descriptions of Bigfoot. In most narratives, the storyteller begins by blending stereotypical physical traits associated with the mixed racial heritage. Negro characteristics are normally evidenced in "krinkly" hair; Native American physical earmarks typically include a "strong-jawed" face or jet-black hair, and Euro-American features generally include blue eyes or fair skin. These racial traits are not presented in random fashion, especially when the descriptions occur in portions of the text following Bigfoot's turn to terror. Rather, trait patternings symbolize Bigfoot's identification with impulsive, uncontrollable nature. The final portrait is one of a man whose associations with his white ancestry are but a dysfunctional survival.

[Bigfoot] was a monster of a man nearly seven feet tall and weighing over 300 pounds. He was dressed only in a breechcloth from which dangled several blobs of rotting human flesh and hair. His own straight black hair hung around his face and shoulders covering a handsome, strong-jawed face with wild, incongruously blue eyes. Across his forehead, cheekbones, chest and shoulders were plastered great smears of red and yellow mud.[51]

Bigfoot becomes the quintessential wild man, familiar in many folk literatures, who belongs neither to the human nor to the animal world.[52] This portrayal parallels, also, one general Euro-American trend of viewing Native Americans as wild savages in close proximity, mentally and physically, to nature.[53] In some texts we find the transformation to half-man, half-animal is complete.

Around Burley there used to live some kind of giant man. They said that his feet were seventeen inches long and for this reason he was called by the name Bigfoot. He was part Indian and part beaver. The beaver part of him enabled him to escape whenever he became surrounded by swimming up the Snake River. It is said that once thirty men set out after him on fast horses and could not run him down. He was faster than any horse alive and he killed men just for the pleasure of killing them. I think it was the Cherokee Indians that worshipped him and he led them into many fights against the early settlers. He was finally outsmarted by some guy and now his spirit is somewhere up in the mountains outside of Boise. People are always telling of some strange large footprints that they run across.[54]

In another legend, the narrator states that Bigfoot lived in the Owyhee Mountains on ants and other desert life.[55] Other characteristics used to identify Bigfoot's bonds to the natural world include primeval animal screams and "monstrous unintelligible yells" after escaping pursuers or committing an act of revenge.[56] Whether the Indian is portrayed as part of the natural (as opposed to civilized) world through physical characteristics or living habits, the emphasis serves to highlight the Red Savage's alignment with uncontrollable nature in the Euro-American world view. Most Euro-Americans — then and now — perceive the frontier as an arena housing the epic battle between savagery and civilization, between nature and culture. Bigfoot in this drama is a self-serving symbol of savagery's fury.[57]

Bigfoot's rein of terror parallels hostilities between the established Native American inhabitants and the white newcomers. An important element in almost all the narratives is Bigfoot's abilities to elude capture and death until 1868. In most texts, his escapes receive more attention than either the depredations for which he is supposedly accountable or his death. Time after time whites are evaded through superhuman efforts. Bigfoot's favorite tactics include outrunning or outdistancing horse-borne pursuers, or swimming across difficult portions of the Snake River. In all cases he is saved by his superior natural abilities, traits that separate Bigfoot from civilization's agents in both pursuit and symbolic significance. Superhuman abilities ascribed to Bigfoot are similar to those traditionally assigned to legendary wild men and mythological mixed human/animal creatures. Among these motifs are prodigious speed, marvelous swimming abilities, extraordinary size, and superhuman strength.[58]

There once lived an Indian named Nampa. He was known to the U.S. government as "Chief." He was a crossbreed between white Indian and Negro Indian. He was 6 feet 8 inches tall and weighed over 300 pounds.

Besides being the hugest man anyone ever saw, he was the strongest also. He could swim across the widest part of the Snake River, and he could outrun and outdistance the entire U.S. Cavalry on horses. Nampa never had any need for horses, but he was a horse thief. He caused the government quite a bit of trouble because he wouldn't stay on the reservation. The law captured him several times. One time he broke out of jail in the hardest of winters and walked barefoot in forty below weather for over one hundred miles to hide out with fellow renegades. The next spring, Nampa and his friends returned to attack the fort where he had been captured and they freed the other prisoners. They all rampaged around the country but Nampa was soon captured and later was shot to death.[59]

There was some fellows—there was two of them in fact—that came there [to Givens Hot Springs] and worked. And this one fellow told this story at the Givens' of course. And I don't know why they would have any reason to lie about it, they weren't the type of people who would lie about anything. You could depend pretty much on what they said. They were good upstanding Christian people. This one fellow that worked for them there around the Givens Spring, and he told this story about he and another fellow had been back in the hills there looking for horses, rounding them up horses or whatever they were doing, ranching for ranchers. They were younger fellows. This was before Bigfoot got killed. They had been up there in the foothills looking for stock. It was getting pretty late in the evening, almost dark, and they were just letting their horses kind of take their heads and going down there, talking and just riding along, not saying much, just going down to somewhere along the river wherever they lived. All of a sudden their horses kind of walked up a little rise and here was a little hollow right there in front of them. And there was Bigfoot and two Indians hunkered around a little fire. Well it startled both parties because one didn't hear the other was a-coming and the other didn't see anything until they come up on this little rise. Well one of the fellows had a gun in his saddle scabbard. Neither one of them had a revolver or a pistol, but this one fellow had a scabbard rifle. Of course, they reigned up right short when the Indians were only ten or twelve feet away, or fifteen, right down this little swell. This one—these two Indians, the little ones, jumped up and run and Bigfoot run up that little hill and grabbed this one fellow. He just bodily grabbed his saddle and him and pulled that horse right over sideways. He was so big and powerful. Well he was the fellow that had the gun and of course the other fellow wheeled his horse and took off. Well as soon as Bigfoot got this fellow down, that would probably give him enough time to get going. So he took off. The fellow, by the time he got unscrambled from his horse and he got up and got the horse up, well the Indians had disappeared. So he hollered at his partner, he said that they were gone. And then they got together again and took off for the ranch. But he said that it was such a surprise that it liked to scare them half to death, especially that Indian being so big and powerful that he just jerked that horse right over sideways with the rider on it. Of course, the horse was probably unsteady and snorting, and that was no great feat, but it did scare the guy. It about scared him half out of his wits.[60]

In another narrative the internationally known motif of ''Marvelous runner catches wild game on the run''[61]

is the focus of a story that provides an idiosyncratic end to Bigfoot's life.

> Though this story concerning Chief Bigfoot may not be altogether true, it must be believed by quite a few people for a monument was erected near Silver City, Idaho, in his honor. It seems that Chief Bigfoot, chief of the Nampa Indians that is, whose feet were a foot and a half long, was the fastest runner, in spite of his big feet, in Idaho. There was this certain brave in this tribe who doubted the Chief's running ability, so in order to prove to the brave how really good he was, Chief Bigfoot said he would run with a deer. Whoever was ahead at the end of five days was the fastest runner in Idaho. So, well of course Chief Bigfoot won, but at the end of five days he came to a cliff. Knowing that he had won, and being thoroughly exhausted, he jumped over the cliff. Thus a monument was put up in honor of Chief Bigfoot of the Nampa tribe, fastest runner in Idaho.[62]

The significance of these episodes is that the Euro-American on the frontier was no match to the Native American in an encounter hinging on purely natural abilities. Even with the aid of domesticated horses, a white innovation adopted by only a portion of southern Idaho Native Americans, Bigfoot proves victorious. It is of interest to note that all of these encounters involve chase scenes with whites as the hunter and Bigfoot as the hunted. As long as the venery approximated man against man with little cultural interference, however, the Native American emerges the winner.

Bigfoot's demise is inevitable in the context of this world view because it includes belief in the natural progress of culture and the eventual replacement of savagery by civilization. Further, the cessation of Bigfoot's activities could not have occurred through either surrender and peaceful removal to a reservation or death from an unidentified or nonhuman force. None of these solutions would be consistent with Euro-American expectations of the ultimate reward for the ungrateful savage nor would they explicitly demonstrate the triumph of culture over nature. The final act of the Bigfoot story as it is played out in most narratives is important in both the manner of Bigfoot's violent death and the white agent carrying out civilization's mission.

The reign of terror ends when John Wheeler, or some other (usually) unidentified white man kills Bigfoot in Owyhee County, normally in the Reynold's Creek area.[63] The instrument of death is always a rifle because, as we have seen, Bigfoot could not be bested in a struggle of natural abilities. The rifle tips the balance of power in the white man's favor; it also allows him to avoid face-to-face struggle with the enemy by allowing the killing to be done from a distance. In many texts, furthermore, the rifle used is the famed Henry repeater. One of the most sought-after weapons by Civil War participants, the Henry represented America's technological advances in weaponry development at that time. Most of these rimfire repeaters held between twelve and eighteen bullets of crushing .44 caliber diameter.[64] On the Western frontier, the Henry was used mainly for protection, especially from bandits and Indians.

Bigfoot's death is symbolic of an attitude in which the technological superiority of settlers and, by extension, western civilization and culture (e.g., the Henry rifle) triumphs over all obstacles on the frontier, Indians and nature (e.g., Bigfoot's size, speed, and strength). Indeed, the morning before the encounter, Anderson-Wheeler reports that a soothsayer warned Bigfoot that he would meet a "white-headed serpent" armed with a "medicine gun."[65] In this small episode the stereotypical power of the Native American prophetic medicine man, a spiritual power close to nature, is contrasted with the more potent power of the white man's medicine — his technological death-dealing arsenal. The use of many bullets, typically twelve to eighteen, to kill Bigfoot is testimony both to the menace of the Indian terror and to the extent of power needed to clear the path for westward expansion.

In many oral accounts the name of Bigfoot's slayer is not mentioned, but some texts, especially those printed in mass media magazines, devote a sizeable portion of the narrative to John Wheeler and his status as outlaw/hero. At first glance Wheeler's standing as a hero does not mix well with known facts concerning his criminal career. Yet the *Statesman*, in 1878, and numerous other storytellers since then, have had no problem in reconciling these two positions. Many Euro-Americans appear to accept Wheeler's status for two reasons, both of which stem more from folk world view than historical events. First, Wheeler fits the model of the solitary hero able to mediate effectively between order (culture) and disorder (nature) because he is a participant in both sides. Wheeler represents an ideal frontier-breaker, the man who carries civilization into areas characterized by savagery. Yet because the frontier man works outside (or ahead, as it were) of civilized norms and institutions, he is given license to temporarily adopt some of the features of the wild. Later, of course, when order is established, the frontier man is expected either to move on to other frontiers or shed his frontier characteristics. The timing of Bigfoot's removal coincides with the latter stages of the frontier period in southwest Idaho and thus provides a suitable context for the outlaw/hero. Second, the scene of Bigfoot's death also reflects an ambiguous area between order and disorder. The Indian is ambushed by a concealed white man hidden in the rocks of a hilly, barren area. This locale makes it possible not only for Wheeler and Bigfoot to engage in one-to-one combat free from any outsiders (except the unobtrusive witness), but also separates the combatants from civilization's customs and requirements. This theme is a familiar one to anybody who reads popular Western novels. The passage of the stage through the area, in the Anderson-Wheeler text and other narratives, is a reminder that civilization is not far away, but the connecting thread is thin. In a context such as this one, the Euro-American hero cannot be the Christian gentleman of a James Fenimore Cooper novel.

There was a wagon train coming west. There was a huge man with the train and he was part Indian and part Negro. He got an awful case on a girl traveling with the train and just her father, no other family. She was engaged to the horse wrangler. The roustabout did odd jobs on the train. One day he went with the man the girl was engaged to to search for some lost horses. When he came back he told that he and the other man had separated to look for the horses and he had lost track of him. They held the train three or four days but the man didn't return. The train finally had to go on, but the girl and her father stopped off at the nearest settlement which was down by Pocatello. They thought that the fellow might show up and the girl wanted to wait for him.

The next spring they started having trouble with Indian raids down by Glenn's Ferry and Mountain Home. Several trains were raided, the people were killed, and the stock driven off. Shoup, who was governor at the time, wanted something done about the raids. An army man was hired to see if he could stop them. He went to the place where the raids had occurred and noticed that at each place there were large footprints. They started calling this man "Chief Bigfoot" and felt that he must be the leader of the raiders since he was at every raid.

It was getting fall and the Indians started going back up into the Owyhees for the winter. The army man was following them and as they broke into smaller groups he always followed the group where he saw the big footprints. It didn't take the Indians long to figure out that it was Bigfoot he was after, and they deserted him. The army man followed him for a long ways, and finally Bigfoot stopped to fight. They shot it out and when Bigfoot was out of bullets he came at the army man with a knife. It took a whole lot of bullets to kill him.

Before he died he told the army man that he had killed the horse-wrangler, and the reason he was leading these raiding parties all summer was because he hoped to find the girl among the immigrants. He never found her, but if he had his plans were to carry her away with him. Then, the army man had a reward coming for capturing Bigfoot. He didn't know how he would carry the big man out, he was so heavy. The snows had already set in. So he took out his knife and cut off one of the huge feet. He took the foot back to Boise with him to prove he had really killed Bigfoot. He flopped the foot down on Governor Shoup's desk.[66]

On August 22, 1974, residents of Parma and the surrounding area gathered at Fort Boise Park to "dedicate a statue to Parma's historical villain Bigfoot."[67] The seven-foot cement figure depicts an angry-faced Indian in threatening posture with a rifle in one hand and a knife in the other. The activities began with a pot-luck supper and "massacre pageant" in which local citizens portrayed Bigfoot's alleged massacre of the Ward party. For the statue unveiling, Governor Cecil Andrus presented a dedicatory address, praising area residents for "preserving Idaho history." The governor noted the "perseverance of our pioneers" in settling the area and the trials the early settlers endured.

Parma's Bigfoot statue is only one of many public testimonials to this figure's established position in regional folk history. There is also a Bigfoot Tavern and Bigfoot Road in Canyon County; horseback clubs in Twin Falls County go on annual Bigfoot trail rides, offering prizes to the best trackers. Whatever the form of the symbolic reference, whether cast in cement or story, the dominant effect of the expression is the same—Bigfoot is an accepted folk figure and his experiences and fate reflect important folk historical elements of the pioneer period. To note, from an academic point of view, that Bigfoot never existed is akin to claiming that there is nothing to learn about American life by examining the importance of the Lone Ranger, Luke Skywalker, or the cast of tall tale characters who have paraded across the American scene.

Bigfoot has a role far more real than anything tangible, and he will outlive any one of us. His perseverance is due to the fact that Idaho citizens have, through their stories and commemorations, attached Bigfoot to an accepted part of their pioneer history. On the surface, this linkage appears to be with local events and identifiable characters. Yet fused to the fluid specifics of a Bigfoot text are the more enduring attitudes and values that people connect with the pioneer experience, especially Native American and Euro-American hostilities. The story of Bigfoot is a tale of Indian depredation and eventual white victory, and Bigfoot will live as long as this larger view of western Idaho settlement remains central to our regional folk history.

Notes

1. *Idaho Tri-Weekly Statesman*, 14 November 1878. I wish here to acknowledge the assistance of the library staff at the Idaho State Historical Society, particularly Elizabeth Jacox and Karin Ford, who helped track down many elusive Bigfoot references and sources.

2. *Idaho Tri-Weekly Statesman*, 16 November 1878.

3. H. N. Eliot, ed., *The History of Idaho Territory* (San Francisco: Wallace W. Eliot, 1884), pp. 144–50.

4. *Idaho Tri-Weekly Statesman*, 16 November 1878.

5. For aid in researching these points, I want to acknowledge the assistance of the Humboldt County Historical Society.

6. *La Grande Sentinel*, 3 September 1868; *Owyhee Avalanche*, 5 September 1868; and *Idaho Tri-Weekly Statesman*, 5 September 1868.

7. *Idaho Tri-Weekly Statesman*, 5 September 1868 and *The Parma Review*, 10 February 1972.

8. John E. Keller, *The Mendocino Outlaws* (Ukiah, Ca.: Mendocino County Historical Society, 1974), p. xi.

9. Ibid., p. 14.

10. Chloral hydrate is a bitter white crystalline drug, $C_2H_3Cl_3O_2$, used at that time as a hypnotic or in knockout drops.

11. Typical accounts during the period include *Idaho Tri-Weekly Statesman*, 1 January 1867, 13 June 1867, 10 October 1867, 2 June 1868, and 4 June 1868.

12. Keller, *The Mendocino Outlaws*, p. 6.

13. *Idaho Tri-Weekly Statesman*, 18 May 1880. In California, Wheeler signed many of his letters with "Caesar's _____."

14. *Idaho Tri-Weekly Statesman*, 22 June 1880. These sentiments also included Wheeler's feelings that the female is superior to the male, a curious trait considering his criminal activities. This characteristic is often attributed to the outlaw/hero of Western dime novels; indeed, a complete psychoanalytical profile of Wheeler's life would, if it were possible, likely shed a great deal of light on his Bigfoot narrative.

15. Keller, *The Mendocino Outlaws*, p. xii.

16. Ibid., p. xi and *Idaho Tri-Weekly Statesman*, 16 December 1879.

17. For example, Keller, *The Mendocino Outlaws*, p. xii, notes Wheeler's claim that his role in the Oregon robberies involved the innocent lending of money and a horse to one of the outlaws. Eyewitness testimonies in the *Idaho Tri-Weekly Statesman*, of 7 September 1868 portray Wheeler as the leader of the gang and an active participant in at least two robberies.

18. *Idaho Tri-Weekly Statesman*, 17 September 1868.

19. Keller, *The Mendocino Outlaws*, pp. 5–6.

20. Ibid., pp. xi–xii; *Idaho Tri-Weekly Statesman*, 16 December 1879; Henry L. Talkington, *Heroes and Heroic Deeds of the Pacific Northwest*, Vol. 1 (Caldwell: The Caxton Printers, Ltd., 1929), p. 158; and the *Idaho Free Press* (Nampa), 30 December 1928.

21. *Idaho Tri-Weekly Statesman*, 16 November 1878.

22. Excellent studies of tall tales and tall tale narrators include C. Richard K. Lunt, "Jones Tracey: Tall Tale Hero from Mount Desert Island," *Northwest Folklore* 10 (1968): 1–75; Roger Welsch, *Shingling the Fog and Other Plains Lies* (Chicago: Swallow Press, 1972); Vance Randolph, *We Always Lie to Strangers: Tall Tales from the Ozarks* (New York: Columbia University Press, 1951); William Hugh Jansen, *Abraham "Oregon" Smith: Pioneer, Folk Hero and Tale-Teller* (New York: Arno Press, 1977); and Gustav Henningsen, "The Art of Perpendicular Lying: Concerning a Commercial Collecting of Norwegian Sailors' Tall Tales," *Journal of the Folklore Institute* 2 (1965): 180–219. Also see Brunvand's contribution on Len Henry in this volume.

23. *Idaho Free Press*, 4 December 1966.

24. A basic introduction to general tall tale style is Jan Brunvand, *The Study of American Folklore*, orig. pub. 1968 (New York: W. W. Norton and Company, 1978), pp. 115–16.

25. *Idaho Tri-Weekly Statesman*, 16 November 1878.

26. Ibid.

27. *Idaho Tri-Weekly Statesman*, 16 December 1879 and 4 June 1880. Speculation that the tale "seems to have evolved among stage robbers imprisoned in Oregon" is offered in *Idaho State Historical Society Reference Series No. 40*, "Bigfoot," rev. ed. 1970. The Oregon location, though, is

likely incorrect as Wheeler was incarcerated, except for a brief period of time, in California.

28. The killings of the Denoiles are covered in the *Owyhee Avalanche* issues of 13 June 1868, 24 October 1867, 26 October 1867 and 17 December 1867. The best discussions of the Scotts' murders is in *The Oregonian* (Portland) on 4, 7 and 9 October 1867.

29. Jacob Ray Gregg, *Pioneer Days in Malheur County* (Los Angeles: Lorrin L. Morrison, 1950), p. 48. Gregg's account of Bigfoot's complicity in the Ward Massacre is suspect as Anderson-Wheeler's account dates Bigfoot's arrival in Idaho as 1856, or four years after the Ward massacre. It is possible, however, that Wheeler used the Ward massacre as his model for Bigfoot's first mass murder. In both events a young unmarried woman is among those killed, and in each case her death is especially gruesome.

30. See, for example, the introductory sentences to the oral texts on p. 20 and pp. 21–22.

31. The most popular example of this process is a cycle of Bigfoot narratives in which Bigfoot's son is kidnapped by soldiers and given to John Kelley, a noted violinist. Kelley, in turn, trains the boy in the art of contortion and mime. The team embarks on a successful European tour that ends with the boy's death from illness. See Dunham Wright, "One Century of Life," unpub. Mss. at Idaho State Historical Society; Dorine Goertzen, *Boise Basin Brocade* (Boise: n.p., 1960), n.p.; William J. McConnell, *Frontier Law: A Story of Vigilante Days* (New York: World Book Co., 1924), pp. 83–85; and *Early History of Idaho* (Caldwell: Caxton Printers, 1913), pp. 139–41 and 180–81.

32. Text collected by Brent Cornell from Jennie Cornell in Middleton, Idaho, on February 8, 1977. Ms. Cornell is Abner Calloway's granddaughter. The College of Idaho Folklore Archives.

33. Text collected by Sharon Lancaster from L. H. Lancaster in Caldwell, Idaho, on April 17, 1964. University of Idaho Special Collections.

34. In the decade following the 1878 *Statesman* articles, a host of related Bigfoot stories appeared. Many of these were aimed at establishing the authenticity of the "Anderson" text. These items included one man's claim that he also witnessed the slaying of Bigfoot (10 December 1878) and the discovery of the half-breed's gun buried by Wheeler (23 December 1878). Other writings capitalized on the tall tale threads; perhaps the most sensational piece appeared on 15 March 1879:

> It now appears that the remains of the bigfooted fiend who was killed by Wheeler on Reynold's Creek in 1868, were completely pertrified and then tumbled to pieces near the place where the body was hidden. Several fragments of different members have been found, leaving only the eyeball unaccounted for, and yesterday, Joe Oldham, who has had Bigfoot on the brain ever since the story was published in the STATESMAN, succeeded in finding the missing eyeball among the archives of the Sheriff's office. This orb of Bigfoot optics is an elongated spheroid of a dark brown color, weighing about five pounds, and is encircled by a groove, making it appear as if it had been worn as an ornament by some inmate of the County jail. The iris and pupil of the eye have been well preserved in the process of petrification, and by looking closely through the pupil, the image of Wheeler and Anderson can be distinctly seen through the crystalized, and now pertrified lenses, painted in miniature on the retina.

35. Most amateur and professional historians base their conclusions on the evidence presented in [Merle Wells], "Bigfoot," *Idaho State Historical Society Reference Series*, No. 40, orig. pub. 1964, rev. ed., 1970.

36. Ibid., p. 1.

37. Attempts to explain newspaper accounts of large footprint sightings offer some interesting, albeit generally unsupported, ideas. The most quoted explanation is that hostile Indians used overstuffed moccasins to terrorize their enemies, both Native American and Euro-American. See Ibid., p. 2 and *Idaho Tri-Weekly Statesman*, 13 August 1868.

38. Bill Gulick, *Snake River Country* (Caldwell, Id.: Caxton Printers, Ltd., 1971), p. 157.

39. This case is made in many publications, especially within the myth-symbol school of American Studies. The first important statement is Henry Nash Smith, *Virgin Land: The American West as Symbol and Myth* (Cambridge: Harvard University Press, 1950). Recent works extending Nash's hypotheses to, respectively, Europe and wider segments of the American population, are Ray A. Billington, *Land of Savagery, Land of Promise: The European Image of the American Frontier* (New York: W. W. Norton and Company, 1981) and Robert Berkhofer, *The White Man's Indian* (New York: Alfred A. Knopf, 1978).

40. The best discussions of this promotional scheme and its impact on local legends are Annie Laurie Bird's *My Home Town* (Caldwell: The Caxton Printers, Ltd., 1978), pp. 70–74; *Idaho State Historical Society Reference Series*, No. 39 (1966); and "Was 'Chief Nampuh' Legend a Festival Publicity Stunt?" *Idaho Free Press* (Nampa), 4 May 1953. Nampa may draw its name from a Northern Paiute leader still recalled in Paiute legends; see [Sven Liljeblad] "Nampa," *Prospector* 5 (1975), p. 6.

41. See references in Note 11.

42. *Owyhee Avalanche*, 1 January 1866.

43. Most of these military outposts were established in the mid-1860s and abandoned by 1870.

44. *Idaho Tri-Weekly Statesman*, 14 August 1868.

45. *Owyhee Avalanche*, 17 February 1866. No bounties were ever paid.

46. The "Snake" designation was used by early citizens in indiscriminate reference to all Shoshone-speaking individuals in the Snake River country.

47. *The Weekly Oregonian*, 23 February 1867.

48. *Owyhee Avalanche*, 14 April 1867. Exactly six months later, the *Idaho Tri-Weekly Statesman*, offered "fifty dollars for the big toe of this babe of the woods," or one hundred dollars for his "top-knot."

49. The "Nigger" insult appears in the Anderson-Wheeler text and many narratives in the popular literature. Few oral texts include this reference. The competitor's derogatory remark could be viewed as sufficient reason for Bigfoot's violent reaction, yet only a few narratives imply that the half-breed's killing of his rival was justified. In these texts, all of which are recent and perhaps shaped by a sense of the white man's guilt, Bigfoot is presented as an Indian Robin Hood, taking from the whites to help his people keep their land and dignity. For example, see Rafe Gibbs, *Beckoning the Bold* (Moscow, Id.: The University of Idaho Press, 1976), pp. 110–12.

50. Text collected by Rutha Mims from Sharon Ireton in Mountain Home, Idaho, on April 2, 1973. The College of Idaho Folklore Archives.

51. Robert Froman, "The Giant and the Gunslinger," *True: The Man's Magazine* 24:9 (September 1957): 58.

52. This character type appears mainly in areas containing inaccessible or remote locations, especially rugged mountains, desert, jungle, or swamps. The other Bigfoot, or Sasquatch, is sighted mainly in the remote Northwest; the Jersey devil noted in publications of Henry Beck and Herbert Halpert lives in the pine swamps along the New Jersey shore.

53. Virtually all stereotypes of Native Americans focus on a culture/nature tension although some prototypes, especially the romantic Noble Savage image, incorporated an idealized view of nature's influence that placed the Native American close to purity and Edenlike innocence. Discussions of the Noble Savage theme are found in the references cited in Note 39. No oral Bigfoot texts portray this figure as a Noble Savage.

54. Text collected by Donna Sylvester from Suzanne Hayes, Riggins, Idaho, on January 30,1973. The College of Idaho Folklore Archives.

55. Text collected by J. Sanford Rikoon from D. W. in Nampa, Idaho, on April 7, 1982. Idaho Folklife Archives.

56. Cross-cultural instances of this characteristic as it is given to "wild men" are noted in Gordon R. Strasenburgh, "Perceptions and Images of the Wild Man," *Northwest Anthropological Research Notes* 9:2 (1975): 288.

57. Louie Attebery places Bigfoot's symbolic significance in similar duality relationships in his "Folklore of the Lower Snake Valley: A Regional Study," unpub. Ph.D. dissertation, University of Denver, 1961, p. 43.

58. Stith Thompson's *Motif-Index of Folk Literature*, orig. pub. 1935–38 (Bloomington: Indiana University Press, 1956) presents international parallels to several motifs found in Bigfoot texts, including F681.9 "Man who is too heavy for any horse runs faster than horseback riders," F696 "Marvelous swimmer," and F681.6 "Marvelous runner catches wild game on the run."

59. Collected by Diana Doan from Eve Owen in Caldwell, Idaho, on January 10, 1973. The College of Idaho Folklore Archives.

60. Collected by J. Sanford Rikoon from Jim Huntley of Marsing, Idaho, on May 17, 1982. Idaho Folklife Archives.

61. See Note 58. This international motif is traceable to Italian novella. References to another Bigfoot narrative with the same motif are found in [Merle Wells], "Bigfoot," and A. B. Meacham, *Wigwam and War-Path* (Boston, 1875), p. 231.

62. Text collected by Julette Cordon, [1943?], Works Progress Administration collection, Idaho State University Archives.

63. It is important to note that Bigfoot's killer, whether John Wheeler or another man, almost always works alone. The one-to-one confrontation with the white man victorious supports, of course, the individualistic ideal of the Western hero and the superiority of the Euro-American male.

64. Ken Swanson, Idaho State Historical Society, is due thanks for instruction on the technology of the Henry rifle. One Bigfoot chronicler, Bennett Williams, significantly describes the Henry as "the atomic bomb weapon of its day." In "Bigfoot's Last Fight," *Statewide* (Boise), 7 October 1948.

65. *Idaho Tri-Weekly Statesman*, 16 November 1878.

66. Text collected by Tony McNevin from Lydie Swinyer of Salmon, Idaho in 1964. Ms. Swinyer learned this narrative from a son of Governor Shoup. University of Idaho Special Collections.

67. *The Parma Review*, 15 August 1974. Other information on the festivities is found in Ibid., 22 August 1974 and *The Idaho Statesman*, 21 August 1974.

Appendix

The appendix contains the complete narrative of Bigfoot transcribed from the original text in the *Idaho Tri-Weekly Statesman*, issues of November 14 and 16, 1878.

THE BIGFOOTED FIEND. A Thrilling Account of the Career of the Notorious Indian Bigfoot and the hand to hand conflict between him and his slayer, J. W. Wheeler. How and when the Terror of Idaho was Killed. BY AN EYEWITNESS OF THE SCENE.

The following narrative will no doubt be interesting to many of the old pioneers of Idaho, who may have had dear relatives, or friends murdered and scalped by the red-handed savages that once infested Idaho Territory to such an extent that the daring and hardy miner was not safe in wandering from his tent, or the teamster from his wagon without his trusty rifle and revolver in hand. Whole trains of emigrants — composed of men, women and children — were slaughtered without mercy; the bones of many of whom were left bleaching on the Boise and Snake rivers, testifying to the deadly hatred of the Snake Indians to the whites.

The leader, and the most desperate of all Indians between Oregon and Utah, was one known as Bigfoot, who, like a gigantic monster, as he truly was, roamed over the plains and mountains of Idaho, with a small band of picked warriors, committing murders and depredations. They ranged from Grande Ronde valley, in Eastern Oregon, to the heads of the Owyhee and Weiser rivers in Idaho. Many stories were told of the giant size of this noted Indian desperado, and about the enormous size of his foot. Whenever a depredation was committed, those large moccasin tracks were certain to be found among the others. He never had but a few Indians with him. While the other Indians were sometimes mounted on ponies, he was always on foot. One reason for this, perhaps, was that no ordinary horse could carry him; and the following account will show that he had but little use for a horse; for the rapidity with which he traveled from place to place was a wonder and surprise to all settlers on the Snake and Boise rivers. One day his fresh tracks would be seen on the Weiser, and the next day he would be heard of on the Owyhee — 75 or 80 miles distant. Once he was chased by Wheeler, Frank Johnson, and a man named Cook, who were all mounted, while Bigfoot, as usual, was traveling on foot with two other Indians. Wheeler and his two companions were camped near the head of the Malheur River. In the night their horses gave indications that Indians were prowling near the camp, so a close watch was kept up until daylight, when, on examination of the ground, it was discovered that old Bigfoot and two other Indians had been within a few yards of the camp during the night. Upon making this discovery all were excited — all were eager for the chase. Bigfoot had been treading on dangerous ground. Here were three as cool and determined men as ever set foot out west, all three of them crack marksmen, and all well accustomed to Indian fighting, and three better horsemen could not have been found in the Territory. Dispatching a hasty breakfast, all mounted their horses and took the trail; Frank Johnson remarking, "Well, Boys, we will make it hot for old Bigfoot today." Wheeler replied laughingly, "Yes, and it will make it hot for our horses to catch up with that old feather-headed devil, if he can travel as far in a day as Enoch Fruit says he can." Enoch Fruit was a noted horse-thief, who once kept a ferry at Farewell Bend, on Snake River, and he had often met Bigfoot and had often talked and traded with him. It was through Fruit that the fact was first known that Bigfoot could speak English, and that it came to be believed that the bigfooted fiend belonged to some other tribe of Indians than the one he was found with, which, in time, proved to be true.

The three men rode on in hot pursuit. A fierce ride of two hours brought them in sight of the Indians, who were going at a rapid rate toward the Snake River. All hands now prepared in earnest for the chase. The big Spanish spurs were applied without mercy to the already bleeding flanks of their faithful and spirited horses. The two smaller Indians were soon overtaken and shot down. They made a determined and desperate resistance, but their horses and arrows and old style guns proved of no avail before the Henry rifle in the hands of men they now had to deal with. By the time these two Indians were dispatched old Bigfoot was at least a mile ahead; running and jumping the sagebrush like a deer; increasing the distance between him and his pursuers where the ground was toughest and losing where the ground was better. The exciting chase was kept up in this way for over thirty miles with about the same result, until at last the huge monster reached the banks of Snake River, where he plunged into the stream and struck out swimming for the opposite shore. He proved himself to be an excellent swimmer as well as a skillful runner, carrying his gun and ammunition above water. The faithful horses were now put down to their very best speed, but only reached the bank in time for their riders to see, much to their disappointment and disgust, the tall and dripping form of Bigfoot clambering out of the water on the other bank. Johnson shouted: "Boys, look there! Don't Bigfoot beat hell?" Cook said, "Yes, and he beat our horses, too." Wheeler quietly remarked that if old Bigfoot did not have the rheumatism after running so far and then swimming that cold river that he deserved to be remembered as a living specimen of health and endurance. In the meantime, Bigfoot having gained the bank of the river and shaken himself, and after giving an unearthly yell, shouted out in plain English: "Come on over, come over, you damned cowards," and then dived into the thick willows. The poor bleeding and foaming horses were completely fagged out; so were their riders; for many times during the day the horses had plunged into badger holes, falling and pitching their reckless riders over their heads. But those were the boys who could not be stopped by trifles; fear and failure were alike unknown to them. It was of course, owing to rocky gul-

lies and rough ground that Bigfoot baffled the horsemen and made his wonderful escape.

Well, the next move was to go some five miles down the river and cross at the nearest ferry, which was then kept by Mr. Packwood, and then come up the river and try to strike the trail of the Indian again. This they did, following his enormous tracks for a few miles to the mouth of the Weiser River. Here, they found that the object of their pursuit had caught two of the largest sized salmon and that he had built a fire and roasted them and had eaten every morsel of them, leaving the bones picked clean. He had then taken the back track and had gone to the Snake River and swam back to the side from which he had been chased.

Night came on and found three of the angriest, sorest, and hungriest men who had ever lain down on the banks of the Snake River. But instead of growling and complaining over their disappointment as most men would have done, the evening was spent in joking and in recounting the many incidents of the day. It was agreed by all that old Bigfoot could outrun and outwind any Indian on record, and that he was the largest man and had the largest foot by half that they had ever seen. That he was a dear lover of fish was evident from the skeleton he had left at his last campfire. Frank Johnson said that he had a mind to have imported a first-class thoroughbred racehorse that would be able to run that old yellow-legged "cuss" down, or send for a pack of bloodhounds. Mr. Cook declared that if Bigfoot should happen to be as fond of dogmeat as he was of fish, that he would eat up a small pack of hounds at one meal, then swim the Snake River a time or two and swallow Johnson's imported horse.

Next morning the chase was for the time abandoned; Wheeler remarking that he would get even on that old son-of-a-cricket-eater if it took him five years, for his having caused him to ruin his fine horse and almost breaking his neck. This resolve was realized, but not until nearly two years afterwards, during which time Bigfoot sent many a poor unfortunate miner and teamster to that land from which no traveler returns.

Bigfoot's favorite field of slaughter was between Boise and Silver City, where the road passes through a narrow defile between table rocks or bluffs, a few miles south of Snake River. It was among these bluffs that this noted chief and his braves lurked and picked off many of Idaho's first settlers. Scarcely a week passed that someone was not killed while traveling to or from the Owyhee country. It was near this place that Bigfoot afterwards met his death in a way that he least expected, just in sight of the spot where he had murdered Mr. Ulman Lamon, a man named Baker, and a partner of Charles Adams. He had also shot Charles Adams through the hand, and had killed a score of others whose names I do not now remember; but the last man known to have been killed by Bigfoot and his little band was a man named Jarvis, who was on his way from Boise Valley to Owyhee with a load of eggs and vegetables. A Chinaman was also killed at the same time who was riding with Jarvis. This occurred in 1868, just a short time before Bigfoot was himself sent to the happy hunting grounds by Wheeler. It thus appears that Jarvis was Bigfoot's last victim before he met his own fate and found more than his match, which was no easy matter, but like all other of his kind he was fated at last to find his man.

As I am, perhaps, the only white man now living — unless Wheeler is still alive — who knows how or when this noted Chief Bigfoot met his death, I will give as true and faithful an account of the thrilling and deadly encounter as possible and the reasons why it was kept secret from the world so long.

In the spring of 1868, I was working at the carpenter's trade in Silver City, Idaho. It was at the time of the great lawsuit and the pitched battle which was fought over the Golden Chariot quartz hole, in which many lives were lost on both sides and which resulted in the death of the two owners of the disputed ground, namely Marion More and Samuel Lockhart. The whole town was in an uproar and a terrible state of excitement existed. Everybody went armed to the teeth. Governor Ballard resolved to place the town under martial law, and many came over from Boise City to assist in the somewhat dangerous undertaking. Among those who came I noticed a tall, fine looking young man of rather slight but handsome build with small hands and feet. He had dark brown hair and a smooth face, with dark steel gray eyes expressive of intelligence and a kind heart. Though there was something striking in the appearance of the man, little did I think that he could look death in the face with a smile or without the slightest change of countenance, but such indeed was the character of the man. I was made acquainted with Wheeler by Capt. Hatch, who was also a carpenter and a refined gentleman. He knew Wheeler well, having been on a prospecting tour with him, and had also mined near him or with him at one time. Wheeler was a good-hearted fellow and was the life of the camp and of every circle into which he came; but he was at the same time one of the bravest and most determined men in the Territory. He was as strong and active as a panther, and a better marksman than any man he ever met in his life. Though a peaceable and temperate man, the desperadoes all knew him, and never offered to infringe upon his rights. This was the last time I saw Wheeler, until I met him on the scene where the terrible combat – Bigfoot's last fight – took place. This happened in the later part of July, 1868. I was going from Silver City to Boise City, traveling alone with a two-horse wagon, when near the dangerous pass where so many had been killed, I being unarmed, concluded to lay over and let my horses graze until I should have company through the canyon; so I foolishly turned my horses loose and set myself to cooking something to eat. While I was thus engaged, the horses got frightened at something and ran off leaving me on foot and alone and frightened half to death. I followed the horses tracks and found that they had gone down Reynold's creek in the direction of the massacre ground. As the creek runs through this bluff of rocks within a few hundred yards of where the road does, I followed them and found that they had started through the canyon, and I had just turned back, afraid to go farther, when, to my horror and surprise, I looked across the creek and saw three Indians coming at full speed. They were painted and feathered, and as they were coming directly toward me, I felt certain that they saw me and I thought my time had come. The tall and terrible looking monster, who could be no other than Bigfoot himself, was some fifty yards ahead of another Indian, while the third was about an equal distance behind the second one. I stood paralyzed with fear. The only chance I saw left was to hide behind the rocks and there await my fate, which I felt certain would in a few minutes be death; so I crouched down behind a ledge of rocks and bid a last farewell to home and friends as I then thought, expecting that in a few minutes my dripping scalp would be hanging to the belt of the most horrible looking monster I had ever beheld. It would be useless for me to attempt to describe my feelings at this moment. In less than a minute old Bigfoot came thundering along like an old buffalo bull within less than thirty yards of me, but did not halt, making straight for the road which was

near us. I looked and saw the stage full of passengers with several females among the number.

[Second installment, *Idaho Tri-Weekly Statesman*, November 16, 1878]

Somewhat to my relief I now discovered that it was the stage and not myself which was the object of Bigfoot's attention. He had evidently resolved to head the stage off and murder the driver and the passengers. He was destined, however, never to do any more scalping on this side of the "dark river." When the Indian who followed next the Chief was nearly opposite my hiding place my blood was chilled by the crack of a rifle which dropped this Indian dead within twenty yards of me. At the report of the gun old Bigfoot jumped behind a large rock and the hindmost Indian broke back over the hill and was not seen again. For a moment all was quiet. I saw Charley Barnes, the noted stage driver, throw the silk gracefully to his horses, as was his habit on entering the canyon; he and his passengers all unconscious of the terrible fate they had just escaped. I afterwards learned that among the passengers were Judge Roseborough, Charley Douglas, the gambler, and Mrs. Record and her daughter. Mr. Record and family were then keeping the stage station and hotel at the 15 mile house, between Boise City and Snake River. There was also among the passengers a young lady named Lib Gardner. These with Charley Barnes, the driver, made up the little company of intended victims. Little did they think that there was one so near them in such a plight as I was, who dared not move or ask for aid, and that the most dreadful and bloody encounter was about to take place that had ever been witnessed by any of us. Those few minutes seemed ages to me. I knew that an Indian had been killed near me; but by whom, or from what direction I could form no idea. I knew not what best to do. From Bigfoot's actions it was evident that he thought the report of the gun came from a tree surrounded by a small clump of willows near the creek some 80 yards distant from where he stood. The sequel proved that he was right. A few minutes after the stage had passed out of sight, Bigfoot commenced practicing a bit of strategy that was new to me. All that I could do was to lie still in dread silence and watch his movements. First he would crawl to one side of the large rock behind which he was hiding, then he would crawl to the other side of the rock and cautiously peep around the side of the rock; but no one shot at him. All was dead quietude. He would then put his ear to the ground and listen, but could not hear the slightest noise. At last he tried another plan of escape. He tied a large bunch of sagebrush to his back and started to crawl away; and to my great horror he was advancing directly towards the spot where I lay hidden behind a ledge of rocks. He came slowly and gently towards me. I was undecided whether to remain where I was a while longer or jump and run towards the clump of willows which Bigfoot had been watching so long, and take the chances of finding a white man. If I remained where I was much longer Bigfoot, who had not yet seen me, could not fail to find me. But this terrible state of suspense was soon brought to an end. When Bigfoot had crawled over about half the distance which had separated his first hiding place from mine, I heard a clear voice ring out on the mountain air in cool deliberate tones, saying, "get up from there, Bigfoot, you old feather-headed, leather-bellied coward. I can see you crawling off like a snake. This is one time that you did not get even a woman's scalp. Here is a scalp, come down and get mine you coward." At this Bigfoot sprang to his feet and leveled a large double-barreled rifle at the willows, and said: "You coward, me no coward. You come out I'll scalp you too." At this Wheeler sprang from among the willows in plain view, saying, "Here I am; now sail in, old rooster." Both men fired at almost the same instant. Bigfoot staggered, but recovered and fired again, and then threw his gun down and started to run toward the dead Indian. He ran but a few yards when another shot caused him to reel again, but he succeeded in reaching the spot where the dead Indian lay, and picking up the gun left by the latter where he had fallen, he leveled it toward Wheeler and fired again just at the moment that Wheeler's gun sent another unerring bullet into his powerful frame. Bigfoot again staggered and came very near falling but again, recovered and drawing a knife gave an unearthly whoop which almost froze my blood and then started toward Wheeler. He had gone but a few yards when another shot staggered him and then another. So rapidly did Wheeler fire that a constant blaze seemed to issue from his rifle. Each shot told that it was doing its part in the deadly work. I was dumb with fear: apprehending that after all the Indian might succeed in reaching Wheeler and then grasp him in his powerful clutches. Wheeler never moved from the spot where he stood, but handling his gun with extraordinary skill continued to fire until at last when within 30 yards of him the huge red demon fell with a broken leg to rise no more. Wheeler, however, emptied the whole sixteen shots into him and then without moving out of his tracks reloaded his rifle and said: "How do you like the way my gun shoots, old boy? I'll bet my scalp against yours that you don't scalp any more white men in this canyon very soon." Bigfoot cried out in plain English: "Don't shoot me any more. You have killed me." Wheeler walked up near the Indian, and pulling out an ivory-handled revolver, gazed for a moment at his fallen foe, then shouted to me: "Come down, whoever you are; there is no danger now." I went to the spot and found Bigfoot bleeding from twelve wounds, both legs and one arm broken. The Indian asked for water when Wheeler said: "Hold on until I break that other arm; then I'll give you a drink." Bigfoot said, "Well, do it quick and give me a drink and let me die." Wheeler leveled his pistol, and at the report the arm fell useless to the ground. This, to some may seem cruel, but I was yet afraid to go near this powerful and desperate savage monster. Wheeler went down to the willows and brought up his canteen full of water, and placed it to the mouth of the Indian, who drank it all. Bigfoot then said he wished he had some whiskey, when Wheeler said he had a small bottle of alcohol and ammonia which he always carried in case of snakebite; that he could have that if he thought it would do him any good. Bigfoot said, "Give it to me, quick! for I am getting blind." Wheeler gave him a pint flask filled with the strong fluid mixed with a little water. The Indian drank it every drop, and then said, "I am sick and blind;" and then fell back apparently dead. After a few minutes, he revived, and said that he was better, and that he wished us to wash the dust and paint from his face and see what a 'good-looking' man he was. We complied with his request, and, to our surprise, we found a fine-looking face, with the handsomest set of teeth we ever beheld. He had large black, but wicked looking eyes. His complexion had been almost white, but was now, of course, badly tanned. He had a heavy shock of long black hair, somewhat inclined to be kinky. He was of enormous size and such hands—and especially feet, I never saw on

any mortal before or since. He soon began to be quite talkative, and expressed a wish that we would make him one promise. Wheeler asked him what it was. He asked that we should not send him nor take him to Boise City after he died; but to drag him in among the willows and pile some rocks upon him and to lay his old gun by his side. "If you will promise me this," said he, "I shall die satisfied." Wheeler told him that if he would tell him who he was and where he came from, he would perhaps promise and do what he wished; but that he must answer all the questions he was asked, and tell the truth. Bigfoot then said:

"I have been a very bad man; and if I tell you all that I have done, I am afraid you will not do what I have asked of you." Wheeler said: "I know you have been a bad man; but if you will tell me everything, I will not tell anyone that you are dead, nor tell anything about you." When Wheeler said this Bigfoot seemed to brighten up and said: "Now, do keep your promise and I will tell you my whole history and all that I have gone through, if I can only live long enough to do so." Wheeler said: "I have been assured by many good and prominent citizens of Boise City that if any one killed you and brought your feet and your scalp to Fort Boise, that at least $1,000 would be paid for them; for you have done a great deal of mischief; killed many white people, and everybody thinks that you were one of the party that killed Mrs. Scott and her husband on Burnt River last fall, as your big tracks were found next day near the scene of the murder, as they have always been found when white people have been killed by Indians in this part of the country. I have now been out here four days waiting for you and the mosquitoes have nearly eaten me up while hiding in the willows; but now if it will do you any good I will hide you, but I will break your gun so that other Indians may not use it again.

BIGFOOT'S HISTORY AND CONFESSION

The following is Bigfoot's account of himself and his career, taken down just as it was recited to Wheeler and myself.

"I was born in the Cherokee Nation. My father was a white man named Archer Wilkinson. He was hanged for murder in the Cherokee Nation when I was a small boy. My mother was part Cherokee and part Negro, so I was told. She was a good Christian woman. My name is Starr Wilkinson. I was thus named after Thomas Starr, a noted desperado in the nation. I was always called Bigfooted Wilkinson as long ago as I can remember. The boys always made fun of me when I was a boy because I was so large for my age and had such big feet. I had a bad temper and got to drinking when quite young and got to be so strong that when anyone would call me by my nickname I would fight him. In this way I came near killing several with my fist. I found out that I would soon be killed if I remained in that country; so I ran away from home and went to Tilaqua, then the capital of the Cherokee Nation. There I fell in with some emigrants, who were going to Oregon in 1856, and drove a team for my board across the plains. The folks I traveled with were very kind to me. I fell in love with a young lady of the company, who thought a good deal of me until we fell in with a train from New York. Along with these new people was an artist, who was a smart goodlooking fellow. He soon cut me out. After this the young lady would hardly notice me or speak to me. I knew then that he had told her something bad about me. He made fun of me several times; and while we were camped near the Goose Creek Mountains, he and I went out one morning to hunt up the stock. We went to the bank of Snake River. I asked him what he intended to do when he got to Oregon. He said he was going to marry my girl and settle down. I told him he should not do so for I thought I had the best right to her. He laughed at me and said: "Do you suppose she would marry a big-footed nigger like you, and throw off on a good-looking fellow like me?" This made me mad, and I told him I was no Negro; and that if he called me that again I would kill him. So he drew his gun on me and repeated it again. I was unarmed, but started at him. He shot me in the side, but had not hurt me much. So I grabbed him and threw him down and choked him to death, then threw him into the Snake River, took his gun, pistol, and knife, and ran off into the hills.

"The emigrants did not break camp for a few days. They were, perhaps, hunting for us. Some of them then went on to Oregon; but the family that I had been traveling with went back with some others to Salt Lake, where they wintered. I made my way to the Boise River, where I found a French trader and trapper and a man named Joe Lewis, who had been with the Indians for many years. This Joe Lewis was one who helped massacre Dr. Whitman and many others near old Fort Walla Walla in 1847. He was a bad man, but he was a good friend to me when I needed a friend. So I went with him and joined the Indians and have remained with them ever since. In 1857 I went with Lewis and some Indians near the emigrant road for the purpose of stealing stock from the emigrants. In one of our raids I found cattle that I knew had belonged to the family I crossed the plains with the year before. So I determined to go to the train and see if my girl was with them and try to get her to run off with me. I found her but she was very mad with me, as were all the rest. They said they thought that I had killed Mr. Hart, the young artist, and that I ought to be hanged for it. They told me to leave the camp. I told the girl that if she did not have me that she would be sorry for it before she got to Oregon. I had to leave, but was determined to have revenge; so I took Joe Lewis and thirty Indians and followed them down Boise River to where it empties into Snake River and massacred them and ran off all their stock. I and several Indians ravished the girl before we killed her. I am sorry for that now, for she was a good girl, but it is too late now to be sorry. I was mad and foolish. I have been in several other massacres. I helped to kill that Scott family on Burnt River. We wanted their horses. I also helped to kill an officer and took his wife prisoner last fall. The officer was on his way to Camp Lyon. His wife got sick, had a child and could not ride; so some of the Indians killed her. I had a squaw for a wife and when Jeff Stanford was out with a lot of men fighting us they killed my wife and carried off my little boy. Since that time I have done all the mischief I could, and am glad of it." Wheeler here asked Bigfoot what became of Joe Lewis. He said that Lewis was shot by a man who carried the express from Auburn to Boise in 1862. While Lewis was trying to steal some horses on the Payette River one night the expressman shot across the river with Buckshot, hitting Lewis in the side and wounding Bigfoot in the leg. As it was dark and neither of the wounded men spoke, the expressman did not know that any one had been hit. "Joe whispered to me," continued Bigfoot, "that he was hurt bad; so I took him on my back and started to run with him, but he soon died and I covered him up in the sand on the bank of the Payette River where he was never found by the whites; and that was the last of poor Joe and I hope you will do that much for me." Wheeler said: "All right, Mr. Wilkinson. I guess I will do it, as I am from the Cherokee Nation myself, and have a little Cherokee blood in my veins, I will not refuse your dying re-

quest." When Wheeler said this and assured him that he would not take his body or any portion of it to the fort, Bigfoot actually wept and asked to know Wheeler's name, and said: "You are a brave man, and I know you will keep your word. I am a brave man too, but you shot a little too quick for me, and you had the best gun and you have killed me. Your shot struck me just as I was pulling the trigger, else I think I should have killed you, as I hardly ever missed anything I ever shot at. I got my old gun at the massacre in 1857. I do not know how many men I have killed with it. I knew I was killed when your first shot struck me; for I could not see to shoot well afterwards."

Bigfoot was throwing up blood every few minutes and bleeding fast from his numerous wounds, half of which would have proved sufficient to kill any ordinary man instantly, but he was possessed of so much vigor and vitality that he lived for nearly two hours after receiving so many mortal wounds. Wheeler asked him where the Indians got their ammunition. He said that some of it was obtained from friendly Indians, who visited the towns and military posts for that purpose. Bigfoot continued: "Nearly all of my little band of warriors are killed off. There are but five left who have been running with me. You have just killed one of the bravest of the band. He has been one of my head braves ever since the Indians recognized me as the leader of the brave little band. His father is the old medicine man, and he told us when we left not to go on this trip for he had dreamed about us. He dreamed that there was a large snake secreted in these bluffs that had a white man's head on, and had a medicine gun; that when he pointed it at the Indians they could not see how to shoot and that after killing them he broke their guns to pieces. He wept when we left camp and said that he would never see us again until we met in the spirit land. He was right. If I had minded him I would not have got killed." Wheeler said: "Well, if you meet the old medicine gentleman in the spirit land tell him he was a good hand at dreaming, if he did call me a snake." Wheeler then asked him where the rest of the Indians were camped. Bigfoot said: "This is something I cannot tell; but I will tell you anything you may ask me. There are but few of them left; and now that we are killed, the rest will soon go into the fort and it would do you no good to kill them. The little band I run with call themselves Piutes; the rest call themselves Fish Indians, because they live by fishing on the Malheur and Snake rivers and do not mix with the Lake Piutes and Bannocks. The other Indians are not friendly towards us, and I care nothing about them; but our little band have been brave Indians. They have always treated me well, and I do not wish to betray them as the last act of a bad me." Wheeler said: "Bully for you, Wilkinson. I think more of you than I did before, for you are not a traitor if you have been a bad man otherwise." Wheeler asked him how tall he was and how much he thought he weighed. Bigfoot said he did not know; for he had grown very much since he joined the Indians; that when he left the whites he was but nineteen years old; that he then measured 6 feet 6 and a half inches in height and weighed 255 pounds. "But I know," said he, "that I must weigh at least 300 pounds now, and there is not a pound of fat on me," which was true. He was a model of strength and endurance. I had a tape line and rule in my pocket with which I took the following exact measurements of this wonderful being: "Around the chest, 59 inches; height 6 feet 8½ inches, length of foot, 17½ inches; around the ball of the foot, 18 inches, around the widest part of the hand, 18 inches." I am now confident that he must have weighed at least three hundred pounds, and all bone and sinew; not a pound of surplus flesh about him. We asked him if he knew how strong he was. He said: "No; but I was very powerful. I have had as many as ten Indians at me trying to throw me down, but never succeeded. I have many times run all day long without being hurt by it; but I have suffered a great deal from hunger, for this is a poor game country." Wheeler asked him if he knew any other white men besides Enoch Fruit, who had been mixed up with the Indians. Bigfoot said that there was a man called Washoe Charley, who had lived with the Indians for a while, and then stole all their best horses and ran off to the whites again. He then began to tell us about assisting in the killing of a man named Jordan, who he said had helped to kill Indian squaws and children because some other Indians had stolen his horses. He said that Jordan was a very bad man, but that he was a good fighter. His voice here failed him, and he fell back saying, "Everything is getting dark," and lay silent for a while, then spoke in husky, rapid tones. "Look! Look! the soldiers are after me! I must go. quick! quick!" He then straightened out and died without a struggle.

We both stood and gazed at the dead body for a moment of silence. Two hours before, this gigantic chief had struck terror to my heart, and now he lay lifeless and harmless at my feet, all covered with blood and the ground all around him saturated by the crimson tide. This being the first time I had ever witnessed such a scene, the reader must be left to imagine my feelings. Wheeler talked the whole affair over as unconcernedly as though nothing unusual had happened, remarking that according to Bigfoot's story, that he was but 31 years old, though he looked to be much older, and that he was quite large enough to be one hundred years old. I asked Wheeler what we should do next. He said: "We will first break their guns to pieces, unless you want one of them." I told him they would be useless to me, as I could not shoot. So Wheeler said, "In order that the old medicine man may not be made out a liar, I will break them over this rock." This he did, and bent

the barrels so that they could not be used again. We then went and looked up my horses, put a rope around Bigfoot's body, to which we hitched the horses, and dragged the body some one hundred and fifty yards to the creek, and put Bigfoot's old broken gun by his side. We then threw some brush and rocks upon him, hid the other broken gun, threw away what little ammunition the dead Indians had left, and left the other Indian lying where he had fallen. Wheeler said the other Indians would probably come and burn what they could find, if they were not afraid to try it.

We left the spot and went to my wagon, where we had something to eat, as Wheeler was very hungry, having eaten nothing for two days. We then started for Boise City, where we arrived the next day. Wheeler made me promise to say nothing about the affair, as he had given his word to Bigfoot, and was resolved not to break the promise he had made. I left Idaho a few days afterward for Nevada; but I still have in my tool chest one of Bigfoot's moccasins, which is a curiosity well worth looking at.

I have never heard of Wheeler since, and never until now mentioned the affair to any one. The day I left Boise City I saw Wheeler very neatly dressed, sitting and conversing quietly with some gentlemen. He did not appear at all like the man who, three days before, had met and killed in fair combat two of the most desperate of all the braves of Idaho, and a deed which would have been proudly boasted of by almost any other man, was kept a secret from the world by the singular but brave Wheeler.

As I have now given as truthful an account of this whole affair as possible, I hope that after so many years have passed that I have done no one any harm in telling what I knew of the terrible encounter between these two fierce and determined men. If the reader has been interested in the account I have given, I am amply repaid for the trouble of writing.

Folklore in Regional Literature: Carol Brink's *Buffalo Coat*

Mary E. Reed

One of the values of folklife research is the light it can shed on literary works. The relationship between folklore and literature is close and complicated: Shakespeare made use of rituals and bawdy songs, Mark Twain's Huckleberry Finn *is full of the superstitions of the southern Midwest, Longfellow's "Hiawatha" mixes Algonquin legends with the metrical pattern of a Finnish epic, and Seba Smith's literary ballad of "Young Charlotte" has entered the repertoire of many traditional folksingers. Two important studies of the development of American literature, Constance Rourke's* American Humor *(1931) and Daniel Hoffman's* Form and Fable in American Fiction *(1961), demonstrate how the use of folklore can help ground a narrative in local culture and at the same time enhance its universal significance. Carol Ryrie Brink's works incorporate stories, beliefs, and attitudes from her family and neighbors in Moscow, Idaho. Though her children's books, like* Caddie Woodlawn, *have remained popular, her adult fiction has been rather neglected. Mary Reed indicates in this article that Brink's* Buffalo Coat *is a significant regional novel, in which a cluster of local legends are reshaped into a powerful and coherent narrative.*

Mary Reed is a free-lance historian from Pullman, Washington, who is investigating the role of women in early Western settlements. She is also currently working with historian Keith Petersen on the history of six communities in the Palouse area of eastern Washington and northern Idaho.

*T*hose who are interested in the history and traditions of Moscow, Idaho, are fortunate to have a novel by a local author who uses stories of actual events which were passed around while she was living there. Carol Ryrie Brink's *Buffalo Coat* is an example of how history and folklore can be skillfully used to create excellent regional fiction. The novel is based on stories of Moscow which Brink heard repeatedly during her childhood in the early 1900s. The existence of these narratives in the oral history collection of the Latah County Historical Society (begun in 1973) proves their persistence in popular memory. Recent taped interviews with the author provide insights into the process of molding folklore and history into fiction.[1] These interviews, completed in 1981, reveal the author's sensitivity to her local roots and her close relationship to and respect for the community. A further comparison of the historical facts (as far as they can be determined) with the popular versions of events and with the author's interpretation suggests the operation of two selective processes. Oral storytellers emphasize particular details and assign motives according to the standards of their community. Likewise the author selects details in an attempt to shape the patterns of choice and circumstance into art.

Brink's success as a regional novelist is partly due to the inspiration of her grandmother, Caroline Woodhouse Watkins, a formidable storyteller who raised Carol after the death of her parents in 1900 and 1904. Caroline Watkins, widowed in 1901 by the murder of her husband, Dr. William Watkins, led thereafter a quiet life. Despite her retiring nature, she avidly read the local newspapers and kept abreast of local affairs. Gram Watkins, according to several accounts, possessed an uncommon ability to recall much of her childhood in Wisconsin. Without brothers, sisters, or parents, Carol Brink relied to an unusual extent on her grandmother's stories and adult companionship for her entertainment. In her autobiographical novel, *Snow in the River*, she recalls how she sat quietly drinking up stories of the past. "I was a quiet spectator, listening and watching, smelling and tasting, storing the troubles and gladnesses of other people away in my mind beside my own. To sit unnoticed at a table where grown people conversed or told old tales had almost never bored me."[2]

Although Carol was surrounded by adult company and conversations, Gram Watkins made a special contribution to Carol's development as a writer because of her talent for relating a story. Unlike Elsie Watkins, an aunt who lived in the household and helped raise Carol, Caroline Watkins knew how to pick out the dramatic elements and establish a relationship between incidents.[3] Unlike the gossip, the conversationalist, or the jokester, the raconteur searches for meaning in the material, perhaps a moral or a thread between events and human characteristics. It is the storyteller who manipulates the pace or the texture of the story to retain the audience's attention.

Brink's most famous book for children, *Caddie Woodlawn*, is based on her grandmother's stories.[4] In the dedication she remembers Gram, "whose tales of her childhood in Wisconsin gave a lonely little girl many happy hours." In the preface Brink acknowledges her debt to her grandmother, the Caddie of the title. "She has a wonderful memory and she has always known just which things made the best stories and how to tell them in the best way."[5] The author explains that she only recorded her grandmother's stories, keeping as close as possible to the original versions; the skillful pacing and realistic dialogue indicate both Caroline Watkins' and Carol Brink's gift for storytelling.

An example of Watkins' influence on her granddaughter's craft is the account of Carol's own birth that she includes in another Idaho novel, *Snow in the River*.[6] Grandmother Watkins told how Dr. Watkins blew his tobacco breath into the newborn baby and brought her to life. Gram Watkins' use of details made this scene, in Carol's words, "as clear as if I could see it."[7]

In the novel Carol vividly describes the arrival of the baby herself, "a little silent thing that did not cry." Gram Watkins, here Mrs. Hedrick, exclaims in a shocked whisper, "Stillborn!" The redoubtable Doctor Hedrick cries, "Not yet, by Godfrey." He then "put his rough bearded mouth to the infant's lips and filled its lungs with his breath, working the tiny arms upward and back as he did so." After a few seconds, "a thin wail rose uncertainly on the air, and a new life was begun." In describing this incident, Brink the novelist tells us of the child who knew this story by heart:

> When I remember that I was that little girl I am sometimes surprised. The story of my birth, and how my grandfather Hedrick blew the breath of life into me, was so often told to me when I was young that it became a legend, the history of a stranger with whom I was not acquainted.[8]

Another storytelling technique Brink learned from her grandmother was the importance of small coincidences connecting separate events. For example, her grandmother had often explained how she had been sitting on a porch shelling peas when Dr. Watkins had proposed to her, and how she had been doing the same thing when they brought word of his death.[9] In Brink's novel *Buffalo Coat*, she uses parallel scenes of pea-shelling to foreshadow the tragedy of Dr. Watkins' murder as well as to draw together the lives of the two characters.

In addition to drawing on her grandmother's oral storytelling techniques, Brink also made use of local traditions, including a "haunted house." Before the Steffen house burned down, it reminded passersby of the murder of Dr. Watkins and the posse's shooting of Will Steffen, the deranged man who lived in that isolated house with his elderly mother. It was popularly believed that Will cruelly beat his frail mother and chased away the neighbors from the property, thus adding to the forbidding aspect of the farmhouse.[10] A longtime resident of Moscow told in her reminiscences how she used to shudder when she passed the bullet-riddled house on the country road.[11]

As a child riding into the countryside, Brink was very conscious of the deserted house and found the bullet holes made by the posse on the unpainted boards. She remembered how it stood up stark and weathered, unrelieved by trees, appearing like a narrow city house in the country of wheat fields where it didn't belong.[12] "It impressed me very much as a child," Brink remarked in an interview, "because I knew the story of how the men had gone out and crept through the wheat fields, and shot and shot at the house, and how he had shot back."[13] In *Buffalo Coat*, the vigilantes pour volley after volley through the weathered clapboards of the house, "standing up so stark and alone without shed or tree." As the siege continues, the number of perforations grows in the gray wood. "They were all over the upper story of the house — holes a little larger than a woodpecker would make."[14]

The house figures prominently throughout the novel as it introduces a sense of horror in the first part and reappears to sustain the current of doom surrounding the unstable Alf Stevens. At the beginning of *Buffalo Coat* Alf's father has hanged himself in the barn and Doc Watkins must go out to attend to the details and assist Alf, then just a boy, who has fallen into a fit after discovering his father's body. Here the house appears to the doctor as Brink remembered it from her childhood, "narrow and bleak and weathered . . . the kind of house a city man would build, not a farmer . . . A man's mind might grow strange and secret here . . . he might be troubled by fantastic thoughts which would not have occurred to him on a high stool in a narrow office . . ." (p. 16). The house becomes a curiosity as rumors circulate about Alf's prowlings at night and brutality toward his horse and his mother. "People avoided them more and more, and began pointing the house out to strangers. 'That's where Alf Stevens lives. Don't go in there, or they'll have the dogs on you'" (pp. 119–20). The final scene of the tragedy is enacted at the house, its windows splintered by the posse's bullets.

Brink's writing talents matched her good memory and sensitivity to the potential literary qualities of the stories she grew up with. In my interviews with her she spoke directly to this point, describing how when growing up she had read enough books to make her realize that the events in Moscow were just as exciting as those she read in novels. After college Brink planned to write the great American novel, but in the back of her mind was the intention to "do something" with the Moscow stories with which she was so intimately associated: "These things I'd heard talked about and told over and over until they got almost like folk stories to me."[15]

Of all Brink's fictional works, *Buffalo Coat* is the most completely based on family and community history. Two stories form an interrelated plot in *Buffalo Coat*: the murder of Dr. Watkins and the double suicide of Dr. Ledbrooke and Winnifred Booth, occurring in 1901 and 1902 respectively. The most reliable sources of facts concerning these incidents are the contemporary newspaper stories about them, although these differ on some details. On Sunday morning, August 4, 1901, Dr. Watkins was returning from a sick call when he encountered William Steffen. Steffen called out, "Hello Doctor," and Watkins stopped, giving Steffen the opportunity to pull out his revolver and shoot Watkins three times, through the heart, the temple, and the back. Watkins let out a piercing scream, and the frightened horse galloped on to the office on Third Street, pulling behind it the buggy containing the body.[16]

Continuing his search of the quiet streets, Steffen met George Creighton, a local merchant, After shooting Creighton in the arm, he raced his horse toward the city limits where he ran into Deputy Sheriff Cool. Steffen shot again, mortally wounding Cool. Someone then succeeded in hitting Steffen's horse, forcing Steffen to flee on foot a quarter mile to his mother's house near the cemetery.

Another version adds that before his encounter with Cool, Steffen stopped at the house of the office deputy sheriff, Charles Jones, who was pumping water. As Jones brought a dipper of water to Steffen, Steffen remarked that he heard there was a warrant out for his arrest. Jones denied it, and Steffen retorted that the city marshal, Langdon, had a warrant but "he won't serve it nearer than a Winchester can shoot." At that point, Sheriff Collins ran up with the news that Watkins had been shot. Steffen then "vaulted into the saddle and, flourishing his revolver, exclaimed dramatically, 'Sheriff, I shot Watkins.' " With Collins cautiously following Steffen's horse, Cool and Gainford Mix rode up on horseback. In the resulting gunfire and chase, Cool was wounded and Steffen's horse crippled.[17]

The pursuers surrounded the Steffen house, and Sheriff Collins sent to town for more men and ammunition. The owners of Moscow's hardware stores opened their doors and distributed arms and bullets to a group of around fifty men. Newspaper reports differ on the part Steffen's mother played in the events. The Spokane *Spokesman-Review*, perhaps more objective because of its distance from Moscow, first gave an account without Steffen's mother pleading for her son, and then added a summary of the version that appeared in the Colfax, Washington, *Weekly Commoner*. Here the mother pleaded twice with the posse to cease shooting so she could enter the house and persuade her son to come out. Whether or not she took this action, the gunfire exchange was heavy; then the shots from inside the house abruptly stopped. Steffen's mother either ran

into the house and discovered her dead son or was inside the house and suddenly opened the front door, shouting to the men outside, "My son is dead. Don't shoot anymore."[18]

Cautiously entering the farmhouse, the men found Steffen's body upstairs near a window with a broken windowpane and casement. There was a large bullet wound in his left breast and a stain on the shirt which the Colfax paper assumed was a powder burn and evidence of his suicide: "in desperation he had turned the weapon against himself." The Palouse *Republic* agreed with this view although it reported that the bullet had pierced his forehead. The official coroner's report listed the cause of death as a self-inflicted wound.

Several envelopes were found on the body. Steffen had written on one the names of his intended victims, which included Watkins. Another message read, "If the inevitable comes, I want to rest in Pullman." Large, printed letters on yet another envelope contained a tortured message, "I didn't get the right ones after all." The Colfax paper reported the existence of two other messages, one listing three small debts Steffen owed, and another with the unfinished sentence, "See that my mother. . . ."

Speculation on motives for the murders occupied a fair portion of the newspaper articles. Apparently Steffen was known as a hard-working man who had never given any indication of being insane although he had a quick and violent temper and was morose, according to the *Spokesman-Review* and the *Commoner*. The Palouse *Republic* flatly stated that Steffen was "violently insane."

His quarrel with former employer August Held and a grudge against Watkins and Elmer Jolly were suggested as possible motives; all three names had been on the list. Watkins had delivered a severe reprimand to Steffen about his mistreatment of his mother, and Jolly had written and printed in the Moscow *Mirror* the story of the trial at which Steffen was fined.

Less than a year later, a second and even more lurid event shocked Moscow, this time involving a romantic tryst between a married doctor and the young and beautiful daughter of the Methodist minister.[19] Francis J. Ledbrooke, a former Presbyterian minister, often officiated at services when ministers were out of town and developed a friendship with Reverend Booth and his family in this way. He had arrived in Moscow shortly after the Watkins murder, taking over the office and the lucrative practice. As physician to Winnifred during her long recovery from a dangerous appendicitis attack and later when she almost drowned, Ledbrooke developed an intimacy with Booth that led to a double suicide. On Saturday, May 10, 1902, Ledbrooke and Booth left the boardinghouse near Kendrick where she had been teaching for a few months. They traveled by train to Orofino and engaged a hotel room for Saturday and Sunday nights. On Sunday night, Ledbrooke paid the hotel bill and early Monday morning left his room to ask for ice water. Then at 10 a.m. the hotel

staff broke into the room after an employee had
reported sounds of unusually heavy breathing. The
couple were discovered in bed, fully clothed and in
each other's arms. Ledbrooke was still alive but unconscious. Efforts by two doctors kept him alive for
several hours.

Numerous letters to friends and relatives and to a
Moscow undertaker specifying funeral arrangements
testified to the deliberate nature of the suicides. One letter to a mutual friend stated that a love stronger than
death had impelled them to the deed because they could
not live, except in sin.

Two of the newspaper accounts disagreed on the
nature of the relationship, with the *Republic* pursuing
the theory that Ledbrooke had hypnotized Booth and
exerted an unnatural influence over her. The paper
reported details of the weekend rendezvous, with Ledbrooke morose and Booth first full of gaiety and then
agitated and weeping. Booth's sister and friends
remembered how anxious she had been to escape Ledbrooke, whom she despised but could not resist, and
how the doctor had taunted her with the fact that she
was in debt to him for saving her life.

The cooler report in the *Spokesman-Review*, perhaps
because of its detachment from local prejudices against
Ledbrooke and sympathies for Booth, ignored or was
unaware of reports of her dislike and fear of the doctor.
It portrayed Ledbrooke as a serious and earnest
scholar, highly respected among church and business
circles and interested in psychology. The only motive
given was that they were desperately in love with each
other.

The newspaper accounts of these events found their
way into scrapbooks just as the oral versions became
part of the community's repertoire. The events, particularly the murder of a leading resident of Moscow,
became points of reference. Moscow citizens remembered what they had been doing on that Sunday when
they learned of the shootings. According to Lola Clyde,
a native of the area and one of its keenest observers,
"They all remembered, 'I was just coming in from a picnic out at Moscow Mountain'; 'I was standing right
there on Main Street and I saw the buggy go by, the
horse going slowly by with the doctor leaning over in it
and didn't know he was dead . . .'; 'I saw George
Creighton and the blood running down his arm.' "[20]

The dramatic elements of these murders, scandals,
and suicides insured their prominent place in the oral
tradition of the Moscow area. Printed versions, first in
the newspapers, then in the journalistic *History of
North Idaho*, published in 1903, and finally in the
fictionalized and personalized account in *Buffalo Coat*,
published in 1944, are all to some degree colored by
oral recountings. The 1903 *History*, like others of its
genre, was written by professionals primarily as a
financial venture. Those who wished to be included in
the biographical section paid a fee and wrote a short
autobiographical sketch to which was added platitudes
about the enterprise and outstanding qualities of these
pioneers. The historical narrative, although fairly accurate in its facts, contained similar glowing phrases
about Moscow, with its "inexhaustible prospects for
prosperity," and its citizens possessed of a "fine public
spirit."[21] Relying on newspapers and accounts by local
residents, the *History* reflects contemporary attitudes
and interests.

In relating the episodes of 1901 and 1902, the *History*
reveals the impact of these unsavory events on the
public mind. It comments that Latah County had never
been the setting for crimes committed in the mining
communities farther north where "red-handed, blazen-
eyed murder stalked unmasked at midday through the
streets of the town."[22] The authors of this popularized
history transmitted other community attitudes. For instance, by linking the deaths of Watkins and Ledbrooke
with the accidental death of the third inhabitant of the
doctor's office, Dr. Parsons, the *History* reinforced the
local belief that the Watkins office was jinxed or hoo-
dooed, a belief that persisted even after Mrs. Watkins
finally found a renter able to disregard this fear.[23]

A comparison of the newspaper accounts of the
Steffen and Ledbrooke affairs with the accounts in the
History indicates that the latter is heavily influenced by
local storytellers' rearrangement of facts to fit their own
ideas. For instance, the *History*, in recording the
murder of Watkins, altered the newspaper account of
Steffen's death. Moscow citizens may have preferred to
believe that Steffen had committed suicide instead of
being murdered by a posse; the *History* concludes its
account by stating that "Steffen had shot himself in the
face of the hopelessness of escape."[24] Similarly, a prominent source of local history wrote in her family history
that Steffen had run out of ammunition, and that he
had killed himself rather than be taken.[25] Members of
the posse were also said to have attributed Steffen's
death to suicide in order to evade their own responsibility in the affair.

Recent interviews with Moscow residents indicate a
continuing concern with the moral issues raised by the
killing. One narrator described Steffen's mother pleading with the men to leave because her son was not in
his right mind: "I'll get him down and see what we can
do about it." The posse refused to leave, and "they
stayed with it until the man was shot. They just had to
take care of this man."[26] It was also believed that some
of those who participated in the Sunday hunt later admitted that they were not proud of their part in it, "but
on that morning, they made no effort to capture Will
alive," this man who was regarded as a "dangerous
wildman."[27]

Descriptions of Steffen tend to condone the posse's
action. Steffen is said to have been a formidable oppo-
nent, a man with great muscular arms, a butcher by
trade, who had been known to beat his mother and
threaten his neighbors. The story is also told how
Steffen once took a meat cleaver and attempted to kill
some men in a lumber camp. So instead of coaxing him
out of the house, "the town threw open all the hard-

ware stores . . . formed a sheriff's posse, and went dashing out through the wheat.''[28]

Less than a year later, the Ledbrooke-Booth affair shocked Moscow with its dramatic plot and intriguing characters lending themselves naturally to oral circulation. The *History* reports the suicides of May 12, 1902, in the fulsome prose style of that age. On that day, Dr. Francis J. Ledbrooke, a respected physician and active worker in the Methodist Church, ''committed a crime that horrified and mystified the community as nothing had ever done before or has done since.'' The *History* recounts how Ledbrooke had ''enticed by deceit and misrepresentation one of the most estimable young ladies of Moscow, over whom he exercised hypnotic influence, to Orofino.'' After placing his lady under his power, Ledbrooke murdered her with an injection of morphine into the arteries in her wrists. Then, ''after commission of that dreadful crime, the doctor died by his own hand and in the same manner as his innocent victim.''[29]

There were few, if any, favorable impressions of Dr. Ledbrooke. Old-timers remember him as a peculiar looking man with dark, bulging eyes that had hypnotized the beautiful and innocent Winnie. Some believe that he was indeed a dope addict who had addicted Winnie when she was under his care with a broken leg. Popular belief gave Winnie a weak character which had been unable to resist Ledbrooke's influence.[30]

As the story goes, Ledbrooke went to fetch Winnifred one Friday afternoon at a boardinghouse near Kendrick. After a tearful good-bye with the landlady, Winnie drove off with Ledbrooke in a buggy pulled by a fancy driving team.[31] The following Monday morning Moscow learned that both were dead. According to popular accounts, the couple left notes, as Steffen had. Ledbrooke asked that they be buried in the same grave (a request that decency would deny), and Booth requested that the hymn, ''There's Not a Friend Like the Lowly Jesus,'' be sung at her funeral. Although the hymn was sung and its title inscribed on her tombstone, ''the good Methodist women were all the more shocked at the death because of this hanky-panky going on.''[32]

Although Lola Clyde remembers that Watkins' murder had a stronger impact on the town because of his profession and social position and the number of people involved,[33] the Ledbrooke-Booth incident excited speculation to a much larger degree. Ledbrooke's appearance and supposed connections with drugs and hypnotic forces heightened the mystery of the affair. One intriguing account of Ledbrooke was told to Lola Clyde by a proprietor of a photograph studio in Moscow, Mrs. Eggan. The studio had displayed in its window a photograph of Winnie Booth in profile, showing her gazing at a rose in her hands. When Ledbrooke saw the photo, he studied it a long time, then went into the shop. He asked that a photograph be

made of him, also in profile, and put into the window so that his image would be looking at Booth's.[34]

The widow, Alice Ledbrooke, seems to have disappeared from public memory. No one knew very much about her, in contrast to Dr. Ledbrooke. ''We knew him, we saw him, we had him, but we never saw Mrs. Ledbrooke.''[35] Some thought that she had returned to England soon after her husband's death, when in reality she lived in Moscow for a few years with the Watkins family before moving to Spokane with them. There she met and married a quiet and respectable widower.

Brink's first attempt to fashion these stories into a novel used the legend of the jinxed doctor's office and the death of the three doctors. When she submitted the draft to Macmillan, they returned it with the comment that she had killed off the most interesting character in the first part of what was not really a novel but a series of short stories. If in *Caddie Woodlawn* Brink had been able to compress with comparative ease Caroline Watkins' several stories into a single book, now she had to radically change some of the facts and relationships to make a good, marketable novel. As she later described this process, ''It remained for me to fictionize the facts and dovetail the events.'' However, she strove to remain true to the accounts of the individuals, keeping them ''about as accurate as anyone living today can make them.'' Brink did change the relationships among the characters and some of their motivations.[36]

The final product published in 1944 received enthusiastic praise from reviewers and appeared for two weeks on the New York *Times* best-seller list. Although a wartime paper shortage and the eclipse of *Buffalo Coat* by the sensational *Forever Amber* soon relegated the author and the novel to a modest position in the ranks, a contemporary review by the *Times* emphasized its contribution to regional literature. The reviewer remarked that *Buffalo Coat* possessed the one prerequisite of a good historical novel, the placement of characters with timeless motives, emotions, and essential humanness in a particular era and environment which molded and determined their destinies.[37]

The strong reaction to the novel in Moscow surprised Brink, who had thought that people would regard *Buffalo Coat* as mere fiction and would have forgotten her during the twenty-five years she had been away. Quite the contrary. *Buffalo Coat* revived interest in these people and events, and in the author. Nor did everyone agree with Brink's interpretation of some of Moscow's most colorful, famous, and infamous characters.

Brink's retelling of these stories from a distance of forty years softened the rather harsh judgments of an earlier age. Brink used the setting of early twentieth-century Moscow to reflect upon universal themes of alienation, passion, and ambition. In setting these themes in the young Idaho town full of restless, aspiring newcomers, Brink provides a framework of opposite forces of savagery and gentility. Here civilization rests lightly upon untamed instincts like a thin pie crust over a mixture of venison and bear meat. The image of a "danger and hidden threat, the lure to suicide, the quick, wild urge to hurt and kill" underlies the plot. The folk stories, the gossip heard on summer porches and around a warm stove in winter are brought together by Brink into a fuller and more complex whole.

Dr. Watkins' murderer is introduced as a young boy, Alf, whom the doctor treated for shock after he found the body of his father hanging from a rafter in the barn. The boy has a "pinched appearance of ill-nourishment and underdevelopment . . . his eyes moving furtively as if searching for something" (p. 18). Dr. Watkins is filled with pity for this shy, unstable child, who lies on the threshold between life and death. Although Alf lives, he avoids the company of others except when he gallops recklessly at full speed through Opportunity (Moscow) delighting in the consternation and fear he causes. Watkins commits Alf to a mental hospital, but Brink cannot believe that Alf is immune from human feeling and sentiment. As the lovely Jenny Walden (Winnie Booth) throws a sprig of juniper to him as his train is departing for Orofino, Alf leans forward to retrieve the "fallen bit of green . . . and suddenly he began to sob, a terrible, hoarse sobbing that shook his shoulders" (p. 122).

By the time he is released a few years later, Alf has succumbed to darker forces. On the morning of August 4, 1901, the members of the posse, incited by the shootings, crowd into the hardware stores to get arms and ammunition, hot and sweaty with dry mouths and red eyes. "They were like hounds who have caught the scent of the fox. They were savages running to the kill" (p. 414). When it is all over, Alf is dead and his mother sits "hunched over on the porch step with her apron over her head crying and sobbing" (p. 417). One of the men replies to another's remark, "I wonder whose bullet?" with the simple statement of contrition: "Pray God we don't never find out" (p. 417).

In fictionalizing the second tragedy, Brink discarded the local belief that Ledbrooke had drugged or hypnotized the young, vulnerable Booth. She preferred to portray these two as victims of their own passion and strict social conventions. As Brink states in the introduction to the new edition of *Buffalo Coat*, "these were two very religious people who believed that because he was married, loving each other was a sin." In an interview, Brink further explains that "it was really a true love match, but in those days there were all the inhibitions that we don't have nowadays. In our own time," Brink remarked, "they would have spent a weekend together somewhere, and everything would have been fine and that would have been the end of it."[38]

Brink used considerable license in creating the character of Jenny Walden as she knew very little about the real Winnifred Booth.[39] Brink depicts Walden as high-strung and intelligent and increasingly frustrated with the desire to escape to somewhere where there were "lovers who would recite poetry . . . and she could be free and beautiful" (p. 110). Her romantic impulses find an object in Dr. Allerton, who represents the wider, sophisticated world beyond Moscow.

In the novel, Allerton (Ledbrooke) — no longer the drug addict with hypnotic eyes of town folklore — is revealed as a serious man with a definite purpose, whose natural passions are frustrated by a sexually repressed wife. In Opportunity, Allerton becomes alive, the thin clear air filling him with a restless excitement, "an almost physical aching for something nameless, something he had missed along the way . . . a pain which was not altogether an unhappiness" (p. 189).

Allerton's wife, lacking courage and imagination, cannot hold her husband from the beautiful and impulsive Jenny Walden. When Walden breaks her ankle, Allerton takes an inordinate interest in her welfare, visiting her daily and reading Browning's poetry to her. They both attempt to subdue their emotions, as "some instinct, or some inner wisdom . . . not quite drowned by the dark surge of happiness warned them of a border beyond which they must not go" (p. 321).

Inevitably the forces of youth, human passion, and desire prevail in these two who had "travelled so far through dissatisfaction and unhappiness and darkness" (p. 328). They see only one alternative to either a life without each other or bringing harm and grief to innocent people. They chose to experience the fullness of their love in one perfect day, "with no regrets afterward, no feeling of shame, no gradual cooling of the wonders" they felt (p. 379).

It is not difficult to understand the considerable excitement *Buffalo Coat* created in Moscow, which had never been the setting for a popular novel. For a long time people talked about the book and attempted to discover the real counterparts to the fictional characters. Old memories and scrapbooks were dusted off as older residents began comparing the novel with their own familiar versions. In many cases the novel was faulted for departing from remembered facts. A nephew of Will Steffen immensely disliked the attention the novel drew to the family. In an interview, Kenneth Steffen strongly disputed the portrayal of William as a man who beat his mother, claiming that he was in fact good to her and took care of her. According to Steffen, feelings against his uncle were due to Watkins' popularity in Moscow, and so this one murder is remembered although there were all kinds of shootings and killings around the area.[40]

Others also disputed Brink's interpretation of William Steffen's character and the reasons for his crime. They remembered Steffen as a big husky man, around thirty-nine years old, with strong, muscular arms, someone who would not have — as Alf Stevens did — put flowers on Winnie Booth's grave.

Nor was popular memory content with Brink's portrayal of Dr. Ledbrooke, having decided that he was a peculiar man and not the "idealist, the dreamer, the reformist," or one "upholding the right and working for the good of the community." Popular sympathies were clearly for the Booth family, headed by the Methodist minister who was "a very fine, gentle, quiet person with a lovely wife and family."[41]

Perhaps the most interesting effect of the novel on folklore was its creation of a new legend based on the

fiction of Alf Stevens' placing flowers on Jenny Walden's grave. After *Buffalo Coat's* publication, it is said that flowers began to appear mysteriously on Winnie Booth's grave every Memorial Day.[42] No one has discovered the identity of this person, or, perhaps, no one wishes to dispel this mystery linking the past to the present.

Notes

1. This article is based on research and interviews with Carol Brink in 1981 funded by a grant from the Association for the Humanities in Idaho. Additional research was conducted in conjunction with a research grant from the National Endowment for the Humanities. The author interviewed Carol Brink at her home in San Diego, July 1981. Copies of the tapes and indexes of the interviews are in the Latah County Historical Society, the University of Idaho Library, and the Idaho Historical Society. A tape and transcript of a previous interview in 1975 in which Brink responded to questions mailed to her by Sam Schrager are also deposited at the Latah County Historical Society and the University of Idaho. Information on Brink in this article is largely from the 1981 interviews. Except for short biographical descriptions in reference works, the only biography of Brink may be that by Mary Reed in the Latah County Historical Society's quarterly, *Latah Legacy*, Spring 1982, pp. 19–26.

2. Carol Brink, *Snow in the River* (New York: Macmillan, 1964), p. 287. This is the third of the Idaho novels which Brink described as a trilogy. *Buffalo Coat* was published in 1944, and *Strangers in the Forest* in 1959, both by Macmillan.

3. Brink interview, Tape 2, Side A.

4. Ibid.

5. Carol Brink, *Caddie Woodlawn* (New York: Macmillan, 1935).

6. Brink explained in her interview that *Snow in the River* was as near an autobiography as she would ever write, and that it included a lot of truth of her own childhood and family. See Tape 4/B.

7. Brink interview, Tape 1, Side A.

8. Brink, *Snow in the River*, p. 119.

9. Brink interview, Tape 5, Side B.

10. Interview with Lola Clyde by Sam Schrager, 1975, transcript of third interview, pp. 5–7. Also in an interview with Ione Adair by Schrager, 1977, transcript of fifth interview, p. 49. This aspect was also mentioned in contemporary newspaper accounts. See, for example, the Colfax (Washington) *Weekly Commoner*, August 9, 1901, which refers to a story of Steffen beating his mother. This story apparently first appeared in the Moscow *Mirror*. However, early copies of that paper are not extant.

11. Alma Taylor-Lauder Keeling, *The Uncovered Wagon*, 1975, p. 197. This family history was privately printed; it is available at the Latah County Historical Society library.

12. Brink interview, Tape 2, Side A.

13. Ibid.

14. Brink, *Buffalo Coat*, pp. 416–17. Quotations from *Buffalo Coat* are drawn from the 1980 edition; hereafter page numbers are given after the quoted text.

15. Brink interviews, see Tape 2, Side A; Tape 3, Side B; and Tape 4, Side A.

16. This account is compiled from local newspaper accounts, including the *Palouse Republican*, August 1, 1901; Spokane *Spokesman-Review*, August 5, 1901; and Colfax *Weekly Commoner*, August 9, 1901. Unfortunately, issues of the Moscow papers describing the shootings are not known to exist.

17. *Weekly Commoner*, August 9, 1901.

18. The article in the *Spokesman-Review* was printed August 5, the day following the incident.

19. This account is based on reports of this event which appeared in the *Spokesman-Review*, April 13, 1902, and *Palouse Republic*, May 16, 1902.

20. Clyde, pp. 40–41.

21. *An Illustrated History of North Idaho Embracing Nez Perces, Idaho, Latah, Kootenai, and Shoshone Counties* (Seattle: Superior Publishing Co., 1903). I have used a reprint from that history on Latah County which was published by Simon K. Benson, Provo, Utah, ca. 1981, p. 114. Reference hereafter will be cited as "*History*."

22. Ibid., p. 29.

23. Ibid., pp. 103–4.

24. Ibid., p. 103.

25. Keeling, *The Uncovered Wagon*, pp. 106–7.

26. Adair, transcript of fifth interview, p. 49.

27. Clyde, p. 6.

28. Ibid., p. 5.

29. *History*, pp. 103–4.

30. Clyde, p. 38.

31. Willa Cummings Carlson, transcript of third interview by Sam Schrager, Latah County Historical Society Oral History Collection, 1974, pp. 75–79.

32. Clyde, pp. 35–37.

33. Ibid., pp. 40–41.

34. Ibid., p. 34.

35. Ibid., p. 48.

36. Brink, note to 1980 edition of *Buffalo Coat*.

37. New York *Times*, Nov. 26, 1944, p. 18.

38. Brink interview, Tape 2, Side A.

39. Ibid., Tape 2, Side A.

40. Kenneth Steffen, transcript of first interview by Sam Schrager, Latah County Historical Society Oral History Collection, 1976, pp. 3–6 and 15–17.

41. Clyde, pp. 38–39.

42. Ibid., p. 47.

Land Use Attitudes and Ethics in Idaho Folklore

BRIAN ATTEBERY

Folklore has both intrinsic and extrinsic values. Intrinsically it is valuable because, like literature, it engages the mind with its narrative, lyric, or dramatic possibilities. That is, folklore is quite as aesthetically and intellectually satisfying as literature is. Extrinsically, folklore is a rich mine of attitudes, mores, values, and beliefs which can be studied by various disciplines to show how a human community responds to the challenges of circumstance and environment.

In this essay, the author combines the perspectives of folklore and American Studies to show that beliefs, superstitions, and traditions about land use, gathered from two widely separated Idaho communities, call for a revision of "conventional wisdom about the exploitative American farmer who farms until the land is exhausted or eroded away and then moves on without a qualm."

Brian Attebery directs the American Studies program at Idaho State University, where he is a professor of English. He is the author of The Fantasy Tradition in American Literature: From Irving to Le Guin *(1980).*

"Land ethic" is a term coined by naturalist Aldo Leopold in his book *A Sand County Almanac* to describe a way of taking into consideration not merely the human community but also the processes of the natural community — the land — in making decisions.[1] Humans have learned over the centuries, says Leopold, to treat one another with a measure of respect: first one's own family, then members of one's tribe, and so on until ultimately the entire human race is considered to belong to the class of things that can no longer be dealt with merely according to the principle of expediency. The next step in this evolution is to grant the same rights, to elements of the biological community that we grant to the human community, and for the same reason — that we are inescapably a part of that community.

The concept of ecology has wandered out of the confines of biology to be applied to such fields as economics and even linguistics, so there is no reason to doubt that folklore too will find useful its ideas of balance, niche, and ecosystem. The folkloric transmission process itself may be described in such terms. In this case, however, I am concerned with the content, rather than the mechanisms of folklore. Leopold's concept of a land ethic seems to be a useful measuring stick to apply to aspects of Idaho folklore. Much of the lore found in the farming communities of Idaho describes or prescribes a relationship between mankind and the land he inhabits. I would not claim that the traditional anecdotes, beliefs, and practices of the two rural communities discussed here represent explicit ethical statements, but I believe they do indicate an underlying pattern of values.

The first of these two communities is the settlement along Mann Creek, also known as Mann's Creek, a tributary of the Weiser River. The valley along Mann Creek is fairly flat and fertile, and the creek, unlike many in the area, has a substantial yearlong flow. Since the earliest days of settlement, beginning in the 1860s, agriculture has been the only important enterprise. The earliest settlers, like John Saling, took up homestead claims along the creek, where small diversion canals would water orchards, pastures, and grain fields. Later homesteaders moved up the sides of the valley, relying on more ambitious irrigation projects and dry land farming. In the 1930s, Mann Creek was populated densely enough to support three schools and a store. Since then, many of the farms have been consolidated, and most of the older residents have moved into Weiser.

The second community is the Sawtooth Valley, a long, high, arid groove in the mountains of central Idaho. The Salmon River has its source in the southern end of the valley and runs the length of it to the town of Stanley, where it turns east and enters a spectacular canyon. To the west of the Sawtooth Valley is the Sawtooth Range from which it takes its name; to the east are the Washington, Boulder, and White Cloud peaks. Valley and mountains are among the most scenic parts of the state, and the entire area has been proposed many times for national park status. Settlement in the Sawtooth Valley consisted of a number of transient or temporary occupations — as a summer encampment for Shoshoni Indians, as a site for fur trapping, and as the scene of placer and hard-rock mining — before the eventual establishment of a number of ranching homesteads at the beginning of this century. Tourism, now surpassing ranching in economic importance, began soon after settlement; many of the early ranchers supplemented their income by running pack trains into the wilderness.

Fieldwork in both communities consisted primarily of tape-recording interviews. [2] In Mann Creek, a team of three collectors sought out and interviewed second- and third-generation residents of the community. A few were still residents of the valley, but most were interviewed in their homes in town. In the Sawtooth Valley, some of the informants were first-generation settlers, and nearly all still lived on ranches or in vacation-style homes in the area. In both studies, the folklore collection was only part of a larger interdisciplinary project, and the emphasis on ecological themes was dictated by the overall goals of the project. Interviews were conducted using an informal questionnaire designed to elicit accounts of farming practices, weather beliefs, settlement legends, personal experience stories or memorates about contacts with Indians, and other items of folklife and folk narrative that might shed light on traditional attitudes about the land and its uses. We attempted not to let preconceived notions limit the kinds of lore collected, and the tapes contain many digressions into play-party games, Baptist-Adventist rivalries, the foibles of early trucks, Forest Service policies, and flavors of homemade jams. Such subjects have an interest of their own and sometimes led in surprising ways to new insights into our topic.

Another technique used, especially in the Sawtooth study, was on-site observation of traditional architecture. The way man builds his shelter reflects the way he perceives the environment, and, particularly in the Sawtooth area, most of the building was done using traditional techniques, so that any attitudes reflected are likewise indicative of a tradition. [3]

Typical of the material collected in the Mann Creek study is a set of descriptions of the landscape in its original uncultivated state. Nearly every person asked had something to say about bunchgrass:

> All these hills in here used to be just big tall bunchgrass, you know, like that, just blowing in the wind; but the cheatgrass in the last fifty-sixty years has come in and taken the place of this bunchgrass. [4]

A similar account comes from a history of the region based on oral sources:

> There was no sagebrush. Bunchgrass four to five feet high covered the hills. It was so tall that the snow did not cover it in winter and the stock could eat it all winter. The valley was covered with tall rye grass which the settlers cut for hay. [5]

Informants differ on whether this bunchgrass was tall or short (perhaps depending on whether they are remembering Idaho fescue or the taller, coarser Great Basin rye) but they all agree that bunchgrass is good feed, that it grew lushly, and that it is largely gone.

Questions about bunchgrass primarily prompted the recounting of traditional beliefs, as in the above description. Questions about sagebrush led not only to description but also to narrative, to memorates and family legends. Bunchgrass need only be appreciated for its value to the rancher, but sagebrush must be confronted: hence a story about finding it, getting lost in it, or grubbing it out with a team of horses or by hand. In these anecdotes, sagebrush plays two roles. Sometimes it is the villain, a symbol of barrenness: "And there it wasn't a thing but desert, you know, just eighty acres there of sagebrush high as this ceiling." At other times it, like bunchgrass, can represent natural bounty. The same informant went on to say that his father "knew it was good soil by the way that brush grew, you know."

Descriptions of bunchgrass glorify the land; anecdotes about sagebrush glorify the man who settles it. Often the same informant will recount both, depending on whether he is trying to create an impression of what a good place to live his land was or to suggest how difficult it was to cultivate.

Henry Nash Smith has suggested that it is typical of American images of the West either to exaggerate its virtues to produce a picture of a new Garden of Eden or to distort the other way and speak of the Great American Desert. [6] Mann Creek lore suggests that we may be able to hold both of these views simultaneously, and that each serves a purpose. The Garden image helps establish ties to the landscape, while the Desert image enables us to view ourselves as cultivators and improvers of it. The first is ethical, in that it ascribes an independent value to natural surroundings — it would be wrong to ravage a garden. The second removes the ethical consideration; it tends to treat the land as a neutral commodity which may be left alone or modified to suit human needs. If the land in question were an area less easily modified to agricultural production than the Mann Creek Valley — say, central Wyoming — the sagebrush image might represent a channel for hostility toward the land. As it is, one gains the impression that the area may have been wayward at one time, but diligent work has "redeemed" it.

The various resources found on the land — trees, game animals, soil, fish, minerals, and especially water — also appear in traditional beliefs and narratives. They tend to follow one side or the other of the bunchgrass/sagebrush split. Depending on the narrator and the context, a collector may be persuaded that the area was either barren of or rich in resources. Here is a set of statements about wild game, for example:

> When I was a boy you never seen a deer in this country anywhere outside the timber.

> Deer were very scarce and timid, and specially in Mann's Creek up there.

Yes, there was lots of wild meat like that; that's what they lived on.

In the case of deer, both beliefs may be true, and may come from different times. The third source is drawn from an older set of stories, since the informant's grandparents were in the area in the 1860s or '70s. But even if both are true, it is important that the two traditions exist simultaneously; they reflect the views which our ancestors had on paucity and plenty. By being retold, these views may still affect our attitudes and actions today.

If one examines stories of mineral wealth, one comes to the conclusion that we would prefer to believe in plenty rather than in paucity. In our study we collected personal memories which indicate the lack of precious minerals in the area; nevertheless, we were told a tale in which the informant's grandfather discovered a plate of gold and silver melted out of the rocks by a campfire. The vein was unfortunately buried under a landslide during the twenty years which elapsed between the initial discovery and the return to the site. The desire to believe in natural bounty seems to outweigh the conspicuous illogic of the legend circumstances.

Water, a vital resource in the West, plays an important part in Western folklore. The most favored of water sources is the spring, with its "good water, softest, best water you ever seen." Popular belief tends to magnify the amount of water that is present. Even place names, like Thousand Springs Valley (not the aptly named Thousand Springs Valley near Hagerman) ignore the general dryness of the area. Many of the water items fall into the category of recommended usage. For example, pumping is frowned upon, since it may lower the water table. Other water lore includes a nearly universal belief in dowsing or water witching. This practice implies that adequate water is there, hidden but available to the person with sensitivity and the right technique. The water witcher is, in a sense, cooperating with the land, responding to its signals and making use of its natural patterns.

Closely tied with water is climate, and climatic changes are felt and remembered by the folk. The five of our Mann Creek informants that we asked about climate all commented on the change since their youth:

Don't get that kind o' moisture any more, or any winters like that.

Oh, we don't have the snow like we used to have.

It used to snow, right down here in town, you know, the snow'd get to two feet deep . . . but it don't do that way any more.

'Bout five feet deep, snow'd always get on Mann's Creek, that high.

Or simply,

We had snow, but they don't have it now.

Surprisingly, snow, which might be considered one of the banes of rural life, is remembered with fondness, for games and sledding. The perceived change in climate to milder winters, whether attributable to the move to town or to the grander scale of childhood memories or even to a real alteration in weather patterns, becomes part of a general nostalgia for an older way of life in close contact with nature, despite its hazards and unpredictability.

Weather, because it is so unpredictable and unalterable, tends to generate the vaguely supernatural beliefs we call superstitions. On Mann Creek, rain was connected with the crescent moon. The moon also appeared in other superstitions: it was said to affect both crops and cattle. One narrator speculated, "I don't know whether it's superstition or whether it's . . . the moon and the tides and so on might have some effect on the weather or the temperament of the animal." Superstitions like these imply an interconnectedness of things—the moon, the earth, the weather, calves, potatoes, or the copper wires, green twigs, and underground springs of water witching—that is not systematic but otherwise not unlike the teachings of ecology. Hidden in the ancestry of such beliefs is a kind of animism, ascribing to all things a life and a soul that mankind, if he obeys the proscriptions and follows the rituals, can communicate with and influence. Though no Mann Creek rancher would sacrifice to the moon or pray to mother earth, still, he is willing to grant that there may be lines of influence that he cannot see, and so he continues to castrate, butcher, and wean "by the sign."

In gauging the settlers' attitudes toward the land, it is useful to see what they have to say about its state when they arrived. Stories about Indians are often part of their conception of that original state. On Mann Creek, Indians show up in narratives about wandering bands who beg food from the ranchers. Although the narrator often speaks of the wife or children being frightened of these visitors, Indians are not described as dangerous, but merely troublesome. Nor are they said to have been really living in the area; rather they were always passing through on their way to the river below or hunting grounds above. They were not considered to have been using the land, as the farmers used it, since use implied change. The Indian life of hunting and food gathering meant that "they was too lazy to farm and really raise their food." Thus their eventual disappearance is understood not as the displacement of one group of inhabitants by another, but as the closing of a thoroughfare and consequent end of casual traffic through what has become a settled community.

Another set of stories that may be interpreted as comments on the natural landscape includes accounts of the original settlement. Why were the first settlers said to have picked the sites they did? We collected three different versions of the coming of the Saling family to the creek, each of which reflects something of the land attitudes of the teller. In the first, the family was heading south after a hard winter in Midvale, a community north of Mann Creek, when they had a runaway. To save the children in case the wagon crashed, the mother threw them out onto the soft mud. When the parents went back to pick up the children, the father spotted the place that he wanted to homestead.

The second legend is similar, except that the Salings simply camped in the proper spot without the intervention of a runaway horse. According to this source, John Saling is supposed to have said, "Well, girls, this is where we stay."

The third account is quite different. In it, the Salings ran out of meat during the winter in Midvale. John Saling went deer hunting on top of Iron Mountain and saw Mann Creek below him, with the snow just melted off. He headed back to Midvale, packed up his family, and moved to the creek.

Each account emphasizes the mildness and attractiveness of Mann Creek as compared with Midvale. The first account puts the land itself, with its soft mud, in the role of receiver and protector. The second merely makes the future homestead a campsite, but reinforces its good qualities with a quotation. The third is a Moses-like discovery of a new and more promising land. All three clearly place a value on the place. The land that rescues you and provides for you is not something to be used and discarded without thought, as pioneers are often said to have used and abandoned farm after farm in their move west. "This is where we stay" shows the intention, at least, to settle permanently in one spot, to tie oneself to the setting. And farming practices remembered by Mann Creek residents seem to reflect this effort at permanence.

To farm the hills above the valley, it was necessary to practice dry-land farming techniques. Here is a description of the process:

> Well, dry-land farming, they had to figure to conserve the natural moisture. And the proper way to do dry-land grain farming is to plow it in the fall, let it lay there rough all winter, just the rougher it lays the better, the clods big as suitcases—it catches all the moisture that way—and as soon as spring comes start cultivating it. Cultivate it all summer, and then sow it that fall to grain.

These techniques—conservation of moisture, rough plowing, lying fallow, and fall sowing—provide for long-term use of hillside land that would otherwise erode away with the first rain. They are traditional techniques, predating governmental conservation programs. Whether or not such practices are better for the land, the farmers believe that they help preserve soil and moisture and that it is important to do so.

With a similar protective aim, many people practiced some form of contour plowing and worked to prevent and allay erosion:

> Two big sand washes, one went right down through the middle of that eighty he bought, deep, you know, deep as this house, you know, and just clear down through. And

he put that sagebrush in there, just kept filling it in, cutting and filling it in and plowing till you can't see it today, couldn't see it then because he had a nice field of hay out over it. It was all done by hand.

Another traditional farming technique concerns the treatment of pests. The smaller fields and more diversified crops of the early days probably brought in fewer pests than one finds in modern farms, but those which existed, like a weevil that infests alfalfa, were dealt with in nonchemical ways: "We just, after we got the first crop off, we'd just use a drag harrow; the dust'd kill 'em." One lived with pests on the farm, just as one lived with flies in the house, keeping them out if possible, killing them when it was convenient, but not considering eradicating them completely. Pests came with the territory. This is not to say they would not have used pesticides if any had been available, but that the absence of all but the crudest insect-killing chemicals led to a certain attitude of tolerance.

Land use folklore in Mann Creek reflects several facts about settlement in the valley: its relatively early date, its stability, the mildness of the climate, and the fertility of the soil. Where tradition seems to provide rival attitudes or ethical stances toward land and environment, as in the stories of sagebrush and bunchgrass, these factors reinforce the more positive side of the tradition. Accordingly, one hears more about John Saling's discovery of beautiful Mann Creek than about years of drought, more about fresh, cold springs than about digging ditches, and more about how to maintain a hillside farm than about how to fatten steers for the highest profit.

It should be remembered that most of this lore was recounted by people who had sold their farms and moved to town, that Mann Creek is farmed or ranched nowadays by the techniques of agribusiness, and that the farming practices described by our informants are borne only passively, remembered rather than passed on through demonstration. There has been a break or alteration in local tradition, and a study of twenty- to forty-year-old residents would undoubtedly produce different results than our study of sixty- to ninety-year-olds. Nevertheless, the tradition described here is the one that was in operation from the time of settlement until quite recently, in some cases into the 1950s.

In the Sawtooth Valley, none of the factors mentioned above was present: most of the agricultural settlement dates back only to the turn of the century; the presence of trapping, mining, and lumbering tended to engender or reinforce feelings of transience rather than a sense of permanent settlement; the climate is harsh, with snowfall possible in any month; and the soil is thin and full of glacial rocks. The growing season is too short for crops. Even alfalfa, the standby of the western rancher, will only survive a single season. Sheep do not winter well and must be taken to lower country in the fall. Ultimately, most of the homesteaders in the valley settled on cattle as the main source of income—dairy cattle, for the most part, because the profit on beef was too low to pay for winter feeding.

Cattle ranching required sufficient land to graze the cattle through the summers while putting away enough hay to last the winter. The first kind of hay used was wild hay, cut in the natural meadows that form wherever the water table is close to the surface of the ground. Later this wild hay was supplemented by clover, but it continued to be used and was highly valued by the ranchers:

> We have a native timothy here, it's a meadow fescue, but it grows wild and matures early, and it gets, oh, sort of dry looking long before the rest of the hay is ready to cut . . . it's a long, high, spindly looking grass that doesn't build up much, but it's awfully good feed when you do get a bunch of it. It's good horse hay, real good horse hay. And any of this wild hay that grows here, I'd rather have a ton if it than I would a ton and a half of alfalfa. It'll go farther and there's more strength in it. And it's wonderful all around hay for sheep, cows, and horses, both, 'cause they could pick what they want, there's so many different varieties: you've got weeds of all kinds, and dandelions now, nut grass, wire grass, slough grass, and every other thing mixed with it.

Such recognition that variety can be a strength is rare in American agriculture. Something of the rancher's view of his environment is revealed by his awareness of the many kinds of grass and herb and the uses of each. Timothy is especially good for horses. Slough grass is good feed, and it can also be used to stuff the packs used on mules.

Just as the main focus of ranch activity was storing cattle feed for the winter, the main domestic activity was acquiring and preparing food, no easy task when a farm might be snowed in for months at a time. Since ranching in the Sawtooth Valley was not a lucrative proposition, the homesteaders tried to buy as little as possible. That required techniques for storing or preserving what little could be raised in gardens—early producers like carrots and lettuce or very hardy perennials like rhubarb—or butchered from the stock. Store-bought items, too, had to be preserved from spoilage, and milk from the dairies, whether intended for sale or for home consumption, had to be put into a form that would last without reliable refrigeration. Therefore, the ranchers drew on a variety of traditional methods of preserving foods. The milk was separated and turned into butter and cheese (often pressed in homemade molds). Homegrown carrots and store-bought potatoes both went into cellars and storehouses, sometimes under layers of sawdust. Meat could be frozen outdoors after winter set in, and so butchering was delayed until November. Other foods were canned or dried.

The ranchers also discovered other sources of food. They went to the forest and mountains and shot game: deer, mountain goat, bighorn sheep, elk, grouse, and sandhill crane. One woman told of shooting a deer by the family woodpile. In the lakes and streams were fish, most notably the migrating salmon from which the river takes it name. Wild berries, too, could add interest to a limited diet:

> There's wild strawberries and raspberries and some gooseberries. My kids used to go gather the wild gooseberries; there are not too many raspberries, but they used to go and gather the gooseberries and I'd make 'em pies or maybe jam. And then if you know where to go there's lots of huckleberries; they'd grow up in the mountains here.

The wild country provided other things besides food for man and beast. The woodpile mentioned above was cut there (and enormous piles they had to be to last the winter, too, stacked in an intricate fashion derived from tradition). Poles of aspen or willow were used for fences and corrals. Aspen, or "quaken asp trees" could also be used as emergency winter feed for cattle. Houses, sheds, and barns were made from douglas fir and lodgepole pine. Counterbalancing these benefits of living near the wilderness were a few dangers and disadvantages. There were predators: coyotes, bears, hawks, and eagles. The coyotes took mostly young lambs and calves, and a certain amount of loss was expected and allowed for. Bears infrequently emerged from the forest, and are spoken of more as a nuisance than as a danger. Hawks occasionally took chickens, but ranchers distinguished between what they called "bullet hawks," which preyed on chickens, and "meadow hawks," which did not. Again, as with the wild hay, there is an awareness of the variety of wild species and a sense that the rancher can profit by knowing as much as possible about each.

Ranchers drew upon the resources of the forest in at least one other way. In order to make a go of things, nearly every ranch required some outside source of income. Many wives taught school while the husbands worked the ranch. In other cases, however, the wives maintained the ranch while the husbands worked outside, either for the Forest Service or as guides and outfitters for hunters and fishermen, and a set of traditions developed to cover packing and trail cooking. Thus the economic survival of most ranches depended upon the continued proximity of the wilderness, and the folklore of the region adapted accordingly.

Although many of the ranches had small sawmills, most of the older buildings in the Sawtooth Valley are built of logs. In nearly all cases the logs are left round. Most are not peeled of their bark, a practice necessary in warmer or moister climates to prevent insect infestation. The gaps between logs are filled with poles, probably aspen, split into quarters and nailed like wedges into the interstices. On the outside the gap is usually covered with a daubing of mud or mud mixed with cement. There is no exterior siding of clapboards or vertical board and batten, nor, for the most part, is there any interior covering except for some use of newspapers.

The logs are held together at the corners with various

kinds of notching. The most common kinds are the simple V- and saddle-notch, sometimes reinforced with nails. Gables are sometimes constructed of sawed planks, but more often of successively shorter lengths of log, supporting log purlins or roof joists that run the length of the building. A common roof type is a row of poles laid over these purlins, from ridgepole to eaves, and a layer of dirt or sod over that.

What is most noticeable about this style of building is the use of native materials in essentially unaltered form. Other building traditions do not leave their materials so raw. One cabin in the Sawtooth Valley contrasts strongly with the dominant building style. This building was made of log timbers squared on the outside and inside so that they formed a smooth wall. The underside of each log was hollowed into a long groove that fit over the curve of the log underneath, so that there were no gaps to fill. The corner notching was full dovetail, a kind of notch that takes skill and a sense of spatial relations to make each cut slant simultaneously inward and upward or downward to match the next log. This type of cabin, usually found among Scandinavian immigrants, seems admirably suited to the Sawtooth Valley environment: it is sturdy, air- and water-tight, and made of available materials. Nevertheless, with this lone exception, all of the ranchers in the valley built with round logs and chinking. With care, such a cabin can also be made sturdy and draft-proof, and it requires less time and skill in its construction. In addition, it ends up looking like what it is made of. Whereas a building of squared timbers or one covered with boards can easily be taken for a building made of finished lumber, a cabin of round, unbarked logs, with a roof of poles and sod, can be mistaken for nothing else. It reveals its origins: the trees, grass, and earth around it. While the primary aim of the Sawtooth builders was not to blend in with the surroundings, that is certainly one of the results of the building technique.

Most of these buildings are adapted to the environment other ways than visually. The typical Sawtooth Valley cabin is square or nearly so, a shape that gives the maximum volume per wall surface and thus is easier to keep heated and also takes less wood than a long rectangle. The typical roof angle is surprisingly low, surprising until one hears the explanation. Whereas one might expect a concern with the roof's ability to shed snow, these roofs were designed to retain a layer of snow, which then added to the insulation of the roof. If the pile got too deep, someone could climb up and shovel some off. Recent, commercially designed chalet-style and A-frame cabins, in contrast, are meant to slough off the snow, and thus must compensate with some other form of insulation if they are to be used in winter. Either system works, but the traditional method works with natural conditions, while the modern style works rather in spite of them.

In both of these communities, certain aspects of the folklore and folklife are compatible with a scientifically derived ecological world view. Other aspects are not.

However, in each community, local conditions support an emphasis on those items of lore that are harmonious with such a world view. In the Sawtooth Valley, proximity to the uncultivated forest and semi-wild meadow led to the selection from folk tradition of a set of practices concerned with the use of wild plants and animals for food and shelter. Great attention was paid to naming each species and cataloguing its virtues. The homesteaders recognized that without these resources, ranching would probably not have been possible; the valley would at best have been fit for summer pasture.

On Mann Creek, fertile soil and a climate relatively milder than that of surrounding areas led to an interest in permanent settlement. Another circumstance that may have influenced the settlers is the fact that many of them had already traveled from the Midwest to Oregon and then, finding the Willamette Valley overcrowded, turned east to find some place back along the trail. People on Mann Creek did not have the knowledge of wilderness and wild species that Sawtooth Valley people did, and their idea of a proper farm was considerably tamer and more humanly altered than the typical Sawtooth ranch. These alterations were fairly major ones, like grubbing the sagebrush, digging ditches and wells, and planting hay or grain or orchards. However, such changes were made cautiously, a step at a time, "by hand," as the farmers like to boast. At each step, attention could be paid to the lay of the land, the quality of the soil, the height of the water table, and so on. There was no wholesale reworking of the landscape, as is possible with modern machinery, and the local farming ethic would not have favored such drastic measures. The valley was a good place to begin with, as evidenced by settlement stories and conventional ways of describing it, and the goal was simply to make it a little better, a little more habitable, without upsetting the basic order. Farmers were willing to work within the limitations of terrain, weather, and the cycles of sun, moon, and earth in return for the opportunity to remain in one spot year after year.

Perhaps this harmony with nature is merely the result of the nostalgia of town-bound farmers. Considerably more data are needed to validate the conclusions drawn above: more fieldwork within the Mann Creek and Sawtooth Valley communities, fieldwork in other settlements, and observation of actual farming techniques, as opposed to remembered practice. In interpreting the evidence, I have had to draw many inferences, supported, I believe, by the lore. Others may view the same materials differently. No clear statement of Thou Shalt or Thou Shalt Not appears in any of the items collected; where a folk land ethic exists, it is not stated outright but buried within a host of sometimes contradictory stories, expressions, and practices.

Despite these reservations, I think that a Leopoldian interpretation of folklore and folk life can reveal previously unnoticed directions and patterns in our rural traditions. The patterns in these two communities seem to contradict conventional wisdom about the exploitative American farmer who farms until the land is exhausted or eroded away and then moves on without a qualm. In other communities, though, such a view may be accurate. A full explanation of such contradic-

tions would require that folklorists work together with historians, geologists, and biologists to write a new kind of history of the West. Further studies, either supporting or amending this one, would be useful steps toward the completion of such a history.

Notes

1. Aldo Leopold, *A Sand County Almanac* (New York: Oxford University Press, 1949). Useful discussions of Leopold's ideas may be found in Roderick Nash, *Wilderness and the American Mind*, Revised Ed. (New Haven and London: Yale University Press, 1973), pp. 182–99, and in Peter Fritzell, "Aldo Leopold's *A Sand County Almanac* and the Conflicts of Ecological Conscience," *Transactions of the Wisconsin Academy of Sciences, Arts and Letters* 64 (1976), 22–46.

2. Mann Creek fieldwork was conducted in 1972 by Jennifer Eastman, John Burch, and Brian Attebery under a grant from the Snake River Regional Studies Center. Sawtooth Valley fieldwork was conducted in 1974 by Jennifer Eastman, Brian Attebery, and James Broich as part of the Sawtooth Interdisciplinary Study of The College of Idaho, under the sponsorship of the National Science Foundation's program of Student Originated Studies. My report on the Mann Creek

study was published under the title, "A Land Ethic in Idaho Folklore," Snake River Regional Studies Center Occasional Paper 10, Part III, 1972.

3. A more detailed account of these log structures may be found in Jennifer Eastman Attebery, "Log Construction in the Sawtooth Valley of Idaho," *Pioneer America* 8 (1976), 36–46.

4. Interview tapes from both projects and transcripts of the Mann Creek interviews are in The College of Idaho Folklore Archive, Caldwell, Idaho, and may be examined with permission. All subsequent unmarked quotations are drawn from these tapes.

5. Charlotte Stanford, "The Eight Water Hogs," manuscript in the library of The College of Idaho, Caldwell, Idaho.

6. Henry Nash Smith, *Virgin Land: The American West as Symbol and Myth* (Cambridge, Mass.: Harvard University Press, 1950, reissued 1970), pp. 123–32 and 174–83.

Appendix

An Annotated Bibliography of Materials on Idaho Folklife
J. SANFORD RIKOON

An Annotated Bibliography of Materials on Idaho Folklife

J. SANFORD RIKOON

INTRODUCTION

The following bibliography is intended to inform researchers of the scope and locations of works on Idaho folklife. The main criteria used in the selection process included the accurate and authentic presentation of folk traditions and the provision of minimal contextual information on the informants and the collection of data. With few exceptions I do not include publications in which the authors obviously tampered with the collected materials. The most common errors in this regard are editing of oral items, combining a number of separate traditions into one tradition, and the misconception that whatever is not historically accurate must be "folklore."

Two caveats concerning the scope of this listing are required. First, although many oral history volumes and essays (e.g., Bert Russell's *Swiftwater People* (1979) and *Hardships and Happy Times* (1975)] and autobiographical accounts contain interesting descriptions of folk culture, these sources are not typically included. All researchers are encouraged, however, to consult both of these sources. Second, publications presenting Native American folk traditions are not cited because of both the compiler's acknowledged unfamiliarity with these works and the pre-existing inventories of publications on Native Americans compiled by historians and anthropologists. Among the recommended bibliographies on this topic are the following:

Dockstader, Frederick J. *The American Indian in Graduate Studies: A Bibliography of Theses and Dissertations*, 2 vols. New York: Museum of the American Indian, Haye Foundation, 1973–74.

Etulain, Richard W. and Merwin Swanson, eds. *Idaho History: A Bibliography*. Pocatello: Idaho State University Press, 1979, pp. 46–51 and 89–94.

Murdock, George Peter. *Ethnographic Bibliography of North America*. New Haven: Human Area Relations File, 1960, Sections VII–1, VII–5, VII–7, VII–11, VIII–2, VIII–7 and VIII–11.

Walker, Deward E. *Indians of Idaho*. Moscow: University of Idaho Press, 1978, pp. 167–82.

Archibald, Edith. "Swedish Folklore from the Idaho White Pines." *Western Folklore* 24:4 (October, 1965): 275–80.
Archibald presents a representative collection of Swedish and Swedish-American lore from the Troy area of eastern Latah County. Little discussion of the materials is included in the author's collection of ethnic and dialect jokes, proverbs and sayings, and play-party songs.

Attebery, Brian. "A Land Ethic in Idaho Folklore." *The Snake River Regional Studies Center Occasional Paper 10, Part III*. Caldwell: The College of Idaho, 1972.
Reprinted and updated in this volume.

Attebery, Jennifer Eastman. "Log Construction in the Sawtooth Valley of Idaho." *Pioneer America* 8 (January, 1976).
Attebery's article focuses on a survey of construction techniques and types of nineteen log structures in the Sawtooth Valley in central Idaho. One of the few good studies of Idaho folk architecture, this essay also includes hypotheses on the relationship of these buildings to log building patterns in the East, Midwest, and Far West. The author concludes that while there are similarities between the surveyed buildings and other traditions, distinct Sawtooth types appear to reflect local ecology and distinct Rocky Mountain patterns.

_____. "The Uses of Oral History in Folklore." *Idaho Humanities Forum* 2:1 (May, 1979) pp. 2, 8.
The focus of this discussion is the differences and similarities of folklore and oral history, and how the folklorist can benefit from the data collected through oral history projects.

_____. "Domestic and Commercial Architecture in Caldwell." *Idaho Yesterdays* 23:4 (Winter, 1980): 2–11.
This survey includes some examples of log structures during the early settlement periods in Caldwell. Later uses of traditional floor plans and space usage with other construction materials are also noted.
Also, see Eastman, Jennifer.

Attebery, Louie W. "Folklore of the Lower Snake Valley: A Regional Study." Ph.D. dissertation, University of Denver, 1961.
This study presents the most complete collection of Idaho folk traditions yet assembled. Major portions are devoted to traditions, mainly oral, associated with gold, Indians, folk remedies and beliefs, the cowboy, entertainment, and regional humor. This work is unfortunately unpublished, but is available at the Idaho State Historical Society Library.

_____. "Home Remedies and Superstitions." In *The Idaho Reader*, edited by Grace Edgington Jordan. Boise: Simms-York, 1963, 92–100.
Attebery's survey of folk beliefs from the Snake River Valley is based on a chapter in the author's dissertation (see Attebery, 1961).

_____. "Rural Traditions of the Snake River Valley," *Northwest Folklore* 1:2 (Winter, 1965): 23–30.
Focusing on pre-World War II folk culture of the Snake River Valley, Attebery touches upon a variety of traditions, including haying and threshing techniques, practical jokes and pranks, and beliefs connected with weather prediction and cosmic signs. The presentation of contextual data aids in placing the folklore within everyday lives and patterns.

Ball, Leona Nessly. "The Play Party in Idaho." *Journal of American Folklore* 44 (1931): 1–26, rpt. in John Greenway, ed., *Folklore of the Great West: Selections from Eighty-Three Years of the Journal of American Folklore*. N.p: American West Publishing Company,1969, pp. 415–24.
This early article focuses on north Idaho social traditions, especially during the winter season. The play-party is described in detail, including organization, structure, and the music and dances of a typical event. Some comparisons are made between play-parties of the 1880s and 1920s.

Beal, Merrill D. "Rustlers and Robbers: Idaho Cattle Thieves in Frontier Days." *Idaho Yesterdays* 7:1 (Spring, 1963): 24–28.
Based on both written and oral sources, this discussion of such "bad men" as the Bob Tarter gang, Ed Harrington and the Devils Corral Crowd includes some legendary materials. Little information on oral sources or analysis of the texts is provided.

Bieter, Pat. "Folklore of the Boise Basques." *Western Folklore* 24:4 (October, 1965): 263–70.
Bieter's article begins with an impressionistic account of a Basque sheepherder's life and then moves toward a more objective survey of Basque culture and cultural change. The article includes discussion of festivals and holiday celebrations, music, language, anecdotes, and card games. Bieter provides a good glimpse of the breadth of Basque culture and some of the impacts of the Idaho experience on Basque life.

Booth, Wayne R. "A History of the Latter-day Saint Settlement of Oakley, Idaho." Unpublished MS., Brigham Young University, 1963.
Chapter VII of this manuscript contains a brief discussion of local legends and tall tales, including stories of the "wild man" of Birch Creek and buried treasure lore.

Brainard, Robert L. "The Jackass that Discovered a Mine." *Seeing Idaho* 1 (May, 1937): 14.
Brainard's text is a legend relating to the 1885 discovery of Noah Kellogg's silver-lead mine (now Bunker Hill mines) because of the fortuitous actions of a mule.

Brunvand, Jan H. " 'The Unfortunate Rake' in Skis." *Western Folklore* 18 (1959): 38.
Brunvand presents a parody of "The Cowboy's Lament" that details the death and last requests of a Sun Valley skier.

_____. "Folklore and Superstition in Idaho." *Idaho Yesterdays* 6:3 (Fall, 1962), 20–24.
This article is a collection and discussion of folk beliefs on such topics as logging, luck, farming, and ranching.

Although there is little analysis of the data, this essay provides a good introduction to folk medicine study and should be read in conjunction with Louie Attebery (1963).

_____. "Miscellany of Idaho Superstitions." *Western Folklore* 12 (1963): 202–3.
Fifteen folk beliefs collected by the author from his students at The University of Idaho are listed in this note. The items are from a variety of locations around the state.

_____. "Spinner of Tall Tales." *Lewiston Morning Tribune* (Sunday, 5 Jan. 1964), Sec. 2, pp. 1, 3.
Brunvand summarizes his research on Len Henry, the tall tale raconteur, and presents some tall tale texts. For a more complete discussion of Len Henry, see Brunvand (1965) and his essay in this volume.

_____. "Have You Heard the Elephant (Joke)?" *Western Folklore* 23:3 (July, 1964): 198–99.
This note contains a collection of nineteen elephant jokes current on the University of Idaho campus in 1963.

_____. "Rodeo Clown Jokes (From Northwest Archives)." *Northwest Folklore* 1:2 (Winter, 1964): 31–32.
From a collection of texts told by Mark Meath and son of Emmett, Idaho are presented several joke exchanges of vaudeville variety and a brief description of the function of rodeo clowns.

_____. "Len Henry: North Idaho Münchausen." *Northwest Folklore* 1:1 (Summer, 1965): 11–19.
Len Henry was a tall tale raconteur and last surviving "pioneer squawman" on the Nez Perce reservation. After briefly tracing Len's life, Brunvand uses information collected from former associates of Len to skillfully reconstruct aspects of Len's repertoire, style, and performance contexts. Of the tales Brunvand collected, some were told by Len himself about his own exploits while others are part of the stock tall-tale variety. This article has been extensively reworked for presentation in this volume.

_____. "Folk Song Studies in Idaho." *Western Folklore* 24:4 (October, 1965), pp. 231–48.
Reprinted in this volume.

_____. "Desk-Top Inscriptions from the University of Idaho." *Northwest Folklore* 1:2 (Winter, 1965): 20–22.
Brunvand categorizes 59 desk-top inscriptions according to content with fraternity-sorority and "sexy sayings" the two most popular classes. This note provides a starting point for research into anonymous lore.

_____. "Some International Folktales from Northwest Tradition." *Northwest Folklore* 1:2 (Winter, 1965): 7–13.
From a corpus of 25 versions of 17 Aarne-Thompson tale types, Brunvand prints a sample of texts and discusses their similarities and differences to tales collected in other areas and among other ethnic groups. He also illustrates processes through which wonder tales become jokes and the localizing of motifs through geographic place names and occupational references.

Bryant, Frank B. "Happy Days and Happy Men." *Idaho Yesterdays* 9:3 (Fall, 1965): 8–15.
This article contains anecdotes, legends, and local character stories based on remembrances of the author's experiences as mine engineer in the Salmon Mountains around 1910.

Cheney, Thomas Edward. "Folk Ballad Characteristics in a Present-Day Collection of Songs." MA thesis, University of Idaho (1936).

This collection and analysis of 71 Idaho songs is important not only for its perceptive insights into changes in folk song style, content, and tradition, but also because it is one of the largest assemblages of field-collected Idaho song texts. Regretfully, Cheney does not present any tunes for the texts. His emphases reflect his literature background; texts are compared to the older Child ballad corpus respecting major characteristics, content, style, and presentation. Cheney also discusses cowboy songs and, most importantly, attempts to relate changes in song traditions to other corresponding changes in American life.

_____. "Facts and Folklore in the Story of John Wilkes Booth," *Western Folklore* 12 (1963), 171–77.
This study focuses on legends from Declo, Idaho, nine miles from Burley. The legend complex surrounds the story of Bill Evans, who claimed to have John Wilkes Booth's body in a railroad car parked in a potato field near Declo in the mid-1930s.

Clark, Ella E. "Watkuese and Lewis and Clark." *Western Folklore* 12 (1953): 175–78.
Clark discusses and presents the Nez Perce narrative on the saving of Lewis and Clark by Watkuese, an Indian woman. Years before, Watkuese had been befriended by some unidentified whites in her long trek home after capture by an eastern Indian group.

Derig, Betty. "Celestials in the Diggings." *Idaho Yesterdays* 16:3 (Fall, 1972): 2–23.
Although Derig focuses on relations between Chinese and white miners, especially anti-Chinese agitations, some attention is given to Chinese traditions in the Boise Basin area. Among the cultural activities treated are festivals, local associations and occupations, food traditions, and religious celebrations.

Eastman, Jennifer. "Mann Creek, Idaho: Recollections of a Western Pioneer Community." *The Snake River Regional Studies Center Occasional Paper 10, Part V.* Caldwell: The College of Idaho, January, 1974.
The author uses recollections of early settlers and portions of their traditional complex to reconstruct patterns characterizing early days in the Mann Creek community. Among the topics discussed are relations with the Indians, early settlement practices, cooperative labor and neighborliness, and the influence of the First-Day Adventist Church.

Ellis, Earl H. "That Word, 'Idaho.'" *Studies in Humanities*, No. 2. Denver: University of Denver Press, 1951.
This short monograph is mainly concerned with the etymology of the state's name and the variety of legends that have been used to account for its derivation. Some of the legends treated include those attributing the name to Native American languages, to politicians naming the state after relatives, and to local place name legends.

_____. "Idaho." *Western Folklore*, 10 (1951): 317–19.
Ellis briefly summarizes his 1951 *Studies in Humanities* publication in this short note.

Fife, Austin. "Folklore of Material Culture on the Rocky Mountain Frontier." *Arizona Quarterly* 13 (1957), 101–11.

_____. (Ed.) "Folklore from Utah, Wyoming, and Southern Idaho," Vol. III. Unpublished MS, Logan, Utah: Utah State University, 1958.
This unpublished collection is housed in the Fife Folklore Archives at Utah State University. Idaho materials, collected mainly by Fife's students, are primarily from Malad River and Bear River valleys. Strengths of the collections include folk medicine, tales of lost treasures and mines, and legends.

Fife, Austin E. and James M. "Hay Derricks of the Great Basin and Upper Snake River Valley." *Western Folklore* 7 (1948), pp. 225–39.
Reprinted in this volume.

_____. "Hay Derricks." *Western Folklore* 10 (1951), pp. 320–22.
This note is an addendum to Fife and Fife (1948) and is reprinted in this volume.

Fisher, Vardis, ed. *Idaho Lore.* American Guide Series, Caldwell: The Caxton Printers, 1939.
Fisher's volume is unfortunately of little value to folk cultural research because of both the editor's tampering with the materials and the amateur collection techniques used by his "correspondents." All items are clearly edited and rewritten, and no information about sources is provided.

Haines, Francis, Sr. "Goldilocks on the Oregon Trail." *Idaho Yesterdays* 9:4 (Winter, 1965–66): 26–30.
In this discussion, Haines attacks the problem of analyzing "historical narratives" for their folklore motifs. His focus is a corpus of Oregon Trail stories in which a group of Indians attempts to purchase a child, normally a fair-haired girl, from the settlers. Haines demonstrates that the story is an international one localized to the Idaho scene.

Halpert, Herbert. "Proverbial Comparisons from Idaho Territory." *Western Folklore* 6 (1947): 379–80.
Halpert lists 33 items collected from Laura Wallace, a Camas Prairie resident from 1883–1909.

Henning, Marion. "Comic Anecdotes from Santa." *Western Folklore* 24:4 (October, 1965): 249–58.
This interesting article focuses on comic anecdotes told about the experiences and activities of Mrs. Sarah Renfro, a well-known local character from Santa in northern Idaho. Interspersed with information about Sarah's life and short biographies of informants are narratives about logging, lumber camps, and other local figures from the Santa area.

Hines, Donald M. *An Index of Archival Resources for a Folklife and Cultural History of the Inland Pacific Northwest Frontier.* Ann Arbor: University Microfilms International, 1976.
This volume is an inventory of largely unpublished materials at the University of Idaho (Special Collections), Eastern Washington State Historical Society, and Washington State University Library (Manuscript–Archive Division). Hines focuses on the materials from the period of 1830–1900 and provides general content descriptions for each manuscript. This work will be of special interest to researchers studying north Idaho cultural traditions and history.

_____. *Frontier Folksay: Proverbial Lore of the Inland Pacific Northwest Frontier.* Norwood, PA: Norwood Editions, 1977.
Based on Hines' dissertation at Indiana University, this volume focuses on proverbs culled from early newspapers, including one from Grangeville. The rich harvest presented demonstrates the virtually untapped veins of information contained in early publications. Hines presents little discussion of the proverbs and lists them in categories similar to those developed by Archer Taylor.

Horvath, Joyce K. "Some Riddles from Idaho." *Western Folklore* 24:4 (October, 1965): 285–86.
Horvath's note is comprised of twenty-three riddles representing all sections of the state. For each item, the author notes the informant, collector, and place of collection, along with providing annotations to Archer Taylor's *English Riddles from Oral Traditions*.

———. "Mining Lore from Kellogg," *Western Folklore* 22:4 (October, 1965): 286–87.
A brief discussion of local legends concerning the famous jackass that discovered the lead-silver veins at Bunker Hill. Also, some mention of beliefs about bad luck held by local miners.

Hult, Ruby E. *Lost Mines and Treasures of the Pacific Northwest*. Portland, Oregon: n.p., 1957.
In her section on Idaho tales (pp. 171–238), Hult relies on previously published sources of varying quality. Readers are urged to consult the originals whenever possible. The majority of her texts are stories of lost mines and other mining experiences.

Humphreys, Alfred Glen. "Peg Leg Smith." *Idaho Yesterdays* 10:2 (Summer, 1966): 28–32.
Humphrey's discussion of horse trader (and sometimes horse thief) Peg Leg Smith relies on both newspaper and legendary accounts. Almost all of the texts are retold or condensed by the author.

Idaho Legend and Story. The Pocatello Chapter of Idaho Writers League. N.p: n.p., 1961.
This volume presents a good cross section of the Idaho oral tradition. It includes sections on Indians, outlaws and highwaymen, town life, and tall tales. Many of the legends, anecdotes, and humorous narratives were collected directly from oral traditions, and the compilers have, usually, left the narratives in their collected form. Focus is southern and eastern Idaho.

Jensen, Paul. "Desert Rats' Word-List from Eastern Idaho." *American Speech* 7:2 (1931): 119–23.
A diverse collection of terms and phrases reflecting the major groups (Mormons, farmers, ranchers) and activities (e.g., hunting and fishing) in the area. Jensen provides local spelling for each term along with, usually, a brief explanation of each item.

Jones, Janice S. "Folk Beliefs Popular in the Lower Snake River Valley." *Northwest Folklore* 3 (Winter, 1968): 12–15.
A collection of folk medicine, home remedies and cures with little discussion.

Kernan, Henry S. "Occupational Nicknames." *Hoosier Folklore Bulletin* 1:3 (1942): 103.
A brief listing from Headquarters, Idaho.

———. "Idaho Lumberjack Nicknames." *California Folklore Quarterly* 4:3 (July, 1945): 239–43.
Gathered in Clearwater County in the white pine forests, these nicknames reflect central themes — occupations, transitory nature ("Three Day Braum"), ethnic background, geographic homeland in United States, striking incidents and physical features. Close to three hundred men's names and fifty women's names are noted.

Kirtley, Bacil F. "Wandering Skull Pursues Man." *Western Folklore* 28:4 (October, 1969): 272–73.
This ghostly yarn, reprinted from an 1978 *Idaho World* edition, concerns a man who witnessed a skull moving across the desert floor. The explanation given in the original is that a prairie dog hidden in the skull caused its

movement. Kirtley discusses the possible truth of this rationalization.

Koch, Elers. "Geographic Names of Western Montana, Northern Idaho." *Oregon Historical Quarterly* 49:1 (March, 1948): 50–62.
Koch traces the origins of local names, focusing mainly on those derived from early homesteaders, the English, geographic names, mines, influence of fur trade, and Lewis and Clark. The author alludes to a large corpus of informal local legends "which have only a local significance" but, unfortunately, does not pursue this topic.

Kramer, Fritz L. *Idaho Town Names* in Twenty-third Biennial Report of the Idaho State Historical Department (1951–52), pp. 14–114.
Originally his thesis at the University of California, Kramer's study focuses on his search for the "true" story behind each town naming. He primarily uses previous historical reports and personal communications. References to local legendary materials are often made, but seldom presented.

———. "Idaho Place Name Records." *Western Folklore* 12 (1953): 283–86.
The author provides useful sources for pre-1953 references which discuss Idaho place names and their etymologies.

———. "More on 'Idaho.'" *Western Folklore* 12 (1953): 208–10.
Kramer discusses some of the legendary materials bearing on the origins of the state's name: the Indian word borrowing; a text purporting that a Congressman Cole heard the name used by an Indian woman to call her daughter; and a reference that the term means "star" in the Walla Walla tongue.

Maloney, Violette G. "Jumping Rope Rhymes from Burley, Idaho." *Hoosier Folklore Bulletin* 3 (1944): 24–25.
This note consists of a brief listing of children's rhymes.

Pethtel, Lillian. "Name Lore Around Kamiah." *Western Folklore* 24:4 (October, 1965): 281–84.
Pethtel presents a collection of nicknames given to machinery used in logging operations near Kamiah in north-central Idaho. She also notes names given to ranching vehicles and tractors in honor of cow camps, logging camps, and ranch homes. For most terms, Pethtel attempts to establish their etymology.

Rees, John E. *Idaho Chronology, Nomenclature Bibliography*. Chicago: W. B. Conkey Company, 1918, pp. 52–118.
Rees' volume contains a collection of town and place names with a discussion of name etymologies presented in nineteenth-century publications. The author does not analyze the stories but includes some reprinting of previously published legends and local anecdote narratives.

"Some Wellerisms from Idaho." *Western Folklore* 25 (1966): 34.
This note includes a listing of fourteen wellerisms, along with brief biographical information on the source of each item.

Swinney, H. J. "The Hacker's Trade." *Western Folklore* 24:4 (October, 1965): 271–73.
Swinney presents a nice introduction to the study of this often-practiced occupation in north Idaho. His focus is railroad tie-making as practiced by Matti ("Big Matt") Heikkola, a Finnish-American living near McCall.

Talbert, Ernest W. "Some Non-English Place Names in Idaho." *American Speech* 13 (1938): 175–78.
Talbert's brief essay focuses on names of foreign and Indian origin in Idaho, along with local pronunciations and the derivation for each name. About twenty foreign-derived (mainly French) and fifteen Indian-derived (mainly Nez Perce) names are included.

Teichert, Minerva Kohlhepp. *Drowned Memories.* N.p.: n.p., n.d.
In this volume a former resident of the Ft. Hall Bottoms area (now covered by the American Falls Reservoir) recalls stories and experiences of her life in the area. The text includes narratives about cattle drives, ranch life, holiday celebrations, rural customs, and local characters. Although not a folklore text, Teichert's autobiography illustrates the rich folk cultural harvest one can glean from this genre.

Thompson, Bonnie. *Folklore in the Bear Lake Valley.* Salt Lake City: Granite Publishing Company, 1972.
This work relies heavily on manuscript sources and other written texts. Some narratives and customs are presented verbatim from their source, while others have been edited or condensed. Major sections deal with anecdotes, legends, customs, fishing tales, Indians, local characters, Mormon folkways, outlaws, and folk and popular verse.

_____. *Flickering Memories* (Vol. II of *Folklore in the Bear Lake Valley*). Salt Lake City: Printers, Inc., 1977.
This second volume is more valuable than the first because it is more faithful to oral tradition and relies more heavily on oral sources. The author's discussions between the texts provide interesting information about the narrators and folk traditions. Major emphases include place-name legends, early folkways, Bear Lake anecdotes, polygamy, medical culture and folk beliefs, and verse and song.

Tinsley, Virginia Ann. "Children's Rhymes in Idaho." Unpublished MA thesis, University of Idaho, 1966.
The primary fieldwork for this study was done in Moscow elementary schools, with supplementary items collected from college students and from schoolteachers around the state. There are two hundred and fourteen rhymes and their variants classified and analyzed in terms of form, style, function, and traditionality.

Toelken, J. Barre. "Northwest Traditional Ballads: A Collector's Dilemma." *Northwest Review* 5 (1962) 9–18.
The dilemma, notes Toelken, is that the formation of a northwest ballad tradition was hindered by the recency of settlement, the heterogeneous nature of settlement patterns, and the isolation of groups due to the physical landscape. Still, there is a small corpus of northwest balladry that reflects some of the diverse heritages and experiences of local groups. Toelken presents ten texts (with no tunes), including five from Idaho.

_____. "Traditional Fiddling in Idaho." *Western Folklore* 24:4 (October, 1965): 259–62.
This article traces the growth of the fiddle contest in Weiser and details activities during the annual festival. Toelken makes some interesting points about festival structure and the place of the event within the community.

Wilgus, D. K. "Again the Benders." *Western Folklore* 15 (1946): 58–59.
Wilgus presents a text from Challis on this noted Western murder legend.

_____. "Folk Beliefs from Boise, Idaho." *Western Folklore* 28:1 (January, 1969): 41–42.
This note includes a collection of thirty-one beliefs collected from Mrs. Ann Stevens of Boise. Several of the items were learned and practiced around 1900.

Williams, Mary E. "Welsh Nicknames, Malad, Idaho." *Western Folklore* 18 (1959): 165–66.
Nicknaming is a common phenomenon in Malad because many of the area Welsh families have the same last name, and parents often name their children after living family members or relatives. Williams discusses names either given or taken by men and the stories behind the nicknaming process.

WPA Writer's Project. *Idaho: A Guide in Word and Picture.* (Caldwell: Caxton Printers, Ltd., 1937).
This volume contains short sections on buried treasure tales (pp. 365–75) and tall tales (pp. 393–402). All texts display the marks of some editing by the book's editors, although the section on tall tales appears more faithful to the oral tradition. No contextual or informant information is provided.